Interventions for Autism

Interventions for Autism: Evidence for Educational and Clinical Practice

Phil Reed

WILEY Blackwell

This edition first published 2016
© 2016 John Wiley & Sons, Ltd.

Registered Office
John Wiley & Sons, Ltd, The Atrium, Southern Gate, Chichester, West Sussex, PO19 8SQ, UK

Editorial Offices
350 Main Street, Malden, MA 02148-5020, USA
9600 Garsington Road, Oxford, OX4 2DQ, UK
The Atrium, Southern Gate, Chichester, West Sussex, PO19 8SQ, UK

For details of our global editorial offices, for customer services, and for information about how
to apply for permission to reuse the copyright material in this book please see our website at
www.wiley.com/wiley-blackwell.

The right of Phil Reed to be identified as the author of this work has been asserted in accordance with
the UK Copyright, Designs and Patents Act 1988.

Library of Congress Cataloging-in-Publication Data

Reed, Phil.
Interventions for autism : evidence for educational and clinical practice / Phil Reed.
     pages   cm
  Includes bibliographical references and index.
  ISBN 978-0-470-66992-1 (cloth) – ISBN 978-0-470-66991-4 (pbk.)
1. Autism spectrum disorders.   2. Autism spectrum disorders–Treatment.
3. Autism in children–Treatment.   I. Title.
  RJ505.P6R44 2016
  618.92′85882–dc23
                                                     2015025663

A catalogue record for this book is available from the British Library.

Cover image: Biology of Tears, illustration by Lisa A.Osborne. Reproduced by kind permission of the artist

Set in 10/12.5pt Galliard by SPi Global, Pondicherry, India
Printed and bound in Malaysia by Vivar Printing Sdn Bhd

1   2016

For Lisa
This above all

Contents

Acknowledgements

My gratitude is due to all of the team at Wiley, especially my project editor Karen Shield, whose help and patience while waiting for an age for the final manuscript was greatly appreciated. More than my thanks to Lisa Osborne who beyond anybody else provided the intellectual support while I put this book together, as well as the cover art. Her patience while I struggled to calculate endless effect sizes and try to make sense of these data was beyond anything that could reasonably be expected.

1
Autism Spectrum Disorders – What is the Problem?

The quest for the 'holy grail' of developing effective interventions to help people who have Autism Spectrum Disorders (ASD) has brought forth the usual clutch of quacks, charlatans and self-publicists, but mingled with the money-seeking snake-oil sellers are highly committed and professional practitioners and researchers, whose efforts have produced important innovations in the treatment of ASD. The many debates that have been produced in this quest for interventions have generated much heat, some little light, certainly much controversy and a great deal of confusion regarding what interventions are actually effective. The current work aims to untangle some of the mass of data regarding interventions for ASD and to provide some suggestions about the circumstances under which particular approaches may offer some help to the key people involved; that is, those affected by ASD, both directly themselves and through their close connection to somebody who is directly affected.

Autism Spectrum Disorders

The precise definition of ASD is and has been, in flux for 50 or more years. Recently, the diagnostic criteria for labelling the disorder have undergone yet another shift, from those contained in the previous Diagnostic and Statistical Manual (DSM) IV-TR, to those outlined in the new DSM-5. The nature of these criteria and some of the implications of these changes, will be discussed in Chapter 2, but it is safe to assert that ASD presents a range of complex and interacting behaviours and deficits that appear early in a person's development and persist, sometimes in differing forms, throughout that person's life impacting a wide range of their functioning. These characteristics mark out ASD from other more specific forms of psychological problems associated with childhood and make complex any intervention.

Interventions for Autism: Evidence for Educational and Clinical Practice, First Edition. Phil Reed.
© 2016 John Wiley & Sons, Ltd. Published 2016 by John Wiley & Sons, Ltd.

These issues will be covered later in terms of developing a characterization of the nature of ASD that presents for treatment (see Chapter 3), but, at this point, it is worth noting a few salient generalizations about the condition. For many, it is the types and quality of social and emotional interactions engaged in by people with ASD, as well as behavioural inflexibility and highly focused attention on aspects of their environment, that are central to its characterization. These key aspects of the disorder typically present together, making this a wide-ranging 'syndrome', with myriad potential causes – genetic, obstetric, physiological and even parenting. In itself, a disorder with multiple causations is often difficult to treat, but these primary problems are often connected with secondary or co-morbid problems for the individual with ASD, such as high levels of challenging behaviour, social isolation, anxiety and depression. The degree to which such secondary symptoms are present differs between each individual, both in the types of symptom present and also in their severity, making ASD a 'spectrum'. Of course, these individual symptoms are not unique to ASD and it has been suggested that all share some of these ASD-typical traits – that is, there is a 'broad autistic phenotype' in the population. This may be true, but it is the presence of all problems together that characterize the disorder as ASD – a syndrome with a spectrum.

It is certainly the case that ASD cannot be recognized physically (despite some recent claims to contrary) and it is also true to say that ASD is found across the entire range of people in society. This consideration raises another issue: given this broad range of people with ASD and given the potential presence of these characteristics in us all, is it a problem to have ASD? This question touches on another, increasingly important, aspect of the theoretical discussion that it is important to raise early: that is, whether the 'core' elements of ASD are always to be regarded as 'impairments' that are in need of 'treatment'. Indeed, some have even queried whether ASD should be 'treated' at all. It has been suggested that some of the behavioural and cognitive differences between people with and without ASD can sometimes confer an enhanced ability to the individual with ASD in some areas of performance (e.g. in terms of attention-based tasks requiring focus on detail) – albeit an ability at the expense of flexibility as circumstances change. However, it is equally important to note that there is by no means a consensus on this issue, either in the academic literature or among those individuals with an ASD themselves. The task of answering this question is made doubly difficult given the variation in behaviours and needs of people with ASD.

In framing a focused understanding of the scope of the present work, it may, thus, help to consider two questions related to these issues: (i) is having ASD a problem and (ii) if so, how and for whom? The first question is rather easier to answer from the perspective of a work on intervention, than from the perspective of a more theoretically based tome – quite simply, there are many, perhaps countless, individuals with ASD and their families who desperately need help – therefore, it is a problem for those people with ASD and for those people who their lives they touch, when it is a problem for them. To deny the existence of such a problem is wrongheaded and, to deny the treatment, is cruel, which is worse. As usual, there are very important provisos to add to this straightforward answer: not all people with ASD do require help and not all people with ASD require help with everything. Thus, interventions for ASD must be flexible enough to accommodate these considerations; that is to say, they must recognize that which was noted previously – that ASD is a spectrum and not a unitary disorder and that interventions will need to be tailored to suit different situations with different individuals. Together, these guiding tenets impact considerably on the focus to be taken regarding understanding the nature of ASD and the development of its interventions.

To answer the second question posed previously – 'whose problem is ASD?' – it can be said that it is not just a problem for the person with ASD, but it is a problem for and of, the community in which that person with ASD resides. The current text takes the view that an important contrast is made between the within-person disability model, which attempts to identify immutable causal structures within the person with ASD and a social-environmental approach, which suggest mutable functional connections between the person's environment and their behaviours (see Chapter 3). Far too much attention and too many resources have been placed on the former view at the expense of the latter, especially when it is seen that almost all scientifically supportable interventions stem from the latter conceptualization of ASD.

Treating ASD

If ASD is to be considered as a problem to be treated, then it is worth saying a few brief words about the nature of 'treatment'. There are a vast range of interventions now championed as being effective for ASD and the current work surveys those on which significant serious research has been conducted. These will be described throughout the text, but it is taken as a truth that it is possible to say that there are some interventions that are better than others and also that it is not in anybody's best interests to accept the claim that any intervention is good merely if is offered and conducted well (Jordan et al., 1998). Too many times has it been suggested at conferences and gatherings of professionals that anything goes in this field. A consequence of the assumed need for a clear evidence-base tilts the approach of this book toward adopting a 'medical model' of evidence assessment – an approach that has met with considerable success in other areas of treatment – hence, the use of the term 'treatment' interchangeably with 'intervention' and in preference to currently more trendy re-labelling of 'treatment'.

With this belief, the current work will take as 'treatments' those interventions that have made it out of the laboratory. This focus has the result of acting rather like a filter, determining which, out of the many potential interventions, will be discussed. Many interventions that have been developed purely in the laboratory, on the basis of particular theories, will not be addressed and neither will those that have been developed on the whim of individual practitioners. However, there are still many intervention programmes that pass this filter. Some of the history of interventions is presented in Chapter 3, where it can be seen that interventions for ASD have a longer history than might be expected. However, from the early 1970s onwards, larger numbers of interventions have emerged. For example, although Applied Behaviour Analysis (ABA) programmes (e.g. Lovaas, 1987; see Chapter 4) are often commented upon in the scientific and popular literature, approaches such as the Treatment and Education of Autistic and Related Communication Handicapped Children (Schopler & Reichler, 1971) and the Denver Health Sciences Programme (Rogers et al., 1986), emerged at least as early as ABA and the last few years have seen the development and proliferation of many more interventions for ASD. Many of these treatment types are

Behavioural approaches

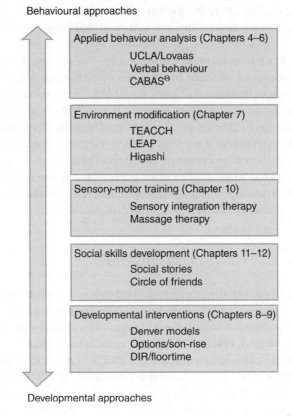

Developmental approaches

Figure 1.1 A schematic representation of a number of individual types of intervention programmes and their broad characterizations (based on Opsina et al., 2008).

mentioned in Figure 1.1, which presents a schematic representation of the interventions that several reviews have suggested as important (Odom et al., 2010; Ospina et al., 2008; Stahmer et al., 2005; Vismara & Rogers, 2010).

The current filter applied to the selection of particular interventions to be considered also has a number of further components. The current survey addresses only those interventions that accept, as their central focus, the individual affected by an ASD. This sounds like a rather odd or obvious thing to state, but too many times the main focus of an intervention has been to support the underlying theory or philosophical beliefs from which the intervention was developed. To this end, the evidence, as it relates to the impact of interventions on the functioning of people with ASD and not how it supports this or that theoretical view of ASD, will be utilized. This approach reinforces two aspects already introduced into the discussion – in addition to the necessity of obtaining good evidence regarding the effectiveness of interventions, emphasis needs to be placed: firstly, on the functionality of the interventions – they must affect change, rather than adhere to any particular theory and secondly, on the essential individuality of people with ASD – the interventions must be adaptable to one of the most individual group of people. Needless to say, this will not be easy.

One way of summarizing these various aspects of the support to be provided by any good intervention is that they are all concerned with producing a better match between the abilities of people with ASD and the environment in which they are placed. This objective is well reflected in a quote from a person with Asperger's syndrome reported by Baron-Cohen (2003, p. 180): 'We are fine if you put us in the right environment. When the person with Asperger's Syndrome and the environment match, the problem goes away... When they do not match, we seem disabled.' That is, interventions need to be targeted at adapting the environment to the person in order to more effectively contact that person's behaviours, develop their skills to their full potential and enhance their chances of success. It is argued in Chapter 3 that this form of treatment philosophy has produced the greatest number of effective interventions for ASD. Thus, there is no tension between such a person-centred psycho-social approach and a hard-core medical model of assessment, as these approaches seem to offer the best way to deal with the size and costs (both human and economic) of the problem posed by ASD.

The Size of the ASD Problem

The importance of developing interventions for ASD can be placed in perspective by a consideration of the scale of the problem (see Williams et al., 2006, for a thorough review). The population prevalence of ASD is generally estimated to be between 0.9 and 1.5% (Baird et al., 2006; Baron-Cohen et al., 2009; Brugha et al., 2009). This sort of estimate has been widely accepted for some time, however, Kim et al. (2011) suggested that a remarkably high number of children may display signs of ASD in diagnostic tests, but do not receive a diagnosis, noting prevalence rates of over 3.5% in males and 1.5% in females. Thus, prevalence estimates vary but, as shall be seen, these estimates depend on a number of factors, such as the definition of the disorder that is employed and the method used to calculate the prevalence.

It is a truism to say that the prevalence of ASD is whatever studies of its prevalence say that it is, but this truism encapsulates an important fact: there is no definitive way of knowing what the prevalence of ASD really is, as all estimates carry with them their own definitions of the disorder. Of course, that is not a particularly helpful thing to point out, as, in developing a view regarding the most appropriate forms of intervention for ASD, of central concern to most service providers are the numbers of individuals who are likely to present with these problems. Crudely put, services can only be delivered if there is the money to pay for those services and those financial calculations will depend on the numbers of people likely to present for treatment. Thus, knowing the prevalence of ASD is important for intervention planning and development.

An ASD epidemic?

As noted previously, most contemporary reports place the prevalence of ASD at about 1% of the population (e.g. Baird et al., 2006; Baron-Cohen et al., 2009). However, an issue that has exercised much current thinking concerning prevalence is that the numbers of people with ASD appear to be rising over time (see Maenner & Durkin, 2010; Williams et al., 2006 and Figure 1.2). Initial estimates, given about 40 years ago, placed ASD prevalence at about 4.5 in every 10 000 (Lotter, 1966), which increased to about 20 in every 10 000 around 30 years ago (Wing & Gould, 1979).

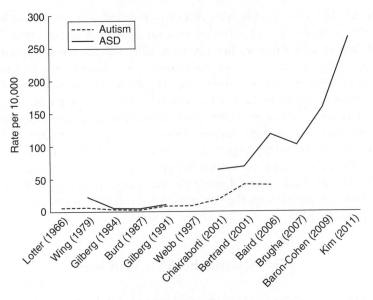

Figure 1.2 Estimation of prevalence rates for typical Autism (Autism) and all Autism Spectrum Disorders (ASD) across the last 40 years. The names refer to the first author of each report (see References for full details). It is unlikely that the increase in prevalence in the later studies reflects a real increase in ASD (see text for discussion).

The prevalence rate was placed at 60 in every 10 000 about 10 years ago (Bertrand et al., 2001; Chakraborti & Fombonne, 2001) and more recent estimates have placed this at around 100 in every 10 000 (Baird et al., 2006; Baron-Cohen et al., 2009).

This rise in the estimated rates of ASD has sparked concerns over the causes of the putative rise and concerns about the existence of an 'epidemic'. However, as shall be seen next, it is unlikely that these figures show anything of the kind (see also Fombonne, 2003; Williams et al., 2006, for similar discussions). Much of the variance in these data can be attributed to differences in the criteria used to define ASD, which have become much less strict and less narrow over time (see Baron-Cohen et al., 2009; Lotter, 1966) and to variation in the methods used to arrive at these prevalence estimates.

Definitional issues

The criteria used to define ASD are clearly critical in impacting estimates of prevalence. In extensive reviews of the literature, both Fombonne (2003) and Williams et al. (2006) have noted that this definitional factor shows the highest degree of association with noted prevalence rates and that this factor is also completely confounded with the time at which the rate was calculated. For example, initial prevalence estimates (e.g. Lotter, 1966), using a set of criteria derived from Kanner (1943), noted a rate of only 4.5 in every 10 000; subsequent rates using the DSM-III criteria tended to produce estimates of around 20 in every 10 000 (see Williams et al., 2006) and estimates based on the DSM-IV-TR vary between 60 in every 10 000 (Bertrand et al., 2001) and 116 in every 10 000 (Baird et al., 2006). The overall impact of these changes has been to increase estimates of the rates of ASD in the population (see Figure 1.2).

A current concern is the impact of changing the criteria for ASD diagnosis from the DSM-IV-TR to the DSM-5. This change might actually buck the trend of increasing rates of ASD, as many of the behaviours previously included in a definition of an ASD in the DSM-IV-TR would result in a reclassification of the person into having another category of disorder. In fact, one study of the potential impact of the proposed change in diagnostic criteria on prevalence by Worley and Matson (2012), has suggested that the DSM-IV-TR to DSM-% change will reduce prevalence estimates by around 33%. Clearly, the criteria used and differences in professional judgements regarding the diagnosis that exist will impact heavily on this aspect of prevalence estimates.

A further related explanation of the increases in estimated prevalence of ASD concerns the concept of 'diagnostic shift': individuals previously diagnosed as falling into one diagnostic category are now placed in another (Shattuck, 2006). The clearest evidence for this suggestion in the context of ASD comes from studies that have noted that as increasing numbers of individuals are diagnosed with ASD, decreasing numbers are diagnosed as having other problems, such as learning difficulties (Croen et al., 2002; King & Bearman, 2009; Matson & Shoemaker, 2009). For example, Croen et al. (2002) noted a 9.1% increase in ASD diagnoses between 1987 and 1994 and a corresponding 9.3% decrease in children diagnosed with mental retardation over the same time period. Although this is the clearest example of diagnostic substitution related to ASD, it is not the only one (see King & Bearman, 2009; Shattuck, 2006). While some have argued that this phenomenon cannot explain the entire increase in ASD prevalence (e.g. Charman et al., 2009; Newschaffer et al., 2005), when coupled with shifts in diagnostic criteria, it is probably sufficient reason to suggest that there is not enough evidence to substantiate the claim that actual levels of ASD are increasing beyond the way that they are calculated and reported.

Methodological issues

Several methods can be employed to estimate the prevalence of ASD, but the two most commonly used are those based on screening particular samples (see Charman et al., 2009; Fombonne, 2003, for discussion) or surveying service and administrative records. Although it is unclear whether one or other of these approaches will systematically produce higher estimates of the numbers of individuals with ASD, emerging evidence has shed some light on this issue. Fombonne (2003) presented data suggesting that during the period 1999–2001, higher rates of prevalence were produced by screening techniques (prevalence rate range: 26.1–62.6 per 10 000), than by survey techniques (prevalence range: 4.8–10.1 per 10 000). This trend is also apparent in some recent estimates of prevalence: Baron-Cohen et al. (2009) suggesting a prevalence of 94 in every 10 000, based on SEN registers in parts of the UK and Baird et al. (2006) suggesting a greater prevalence of 116 in every 10 000, based on a screening procedure.

Screening methods   The screening method is considered a more standard technique for prevalence estimates. It involves initially screening a population for cases of actual or suspected ASD and then following-up this initial screen by an intensive screen conducted on a sample of those individuals identified as having a diagnosis or being at risk of such (e.g. Baird et al., 2006; Chakrabarti & Fombonne, 2001). However, the screening approach presents problems at several points in the procedure that require careful consideration and which have been reviewed (Fombonne, 2003; Williams et al., 2006).

The type of information initially sent out to those identifying the suspected cases of ASD will have an effect on the identification rates, as will the subsequent participation rate (i.e. not all screening letters that are sent out will receive a response). The age of the sample being screened may also play a role. Williams et al. (2006) suggest that greater numbers of individuals are noted in samples that target a younger age group, compared to those samples targeting an older population. The coverage of the initial sample needs consideration in terms of its size relative to the population under consideration. Often these samples are very large: for example, Chakrabarti and Fombonne (2001) covered all 15 500 pre-school children in one UK authority and Baird et al. (2006) sampled over 56 000 individuals in 12 districts in the UK. In some cases, however, the sample is based only on a subset of the entire population to be screened, such as those conducted by Taylor et al. (1999), who sampled around 500 known cases of ASD from a population of around 500 000. In general, prevalence estimates are higher the lower the sample size screened. Similar problems also exist at the intense screening stage of the process, although participation rates typically appear to be relatively high among those who return the initial screening questionnaires (Fombonne, 2003).

Survey methods In terms of the survey approach, typically, the records for an educational authority or service provider are searched in order to note the numbers of children recorded with ASD (see Baron-Cohen et al., 2009). However, it has been noted that there are a number of problems with this, seemingly simple, approach. Such an approach is clearly dependent upon the manner in which an individual's need is assessed in a particular area, which may depend, not only upon their symptoms, but also on the degree to which help and finances are available in that area (see Charman et al., 2009). An example will serve to illustrate this point. Laidler (2005) examined national administrative data from the USA and concluded that such records may not suitable for tracking prevalence rates due to a number of peculiarities in this set, such as the flat profile of diagnosis across the age range of children from 1 to 17 years, with a dip between 11 and 12 years old (a transition point in the school system). These data seemed more likely to reflect the needs and constraints of the educational system than reflecting the numbers of children with ASD.

The Economic Cost of ASD

The extent of the economic cost of ASD is, of course, a key issue to service managers with an eye on the budget and is a key issue for interventions in two additional regards. Firstly, such service managers often ask whether any condition is financially important enough to warrant special consideration, over and above the many other conditions that vie for funding. Secondly, if it is an economically important condition, any intervention will not only be assessed against its performance in improving functioning and prognosis of individuals with ASD, but also against its cost effectiveness. It may be that the intervention that produces the best prognosis and functioning does not produce the best economic return. To answer these questions, it is necessary to turn to health economics.

Unfortunately, health economics is a wretchedly unreliable discipline that relies on assumptions at every level and builds its cost calculations on extremely shaky foundations. Given this, only a short analysis of these findings will be given to offer a flavour of the costs and arguments involved in the treatment of ASD. In a typical analysis of the costs of ASD, assumptions will be made about the prevalence of the disorder, the characteristics of the individuals with ASD and then issues about the associated costs of the lifestyle and services resultant from the disorder, such as residence (supported or not), special education, health and social care, will be made. Additionally, attempts will be made to assess the costs in terms of lost economic productivity for the individual and their families (see Järbrink & Knapp, 2001; Knapp et al., 2009). Once the potential costs have been identified, then figures relating to the costs of these services and so on will be gleaned from existing data or from small samples. Of course, any one of these estimations can be incorrect.

In the UK there have been a number of estimates of the cost of ASD. Järbrink and Knapp (2001) made an assumption that the prevalence of ASD was 5 in every 10 000 and, on this basis, estimated that the annual cost to the country was around £1bn, with a lifetime cost of ASD of around £2.4 mn per individual. However, close to a decade later, with a prevalence assumption that was 20 times higher (100/10 000), Knapp et al. (2009) suggested that the costs to the UK of supporting children with ASD was £2.7 bn per year and £25 bn per year for supporting adults, with a lifetime cost for individuals with ASD of £0.8–1.23 mn if they had associated intellectual problems. An additional cost study, conducted in the USA by Ganz (2007), placed the lifetime cost of ASD at about $3.2 mn per individual. Thus, these later estimates of the cost appear to be fairly consistent, which may just reflect their use of common assumptions that may or may not, in themselves, be correct.

One area of contention in these figures is the associated economic costs to the family. In their estimation of cost, Järbrink and Knapp (2001) suggested that the overall costs of ASD had only a small component that could be related to the family, estimated to be only 2.3% of the total cost. However, the true cost to the family is particularly difficult to assess and Sharpe and Baker (2007) place the cost to the family as being extremely and often ruinously, high. In fact, Arno et al. (1999) attempted to compare the actual cost of care provided to individuals with chronic conditions in the USA and found these costs fell to a substantially greater extent on the family than on the professional services (see Figure 1.3). Although these data were collected in 1999 and in the USA, it is unlikely that the situation is very different in other countries or that subsequent governments have done anything to rectify this situation. Clearly, this is an area in need of further study.

If it is accepted that the cost of ASD is high, then it follows that one outcome of a successful intervention would be to reduce this cost as the individual begins to function more effectively and requires less support. In health economics, this is typically estimated by examining the impact of the treatment on the quality of life of the individual and assessing what the consequent reduction in cost to society will be

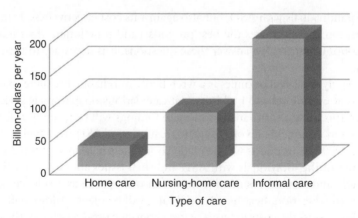

Figure 1.3 Estimated costs of types of care for disabled adults in the USA during 1997 (Arno et al., 1999). 'Home care' and 'Nursing-home care' refer to professional provided services, and 'Informal care' refers to the cost to families of caring for the individual.

of this improved quality of life for that individual (with the consequent reduction in need for support). This is usually assessed by reference to the effects of the treatment on the results obtained from a measurement tool such as the EQ-5D (Gusi et al., 2010). Unfortunately, there has been very few such quality of life studies conducted for ASD. Whether or not tools such as the EQ-5D actually measure anything important is another question (see Osborne et al., 2014, for a review in different context), but they are current currency in the field and their relative absence in relation to ASD makes it difficult to argue for the financial effectiveness of treatment in the same language as is spoken when discussing the health economics of other disorders and their treatments. Irrespective of which tools are used to estimate issues such as quality of life, it is worth keeping in mind when reading the subsequent chapters that virtually none of the studies of treatment outcome for ASD includes any measures of this area.

Nevertheless, there are some studies that have attempted to estimate the cost benefits of some interventions for ASD. For example, Jacobson et al. (1998) estimated that there was a lifetime saving, for an individual with ASD who had undergone an Applied Behaviour Analytic (ABA) intervention, of between $656 000 and $1 082 000, depending on the effectiveness of the treatment. However, this suggestion was criticized by Marcus et al. (2000), both on the grounds of being overly speculative and optimistic in terms of the assumptions made about the costs and outcomes of ABA programmes and also as no alternative interventions were studied. The latter problem was remedied, to some extent, by Chasson et al. (2007), who estimated the savings of employing an ABA approach, compared to 'treatment as usual' (in practice placement in special educational settings), of $208 000 between the ages of 3 and 22 years (i.e. about £11 000 a year). A similar study conducted in Holland by Peters-Sheffer et al. (2012) estimated a comparative saving of €1.1 mn between the ages of 3 and 65 years for each individual treated with ABA (i.e. about £14 500 a year). Again, these estimates are similar to one another, but these figures are based on assumptions of uncertain validity concerning the impact of such intervention programmes.

Prognosis for Individuals with ASD

Ultimately, an intervention aims to improve the prognosis for the individual affected and perhaps the best descriptor that can be applied to the findings from the research that has focused on the long-term prognosis for individuals with ASD is 'variable' (see Gillberg, 1990; Levy & Parry, 2011). There are a wide range of metrics that can be used in long-term prognosis studies, but these mainly focus on clinically relevant issues (such as independence of functioning and social and economic integration) rather than on the more basic assessments of functioning that are used in outcome-effectiveness studies (such as standardized assessment of intellectual functioning, language skills or adaptive-social behaviours). However, it is difficult to come to any definitive conclusions on this point due to the wide range of outcome measures and techniques used to assess the long-term prognosis for individuals with ASD and also due to the wide range of samples studied, which make it extremely difficult to compare results across reports.

Early reports of the prognosis for individuals with ASD were unremittingly bleak (see Howlin, 1997; Levy & Perry, 2011). For example, Rutter and Lockyer (1967; see also Lockyer & Rutter, 1969; Rutter et al., 1967) reported a series of studies that followed a sample of individuals diagnosed with ASD (using a rather strict definition) and found that over 50% of these individuals were institutionalized 10 years after diagnosis. Similarly, DeMyer et al. (1973) followed individuals with ASD between the ages of 5 and 12 years old and found that 42% were institutionalized at the end of the study. This figure corresponds broadly to that produced by Lotter (1974a; 1974b), who noted that 50% of the somewhat older sample in that study were in hospital and only 1 out of 29 was in employment, at the end of the study period.

However, these rather depressing figures on longer-term prognosis concerning hospitalization have improved over time. In a review of the literature, 20 years after these initial studies were published, Howlin (1997) noted that rates of hospitalization or institutionalization, in studies published after 1980, had dropped to less than 10%. Howlin (1997) relates this improvement to the increase in the number of interventions that had become available to those with ASD in this period. This may well be true (see current Chapter 3), but it has to be noted that this figure may not represent anything as simple or hopeful as intervention-promoted improved prognosis. The change in this figure also corresponds with a closure of many institutions for people with mental problems (see DHSS, 1981, *The Harding Report, 'Care in the Community'*) – there were fewer hospitals in which to place people with ASD. Consistent with this view, Gillberg (1990) noted that, while not institutionalized or hospitalized, 66% of the sample with ASD studied was still dependent upon others (i.e. the care cost had just been out-sourced by the government to the family!). Moreover, the decline in institutionalization also corresponds with the introduction of a broader definition of ASD, meaning those with less typical symptoms (and perhaps less severe symptoms) than employed in Kanner's definition, were also studied in those later reports and for whom prognosis may be better.

In order to give a comparison that has a chance of examining trends in time and to see if the increase in available interventions may have had an impact on prognosis, the notion of the 'summative' outcome can be employed (Lockyer & Rutter, 1970; see Levy & Perry, 2011, for a discussion). Most studies will assess whether the individuals have had a 'good', 'fair' or 'poor', outcome. These categories will be based on a range of indices

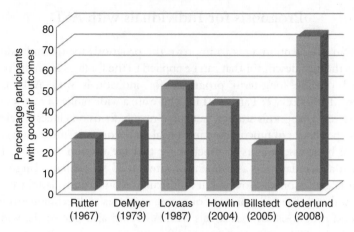

Figure 1.4   Percentages of participants in selected reports displaying 'good' or 'fair' outcomes. The names refer to the first author of each report (see References for full details). On this basis, there has been little noticeable improvement in prognosis over time.

including: independence, employment, functioning and so on, although these may differ from study to study. Pre-1980, a number of reviews have noted that the average of individuals with ASD with a 'good' prognosis typically was around 10% (see Howlin, 1997; Levy & Parry, 2011), whereas an average of 60% of outcomes could be said to be 'poor' (Howlin, 1997). For example, DeMyer et al. (1973) found that up to 15% of the individuals assessed displayed 'good' or 'borderline' levels of 'recovery' (where functioning was rated as similar to individuals without ASD), 16–25% showed 'fair' recovery and 60–75% had 'poor' recovery. Inspection of these data post-1980 (i.e. Billstedt et al., 2005; Cederlund et al., 2008; Howlin et al., 2004; Lovaas, 1987), suggests that about 20% of outcomes can now be regarded as 'good' (or better) and 50% as 'poor' or worse.

Of course, these figures are based on quite different data across studies and also are subject to changes in expectations over time of how an individual with ASD should be able to function in society. When the more positive outcomes (good and fair) are grouped to provide a less fine-tuned distinction, these differences are somewhat less pronounced than when the more subtle distinctions between 'good' and 'fair' imply. Figure 1.4 shows the percentage of individuals with a fair or good outcome for a number of studies organized across time, where such summative outcomes can be determined and these data make for some salutatory reading.

Thus, although there has been some improvement in the prognosis from the initial reports, including fewer hospitalizations and a doubling of 'good' prognosis outcomes, this latter figure suggesting improvement only takes into account about 20% of all ASD cases. Indeed, beyond the broad categorization of prognosis into 'good' or 'poor', there are still concerning issues for ASD prognosis. For instance, Hofvander et al. (2009) found that 60% of individuals with ASDs were unemployed and 84% of their sample had no significant social relationships. These figures are mirrored by those presented by Mordre et al. (2012), who noted that 80% of their sample was unemployed and 92% had no relationship. These poor economic and social integration outcomes are also consistent with the findings of UK Adult Psychiatric Morbidity Survey conducted for people with ASD (Brugha et al., 2009). In fact, the data from

Mordre et al. (2012) show little difference in these figures from those presented nearly half a century earlier by Rutter and Lockyer (1967).

There are two caveats to these rather unsatisfying conclusions on the change in prognosis for people with ASD over the years. The previous figures show the collective outcomes for all cases of ASD studied in these reports. There are, of course, differences in prognosis depending on the severity of ASD and the level of intellectual functioning (see Levy & Perry, 2011), although the literature on this is again mixed. For instance, Mordre et al. (2012) found prognosis was better for those with less severe forms of ASD (i.e. non-typical autism compared to Autistic Disorder according to the DSM-IV); whereas Billstedt et al. (2005), using a similar sample, failed to find a difference between individuals with atypical ASD and Autism Disorder in terms of prognosis, although it was noted that prognosis was better for those with Asperger's Syndrome relative to Autistic Disorder. In terms of IQ, Farley et al. (2009) noted that 50% of individuals with ASD with IQ scores of 100 or greater achieve independence (a level of intellectual functioning that often corresponds to those with Asperger's Syndrome under the DSM-IV criteria). Carbone et al. (2010) also suggest prognosis for higher intellectually functioning individuals with ASD is better than for more severe cases – although these positive results, in terms of better social and economic prognoses, should be weighed against the higher prevalence of depression in higher functioning individuals with ASD (see Ghaziuddin et al., 1998; Chapter 2).

It should also be borne in mind that it is actually quite unclear what experiences and interventions the individuals in these prognosis studies have undergone. Carbone et al. (2010) notes that prognosis, especially among the less high functioning, can be improved by intervention and, as noted earlier, this is the point made by Howlin (1997) in examining the change in prognosis figures over time. In fact, it is the role of intervention in improving prognosis that sparked one of the most important debates in this field and, in some ways can be considered pivotal in the development of treatment for ASD. Lovaas (1987; see Figure 1.4) published data from a study of an ABA intervention conducted on young children that showed 50% of the sample having 'recovered' (i.e. being indistinguishable from their peers without ASD). These claims were made largely on the basis of the impact of the intervention on the children's IQ and on their school placement. While this claim has been disputed by subsequent reports (see Chapter 4), it does point to the importance of intervention in developing functioning and potentially highlights one route to improvement of prognosis, in terms of impacting on one area of functioning (such as IQ) and hoping for a knock-on effect to the more clinically relevant variables.

Treatment Approaches to be Included

The preceding three sections have highlighted the size of the problem facing those who would develop interventions for ASD. If these human and economic costs are to be addressed, then the discussion must revert to that of effective treatment programmes and which treatments should be given consideration. As noted previously, there are huge numbers of intervention strategies that have been used in an attempt to help individuals with ASD and it is impossible to detail within one text the evidence for all of these strategies.

To focus the discussion, some selection criteria were outlined in a previous section of this chapter, but the following sections give more detail about the approach to be taken to the selection and assessment of treatments. In particular, the current survey will focus on treatments that are 'comprehensive' in nature. There are many views on exactly what a 'comprehensive' approach should look like (see Odom et al., 2010; Vismara & Rogers, 2010), but there are certainly three features that need to be present: (i) the intervention must potentially cover the full range of problems associated with ASD; (ii) the approach must be based on some underlying philosophy of treatment that unites the intervention's strategies and (iii) there must be sufficient evidence from good quality studies on which the assess the impact of the approach.

Wide-ranging nature

A comprehensive approach must attempt to deal with the full range of problems that can present with ASD and they certainly must cover the core problems of ASD. Moreover, any intervention programme that lays claim to the term 'comprehensive' should also be capable of being the only from of treatment provided for the individual. That is not to say that such an intervention could not be offered alongside other interventions, if that is desired, but, theoretically, to be termed 'comprehensive' it has the potential to be used on its own to provide an encompassing treatment package.

This definition would differentiate a comprehensive intervention approach from a component strategy of that intervention. Although the component strategy might contribute to the operation and success of the overall intervention, it would not, in itself, be used as a treatment. For example, many intervention packages for ASD employ a visual prompt (see Dettmer et al., 2000; Hayes et al., 2010) to help guide the learning of a person with ASD, but, while that visual prompt is clearly part of the intervention, it would not be considered itself as an entire intervention programme.

This criterion also differentiates a comprehensive intervention from approaches that are designed to improve just one aspect of functioning for people with ASD – such as social functioning (e.g. Social Stories™ by Karkhaneh et al., 2010) or communication abilities (e.g. Picture Exchange Communication System by Frost & Bondy, 2002). These domain-focused interventions may employ only a single intervention strategy, focused on one aspect of functioning or they may employ multiple strategies in dealing with this aspect of the individual's functioning, but, either way, these focused interventions do not attempt cover the whole range of problems that a person with ASD may exhibit. For example, the 'Circle of Friends' approach (e.g. Whitaker et al., 1998) is a rather complex intervention, involving a number of elements that has been employed for individuals with ASD (James, 2011), but it focuses only on developing the social functioning of the individual and not the restricted and repetitive behaviours or sensory problems, of the individual, so does not qualify as a 'comprehensive' intervention.

Cohesive principles of treatment

In addition to providing treatment strategies that impact on a wide range of ASD symptoms, in order to be truly comprehensive an intervention must be based on a cohesive set of principles. In considering what such unifying principles could be, it is important to understand that these principles can be quite different in form from one another. They may be based on psychological assumptions regarding the controlling variables of behaviour (as in the behavioural approaches to be discussed in Chapter 4 to 6) or the developmental needs of the individual (as in the developmental approaches, to be discussed in Chapters 8 and 9). For example, the model presented by Ospina et al. (2008) places 'behavioural' approaches or treatments based around the impact of learning about the environment at one end of a spectrum and 'developmental' approaches or treatments organized around within-person characteristics at the other end of this spectrum.

However, it should not be assumed that these principles must fall along some kind of psychological continuum, rather they could relate to other important treatment considerations. Other sets of principles could be established around the core problems that are believed to be important in ASD. Such views suggest that by targeting the 'core' deficit of ASD, the symptoms resulting from this central deficit will be remedied (as in some sensory-physical treatments, discussed in Chapter 10). For other approaches, the unifying principle is that the interventions are professionally driven – based on a set of beliefs concerning the best ways to optimize the coherence of the delivery system involved (e.g. the school-parent partnership). These professionally driven programmes focus on a 'systems-based' approach to the intervention delivery – and they have a cohesive and coherent view about how the elements in the intervention fit together with one another and have a developed philosophy of education (see Chapter 7). Yet other comprehensive approaches comprise component elements that may have little in common other with one another, other than they are included due to the belief that together they will have a positive impact on the individual with ASD (often termed 'eclectic' models and analysed in Chapter 11).

Strength of evidence

Any book focused on assessing the evidence for ASD interventions needs to consider whether there is enough strength of evidence to get these interventions to the wicket in the evaluation game. Thus, the final criterion is that there must have been a reasonable number of good quality studies conducted on the intervention to allow conclusions to be reached or, at least, tentatively suggested. That does not mean that the other approaches than those assessed are ineffective – absence of evidence, is not evidence of absence – but it does mean that these interventions cannot draw on evaluation evidence in their support. If these interventions were drugs, of course, they would not have been released on the market.

It has to be noted that there are many respectable arguments in favour of assessing an intervention from practice; that is, a particular strategy has been used by practitioners and they anecdotally report its success (see Baranek, 2002). These reports are very useful aids to professionals and certainly can be just as helpful as outcome-effectiveness studies in furthering the field. Moreover, this practice-led argument should not be confused with the view that 'anything should go' or that, somehow, evaluation in the field is unnecessary (Jordan et al., 1998) or even impossible (see Lord & McGee, 2001, for a discussion of many assessment problems). However, for others to be able to ultimately assess whether a particular intervention should be used, especially one with potentially large resource implications, more

Table 1.1 Categorization of the scientific merit of outcome-effectiveness studies for ASD interventions, based on Eikeseth (2009).

	Diagnosis	*Design*	*Measures*	*Fidelity*
Level 1	DSM criteria. Independent assessment. Blind assessor.	Randomized Control Trial.	Full range of domains. Standardized measures. Blind assessors	Assessed.
Level 2	DSM criteria. Independent assessment. Blind Assessor.	Controlled Study.	Full range of domains. Standardized measures. Blind assessor.	Assessed.
Level 3	DSM criteria.	Observational Study. Retrospective Controls	Partial range of domains. Standardized measures. Blind assessor.	Assessed.
Level 4	Insufficient scientific value			

than anecdotal reports or even case reports, are needed. This book will mention some such studies, but only to illuminate the stronger evidence regarding the intervention. Interpretation of the evidence provided by any study is dependent upon its scientific quality.

There are now a substantial number of studies that have assessed the impact of interventions for ASD, however, these studies vary considerably in their quality and hence, in the extent to which any weight can be placed on their conclusions. In considering this issue, Eikeseth (2009; see also Makrygianni & Reed, 2010a; Reichow & Wolery, 2009) outlined four general levels of scientific merit and these are shown in Table 1.1. Levels 1–3 would allow some degree of evidence to be derived from the results and Level 4 would not and only studies with the first three levels of quality have been included in the current book. Thus, these studies have used appropriate research strategies (e.g. randomized control trials, controlled studies and observational studies), assessment across a range of ASD-related behaviours (e.g. cognition, language and communication, social abilities and behavioural problems) and well-validated tools (e.g. standardized intelligence/language tests, Vineland Adaptive Behaviour Scales etc.). Unfortunately, many interventions have not really adhered to these basic needs – often presenting anecdotal case reports or using idiosyncratic assessment tools. These problems reduce the numbers of interventions that can be reasonably assessed quite dramatically.

It should be noted that the treatment approaches that are most often assessed are not necessarily the interventions that are most often employed. Figure 1.5 shows the relative levels of employment of interventions for ASD, as documented by Stahmer et al. (2005) and Green et al. (2006). Apart from illustrating the difficulty in accurately assessing the actual levels of usage of interventions (the results from the two studies

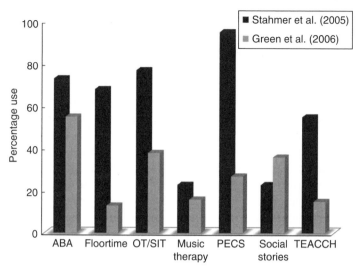

Figure 1.5 Percentages of respondents in two studies reporting the use of particular types of interventions (OT = Occupational Therapy; SIT = Sensory Integration Therapy; PECS = Picture Exchange Communication System; TEACCH = Treatment and Education of Autistic and Related Communication Handicapped Children).

are quite dissimilar to one another), these data also serve to show that, although many of these approaches are listed also in Figure 1.1 they have not been assessed by quality studies to any large degree. This contrast is presented not only to illustrate that the adoption of evidence-led practice still has some way to go, but also to suggest that outcome-effectiveness studies are not the only driver of the perceived usefulness of an intervention strategy.

The relatively high prevalence of behavioural approaches (54% of all interventions adopted by parents of children with ASD, as noted by Green et al., 2006), is reflected in the high numbers of outcome-effectiveness studies conducted regarding this approach. In the most wide-ranging of the meta-analyses, Ospina et al. (2008) recorded 101 outcome-effectiveness studies and categorized 53% of them as targeting behavioural aspects of ASD. In contrast, Green et al. (2006) note that almost 10% of parents report using facilitated communication procedures, but this technique does not register high in terms of number of studies conducted.

There is one final caveat that the data reported by Green et al. (2006) also highlight and which is important to keep in mind when translating the findings reported here to real world situations. Although 54% of parents use a behavioural intervention of some description, they will also use a variety of other approaches in addition. In fact, Green et al. (2006) report that the average number of interventions employed by parents was seven. This number differed across the type and severity of the ASD noted, with a mean of 4.5 interventions being used for individuals with Asperger Syndrome, 7.2 interventions being employed for mild ASD severities and 8.7 approaches being used for severe ASD. Thus, while much of the research effort recorded in this text has been directed as isolating the impact of comprehensive approaches when performed in isolation, this does not necessarily correspond to what actually happens in most cases.

Structure of the Present Chapters

Based on these considerations, the current book assesses comprehensive treatments for ASD that share the characteristics of addressing the full range of ASD problems, being able to be applied on their own, having a coherent underlying treatment approach and having sufficient quality research to allow conclusions to be drawn. It is organized to describe and evaluate five categories of comprehensive interventions, although it should be noted that these are only broad groupings and that they do have some overlap with one another: (i) behavioural approaches (Chapters 4–6); (ii) environmental-systems approaches (Chapter 7); (iii) developmental approaches (Chapters 8 and 9); (iv) core-deficit treatments (Chapter 10) and (v) eclectic treatments (Chapter 11). Each set of chapters sets out and discusses the conclusions that might be drawn from these studies – examining the evidence for the intervention's success and the range of situations where it might reasonably be applied. In developing such an evidence base, each chapter is based on reports that have adopted certain study designs: either various forms of outcome-effectiveness studies or descriptive and meta-analytic reviews of these outcome-effectiveness studies.

Outcome-effectiveness studies

There are three broad categories of outcome-effectiveness studies that can be considered as providing evidence of, at least, Level 3 standard (see Table 1.1): Randomized Control Trials; Controlled Studies and Observational Studies. Each of these types of study concentrates on examining the impact of an intervention for ASD on the participants' functioning over a period of time and they do so by taking both a baseline measure prior to the introduction of the intervention (i.e. a pre-intervention measure) and at least one follow-up (post-intervention) measure after a period of application of the intervention. However, each form of design has its own strengths and weaknesses that need to be borne in mind while assessing these data.

Randomized control trials This form of evaluation evidence is often thought to be of major importance in the assessment of outcomes for any intervention. Participants in a randomized control trial (RCT) are randomly allocated to either the treatment group (i.e. the targeted intervention for ASD) or to a control/comparison group (which could be an alternative treatment, a waiting list control or a no-treatment group). The RCT aims to overcome any potential selection bias in the samples at the start of the programme through such a random allocation. If participants are assigned to a group for non-random reasons, then the groups may well differ from one another at baseline along some critical dimension and the difference along this dimension, rather than the treatment itself, may be the critical factor. The groups in the RCT are then given a pre- and post-test measure and the relative change between them is taken to indicate the impact of the intervention in the absence of any other confounding variable.

Although sometimes thought of as a 'gold standard' of evaluation, the RCT study does have some drawbacks. A practical limitation is that it can be very difficult to obtain high numbers of individuals for such studies as they require recruitment *de nova*, rather than utilizing existing programmes. Also, it may not be ethical to randomly allocate people to treatment alternatives, especially if one possible alternative is to receive no treatment. Finally and importantly, individuals do not choose treatments randomly and violation of this aspect of the process can reduce both the external validity of such studies and the estimation of the effectiveness of the treatment: if a treatment relies to some extent on patient compliance, as most psychological treatments do, then denial of patient choice may reduce this factor and the efficacy of the programme.

Controlled studies Controlled studies offer an alternative to the RCT and they attempt to compare two or more interventions across pre- and post-intervention tests. The major difference from an RCT is that there is no randomization of participants into groups prior to the start of the intervention. As noted previously, this could introduce a number of confounds into the study, such a baseline differences between the groups of participants. Although most of these studies do attempt to examine whether there are any baseline differences in the participants in the various groups, the critical differences may not be measured. However, while this consideration does reflect a limitation of the controlled study, it also produces an opportunity to study the impact of the 'real world' effectiveness of the interventions and this may well offer external-validity advantages over the RCT, as discussed earlier. The other key advantage of a controlled study is that can utilize pre-existing interventions more readily than a RCT and, consequently, it may be able to recruit greater numbers of participants in each study.

Observational studies Both the RCT and the controlled study offer opportunities to compare the effectiveness of two or more interventions over a period of time. This allows both an assessment of the impact of the target programme over time and of its relative impact compared to an alternative programme. However, it may not always be possible to compare two programmes (or indeed ethically desirable to do so) and the final form of outcome-effectiveness study to be discussed is the observational study. In this type of study, participants are measured at baseline and at a follow-up point and the change in their functioning is calculated, but no control group is included. The outcome data from observational studies are almost always collected on participants undergoing an existing intervention, rather than an experimental approach and, as such, represent an accurate real world effectiveness of a treatment.

The observational study allows an idea of the change over time as a result of exposure to an intervention, but a major problem with the interpretation of such change is that it may have occurred anyway with time in the absence of the intervention. However, as with the controlled study, an observational study can utilize existing interventions and can recruit significant numbers of participants. This recruitment can be even greater than in a controlled study, as there is no requirement for a comparison group and this presents another opportunity; with sufficient numbers of participants, the potential impact of those baseline characteristics on the treatment outcomes can be more easily established. That is not to say that this cannot be done with these two sorts of study design, but it is easier with more participants.

Assessing the collective evidence

The conclusions that can be drawn on the bases of these individual outcome-effectiveness studies are obviously limited by the particular characteristics of the study and the sample involved. For this reason, two additional forms of analysis of the impact of interventions for ASD often have been employed, which combine the results of individual studies and the current book draws on both techniques.

One method of combining and integrating the results of individual studies is through the traditional descriptive review of the literature. This provides an opportunity to describe and characterize the area. However, a problem with such descriptive reviews is that they tend to be somewhat selective and potentially idiosyncratic, in their inclusion of studies. Nevertheless, where there are relatively few studies of a particular intervention and where these studies each measure quite different areas of functioning from one another, this narrative technique will be employed.

However, in an attempt to become more systematic in the analysis of outcome-effectiveness studies and to overcome some of the problems of a narrative review, the meta-analysis (see Wilson & Lipsey, 2001) has been developed. The meta-analysis attempts to give specific criteria for inclusion of studies and gives quantitative aggregate summaries of the outcomes of the individual studies. The current book will perform its own meta-analyses on each sort of intervention included where the data permit. These will be conducted to assess the overall effectiveness of an intervention and also to allow potential predictors of its success to be established.

A critical aspect of any meta-analysis is the calculation of effect sizes and these metrics will form a large part of the subsequent evaluation of the interventions. 'Effect size' is the name given to an index of the magnitude of a treatment effect and there are many ways in which these can be calculated (see Wilson & Lipsey, 2001). The current text will employ Cohen's *d* as the effect size statistic of analysis (see Cohen, 1988), as it is relatively straightforward to understand and can be calculated from basic data contained in many articles or estimated from the results of reported statistical tests or from reports of other effect sizes.

In general, for the interpretation of effect sizes, Cohen's (1988) suggestions are followed here: an effect size of 0.30 or less is taken to be small (and clinically insignificant); an effect size of between 0.31 and 0.69 is of medium size (and clinically relevant) and an effect size of above 0.70 is taken to be large (and clinically important). However, one important proviso should be given in the interpretation of these effect sizes: not all studies give adequate descriptions of the data to allow such calculations and, in some instances, the effect sizes are only approximations. However, since the goal is not to establish *the exact effect size*, but to give indications of effectiveness and predictors, this approach seemed satisfactory.

It is possible to produce two expressions of the effectiveness of interventions using effect size as a metric (Wilson & Lipsey, 2001). Firstly, the change between the pre- and post-treatment performances of the individuals can be calculated and this is the only type of effect size that can be performed for an observational study. This effect size is typically expressed by the change in the group mean produced by the intervention divided by the standard deviation of the scores at baseline. The method used to calculate this metric throughout the current text is shown in Table 1.2, but also may be illustrated by a simple example: if an IQ measure had changed by 9 points at the

Table 1.2 Formulas used where possible for the calculation of the different effect sizes (ES_1 = change from baseline to follow-up; ES_2 = change for intervention group relative to control group).

$$ES_1 = \frac{\overline{x}_{post} - \overline{x}_{pre}}{SD_d / \sqrt{2(1-r)}}$$

Where: $\overline{x}_{post}$ and $\overline{x}_{pre}$ are the means of the post-treatment and pre-treatment assessments, respectively; r is the correlation between the pre-treatment and post-treatment scores; and SD_d is the standard deviation of the gain scores.

$$ES_2 = \frac{\overline{x}_1 - \overline{x}_2}{\sqrt{\dfrac{(n_1-1)SD_1^2 + (n_2-1)SD_2^2}{(n_1-1)+(n_2-1)}}} \times \left[1 - \frac{3}{4(n_1+n_2)-9}\right]$$

Where: $\overline{x}_1$ and $\overline{x}_2$ are the mean standard scores for behavioral and control groups, respectively; SD_1 and SD_2 are their standard deviations, respectively; and n_1 and n_2 are the numbers of children in the groups, respectively.

post-test compared to the pre-test and the standard deviation of the samples' IQ at baseline was 15, then this would give an effect size of 0.66 (i.e. 9/15).

Secondly, the performances of individuals in an intervention programme and in a control group can be compared with one another and this analysis can be performed for controlled studies and RCTs. The calculation for this metric may also be illustrated by an example: if IQ improved by 9 points over treatment for the intervention group and by 3 points for the control group, then the difference would be 6 points in favour for the intervention group. If the pooled standard deviation of the two groups at baseline was 15, then this effect size would be 0.4 (i.e. 6/15). This is a simple example and the calculation gets somewhat more complicated if the standard deviations of the two groups are different at baseline or the sample sizes are different (see Wilson & Lipsey, 2001; Makrygianni & Reed, 2010a). Nevertheless, the basic calculation is quite clear.

Both of these types of effect size will be employed in the current assessments. However, in terms of comparing one intervention against another, effect sizes derived from the first type of analysis are often most useful. While the effectiveness of an individual programme against a control needs the second type of effect size – when combining across different studies, for different interventions, the control conditions might show radical differences from one another. Differences in the control groups used would impact on the relative sizes of the second effect size, in a way that it will not impact the first.

2

Autism Spectrum Disorders

Autism Spectrum Disorders (ASD) represent a syndrome of connected behaviours and problems with a spectrum of severities that persist across the individual's lifetime and impact on multiple areas of their functioning. Undoubtedly, ASD is one of the most complex syndromes that presents but, despite its complexity, there are alterations in functioning across key domains that are very common to the disorder. Broadly, these key areas in which the functioning of the person with ASD is altered include their social and emotional interactions with others and a relative behavioural and/or psychological flexibility in response to change. Although there are continuing debates regarding the behaviours that should be 'central' to the definition and diagnosis of an ASD, these areas of functioning are important for interventions to target.

The 'core' behaviours and deficits associated with ASD also generate further problems for individuals with the condition, which can be considered to be 'secondary' consequences of the disorder. These secondary and co-morbid problems often involve the impacts of the condition on the psychological adjustment of the individual with ASD and certainly include depression and mood disorders, as well as many forms of anxiety disorder. In addition, there is a wide range problems often noted with ASD, such as learning disabilities and physical disorders (such as gastric problems), which may further complicate the picture in terms of developing an appropriate treatment package. Although these issues do not necessarily form part of 'core' definition of ASD, these are problems that will concern those with ASD and those trying to help them. Thus, ASD presents a truly complex pattern of physical, behavioural and cognitive issues for any intervention to tackle.

It should be noted that the nature of ASD itself is conceptualized quite differently by different psychologists depending upon the approach being taken to understanding the condition (see Chapter 3). An increasingly important aspect of this theoretical debate revolves around specifying the core elements of ASD, if, indeed, there are such central elements to the disorder that can be identified and determining which of these

Interventions for Autism: Evidence for Educational and Clinical Practice, First Edition. Phil Reed.
© 2016 John Wiley & Sons, Ltd. Published 2016 by John Wiley & Sons, Ltd.

'core' elements of ASD should be treated by an intervention. However, it is equally important to note that there is by no means a consensus on this issue and the identified core elements in the research literature are not always the same as those held to be important by the individuals with ASD or their families. For example, families of children with ASD are often more concerned about the levels of externalizing behaviours exhibited by their children, which are not always regarded as central deficits for ASD (see the DSM-5 and ICD-10 classifications). Similarly, there are aspects of functioning that are not listed as central to the diagnosis of ASD, such as the individual's intellectual abilities and levels of emotional distress, which are certainly of concern to those with ASD and their families. Thus, the academic, research and personal perspectives regarding ASD do not always correspond to one another and developing the widest understanding of the diverse and personal nature of ASD is also a key goal for those attempting to offer help and intervention.

This brief introduction to the issues involved in the characterization of ASD shows that the questions regarding how ASD is to be defined and, hence, how its treatment is to be best affected, actually produces a series of interlocking and interacting issues. Some of these issues, although by no means all, are addressed in this chapter and they cover: (i) which behaviours and cognitions associated with ASD are 'core' characteristics and which are secondary consequences of the condition, and (ii) how these key behaviours are to be grouped or categorized into clusters so that ASD can be identified and whether ASD is actually a unitary condition at all. The answers to these issues will, in part, determine the types of intervention that are thought to be most appropriate. The answer to this question will also depend on the nature of the ASD unique to the individual in question and also, to the theoretical perspective of the person delivering the intervention.

Core Functioning Domains Implicated in ASD

At the outset, it is wisest for any text primarily concerned with interventions to state that there are probably as many behaviours exhibited by those with ASD as there are people with ASD and that these behaviours display a wide range of individualized clusters across the entire population of people with ASD. That is, the prime objective of a practical approach to intervention is to assess the needs of the individual and not to treat the individual as identical to a perceived disorder – good interventions, as shall be seen throughout the text, place individualized assessment of difficulties at their core. However, this truism is not particularly helpful for those attempting to understand the reasons why particular interventions for ASD have been developed, nor does it help very much in gaining an overview of the potential difficulties that a person with ASD might encounter. To aid in this understanding, the fullest range of functioning domains implicated as important for ASD needs to be documented.

A good starting point in documenting the domains commonly taken to be central to the definition of ASD is to examine the kinds of areas of functioning outlined by the various classification systems for the condition. Four such methods of classifying and identifying ASD are displayed in Table 2.1. These methods are derived from the systems for diagnosing an ASD suggested by Kanner (1944), the DSM-IV-TR, the DSM-5 and the ICD-10. Two of these systems, Kanner's and the DSM-IV-TR, are now theoretically 'out-of-date', the ICD-10 will become out-of-date in 2015 and the

Table 2.1 Four different classification systems for diagnosing Autism and Autism Spectrum Disorders.

Kanner Kanner & Eisenberg (1956)	DSM-IV-TR APA (1994)	DSM-5 APA (2013)	ICD-10 WHO (1992)
Profound lack of affective contact with other people.	Impairment in social interaction.	Deficits in social communication and social interaction across contexts.	Impairment in reciprocal social interaction.
Anxiously obsessive desire for the preservation of sameness.	Impairments in communication.	Restricted, repetitive patterns of behaviour, interests, or activities.	Impairments in communication.
Fascination for objects.	Restricted repetitive and stereotyped patterns of behaviour, interests, and activities.	Symptoms present in early childhood.	Restricted repetitive and stereotyped patterns of behaviour, interests and activities.
Mutism or language not intended for inter-personal communication.		Symptoms together limit and impair everyday functioning.	
Cognitive potential in memory or skills on performance tests.			Developmental abnormalities present in the first three years.
Onset from birth or before 30 months.			Clinical picture not attributable to other disorders.

DSM-5 will, one day, become out-of-date. Nevertheless, they offer a good starting point to show the features thought important for ASD, as well as offering both a brief history of the condition and a *memento mori* for all who would develop such classification systems. However, despite the differences between them, all four systems highlight several common aspects in identifying ASD: (i) social and emotional interactions; (ii) communication; (iii) behavioural and psychological inflexibility; (iv) sensory responsiveness and (iv) externalizing behaviours, which are discussed next and which are all critical for interventions to target.

Social and emotional interactions

Out of necessity, everybody with a diagnosis of ASD displays some difficulty with social interaction and emotional understanding, as this is part of the diagnostic criteria for the disorder (e.g. DSM-5; ICD-10). However, the range and severity of these behaviours can vary markedly across individuals and the current section highlights a few potentially problematic areas in this functioning domain – there will be many other variants. On the whole, the behaviours involved in this domain are those connected with interpreting the social and emotional actions of others (and sometimes of the self). Difficulties in these areas can also be manifest in a lack of ability and/or pleasure in maintaining social contact with others (Lord et al., 1994). A range of potential problems in this domain, as specified by the DSM-IV-TR and DSM-5, can be seen in Table 2.1.

Although it is not the focus of the current section to provide theoretical explanations for differences in functioning between people with and without ASD, it is almost impossible not to mention that problems in the social domain have often been connected with particular cognitive deficits, such as a failure to be able understand what another person may be thinking or what that other person may be attempting to do. This has been termed 'mind-blindness' by Baron-Cohen (2000; 2003) and that theory describes much of what can be seen in those with ASD when they are socially interacting with others. Such 'high-level' deficits are often characterized by positing that the person with ASD lacks an adequate 'theory of mind' (e.g. Baron-Cohen et al., 1985) or a lack of understanding of 'folk psychology' (Baron-Cohen & Wheelwright, 1999). For example, sometimes those with ASD have difficulty understanding that all people do not have the same thoughts as themselves or have different perspectives on an event from themselves (e.g. Dawson & Fernald, 1987; see Baron-Cohen, 2000, for a review). This deficit is suggested to underlie many of the social-emotional problems observed in ASD. However, it should be mentioned that such difficulties are certainly not limited to those with ASD (see Korkmaz, 2011) and, indeed, are not noted across all situations for people with ASD (e.g. Carpenter et al., 2001), leading some to suggest that a full understanding of this aspect of the social–emotional difficulties connected with ASD may, unfortunately, have overshadowed by the publicity and focus given to this theoretical interpretation of these problems (see Tager-Flusberg, 2007, for a discussion).

Whatever the eventual resolution of this theoretical debate, it is the case that social interactions involving individuals with ASD sometimes do not follow typical conventions. In extreme cases, there may be no response made by the person with ASD when they are addressed directly (see Dewey & Everard, 1974). For those individuals with ASD who do engage in social interactions, their eye contact with others can be over-long and somewhat disturbing (e.g. Senju & Johnson, 2009); alternatively, there can be an excessive politeness in the forms of address made by the person with ASD (Sirota, 2004). These latter two behaviours can result from a rigid adherence to learned social rules or conventions (pragmatics) on the part of the person with ASD, but without the person with ASD being fully aware of the reasons for these arbitrary social rules (see Baron-Cohen, 1988, for a discussion of pragmatic issues for ASD). In fact, if and when a person with ASD does come to develop recognition of the existence of differences in social behaviours between themselves and others, this can prompt the development of depression and mood disorders (see Browning et al., 2009, for a discussion). Thus, whether to include the teaching of simple pragmatic rules for social situations in an intervention for people with ASD is an issue not to be taken lightly.

A further area of difficulty for individuals with ASD is connected to the recognition of emotions in others, often through their facial expressions (e.g. Hobson et al., 1988; Hubert et al., 2007; but see Grossman et al., 2000, for an alternative view). For example, in the study reported by Hobson et al. (1988) groups of individuals, who either had ASD or did not have ASD (but who were similar to the ASD group in many other ways) were presented with photographs of various emotions or non-emotional situations and had to state what the pictures represented. The group without ASD recognized many more of the emotions correctly than the group with ASD did. Examples of the types of stimuli employed and the results of the recognition test are shown in Figure 2.1 – where high scores reflect better recognition of the sets of pictures.

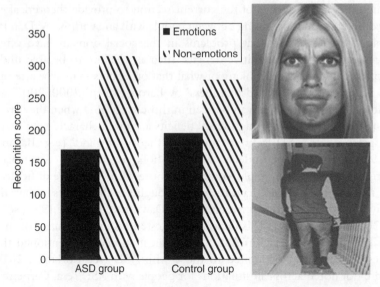

Figure 2.1   Results from the study reported by Hobson et al. (1988) on the recognition of photographs of emotions and non-emotions by a group with ASD and a matched control group (left side), along with example photographs of the emotional and non-emotional stimuli (right side). Note that the ASD group recognized more non-emotions but fewer emotions than the controls.

This difficulty with recognizing emotion has obvious and potentially serious implications for social interactions – for example, if the emotion of another cannot be easily identified, then it is hard to adjust any interaction accordingly. While it is certainly true that this plays a role in the problems experienced by people with ASD, it should be pointed out that it is not the case that individuals with ASD do not understand the existence of emotions in others, nor their implications for those other people; rather individuals with ASD just have difficulty in recognizing the nature of these emotions and why they may be felt at that time (Begeer et al., 2006; Hobson, 1986) – that is to say, individuals with ASD do not display psychopathic tendencies just because of a problem with emotional recognition in others.

It is also becoming increasingly clear that emotional-recognition deficits in ASD are not as straightforward as was once believed, with much recent literature demonstrating that such problems are highly paradigm-dependent (see Jemel et al., 2006). For example, data suggests that the use of dynamic stimuli (e.g. moving images) may give a more accurate measure of emotion recognition in those with ASD and the use static stimuli (e.g. photographs) could underestimate ability in this area. Dynamic stimuli may offer additional information (such as temporal cues), that is absent in static photographs and this may facilitate the recognition of emotions (Moore, 2001). One study has explored recognition of emotions from dynamic facial stimuli in children with ASD (Gepner et al., 2001) and noted that these children performed similarly to control groups in recognizing basic mental states. Similarly, when additional situational information (i.e. what the context of the emotion was) is made available, emotional recognition in those with ASD is improved (Klin et al., 2002). Thus, as dynamic stimuli bear a greater similarity to what we experience in everyday life, they may allow a better estimation of emotional recognition (see Hubert et al., 2007; Klin et al., 2002; Moore, 2001). Of course, this set of findings begs the question of why individuals with ASD have difficulty with static stimuli, but, whatever the reason for this, it may not be primarily an emotional recognition problem – but could be a problem with generalizing from one situation in which an emotion is recognized (real life) to another (and experiment).

A 'lower-level' processing problem that may explain some of difficulties that people with ASD have in recognizing facial expressions of emotion is that their eye contact is often not maintained or is very poor by typical standards (Zwaigenbaum et al., 2005). Additionally, there often is difficulty attending to the expressions of emotion displayed in the eye region (see Baron-Cohen et al., 2001). Of course, it could be that eye contact is a secondary problem, resulting from social phobias and some researchers have suggested that individuals with ASD may actively avoid eye contact (Buitelaar, 1995; Volkmar & Mayes, 1990). Whether the eye-contact problems precede or are a result of, social interaction deficits, they may increase problems in the emotional recognition domain for those with ASD, as much emotional information is contained in the eye region (see Bal et al., 2010; Song et al., 2012).

Communication – verbal and nonverbal

Problems in this domain of functioning are experienced by all people diagnosed with ASD as this also forms a necessary part of the diagnostic criteria. Of course, 'communication' as a set of behaviours is difficult to distinguish from 'social interaction' and, partly for this reason, the DSM-5 has merged these two categories that were separate in the DSM-IV-TR. However, this is merely a clustering or categorization problem that will be discussed in more detail next and it does not negate the fact that there are differences in functioning across these behaviours in ASD. In fact, this set of behaviours involves impairments in the individuals' being able to 'converse' with another person and to share ideas with them. It should be noted that such interactions do not necessarily have to be verbal in nature (although deficits in social language formed part of the DSM-IV-TR, only nonverbal communication forms part of the DSM-5). However, it is clear that both areas of functioning are associated with ASD.

In terms of nonverbal communication, there are numerous behaviours that are altered or deficient in those with ASD and which may impact on their ability to communicate with others. For example, as noted previously, initiating and maintaining eye-contact (Baron-Cohen et al., 2001; Zwaigenbaum et al., 2005) and joint attention (Mundy et al., 1994) is less pronounced in individuals with ASD. Pre-verbal and very young children with ASD are less likely to communicate through pointing, looking or physically interacting with another person (Stone et al., 1997). The behavioural differences related to nonverbal communication can often persist into adulthood. Deficits in nonverbal communication are even noted in verbally able individuals with ASD (notably those with the diagnosis of Asperger syndrome); for example there are differences in body posture (body language) during communication in these individuals (Gillberg, 1998; Szatmari et al., 1995).

In terms of verbal communication, in extreme cases, there may be no speech at all. Rapin (1996a) noted that around 50% of individuals with low-functioning ASD were non-verbal, but also noted that only 6% of high-functioning individuals were similarly non-verbal. Other individuals with ASD display 'echolalia', which involves the repetition of words or phrases, often out of context. This phenomenon has been noted in up to 75% of all persons with ASD (Rutter, 1968), although it is important to note that the function of this behaviour may differ across individuals with ASD (Schuler, 1979).

Those individuals with ASD who are verbal and do engage in verbal conversations may produce inappropriately long responses to questions, as if reciting from a book or learned text (see Capps et al., 1998, for a discussion of narrative structure in those with ASD). The speech patterns of individuals with ASD also may contain nonstandard semantics and pragmatics (see Baron-Cohen, 1988; de Villiers et al., 2010; Tager-Flusberg, 1981, for further discussion). Spoken-sentence construction can often involve missing words, most often those words that serve a 'linking' function (e.g. instead of: 'I want to go to the shop', individuals with ASD might say: 'want go shop') and there can be difficulties with employing appropriate pronouns, such as 'I' or 'you' (Bartak & Rutter, 1974; Hobson et al., 2010). Problems may also occur with understanding ambiguous statements, such as that contained in the classic example: 'there was a tear in her eye' (see Happé, 1997); in this case, the word 'tear', can have two meanings (a saline liquid or an injury) that are often determined by the context in which the word occurs and some theories, for example, weak central coherence theory (Happé, 1995), posit a difficulty with contextual control of behaviours for people with ASD (see Chapter 3).

For those individuals who do possess highly functional speech, this speech can be defined as: idiosyncratic – involving odd linguistic constructions; neologistic – involving the use of new/nonexistent words and dysprosdic – being unable to utilize typical speech patterns (Schreibman, 2005). For instance, people with ASD can display odd enunciation of words, often tending to over-emphasize some words in their speech. They also may well as have non-typical intonation in their speech (Sharda et al., 2010) and prosody or speech rhythm problems (Grossman et al., 2010; Peppé et al., 2011).

However, it is in the area of social language that many high-functioning individuals with ASD show quite different patterns of speech to people without ASD, particularly with respect to the range of social language that they possess (Rutter, 1978; Sigman et al., 1992). These individuals have also been shown to struggle socially when they are required to respond to questions and comments and typically contribute fewer narratives of personal experience, compared to than typically developing children (Capps et al., 1998; Losh & Capps, 2006).

Behavioural and cognitive flexibility

This area covers a wide range of problems, is displayed by almost all with ASD and predicts its severity (Bodfish et al., 2000); a lack of flexibility, in some form, being required for the diagnosis of ASD (DSM-IV-TR, DSM-5). This lack of flexibility (rigidity) can be manifest either in the emission of stereotyped behaviours (Bodfish et al., 2000), in terms of the range of behaviours that they are willing and/or able to emit (Hughes et al., 1994) or in terms of an ability to adapt to changing circumstance (Dover & LeCouteur, 2007). Such behaviours are not unique to ASD, but are seen up to three times more often in those with ASD than in those with developmental delays or intellectual disabilities (Bodfish et al., 2000; Matson et al., 1996). This is true for any age group at which the comparison is made: children (Militerni et al., 2002), adolescents (Bradley et al., 2004) or adults (Bodfish et al., 2000). However, the nature of the repetitive behaviour displayed alters with age and intellectual impairment (Militerni et al., 2002).

In younger children with ASD, these repetitive tendencies are often manifest by the emission of highly stereotyped behaviours, such as hand flapping (Ornitz, 1974) or other movement disorders (Matson et al., 1996; Militerni et al., 2002). For example, Militerni et al. (2002) noted between 62–76% of younger children with ASD evidenced some form of movement disturbance (see also Bradley et al., 2004, for a similar estimate). These levels are much higher for almost all forms of movement disturbance than in matched controls with other disorders, with the exception of dyskinetic or involuntary movement problems (Matson et al., 1996).

Over time, these simple stereotyped behaviours can be replaced by complex routines or rituals (see Turner-Brown et al., 2011), with Militerni et al. (2002) noting that only 23% of older children with ASD displayed movement disturbances, a figure that corresponds closely with that suggested by Bodfish et al. (2000). This can result in behaviours that appear akin to those noted in obsessive compulsive problems (see the section that follows on co-morbidities), with 94% of adults with ASD displaying some compulsive behaviour (see Bodfish et al., 2000; Bradley et al., 2004). Thus, adults with ASD often have a tendency to display highly repetitive and complex chains of behaviours (Bodfish et al., 2000; Lopez et al., 2005), have a marked preference for sameness over change (Rutter, 1978) and do not cope very well with changes in their environment (see Dover & LeCouteur, 2007, for a description of this problem). This complex set of repetitive behaviours is more likely to be seen in those with higher levels of intellectual functioning (Militerni et al., 2002).

Problems with behavioural flexibility can also be manifest in a disrupted ability to alter behaviours that been previously learned when the rule governing the outcome of that behaviour changes (Hughes et al., 1994; Lopez et al., 2005), often resulting in poor ability to adapt to novelty and learn new ways of doing things (Reed et al., 2013a). However, individuals with ASD can also develop intense nonclinical fascinations with particular areas of interest: in younger children this could be an extreme interest in *Thomas the Tank Engine* and the like (Lord et al., 2011); but, as the person gets older, this can also involve developing a great and detailed knowledge of systems, such as the weather, timetables or the functions of numbers (e.g. Rapin & Dunn, 1997). Clearly, rather than being an impairment, this knowledge could sometimes can be an advantage. However, its association with a range of other co-morbid problems suggests that this 'processing advantage', in some circumstances, also comes at some cost to the individual (see Bradley et al., 2004 and next, for a list of conditions associated with stereotypy and ASD, such as anxiety, self-injury and depression).

Sensory responsiveness

Individuals with ASD often display differentially sensitized reactions to particular stimuli drawn from particular modalities (Donnellan et al., 2012; Robertson & Simmons, 2013; Wing et al., 2011). These altered sensory sensitivities can take the form of either: hyper-sensitivity, which is an increased reaction to a stimulus, such as agitation, distress or withdrawal in response to certain cues or a hypo-sensitivity, which

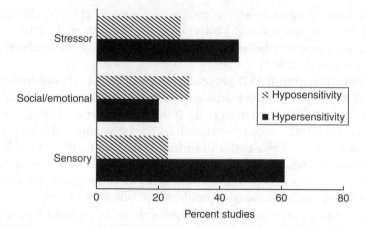

Figure 2.2   Percentage of studies whose participants with ASD showed an increased (hypersensitivity) or a decreased (hyposensitivity) physiological reaction to various kinds of stimuli (from data presented by Lydon et al., 2015).

is a diminished reaction to a cue, such as a lack of reaction to speech or pain (Liss et al., 2006). Although now included as a diagnostic indicator of ASD in the DSM-5, whereas it was not included in the DSM-IV-TR or the ICD-10, it should be noted that this area of altered functioning is not an essential request for the presence of ASD. Nevertheless, the prevalence of such differential sensory sensitivity in those with ASD is high: Leekam et al. (2007) noting that 90% of young individuals with ASD in their sample displayed at least one sensory problem and Billstedt et al. (2007) noting that such sensory sensitivities endured into adult, with 95% of their sample still displaying differential sensitivity at 30 years old (although other reports have noted that sensory problems are more typical in younger individuals, see Militerni et al., 2002).

Figure 2.2 shows the percentage of studies that have shown either hyper- or hyposensitivity to a range of different types of stimuli. Inspection of these data from a review of physiological reactions to stimuli conducted by Lydon et al. (2015) shows that enhanced or diminished sensory responsiveness have been shown to stimuli drawn from almost any modality (see also Donnellan et al., 2010; Liss et al., 2006). For example, they may develop either aversions or a lack of responsiveness to loud noises (Khalfa et al., 2004), bright lights (see Simmons et al., 2009, for a review of vision in individuals with ASD) or touch (Cascio et al., 2008). Although either hyper- or hyposensitivity to sensory input can be seen, Woodard et al. (2012) noted that hyperreactivity to sensory stimuli appears to be more common and Lydon et al. (2015) in a review noted that hyper-sensitivity was noted in around 60% of studies, hypo-reactivity in 20% of studies and qualitatively different sensitivity and reactions in 20% of reports. Certainly, many people with ASD are more sensitive than controls to slight differences in the salience of stimuli (Leader et al., 2009; Plaisted et al., 1998). In terms of painful stimuli, the literature throws out an apparent contradiction (see Lydon et al., 2015), in that Tordjman et al. (2009) noted reduced (hypo-sensitive) behavioural responsiveness to pain, but Spratt et al. (2012) noting increased (hyper-sensitive) physiological responses to pain. Of course the former reaction may be muted by the lack of need to socially interact (see section previously), but this discrepancy remains to be resolved.

In addition to hyper- and hypo-sensitivity to physical stimulation, Donnellan et al. (2010), in reviewing the self-report literature form individuals with ASD, noted that there are many descriptions of a lack of sensation from social cues. Lydon et al. (2015) suggested that, where a sensory abnormality to a social cue is noted using physiological measures (heart rate, blood pressure etc.), the difference is typically in the direction of hypo-sensitivity. Given the discussion previously, these results are, perhaps, not overly surprising.

It is unclear whether such sensory reactivities are unique to individuals with ASD. On the one hand, abnormal sensory reactions are heightened in ASD compared to other developmental disorders (e.g. Klintwall et al., 2011; Wiggins et al., 2009); whereas on the other, Rogers and Ozonoff (2005) have noted the presence of sensory sensitivities in many groups of children with different developmental- and physical-disabilities. This issue of the relative specificity of sensory reactivity for ASD has yet to be resolved.

Externalizing behaviours

A high proportion of individuals with ASD display behaviours, such as aggression, that are problematic for themselves and others. Such problem or challenging behaviours are not uniquely predictive of ASD, but these behaviours are a core ASD symptom according to the ICD-10 (if not the DSM-5). For example, self-injurious behaviours or self-harm occurs in around 10% of individuals with ASD (Schroeder et al., 1978) and over 30% of individuals with ASD display aggressive behaviours directed at others (Hartley et al., 2008; Matson & Rivet, 2008). Externalizing behaviours can also include disturbances in sleep patterns (Bradley et al., 2004), which are very common in children with ASD – occurring among between 40 and 80% of children with ASD (Couturier et al., 2005) and also in disordered eating patterns and studies have suggested that 58% of people with ASD have an eating disorder (Bradley et al., 2004) and that people with ASD account for around 25% of adults (especially adolescent females) with an eating disorder (Råstam et al., 2003).

Externalizing behaviours can cause severe problems for the families of children with ASD and they are one of the factors most strongly related to high levels of parenting stress (see Osborne, 2009; Osborne & Reed, 2009a, for reviews). In slightly older children, these behaviours can lead to high levels of school exclusion or prevent a child with ASD from gaining a school placement at all (Kupersmidt & DeRosier, 2004). Although these problems tend to disappear over time, as they do with most children (Taylor & Seltzer, 2011), if they are not addressed in those with ASD early in their development then they can be extremely problematic as the child grows larger and stronger (see Osborne & Reed, 2009b). While there is some suggestion that these behaviours may lead to problems with the criminal justice system for some individuals with ASD, especially in terms of crimes against the person (see Cheely et al., 2012), such occurrences are actually quite rare and, in fact, there is little evidence that individuals with ASD are over-represented in the prison system (e.g. Ghaziuddin et al., 1991; Mouridsen, 2012).

Summary

The preceding text has been a brief overview of the types of problem commonly seen in those with ASD and also of the key areas of functioning that any intervention will need to consider. Of course, the existence of a deficit in any one of these domains, on

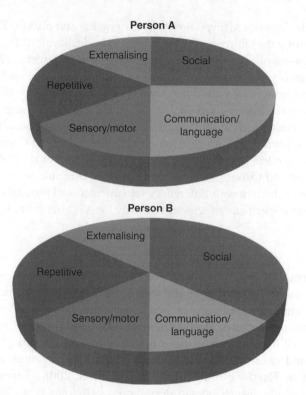

Figure 2.3 Schematic representation of the distribution of symptoms across two hypothetical people diagnosed with ASD. The person represented in the top panel has typical autism, the person at the bottom has Asperger Syndrome (DSM-IV) or Social Communication Disorder (DSM-5).

its own, does not indicate the presence of ASD – ASD is a syndrome of associated problems. However, individuals with ASD will each display some subset of these problems, although, on such an individual level, the behaviours and deficits displayed by those with ASD manifest enormous variation and aspects of ASD may vary in the degree to which they are present in one individual compared to another.

The degree to which these behaviours/deficits are present can make individuals display very different forms of ASD. Figure 2.3 presents a conceptualization of the way in which two hypothetical individuals diagnosed with ASD display quite different patterns of behaviours from one another – the larger the slice of the pie chart, the greater the level of problem experienced in that domain. In this example, the individual represented in the top panel of Figure 2.3 has a range of difficulties across the social, communication/language, repetitive interests, sensory/motor and externalizing behaviour problems domains; whereas the individual represented in the bottom panel experiences great difficulty in dealing with social interactions, has high levels of behavioural inflexibility and motor problems, but has relatively good communication/language ability and few externalizing behaviour problems. According to previous methods of classifying these individuals (e.g. DSM-IV-TR), the person reflected on the top panel would have been given a label of 'autism' and the person on the bottom would have received a label of 'Asperger syndrome', according to newer methods (DSM-5) both would have ASD but with different descriptors. Whatever the method of classification – both have radically different presenting symptoms, but both have an ASD. It is also important to note that these key elements can also vary according to the changes or pressures that the individual with ASD undergoes, such as their physical and psychological maturation and, of course, the behaviours that are displayed will alter according to the circumstances and experiences of the individual with an ASD.

The presence of these central issues for individuals with ASD is reflected in the many psychometric tools that have been developed to help in the assessment, diagnosis and measurement of ASD. Table 2.2 displays a range of these tools and highlights the domains that they cover. In addition, it displays the psychometric properties of the tools, such as their: reliability (freedom from error), validity (whether they assess ASD like other measures), sensitivity (whether they identify all cases of ASD) and specificity (whether they only identify cases of ASD and exclude other disorders). Their performance on these aspects can be evaluated by using criteria (Osborne et al., 2014): less than 0.30 is poor, 0.30–0.69 is moderate and more than 0.70 is good. It can be seen that there is a great variation in the domains covered by the tools and different evaluations of a person's ASD will be obtained through the use of each tool. Some directly examine the child (e.g. ADOS) and some rely on informant-observations, such as a parent (ADI or GARS) or a teacher (DISCO). The different methods of obtaining data – through rating by observer, teacher or parent, will also introduce differences in the extent to which various behaviours are reported. For example, Reed and Osborne (2013) noted differences in ratings given to the behaviours of children with ASD by parents and teachers, in the same context. Thus, as well as the range of functioning domains covered and the psychometric properties, of these instruments, attention also needs to be given to who is doing the assessment.

Co-Morbid and Secondary Symptoms of ASD

In addition to these core areas of altered functioning for individuals with ASD, there are many co-morbid and secondary conditions. 'Co-morbidity' refers to the co-existence of two or more psychiatric or psychological diagnoses for the same individual. These conditions are not part of the disorder itself and would not form part of any clinical assessment of the severity of type of ASD, but they are commonly exhibited by individuals with ASD. Some of these co-morbid problems are highly correlated ASD (such as intellectual disability, motor problems) and some seem to emerge as a result of ASD (e.g. depression and anxiety) – this latter group of co-morbidities could also be termed as 'secondary' problems as they appear to be a product of ASD. The current section focuses on some of the more commonly occurring of these co-morbid/secondary problems and also attempts to differentiate which of these problems co-occur with ASD and which may be a secondary problem of ASD.

There have been numerous reviews of the typical co-morbid problems facing individuals with ASD (e.g. Billstedt, 2000; Bradley et al., 2004; Hayashida et al., 2010; Leyfer et al. 2006; Matson & Nebel-Schwalm, 2007; Simonoff et al., 2008). In fact, the range of co-morbid disorders often found along with ASD is very wide and includes many general medical or physiological conditions, such as bowel problems,

Table 2.2 A sample of common assessment tools for ASD, showing the domains covered, along with an indication of the psychometric properties of each tool (derived from their manuals and a variety of assessment articles).

Measure	Domains	Type of Test	Internal Reliability	Inter-rater Reliability	Sensitivity	Specificity
Autism Diagnosis Observation Schedule *Lord et al.* (1999)	communication reciprocal social interaction	professional observation of child 30–60 min	Moderate–Good	Good	Good	Good
Autism Diagnostic Interview *Lord et al.* (1994)	social communication repetitive	professional interview with parent 90–150 min	Moderate–Good	Good	Good	Moderate
Childhood Autism Rating Scale *Schopler et al.* (1988)	autism	parent completed questionnaire 5–10 min	Good	Good	Good	Good
Social Communication Questionnaire *Rutter et al.* (2003)	social communication repetitive	parent completed questionnaire 10 min	Good		Good	Good
Gilliam Autism Rating Scale *Gilliam* (1995)	social interaction communication stereotyped behaviour developmental disturbances	parent completed questionnaire 10–15 min	Good		Good	Moderate
Autism Behaviour Checklist *Krug et al.* (1980)	sensory relating body/object use language social self-help	parent completed questionnaire 10–15 min	Good	Good	Good	Good
Diagnostic Interview for Social and Communication Disorders *Wing et al.* (2002)	core symptoms plus many associated problems	professional semi-structured interview with parent 120–180 min		Good	Good	Good

White = strong effect; light grey = moderate effect; dark grey = weak effect; black = no data.

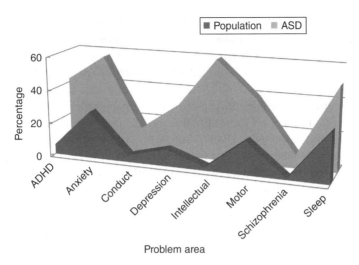

Figure 2.4 Estimated prevalence of co-morbidities of ASD, along with the prevalence of those disorders in the general population. In almost all cases, those with ASD have a greater chance of displaying the problem than those in the general population.

(Wang et al., 2011), Fragile-X syndrome (Hatton et al., 2006), auto-immune problems (Ashwood & Van de Water, 2004) and epilepsy (Canitano, 2007). In addition, there are a range of co-morbid issues that are more commonly covered by psychological approaches to ASD: including motor problems (Ming et al., 2007) and learning disabilities (Matson & Nebel-Schwalm, 2007), as well as emergent secondary psychological problems, including depression and mood disorders (Bradley et al., 2004; Ghaziuddin et al., 1998) and anxiety disorders (Bradley et al., 2004; White et al., 2009).

It is currently estimated that around 70% of people with an ASD have at least one co-morbid disorder (Bradley et al., 2004) and that over 40% have more than one co-morbidity (Simonoff et al., 2008). Unfortunately, there is little research on the co-occurrence of various co-morbidities. It should also quickly be noted that these figures are subject to quite large variation, depending on the criteria adopted for diagnosing such problems (including those criteria used for diagnosing an ASD). An estimate of the prevalence of these co-morbidities for ASD derived from combining the results of several reviews of the area (Bradley et al., 2004; Hayashida et al., 2010; Leyfer et al., 2006; Simonoff et al., 2008) are shown in Figure 2.4 and these prevalence figures suggest a high chance of additional problems being experienced by individuals with ASD. The current section focuses on those co-morbidities more typically falling under the remit of psycho-social treatments and their implications for such interventions for ASD.

Motor and coordination problems

A relatively high proportion of individuals with ASD exhibit pronounced motor deficits and physical problems with coordination (Ming et al., 2007; Rapin, 1996a). For example, Ming et al. (2007) noted that between 20 and 40% of children with ASD displayed some form of motor problem. Similarly, Rapin (1996a) found that about

25% of children with ASD presented with hypotonia (a decreased muscle tone) and that around 30% of high-functioning and 75% of low-functioning, children with ASD exhibited limb apraxia (an inability to execute learned movements).

The existence of motor problems can reflect an atypical neurological development pattern and include disruptions in the achievement of motor-milestones (Teitelbaum et al., 1988) and the prolonged presence of primary reflex responses (Minderaa et al., 1985). Such motor co-morbidity was initially commented on by both Kanner (1943; 1944) and Asperger (1944), but, since these initial descriptions of the condition, motor problems have not found its way into the classification systems and it should be noted that individuals with several other developmental and intellectual disorders display associated motor problems to a greater extent than those with ASD (Bodfish et al., 2000).

The most prevalent motor problems for people with ASD are clumsiness (Miyahara et al., 1997), disturbances in grasping movements (Ghaziuddin & Butler, 1998; Mari et al., 2003) and dyspraxia and gross and fine motor movement deficits (Dziuk et al., 2007; Noterdaeme et al., 2002), as well as impaired postural control (Kohen-Raz et al., 1992; Minshew et al., 2004) and gait disturbances (Rinehart et al., 2006) such as 'toe-walking', which is not entirely uncommon as walking develops (Ming et al., 2007; Weber, 1978).

Learning disabilities

A learning disability is taken to be present if a person's IQ is lower than 70 and there are also poor adaptive behavioural abilities that have persisted since before the age of 18 years (see Matson & Nebel-Schwalm, 2007). It is estimated that between 65 and 85% of persons with ASD have such a learning disability (Gillberg & Coleman, 2000; LaMalfa et al., 2004; Matson & Shoemaker, 2009; O'Brien & Pearson, 2004). The co-morbidity of ASD with learning disabilities is important in the context of intervention, as Eaves and Ho (2008) noted that there was a better prognosis in adulthood for those individuals with ASD who had higher IQ scores and Shattuck et al. (2007) noted worse prognosis for those with poorer IQ scores. Quite clearly, the presence of a learning disability will impact on the choice of intervention and will also impact on the prognosis for the person with ASD (these issues will be taken up in further detail in later chapters).

The distribution of this co-morbidity differs across the different severities and types of ASD: around 70% of those diagnosed with 'autism' (according to the DSM-IV-TR) also have a learning disability; but only around 25–40% of those with Pervasive Developmental Disorder Not Otherwise Specified (PDD:NOS) have such a low IQ (Baird et al., 2000; Chakrabarti & Fombonne, 2001). The DSM-IV-TR diagnosis of Asperger syndrome specifically excluded the possibility of a learning disability. The presence of a co-morbid learning disability may also impact the form of behaviours that are exhibited by the individual with ASD. Those with lower IQs being more likely to display motor stereotypy, poor language and worse social abilities; whereas, individuals with higher IQs tend to display more complex rituals and abnormal language patterns (O'Brien & Pearson, 2004). These groups of individuals with high- and low-functioning ASD are also differentially susceptible to typical/atypical depression and various form of anxiety disorder (see sections that follow).

Depression and mood disorders

Depression is now recognized as a major co-morbid problem for those with ASD (Bradley et al., 2004; Ghaziuddin et al., 1998). It occurs with a variety of probabilities, depending on the presence of a number of factors, such as the severity of ASD and the presence of other co-morbidities such as intellectual disabilities. In fact, the two factors that appear to contribute to the emergence of co-morbid depression are the person's age and their level of functioning; depression being more likely to be diagnosed higher-functioning and older individuals (Ghaziuddin et al., 1998).

In terms of level of functioning, around only 2% of those who were given a DSM-IV-TR diagnosis of 'autism' and who could be characterized as 'lower-functioning', display depression (Ghaziuddin et al., 1992). In contrast, co-morbid depression has been noted in between 30 and 50% of those who could be characterized as 'higher-functioning' (Bradley et al., 2004; Ghaziuddin et al., 1992) – a figure much in excess of the rates of depression noted for 'typical' community samples (Ghaziuddin et al., 1998). The association of depression with levels of ASD functioning, being greater in those with higher IQs and those with Asperger syndrome, is consistent with the literature showing depression is not found so strongly in those with intellectual disabilities (Matson et al., 1998).

It should be noted that the higher rate of co-morbid depression for those with higher-functioning ASD may be, at least in part, due to the difficulties in measuring depression in lower-functioning individuals, who tend to be nonverbal and who find it more difficult to report such internalizing problems. In these individuals, it may also be that the presentation of depression is atypical (Lainhart & Folstein, 1994) and consequently is under-diagnosed (Magnuson & Constantino, 2011). In response to this problem, Matson and Nebel-Schwalm (2007) have suggested an enhanced focus on the somatic symptoms of depression as an indicator of its presence for the low-functioning ASD population, rather than use of traditional methods that often rely on self-report and insight (see also Deprey & Ozonoff, 2009).

Depression is also taken to rise with age for higher-functioning individuals with ASD and ranges from around 15% in 9–14 year olds, to around 30% in older individuals (see Ghaziuddin et al., 1998; Leyfer et al., 2006). Of course, depression in children may be atypically expressed, being more closely linked with externalizing behaviours (see Kim et al., 2000), a finding that has certainly been noted for those with ASD (Ghaziuddin et al., 2002). When taking account of symptoms such as irritability, Hayashida et al. (2010) noted that around 20% of pre-school children with ASD displayed some signs of depression. It is hard to dissociate irritability from other externalizing behaviours, which may in itself, lead to diagnostic over-shadowing, but this potential under-reporting of depression, due to focusing on age-inappropriate symptoms, must be considered a possibility in accounting for age-differential rates of reported depression in ASD.

Tantam (1991; Adreau & Stella, 2001) noted that the impact of levels of ASD severity in relation to the development of co-morbid depression, was greatest on transition from one school to another (typically, from primary to secondary schools). In line with this observation, Ghaziuddin and Greden (1998) suggested that stress-related life events, which occur with a greater frequency as individual get older, such as a change of educational programme, are one trigger of depression for those with

ASD. Indeed, such transitions may be linked with changes in routine and the range of social coping skills required by an individual's situation, both of which are associated with the development of anxiety in individuals with ASD (Bellini, 2006; Browning et al., 2009).

Anxiety

Anxiety disorders are a very common co-morbid problem for those with ASD (see MacNeil, et al., 2009; White et al., 2009, for reviews and discussion) and levels of anxiety are elevated in those with ASD relative to the general population (Bellini, 2004; Kim et al., 2000). The range of types of anxiety experienced by those with ASD is also great and includes: specific phobias, general anxiety, separation anxiety, obsessive-compulsive disorder and social anxiety (see Leyfer et al., 2006). Again, some of these forms of anxiety disorder are difficult to disentangle from the core symptoms of ASD, such as ritualistic behaviours and avoidance of social contact (see Tantam, 2000), making precise estimations of co-morbidity difficult.

In younger individuals with ASD, anywhere between 20% (reported by Kim et al., 2000, for 4–6 year-olds) and 30–45% (reported by Hayashida et al., 2010, for 3–6 year-olds), display some form of anxiety disorder. In older individuals with ASD, these prevalence values are higher and can vary from between 42% (Bradley et al., 2004; Simonoff et al., 2008) and 55% (de Bruin et al., 2007) of the population. Obviously, the types of measurement taken and the specific anxieties targeted, play a substantial role in generating this variation in rate.

In terms of the impact of the type of ASD on the likelihood of observing an anxiety disorder, there is some evidence that such co-morbid problems are more often seen in those with higher-functioning ASD (or the previous Asperger syndrome diagnosis) than in lower-functioning ASD and that anxieties co-vary with cognitive functioning levels (see Matson & Shoemaker, 2009). However, as with depression, the form of the anxiety displayed can alter across groups with different levels of functioning. Higher functioning individuals with ASD are more likely to display typical signs of anxiety disorder, while those who have lower levels of functioning, tend to display externalizing behaviours associated with their anxiety (see White et al., 2009), which may mask the occurrence of anxiety in these latter groups.

Summary

The presence of co-morbidities and secondary problems is an increasingly recognized issue for understanding the nature and treatment of ASD. For individuals with ASD, there is a very high chance that they will have a co-morbid problem – for lower-functioning individuals this is likely to be an intellectual disability or motor problem and for higher-functioning individuals this is likely to be a secondary psychological issue, such as depression or anxiety. In fact, rates of occurrence of the co-morbid disorder (e.g. depression) are often higher in those with ASD than they are in the general population (see Gillott & Standen, 2007; Kim et al., 2000). Despite this high level of psychological disorder, there is no greater take-up of services by those with ASD than by individuals without the condition (Brugha et al., 2009). This suggests that these co-morbid problems may exert a long-lasting and deleterious impact on prognosis for

ASD. Moreover, the presence of a co-morbid disorder can present difficulties for the diagnosis and assessment of an ASD and also for selecting the most appropriate intervention for that individual – although as shall be seen in subsequent chapters, few comprehensive interventions for ASD actually tackle such co-morbid problems directly.

Despite a growing amount being known about the nature of the conditions that are co-morbid with ASD, there remain significant difficulties in detecting co-morbid conditions (see Deprey & Ozonoff, 2009, for an overview). For example, when the presenting symptoms of two disorders are similar to one another (e.g. rituals in ASD and in OCD), those presenting symptoms are attributed to one of the disorders. This can lead to an under-reporting of co-morbid conditions, as the symptoms are attributed to one disorder only, which prevents the other disorder from being recognized – that is, 'diagnostic overshadowing' occurs (Mason & Scior, 2004). In extreme cases, the diagnostic criteria for ASD preclude the co-diagnosis of other problems, such as attention deficit hyperactivity disorder (Reiersen & Todd, 2008; Volkmer et al., 1997), even though these two disorders are thought to co-exist in around 26% of those with ASD (Goldstein & Schwebach, 2004; see Billstedt, 2000, for a review).

Additionally, the presence of one disorder can distort the symptoms that would typically occur as the result of a second, co-exiting, disorder (see Kim et al., 2000; Lainhart & Folstein, 1994), which, again, can lead to under-reporting of co-morbid problems, as the symptoms resulting from the co-morbidity often fail to be recognized (Magnuson & Constantino, 2011).

These issues raise numerous problems for the measurement of symptoms in particular groups of individuals with ASD (Leyfer et al., 2006; Matson & Nebel-Schwalm, 2007) and the reliability and validity of measurement instruments for the co-morbid problem should always be noted for the ASD population.

The Unitary Nature of Autism Spectrum Disorders

The current section now turns to address the issue of such as how ASD-related behaviours should be clustered. That is, it considers the issue of how ASD should be defined and, whether it can be considered to be a unitary disorder. This debate has practical relevance to those concerned with offering treatment, as the delivery of an intervention, certainly in many educational settings, is often dependent on a diagnosis of ASD being obtained. Thus, the way in which ASD is conceptualized will impact how and when, treatment is offered.

Identifying the manner in which the individual behaviours connected with ASD should be formulated to indicate the presence of the syndrome, as opposed to a collection of unrelated problems, actually proves to be a difficult thing to achieve. Firstly, there is considerable debate as to whether ASD should be considered as a disorder with a common core or as a group of separate, though somewhat similar, problems. It has even been suggested that these key behaviours are sometimes not strongly related to one another, leading to the suggestion that ASD is not a unitary condition (see Skuse, 2009; Verhoeff, 2012; for discussions). The move from the five different disorders detailed in the DSM-IV-TR (Autism, Asperger syndrome, Rett syndrome, Childhood Disintegrative Disorder and PDD:NOS) to the one spectrum condition – Autism Spectrum Disorders – in the DSM-5, suggests one solution to this problem, that is, to define it away. Secondly, while it is true that across the population of individuals with ASD as a whole, there are some consistencies in the manifestation of these behaviours (Mandy & Skuse, 2008; Wing & Gould, 1979), the way in which these behaviours are clustered in the definition of ASD has changed over time – and there is no reason to suppose that this protean nature will not continue into the future. The current section presents a range of alternative conceptions of the relationship of these behaviours in the definition of the ASD syndrome.

The dyad versus the triad

The assumption that there is a tendency for the problems central to ASD to occur together has formed the basis for most views of the nature of ASD and has exerted a strong influence over classification systems and practice. The two most commonly accepted views of the key clusters of symptoms that define ASD can be referred to as the 'dyad' (e.g. DSM-5; Kanner, 1944) and the 'triad' (DSM-IV-TR; Wing & Gould, 1979). The suggestion of two potential conceptions of ASD may come as a surprise to many whose thinking about these conditions and their treatment has long been embedded in the notion of a 'triad' of impairments (after Wing & Gould, 1979). However, while the 'triad' model has been an extremely important conception for ASD, it should be remembered that this is just one of many possible conceptions (another being that there is no need for a belief in the unitary nature of ASD at all). In fact, the 'triad' is not the only view, nor is it necessarily the most contemporarily supported model for characterizing ASD (see DSM-5; Wing et al., 2011). At various times, one or other of these conceptions has held sway (see Figure 2.5 for a schematic representation).

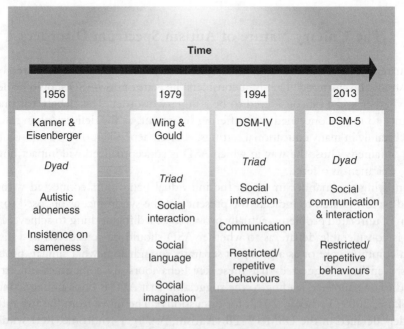

Figure 2.5　Schematic representation of the changing conception of ASD, note how the conceptualization seems to alter between a 'dyadic' and a 'triadic' view of the disorder.

Historically, the Kannerian conception of 'autism' involved the presence two key-clusters of behaviours: an 'autistic aloneness' and an 'insistence on sameness' (Kanner & Eisenberg, 1956). It was only later in the development of the field that the notion of a 'triad of impairments' gained currency, mainly as the result of the seminal work of Wing and Gould (1979). This triad of impairments being in: social interaction, social language (speech and symbolic representation) and social imagination.

It is worth noting that the triad conception was developed on the basis of a particular sample and using classification systems that may not be in contemporary use. Wing and Gould (1979) screened the records of 914 children (aged 2–18 years) out of a total of about 35 000 records in a London borough. Of these children, 132, who were in special education, were identified as having one of the three of problems of the triad. Of these 132 children, 78 were identified as displaying inappropriate social interactions and 54 had appropriate interactions. Of the 78 children with inappropriate social interactions, 55% also displayed symbolic problems, 55% displayed speech difficulties and 75% exhibited repetitive behaviours. These percentages compared to: 16, 33 and 7%, respectively, having these problems, for the 54 children with appropriate social interactions. These results suggested to Wing and Gould (1979) that these three symptoms tended to cluster together and that this triadic cluster could be termed ASD.

Although this view of the nature of ASD gained strong acceptance in the field and heavily influenced thinking about the development of diagnostic systems (e.g. DSM-IV-TR), the limitations of the Wing and Gould (1979) study have not gone unnoticed. For example, the sampling techniques, the diagnostic approach employed to categorize pupils as having an ASD (Happé & Ronald, 2008) and the rather primitive statistical techniques used to produce this clustering (see Eaves et al., 1994; van Lang et al., 2006), are just two methodological problems raised concerning the initial work and which have fed into a re-examination of the 'triad' conception. For instance, it has been recognized that the degree to which these clusters of behaviours actually co-occur with one another will depend upon the nature of the samples employed (Caron & Rutter, 1991) and also on the measurement tools used to assess them (Ozonoff et al., 2005).

There are several strong sets of considerations that produce cause for re-consideration of the triad view of ASD. Firstly, from a practical-intervention perspective, the triad approach does little to encompass the wide range of core and co-morbid issues related to ASD. Secondly, it is not clear that the three aspects of ASD are as strongly connected with one another as was suggested by Wing and Gould (1979). For example, Happé et al. (2006) found little evidence in a nonclinical sample that the three sets of behaviours noted in the triad were strongly related to one another. There often being a separation between the socially related behaviours and those concerned with repetitive behaviours. For example, Ronald et al. (2006) noted only moderate correlations between socially related behaviours and repetitive behaviours and also similar modest correlations between social behaviours and language (see Happé & Ronald, 2008, for a review). Of course, the fact that the different aspects of the triad may be fractionable, exist in isolation from one another and have different causes, does not necessarily mean that they cannot co-occur in some individuals to produce ASD, but it is becoming increasingly clear that these behaviours often are present separate from one another.

Thirdly, notwithstanding the data presented by Ronald et al. (2006), several authors have suggested that the conceptions of impairments in social interaction and social communication are not easily dissociable from one another, with particular symptoms being categorized almost randomly into either of these two domains (Lord et al., 2012). Moreover, it is unclear whether one of these two areas of problem is not responsible for the presence of the other. There is a growing body of evidence that suggests that individuals with ASD, rather than lacking social insight, may lack the necessary language to talk about how they experience the social world (see Tager-Flusberg, 1992). This suggests that those with ASD may not be socially impaired, but, instead, may be impaired only by a lack of appropriate language through which to talk about emotional and cognitive states (see also Sigman et al., 1992). Such a view implies that ASD should not be defined in terms of a 'poverty of emotional understanding' (e.g. Frith, 1991), but should instead be characterized as expressing emotion unconventionally due to language deficits (e.g. Sigman et al., 1992).

For such reasons, among others, the DSM-5 has reduced the triad of impairments to a binary set – social communication impairments (involving both social interaction and communication) and behavioural rigidity. In this, it is an irony that, after over half a century of debate, with the literature suggesting a broader and broader range of problems implicated in ASD, the diagnostic conceptualisation of ASD has returned to the rather narrower view suggested by Kanner and Eisenberger (1956).

Beyond the dyad and triad

As implied previously, while the DSM-5 has retreated from three to two behavioural clusters by which to characterize ASD, developments in the behaviours that interventions for people with ASD focus upon (e.g. Hess et al., 2008; Lovaas, 1987) and the evidence on the prevalence of different problems associated with ASD (see the previous sections of this chapter), suggests a need to expand, rather than contract, the conception of the behaviours considered as being relevant to ASD. The issue of importance in the current context is that the 'dyad' or 'triad' are only two possible methods of combining these behavioural sets.

A range of factor-analytic studies have shown anything from one (Constantino et al., 2004) to eight (Siegel et al., 1986) clusters of behaviours associated with ASD (see Happé & Roland, 2008; Mandy & Skuse, 2008, for reviews). In fairness, most of these factor-analytic studies do suggest two factors: a social factor and a nonsocial factor (Mandy & Skuse, 2008), supporting the DSM-5 system, over the DSM-IV-TR system (see also Lord et al., 2012, for further support of the DSM-5). Of course, this is not necessarily saying too much, as these categories are so broad to be largely unhelpful in practical terms. For example, language ability and eye-gaze both count as social behaviours in many of these factor analytic studies, but would be treated very differently in intervention terms. Moreover, the factor-analytic approach is fraught with considerable problems and is hugely dependent on the measurement scales used (some will show more overlap with one another than other) and on the factor analytic techniques employed.

It has been suggested that the 'triad' could actually be a 'square' (see Table 2.1; nobody has yet suggested a pentangle or other polygonal-shaped model!), but there is less consensus about which behaviours should form the other corner stone of the square; some have suggested that it could be sensory problems (e.g. Cashin et al., 2009; Donnellan et al., 2012) and some have suggested that it should be behavioural problems (e.g. ICD 10; Matson et al., 2008). However, it is unclear that other problems should not be included also, such as motor and sensory problems (see Donnellan et al., 2012; Ming et al., 2007; Miyahara et al., 1997). According to Wing and Gould (1979) these problems were not extensive enough to warrant inclusion in the triad used for diagnosis. However, recent evidence has suggested otherwise and has indicated that many such behaviours are often present in ASD (Donnellan et al., 2012; Matson et al., 2008; Ming et al., 2007). These additional problem behaviours provide some of the most serious causes for concern for interventions (see Lovaas, 1987). For example, clinically significant levels of externalizing behaviour problems, such as aggression, have been noted in one third of children with ASD (Hartley et al., 2008; Matson et al., 2008) and are a common source of family stress (see Osborne, 2009). Similarly, sensory sensitivities are seen in around 70% individuals with ASD (Baranek et al., 2006) and there are strong correlations between the presence of sensory problems and ASD traits (Robertson & Simmons, 2013).

From this discussion, one conclusion seems unavoidable – it is completely unclear which behaviours should be considered as core to ASD, how these behaviour interact with one another and which are a product of those core behaviours. In a sense, one cannot help but agree with Baron (2008, p. 271) that: '…a prolific literature made possible by an expenditure of enormous professional and financial resources has not yet yielded a clearer picture of core aspects…'

Implications for ASD Interventions

It can be seen that the extremely wide range of behaviours associated with ASD extends way beyond the typical triad or dyad. Indeed, the existence of so many associated behaviours has placed considerable pressure on the notion that ASD is a unitary condition (see Happé et al., 2006; Skuse, 2009). Moreover, any attempt to produce a greater degree of unity regarding the nature of ASD may prompt a search for a single cause, which is now regarded as somewhat futile and wasteful exercise, certainly in the context of interventions (e.g. Happé et al., 2006; Skuse, 2009).

Nevertheless, it has to be acknowledged that it is the presence of such clusters of behaviours that is critical in identifying an individual as having an ASD and it is important to note that no one of these behaviours or deficits, in themselves, is unique to ASD. Thus, as a term, 'Autism Spectrum Disorders' is a helpful heuristic for thinking about the types of problem that an individual might have, but, at a practical level, this is as far as the notion that ASD as single entity goes. Instead, for development of an intervention, ASD may best be regarded as a set of individual presentations of behaviours, of great variety and variation, which bear some family resemblance to one another across individuals.

It may be wisest to note that, while ASD is not solely characterized by the presence of particular behaviours and deficits, it is these individual behaviours that require intervention, not the clusters. This is not a condition with a particular cause, like a virus, but one that may have myriad causes and manifestations and whose disparate symptoms are those that require intervention.

3

The Relationship of Theory and Interventions for ASD

Separate from the clinical goal of specifying the problems that an intervention must address (see Chapter 2), it has been a research goal to discover the 'root' problem of ASD through exploring the putative core deficits of the condition. This approach has been sold mostly on the hope that developing such an understanding will facilitate a cure for ASD or, at least, more effective management strategies. Much of this effort has been devoted to discovering what might be termed 'within-person' deficits – that is, identifying the nature of the cognitive, genetic and neuro-physiological structure of an individual with ASD (see Rimland, 1964, for an early example). However, such a within-person perspective stands in contrast to many approaches that have provided techniques for ASD intervention and which tend to focus on 'extra-person' or 'environmental' factors (see Chapter 1). This contrast pits two great conceptions of developmental psychology against one another and the aetiologies of these approaches to development are informative in the context of understanding interventions for ASD.

The central European 'structural' approach, including that of Piaget, has dominated almost all contemporary theoretical thinking about ASD. This conception resonates well with the developmental-stage (or modularity) accounts (e.g. Fodor, 1983; Leslie, 1987) that underlay theory of mind views of ASD (Baron-Cohen et al., 1985) and also with some aspects of the original Kanner/Asperger conceptualizations of the condition. In contrast, the eastern European learning-social approach of Pavlov and Vygotsky, although not widely applied by western psychology to ASD, reflects earlier conceptions of a childhood developmental problem, highly similar to ASD, that was first noted and described by Yarmolenko (1926). This learning approach later finds echoes in the behavioural-based approaches for ASD that are currently dominant in interventions for the condition (e.g. Greer, 1997; Lovaas, 1987).

Thus, there is a tension between these two views – one dominant in terms of understanding the nature of ASD (the within-person cognitive account) and the other

Interventions for Autism: Evidence for Educational and Clinical Practice, First Edition. Phil Reed.
© 2016 John Wiley & Sons, Ltd. Published 2016 by John Wiley & Sons, Ltd.

dominant in terms of interventions to manage the condition (the 'learning-social' approach). To help understand some of the points of contention between these approaches in the context of the treatment of ASD, the current chapter places this discussion within a brief historical analysis of ASD. This is important, not only to place the interventions to be discussed later in this text into context, but also in order to aid subsequent understanding of such interventions and their associated controversies.

Within-Person Theories of ASD

The within-person cognitive view of ASD is associated with the current interpretations that have been placed on the works of Kanner (1943; 1944) and Asperger (1944), which are generally taken as the genesis of modern understanding of ASD (see Frith, 1989; Wing, 1981). Although it is not entirely clear that these undoubted pioneers did always view ASD as a 'within-child' problem (see Kanner, 1949), the work of Kanner and Asperger has certainly come to be viewed from the perspective of a developmental psychology that places emphasis on structural changes 'within' the child to explain developmental trends (e.g. Genetic Epistemology; Piaget, 1968; but see Drash & Tudor, 2004; Osborne & Reed, 2009a, for different alternative discussions in the context of ASD). Certainly, such perceptions have exerted an influence over views such as the 'Modularity of Mind' hypothesis (Fodor, 1983; Leslie, 1987), which, in turn, have impacted on much contemporary theorizing about ASD (see Baron-Cohen et al., 1985).

This is not to say that there is only one within-person view of ASD; in fact, there are many types of within-person theory. Firstly, there are views that may be termed 'higher-level' accounts and which often place social and communication deficits at their core (Baron-Cohen et al., 1985; Hobson, 1986). Secondly, 'low-level' views often suggest that the myriad behaviours exhibited by individuals with ASD (Chapter 2) are the product of simple alterations in cognitive processing (Happé, 1997; Hughes et al., 1984). The current section briefly outlines the basic tenets of several of the most commonly cited such theories and documents the relationship between these theories and the interventions derived directly from them.

High-level theories

High-level views focus on the complex behaviours and abilities that are often present with ASD and assume that these deficits and differences are the result of a mechanism that controls these high-level or complex behaviours, rather than resulting from simpler processing problems (see Gomez, 2009 and Reed, 2014, for debates). Although there are many such 'high-level' theories of ASD, some of which are very specific to particular skills, such as imitation (e.g. the 'broken mirror' hypothesis; Williams et al., 2001), two high-level views in particular have been widely researched: (i) the notion of specific social-emotional deficits (e.g. Hobson, 1986) and (ii) the notion of a 'theory of mind' deficit (e.g. Baron-Cohen et al., 1985).

Social-affective impairments   Theories in this category hold that ASD is the result of an inability to process social-emotional information (Hobson, 1986) and that a lack of ability to understand the publically observable correlates of an emotion in others could be central to the difficulties experienced by individuals with ASD (Grelotti et al., 2002). Failing to accurately recognize and/or label these emotions from the visual cues available, not only could result in deficits in social communication and social awkwardness, but also could provoke isolation and drive the interests of the individual with these difficulties toward the non-social (Dawson et al., 2005).

The data generated by Hobson et al. (1988) regarding the reduced of adolescents with ASD to recognize emotions from photographs (discussed in Chapter 2) is often cited in support of this view. Also in support of this views are findings from a range of other studies. For example, young people with ASD have been shown to have a reduced ability to mimic emotions (McIntosh et al., 2006) and they are poor at matching emotional expressions (Celani et al., 1999), especially when they are incongruent to any semantic content that accompanies the expression (Stewart et al., 2013).

However, the central findings underlying this theory have not gone unchallenged. Both Grecucci et al. (2013) and Hubert et al. (2009) found no particular differences in the abilities of individuals with ASD to recognize emotion. Similarly, Gepner et al. (2001) found that a group of individuals with ASD performed as well as a control group in recognizing basic mental states, when they were presented with moving faces as opposed to static images. In general, it has been found that situations with more ecological validity facilitate emotional recognition in those with ASD (Klin et al., 2002; Moore, 2001; see Jemel et al., 2006, for a review). For example, whereas many early studies of the ability of people with ASD to recognize emotions relied on static stimuli (photographs and line drawings; e.g. Hobson et al., 1998), it is now thought that dynamic stimuli (video clips) may give a more accurate measure of emotional recognition abilities in those with ASD (Klin et al., 2002; Moore, 2001). Indeed, when there are other sources of information about the emotion, such as contextual or semantic (see Stewart et al., 2013), the presumed deficit does not appear to be readily apparent. Thus, the status of this formally widespread theoretical view of ASD is currently unclear

Theory of mind deficits   Theory of mind refers to the ability to understand what others are thinking (see Baron-Cohen, 2000, for a discussion). The notion originally derives from work conducted with non-human primates (Premack & Woodruff, 1978), conducted in order to determine whether chimpanzees could understand what a person was thinking. The notion that one organism can have insight into what another organism was thinking was subsequently applied to humans by Wimmer and Perner (1983), who showed that this ability, typically, develops by about 3 years old (see Tager-Flusberg, 2007, for a review relative to ASD). The development of these theory-of-mind abilities was integrated into the 'modularity of mind' hypothesis by Leslie (1987). Modularity of mind suggests that 'mind' consists of separate innate structures that have established evolutionary-developed functional purposes (see Fodor, 1983) and that these modules are engaged at certain points in an individual's development. In respect to ASD, Baron-Cohen et al. (1985) suggested the module responsible for theory-of-mind abilities was not activated, resulting in a social-understanding deficit in these individuals.

There are a number of ways in which a theory-of-mind ability is tested, which are important for understanding the literature relating to ASD. The 'false belief task' attempts to assess if one individual can understand that a second individual may hold a different (and false) view from that held by the first individual. An example of such a test is the 'Sally-Ann' task (e.g. Wimmer & Perner, 1983). Here, the participant witnesses one puppet (Sally) place a marble under a particular cup. Sally then is taken away and a second puppet, Ann, is shown moving the marble from the original cup and placing it under a different cup. The participant is then asked where Sally will look for the marble when she comes back. If the participant can think like Sally, then they will indicate the original cup, but, if they cannot place themselves in the mental position of Sally and, instead, rely only on the information that they themselves have (but which Sally does not), then the participant will indicate the second cup where they know the marble to be.

A further method of assessing theory-of-mind ability is the 'appearance-reality' task (e.g. Gopnik & Astington, 1988). In one variant of this task, a participant is shown a tube of Smarties® and is asked to say what is in the tube. After they have responded, usually by saying 'Smarties', they are shown that it actually contains pencils. The participant is then asked what somebody else would say was in the tube. If they are able to understand the perspective of another, the participant will say 'Smarties'; but, they will say 'pencils', if they do not have the ability to understand that somebody else does not have the knowledge that they, themselves, possess.

In applying tests such as the Sally-Ann task to individuals with ASD, Baron-Cohen et al. (1985) found children with ASD do not pass such tests as easily as controls and suggested that these results support the view that the theory of mind modules were not activated in these individuals, producing the social and emotional difficulties noted in ASD. This view has achieved a large degree of acceptance and discussion in relation to the theoretical understanding of ASD.

However, in response to a number of subsequent criticisms, this view has undergone some modification from its original form. In response to the suggestion that the view is actually rather circular (i.e. it essentially re-describes a central problem for ASD and then suggests that this problem is the cause of ASD), Baron-Cohen (2002) postulated the 'extreme male brain' theory, which attempts to suggest why theory-of-mind deficits emerge. This theory postulates that the mechanisms responsible for theory-of-mind abilities are impaired by too much pre-natal testosterone. In support of this view, Lutchmaya et al. (2002) correlated levels of eye-contact made by children and their pre-natal testosterone levels in their mothers and found a negative relationship between the two; the more testosterone, the worse was the eye-contact and these data are shown in Figure 3.1. However, examination of these shows that this effect is stronger in males than females – suggesting that these data, at best, indicate that males suffer more from ASD like symptoms (i.e. lower levels of eye-contact) and also tend to have more testosterone, than females. Moreover, Falter et al. (2008) found no relationship between enhanced visual search for details (another ASD trait) and pre-natal testosterone levels, which would have been expected. Thus, it is difficult to draw strong conclusions about this view (see Baron-Cohen, 2009, for a summary of the problems and issues associated with this view).

It should also be noted that, although the theory-of-mind view is able to accommodate (or, at least, describe) the social and emotional problems noted in ASD, a number of problems remain associated with this theory. Firstly, it struggles to

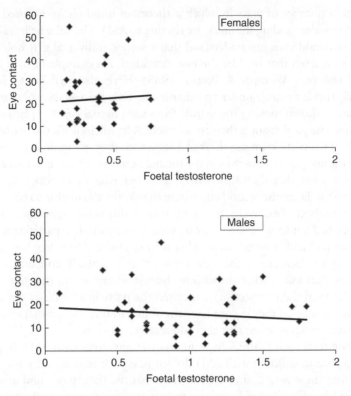

Figure 3.1 Data from study reported by Lutchmaya et al. (2002) showing the relationship between foetal testosterone levels and eye-contact at 12 months of age for females (top) and for males (bottom). Note that the negative relationship only holds for males.

accommodate directly many other aspects of ASD outlined in the current Chapter 2, such as the restricted range of interests and areas of enhanced processing that can occur (see Frith & Happé, 1994; Hobson, 2005). Moreover, such theory-of-mind problems are not limited to individuals with ASD and they occur in many other disorders, such as schizophrenia, with very different presenting symptoms (see Tager-Flusberg, 2007). This makes an appeal to theory-of-mind deficits as a cause of the unique symptoms of ASD less attractive from a theoretical perspective.

Interventions In terms of the development of interventions to help people with ASD, the two sets of high-level views mentioned previously are so similar in terms of the behaviours that they attempt to explain, that discussion of the interventions derived from these accounts is easier to present combined. Of course, there are a vast array of treatments targeted at the social-skills deficits of individuals with ASD (see White et al., 2007, for a review) and many of these interventions have had some success when implemented outside of the clinic or laboratory setting (see Kasari & Patterson, 2012; McConnell, 2002, for reviews). However, it is completely unclear that these interventions owe anything to the specific high-level theoretical perspectives outlined previously and these treatments cannot reasonably be said to suggest that high-level views have promoted the development of interventions for ASD.

There have been some attempts to develop interventions based directly on the view that there is an emotional-recognition deficit in individuals with ASD (see Baron-Cohen et al., 2012, for an overview). For example, LaCava et al. (2010) reported some success in using computers to teach emotional recognition in children with ASD. Similarly, Golan et al. (2010) reported that watching an animation designed to enhance emotional understanding, improved the emotional recognition of children with ASD, compared to similar children with ASD who had not seen the animation. However, it not clear whether such interventions are effective because they impact directly on the child's emotional recognition or whether the improvements come about through some nonspecific effects on the child's ability to complete the experimental tasks; that is, there is almost no evidence about the generalized impacts of the task beyond the experimental test. Neither is it clear whether such improvements in emotional recognition would be seen outside the very narrow range of high-functioning individuals that have been tested (i.e. the verbal IQs of the participants were about 100 or average for the population as a whole, which is clearly not the case for most individuals with ASD).

There also have been a few attempts to develop teaching interventions directly to overcome theory-of-mind problems. As an aside, it may be worth noting that the relative lack of intervention development may reflect the view implicit to this theory that the deficit it is innate and not necessarily subject to remediation through learning processes (see Gómez, 2009; Leslie, 1987). However, Fisher and Happé (2005) examined specific training procedures to develop a theory-of-mind ability in individuals with ASD, but found that, while this specific ability could be improved, it led to no improvements in the participants' performance on other related tasks. Similarly, Begeer et al. (2011) noted that a specific theory-of-mind training programme could produce improvements in the children's theory-of-mind abilities, but that this did not lead to any improvements in empathy or in their social behaviours outside of the test context. This lack of generalization in improvements was also noted by McGregory et al. (1998). Thus, these almost entirely laboratory-based efforts have shown only limited effectiveness, with little evidence for any impact beyond the confines of the task employed.

In summary, there is little strong evidence regarding the impacts of such interventions. Moreover, although some of this intervention work has cited these higher-level theories, it is unclear whether these theories were at all necessary for the development of these interventions; it cannot be said with any degree of conviction that these interventions have been the direct result of either of these two theories. Rather, there are many interventions targeting social skills in those with ASD, such as social stories (e.g. Chan et al., 2011) or naturalistic behavioural interventions (e.g. Ingersoll, 2012), that have resulted from the simple recognition of the problems displayed by persons with ASD and which did not require such high-level theories for their development.

Low-level theories

There are a large number of views regarding the ways in which cognitive processing could be disrupted or different in individuals with ASD. In fact, it is possible to point to disturbances at almost every stage of the processing channel (see Figure 3.2):

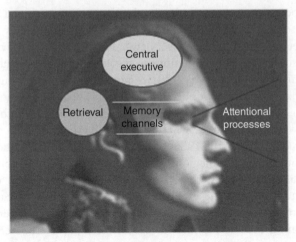

Figure 3.2 Different aspects of the processing channel that have been implicated in ASD – from problems with attention, through issues with memory, and central executive control of information, to issues with storage and retrieval of information.

from early attention problems connected with eye gaze (e.g. Dube & McIlvane, 1999), through restrictions to working memory capacity (e.g. Boucher et al., 2012) and central executive control of working memory processing (e.g. Hughes et al., 1994), to late-stage retrieval problems, involving both the formation of connection between individual elements of complex stimuli (e.g. Happé, 1997) and the potential for over-generalized suppression of non-target material during retrieval (e.g. Reed, 2011).

What all of these views share is the assumption that a simple (or several simple) deficits in basic learning and memory mechanisms might underlie the range of problems seen in ASD. Perhaps the two most developed of these views are the Executive Dysfunction view (see Hughes et al., 1994) and the Weak Central Coherence view (Happé, 1997). These will be discussed here, mainly with respect to their impact on the development of interventions. Perhaps from the outset it should be stated that, despite having some aspects to recommend them, unfortunately neither of these low-level views has led to the development of a specific intervention.

Executive dysfunction 'Executive function' is a term used to refer to a very wide set of cognitive processes: for example, planning actions, impulse control, working memory, behaviour inhibition, flexibility and action monitoring (Miyake et al., 2000). Individuals with ASD have been noted to display problems with many aspects of their executive function (see Hill, 2004, for a review) and perform worse in tasks that are assumed to need executive function compared to matched control groups (Hughes et al., 1994; Ozonoff et al., 1991). In particular, many of these tasks involve either problem-solving abilities (Ozonoff et al., 1991) or displaying mental or behavioural flexibility (Reed et al., 2011; Yerys et al., 2009).

Hill (2004) has reviewed the evidence relating to such problems in people with ASD, especially from procedures involving tests for cognitive and behavioural flexibility; such as extra-dimensional shift and the Wisconsin card sort, tasks. In a typical card-sorting test, individuals are asked to learn to perform a task according to one rule and then the rule is changed without telling the participant. Usually, individuals with ASD take longer to learn the new task than matched controls (e.g. Reed et al., 2011; Yerys et al., 2009).

It has been suggested that this underlying central deficit may be associated with the development of repetitive behaviours (Yerys et al., 2009) and may also be the source of some higher-order deficits, such as language and social-affective, problems, which are taken to require good executive function (see Hill, 2004). However, a major problem for this view (as with the theory of mind view) is that many clinical groups also show executive dysfunction, such as individuals with schizophrenia and also those with acquired brain injury, but these groups do not always show the precise social deficits seen in those with ASD. Again, this makes the attribution of ASD symptoms to this deficit less than compelling

Weak Central Coherence Theory   This view suggests that individuals with ASD display difficulties in utilizing the whole context of a situation in controlling their behaviour. It is thought that this processing difference can explain both impaired functioning in situations where many cues are needed to control behaviour appropriately, such as in social situations and it may also explain the enhanced performances sometimes seen in those with ASD, such as in tasks where attention to detail is needed (Frith & Happé, 1994).

In support of this view, Happé (1997) reported that individuals with ASD often mispronounce homophones, apparently not being able to utilize the context in which the word appears to determine the correct pronunciation. For example, in the phrase: 'there was a tear in her eye', the errors noted in pronouncing the word 'tear', depend on not using the context of the whole sentence. However, as noted previously, this difference in processing also can mean that, in some circumstances, individuals with ASD show a performance advantage: for example, in tasks that depend on specific aspects of a situation to control behaviour, such as search for embedded figures, individuals with ASD often show enhanced speed of recognition (Shah & Frith, 1983).

A key problematic issue for Weak Central Coherence theory is that the mechanism that produces this processing style is not clear. It is not specified whether central coherence problems result from a deficit in contextual control *per se* or whether they reflect an enhancement of elemental control. Moreover, while it is assumed that such processing differences underlie the complex social and emotional difficulties experienced by people with ASD, there is no strong direct evidence that this is the case. There are equally plausible explanations in the literature, some of which have been discussed previously. Nevertheless, the Weak Central Coherence theory does offer an explanation of both attenuated and enhanced processing patterns in ASD.

Evaluation of within-person views of ASD

The problems with the 'higher-level' views is that they struggle to explain the range of issues involved in ASD beyond the social-emotional problems; whereas, the 'low-level' theories often struggle to offer a convincing case that the myriad of issues seen in ASD can be reduced to such a simple problem. It may be the case that the very notion that ASD can be related to a single deficit has had its moment in time. While it is certainly true that many interesting experiments have been conducted to examine this issue, most of this attempt has been flawed in both conception and conclusion: conception, as these views typically assume that there is a single deficit that will explain the problem of ASD, whereas it is highly unlikely that this is true and conclusion, because the resultant theories never accommodate the full picture of ASD. Even the most originally vociferous of proponents of such single within-person theories now admit that the search for a single cause or discovery of the unitary nature of ASD, has failed or is misguided (see Happé et al., 2006; Skuse, 2009, for discussions).

More importantly for the current context, these within-person deficit-approaches have strikingly failed to provide the promised therapeutic breakthroughs. Such 'within-child' conceptualizations of ASD make manipulations to alleviate any difficulties resulting from ASD particularly problematic. Not only are there uncertainties in accurate identification of the putative structures that may have 'mal-functioned' to produce the ASD (see Levy et al., 2009, for a review of the myriad of suggested genetic and physiological associations with ASD), but also, if such 'within-child' issues were to be identified, it is far from clear what could be done to remedy any such a 'faulty' structures. Given these considerations, the current chapter next turns to the alternative conception of ASD – that which relates it to the environment.

Learning-Social and Behavioural Views of ASD

In contrast to the within-person view, there is another history to the understanding ASD that is not much discussed and has its roots in Soviet Psychology (Vygotsky, 1987; Yarmelenko, 1926), American Behaviourism (Skinner, 1938; Watson, 1913) and British Empiricism and Common Sense Philosophy (Hume, 1748; Reid, 1785). All of these views place the drivers and causes of an individual's development in the environment and, thus, within easier range of an intervention.

This learning-social conceptualization offers a different and perhaps more liberating, view of ASD, certainly in terms of the development of possible treatments. This view suggests that the problems often associated with ASD result, at least in part, from the interactions between the individual with ASD with their environment and produces the consequent hope that an alteration in that environment will aid the individual's ability to function. It is certainly true to say that, in contrast to the previous within-person views, the leaning-social approach and learning theory in general (see Boakes, 1984; Bolles, 1979, for reviews), has facilitated the development of many interventions for ASD (e.g. Greer, 1997; Lovaas, 1987; 2003; Sundberg & Michael, 2001; Sundberg & Partington, 1998).

Appreciating why a learning-social approach has produced such a number of interventions, whereas other approaches have not, involves appreciating some fundamental conceptual and historical contrasts between the views of ASD taken by learning-social and within-person psychological approaches. There are three areas of importance in this regard: (i) the theoretical and conceptual differences between these approaches – most notably in terms of the focus of the learning-social views on an environmental explanation of behaviour; (ii) differences in the conception of the nature of ASD – especially in relation to whether ASD is regarded as a single entity or a collection of fractionable behaviours and (iii) the relationship between basic and applied work in the two domains. These issues will be discussed, in turn, as the conceptual issues raised are important to understand for the following chapters that deal with interventions in detail.

Environment and learning

The extent to which environmental determinants are brought to the fore in learning-social thinking (especially by behavioural approaches), compared to the role given to such factors in 'within-child' deficits approaches, is clearly a prime area that can be used to explain the differences in the development of interventions based on these approaches. However, it should also be noted that the focus on individual behaviours, rather than on a single central cause of ASD, is also important in the greater development of interventions by the learning-social approaches.

The view that ASD can be manageable through environmental alterations is important to many contemporary interventions, whether behavioural (e.g. Lovaas, 2003) or more generally learning–social in nature (e.g. Mesibov et al., 2004; Rogers et al., 1986). Certainly, focus on this relationship was of critical importance in developing behavioural approaches to the treatment of the condition (see Ferster, 1961; Lovaas, 1987; 2003). As shall be seen, a key characteristic of a behavioural approach to intervention is a focus on identifying the environmental variables that control behaviours (see Chapter 4). This view is a radical departure from 'traditional' approaches to ASD that place the deficits firmly 'within' the child.

In addition, much learning-social and behavioural work conducted on ASD has focused on investigating the control of specific behaviours associated with ASD, rather than addressing a putative central core underlying the condition. Thus, a key difference between behavioural and cognitive approaches is that the former characterize ASD *de facto* as a collection of potentially separable behaviours rather than as a unitary disorder (see Chapter 2 for discussion of this general issue). Such a focus on individual behaviours may also facilitate the development of interventions, as a focus on a complex and diffuse unitary disorder may obscure and make intervention development practically difficult.

In support of the view that a focus on manipulable relationships between ASD-associated behaviours and the environment is a more practical route to travel for those seeking an intervention, it is easy to point to the far greater amount of research regarding interventions stemming from behavioural learning theory (see Chapters 4–6), compared to that stemming from a 'within-child' view (see previously). Moreover, in those interventions used for ASD that have a non-behavioural background and that have been reasonably well researched (see Chapters 7–11), there is little in the way of particular theoretical underpinning that demands the adoption of a within-person deficit view of ASD.

Historical behavioural conceptions of ASD

The current section aims to give a selective overview of the historical development of ASD research in order to demonstrate the important early influences of learning-social and behavioural psychology to the field and the subsequent focus by learning theorists on understanding the key components of ASD as separable behaviours. The numbers of papers that contain the term 'autism' increased over the hundred years from 1870 (when publishing in psychology started in relative earnest) to mid-1960s (when the 'within-child' view of ASD came to be more widely accepted). This increase is as nothing compared to the subsequent 'autism industry' in publishing that has occurred since this period. However, the first mentions of 'autism' within the developmental and learning research literature are made remarkably early and predate the often stated attribution (e.g. see Frith, 1989) of the identification of what is now known as ASD to Kanner (1943) and Asperger (1944). Thus, as well as offering support for the previous 'alternative' conception of ASD, this brief history also charts the initial rise and fall of behavioural theorizing about ASD, prior to its phoenix-like re-emergence in the 1980s as a much-used intervention strategy.

Early learning theory views of ASD   The articles published during the early (pre-Kanner) period largely use the term 'autism' in the context of adult schizophrenic behaviours and these articles relate little to the contemporary conceptual understanding of ASD. However, it should be noted that many early mentions of 'autism' from researchers from a social-learning or behavioural background do appear to offer insights of relevance today. Notably, these mentions are made by psychologists working in the Soviet Union (see McLeish, 1975, for a review of this tradition), in which the behaviour described in relation to 'autism' is extremely relevant to contemporary ideas of ASD.

Possibly the first article to use the term 'autism' in a context that is clearly separable from its connection to schizophrenia and that shows clear connection with the childhood problems that are conceptualized as ASD today, is that by Yarmolenko (1926). This article presents a three-stage model of learning in children, based on the associative-learning principles of Pavlovian or Classical Conditioning (Pavlov, 1926; see Gray, 1980, for a review).

The left panel of Figure 3.3 shows a representation of a classical conditioning procedure. The pairings of an initially neutral stimulus (a 'conditioned stimulus' that does not evoke a particular response), with a subsequent biologically important stimulus (an 'unconditioned stimulus' that does produce a particular response), come to allow the conditioned stimulus to provoke the same types of responses as the unconditioned stimulus. In Yarmolenko's model, there is a period of positive generalized responding to all stimuli that are similar to the conditioned stimulus (i.e. the stimulus that has been learned about). Following this initial generalization from the learned about stimulus, there is a period of generalized inhibition of responding to all stimuli, including the target conditioned stimulus. Finally, a specifically differentiated response develops to the target conditioned stimulus only. Yarmolenko's (1926) model proposes that, in the case of childhood autism, 'unsettled' and/or 'highly changeable' environments disrupt this developmental progress and halt the development at the stage of generalized inhibition. This severely inhibits the range of the child's responsiveness to stimuli and this arrested and restricted development characterizes the reactions noted in children with autism (see the right panel of Figure 3.3 for a conceptualization of this model).

Three things mark out Yarmolenko's (1926) paper as an early example of a learning–theoretic approach to ASD. Firstly, the focus on the environment as a cause of the problem is a key factor in learning theory and this view certainly was heavily

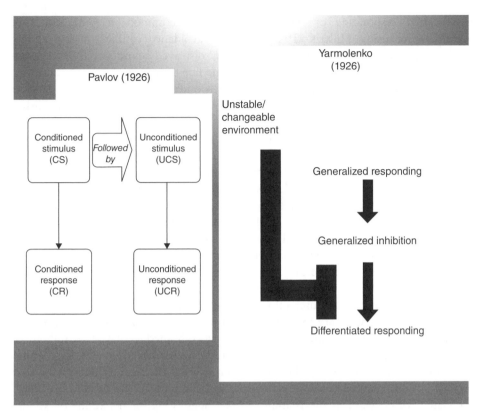

Figure 3.3 The left panel shows a representation of the classical conditioning procedure – responding to a conditioned stimulus (CS) is produced by pairing it with an unconditioned stimulus (UCS) which already produced a response (Pavlov). The right panel shows the suggestion by Yarmolenko regarding how 'unstable environments' can prevent accurate learning about which stimuli to respond to – people in these environments are taken to be blocked at the stage of a generalized inhibition of the CR.

influenced by Bekhterev's concepts of conditioning and generalization (see Hergenhahn, 2009, for an elaboration). Secondly, the focus of the theory on disruptions to typical stimulus control as a key-element of ASD is a mainstay of many recent accounts of ASD given by both contemporary behavioural (see Dube, 2009; Lovaas & Smith, 1989) and cognitive (see Frith & Happé, 1994; Happé, 1997) theorists. Finally, it is marked out as a model of ASD, as understood today, by its focus on particular aspects of behaviour, such as disrupted attention, challenging behaviours and aberrant motor responses that were subsequently developed across Yarmolenko's later career (e.g. Yarmolenko, 1930; 1935a; 1935b). The former two issues are central to several contemporary diagnostic systems (e.g. DSM-V; ICD-10) and motor coordination is a problem for many children with ASD (see Chapter 2).

Following this early Soviet work, there followed a number of papers (e.g. Phillips, 1957; Schafer & Murphy, 1943; Walters, 1958) that attempted to relate specific features of ASD to various aspects of learning. Some of these offered a theoretical interpretation of ASD and, of particular note, Phillips (1957) suggested that the perseverative responding or repetitive behaviours, common in ASD, could be accounted for using Miller's (1944) approach-avoidance conflict theory. Phillips (1957) hypothesized that children with 'autism' displayed a tendency to learn 'over-assertiveness' (a tendency to continue along one line of behaviour) due to an excessive, rather than a deficient, motivation to respond. The theory clearly identifies central problems for ASD as understood today and relates them to well-established principles of learning.

This view of ASD as being connected with an 'excess of motivation', underlay a number of further experimental investigations of the condition and laid some of the foundations for the contemporary views of restricted attention in ASD (e.g. Dube, 2009; Happé, 1997; Lovaas, 1966; Reed & Gibson, 2005). Consideration of a brief sample of these papers demonstrates the importance of learning theory in the research. For example, Schafer and Murphy (1943; see also Walters, 1958) examined the role of 'autism' in responses to a visual figure-ground relationship. This experiment was designed to show whether over-selectivity (a tendency to respond to only one aspect of the environment) could be explained on the basis of an over-sensitivity to reward (see Reed et al., 2011, for a contemporary re-examination of this view). In an ingenious study predating computer morphing, Schafer and Murphy (1943) presented four facial profiles: two were followed by a monetary reward and two by a monetary penalty. Following this training, the profiles were combined to make two ambiguous figures, each containing a profile that had been previously rewarded and one that had previously yielded punishment. The participants were then asked to identify the faces and 80% of the merged faces were reported as belonging to the profiles previously associated with reward in the training series – suggesting, in the terms of Miller's (1944) approach-avoidance theory, that for individuals with autism, it is the reward and not punishment, that was more powerful in driving learning.

Apart from sharing a focus on the role of over-selective responding with contemporary investigations of ASD (see Dube, 2009), these papers show that learning theory played a prominent role in the early theoretical and empirical conceptualizations of ASD. Indeed, some of these studies were conducted on the central aspects of ASD that were clearly initiated prior to the advent of Kanner's seminal work in 1943.

The impact of Kanner   After the publication of Kanner's (1943) description of autism, a much broader variety of theoretical approaches began to offer interpretations of the disorder. In contrast to the early behavioural work, these attempts appear to try to account for the central deficits underlying the problems seen in those with ASD, rather than attempting to account for each specific problem individually. Nevertheless, despite the oft recited impact of the 'cognitive revolution' that occurred just after Kanner's observations (see Mandler, 2002, for an analysis and discussion), behavioural work remained prominent in the analysis of ASD during this period, particularly in stressing the importance of the environment in contributing to the key ASD problems of language and restricted behaviours and attention. Importantly, the idea that these problems were associated with environmental impacts promoted the view that, if some of the problems experienced by those with ASD were related to the environment, then it could be managed by manipulating that environment.

Language   A post-Kannerian behavioural view of ASD was developed by the learning theorist Mowrer (1958) and was related to the apparent reduced levels of communication by individuals with ASD. According to Mowrer (1952), birds developed a 'self-satisfaction' based on their vocal performance, because of the 'subjective comfort' provided by such vocalizing. That is, vocalizing served as 'self-reinforcing' (i.e. a conditioned reinforcer) for the birds, as such noises had been previously associated with a reward, for example, interactions with/feeding by their keeper). Mowrer (1958) suggested that there were a number of applications of this view of the 'self-reinforcing' properties of language to the speech pathologies observed in individuals with ASD. He speculated that the learning processes of human babies may be dependent, to a considerable extent, on the 'reassuring' and 'secondary-reinforcing' properties of the language sounds that they heard and made. If the child with ASD does not gain satisfaction from the contact with others that their vocalizations produce, then language will not become reinforcing and the child will fail to acquire language to any notable degree – that language is simply not reinforcing. Indeed, such observations had fuelled a number of early educational interventions that attempted to make social contact more reinforcing for children with ASD (e.g. Prinsen, 1954) and led to the development of a number of interventions that were developed within schools (e.g. Davison, 1965; Hewett, 1966). In fact, the literature on teaching language to non-humans has proved productive in the development of emotional private event language in children with ASD (see Conallen & Reed, 2012).

Restricted attention and behaviours   Differences in the attention capacities of individuals with ASD also were identified early in the investigation of this area (e.g. Ionasiu et al., 1936; Schafer, & Murphy, 1943; Yarmalenko, 1926). As with the communication deficits, the role of the environment in impacting these behaviours was suggested by many behavioural workers during the immediate post-Kannerian period. Importantly, the investigation of this aspect of ASD corresponded with a strong focus on perceptual learning that was current in learning theory at the time (e.g. Gibson & Walk, 1956). Indeed, the view that there may be individuals who display attention to only a very restricted range of stimuli as a result of their early experiences was a main thrust of early learning theory investigations.

A number of attempts to model the restricted attention to stimuli paid by individuals with ASD were made through various conditioning procedures (e.g. Reynolds, 1961; Smith & Hochberg, 1954; Solley, & Engel, 1960; Walters, 1958). These attempts often did not employ participants with ASD, but tried to show that the behaviours that are typically displayed by such individuals can be seen in the general population under the correct conditions (and, indeed, in other species under those conditions). For example, Walters (1958) conducted an experiment to demonstrate the production of 'autistic-like' effects in problem-solving by generating an over-focus on restricted aspects of complex cues. The task was to locate a simple figure within a larger complex coloured figure (see Figure 3.4). The simple figure could be located in one of two differently coloured areas within the complex figure. During an intervening training period, certain colours were rewarded and other colours were punished. The complex figures were presented again and changes in the responses were observed. There was a significant change in the number of subjects altering their

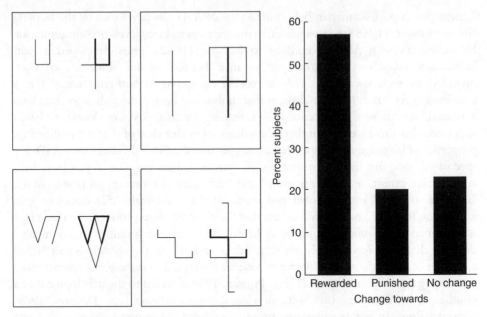

Figure 3.4   Results from the study reported by Walters (1958) in which subjects performed a visual search for patterns (left panel) that were embedded (in bold) in certain colours. Subjects were then rewarded or punished in the presence of those colours. After the conditioning subjects altered their search to the rewarded colours (right panel) – and were shown to be over-selective in their search strategy.

responses toward choosing the location of the rewarded colours, but not away from the punished colours (see also Schafer & Murphy, 1943).

This post-Kannerian learning theory work on restricted attention to environmental stimuli was developed in new and not necessarily helpful, directions by the discovery of the relationship between imprinting (early learning about stimuli) and perceptual learning processes (see Kovach et al., 1966; Sluckin, & Salzen, 1961). Around the same time as the rise of interest in perceptual learning (see Gibson, 1969), Tinbergen and Tinbergen (1972) were exploring an ethological approach to ASD and suggested that learning about which aspects of the social world to respond to was influenced by the feedback that responses to those stimuli received. Tinbergen and Tinbergen (1972) had noted previously that if gull chick's responses to the parent's red beak-spot were not reinforced by the parent gull, then those chicks stopped responding to that parent stimulus and tended to become more and more socially isolated. Tinbergen and Tinbergen (1983) argued that some aspects of ASD also may be produced by a lack of reinforcement for socially directed responses (sometimes characterized as inadequate bonding between child and mother) and could be treated by re-establishing this bond through a 'holding therapy' (see Welsh, 1989, and the current Chapter 10).

From these studies, it can be seen that the interaction between the person with ASD and others was placed quite centrally by many of the early learning-theory conceptions of ASD (e.g. Ferster, 1961; Mowrer, 1958; Tinbergen & Tinbergen, 1983; see also Drash & Tudor, 2004, for a recent example of such a view). It is almost certainly the case that this view created an impression that behavioural psychologists were somehow similar to psychoanalysts (e.g. Bettelheim, 1967), who were perceived as 'blaming' the parent for the child's ASD (see Schopler, 1971). However, it is important to be very clear that the view outlined by Ferster (1961) did not 'blame' the parent for creating the individual's ASD, but holds that the parents' behaviour is just as much a product of the child's as vice versa. This issue is of more than just historical concern. As often happens, a subject's history impacts on the current research imperatives. In this case, it is to be regretted that the focus on the child as the site of the ASD (perhaps stemming from Rimland, 1964) has, until recently, stifled an important area of work – a focus and understanding of the role of family variables. Happily such work is progressing again, often driven by behavioural workers, investigating stress in families (e.g. Lecavalier et al., 2006; Osborne, 2009) or the role of parents (both positive and negative) in the development of their children's behaviours (Osborne et al., 2008a).

Historical primacy of behavioural interventions

The strong link between the aetiology and the treatment of ASD that is clear in the behavioural approach is reflected in the fact that many pieces of behavioural research into ASD are *inter alia* pieces of applied work and the strong theory-action link has facilitated development of behavioural interventions. Although a review of the field's history shows treatments being suggested from many perspectives, the causal understanding regarding particular behaviours gives behavioural psychology some claim to historical precedent for effective ASD treatment. Indeed, some researchers have perceived the prospects for individuals with ASD as being transformed by the development of behavioural interventions. For example, both Lovaas (1987) and McEachlin et al. (1993) quote results from previous intervention studies (e.g. Lotter, 1978; Rutter, 1970; see the current Chapter 1) to support claims that, until the advent of behavioural interventions, the prognosis for children with ASD was very poor.

It might be argued, however, that while it appears to be the case that the earliest *effective* interventions for ASD were derived from a behavioural background, claims for historical precedence *per se* may not be entirely supportable. In fact, examination of the type of interventions discussed in applied papers from the pre-Lovaas (1987) period show an approximately even split between behavioural interventions (behaviour therapy and modification), physiological treatments (pharmacological and psychosurgery; Sauri & De-Onorato, 1955) and cognitive-social interventions (often involving family therapy; Scanlon et al., 1963).

Rather than dating back to the work of Mowrer (1952), many contemporary behavioural interventions actually stem more directly from the work of Ferster (1961), who applied the basic principles of operant conditioning to produce an analysis of the behavioural deficits seen in a child with ASD. Following this analysis, Ferster and Demyer (1962) described how operant conditioning could be used to alter the behavioural repertoires of such children in a controlled environment. In addition, several studies reported the use of learning-social techniques to promote the amelioration of some ASD-related problems. For example, Davison (1965) noted that the treatment of ASD must involve endowing social stimuli with meaning for individuals with ASD.

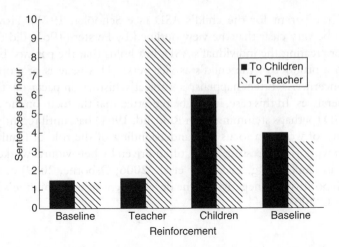

Figure 3.5   Average number of sentences emitted per hour directed towards teachers or towards other children by the pupils in the study reported by Hart and Risley (1975). Experimental conditions were: Baseline = no reinforcement; Teacher = incidental teaching of compound sentences directed to teachers; Children = incidental teaching of compound sentences directed to children.

An important area of concern among early behavioural workers in the field was the deficits in the linguistic abilities of children with ASD and their alleviation (see Mowrer, 1952; 1958). A seminal study in this regard was reported by Lovaas and Newson (1976), who developed a training regime aimed at establishing a verbal repertoire in children with ASD. This regime included the teaching of imitation as an important technique in developing linguistic skills. In Phase 1, food reinforcement was given for any noise made by the child within 5 s of the tutor making a noise. Once verbal behaviour was being emitted a level high enough, the food reward was presented only if, say, the sound 'd' was made within 5 s of the therapist making that sound. Gradually, the temporal window for reinforcement of the subject's imitation of the 'd' verbalization was reduced. Once this sound was acquired, other sounds were gradually added to the repertoire and speech was built up in this manner. There are many such variants in teaching language through the use of reinforcement, which can become quite detailed and sophisticated. Figure 3.5 shows a graphical representation of the results of study of the reinforcement of language by Hart and Risley (1975).

Thus, there is strong evidence for the early development of behaviourally based intervention for ASD. Nevertheless, there were treatments developed that did not stem from this background, which limits the claim for temporal primacy for the behavioural view. As mentioned previously, there are some reports of non-behavioural interventions being developed contemporaneously with these behavioural treatments. However, it is clear that these interventions did not derive from a particular theoretical set of principles, but were more isolated attempts at tackling the disorder. For example, a number of pharmacological interventions were tried for ASD. Ferster and Demyer (1961) noted increased performances of a child with ASD when given prochlorperizine. Freeman et al. (1962; see also Sauri & De-Onorato, 1955; Simmons et al., 1966) discussed experiments with LSD on children with ASD, who were given the drug in their preferred liquid. The effects of administration included facial flush, dilation of pupils, catatonia, ataxia, loss of appetite, desire for physical contact, rapid mood swings from elation to depression, flattening of affect, auditory and visual hallucinations, decreased alertness and increased remoteness. However, the hoped-for change from muteness to speech did not occur.

There were also a number of early approaches to the treatment of ASD that can be said to fall into the 'cognitive-social' category. For example, Scanlon et al. (1963) reported a study to determine the effect of speech therapy on the development of communication and 'unrelatedness', in a group of nonverbal children with ASD. The results suggested that the inclusion of language and speech therapy techniques be considered in developing a treatment program for such children. Similarly, Speers and Lansing (1965) describe a group-approach to the treatment of pre-school children and Kestenberg (1954) presented a case history including details of a social therapy over a several-year period for a child with ASD.

The present section has focused on a brief and selective review of the development of research into ASD in order to try to highlight some conceptual differences between the learning-social-behavioural and within-person approaches to ASD. Although claims to any absolute historical primacy of behavioural psychology in terms of intervention development for ASD may not be supportable as these behavioural approaches were developed at about the same time as many other approaches, there is evidence that claims to intervention effectiveness may have some support. It does appear to be the case that the learning–social–behavioural approach has lent itself much more effectively to the development of effective interventions. Few of the early techniques derived from alternative approaches demonstrated the effectiveness of learning-social approaches, as suggested by Lovaas (1987) and McEachlin et al. (1993). This difference in relative efficacy may reflect the emphasis placed on relating behaviours to the environment and learning; hence, placing them in the arena of the manipulatable. In this regard, it may well be the case that behavioural approaches do have some claim to primacy in terms of demonstrable effectiveness.

Overview

The current chapter has highlighted some of the within-person and 'environmental' approaches to ASD and its treatment. In doing so, a number of issues have been thrown into some focus. In particular, researchers from a cognitive – or within-person perspective – have often attempted to uncover a central core problem from which all of the other symptoms presented by ASD arise. As a consequence, such researchers may often view ASD as a 'unitary' disorder with a common set of defining deficits. However, this approach has not led to the development of many intervention strategies and those which have been developed purportedly based on such theories struggle to demonstrate a strong theory–intervention nexus. A harsh critic might suggest that this approach tends to reduce to the 'academic', in the worst sense of that term; debates about the nature and causes of ASD, being not dissimilar to those medieval debates about 'angels on the heads of pins'.

In contrast, the learning–social view has largely eschewed such debates and conceptions and, by doing so, has provided the hope of improvement and help to those people with ASD and their families. This approach may sit more comfortably with those involved in planning interventions. These practitioners will, necessarily, focus on the behaviours that are displayed by particular individuals and which are causing problems for that individual and their families, irrespective of the conception of the disorder. The history of the topic implies that this learning-social conception appears to be better suited to the development of interventions. Of course, there is an irony in suggesting that, for those most individualistic of people – those with ASD – a 'social' solution is necessary, but perhaps that is the very point of an intervention for this condition.

4

Behavioural Approaches to ASD

Behavioural approaches have provided a rich set of principles and techniques that underlie many widely practiced interventions for Autism Spectrum Disorders (ASD). The past 30 years have seen the emergence of a wide range of such interventions and the current chapter focuses on the more well-established comprehensive behavioural packages that practitioners are likely to come across. These comprehensive approaches employ a wide range of behavioural techniques and attempt to address the full range of behaviours identified as problematic for ASD (see Eikeseth, 2009). They all comprise sets of techniques derived from Applied Behaviour Analysis (ABA), but often place different emphasis on the types of ASD-related behaviours to be targeted.

The range of individual ABA techniques has been very ably set out in numerous texts and manuals (e.g. Catania, 2007; Cooper et al., 2007; Greer, 1997; Reed, 2009; Sarafino, 1996) and the principles that characterize ABA as a discipline were first set out by Baer et al. (1968; see Table 4.1). Comprehensive behavioural approaches (e.g. Greer, 1997; Lovaas, 1981; Sundberg & Partington, 1998) adopt the principles outlined in Table 4.1 as a central guiding tenet, placing them in contrast to other forms of treatment that may use behavioural techniques as part of their approach to ASD or to focus on only one aspect of ASD (see Ospina et al., 2008; Peters-Scheffer et al., 2011; Chapter 1, for discussion). Such single behaviourally based techniques could be integrated into almost any programme of treatment of ASD (see Ospina et al., 2008). Just in terms of behavioural techniques, it is worth noting that Peters-Scheffer et al. (2011) estimated that there over 2000 examples of the use of this approach documented in the literature to help people with ASD. However, the current chapter outlines three well-established forms of comprehensive behavioural treatment package for ASD: the 'UCLA/Lovaas', 'Verbal Behaviour' and 'CABAS®' approaches.

Interventions for Autism: Evidence for Educational and Clinical Practice, First Edition. Phil Reed.
© 2016 John Wiley & Sons, Ltd. Published 2016 by John Wiley & Sons, Ltd.

Table 4.1   Characteristics of Applied Behaviour Analysis, as outlined by Baer, Wolf, and Risley (1968).

Principle	Description
Applied	Targeted behaviours should have social significance for the individual involved.
Behavioural	Environmental alterations and physical actions involved should be systematically and precisely recorded.
Analytic	Carefully collected data should provide clear and convincing evidence that the intervention is responsible for any behaviour change.
Technological	Techniques used should be completely and precisely described and capable of replication by another.
Conceptually Systematic	The programme must be relevant to, and associated with, current established and accepted principles (evidence based).
Effective	Alterations in the targeted behaviour should be 'momentous' to the individual.
Generality	Behaviour change should occur across many settings and environments, and be emitted in the presence of multiple audiences, or should also occur with similar or comparable behaviours.

The UCLA/Lovaas Approach

Despite the number and variety of behavioural interventions for ASD, the programme developed by Lovaas and colleagues at UCLA (e.g. Lovaas, 1987; 2003; Lovaas & Smith, 1989; see Eldevik et al., 2009, for a review) has achieved the greatest degree of evaluation and discussion (see Connor, 1998; Eldevik et al., 2009; Gresham & MacMillan, 1997; Reichow, 2012; Schopler et al., 1989; Smith, 1999). This intervention programme for ASD has provided both hope for parents and a great deal of controversy – and the claims of sometimes spectacular improvements for some children with ASD (e.g. Lovaas, 1987) have been the subject of numerous fierce debates and tirades (see Boyd, 1998; Gresham & MacMillan, 1997).

This approach is sometimes referred to as the 'early intensive behavioural intervention (EIBI)' programme. However, this may be something of a misnomer, as the programme is not necessarily always applied early for younger children (e.g. Eikeseth et al., 2002; Fenske et al., 1985), nor is it always applied intensively for long periods of time (see Reed et al., 2007a). Moreover, other educationally based approaches to treat ASD also are sometimes also applied early and intensively (e.g. Rogers & DiLalla, 1991; Sundberg & Pennington, 1998). For these reasons, the current text will use the more colloquial, but ubiquitous, nomenclature of the 'Lovaas' or UCLA approach to describe this programme.

Apart from the sheer volume of studies focusing on the Lovaas approach, there are additional reasons why this programme requires somewhat special attention compared with other behaviourally oriented interventions (see Jocelyn et al., 1998; Weiss, 1999). Setting aside the wider issues regarding the degree to which the Lovaas programme produces improvements for children with ASD (see Eldevik et al., 2009; Makrygianni & Reed, 2010a; Reichow, 2012, for reviews), the initial outcome-effectiveness study of this programme reported by Lovaas (1987) undoubtedly became the point at which greater attention was paid to interventions for young children with ASD. Moreover, study of the Lovaas programme allows assessment of some of the methodological problems that are inherent in assessing the impact of such interventions.

The current section, therefore, attempts to outline the background of this behavioural approach in order to more fully understand the current status of this intervention and to suggest areas where future research needs to be directed. An examination of the background to the development of this intervention may also help to explain the distinctive nature of the Lovaas approach and the divergences of other behavioural strategies (such as the Verbal Behaviour and CABAS® programmes) from this intervention.

Outline of the UCLA discrete-trial approach

The suggested programme for the Lovaas intervention is specified in a number of places, such as the *The ME Book* (Lovaas, 1981; see also Lovaas, 2003; Lovaas & Smith, 1989). The intervention is typically conducted through 1:1 teaching, using a variety of adult tutors (often termed 'therapists') to deliver the programme to the child with ASD. The programme was designed to operate for a 3-year period (preferably starting with a child around 2–3 years old). The teaching was to be delivered for around 40 hours a week (although in many contemporary instances, this total may include time spent in other interventions; e.g. speech and language therapy, occupational therapy, sensory-integration therapy etc.). The weekly intervention time is typically divided into a number of 2- or 3-hour daily sessions. The teaching in each daily session is highly structured and, during a teaching session, there are about 8–14 tasks presented for the child to learn (e.g. matching pictures, vocabulary, imitation). These tasks have often been termed 'drills'; each of the 'drills' is taught for about 5–10 minutes and is followed by about 5 minutes 'down-time' for the child between each successive task.

Each task is taught through a discrete-trial reinforcement-based method that has a number of clearly identifiable components, which are displayed in Figure 4.1 and these include: (i) the production of a question or task, by the tutor for the child to tackle; (ii) the emission of a response by the child, which can be prompted if necessary (see MacDuff et al., 2001, for an overview of prompting techniques) and then (iii) the delivery of a consequence for that response by the tutor (see Cooper et al., 2007; Miltenberger, 2011, for a discussion). It should be emphasized that while this provides the basic structure of a Lovaas teaching episode, there are a wide variety of techniques that can be used within this structure to deliver the teaching question, to prompt the child's response and to deliver the reinforcer; and these techniques are also highlighted in a number of manuals (see Lovaas, 1981; 2003; Smith, 2001).

The precise behaviours that are targeted for a particular child are tailored in accordance with that child's needs and this is established through task- and functional-analyses of the behaviours. That is, the behaviours lacking in particular

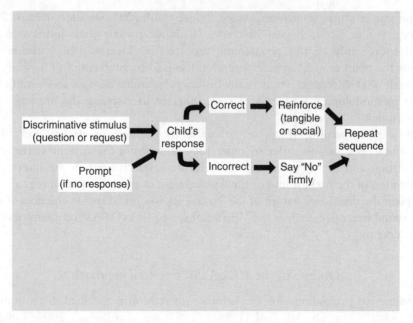

Figure 4.1   Schematic representation of the stages in a single trial ('drill') of a UCLA/Lovaas teaching intervention.

Table 4.2   Overview of the UCLA/Lovaas teaching programme. Left panel shows the basic structure of the sessions during a week. Right panel shows the broad overview of the three-year curriculum.

Intervention Overview	*Curriculum Overview*
40 hours per week. 2–3 hours per session. 8–14 drills (tasks) per session. 5–10 minutes per drill (task). 5 minutes downtime between drills (tasks).	*Year 1:* Aims to reduce self-stimulation and aggression; and to develop 'compliance' with commands, imitation and play. *Year 2:* Focuses on expressive language and interactive play. *Year 3:* Deals with emotional expression, pre-academic skills and observational learning.

contexts, the contexts that provoke problematic behaviours and the most effective reinforcers for an individual child, are all carefully analysed and studied (see Hanley et al., 2003; Mace, 1994, for discussions of functional analysis). These targeted behaviours alter over time for the children in the programme according to need and to the broad curriculum (see Table 4.2 for a general outline of this curriculum). Typically, the teaching delivered in Year 1 aims to reduce self-stimulatory and aggressive behaviours and to develop compliance with commands, imitation abilities and play behaviours. The second year of the programme focuses on teaching expressive language and developing interactive play. Finally, the teaching in the third year deals with the child's emotional expression, pre-academic skills and observational learning abilities.

Background development

A number of interventions were developed to help people with ASD prior to the Lovaas approach (see Chapter 3) and many of these approaches influenced the development of the Lovaas programme. Certainly, the pioneering work of Ferster and colleagues (e.g. Ferster, 1961; Ferster & Demyer, 1962) highlighted the potential of reinforcement-based learning theory to aid treatment of ASD. However, the particular form that the Lovaas approach has taken, especially its reliance on discrete-trial teaching techniques, can be traced to the pronounced influence of Mowrer (1939; 1944; 1958). The conditioning-based explanations produced by Mowrer for phenomena such as language learning (Mowrer, 1958) and anxiety (Mowrer, 1939; 1944) – an area in which Lovaas, himself, first published (see Lovaas, 1960) – would have had a strong impact on Lovaas at the start of his interest in ASD and the predominant 'discrete-trial' approach to conditioning often used in this early learning-theory work seems to have had a lasting effect on the development of the Lovaas teaching approach.

In the discrete trial approach described previously (see Figure 4.1), the child's response to the therapists question has little impact on the subsequent behaviour of the tutor (other than eliciting a consequence). In contrast, other behavioural approaches (e.g. CABAS®; Greer, 1997), are derived from a more 'free-operant' background (see Ferster & Skinner, 1957) of reinforcing behaviour as it naturally occurs, rather than forcing behaviour to occur through a discrete-trial or 'drill'. Thus, the effect of Lovaas' early learning-theory influenced studies (e.g. Lovaas, 1960) helps to understand the lines of fracture between the discrete-trial approaches, as embodied by the UCLA intervention (Lovaas, 1987) and various alternative behavioural approaches (see the following).

Lovaas initially started to develop what became the UCLA programme throughout the 1960s (see Lovaas, 1993, for a personal history). However, while there were gains made in the functioning of children who had undergone these early teaching programmes, the follow-up results were not as striking as the original outcomes. For example, Lovaas et al. (1973) found that nearly all of the gains made by two children with ASD who had undergone the programme 6 years earlier had slipped back: 'When we discharged the clients to the State hospital from which they had come, they inevitably regressed. It was heartbreaking to observe Pam and Rick…slowly but surely lose the skills they had acquired.' (Lovaas, 1993, p. 623). These early disappointments brought reflection on the intervention and the reasons for the long-term failure and this reflection shaped the development of the subsequent Lovaas early intervention programme.

In response to these concerns, the programme was moved from being a home-based approach, to being delivered an institutional-care setting, as it was thought that this would add rigour to the intervention. Thus, the report issued by Lovaas (1987) on the outcome-effectiveness of the UCLA programme is about a clinic-based approach, which stands in contrast to the way that the programme is often delivered in practice at the child's home (see Love et al., 2009; Mudford et al., 2001, for discussions of the predominant characteristics of ABA programmes). It was also thought that increasing the amount of training received by the child would generate sufficient strength of behavioural change to ensure that any improvements would not fade with time. Additionally, employing a range of tutors, including parents and peers, to teach a wide range of skills on the programme, was suggested in order to promote generality for the learned behaviours. Finally, younger verbal children were targeted than in the original reports and the focus on language was stressed, as it was believed that this would also to aid generalization and the chances of success.

Initial outcome evaluation study

Although it had been employed for some time, the Lovaas approach to the treatment of ASD came to a more general prominence through the results and subsequent reporting, of the first large-scale evaluation study for the intervention (Lovaas, 1987; McEachin et al., 1993). This study was conducted on 38 young individuals with ASD and there is little doubt that the results of this study prompted the re-emergence of behavioural interventions into the mainstream of professional and parental consciousness.

The criterion for the inclusion of children in this study were that they must have an independent diagnosis of ASD, their chronological age must be less than 40 months and their mental age must be greater than 11 months. In addition, the participants selected did not have language difficulties, such as echolalia and they had to live within one hour of the centre that was providing the intervention. The participants were placed into one of two groups: one group received the Lovaas programme, described earlier, for 40 hours a week and the other group received a similar treatment for a less intensive regime (10 hours a week). The group allocation of the participants was determined by the availability of staff to provide the treatment. The data from a further 21 individuals with ASD were collected from the records of another study and these participants were termed 'no treatment', but they many may well have received some form of alternative intervention.

The results of the study reported by Lovaas (1987) revealed considerable improvement in the overall intellectual functioning of the children in the intensive intervention group (see Figure 4.2). This improvement in IQ functioning for the full treatment (i.e. 40 hours a week) was dramatic in itself and also in comparison to the relative lack of gains seen in the two other groups. In an additional study, these gains appeared to be maintained at a 5-year follow-up assessment (McEachin et al., 1993). However, the claim that sparked much controversy was that of 'recovery' for some children in the intensive-treatment group. These data were based on the children's subsequent school placement and it was reported that 50% of the children undergoing the intensive intervention had a mainstream school placement and could not reliably be discriminated from their typically developing peers, which was taken to indicate 'recovery'.

There have been numerous replications of this study, which will be fully analysed in Chapter 5; however, the initial concerns centred on whether these results should be taken as a valid basis for the full-scale implementation of behaviourally based treatments for ASD (see Connor, 1998). These debates revolved around the criticisms of the initial study (e.g. Gresham & MacMillan, 1997; Schopler et al., 1989) and their resolutions, which are also instructive in terms of the types of criteria that need to be employed in evaluating evidence in this area. Indeed, consideration of these criticisms allows a good understanding of the difficulties facing any outcome-effectiveness investigation of a treatment for ASD.

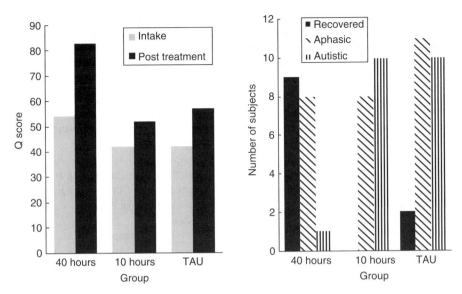

Figure 4.2 Results from the study of the UCLA programme reported by Lovaas (1987). Left panel shows the IQ score before and after treatment for the groups receiving 40 hours of treatment (full treatment), 10 hours of treatment (a control) and treatment as usual (TAU). Right panel shows the final classification of those subjects according to Lovaas (1987).

Major criticisms of Lovaas (1987)

Despite the impressive gains shown by the children in the intensive intervention group reported by Lovaas (1987; McEachin et al., 1993), there are problems with the design of the study that mean these findings are not definitive. Although no one study can ever be definitive, much effort has been devoted to arguing the extent to which these findings should be taken as indicative of the effectiveness of this behavioural approach. The major problems associated with the Lovaas (1987) study have been well rehearsed in numerous critiques of this work (e.g. Boyd, 1998; Connor, 1999; Gresham & MacMillan, 1997; 1998; Schopler et al., 1989). Several of these commentaries have pointed out the threats to the validity of this work (Boyd, 1998; Gresham & MacMillan, 1997; 1998; Schopler et al., 1989) and have offered reasoned caution against too quick an acceptance of this behavioural model (Connor, 1998). Subsequent reviews have made similar comments about intervention studies for ASD in general (e.g. Kasari, 2002). In the light of these concerns, a number of articles have suggested criteria by which intervention studies should be judged (e.g. Reichow, 2012; Wheeler et al., 2006; Wolery & Garfinkle, 2002) and a summary of these can be seen in Table 4.3.

Threats to internal validity The first set of threats to the strength of the results reported by Lovaas (1987) and subsequently by other studies of the UCLA approach, relate to threats to the 'internal validity' of the study. These threats concern the manner in which the study was conceived and conducted, in itself, rather than its applicability to other children with ASD (although, of course, such 'internal problems' also impact the generalizability of the data as well). In terms

Table 4.3 Summary of the criticisms made of the study reported by Lovaas (1987) concerning ABA treatment for children with ASD. Left panel describes some of the salient problems relating to the design of the study itself. Right panel outlines some of the problems in generalizing the results from this study.

Threats to internal validity	*Threats to external validity*
Instrumentation Different tests used at baseline and at follow-up – not perfectly compatible.	*Outcome measures* Is IQ the appropriate measure for this population?
Participant allocation Participants were not randomly allocated to groups, potentially introducing biases into the samples.	*Samples* Relatively high-functioning and more linguistically able children are not representative of ASD as a whole.
Control groups Participants not equated to experimental groups for prognosis (e.g. gender imbalances).	*Location* Clinic-based samples may not reflect the gains made in 'typical' home-based intervention programmes.

of the original study reported by Lovaas (1987), there are four important threats to its 'internal' validity: its particular use of measures or instrumentation; its allocation of participants to groups; the nature of the control groups and the integrity of the treatment.

Instrumentation   Many studies of the outcome-effectiveness of the UCLA approach, including that of Lovaas (1987), have focused on intellectual ability (IQ) as a main index of functioning (e.g. Sheinkopf & Siegel, 1998; Smith et al., 1997). The choice of this measure as appropriate for this population will be discussed in detail in the section dealing with threats to external validity (next), however, it is not just the type of test employed that is employed as an outcome assessment that is in question, but rather it is the manner of their employment that causes concern for some commentators.

  In many studies, different tests of intellectual ability have been used at the intake (baseline) and at the follow-up assessments. Sometimes these IQ tests are not perfectly compatible with one another and this may impact the reliability of the results (see Magiati & Howlin, 2001). For example, Lovaas (1987) used a range of different IQ tests for different children and also employed different tests at baseline and follow-up assessments for the same children. Another study of the UCLA technique, reported by Smith et al. (2000), used the Stanford–Binet Intelligence Scale, the Bayley Scale of Infant Development and the Merrill–Palmer Scale of Mental Tests. The particular test that was used depended on the ability of the participant at the time of the test (see also Remington et al., 2007, for similar use of multiple tests). This meant that the participants were sometimes given different tests at the initial and final assessment points. Similarly, Sheinkopf and Siegel (1998) used five different combinations of the Bayley, Cattell, Merrill-Palmer and the Wechsler scales, for their participants at intake and follow up assessments. Before discussing the problems that such combinations produce, it should be noted that this was not the case for all of the studies of the Lovaas intervention. For example, both the reports by Smith et al. (1997) and Reed et al. (2007a; 2007b) employed the same test for all participants at all measurement points.

Magiati and Howlin (2001) examined how conclusions about the progress of children on early intervention programmes may be influenced by the use of different cognitive assessment tools. They studied 24 children (aged 27–58 months) who were each tested on the Bayley Scales of Infant Development, the Merrill–Palmer Scales of Early Learning and the Vineland Adaptive Behavior scales. The results demonstrated that, although the scores on the different tests were correlated with one another, the actual indications of functioning derived from the specific tests varied considerably; the Bayley produced the lowest estimates of IQ and the Merrill–Palmer test the highest. Magiati and Howlin (2001) also suggested that judgements about interventions may be influenced by the selection of different tests for pre- and post-treatment assessments: for example, a move from the Bayley to the Merrill–Palmer (often occasioned by maturation) may, in itself, be enough to produce an increase in functioning, even when one may not have occurred.

It is actually simple to illustrate the impact of the use of mixed tests at initial and follow-up assessment on the possible error introduced in assessing intellectual ability. For example, the correlation between the Bayley's and Merill–Palmer scores in the Magiati and Howlin (2001) study was 0.82. A correlation of this value would produce a standard error of measurement of 0.57 standard deviations, if the two tests were used together. In terms of IQ scores, this would represent the introduction of an additional possible error of around 8 points in the measurement of the child's intellectual ability just by using two different tests. Thus, to be 95% certain of an accurate difference score, a range of 32 points would need to be given, introducing a margin of error than would not be there if just one test had been used at both assessment points.

Participant allocation Many authors have commented that the selection of participants for the various groups by Lovaas (1987) was not random (Connor, 1998; Spreckley & Boyd, 2009). In particular, these critics make the points that there were biases in participant allocation between the groups (Reichow, 2012; Wheeler et al., 2006) that the use of a randomize control trial (RCT) would have overcome. Hence, some form of random allocation to groups is one of the main platforms of any controlled study of outcome-effectiveness (see Table 4.3; but see Chapter 1 for a discussion of the advantages and disadvantages of an RCT).

The non-random allocation of participants by Lovaas (1987) is especially troubling for many, as the characteristics of the group receiving the intensive behavioural intervention meant that they may have had a better prognosis than the control groups. For example, the intensive group was younger (34 months) than the less intensive group (41 months) and it is generally thought that a treatment is more effective if delivered earlier than later (see Harris & Handleman, 2000). However, subsequent studies have shown that the Lovaas approach shows positive results when the ages of the treatment and comparison groups are matched (e.g. Reed et al., 2007b; Sheinkopf & Siegel, 1998; see Chapter 5).

Additionally, the gender ratio was also different between the groups in the Lovaas (1987) report: there were more boys in the intensive intervention group than in the control group. Such a difference might have conferred a prognostic advantage to the intervention group, as girls often are more severe in their symptoms (Boyd, 1998; Connor, 1998) and have a worse outcome prognosis (Boyd, 1998). Unfortunately, a gender imbalance is sometimes contained in other studies of the UCLA intervention and always in favour of the intervention group (e.g. Smith et al., 1997). However, there are studies that do contain an even gender split (e.g. Reed et al., 2007b; Smith et al., 2000) or study entirely boys (Luiselli et al., 2000) and these reports show an advantage to the intervention group as well. Such potential predictors of outcome for behavioural approaches related to the participants are discussed in some detail in Chapter 6.

The problem of non-random allocation of participants to groups is not just limited to the initial study of the UCLA approach (Lovaas, 1987. In fact, group allocation in reports of intervention effectiveness is very rarely random (see Reichow, 2012; Spreckley & Boyd, 2009). For instance, Spreckley and Boyd (2009) identified only six randomized control trials for behavioural procedures. In many studies, selection criteria are used to allocate children to groups, often for reason of practical constraints: common criteria being the location of the child's home (e.g. Lovaas, 1987; Reed et al., 2007b) or the therapist's availability (e.g. Smith et al., 1997). However, it should be pointed out that many studies have at least shown that the groups were matched at baseline in terms of their key characteristics (e.g. Reed et al., 2007b; Sheinkopf & Siegel, 1998).

Control groups   Apart from the nature of the participants in the different groups, the types of treatment received by those groups is also a potential area of criticism – that is, does the study offer a fair comparison? For example, groups may differ not only in terms of the specified nature of the intervention received (if any), but also in terms of the intensity of the intervention or level of attention given, making it difficult to conclude whether the programme or the attention received caused differences in the outcomes. For example, the initial studies of the UCLA approach (Lovaas, 1987; McEachin et al., 1993) deliberately chose hours input as a key difference between the groups: the intensive intervention group receiving a greater number of hours of intervention than the control group and the 'no treatment' group. The latter comparison means the difference could be a product of the intervention or just of the higher amount of attention received. However, several more recent studies of the UCLA intervention have addressed this issue. Eikeseth et al. (2002; Howard et al., 2005) compared a group receiving around 30 hours of discrete-trial intervention with one receiving 30 hours of eclectic therapy and noted that the former treatment regime produced greater gains than the latter.

In addition to the intensity of the programme in terms of hours a week, sometimes it is unclear exactly how long the groups received their intervention, especially in the control groups that have been created from retrospective analysis of the records (e.g. Lovaas, 1987). In addition to the Lovaas (1987) report, two other examples can be given to illustrate this issue. In the study reported by Smith et al. (1997), the discrete-trial intervention group received an initial assessment when 36 months old and a follow-up at 71 months old; in contrast, the control group received their initial assessment at 38 months of age and follow-up at 64 months. This means there was a 9-month advantage to the discrete trail group. Similarly, Luiselli et al. (2000) compared children under and over the age of three years, the older group received less therapy than the younger group (although they received more hours a week). Such differences make direct between group comparisons between groups problematic.

Of course, it is important to remember that there are two quite separate questions that can be asked of any intervention study: (i) does it work? and (ii) how does it work? Criticisms about whether the intensity of the programme is important begins to change the nature of the study, from one that addresses the former question, which is a true outcome-effectiveness question, to the latter question, which is a question about the mechanism of action. However, the question: 'could any intervention do as well with the same time input?' is key for local authority planning. One way of addressing this issue is to use an alternative treatment design with matched intervention inputs (see Dawson & Osterling, 1997; Eikeseth et al., 2002; Howard et al., 2005) and this issue is addressed in some detail in Chapter 6.

Treatment integrity   The degree to which the intervention is conducted as claimed (its integrity) is critical to the understanding of the results of any outcome-effectiveness study. That is, it is important to have some indication of precisely what occurred during the intervention sessions. Without this knowledge, results cannot be generalized to other situations and no indication of the 'active' component of the intervention can be made (see Kasari, 2002; Wolery & Garfinkle, 2002). A variety of methods have been used to assess the integrity of the programme, such as the use of a manual (Eikeseth et al., 2002; Lovaas, 1987; Reed et al., 2007b), therapist training (Sheinkopf & Siegel, 1998) and detailed forms (Smith et al., 2000).

Within a complex intervention such as the UCLA programme, guaranteeing the integrity of the treatment is fraught with problems. Lovaas (1987) reported no direct data on this aspect of the programme, although it should be noted that all therapists were trained in the programme and were supervised frequently – it being delivered in a clinic setting. However, this does not ensure compliance with the explicit techniques espoused.

In fact, very few studies have reported observation data from the intervention to verify the manner of delivery, either within- or between-participants, and most reports, similarly to Lovaas (1987), have relied on adherence on the programme manual and staff training. However, Mudford et al. (2001) noted that many home-based programmes received relatively infrequent supervision; only 21% of programmes received supervision from individuals currently accredited as competent to provide UCLA treatment. Thus, one manner in which the intervention integrity might be improved is via staff training and this aspect is key in some of the newer behavioural approaches (e.g. Greer, 1997; Greer & Keohane, 2009). Schreibman (2000) has called for such training as an important aspect of these interventions (see also Salt et al., 2002) and most of the more recent outcome-effectiveness studies of Lovaas approaches do show some aspect of staff training (see Chapter 5).

Threats to external validity   In addition to the problems created by the previous methodological issues, a number of criticisms of the Lovaas (1987) study suggest that the results may not necessarily generalize beyond the sample on which the study was conducted. Such limitations to the degree of applicability to the general population can be termed threats to external validity. Three issues in particular warrant some mention in respect to the Lovaas (1987) report: (i) the choice of outcome measures; (ii) the nature of the sample studied and (iii) the location of the treatment programme.

Outcome measures   Most outcome-effectiveness studies concerned with the Lovaas programme have used some form of IQ score measure as a main index of the impact of the intervention (e.g. Lovaas, 1987; Remington et al., 2007; Smith et al., 1997). The impact of behavioural (or any) programmes on intellectual functioning remains, at once, a key take-home message that many studies wish to give to prospective users of the service, but also somewhat controversial, in that it can be argued that this outcome is not a key part of ASD (e.g. Connor, 1998).

The particular reliance of IQ tests in several high-profile studies of the Lovaas approach (including that of Lovaas, 1987) has raised some questions about the external validity of the results. The problems with the use of general IQ tests for specific problems are well rehearsed elsewhere (see Reed, 1999). However, the reliance on IQ as a measure has been questioned in terms of its relevance to ASD, as this is not taken as a core ASD problem (see Connor, 1998). As noted in Chapter 2, for individuals with ASD the main difficulties are regarded as being related to communication, socialization and repetitive behaviours (see Wing & Gould, 1979). Given this, it is suggested that the results of studies with a heavy reliance on IQ as an outcome measure may have limited application to assessing the important impact of the intervention on children with ASD.

However, despite this reasonable concern, there are good reasons to examine this outcome domain for an ASD population: (i) it is a well-understood and ubiquitous standardized metric of relevance to many educationalists and a domain that will impact on functioning; (ii) many individuals with ASD show co-morbid intellectual impairments (e.g. LaMalfa et al., 2004; Matson & Shoemaker, 2009) and (iii) IQ tests covers a broad spectrum of ability (including language use). Although Lovaas (1987) did not report these scales in detail, several more recent studies do present the results from the separate sub-scales of the IQ tests (e.g. Eikeseth et al., 2002; Howard et al., 2005; McEachin et al., 1993). Also, many subsequent studies of the UCLA approach have adopted the use of measures other than IQ tests (see Chapter 5); employing tools such as the Vineland Adaptive Behaviour Scales (Cohen et al., 2006; Eldevik et al., 2006; Reed et al., 2007a; Smith et al., 1997; 2000). Others have abandoned the use of global IQ scores altogether and have focused on the use of standardized tests of behavioural function as their primary measure of impact (e.g. Luiselli et al., 2000). In many of these studies, there have been considerable gains noted for children as a result of the Lovaas programme (see Chapter 5).

A set of measures that are largely missing from the controlled-study reports concern the impact of such interventions on the family's functioning (see Wolery & Garfinkle, 2002, for a critique of this omission). It has been suggested that the large scale time involvement of the Lovaas programme may prove a burden on the family and there are clear impacts of family functioning on the effectiveness of the intervention (e.g. Osborne et al., 2008a; Robbins et al., 1991). This omission has begun to be addressed in a number of uncontrolled assessments (e.g. Hastings & Johnson, 2001) and in a few controlled study of the outcome-effectiveness of this approach (see Remington et al., 2007; Salt et al., 2002).

Samples   In the Lovaas report (1987), the participants studied were relatively high functioning compared to children with ASD in general, both in terms of their intellectual and language abilities. It has been suggested that such a group would do well whatever the intervention employed, but it is also important to note that such a sample may not be representative of all children with ASD. For example, Schopler et al. (1989) claimed that the IQ criteria alone used by Lovaas (1987) would have excluded 25% of children with ASD in a standard school sample (see also the section on co-morbid problems in the present Chapter 2). Moreover, the additional echolalia exclusion criteria would have excluded up to 57% of children with ASD (see Rutter, 1968). This criticism makes a good point regarding the generalization of the results from the Lovaas (1987) report to the population of people with ASD, in general. However, it should quickly be noted that there are several subsequent studies involving the UCLA approach that have included participants of a much lower functioning (e.g. Eldevik et al., 2006; Reed et al., 2007b) and have found reasonable effectiveness of the approach (see Chapter 6).

Location   The Lovaas (1987) study was conducted in a clinic-setting and this has suggested to some that the results may not be generalized to the application of the UCLA approach in settings outside a clinic such as the home (Connor, 1998). This issue has been highlighted in a review by Bibby et al. (2001; see also Boyd & Corley, 2001) of home-based ABA programmes. They analysed data from 66 children, who were served by 25 different early intervention consultants. After a mean of about 32 months of UCLA type intervention, the IQ scores of these children had not changed and Bibby et al. (2001) concluded that these home-based interventions did not reproduce the results from the clinic-based professionally directed programmes.

Although studies, such as that by Bibby et al. (2001), appear to point to the importance of the location of the programme, there have been a number of controlled studies that have addressed this issue and suggested that location itself is not the prime concern. Sheinkopf and Siegel (1998; Sallows & Graupner, 2005) both noted gains in functioning for children undergoing parent-led Lovaas programmes. Moreover, Howard et al. (2005; Reed et al., 2007b; Remington et al., 2007) noted that Lovaas interventions conducted in the community produced significantly greater outcomes than other approaches (see Chapter 5 for a fuller discussion). In these latter studies, the programmes were directed by appropriately qualified consultants and imply that the issue may not be the location of the programme, but rather the training and competence of the staff delivering the treatment.

Summary

This section has outlined the characteristics of the UCLA approach (Lovaas, 1981) has highlighted the impact that this intervention has had on the field: both in terms of re-generating thinking about how to help individuals with ASD – the volume of studies conducted on its effectiveness attests to its importance in the development of treatment interventions (see Chapters 5 and 6) and in terms of refining the ways in which such studies are conducted. The criticisms of the Lovaas (1987) study also highlight that, while that study did revolutionize the field of ASD treatment, it was not without its methodological problems. Nevertheless, many of the original problems connected with this approach have been addressed by subsequent studies and this approach remains a viable and much supported programme.

Verbal Behaviour Programme

A largely home-based behavioural approach, that is rapidly becoming as popular among parents as the original Lovaas intervention, has been termed the 'Verbal Behavior' approach (Sundberg & Partington, 1998; Verbal Behaviour, in this book). According to a recent survey of parents and practitioners who are associated with ABA approaches, well over 50% of behavioural programmes now employ the Verbal Behaviour approach, either as the sole intervention or as part of the behavioural package delivered to the child (Love et al., 2009).

As a behaviourally based intervention, Verbal Behaviour shares many characteristics with the Lovaas approach (see Carr & Firth, 2005). Both focus on carefully organized and defined training events, both emphasize the need for early intervention and for frequent and specific training – every day if possible. Also, both use highly preferred, tangible rewards as consequences (although the two approaches may choose their rewards differently, see the following). However, the Verbal Behaviour intervention differs in two main aspects from the Lovaas approach. Firstly, somewhat obviously, in its emphasis on the importance of teaching Verbal Behaviour through the techniques specified in Skinner's (1957) book *Verbal Behavior*. Secondly, it differs from the Lovaas programme in its focus on 'Natural Environment Training', rather than discrete-trial teaching.

Programme background principles

The major premise of the Verbal Behaviour approach (Sundberg & Partington, 1998; see Sundberg & Michael, 2001) is the view that language underlies much of the typical development of children, but is absent or reduced in those individuals with ASD. This makes teaching language and communication skills a priority for these individuals for the Verbal Behaviour approach. In this broad focus on language, it follows the suggestions of the Lovaas approach (see Lovaas, 1981; 1993). However, there are three areas of clear demarcation between a Verbal Behaviour programme and a traditional Lovaas behavioural programme (see Carr & Firth, 2005).

Firstly, Sundberg and Michael (2001) note that the type of methods employed in traditional language teaching programmes, including that of Lovaas (1987), focus on developing highly structured forms of language; such as teaching expressive- and receptive-repertoires through discrete trial procedures, instead of a focus on instructing language as a functional communication system in its natural settings (Leaf & McEachin, 1999). These former systems tend to divide language purely into either expressive (speaker) language or receptive (listener) behaviours and they assume that these responses can be taught in the abstract, quite apart from the settings or functions that they may typically have in everyday life (see Carr & Firth, 2005). In fact, placing emphasis on the functionality of language corresponds with many non-behavioural views of the role of language teaching in ASD (see Ogletree et al., 2007).

Secondly, the Verbal Behaviour programme involves a different conception of language itself, from that typically noted in many traditional training programmes for children with ASD, including the Lovaas approach. The Verbal Behaviour approach draws on the principles outlined in *Verbal Behavior* (Skinner, 1957) for its language/communication teaching. This behaviour analytic account (i.e. Skinner, 1957) treats language as a form of behaviour like any other, but one that is mediated (reinforced) entirely by the behaviours of others. That is, language is taken as serving a social-communication function; but the form (function) of communication differs across different types of Verbal Behaviour and the Verbal Behaviour programme suggests that it is these functions that need to be taught in any programme for individuals with ASD. According to Skinner (1957; see also MacCorquodale, 1969; 1970; Place, 1981; Sundberg, 2007), there are a number of types of verbal behaviours that differ from one another in their communication function and are performed in different contexts and receive different types of reinforcement (see Table 4.4 for a description of these forms). The aim of the Verbal Behaviour approach is to utilize this theoretical approach to verbal behaviour (i.e. Skinner, 1957) and apply it to the behaviours of the child with ASD in order to develop a functional communication system, which should also help to reduce the levels of disruptive behaviour.

Finally and related to the previous two points, the Verbal Behaviour programme uses a 'Natural Environment Training' approach. That is, it teaches these behaviours in the appropriate situations and contexts, in the hope of affording a greater chance of generalization to these contexts after training. Such a teaching technique was initially developed by behavioural approaches, such as that outlined by Stokes and Baer (1977). It has also been called by a number of different names, such as: 'Incidental Training' (Fenske et al., 2001), the 'Mand-Model' approach (Rogers-Warren & Warren, 1980); the 'Natural Language Paradigm' (Koegel et al., 1987) and 'Pivotal Response Training' (Koegel et al., 2003). In essence, all of these views suggest that behaviour needs to be taught in the setting in which it is most naturally likely to occur in order to optimize chances of responses contacting 'natural', rather than artificial, reinforcing consequences. For example, training a request for a specific food during a designated 'snack time' and reinforcing that request/response with the food, is taken to be more likely to be successful than arbitrarily asking the child to name food types when the child is not hungry and reinforcing with arbitrary reinforcers (see Charlop-Christy et al., 1999).

Outline of teaching procedures

The precise techniques to be employed in a Verbal Behaviour programme have been outlined in many manuals (e.g. Barbera & Rasmussen, 2007; Sundberg & Partington, 1988). In general, the intervention can be taken to fall into five major stages, which have been described by Sundberg and Michael (2001; see also LeBlanc et al., 2006; McGreevey, 2009) and are outlined in Table 4.5.

Initially, levels of appropriate control over the various different forms of verbal behaviours displayed by the individual with ASD are assessed. Once the individual needs of the child in this regard are established, the programme usually focuses on developing the use of 'mands' by the child (i.e. requesting behaviours). This form of

Table 4.4   Summary of some forms of verbal behaviour, as described by Skinner (1957).

Verbal behaviour	Precondition	Consequence	Description
Mand	Motivating Operation (a need).	Achieves need	Typically a demand, command, or request. A person says: 'I want a drink' and is reinforced by somebody getting them a drink.
Tact	Feature of the environment.	Social	Makes contact with the world, and refers to behaviour under control of non-verbal stimuli – expressive labelling. A person looks into a room, and says: 'There is a cat on the mat' and is reinforced by another person saying: 'Yes, you are right!'.
Intraverbal	Verbal behaviour of another person.	Social	Verbal responses to verbal stimuli showing no formal similarity with the evoking verbal stimuli, and includes: small talk and serious conversation. A person asks another: 'What did you think of that presentation?'. The other says: 'Rubbish!'.
Echoic	Verbal behaviour of another person.	Social	Behaviour controlled by a verbal stimulus that shares similarity with the evoking stimulus – repeating what somebody has just said. A person says: 'Behaviour in French is "comportement"', the other person says 'Behaviour is "comportement"', and the first persons says 'Correct!'
Autoclitic	A person's own verbal behaviour.	Directly Effective	Verbal responses that describe their own behaviour or modify the effect of their verbal behaviour on others. A person says 'I think I *might* be ill', which may make another find out more before taking them to the doctor.
Textual	Verbal behaviour of another.	Social	A vocal response is controlled by a verbal stimulus that is not heard – reading or writing.

communication behaviour is tackled initially for two reasons. Firstly, it is thought that this will bring the behaviour of the child most quickly into contact with the social environment – asking for something is reinforced by somebody giving you that something; whereas naming ('tacting') does not necessarily produce such close social contact (Sundberg & Michael, 2001). Secondly, it is hoped that such mand training will allow replacement of particular forms of problem behaviour with a more functional form of communication (e.g. Functional Communication Training).

Table 4.5 The areas targeted by a 'Verbal Behavior' ABA programme.

Area	Description
Individual assessment	Assessing the level and type of linguistic and behavioural needs.
Mand training	Focuses on the acquisition of functional communication for specific objects, rather than naming objects, as this allows a repertoire that specifies a relevant and effective consequence.
Functional communication training	The mands can be used to replace externalizing or problem behaviours that result from not being able to have a need satisfied.
Establishing operations	Teaching strategies are used in naturally occurring situation across a variety of contexts and with many different people. This allows appropriate circumstances to lead to the training of appropriate mands (e.g. a mand for certain foods can be trained at meal times) – using naturally occurring establishing operations that will make naturally occurring items appropriately reinforcing.
Intraverbal training	Responses to other words, rather than environmental events, are trained that is facilitated by using relationships that the child already knows.
Automatic reinforcement	Associating verbal behaviours with positive consequences develops a positive valance for those behaviours, making them more likely to spontaneously – the association of verbal behaviour with positive consequences makes verbal behaviour reinforcing in itself.

The latter of the two suggestions is derived from the analysis of the factors that typically control problem behaviours like self-injurious behaviours (Carr & Durand, 1985). There are many examples of replacing such problem behaviours in children with ASD in Verbal Behaviour programmes by functional mand training (e.g. Bartman & Freeman, 2003; Marion et al., 2011). This teaching phase tends to follow a programme of identifying the contexts in which problem behaviours emerge as well as their reinforcers and then reinforcing the child for the emission of a mand in those circumstances (rather than the problem behaviour), but using the same reinforcer that maintains the problem behaviour. A focus on increasing a person's linguistic competence to reduce problem behaviours certainly fits with the literature on ASD concerning the potential deleterious impacts of a lack of language on emotional understanding and communication (Durkin & Conti-Ramsden, 2007; Scattone et al., 2002; Tager-Flusberg, 2000). However, it might be questioned whether it is always necessary to train a mand in preference to any other form of communication. For example, Conallen and Reed (2012) used a training procedure that attempted to teach children with ASD 'tacts' for private events (emotions) and found an increase in their ability to 'tact' emotions was associated with a reduction in problem behaviour.

The third focus of a typical Verbal Behaviour programme is the use of 'establishing operations' to help teach mands (Bartman & Freeman, 2003; Drasgow et al., 1999; Eikeseth & Smith, 2013). An 'establishing operation' is the term given to the situations in which particular stimuli become effective as reinforcers. For example, after a period of food deprivation, food will become an effective reinforcer (see Catania, 2007; Tapper, 2005). By programming teaching opportunities according to the prevailing situation, it is hoped that this will increase the likelihood of obtaining appropriate mands that can be reinforced with the types of stimuli that may serve to maintain that behaviour after the training – e.g. food when the child is hungry (see Drasgow et al., 1999; Hall & Sundberg, 1987). This stands in contrast to the type of training often used in the Lovaas approach, in which a child is required to ask for a particular object or to name a particular object, irrespective of whether that child might actually want that object at the time.

Following the development of a strong mand repertoire and the establishment of functional communication, a Verbal Behaviour programme may then begin to focus on the development of 'intraverbal' responses (Drash et al., 1999; Sautter & LeBlac, 2006). These are responses to other words, rather than to other environmental stimuli; such an 'intraverbal' might involve the child in completing a list of items: 'one, two, three… (answer = four)' or responding with a word that is related to the word given to them, for example: 'animal (response = horse)'. The training procedures for teaching 'intraverbals' have been outlined and reviewed by Goldsmith et al. (2007) and there are a number of demonstrations of the way in which this ability can be enhanced by drawing on relationships that the child already knows (May & Dymond, 2014) to enhance the range of 'intraverbal' responses achieved.

Finally, it is hoped that the association of such verbal behaviours with positive consequences will develop an automatic reinforcement for verbal behaviour (Sundberg & Michael, 2001). That is, the association of the emission of verbal behaviour with positive consequences will make the act of verbal behaviours, in themselves, reinforcing (see also Mowrer, 1958; Chapter 3). An example of this aspect of the training procedure is given by Sundberg et al. (1996), who taught children a number of vocalizations by following them with a reinforcer such as tickling. When these verbalizations had been learned, Sundberg et al. (1996) noted that additional vocalizations were subsequently acquired without the need for the use of direct reinforcement. They suggest that the act of vocalization, in the general, had become self-reinforcing due to its pairing with a reinforcer.

Effectiveness of Verbal Behaviour programmes

There are several issues that need to be considered when assessing the effectiveness of Verbal Behaviour programmes: firstly, the extent to which the Skinnerian approach to understanding and teaching language will or will not, produce better results than other approaches; secondly, the level of evidence that Verbal Behaviour is, itself, effective as a programme and finally, the extent to which the Verbal Behaviour approach will outperform other traditional behavioural approaches.

Skinner's Verbal Behaviour   There are many controversies surrounding the correct interpretation of language development that remain unresolved in the literature. The predominant views of language learning are still based on structuralist/nativist views (e.g. Chomsky, 1957; Pinker, 1994). However, as noted in Chapter 3, the extent to which these views have actually impacted on applied or practical problems, such as the education children with ASD, is negligible. To this extent, the Skinnerian functional approach to communication is much more in line with many contemporary views of the role of teaching language for people with ASD, such as the functional communication movement that stresses teaching of communication based on the child's needs (e.g. Ogletree et al., 2007). However, this still does not necessarily imply that the Skinnerian approach to language is correct – after all, there are other non-nativist approaches to language that could also be correct (e.g. Osgood, 1979).

In response to such concerns, the proponents of Verbal Behaviour programmes (e.g. McGreevey, 2009) often point to the increase in the amount of behaviour-analytic research on language being conducted as evidence of the increasing impact of this view (e.g. Sautter & LeBlanc, 2006). This increase is undoubtedly happening, but, just because many people or doing and citing, such work does not make it correct. In fact, many of the presuppositions of Verbal Behaviour remain speculative theoretical works and not necessarily grounded in great numbers of empirical proofs. This issue is still in need for further evidence before it can be adequately addressed.

Overall effectiveness   Although there are many instances showing that the types of technique advocated by Verbal Behaviour approach can be effective in producing gains in language (e.g. Bartman & Freeman, 2003; Sautter & LeBlanc, 2006) and reductions in problem behaviours (Jennett et al., 2008; Sundberg & Partington, 1998), the key issue is whether the approach impacts on the overall functioning of the child with ASD. Despite the focus on the key issue of language and communication by this approach (Sundberg & Michael, 2001), ASD is more than a communication disorder. It is in this latter area of overall functioning that the evidence for Verbal Behaviour programmes is not particularly compelling – in part, as there are very few studies of its impact on overall functioning (Green, 2004; but see Stock et al., 2013).

Although studies, such as that reported by Williams and Greer (1993), have shown greater improvements in language in children with ASD on a Verbal Behaviour programme compared to other programmes, they do not use standard-ized measures of global functioning that would allow comparison across studies. To date, there are only three reports that have employed standardized measures of cognitive and adaptive behavioural function to assess Verbal Behaviour programmes. Green et al. (2002) noted improvements in standardized tests of cognitive function, but this was based on a case study of one child. Reed et al. (2007a) noted improve-ments in IQ and educational functioning as a result of a Verbal Behaviour programme over a 9–10 month period, in four children, but did not note any improvement in adaptive behaviours. However, both of these studies included only few participants and caution needs to be applied in interpreting these data. The final of the three studies was reported by Stock et al. (2013) and was a relatively large-scale study of 14 children with ASD over a 12-month period on a Verbal Behaviour programme. This article noted a mean 8-point increase in IQ, a gain of 10 months in receptive language and a gain of 7 months in expressive language, but no gains in adaptive behaviour. These data are similar to those noted by Reed et al. (2007a) based on their smaller sample.

Verbal Behaviour versus UCLA/Lovaas The distinctions between the Verbal Behaviour and Lovaas approaches have been outlined at a conceptual/theoretical level previously (see also Carr & Firth, 2005; LeBlanc et al., 2006; Sundberg & Michael, 2001). However, there is little direct evidence relating to the relative efficacy of the various programmes (but see Reed et al., 2007a; Stock et al., 2013). There is much evidence that the Natural Environment Training, and a functional approach to teaching mands, can be effectively used to teach verbal behaviour and communication skills (see McGreevey, 2009, for a range of such evidence). However, it is not clear whether these approaches are any more effective that a traditional discrete-trial approach that is concerned purely with reception and expression of words.

One of the only studies to have compared the Verbal Behaviour and traditional discrete-trial approaches was reported by Williams and Geer (1993). This study noted that the Verbal Behaviour approach led to the children using more words, than when they were taught through traditional means. Moreover, the words that were taught through the Verbal Behaviour approach were better maintained after the teaching programme.

The suggestion that the use of Natural Environment Training is more efficient than discrete-trial training for the development of language is a harder claim to substantiate empirically. Again, there are many examples of the success of such programmes in themselves (see Bartman & Freeman, 2003; May & Dymond, 2014; Marion et al., 2011; see McGreevey, 2009, for a review), but there are few direct comparisons between the Natural Environment Training approach and the discrete-trial approach.

Several studies have compared the two teaching styles directly was reported by Koegel et al. (1987). This study noted an advantage of the Natural Environment Training approach over the discrete trial approach in terms of the amount of language learned by children in the respective programmes. Similarly, Jennett et al. (2008) compared the mand training approach, outlined in the Verbal Behaviour approach to discrete trial teaching and noted that five or six of the participants made better progress in requesting items using the mand procedure, as well as showing greater reductions in problem behaviours. However, both Reed et al. (2007a) and Stock et al. (2013) noted no particular improvement after exposure to a Verbal Behaviour programme in standardized measures of language and intellectual functioning compared to a discrete trial approach.

The situation may be a little more complicated than the simple suggestion that one approach is universally better than the other. For example, Sundberg and Michael (2001) suggest that the Natural Environment Training paradigm may well offer advantages in terms of developing mands or expressive language, but they suggest that the discrete-trial approach may have an advantage in terms of developing tacts or receptive language behaviours. Again, much more research is required before this question can be adequately addressed.

Summary

Overall, it is probably safest to conclude that the Verbal Behaviour approach is increasingly being employed in home-programmes and this suggests that it has high acceptability among some parents. It is also clear that the techniques the intervention employs, in themselves, can be very effective and the use of Natural Environment Training methods appears to facilitate maintenance of gains (see also Chapters 8 and 9 on Developmental Approaches to ASD). However, there is still little evidence that that the Verbal Behaviour programme impacts on global levels of functioning (e.g. intellectual functioning, adaptive behaviours), outside of specific behaviours that are targeted, to any greater extent than the Lovaas programme. Until such data are more fully and abundantly collected, it may be wiser to view the Verbal Behaviour approach as a useful set of tools to deal with particular behaviours, than as a fully validated programme for ASD.

Complete Application of Behaviour Analysis to Schools (CABAS®)

The final of the three behavioural programmes to have achieved a degree of wide-spread usage, as well as a growing evidence base, is the behavioural-systems approach named the: 'Complete Application of Behaviour Analysis to Schools' (CABAS®). In this programme, all aspects of the education system employed (be it in a school or at home) are subject to analysis and monitoring (see Greer & Keohane, 2009); that is, not only the behaviours of the children, but also the behaviours of the teachers are seen as part of the programme (see Greer, 1997; Greer & Ross, 2008; Greer & Keohane, 2004; Hawkins et al., 2007). It is important to note that this approach should not necessarily be thought of as only appropriate to children with ASD, in theory it could apply to all schooling – broadly defined to include home schooling, although, to date, it has found most application for children with ASD (see Greer, 1997). In fact, recent reviews have noted that there are now 14 schools in the UK working on such ABA principles (Griffith et al., 2012) and this approach also has been very influential in developing education programmes in Ireland (see Healy et al., 2009).

Overview of CABAS® The CABAS® programme involves the development of a systems approach to education, where the parents and teachers are involved in developing assessment plans for the children and also are instructed in approaches to the management of the behaviours displayed by their children (Greer & Keohane, 2009). These evaluations feed into the objectives specified for each child, which are assessed in an ongoing manner according to the child's progress through a 'curriculum' termed the 'The Preschool Inventory of Repertoires for Kindergarten' (PIRK®; Greer & McCorkle, 2003).

The PIRK® sets out the objectives for teaching the each of repertoires that are believed to be necessary for a child to succeed in a mainstream reception class (Greer, 2002; see also Waddington & Reed, 2009 for a fuller outline of these objectives). As well as serving as a protocol for success in mainstream education, the PIRK® claims to indicate areas where instruction is needed to achieve these goals. There are a total of 491 behavioural targets contained in the PIRK® and these targets are divided into six repertoires: (i) The academic literacy repertoire (224 targets) – largely comprising pre-academic skills such as literacy and mathematics; (ii) the communication repertoire (101 targets) – being largely co-extensive with the issues raised in the previous section on verbal behaviour and certainly drawing on contemporary behavioural theorizing in this area (see Greer & Keohane, 2009); (iii) the community of reinforcers repertoire (25 targets) – dealing with behaviours that will allow contact with naturally occurring reinforcers outside the school setting; (iv) the self-management for school repertoire (44 targets) – aimed at facilitating inclusion in schools; (v) the social self-management repertoire (38 targets) – being targeted at social skills and (vi) the physical/motor repertoire (59 targets).

Once the behaviours needed by an individual child to complete the PIRK® are identified, they are targeted through a series of well-established behavioural techniques, outlined in the overview of CABAS® given by Greer (1997). These teaching procedures include: Direct Instruction (Engelmann & Carnine, 1982); Precision Teaching (Lindsley, 1990); Eco-Behavioural Analysis (Sulzer-Azaroff & Mayer, 1986); Personalized Instruction (Keller, 1968) and Programmed Instruction (Skinner, 1984).

At the heart of all of these behavioural teaching approaches is the conception of the 'learn-unit' (i.e. an opportunity to learn). In analysing learning through such learn-units, the CABAS® programme emphasizes the interaction of teacher and student as the unit of analysis, rather than focusing solely on the child's response to a discrete-trial prompt (Greer, 1997; 2002). A learn unit is taken as a teacher-pupil interaction that is not further divisible into sub-tasks (see Greer et al., 2002).

Effectiveness of CABAS®   There is a wealth of data relating to the success of the CABAS® approach within its own framework (see Greer & Ross, 2008). These reports usually involve an analysis of the numbers of learning objectives, derived from the PIRK®, that have been achieved by the pupils in the system. For example, Selinske et al. (1991) reported a 2.5-times increase in the number of objectives reached by children during CABAS® training, relative a baseline phase without such training. Other studies have related the objectives obtained to a variety of factors, such as the number of 'learn-units' presented (Albers & Greer, 1991), teacher observations (Ingham & Greer, 1992) and the accuracy of the teacher in identifying correct pupil behaviours (Greer et al., 1989).

In terms of the overall development of the children, Pérez-González and Williams (2006) reported three case studies in which children undergoing CABAS® education made strong gains in terms of the numbers of behaviours mastered over a 3-year period. However, although these reports are encouraging, they do not always allow direct comparison with other forms of teaching approach for children with ASD, as they focus on particular specific behaviours rather than overall functioning (e.g. Pérez- González& Williams, 2006) and they do not use standardized assessment tests to determine the global gains made by the children.

There are four studies regarding the impact of the CABAS® approach on the overall development of children with ASD that have employed standardized measured and these studies begin to tell a reasonably uniform story. McGarrell et al. (2009) conducted on observational study on six children undergoing CABAS® treatment in a special school for pupils with ASD. The children were all assessed on standardized IQ tests (albeit different ones to one another and, often, different ones at baseline and follow-up) and some of the children also were also given a Vineland Adaptive Behaviour test assessment for their adaptive social and daily living skills. Reconstructing the data presented in this paper allows the impact of the CABAS® treatment over the first 2 years of its application to each child to be assessed. In terms of IQ, there was a change from a mean score of 74 at baseline to 100 after 2 years (which was statistically significant). For the four children with a VABS assessment, this mean score increased from 57 to 74, which was not statistically significant.

In a similar small-scale study of five children on a CABAS® home-programme and that employed a measure of general intellectual functioning and also the VABS, Reed et al. (2007a) noted a mean increase in IQ, over 9–10 months, from 50 to 65 (which was statistically significant) and a small and statistically insignificant, increase in adaptive behaviour skills from 58 to 63. This study also measured improvement in educational achievements and found a 20 point gain in these skills using the British Abilities Scale. Thus, both studies have noted similar significant improvements in intellectual functioning, but no increases in adaptive behaviours.

The fact that intellectual and educational attainments may be impacted strongly by the CABAS® programme, but social-adaptive skills are not so greatly impacted, may be a reflection of the numbers of objectives associated with these respective skills in the PIRK®, which have a ratio of 224:38 objectives in those curricula, respectively. A consequence of this potential imbalance in training is the impact on the child's functioning once the programme has been terminated. It is quite clear (see also Chapter 12) that control over behaviours and educational skills are critical for successful school placement (Frederickson et al., 2004) and this is reflected in the statistics reported on this topic following CABAS® training.

Greer (1997) reported that 55–75% of pupils with ASD are educated in mainstream settings after CABAS® training. This placement success is impressive and mirrors that from the original outcome-effectiveness study of Lovaas (1987). However, two studies have also followed up such children, not only in terms of their school placement and behaviour, but also in terms of their social-emotional functioning. O'Connor and Healy (2010) reported a follow-up to the paper by McGarrel et al. (2009) and assessed the children once they had left the CABAS® programme. They found that five out of six of these children were in a mainstream school placement, a better average than is typical for children with ASD – currently around 50–60% (Waddington & Reed, 2015). Moreover, the IQ and academic performance of the children, as rated by their teachers, was found to be satisfactory in four out of five of these cases. However, O'Connor and Healy (2010) also noted some concerns over the social skills of the children and in terms of the apparent development of a number of co-morbid disorder issues.

A similar pattern of data was reported by Waddington and Reed (2009), who reported the impact of CABAS® training in children in a special school ($N = 53$). The children with ASD were assessed over a 9–10 month period using the Strengths and Difficulties Scale, which measures problem behaviours across a number of domains. It was found that the pupils who had undergone CABAS® training showed better performance in terms of conduct problems and hyperactivity, relative to a group of children with only special nursery training. However, this latter group showed fewer emotional and social-relationship problems than the CABAS® group. These data are shown in Figure 4.3.

Summary

There is reasonable evidence that the CABAS® approach and its associated curriculum (PIRK®), can impact well on intellectual and educational functioning of children with ASD. However, there are questions regarding the impact of the CABAS® training on

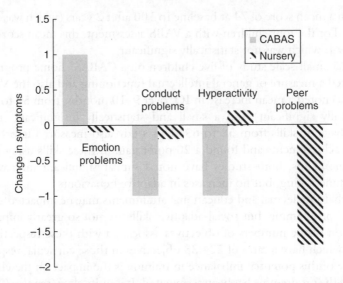

Figure 4.3 Mean change scores for problem behaviours (measured by the SDQ) for pupils with ASD who had either CABAS® or Nursery training prior to placement in special school (Waddington & Reed, 2009). A *decrease* on the SDQ subscales suggests an improvement – showing that the ABA training improves problem behaviours but not emotional problems.

the social and emotional development of the children. The relative lack of impact on the latter aspects of functioning may well be related to the weights given to these skills by the programme and this aspect of the approach may well require some development and certainly further study.

Overview

There have clearly been a wide range of developments in behaviourally based programmes for ASD – the 'UCLA/Lovaas' programme (Lovaas, 2003), the Verbal Behaviour programme (Sundberg & Michael, 2001) and the CABAS® approach (Greer, 1997), are three examples of this form of intervention. Of these programmes, the Lovaas approach is the earliest developed and most widely investigated. However, in the eyes of many, this is one of the less sophisticated behavioural programmes, providing a main focus on basic skills being taught through repetition of training trials. The newer behavioural approaches (e.g. Verbal Behaviour and CABAS®) now focus on teaching complex skills, such as functional language (Sundberg & Michael, 2001) and socialization (e.g. Strain & Schwartz, 2001). These newer techniques also have moved beyond the discrete-trial teaching 'drills' of the Lovaas approach (e.g. Fenske et al., 2001; Koegel et al., 1987) and have been designed to fit into the school curriculum (e.g. Greer, 1997; Hawkins et al., 2007).

Nevertheless, there is still debate as to the precise degree to which they will improve functioning in children with ASD and this will be the subject of Chapters 5 and 6. However, it is still necessary to point out that the fact that these interventions 'dare to speak their behavioural name' provokes episodes of rage and misrepresentation in many (see Morris, 2009, for a commentary on such misrepresentation). The ongoing prejudices against behavioural approaches (see Keenan, 2004; Morris, 2009), also remains an obstacle to progress in the field. In truth, these points of contention have sparked much argument, which has added much heat, but not much illumination, to the debate. However, a period of truce between the proponents of behavioural approaches and their critics now appears to have settled over what Keenan (2004) refers to as the 'autism wars' and this truce has facilitated a period of rather more sober analysis of the effectiveness of behavioural approaches than has previously been observed.

5

Evaluation of Comprehensive Behavioural Interventions

A very large number of investigations have examined the impact of behavioural interventions on the functioning of individuals with Autism Spectrum Disorders (ASD). The current chapter examines the evidence derived from reports concerning the effectiveness of 'comprehensive behavioural programmes' (see Chapter 4) on the overall functioning of individuals with ASD (see Chapter 1 for further discussion of this focus). These programmes include the 'UCLA/Lovaas' (Lovaas, 1981; 2003), 'Verbal Behaviour' (Sundberg & Partington, 1998) and the 'Comprehensive Application of Behaviour Analysis to Schools' (CABAS®; Greer, 1997) approaches. The individual characteristics of these programmes were discussed in Chapter 4 and have been outlined by numerous authors (e.g. Eikeseth, 2009; Peters-Scheffer et al., 2011; Virues-Ortega, 2010).

Characteristics of Comprehensive Behavioural Interventions

In interpreting the data obtained from such outcome-effectiveness studies it is important to consider the types and characteristics of the programmes that these studies assess. This information is critical as it determines the degree to which the results can be generalized to other populations. As noted in Chapter 4, concerns regarding the details of the studies methodologies can lead some question of their external validity or generalizability (see Boyd, 1988; Connor, 1998).

In conjunction with the increasing number of reviews concerning the effectiveness of behavioural interventions, both descriptive (Eldevik et al., 2009; Granpeesheh et al., 2009; Howlin, et al., 2009; Matson & Smith, 2008; Rogers & Vismara, 2008) and meta-analytic (Eikeseth, 2009; Makrygianni & Reed, 2010a; Ospina et al., 2008; Peters-Scheffer et al., 2011; Reichow & Wolery, 2009; Spechley & Boyd, 2009; Straus et al., 2013; Virués-Ortega, 2010), it is possible to identify outcome-effectiveness studies concerning comprehensive behavioural interventions for ASD. The current analysis

Interventions for Autism: Evidence for Educational and Clinical Practice, First Edition. Phil Reed.
© 2016 John Wiley & Sons, Ltd. Published 2016 by John Wiley & Sons, Ltd.

includes data from 33 studies, involving 38 separate behavioural intervention programmes, as some studies include more than one condition (e.g. Sallows & Graupner, 2005; Stock et al., 2013). All of these studies satisfy the basic quality criteria set out in Chapter 1.

Table 5.1 gives a description of the characteristics of the intervention conditions from the various studies included in the current meta-analyses and described their: sample size, type of programme studied (divided into 'Lovaas' or 'Generic ABA'), location (clinic or home), duration in months, intensity (hours of intervention per week) and total hours of intervention given.

Inspection of Table 5.1 shows that these studies have a wide range of characteristics, meaning that the results of any meta-analyses are based on a very broad set of programmes. This reflects the conclusions reached by previous analyses of this area (Eikeseth, 2009; Makrygianni & Reed, 2010a; Ospina et al., 2008; Peters-Scheffer et al., 2011; Reichow & Wolery, 2009; Spreckley & Boyd, 2009; Virués-Ortega, 2010) and suggests that the database for behavioural interventions is already substantial and allows for a thorough analysis of its effectiveness.

The typical sample size for these programmes was around 28 participants (standard deviation = ± 27.9; range 7–158). These participants were predominately male (mean per study = 84%) and had a mean age of 42.79 months (±11.75, range = 25–89). The mean intellectual functioning of participants in these studies at baseline, measured by standardized IQ tests, was: 53.41 (±13.39, range = 15–76); their mean standardized language functioning was slightly lower than their intellectual functioning and was: 41.87 (±15.22, range = 12–63) and they had a mean standardized (Vineland Adaptive Behaviour Scales; VABS) adaptive and social behaviour score of 58.21 (±5.88, range = 50–70).

There were examples of each of the three study designs suggested in Chapter 1: Randomized control trials (RCTs) accounted for 15% (five) of the conditions included (e.g. Eikeseth et al., 2002; Sallows & Graupner, 2005); there were more programmes drawn from controlled studies (45%; 17; e.g. Howard et al., 2005; Reed et al., 2007b; Remington et al., 2007) and 42% (16) were observational studies (e.g. Anderson et al., 1987; Harris & Handlemann, 2000). Where a study included two different behavioural programmes (e.g. Hayward et al., 2009; Perry et al., 2013), then these studies were treated as observational with respect to each of the programmes, rather than comparing the two programmes with one another.

About 58% (22) of the reports concerned clinic-based (including school-based) or professional-led programmes compared to programmes that were conducted in the home and led by parents. This is smaller number of clinic-based conditions than reported by Virués-Ortega (2010), who noted that 80% of behavioural-intervention studies were clinic-based programmes and this difference may reflect a shift in the type of study conducted over the last few years. These data are important to note as they suggest the majority of studies are conducted on professionally led programmes, but a survey reported by Love et al. (2009) noted that most individuals receive the majority of their behavioural intervention at home (58%), with only 20% of people indicating that school and 13% that clinics, provided most of the behavioural programme. Thus, the reality of delivery of behavioural programmes contrasts somewhat with the settings for the outcome-effectiveness studies. This discrepancy between where most programmes are actually conducted and the data from outcome-effectiveness studies has been noted previously as a possible limitation of this data set on the external validity of these studies (Connor, 1998; Mudford et al., 2000).

Table 5.1 Characteristics of studies assessing ABA programmes, showing the number of participants (N), type of trial (Obs = observational; Cont = controlled; RCT = randomized control trial), type of programme (Lovaas/UCLA versus generic ABA), who the programme was led by (Par = parent; Clin = clinician), as well as the duration, weekly intensity, and total hours of intervention.

Study	Year	N	Trial type	Programme	Lead by	Duration (weeks)	Intensity (h/week)	Total Hours
Anan et al.	2008	72	Obs	ABA	Par	12	15	180
Anderson et al.	1987	13	Obs	ABA	Par	53	20	1060
Baker-Ericzen	2007	158	Obs	ABA	Par	12		
Ben-Itzchak et al.	2008	44	Obs	ABA	Clin	53	45	2385
Ben-Itzchak & Zachor	2007	25	Obs	ABA	Clin	53	35	1855
Bibby et al.	2001	66	Obs	Lovaas	Par	32	6	192
Birnbauer & Leach	1993	9	Cont	Lovaas	Clin	105	19	1995
Boyd & Corley	2001	22	Obs	Lovaas		23		
Cohen et al.	2006	21	Cont	Lovaas	Clin	141	37	5217
Eikeseth et al.	2002	13	RCT	Lovaas	Clin	52	28	1456
Eikeseth et al.	2007	13	RCT	Lovaas	Clin	387	18	6966
Eldevik et al.	2012	31	Cont	ABA	Clin	108	13	1404
Eldevik et al.	2006	13	Cont	ABA	Clin	89	12	1068
Farell et al.	2005	7	Cont	Lovaas	Par	110	30	3300
Flanagan et al.	2012	61	Cont	ABA	Clin	118	25	2950
Harris & Handleman	2000	27	Obs	ABA	Clin	407	40	16280
Harris et al.	1991	16	Cont	Lovaas	Clin	49		
Hayward et al.	2009	21	Obs	Lovaas	Par	52	34	1768
Hayward et al.	2009	23	Obs	Lovaas	Clin	52	37	1924
Howard et al.	2005	29	Cont	ABA	Clin	62	32	1984
Lovaas	1987	19	Cont	Lovaas	Clin	106	40	4240
Magiati et al.	2007	28	Cont	Lovaas	Clin	109	32	3488
Matos & Mustaca	2005	9	Obs	ABA	Clin	48	40	1920
Perry et al.	2013	60	Obs	ABA	Par	86	30	2580
Perry et al.	2013	60	Obs	ABA	Par	86	30	2580
Reed et al.	2007a	13	Cont	ABA	Par	42	13	546
Reed et al.	2007a	14	Cont	ABA	Par	42	30	1260
Reed et al.	2007b	12	Cont	ABA	Par	42	30	1260
Remington et al.	2007	23	Cont	ABA	Clin	105	26	2730
Sallows & Graupner	2005	13	RCT	Lovaas	Clin	211	38	8018
Sallows & Graupner	2005	10	RCT	Lovaas	Par	199	31	6169
Sheinkopf & Siegel	1998	11	Cont	Lovaas	Par	69	19	1311

Table 5.1   (*Continued*)

Study	Year	N	Trial type	Programme	Lead by	Duration (weeks)	Intensity (h/week)	Total Hours
Smith et al.	2000	15	RCT	Lovaas	Clin	250	25	6250
Smith et al.	1997	11	Cont	Lovaas	Clin	53	30	1590
Stock et al.	2013	14	Obs	ABA	Par	52	13	676
Stock et al.	2013	14	Obs	ABA	Par	48	20	960
Weiss	1999	20	Obs	ABA	Clin	106	40	4240
Zachor & Ben-Itzchak	2010	45	Cont	ABA	Clin	52	20	1040

Reichow and Wolery (2009) noted that around 60% of studies were of a Lovaas programme, which corresponds broadly with the data presented by Ospina et al. (2008). The current study found that about 47% of the studies were of a Lovaas type, possibly reflecting a move towards newer behavioural programmes over the last few years (see Chapter 4). However, unless the intervention is delivered in a clinic setting where all aspects of the programme delivery can be controlled and described (see Ben-Itzchak et al., 2008; Lovaas, 1987), then the exact type of behavioural approach delivered can be difficult to untangle. For example, when asked to specify the type of behavioural approach that was being used with their children, Love et al. (2009) found that 29% of parents said 'Early Intensive Behavioural Intervention', 25% indicated 'Applied Behaviour Analysis', 23% picked Verbal Behaviour, 19% indicated 'Discrete Trial Instruction' and only 4% indicated Lovaas. However, when asked about the curriculum that was being followed on the programme, 59% of parents selected Lovaas and 57% indicated Verbal Behaviour and 48% of parents also indicated that their treatment was based on more than one published curricula. Thus, there appears to be substantial overlap between these programmes.

The duration of the behavioural programmes reported in Table 5.1 varied from short applications of 12 weeks (Anan et al., 2008) to, in the extreme, long programmes of 407 weeks (Harris & Handleman, 2000), with a mean duration of around 97 weeks (see also Makrygianni & Reed, 2010a; Reichow, 2012). This mean programme duration suggests that much of the data collected from these outcome-effectiveness studies is based on programmes of 2 years' duration; somewhat shorter than that initially implied by Lovaas (1987) as being necessary for producing gains.

The temporal intensity of the programme (hours per week) ranged from 6 (Bibby et al., 2001) to 45 (Ben-Itzchak et al., 2008), with a mean of about 27 hours a week (see Makrygianni & Reed, 2010a) and a modal value in the 28–30 hours a week range (similar to that noted by Reichow, 2012). Reichow and Wolery (2009) note that the various combinations of the overall duration of the programme and the weekly time intensity, gives a very wide range of total hours of intervention input, in the current case from less than 180 hours (Anan et al., 2008), to over 16 000 hours spent on the programme (Harris & Handlemann, 2000).

In addition to the data on the programme and child characteristics, it has also been noted that there were about four staff (range 2–7) involved in delivering each of these programmes (Makrygianni & Reed, 2010a), with around 60% of the interventions being delivered by undergraduate students who were employed as tutors (Reichow & Wolery, 2009). Almost all of the programmes studies were supervised by a qualified Behaviour Analyst.

Overall Outcomes

The studies documented in Table 5.1 have employed a wide range of measures to indicate outcomes, but have mainly focused on standardized measures of intellectual functioning, language ability and the adaptive and challenging behaviours of the participants. In addition, some of the studies also attempted to document the intervention outcomes in terms of the school placements of the participants following the programme.

The results for the individual outcome-effectiveness studies are presented in Table 5.2. These data show the change in the levels of functioning that were measured in those studies, in terms of the change in the standard score of the measure in question and the associated effect size. The latter measure gives an indication of the strength of the impact of the programme that is, broadly, independent of the sample size and measure used. The table is shaded so that strong effects (increase of 15 points in the standard score or greater than 0.8 in terms of the effect size), are seen in cells with lighter shaded backgrounds – these can be taken as practically important changes; moderate impacts (changes of between 10 and 14 points and effect sizes of between 0.4 and 0.7) are shown with medium shaded backgrounds and weak impacts (changes of less than 10 or effect sizes of less than 0.3) are shown in dark shaded cells; these suggest little important change as a result of the programme.

These two sorts of impact are shown for two metrics of the programme's effectiveness: (i) changes between the baseline (pre-test) and follow-up (post-test) measures that indicate the effect of the programme, itself, on the participants' functioning and (ii) where it is available, the difference in the pre- to post-test scores in the behavioural programme group compared to any control groups included in the report (see Chapter 1 for further discussion).

The first of these metrics of impact (the change in participants' functioning over the course of the programme) is a straightforward measure to interpret. However, the comparison with control groups is not, as this needs consideration of exactly what the control group received (see Chapter 1), which varies between studies. Of the 38 conditions discussed here, 19 provide comparison data from a control group other than another behavioural programme. In all cases, the control group was assessed over the same time period as the behavioural intervention group, however, what they received during that period varied widely. In some cases, the control group was produced retrospectively from the records of children not on the behavioural programme (e.g. Lovaas, 1987). In many cases, the comparison group was recorded as receiving 'eclectic' or 'treatment as usual' (Eikeseth et al., 2002; Eldevik et al., 2006), which probably means that they received whatever interventions were offered by their local schools. There were very few instances where the control group was receiving a fully specified alternative treatment (e.g. Reed et al., 2007b) or where the control group was matched in terms of hours of intervention (Howard et al., 2005).

These data form the bases for many of the previously conducted meta-analyses (although are more extensive than most) and most of these meta-analyses have come to the same conclusions (see Reichow, 2012). Of these meta-analyses, six (Eikeseth, 2009;

Table 5.2 Outcomes of studies of ABA showing the pre-to-post intervention changes in standard scores and effect sizes (ES₁), and comparisons with control groups in standard scores and effect sizes (ES₂).

Study (Year)	Pre to Post Change						Comparison with Control					
	IQ	Lang	ASB	IQ ES$_1$	Lang ES$_1$	ASB ES$_1$	IQ	Lang	ASB	IQ ES$_2$	Lang ES$_2$	ASB ES$_2$
Anan et al. (2008)	8.00		5.00	1.27		0.70						
Anderson et al. (1987)				0.35	0.65	1.04						
Baker-Ericzen (2007)												
Ben-Itzchak et al. (2008)	14.82			2.23								
Ben-Itzchak & Zachor (2007)	17.30			0.98	0.78							
Bibby et al. (2001)	6.00		6.90	0.25		0.60						
Birnbauer & Leach (1993)				1.60	1.33	−0.78				0.59	0.56	−0.15
Boyd & Corley (2001)												
Cohen et al. (2006)	25.00	20.00	9.00	0.88	0.75	1.43	11.00	11.00	15.00	0.71	0.53	0.85
Eikeseth et al. (2002)	17.00	27.00	11.00	1.34	1.08	1.96	12.00	26.00	11.00	1.45	5.60	1.09
Eikeseth et al. (2007)	21.00		12.00	1.25		0.86	15.00		23.00	1.14		2.08
Eldevik et al. (2012)	15.00		6.00	0.94		0.72	14.00		7.00	0.80		0.87
Eldevik et al. (2006)	8.00	9.00	−0.02	0.53	0.82	−0.05	11.00	18.00	5.00	1.01	1.43	0.86
Farrell et al. (2005)				0.41						−0.32		
Flanagan et al. (2012)			2.00			0.86			9.00			1.29
Harris & Handleman (2000)	18.00			0.63								
Harris et al. (1991)	19.00	8.00		1.42	0.02							
Hayward et al. (2009)	15.00	7.30	7.40	0.98	0.49	0.71						

(Continued)

Table 5.2 (Continued)

Study (Year)	Pre to Post Change						Comparison with Control					
	IQ	Lang	ASB	IQ ES₁	Lang ES₁	ASB ES₁	IQ	Lang	ASB	IQ ES₂	Lang ES₂	ASB ES₂
Hayward et al. (2009)	17.00	6.00	6.00	1.15	0.40	0.88						
Howard et al. (2005)	33.00	19.00	11.00	1.32	1.02	0.93	23.00	17.00	13.00	1.33	0.97	1.41
Lovaas (1987)	29.00			1.10			18.00			1.24		
Magiati et al. (2007)	-11.00		-2.80	-0.35	0.64	-0.35	-4.70		4.70	-0.23	0.27	0.96
Matos & Mustaca (2006)				1.56	2.38	1.34						
Perry et al. (2013)	17.00		4.00	0.80		0.34						
Perry et al. (2013)	2.00		5.00	0.08		0.49						
Reed et al. (2007a)	6.00		-1.00	0.46		-0.23						
Reed et al. (2007a)	14.00		3.00	0.94		0.40	7.00		1.90	2.06		0.72
Reed et al. (2007b)	15.00		2.00	0.84		0.20	9.00		3.00	0.92		0.30
Remington et al. (2007)	12.00			0.85		0.65	14.00			0.73		
Sallows & Graupner (2005)	23.00	11.00	16.00	1.21	0.87	0.79	-5.00	-8.00	3.70	-0.28	-0.30	0.20
Sallows & Graupner (2005)	27.00	16.00	18.00	1.90	1.13	0.56						
Sheinkopf & Siegel (1998)	27.00			1.07			24.00			1.12		
Smith et al. (2000)	16.00	59.00	2.00	1.00	1.60	-0.11	10.00	28.00	4.40	1.25	0.47	0.19
Smith et al. (1997)	8.00	5.00	2.00	1.71	1.56	0.25	11.00			1.39		
Stock et al. (2013)	13.00	6.00	5.00	0.57	0.40	0.54						
Stock et al. (2013)	8.00	4.00	3.00	0.33	0.27	0.18						
Weiss (1999)	0		33.60	0		4.13						
Zachor & Ben-Itzchak (2010)	0	6.00	4.00	0	0.46	0.50	-2.00	-4.00	0	-0.15	-0.30	0

IQ = intellectual function, Lang = language function; ASB = adaptive-social behaviour. White = strong effect; light grey = moderate effect; dark grey = weak effect; black = no data.

Makrygianni & Reed, 2010a; Peters-Scheffer et al., 2011; Reichow & Wolery, 2009; Straus et al., 2013 Virués-Ortega, 2010) have been broadly supportive of the impact of such behavioural programmes, one (Ospina et al., 2008) suggested that there is growing evidence for the impact of the technique, although it is not the only intervention that offers advantages and one meta-analysis (Spreckley & Boyd, 2009) suggested that there was no evidence for the effectiveness of behavioural interventions.

Given that the meta-analyses all employed variants of the same studies in their analysis, the discrepancy in their findings may come as a surprise. The reasons for this have been reviewed by Reichow (2012) and can largely be attributed to differences in the selection criteria employed by the analyses. The two which did not support the effectiveness of behavioural interventions to the same extent as the others, either employed a much wider inclusion criteria (Ospina et al., 2008) or a very much narrower set of inclusion criteria (Spreckley & Boyd, 2009). Nevertheless, in summarizing these data, Reichow (2012) concluded that the meta-analyses have shown moderate to large average effect sizes in favour of ABA compared to control groups in terms of both intellectual functioning and adaptive behavioural functioning.

However, this rather sweeping generalization hides at least two provisos that need careful assessment in deciding whether any particular behavioural intervention will have this level of impact. Firstly, there are differences in the extent to which these programmes impact on the various domains of functioning (intellectual, linguistic and adaptive behavioural) and each of these domains will be considered in turn. Secondly, the studies included in the meta-analyses also show a variation along a number of dimensions, such as the type of programme employed (i.e. Lovaas versus 'generic ABA'), the location of the programme (i.e. school/clinic-led or parent-led), in their quality (i.e. both in the level of training provided to staff and parents and in the rigour of the studies' methodologies), all of which will receive comment in the sections that follow.

In addition, the programmes also differed in terms of the amount of intervention that was given to the participants, which can be divided into: the duration of the study (how long the programme was conducted); the intensity of the intervention (how many hours per week the intervention was delivered) and the total hours (duration × intensity). The impact of each these three quantifiable variables on the change in the standard scores of the three functioning domains can be seen in the scatterplots shown in Figure 5.1 and these data will be discussed in detail next as they relate to each functioning domain section.

Intellectual functioning

The impact of behavioural programmes on intellectual functioning is a key take-home message for prospective users of the service, but is also somewhat controversial, in that it can be argued that this outcome is not a key part of ASD (e.g. Connor, 1998). However, as noted in Chapter 2, tests of intellectual functioning measure encompass a very broad spectrum of important abilities, potentially giving a comprehensive snapshot of the impact of behavioural programmes on cognitive functioning. According to Virués-Ortega (2010), seven different standardized tests of intellectual functioning have been employed in these studies and Table 5.3 outlines the various domains of functioning that they cover.

Some of these tests measure both verbal and nonverbal intellectual functioning and the current review takes the composite of these two measures – there being relatively

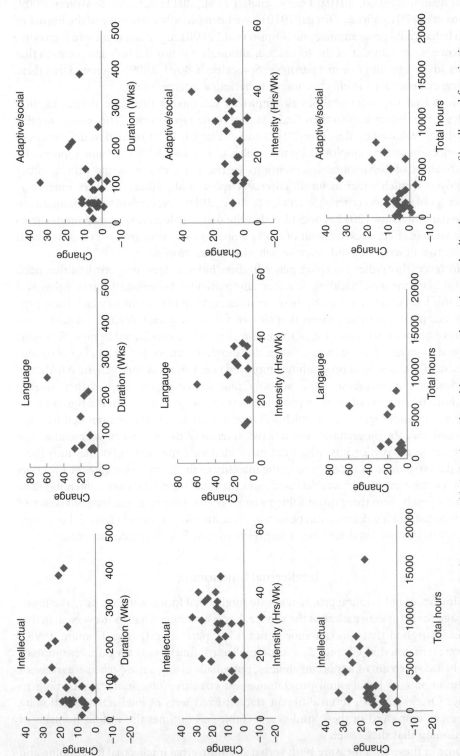

Figure 5.1 Impact of programme duration, weekly intensity and total hours on change in standardized measures of intellectual functioning, language and adaptive-social behaviour (see text for discussion).

Table 5.3 Summary of some commonly-used standardized assessment tools for measuring intellectual functioning.

Scale	Domains	Test time	Age range
Bayley Scales of Infant Development	Three scales administered to child – cognitive, motor and language function. Two questionnaires conducted with parent – social-emotional and adaptive behaviour.	30–90	1–42 months
Cattell Infant Intelligence Scale	Evaluates child's motor control and verbalizations. Motor control is assessed by tasks involving manipulating various objects. The child's communication attempts are also evaluated.	20–30 min	Birth– 12:13 years
Developmental Profile	Five areas assessed to provide age equivalent scores – physical, self-help, social, academic and communication.	20–40 min	
Leiter International Performance Scale	Nonverbal measure of intelligence assesses cognitive, attentional, and neuropsychological abilities across four domains – reasoning, visualization, memory and attention.	20–45 min	3–75 years
Merrill-Palmer Scales of Mental Test	Intelligence test requiring oral and non-oral responses. Covers language skills, motor skills, manual dexterity and matching ability.	45 min	18 months– 4 years
Mullen Scales of Early Learning	Measures learning ability and patterns, and identifies learning disabilities. Provides scores in four areas – visual receptive organization, visual expressive organization, language receptive organization and language expressive organization.	15–60 min	1–69 months
Psycho-educational Profile (revised)	Behavioural observation of performance and a caregiver report provide 10 subtest scores plus 3 composites – communication, motor and maladaptive behaviours.	45–90 min	6 months– years
Wechsler Preschool and Primary Scale of Intelligence	Intelligence test contains a wide range of subtests including – verbal comprehension, visual spatial, working memory, fluid reasoning, processing speed.	30–60 min	3–7 years

little data available by which to provide independent assessments of the impact of behavioural programmes on each area, separately. It might be noted that two previous reviews have attempted to provide differentiation between the impact of behavioural programmes on nonverbal and verbal functioning (Peters-Scheffer et al., 2011; Virués-Ortega, 2010) and have noted broadly similar effects of these two aspects of intellectual functioning, but with slightly higher effect sizes for the verbal compared to nonverbal aspects of intellectual functioning.

Change in functioning

Basic findings   The data in Table 5.2 shows a largely consistent trend across the studies in the improvement of the standardized intellectual functioning scores from baseline to follow-up. The mean increase in intellectual functioning after the behavioural programmes was 14.7 (±9.3; range = –11–33) points. This improvement mirrors the conclusions of the meta-analysis of meta-analyses conducted by Reichow (2012). There are two issues to note in respect to these data: (i) this represents an improvement in intellectual functioning of around one standard deviation on the IQ scale, which would move an individual from one classification of intellectual functioning to another (e.g. from moderately to mildly learning disabled) and, thus, must be regarded as practically important; but also (ii) there is a large degree of variation in these results across the studies, with a range of change scores of 44 points, suggesting that many factors are impacting to modulate this improvement. A similar pattern of impact emerges when the effect sizes are considered. This metric shows a mean effect size of 0.93 (±0.56, range: –0.35–2.23), which falls into the 'large' effect size category (see Cohen, 1988) – although, as with the change in the standard scores, there is a substantial range in these effect sizes.

Analysis of these data by the manner in which the programme was delivered (clinic/school versus home/parent) show a marginal benefit from the programme being led by a clinic/school (mean intellectual functioning change = 15.7, mean effect size = 1.07), compared to when it was home/parent-led (intellectual functioning = 13.2, ES = 0.73). Beyond these current data, three controlled studies have specifically addressed this topic with a mixed pattern of results. Sallows and Graupner (2005) studied children of between 24 and 42 months and an IQ greater than 35 at the start of the study. The participants were either in a clinic- or a parent-led group, which both produced similar IQ gains to one another at a 1-year follow-up assessment. Very similar results were reported by Hayward et al. (2009) in a study of clinic- versus parent-led Lovaas type programmes, for children aged between 24 and 42 months, over 1 year. Both groups produced gains, with no significant differences in those gains depending on group. However, Smith et al. (2000) examined a clinic-led versus a parent-led intervention over a 2-year period. The chronological age of the participants at the start of this study was between 18 and 42 months and their IQ scores were between 35 and 75. The results were quite clear, in that the clinic-led group performed better in terms of IQ gain, but it should be noted that the former group had substantially greater time input on the intervention.

There was a slight advantage in terms of intellectual functioning gain when the programme was primarily a Lovaas intervention (IQ = 17.1, ES = 1.06), compared to a more 'generic ABA' intervention (IQ = 12.6, ES = 0.82). Two reports have examined this issue directly (Reed et al., 2007a; Stock et al., 2013) and both of these reports also noted a numeric advantage for Lovaas programmes in this functioning domain.

Although difficult to assess quantitatively, the rigor of the study (as outlined in Chapter 1) has also been examined as a potential predictor of the outcome across a number of reviews. For example, Reichow and Wolery (2009) found a weak positive relationship between the rigor of the study and its impact on intellectual functioning and Makrygianni and Reed (2010a) who found a similar weak (but statistically insignificant) relationship between the quality of the study of its impact on intellectual functioning.

Programme factors   In terms of the aspects of the behavioural programmes (duration, intensity and total hours), the left panel of Figure 5.1 shows their impact on the change in intellectual functioning (measured by standard score change). Initial inspection of these data shows that all three variables had a moderate positive relationship with the gain in intellectual functioning points. However, this simple summary actually masks a more complex relationship between these variables. In order to study these relationships further, the studies were divided into groups that had different values for these characteristics and the impact of the different groups on intellectual functioning was noted.

In terms of overall programme duration, the studies were divided into those that lasted up to 12 months, those lasting between 13 and 24 months, those between 25 and 36 months and those lasting longer than 36 months. For weekly intensity, the groups created had less than 15 hours a week, between 15 and 24 hours a week, 25 and 34 hours a week and over 35 hours a week. Finally, in terms of total hours of intervention, fours groups were created at the quartile points for total hours: with up to 1164 hours; between 1165 and 1984 hours; between 1985 and 3864 hours and over 3865 hours a week.

Figure 5.2 shows the gains in intellectual functioning standard scores for each group for each programme-characteristic domain, as well as the additional gains in standardized scores per year for each group, calculated by subtracting the previous groups' gain from the target groups' gain – giving the value added in terms of IQ points per year. In a broad aspect, these data could be used to determine the appropriate programme for an individual based on the projected need for gain in intellectual functioning, although, as shall be seen in Chapter 6, there are other factors that also modulate the rates of gain.

For all three of the programme characteristics, there is a tendency to show greater gains as the temporal input increases. Specific studies on this topic have tended to present a rather mixed pattern of results, with some studies showing greater time inputs being more successful (Lovaas, 1987; Reed et al., 2007a) but other studies do not show this pattern – including a very large-scale observational study of over 200 children (Fernell et al., 2011). However, the added value of the standardized points gained per additional year data reflects the previously noted complexity. For the duration of the study (top left panel), this added value tends to be flat after the first year. This suggests that a 3-year programme (Lovaas, 1987; Smith et al., 2000) may only be needed for very severely intellectually impaired cases and milder cases may need less time on the programme. The weekly intensity (top right panel) shows some degree of decrease after the initial 15 hours a week input, but also a diminishing return after this initial input. This profile of diminishing returns was also noted in some (Makrygianni & Reed, 2010a), but not all (Reichow & Wolery, 2009; Virués-Ortega, 2010), of the previously reported meta-analyses. However, precisely where the diminishing returns start is a matter for how the data are split up.

The total programme hours (bottom left panel) show a somewhat more erratic profile of added value. In order to determine if it is better to devote time intensively within a week or have the programme run for a longer period, the bottom right panel of Figure 5.2 displays the data for IQ gain in four groups created by splitting duration and intensity at the median value, to create four groups – low duration and low intensity, high duration and low intensity, low duration and high intensity and high duration and intensity. These data show that, apart from the low

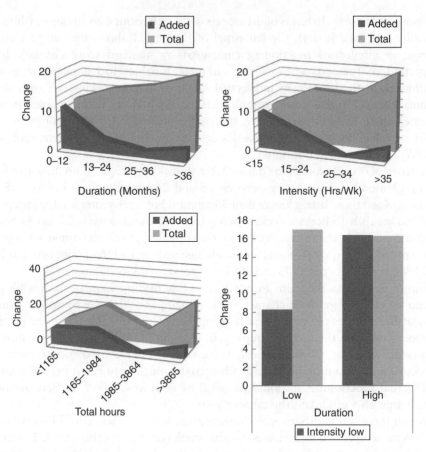

Figure 5.2 Change in standardized intellectual functioning as a product of programme duration (top left), weekly intensity (top right), and total programme hours (bottom right). Grey area is the total gain, and the dark grey area is additional gain for each added period of time. Bottom right panel shows total gains in programmes of low and high duration and intensity.

duration and low intensity programmes, the other ways of combining hours of input – longer programmes or more time per week, show equivalent gains to one another – with there being no particular advantage for very long and very intensive programmes.

Comparison with control groups　The second key metric to consider in evaluating behavioural programmes is how they fare compared to participants without the programme. This is assessed by comparing the outcome for the behavioural programme with that of a comparison group who did not receive that programme. Perhaps not surprisingly, these comparisons show that the impact of the behavioural programme is not as great as suggested by examining the change from baseline to follow-up. Nevertheless, the overall pattern of data from the studies displayed in Table 5.2 is (with few exceptions) that the participants' intellectual functioning increases more on the behavioural programme than it does in the comparison group. The mean improvement over time for the behavioural programmes compared to the comparison conditions in terms of the standard scores was 10.5 (±8.5, range: –5–24) points, with a mean effect size in favour of the behavioural programme of 0.82 ($\pm$0.68, range: −0.32–2.06). These relative improvements can be categorized as being a strong effect of practically significance and suggest that behavioural programmes are more effective than the comparison in elevating the participants' intellectual functioning.

There were some differences observed across the programme types, with programmes conducted at home (IQ = 13.3, ES = 0.94) showing greater relative gains than programmes run at by a school/clinic (IQ = 9.8, ES = 0.78). Generic ABA programmes (IQ = 10.8, ES = 0.96) produced similar relative gains to the Lovaas programmes (IQ = 10.1, ES = 0.73).

These differences do not necessarily mirror the changes seen in the change from baseline to follow-up, previously, but may actually reflect little more that differences in the 'strength' or 'quality' of the comparison group that was employed in the study, as well as the rigour of that study's methodology. Reichow and Wolery (2009) noted the greatest effect sizes in studies that compared behavioural programmes to other less time-intense behavioural programmes (e.g. Lovaas, 1987; Reed et al., 2007a). However, this pattern is not always observed at the level of the individual study. For example, Howard et al. (2005) noted one of the largest effect sizes when comparing a behavioural treatment conducted in school, to a 'generic' programme receiving the same amount of teaching input.

Summary There is little doubt that participants on a behavioural programme tend to benefit in terms of their intellectual functioning. The extent of this benefit seems to depend on the intensity of the weekly teaching on the programme; with the studies showing the greatest gains being made on programmes with longer and more intense teaching – although there may be an upper limit to this relationship. Additionally, the size of these benefits are reduced when the behavioural programme is compared with the gains made on another programme, although, even in these cases, the behavioural programme does impact to a greater extent on the intellectual functioning of the children than the comparison treatment (Howard et al., 2005; Reed et al., 2007b). However, there are still unanswered questions about whether the nature of the comparison groups would moderate this impact and very few studies have compared behavioural programmes with equally intensive alternative programmes.

Language functioning

The language abilities of individuals with ASD are related to the core difficulties and differences exhibited by individuals with ASD (see Chapter 2) in so far as they impact on the ability to communicate and maintain relationships (see DSM-5). Improvements in this aspect of functioning have been taken to be central to improving the prognosis for individuals with ASD (see Luyster et al., 2008; Chapter 1). Given this, the assessment of the impact of the intervention programme on the participants' language functioning has played a large role in many of the evaluations of behavioural programmes (with around 50% of the outcome-effectiveness studies employing a language measure).

Language ability has been assessed with a variety of standardized instruments in studies of outcome-effectiveness (see Virués-Ortega, 2010), including the: Peabody Picture Vocabulary Test/British Picture Language Scale; Clinical Evaluation of

Language Fundamentals; Mullen Scales of Early Learning; Reynell Developmental Language Scales; Receptive-Expressive Emergence Language Scale and Sequenced Inventory of Communication Development. These scales tend to focus on two areas of the participants' linguistic functioning: (i) receptive language ability – that is, their ability to understand what is being said to them and (ii) expressive language ability – which reflects their ability to use language. However, the assessment of functional communication is not assessed to any great extent by these measures. A range of alternative assessments are available that do focus on this aspect of language and these often rely on parent-reports of their child's language ability, such as the MacArthur–Bates Communicative Development Inventories or the communication sub-scale of the Vineland Adaptive Behavior Scales (VABS). However, these are not widely used as assessments of language.

Notwithstanding the previous discussion, the two main aspects of language (receptive and expressive) ability have been used extensively in outcome-effectiveness studies of behavioural programmes. The data in Table 5.2 and the middle panel of Figure 5.1 are a composite of these two aspects of language. In fact, when these aspects of language are considered separately, there appears to be little differential impact of behavioural programmes, with the reviews by Virués-Ortega (2010) and Reichow and Wolery (2009) noting little difference between the two, whereas Peters-Scheffer et al. (2011) found a marginally greater impact of behavioural programmes on receptive language compared to expressive language.

Change in functioning

Basic findings   Studies have typically noted a large improvement in the language standard score of the participants after exposure to a behavioural programme (mean standard score improvement = 14.5 ± 14.5; range 4–59). This improvement is also reflected in the mean effect size from baseline to follow-up, which is 0.88 (±0.56; range: 0.02–2.38). The comparisons between the clinic/school-based programmes and those conducted in the home show that programmes conducted in schools/clinics produced a greater mean increase in standardized language ability than those at home (17.0 to 8.3, respectively) and a greater effect size (clinic = 0.98; home = 0.59). This finding was also noted in the meta-analysis reported by Straus et al. (2013), which found that parent-mediated programme have substantially lower effect sizes in terms of language outcomes.

Of the two forms of behavioural programme, the Lovaas approach (standard score = 17.7, ES = 0.90) seems to offer an advantage over 'generic ABA' approaches (standard score = 8.8, ES = 0.85). However, this may reflect a combination of the type of language training that occurs on the programme (naming, matching to verbal sample in the Lovaas approach, versus functional mand raining on other behavioural programmes – see Chapter 4) and the nature of the language tests used to assess this ability, which tend to focus on the former (Lovaas favouring) measure, rather than the latter type of functional language ability.

Programme characteristics   Inspection of the middle panel of Figure 5.1 shows that there is a strong positive relationship between both the duration of the programme and the total programme hours, with language functioning. The weekly intensity of the programme was also positively related to language outcome, but not

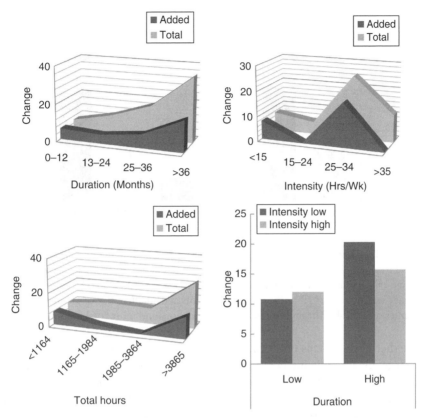

Figure 5.3 Change in standardized language score as a product of programme duration (top left), weekly intensity (top right), and total programme hours (bottom right). Grey area is the total gain, and the dark grey area is additional gain for each added period of time. Bottom right panel shows total gain by programmes of low and high duration and intensity.

as strikingly as the other two variables. This finding was also noted in the meta-analyses reported by Reichow and Wolery (2009) and Virués-Ortega (2010).

The importance of the programme duration and the total number of programme hours can also be seen when the studies were divided into groups based in their temporal characteristics, as described previously for intellectual functioning (see Figure 5.2). In terms of the overall duration of the programme (top panel), both total gains in language standard score and the extra value added per year, increased as the duration increased: that is, this was smallest in studies lasting up to 12 months and increased through studies lasting between 13 and 24 months, those lasting between 25 and 36 months and were greatest in those studies lasting longer than 36 months. This pattern was also true for the total programme hours (bottom panel), with studies grouped into those with up to 1164 hours, those with between 1165 and 1984 hours, between 1985 and 3864 hours and those with over 3865 hours. However, in terms of the weekly intensity (middle panel) – studies with less than 15 hours a week, between 15 and 24 hours a week, 25 and 34 hours a week and over 35 hours a week – there was a less clear relationship between this variable and outcomes and added value per month.

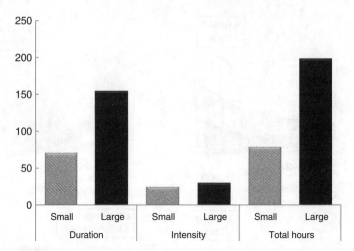

Figure 5.4 Temporal characteristics of programmes (duration in weeks, intensity in weekly hours, and total days input) for ABA programmes that produced a small impact on language (an increase of less than 15 standard points, and an effect size of less than 0.8) and a large impact on language (an increase of 15 or more standard points and an effect size of greater the 0.8). Programmes successful with language have longer durations and more total input time.

To further illustrate this effect, a criteria was adopted to classify studies into those with a large impact on language (an increase in 15 standard points and an effect size of greater the 0.8). There were five outcome-effectiveness studies that had such a substantial improvement in language (Eikeseth et al., 2002; Howard et al., 2005; Sallows & Graupner, 2005; Sheinkopf & Siegel, 1998; Smith et al., 2000). When comparing these large-impact studies to the remaining nine studies that measured language functioning (see Figure 5.4), in terms of their temporal characteristics, the only differences between the high-impact and low-impact studies appeared to be the programme duration and overall total hours of the programme (represented as days of teaching to maintain the integrity of the *y*-axis). There was little difference in the weekly intervention intensity of these two groups of studies.

Comparison with control groups The mean improvement in language standard scores of participants undergoing a behavioural programme, relative to that achieved by a comparison group, was 12.5 points (±14.0, range –8–28) and the mean effect size advantage of a behavioural programme was 1.03 (±1.80, range –0.30–5.60). Both of these metrics suggest that behavioural programmes offer a strong and practically relevant, improvement in language over the various comparisons that have been employed.

However, there was a substantial range in these improvements and this may well reflect the finding reported by Reichow and Wolery (2009) that the type of comparison employed has a substantial influence on the size of the effect noted. This finding was mirrored by Makrygianni and Reed (2010), who noted twice the effect sizes in less-well controlled studies (i.e. those with weaker methodologies and poorer comparison groups) than in stronger controlled studies – the advantage for behavioural programmes reducing from large, in the less-well controlled studies, to moderate in the better controlled studies.

Summary   The overall pattern of data for the impact of behavioural programmes on linguistic function of individuals with ASD is that such programmes impact well on this domain and that it appears to be the overall duration of the intervention that is important for producing this effect. However there are still some important questions that remain to be answered, it is not clear whether this reflects more than the role of the specific type of instruction that occurs on behavioural programmes, which tends to be very similar to the nature of the tests used to assess this area of functioning. Moreover, the relative benefits on language of behavioural to comparison programmes are less easy to assess. Behavioural programmes clearly do improve language to a considerable extent relative to the other programmes, but this might reflect a combination of the previous consideration and the quality of the intervention being offered as a comparison.

Adaptive functioning

The adaptive behavioural skills of an individual with ASD have typically been assessed using the VABS (Sparrow et al., 1984). This is a very widely used and accepted measure of the personal and social skills that are required for everyday living. The scales reflect the individual's abilities in communication, daily living skills and socialization of the individual, as assessed by a parent or caregiver who knows the individual well (two other scales are less often used – motor skills and maladaptive behaviours). These scales can be combined to provide an overall estimate of the individual's adaptive behavioural skills. In addition to the VABS, there are alternative assessment tools for this domain, such as the Scales of Independent Behavior and the Adaptive Behavior Scale-School, but the VABS is by far the most commonly used.

Although there are clear reasons why this measure is important to ASD, there are other reasons to treat these outcomes in a somewhat different light than the two domains discussed previously. The adaptive behaviour ability is assessed almost exclusively by parent report. There is no particular reason to assume that the results will not be valid for outcome-effectiveness studies (see Charman et al., 2004), but there are known differences between the ratings given by parents to behaviours and those given by teachers or therapists – for example, parents often tend to rate these behaviours more negatively than teachers (Reed & Osborne, 2013, for a discussion). However, this measure is an important one to consider in that, unlike the previously mentioned domains of intellectual functioning and language, many of the domains contained in the VABS overlap with those areas that are deemed central to the definition of ASD – such as communication and socialization.

Change in functioning
Basic findings   The studies that have examined adaptive behaviour have typically noted only small to moderate improvements in the adaptive behaviours of the participants after a behavioural programme (mean standard improvement = 6.8 ± 7.5; range –2.8–33.6), with a mean effect size from baseline to follow-up of 0.67 (±0.87, range: –0.78–4.13). These effects are smaller than those noted for the intellectual or language functioning scores.

The comparisons between the clinic/school-based programmes and those conducted in the home suggest that the former is much more effective in terms of improving the adaptive behaviours of participant than the latter location. Programmes conducted in clinics-schools produced a greater mean increase in standardized adaptive ability than those at home (8.0 to 5.3, respectively), with the effect sizes being approximately twice as large in school/clinic-led programmes than parent-led programmes (clinic-school = 0.82; home = 0.46). A similar finding was noted in the meta-analysis provided by Straus et al. (2013).

There is little to differentiate the two forms of behavioural programme in terms of the standardized score improvement (Lovaas = 8.0; 'Generic ABA' = 5.9), but there were greater effect size improvements for the 'Generic ABA' programmes (0.75) compared to the Lovaas programmes (0.57). This may reflect the greater variety of training procedures adopted in non-Lovaas approaches (see Chapter 4), especially those involving functional communication training.

The right panel of Figure 5.1 shows the impact of the programme duration, weekly intensity and total hours of the programme, on the improvement of the standard adaptive behaviour score. These data show that the intensity of the weekly teaching and the overall number of hours, show the greatest impact on the adaptive behaviour scores, with the duration of the programme having a less substantial effect.

Figure 5.5 shows the comparison of dividing the studies in terms of the programme characteristics: overall duration (top left panel) – studies lasting up to 12 months, between 13 and 24 months, between 25 and 36 months and longer than 36 months; weekly intensity (top right panel) – studies with less than 15 hours a week, between 15 and 24 hours a week, 25 to 34 hours a week and over 35 hours a week and total hours (bottom left panel) – up to 1164 hours; between 1165 and 1984 hours; between 1985 and 3864 hours and over 3865 hours a week. Both in terms of the mean standard score gains and in terms of the added adaptive points per year, the temporal variables demonstrated a generally positive relationship to gains. The combination of higher duration and intensity (bottom right panel), demonstrated that, by far, the best method of developing adaptive behaviour. However, it should be noted that Fernell et al. (2011) found little impact of weekly intensity of a behavioural programme (comparing programmes of over 15 hours a week with programmes with minimal behavioural input) on the adaptive behavioural functioning of the participants; although it should be noted that neither group demonstrated great changes in this domain of functioning over the 2-year period studied.

Comparison with control groups The mean improvement in the adaptive behaviour standard scores of participants on a behavioural programme relative to those in a comparison group was 7.8 points (±6.4, range 0–23) and the mean effect size advantage of a behavioural programme was 0.76 (±0.61, range –0.15–2.08). Both of these metrics suggest that behavioural programmes offered a moderate to strong improvement in adaptive behaviour relative to the various comparisons employed.

As with the change relative to baseline improvements, these improvements were much more pronounced for the school/clinic-led approaches (standard score = 8.7, ES = 0.80), relative to the home-based programmes (standard score = 2.5, ES = 0.51). The relative weakness of parent-led approaches in this domain may be mediated by the level of prior training and support that they receive; as the

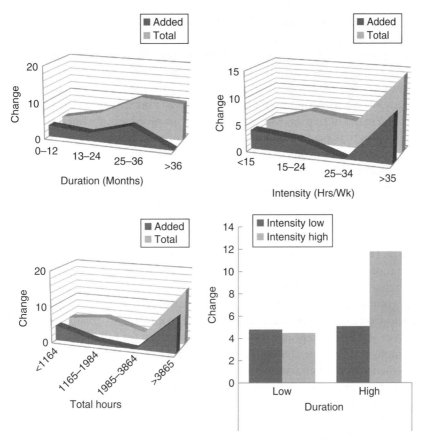

Figure 5.5 Change in standardized adaptive-social behaviour (VABS) as a product of programme duration (top left), weekly intensity (top right) and total programme hours (bottom right). Grey area is the total gain and the dark grey area is additional gain for each added period of time. Bottom right panel shows total gains by programmes of low and high duration and intensity.

meta-analyses reported by Reichow and Wolery (2009) and by Makrygianni and Reed (2010a), found a relationship between the support and parent training offered and the impact of the programmes on adaptive behavioural functioning (relative to comparison groups).

The Lovaas programmes had a greater impact on the relative improvement of the adaptive behaviour standard scores than the Generic ABA approaches (10.3 versus 5.6 points), but not in terms of the effect sizes (0.75 versus 0.78). This may be due to the larger impact on the outcome of the studies quality, noted by Makrygianni and Reed (2010a). This latter analysis noted that in well-controlled studies there was an effect size of 0.60 in favour of behavioural programmes relative to comparisons, which rose to 0.90 in less-well controlled studies.

Challenging behaviours   Despite the enormous literature of the role of ABA in the reduction of specific problem or challenging behaviours and that such behaviours are often associated with individuals with ASD (Hartley et al., 2008; Matson et al., 2008; Chapter 2), the impact of comprehensive behavioural programmes on such behaviours in individuals with ASD are often not specifically or systematically assessed in outcome-effectiveness studies.

This might reflect the previously mentioned difficulties or prejudices about using informant reports, rather than direct observations of behaviours, which are necessary to the measure of this domain, as it is difficult to imagine how such behaviours could be directly observed with any degree of accuracy. This situation is made somewhat more problematic in that assessments of behaviour problems obtained from different informants, such as parents and therapists, do not always cohere with one another (Johnson et al., 2009; Koning & Magill-Evans, 2001; see Reed and Osborne, 2013, for a discussion). Nevertheless, there are a number of well-used scales to assess this area (such as the Child Behaviour Checklist or the Strengths and Difficulties Questionnaire or the Maladaptive Behaviour Scale of the VABS).

The meta-analysis by Reichow and Wolery (2009) suggested that around 77% of the studies reported improvements in some of the behavioural problems associated with ASD. However, this overall figure for improvement in challenging behaviours somewhat obscures the very wide range of impacts that the studies of the outcomes of the behavioural programmes report. A group of six studies report significant reductions in behaviour problems following exposure to a behavioural programme, often showing improvements relative to the comparison groups. For example, Eikeseth et al. (2007) report a 54% reduction in the level of behaviour problems in their sample and Reed et al. (2007b; see also Stock et al., 2013) showed significant improvements in the behaviour problems of their sample, including improvements relative to the comparison groups. Similarly, Sheinkopf and Siegel (1998) reported reductions in the levels of some problem behaviours that were related to the symptoms of ASD (such as stereotyped behaviours), as did Ben-Itzchak et al. (2008) and Eldevik et al. (2006).

However, in contrast to this group of studies, a further four studies noted no improvement in behaviour problems or no improvement relative to a comparison group. For example, Smith et al. (1997 and 2000) reported no differential impact of the behavioural programme on either tantrums or self-stimulation in their samples. Remington et al. (2007) showed no reliable impact of a behavioural programme on the problem behaviours of the participants undergoing a behaviour intervention and Sallows and Graupner (2005) similarly reported that repetitive behaviour problems were not impacted by the behavioural programme.

In summary, although the one meta-analysis to consider this issue (Reichow & Wolery, 2009) does suggest a role for behavioural programmes in reducing these maladaptive behaviours, this detailed analysis of the pattern of data, presents a less compelling picture. This is somewhat surprising, in that it is clearly the case that, when a particular behaviour is targeted, not necessarily in the context of a comprehensive behavioural programme for ASD, the effect of ABA is very well established: thus, the question remains as to why this is not a key area of success for comprehensive behavioural programmes for ASD? Potentially, it may be an issue with the way this behavioural domain is assessed – parent reports in particular tend to rate such behaviours as more severe (Reed & Osborne, 2013), which may obscure the impact of the programme. Nevertheless, the lack of overwhelming evidence in this domain is a surprise.

Summary   Of the three areas of functioning that are most often assessed in outcome-effectiveness studies of behavioural programmes, the adaptive behavioural domain is the one that is impacted to the smallest degree. Of course, the data available suggest that these programmes do have some positive effect on adaptive skills and that they can produce better effects than some other programmes. However, it is clearly the case that the differences in this domain are not as clear cut as they are for intellectual functioning or language. This relative lack of impact on social-adaptive skills was also noted in Chapter 4, when considering the differing effects of the CABAS® programme on various domains of functioning.

It may be that the only moderate impact of behavioural programmes in this domain is a product of this being the least easily definable set of behaviours of those considered and that behavioural programmes work best when targeted at specific definable sets of behaviours. It may also reflect the types of assessments tools employed, which tend to be parent-rated instruments and which may not ask questions pertaining to behaviours that are recent, but include all the developmental history of the child (such as the VABS), which, of course, will not be impacted by a programme instigated after the event. However, that this domain is possibly the closest to the core features of ASD and is the one least impacted by behavioural programmes, suggests that some more work is needed in this area by those programmes or that a combination of approaches may be needed to tackle the full range of issues associated with treating ASD.

Autism severity and placement outcomes

In addition to the three functioning domains discussed so far, some outcome-effectiveness studies have attempted to address the impact of behavioural programmes on either the core symptoms of ASD themselves or in terms of the subsequent educational placement of the child. Paradoxically, while these two domains may be a prime concern to parents (Osborne & Reed, 2009a) and to individuals with ASD (Humphrey & Lewis, 2008) and it, at least to some extent, can be said to be the headline findings from the study by Lovaas (1987) that triggered interest in interventions for ASD, these are the domains with the least well-documented outcomes. In fact, longer-term outcomes after behavioural programmes for ASD (indeed, after any programmes for ASD) have received scant attention in the literature (see Matson & Smith, 2008) The following section will briefly outline the findings relating to both objectively assessed ASD symptoms and also in terms of educational placement.

Autism severity   Reichow and Wolery (2009) noted that there was no particular relationship between undergoing a behavioural programme and having a diagnostic reclassification. Of the studies that assessed this impact of a behavioural programme, 57% of studies showed no impact on the diagnostic category of the participants, 28% showed an improvement in classification but 15% actually showed a worsening in the diagnosis over the period of the study.

Of the studies that demonstrated an improvement in the diagnostic classification of the participants, only the study reported by Weiss (1999) noted a similar change in diagnostic category to that reported by Lovaas (1987). Weiss (1999) reported that 45%

of the participants in this investigation moved from an ASD diagnosis to not qualifying for such a label after the behavioural programme and only 15% of participants remained classified as having ASD. The other studies that have reported improvements in ASD status tend to offer a more limited set of improvement. For example, Zachor et al. (2007) noted that only 20% of the participants could no longer be diagnosed with ASD following the intervention. Ben-Itzchak et al. (2008) noted that the diagnostic classification improved following behavioural intervention, but only in terms of stereo-typed and repetitive behaviours; a finding which contrasts with that of Sallows and Graupner (2005), who found diagnostic improvements, but only in social and communication behaviours and not in stereotypical and repetitive behaviours.

In contrast to these reports, four other reports noted no evidence of any recovery from ASD after the programme (Boyd & Corley, 2001; Reed et al., 2007b; Remington et al., 2007; Sheinkopf & Siegel, 1998). These reports used a variety of methods and instruments (both direct observational and informant) to classify the participants as having ASD. This pattern of results from the outcome-effectiveness studies is in line with other findings which show that most individuals with an ASD diagnosis continue to meet the criteria over the longer term (see Bölte & Poustka, 2000; O'Connor & Healy, 2010).

Given the variety of outcomes reported and the fact that only one subsequent study has come anywhere close to replicating the outcomes reported by Lovaas (1987), it may be safest to conclude that recovery from ASD (as opposed to an improvement in symptoms – placed at around 77% of participants by Reichow & Wolery, 2009) – is unlikely to be produced by behavioural intervention. It remains a possibility that those cases of recovery that have been reported may not have been appropriately diagnosed with ASD initially, as the stability of an ASD diagnosis may not be as strong as previously noted, especially in relatively higher functioning individuals (Turner & Stone, 2007).

School placement   The original study by Lovaas (1987) sparked controversy by reporting that, of the 19 participants receiving the full UCLA/Lovaas treatment, only two (11%) could still be classified as having the same level of ASD as they had originally; eight participants (42%) had a milder level of diagnosis and nine (47%) could be said to be 'recovered'. These judgements over classification were not on the classroom placement of the children (i.e. whether they were placed in a class for pupils with ASD) and this outcome is of some importance to educational providers.

This claim produced some heated debate and has occasionally been revisited in some of the outcome-effectiveness studies noted in Table 5.2, which have produced rather inconsistent results. For example, McEachin et al. (1993) reviewed nine children who, following their original behavioural programme in the Lovaas (1987) report, were placed in mainstream educational settings. The longer-term outcomes for these children reported by McEachin et al. (1993) suggested that eight out of nine of these participants were still in mainstream schools, with one placed in a special class. Similarly, O'Connor and Healy (2010) noted that all of the children in their report who had received behavioural interventions remained in mainstream placements after a minimum of 2 years.

However, despite these successes, Reichow and Wolery (2009) and Makrygianni and Reed (2010a), summarized the available data from outcome-effectiveness studies relating to behavioural programmes and found that, overall, only about 50% of the participants were placed in regular educational classes following these interventions. This average figure obscures a very large range, from 7% of children in mainstream settings (Anderson et al., 1997) to 80% (Cohen et al., 2006). This variation, of course, may reflect the impact of the child-characteristics. For example, Harris and Handleman (2000) found that individuals who received early behavioural intervention (prior to 4 years of age) and who had higher IQ scores at the end of the programme were more likely to be in mainstream settings.

Although mainstream school placement is a prized achievement for their child with ASD for many parents and educators (see Chapter 12), it is not without some difficulties as an outcome measure. Importantly, it is unclear what functioning variables it assesses – it could be due to intellectual, language, adaptive social behaviours or a lack of challenging behaviour (see Frederickson et al., 2004; Chapter 12). Additionally, it is important to note that educational placement, in itself, is not necessarily an index of the participant's functioning. This would imply that those pupils who were placed in special educational classes were somehow performing at a lower or worse level than those pupils who are educated in a mainstream class. This may be the case, but it is not *necessarily* so (see the discussion in Chapter 12). Moreover, the use of placement in this way could be taken to be rather pejorative with respect to special education. Furthermore, with the introduction of a drive to inclusive mainstream education for pupils with ASD (see Chapter 12), this metric is not always indicative of anything other the policy of the educational authorities involved. Apart from these data there are very few long-term indices of prognoses following behavioural treatment available.

Overall Effectiveness

The previous considerations regarding the impact of behavioural programmes on individuals with ASD can be summarized along the following lines:

1. There is little consistent evidence that can be said to imply 'recovery' from ASD following a behavioural intervention.
2. Behavioural programmes are effective for improving intellectual, linguistic and adaptive functioning, but are more effective at the former two areas of functioning than the latter domain.
3. In comparison to other approaches, behavioural interventions appear to be more effective in terms of intellectual functioning and language development, but the situation for adaptive behaviours is less clear, with milder advantages accruing after a behavioural programme than after comparison conditions.
4. The weekly intensity of the programme is important for the development of intellectual functioning, but only up to a point, after which there are severely diminishing returns. The situation for language and adaptive behaviour appears a little different, in that increasing the intensity seems to produce increases in gains
5. The duration of the programme impacts on the language and adaptive behaviour gains that are observed, but less so on intellectual functioning, which appears to reach an asymptote.
6. The available evidence tends to favour Lovaas approaches that are conducted or led by clinics or schools over home programmes.

There are two caveats to these generalizations that do need to be considered: the role of staff training and the quality of the study. The role of staff training has not been mentioned greatly so far, however, Reichow and Wolery (2009; see also Makrygianni & Reed, 2010a; Straus et al., 2013) pointed this factor as a key predictor of outcomes. This factor may be responsible for some of the differences in the types of programme noted previously, in that school-led approaches may offer better training and supervision than home-led behavioural programmes (Bibby et al., 2001) and that specific challenging behaviours require sophisticated techniques for their removal. The role of training in behavioural programmes has been well discussed in a number of articles (Healy et al., 2009). This point is also worth considering in relation to the comparisons between behavioural programmes and alternative treatments.

The few programmes that give a negative effect size (i.e. which favour the comparison) are found in studies where the comparison is a well-organized professionally run school-based system (Farrell et al., 2005; Magiati et al., 2007; Zachor & Ben-Itzchak, 2010). Similar findings have also been reported in a number of studies looking at the later progress of children who have been enrolled for some time on a programme, which shows no great advantage of behavioural programmes over special nursery placements (Makrygianni et al., 2010a; Makrygianni & Reed, 2010b). However, this is not always the case (see Howard et al., 2005). The trend was noted by Ospina et al. (2008), who noted that behavioural programmes show short-to-medium term (but not long-term) advantages over no treatment or usual special-educational classes, controls, but not against well-developed approaches (such as TEACCH). These issues will be revisited in subsequent chapters.

Throughout this review, several mentions have been made to the quality of the study and the impact that this has on the findings; generally, the stronger the study, the weaker the support for behavioural programmes. For example, the one meta-analysis that only included RCTs (Spreckley & Boyd, 2009), found only weak effect sizes in favour of behavioural programmes (of the order of 0.30 for all domains). Similarly, Ospina et al. (2008) noted that behavioural programmes were shown to be more effective in 85% of controlled studies, but in only 25% of RCTs. Notwithstanding these caveats, it is clear that behavioural programmes do have much to offer in the treatment of ASD, but that their outcomes may be impacted by a number of intervention characteristics and child characteristics, which will be discussed in the next chapter, Chapter 6.

6

Child Predictors for Comprehensive Behavioural Intervention Outcomes

In Chapter 5 it was seen that comprehensive behavioural interventions for Autism Spectrum Disorders (ASD) can be effective and that a number of programme characteristics were associated with this success. However, as discussed in Chapter 4, when debating the impact of Lovaas' seminal study (i.e. Lovaas, 1987), much of the original furore caused by this article concerned the extent to which the striking findings reported might be seen in children with characteristics other than those children contained in that sample. It was widely assumed at the time that the strict inclusion criteria adopted by Lovaas (1987); namely the need for younger, relatively high-functioning and linguistically able individuals with ASD, may limit the generality of the behavioural programme's success (see Boyd, 1998; Connor, 1998; Gresham & MacMillan, 1998). Although the data reported in Chapter 5 show that the benefits of such behavioural programmes can be broadly replicated and that they appear to have good impact across many different studies, it has become almost 'folklore' among those administering these interventions that these child characteristics are the optimal participant characteristics for the success of a behavioural (or, indeed, any) programme (Mudford et al., 2001; Perry et al., 2011; 2013).

Mudford et al. (2001; see also Bibby et al., 2001) have claimed that variation from the strict recruitment and treatment variables proposed by Lovaas (1987) may undermine the apparent effectiveness of the 'UCLA/Lovaas' approach. Mudford et al. (2001) summarized the child and programme data from 75 children with ASD (mean age 66 months), who were receiving behavioural programmes in the UK and found that the majority of those children (57%) had started treatment at an older age than those in the Lovaas (1987) study and 16% of them did not exceed his minimum IQ criterion. These observations lead Mudford et al. (2001) to suggest that these variations from the 'Lovaas' model would mean that the original findings are unlikely to be replicated.

Interventions for Autism: Evidence for Educational and Clinical Practice, First Edition. Phil Reed.
© 2016 John Wiley & Sons, Ltd. Published 2016 by John Wiley & Sons, Ltd.

Several studies have attempted to explore this type of claim and have generally noted some degree of association between the child characteristics at the start of the programme and the outcome of the intervention. For example, Perry et al. (2013), in a sample of 207 children, Fernell et al. (2011), with a sample of 208 children and Virués-Ortega et al. (2013), in a smaller-scale study of 20 children, all noted that a younger age and a higher cognitive ability were moderately associated with greater improvements in the children after a behavioural intervention. However, the results from any such individual studies are always difficult to interpret in the context of the ASD population as a whole, especially as a range of different relationships between the various predictors (child age, cognitive ability) and outcome variables (e.g. intellectual, linguistic and adaptive functioning) were found across these reports.

To address issues such as these, two meta-analyses have examined the association between child factors and outcomes, but these reports have come to slightly different conclusions from one another. Makrygianni and Reed (2010) noted a small and statistically significant relationship between both child age and intellectual functioning at the start of a programme and the outcome of the intervention; whereas Reichow and Wolery (2009) noted a small but insignificant relationship between these variables. The difference in report of statistical significance may be due to the differing numbers of studies included in the two reports, but both of these reviews suggest, when combined across all reports, that there appears to be a less consistent trend in these data when taken as a whole than implied by a few individual studies (e.g. Fernell et al., 2011; Perry et al., 2013).

Given the importance of being able to match appropriate treatment to particular individuals, the current chapter explores, in more detail, the impact of some key child predictors of outcome for behavioural programmes. The following sections examine the evidence concerning the predictors of success of behavioural programmes, across a range of participant characteristics and whether the previously mentioned folklore has any basis in reality. As shall be seen, there is actually little strong evidence that could be used to support any of the previous widely held prejudices about when behavioural programmes will be successful and that the various predictors (age, ASD severity, intellectual, linguistic and adaptive behavioural function) often have complex relationship to the outcomes achieved.

Child Characteristics in Behavioural Programmes

The studies included in the analyses reported in Chapter 5 with respect to the outcomes of behavioural interventions can also be described in terms of the characteristics of their participants. The types of individuals who were involved in the 38 programmes that have studied behavioural interventions for ASD can be seen in Table 6.1. This table shows the gender distribution of the sample for each study, along with the age of the children at intake and, where they are available, their baseline intellectual functioning (IQ), language ability and adaptive behaviour standard scores. These data allow an understanding of the nature of the participants on which the claims about behavioural interventions are made – thus, allowing judgements to be made as to

Table 6.1 Baseline characteristics of participants in studies examining ABA interventions.

Study	Year	N	Age (months)	% male	IQ baseline	Language baseline	VABS baseline
Anan et al.	2008	72	44	85	52		53
Anderson et al.	1987	13	43	77	58	52	50
Baker-Ericzen	2007	158	49	83			
Ben-Itzchak et al.	2008	44	27	98	75		
Ben-Itzchak & Zachor	2007	25	27	92	71		
Bibby et al.	2001	66	43	83	51		54
Birnbauer & Leach	1993	9	39	56	51		
Boyd & Corley	2001	22	41	72			
Cohen et al.	2006	21	32	83	61	52	70
Eikeseth et al.	2002	13	66	80	66	52	56
Eikeseth et al.	2007	13	66	80	66	52	56
Eldevik et al.	2012	31	42	81	51		62
Eldevik et al.	2006	13	51	86	41	35	52
Farrell et al.	2005	7	50	75	32		
Flanagan et al.	2012	61	42	87			55
Harris & Handleman	2000	27	49	85	59		
Harris et al.	1991	16	47	88	66		
Hayward et al.	2009	21	34	71	54	21	65
Hayward et al.	2009	23	36	83	54	20	62
Howard et al.	2005	29	33	84	57	52	70
Lovaas	1987	19	35	84	54		
Magiati et al.	2007	28	40	89	76		60
Matos & Mustaca	2006	9	42	89	15		
Perry et al.	2013	60	51	81	41		56
Perry et al.	2013	60	89	81	41		53
Reed et al.	2007a	13	41	100	49		56
Reed et al.	2007a	14	43	90	55		58
Reed et al.	2007b	12	43	100	57		59
Remington et al.	2007	23	47		62		
Sallows & Graupner	2005	13	33	84	51	43	60
Sallows & Graupner	2005	10	34	80	52	43	61
Sheinkopf & Siegel	1998	11	34		62		
Smith et al.	2000	15	36	82	51	27	63
Smith et al.	1997	11	37	90	28	12	50
Stock et al.	2013	14	47	85	42	53	
Stock et al.	2013	14	46	85	40	51	
Weiss	1999	20	42	95			50
Zachor & Ben-Itzchak	2010	45	25	88	75	63	66

whether they are representative of individuals with ASD in general (see Boyd, 1998; Connor, 1998; Gresham & MacMillan, 1998). However, when combined with the outcome data represented in Table 5.2, these data also allow some analyses of the predictors of outcomes for behavioural programmes across a range of different child characteristics.

All of the behavioural outcome-effectiveness studies were delivered to individuals with a confirmed diagnosis of ASD; with the most common diagnoses being autism or pervasive developmental disorder not otherwise specified (mainly based on the DSM-IV criteria). The gender ratio of the samples was, as would be expected, heavily biased toward males: there was a mean percentage male participants of around 84%, with a range of 56% (Birnbrauer & Leach, 1993) to 100% (Reed et al., 2007a) male. The mean age of the participants at intake was 42.8 (standard deviation = 11.8) months. As indicated by the standard deviation, there was a fairly large range in this age value, from 25 months (Zachor & Ben-Itzchak, 2010) to 89 months (Perry et al., 2013). The other feature of note in terms of the mean age of the participants at intake is that most of the children enrolled on these programmes were older than the mean of the participants in the Lovaas (1987) study, which was 35 months.

The participants' levels of functioning at baseline were mainly assessed through the use of standardized IQ tests (measured in 34 or 90%, of the programmes studied), but there are also some data on baseline language (15 or 40%, of the studies) and adaptive-social behavioural functioning (24 or 63%, of the studies). The mean IQ of the participants at intake ranged from 15 (Matos & Mustaca, 2005) to over 76 (Magiati et al., 2007), with a mean of around 53 (see also Makrygianni & Reed, 2010a; Reichow & Wolery, 2009). This was somewhat lower than in the initial Lovaas (1987) study and presents a set of participants that broadly conform to that which would be expected on the basis of the rates of co-morbidity of ASD with intellectual disabilities (LaMalfa et al., 2004; Matson & Shoemaker, 2009; Chapter 2).

The assessments of participants' adaptive behaviour functioning, through the Vineland Adaptive Behavior Scales (VABS), found similar standard scores in adaptive functioning to that of IQ, with the mean standardized VABS values in these studies being around 58, but with a range of 50 (Anderson et al., 1987) to 70 (Howard et al., 2005). This profile of adaptive-social is broadly consistent with that noted by previous meta-analyses of comprehensive behavioural interventions (Makrygianni & Reed, 2010a; Reichow & Wolery, 2009).

In contrast to these two domains, the linguistic functioning of the children with ASD at intake was included by fewer studies and tended to produce standard scores (for receptive and expressive ability combined) lower than those for the intellectual functioning and adaptive behaviour values. There was a mean standardized score for language ability of 42, with a range of 12 (Smith et al., 1997) to 63 (Zachor & Ben-Itzchak, 2010). Again, this pattern of data is consistent with that reported in previous meta-analyses (Makrygianni & Reed, 2010a; Reichow & Wolery, 2009) and with what might be expected given the nature of ASD (Chapter 2).

The data shown in Table 6.2 present the correlations between a range of child-characteristics that are typically thought of as important (e.g. age at intake, intellectual functioning, linguistic ability and adaptive behaviour skills – see Table 6.1) and the gains made in intellectual, linguistic and adaptive behavioural functioning between

Table 6.2 Correlations between various baseline child characteristics and the post-intervention gains in standardised scores across three functioning domains.

Baseline domain	Intellectual change	Language change	Adaptive-social change
Age	–0.231	0.046	–0.036
Intellectual	0.029	0.167	0.144
Language	0.111	–0.048	0.312
Adaptive-Social	0.443	0.179	–0.049

White = strong effect; light grey = moderate effect; dark grey = weak effect. No relationship is particularly strong.

baseline and follow-up on exposure to the behavioural programmes (presented in Table 5.2). These correlations are coded in terms of their strength, with strong relationship (r > 0.70) being shown in lighter cells; moderate relationships (r = 0.31 to 0.69) in medium cells and weak relationships (r < 0.30) being presented in darker cells. It can be seen that virtually none of the associations are practically important (i.e. few have even a moderate correlation with the outcome gain, which would be typically thought of practically significant in these circumstances, see Cohen, 1988). These rather weak overall correlations confirm what has been noted in a number of other meta-analyses (Makrygianni & Reed, 2010a; Reichow & Wolery, 2009), which should not be surprising, as all of these analyses are based on similar sets of studies. However, this overall assessment hides a number of subtler findings and these individual relationships are the subject of the next sections

Autism Severity

A key concern regarding the impact of behavioural programmes is the level and type of ASD displayed by the participant at intake, as the prognosis for any intervention is often taken to depend on the severity of the problems faced by the individual. Unfortunately, none of the meta-analyses conducted regarding the outcomes of behavioural programmes have directly examined such issues. Mainly this 'omission' is the result of the difficulties in making direct comparisons across the various studies due to the variation in instruments and diagnostic criteria across studies, making pooling of the data problematic.

A number of the individual studies have attempted to address the issue of ASD severity and outcomes, but have come to somewhat different conclusions from one another. Both Remington et al. (2007) and Reed and Osborne (2013), provided post hoc analyses of outcome data from behavioural interventions, based on the severity of the ASD noted at intake. In both of these cases, the ASD symptoms were parent-rated. Both of these two reports noted that the children with ASD (aged 2–4 years at intake, in both cases) undergoing a behavioural programme responded more positively to the intervention, either in terms of IQ change (Remington et al., 2007) and across a composite of standardized outcome measures (Reed & Osborne, 2012), if they had more severe ASD symptoms at baseline. These results stand in contrast to the folklore suggestions based on the initial discussion of Lovaas (1987; see Chapter 4) that imply a better prognosis for less severe ASD cases. Of course, the results reported by Remington et al. (2007) and by Reed and Osborne (2012), may reflect that IQ scores (used as part of the outcome measure) will tend to vary with ASD severity (Ben-Itzchak et al., 2008). This would mean that, the more severe ASD cases would have more scope for improvement from baseline in terms of their IQ and, hence, outcomes may appear to be greater in these cases.

These results also stand in contrast to those reported by Sallows and Graupner (2005) who used the Autism Diagnosis Interview (ADI-R) to classify their sample in terms of their intake ASD severity. This report noted that lower socialization and communication problems (but not the restricted-repetitive interests) best predicted a positive change in IQ after exposure to the behavioural programme. It was also noted that language ability at intake was similarly correlated with a positive change in IQ. This combination of results makes it unclear whether socialization and communication, based on the ADI measure, were related to ASD symptoms per se or whether their importance of language for functioning in both domains was the key element in predicting change. This suggestion is made somewhat more likely by the fact that the communication and socialization scales of the VABS did not strongly predict IQ outcomes in this study and these VABS scores measure these key abilities without over-reliance on the assessment of linguistic abilities. Moreover, Ben-Itzchak and Zachor (2007) found no predictive relationship between social and communication domains at intake and the change in IQ over the period of the intervention when the impact of other developmental domains, such as language, was controlled.

Thus, the existent data with respect to ASD severity and the outcome of behavioural programmes does not allow any clear message to be generated. However, it can be said that the notion of an inverse relationship between ASD severity and outcome for a behavioural programme is not necessarily supported by these data. It might also be noted that ASD severity may also be confounded and exacerbated by co-morbid medical and neuro-psychiatric conditions that are often associated with ASD (as discussed in Chapter 2) and which are hardly ever measured in such studies. Further the relationship between ASD severity and intellectual functioning, a key aspect of co-morbidity (Chapter 2), may further complicate these findings, as shall be discussed in detail next when considering intake-IQ as a predictor of outcomes.

Age at Intake

A quick scan of the many websites that are devoted to the treatment of ASD will show that the commonly held view is that the younger a child starts a behavioural intervention, the more successful will be the outcome. This view is also reflected in many research papers, for example Dawson (2008; Perry et al., 2013) outlines the positive impact of behavioural interventions for younger children, both with ASD and also 'at risk' of developing ASD. The putative importance of starting a programme at a younger age was also discussed by Perry et al. (1995) in terms of younger children having greater neural and behavioural plasticity. Thus, it has been suggested that *early* intervention for ASD is essential for an improved prognosis for the treatment (Connor, 1998; Lovaas, 1993; Nordin & Gillberg, 1998).

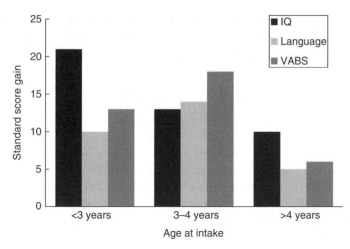

Figure 6.1 Gain in standard scores across three outcome domains for studies of ABA interventions that used participants in different age bands. IQ = intellectual functioning; Language = language ability; VAB = adaptive-social behaviours.

Despite this being a widely held view, inspection of the correlations between age and outcomes, shown Table 6.2, reveals that there is actually little impact of age on any of the outcome domains. This lack of straightforward relationship can further be illustrated by inspection of Figure 6.1, which presents the gains made in the three functioning domains (intellectual, language and adaptive behaviour) for the studies whose participants had a mean intake age of below 3 years old (10 studies), between 3 and 4 years old (20 studies) and greater than 4 years old (8 studies). These data reveal that, while IQ gains are certainly better for the two youngest groups of children, compared to the other two groups, which is broadly true for adaptive functioning, there is a converse relationship for language. Thus, there appears to be an inconsistent impact of age on outcomes of behavioural programmes. In summarizing such data, Makrygianni and Reed (2010a) suggested that, although there are no clear indications of strong correlations between age and outcomes, interventions for children attending before 40 months seem to be offer better opportunities for gain in terms of IQ, although the case of language and adaptive behavioural functioning was far from clear in that meta-analysis.

It has to be noted that conclusions drawn on the basis of such amalgamated data (albeit supported by many similar meta-analyses; Makrygianni & Reed, 2010a; Reichow & Wolery, 2009; Virués-Ortega, 2010) suffer from a problem, in that they result from combining many different studies that each have substantially different methodologies. This combination across quite different studies might introduce extraneous variables that will add 'noise' to the system and potentially reduce the true value of the observed associations.

Unfortunately, only a few studies have explicitly examined the impact of age on outcomes (rather than including simply correlating this factor with outcome). Fenske et al. (1985) compared nine children who started a behavioural programme prior to 60 months of age, with nine children who started after 60 months of age. Of the group who started younger, 67% achieved 'positive outcomes' (i.e. living at home rather than being hospitalized, being placed in mainstream rather than special education), but only 11% of the older-starting children attained such a positive outcome. However, there are questions to be raised about the validity of the outcomes used in this study, as living at home or being placed in a mainstream school, may well depend on factors other than the child's functioning (such as the existence of alternative provision in the child's area). Luiselli et al. (2000) formed a group of participants from children under 3 years old and another group from participants over 3 years old. All participants received less than 20 hours a week of a home-based behavioural intervention for about one year. The results indicated that communication, cognitive and socio-emotional performance did not differ on the basis of age at intake. However, in a larger-scale study, Perry et al. (2013) created two groups of 60 IQ-matched children: a younger group (2–5 years old at intake) and an older group (6–13 years at intake). After about a year and a half, the younger group had demonstrated greater improvements in intellectual functioning than the older group, but there was no difference in improvements in adaptive behavioural functioning between the two groups.

In addition to these controlled studies, three observational studies also have examined the relationship between age at intake and outcome in their cohorts, but have produced quite different results from one another. Harris and Handleman (2000) studied 27 children over a 7-year period and who had mean age at intake of 49 months (range 31–65 months). The report noted that children who were younger at treatment admission were more likely to be in mainstream education and that the younger children had higher and more positively changed IQs at the end of the programme, than those who entered at an older age. Virués-Ortega et al. (2013b) reported the results from 24 children, with a mean age of 51 months, who underwent behavioural treatment for just under 2 years. They noted that age at intake was related to outcome. However, Makrygianni and Reed (2010b) studied 86 children, with a much wider age range (2–14 years) and their developmental progress was assessed over a period of 9 months. However, in this latter study, age at intake did not impact any of the outcome domains.

The difficulty in comparing across studies is compounded when it is noted that these studies employed a wide range of programme durations and weekly intensities of treatment. In fact, when the sample is divided into studies whose participants had a mean age of below and above 3 years old; as well as into those studies that employed shorter (<57 months) or longer (>57 month) durations and also lesser (>30 hours) or greater (>30 hours) weekly intensities, the impact of age on outcome can be seen to differs. The mean gains in three outcome domains are shown in Figure 6.2 for the groups of younger and older children undergoing different durations and intensities of the programmes. Inspection of these data for the programme durations shows that younger children performed better in terms of intellectual functioning and adaptive-social behaviour than older children at both durations. However, older children outperform younger children in terms of language, when the duration of the programme is longer. The data for weekly intensity shows that when the programme is intensive, then younger children fare better across the outcome domains, but when the programme is less intensive, children who start the programme at an older age tend to show better gains.

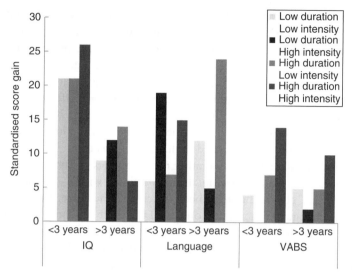

Figure 6.2 Gains in standardised scores in three areas of function reported in studies of ABA that used children below and above 3 years old at intake; either low (<57 months) or high (>57 months) durations; and either low (<30 h/week) or high (>30 h/week) weekly intensities.

Thus, the overall pattern of data relating to the impact of age at the start of a behavioural programme is complex and undoubtedly will be moderated by a number of variables (such as the programme characteristics), many of which will not have been adequately assessed at the moment. Moreover, it should also be borne in mind that there a potential confound between age at intake and the severity of the child's ASD. It is likely that those children who are placed onto a programme at an earlier age will have more recognizable ASD symptoms – and are likely to have greater ASD severity – than those who are placed on programmes later. If it is the case that behavioural programmes work well for more severe cases, then it is hard to determine if the impact of age is acting alone to produce these results or whether it is the associated greater ASD symptoms that lead to any benefits for younger children.

Intellectual Functioning

It has been suggested that those individuals with higher levels of intellectual functioning will fare better on an intervention programme for ASD. This may be true whether the programme is behavioural in nature or not – in fact, an IQ below 50 at the start of school predicts severe restriction of social and adaptive functioning in adult life (Nordin & Gilberg, 1998). However, this relationship between levels of intellectual functioning at the start of the programme and outcomes is thought to be especially strong on behavioural programmes (Lovaas, 1987; Mudford et al., 2001; Perry et al., 2013; Virués-Ortega et al., 2013b).

Following the suggestions made by Lovaas (1987) in respect to the importance of intake-IQ, a report by Smith et al. (1997) attempted to address the issue of severity of intellectual impairment and its impact on outcome. They conducted a study on 11 participants with ASD, who were not more than 46 months old at the start of the intervention, with an IQ of less than 35. After 2 years on the programme, the participants were followed up and the results showed that the IQ gain was nowhere near as great as in the original Lovaas study. These data (among others) have been used to suggest that the Lovaas treatment may have the greatest effect for children with slightly higher intellectual functioning (see Perry et al., 2005; 2013).

This issue has been taken up in other reviews of the area and in a number of studies, but none have attempted a controlled evaluation of this topic. However, as we shall see, the existing literature presents a rather more complex picture of the role of IQ in generating outcomes from behavioural interventions, with a number of suggested mechanisms for the effects that have been observed. The correlations between IQ at intake and the change in functioning on any of the three outcome domains displayed in Table 6.2, shows little overall relationship between intake IQ and any of these variables. In fact, this relative lack of predictive validity of intake IQ and the effectiveness of the behavioural programme has been noted in two previous meta-analyses (Makrygianni & Reed, 2010a; Reichow & Wolery, 2009). Detailed inspection of the individual studies that allow exploration of this relationship (from both observational and quasi-experimental studies) actually reinforces the conclusion that there is no simple answer to the degree of association between intellectual functioning and outcome on behavioural interventions.

Four relatively large-scale observational studies have looked that the relationship between intake IQ and the outcome-effectiveness of behavioural programmes (Fernell et al., 2011; Harris & Handleman, 2000; Makrygianni & Reed, 2010b; Perry et al., 2013). In the report by Harris and Handleman (2000), which is often cited as a key source of evidence for the importance of this relationship, IQ at intake was found to predict educational placement on termination of the programme. Apart from the usual caveat about interpreting educational placement as an outcome, it should be note that IQ in this study was measured by the Fourth Edition Standford–Binet test, which is really a measure of verbal IQ and, it may well be, that verbal IQ is a reflection of linguistic ability, rather than intellectual functioning.

Perry et al. (2013) reported the data from a large sample and employed nonverbal IQ measures and standardized outcome assessments. They found a linear relationship between intake-IQ and the IQ of the participants at the end of the behavioural programme. However, inspection of these data shows that the linear intake largely reflected the children exiting the programme with the same IQ score as they entered with – suggesting that there was little relationship between the intake intellectual functioning and the gains made in this functioning domain.

The study by Makrygianni and Reed (2010b) used a nonverbal IQ scale (Leiter International Performance Scale) and found relationships between intake IQ and advances in language ability and in adaptive behaviour (but not changes in IQ itself). However, the authors emphasize that older children and those with lower IQ scores, did show measurable gains in IQ from the treatment. However, these data were derived from a sample of children who had been in a programme for some time prior to the initial measurements being taken.

The clearest data relating to the impact of intellectual functioning comes from Fernell et al. (2011) in a report of an observational study of 208 children with ASD,

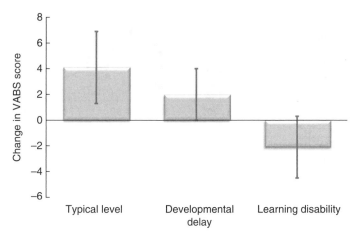

Figure 6.3 Data from study reported by Fernell et al. (2011) concerning changes in adaptive-social behaviour (and 95% confidence limits) over the course of an ABA intervention for children with different types of intellectual functioning at baseline.

who were classified into three levels of intellectual functioning: 'normal' functioning, developmentally delayed and learning disabled. The study noted that the greatest gains in terms of adaptive behaviour were found in the group whose intellectual functioning was in the normal range (see Figure 6.3), although the relationship to other outcome measures were not presented.

A number outcome-effectiveness studies have adopted a quasi-experimental approach to assess this issue (Ben-Itzchak et al., 2008; Eldevik et al., 2006; Remington et al., 2007; Sallows & Graupner, 2005; Zachor et al., 2007). Three of these studies (Eldevik et al., 2006; Remington et al., 2007; Sallows & Graupner, 2005; more will be discussed of the remaining two studies later in this section) divided their sample, *post hoc*, into those individuals who responded well to the behavioural intervention and those that did not and then compared these two groups on their intake variables. All of these studies found that the 'good responders' had higher IQ scores at intake than the 'poor-responding' group. While the study reported by Eldevik et al. (2006) noted that this was only true for verbal intelligence measures, the other two reports (Remington et al., 2007; Sallows & Graupner, 2005) obtained this result with an IQ test suitable for nonverbal children (Bayley Scale of Infant Development). On the face of these data, the suggestion is that there is a relationship between intake IQ and the effectiveness of the behavioural programme; with those having higher IQ faring better in terms of their outcome (certainly, in terms of their IQ outcome).

However, a closer inspection of these data suggests that the situation is not quite as simple as these studies and the general folklore (Mudford et al., 2001), seem to imply. Most of these studies have employed samples that have an IQ score less than the median for the full range of IQs across all of the outcome-effectiveness studies for behavioural interventions (the median of which is 54): the means of the sample being: Eldevik et al. (2006) = 41 months; Sallows and Graupner (2005) = 51 months; the exception being Remington et al. (2007) = 61 months. In fact, a more detailed analysis of the relationship between IQ and outcomes reveals that this is general trend: studies with a sample mean IQ of less than the median (54) present moderate positive

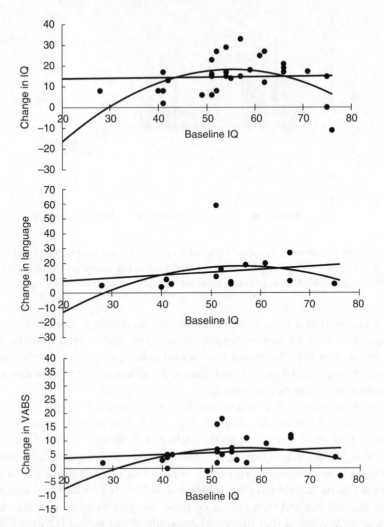

Figure 6.4 Relationship between intellectual functioning at baseline and change in standardized scores in three areas of functioning after an ABA programme. Top panel = intellectual functioning; middle panel = language ability; bottom panel = adaptive-social behaviours. The superimposed lines show the linear and quadratic relationship between these variables – the quadratic relationship explains more of these data (see text for discussion).

correlation between mean intake-IQ and all outcome variables; but, in stark contrast, the studies with samples with greater than median intake-IQ display moderate to strong negative correlations between mean intake-IQ and outcomes

Figure 6.4 presents the scatterplots relating intake IQ and outcomes (baseline to follow-up change) to one another. Superimposed on these data are both the linear and the bitonic relationships between these variables. It is worth noting that the former relationship is not statistically significant, whereas the latter (quadratic curve) is significant. In fact, looking at the peak intake IQ for obtaining an optimal outcome, based on these graphs, it can be seen that this value (i.e. 70) is exactly that chosen as the cut-off point for Lovaas (1987) intake pro-rated mental age, perhaps explaining the strong levels of success noted in this study.

The issue is, then, to explain the inverse-U curve relationship between intake-IQ and IQ-outcome. Firstly, it needs to be noted that there is a relatively psychologically trivial explanation of this effect that may contribute to this pattern of data. Those with lower IQs at baseline simply have more room for improvement over the course of the intervention than those with higher IQs at intake and those with higher IQs at intake have less room for improvement.

Potentially of more importance and certainly of more psychological interest, especially given the previously noted relationship between ASD severity and outcomes, is to consider the relationship between IQ and ASD severity. Many individuals with ASD also display intellectual disabilities (e.g. Matson & Shoemaker, 2010; Chapter 2), but there is also a huge variability in this relationship (see Ben-Itzchak et al., 2008). One of the largest studies conducted concerning this association ($N > 450$) was reported by Munson et al. (2008) and the relationships reported as the result of their analysis, may throw some light on the previous bitonic relationship between intake-IQ and IQ outcomes. In the report by Munson et al. (2008), four clusters of individuals with ASD were found in terms of their intellectual functioning: a low functioning group; a low functioning group with higher nonverbal IQ than verbal IQ; a moderately functioning group (in the high/moderate intellectual disability rage) and a higher functioning group (in the low average range). Interestingly, for the current purposes, there was a strong relationship between IQ and ASD severity for the three groups with some degree of lower intellectual functioning. In these groups, the lower the participant's IQ, the greater the level of ASD symptoms. These three groups covered the vast majority of the levels of intellectual functioning noted in the samples reported in the behavioural intervention outcome-effectiveness studies (Table 6.1). In contrast, there was not a striking difference between the ASD-severity of the moderate-functioning group and the higher intellectually functioning group; suggesting that IQ and ASD scores parallel each other in more closely in severely intellectually disabled cases, but are more variably related to one another in higher intellectually functioning individuals. This more variable relationship for higher intellectually functioning individuals may also explain why the 'good responders' reported by Remington et al. (2007), who used a relatively higher-functioning sample than most, had both higher intellectual functioning and higher severity ASD, which would not normally be thought to go together.

Bearing in mind the evidence that ASD severity and IQ will tend to parallel each over the ascending arm of the bitonic relationship noted in Figure 6.4, this might suggest that any putative effect of intake-IQ on outcomes might, in large part, reflect the severity of ASD for this range of IQ scores. The results from the other two quasi-experimentally analysed studies, mentioned earlier (Ben-Itzchak et al., 2008; Zachor et al., 2007), further strengthen such a suggestion. When controlling for ASD severity, neither report found a relationship between nonverbal IQ at intake and change in intellectual functioning. The major difference between these latter two studies and the former three reports (Eldevik et al., 2006; Remington et al., 2007; Sallows & Graupner, 2005), is that the former studies controlled for the impact of ASD severity in performing this calculation and also did not select their sample into responders and non-responders, but rather divided their sample into high- and low-IQ at baseline and then tested the differences between those groups (potentially including more cases in the analyses).

Taken together, these data suggest that any positive relationship between IQ and outcome on the ascending arm of the curve may, in fact, be mediated by ASD severity. However, the descending arm, involving participants with higher IQs, may not be subject to such a strong mediating effect of ASD severity, as there is a less striking relationship between these variables. However, the parallels between the impact of ASD severity and IQ functioning on outcomes clearly imply that these variables are not entirely separable in their effects.

Language Functioning

The relationship between the initial linguistic abilities of the participants undergoing the behavioural interventions and the outcomes of those interventions is relatively clear in terms of demonstrating a mediating impact. The correlations between intake levels of language functioning (based on a composite of receptive and expressive language) and the three outcome domains, shown in Table 6.2, reveal moderate positive relationships for intake-language with improvements in adaptive and behavioural functioning and, to a lesser extent, with gains in intellectual functioning.

When the studies are split at their median for language ability at intake (a language standard score of 51), the gains in terms of the three outcome domains for the lower- and higher-language functioning groups can be seen in Figure 6.5. These data show that those children with higher-language abilities at intake produce higher gains in the three domains, compared to the children with less developed language skills at intake (although it should be noted that these differences are not astonishingly pronounced).

Although a relationship between language ability at intake and intellectual and adaptive behaviour outcomes was only partly shown in previous meta-analyses that have examined behavioural interventions (Makrygianni & Reed, 2010a; Reichow &

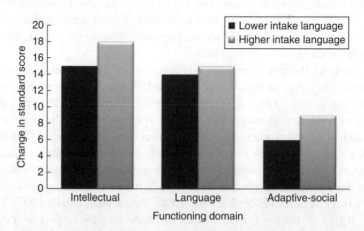

Figure 6.5 Gains in standard scores for three functioning domains after an ABA programme for studies using children with lower (<51) and higher (>51) language functioning at intake. Better language at baseline predicts greater improvements in intellectual and adaptive-social behaviours.

Table 6.3 Correlations between intake standardised language ability and three outcome domains.

	Intellectual change	*Language change*	*Adaptive-social change*
Younger children	−0.165	0.233	−0.206
Older children	0.247	−0.063	0.523
	Intellectual change	*Language change*	*Adaptive-social change*
Shorter duration	−0.036	0.329	0.242
Longer duration	0.628	−0.623	0.600

Top panel = children who were younger (<3 years) and older (>3 years) at baseline (top panel). Any positive relationships are more pronounced for older children. Bottom panel = programmes with shorter than 52 weeks or longer than 52 weeks duration (bottom panel). The relationships are more pronounced for longer programmes.

Wolery, 2009), it should be noted that the current analyses does include a wider range of studies than in those previous reports. Moreover, the results of the current analysis coincide with the impact of intake language functioning that have been noted in several individual studies (e.g. Eldevik et al., 2006; Sallows & Graupner, 2005). In terms of the few individual studies that have examined this relationship between intake-language ability and outcome, Sallows and Graupner (2005) noted that improvements in all aspects of the participants' functioning were associated with the participants' receptive language ability at baseline (as well as a range of their social skills). Similarly, Eldevik et al. (2006) noted that receptive language was associated with positive outcomes across all domains and that the baseline expressive language ability was associated with improvements in intellectual functioning over the course of the behavioural intervention.

It is also important to know that the relationship between language skills at intake and the outcomes of the interventions appears to be mediated by the age of the child at intake. If the studies of behavioural interventions are divided into those whose mean child-age at intake was 3 years old or less and those whose participants were older than three years at intake and the correlation between intake-language and the three outcome domains are recalculated, there are only strong relationships for the older children. These data can be seen in the top panel of Table 6.3, which shows, for the younger and older participant groups, the correlations between language ability at intake and the changes in the three outcome domains. These associations are typically higher for older children, but this does not necessarily mean that the older children often do better than the younger children, but that the gains that they do make are often more strongly related to their intake language ability (the exception is in the domain of language outcome itself)

Similarly, if the studies are split at the mean into those of a relatively shorter duration (less than 52 weeks) and those of a relatively longer duration (>52 weeks), the impact of intake language ability on outcomes can be seen only in those studies of longer duration. The bottom panel of Table 6.3 shows these data and reveal that intake language-ability is only a predictor in programmes running for greater than 2 years. A similar relationship is seen if the studies are divided into lesser and greater weekly intensities, with language only impacting outcome in those studies of greater than median weekly intensity.

Although the overall relationships between intake-language and outcomes are broadly clear and there are a number of important mediators of this effect, one finding is quite apparent: there is a lack of a clear relationship between language functioning at baseline and language outcomes. This finding may, of course, be a product of baseline effects: higher language scores at baseline would allow less room for change, which would tend to limit the strength of the overall associations noted. Alternatively, there are often differences in the receptive and expressive language abilities of people with ASD (Peters-Scheffer et al., 2011; Virués-Ortega, 2010) – with receptive-language scores tending to be higher than expressive-language abilities (see Chapters 2 and 5). It may well be that, while expressive language ability remains low, receptive language is impacted by the programme, but that the particular impact is obscured by the current use of the composite score. The lack of relationship between intake-language ability and language gains may also reflect another aspect of the approaches adopted by behavioural programmes. Many individuals with ASD receiving behavioural programmes are not explicitly taught the use of verbal language, but rather are taught to express themselves through the use of sign language of some form, which would not necessarily be reflected in these tests of language (see Chapter 5 for discussion). This suggests that a range of other communication abilities and non-verbal skills that are related to expressive language should also be considered. Indeed, the relative lack of tools to assess nonverbal communication may be a limitation in developing a fuller understanding of the role of language in predicting outcomes.

There are a number of issues that need to be discussed in this context to allow further understanding of the potential role of language at intake. One question that remains to be answered is whether receptive- or expressive-language abilities are key in predicting gains. Eldevik et al. (2006) suggested that expressive-language abilities at baseline had a greater impact on intellectual functioning gains at the end of the programme than baseline receptive language. Unfortunately, there are few other data on the differential impacts of receptive and expressive language on these outcome domains.

It is possible to construct a number of mechanisms through which either form of language ability may impact on the gains made across the outcome domains. For instance, a simple role of receptive language in allowing more positive outcomes is that understanding verbal requests to perform actions will make the teaching intervention easier to perform and allow for more learning opportunities per unit time, which is correlated with better outcomes (Albers & Greer, 1991; see Chapter 4).

The role of expressive language is still debated, but its establishment may allow replacement of escape-maintained problem behaviours that could otherwise interfere with the ability of the programme to help the child; that is, an individual can end a frustrating or aversive situation simply by commenting on the situation, rather than by engaging challenging behaviour (Carr et al., 1980). Moreover, it may also be that expressive language may be predictive of better emotional and social functioning for individuals with ASD (Clark et al., 2008; Steel et al., 2003). Such considerations point to the importance of developing nonverbal manding and tacting, as now practiced in a number of behavioural programmes (see Chapter 4).

Recently, it has become apparent that language skills, themselves, are predicated by the development of a range of other pre-linguistic behaviours and it should be considered whether these skills might predict outcomes. For example, Ben- Itzchak and

Zachor (2007) noted that expressive language was related to the participants' abilities in nonverbal social functioning. In fact, there are a range of earlier behaviours that have been shown to be related to the development of language abilities: preverbal commenting (McDuffie et al., 2005), requesting (Wetherby et al., 2007), imitation (Ben-Itzchak & Zachor, 2007; Smith et al., 2007) and joint attention (Mundy et al., 1990; Rogers et al., 2003; Thrum et al., 2007). Smith and von Tetzchner (1986; see also Mundy et al., 1988) documented the associations between nonverbal communication and language development and noted that it was nonverbal requesting that was predictive of expressive language in a sample of children with Down's syndrome. This finding that has been partly replicated for children with ASD. Luyster et al. (2008) found that the strongest predictors of expressive language were non-verbal cognitive ability, gestures and imitation, while the best predictors of receptive language were gestures, non-verbal cognitive ability and joint attention.

Taken together, these data imply that developing the language abilities of an individual with ASD is important, both in itself and because these abilities predict a range of other outcomes. There is amble evidence of the relationship between language competence and reductions in problem behaviours exhibited by individuals with ASD (see Conallen & Reed, 2012, for discussion). This relationship was also noted by Makrygianni and Reed (2010b) in the observational study of the developmental of individuals with ASD over the course of 1 year undergoing a range of behavioural interventions. In addition to showing a mediating relationship of language, these data also provide some corroboration of the validity of the curricula suggested in many behavioural approaches (see Chapter 4), as well as some of the recent developments connected to language that have been developed by the 'Verbal Behaviour' (Sundberg & Partington, 1998) and 'CABAS®' (Greer, 1997) behavioural approaches.

Adaptive Behaviours

This measure has a number of important aspects to the prediction of outcomes that the other measures discussed previously do not possess. Firstly, the domains covered in this assessment (made by the VABS) cover many of the nonverbal aspects of functioning (social behaviours, imitation) that have been mentioned previously in relation to language development and, as these are important precursors of language, they should give important insights into whether behavioural programmes are effective across a range of verbal and nonverbal children. Secondly, many of the domains of this assessment are directly related to the core deficits of ASD (e.g. communication, socialization) in a way that IQ and language per se, are not (see DSM-5). In this, adaptive behaviours may give further important insights into the likely range of ASD severities that behavioural interventions may be expected to successfully treat.

In terms of the impact of the child's adaptive behavioural skills at intake on outcomes following behavioural interventions, the pattern noted in the correlations displayed in Table 6.2 is reasonably straightforward. Individuals with greater adaptive behaviour skills at intake develop greater intellectual functioning over the course of the intervention and, to a slightly lesser extent, also develop better language skills (see also Makrygianni & Reed, 2010a).

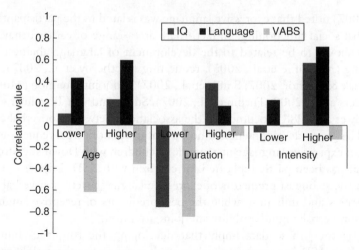

Figure 6.6 Correlations between intake adaptive-social behaviour (VABS) and three outcome domains for various programme characteristics (child intake age, programme duration and weekly intensity).

These relationships are consistent with those reported in several individual studies that have examined the association between intake adaptive behaviours and outcomes. For example, both the study by Eikeseth et al. (2007) and that by Sallows and Graupner (2005), noted this relationship. A recent large-scale study that focused, primarily, on the impact of adaptive behaviour skills at intake on the outcome of a behavioural treatment, also noted a positive association (Flanagan et al., 2012). This latter study reported that adaptive behaviour skills at baseline predicted intellectual functioning and adaptive behaviour scores after two years on the intervention, even when the age of the participant and the duration of the intervention were controlled. This effect was partly noted by the meta-analyses reported by Makrygianni and Reed (2010a).

These positive relationships between adaptive behaviour and outcomes may be taken to reflect the relationship between the adaptive behavioural measure and the ASD severity – as already noted, the VABS covers much of the same ground as many of the measures of ASD severity. That the relationship between VABS and outcomes seems more straightforward than that of ASD severity and outcome (as discussed earlier) may reflect that the VABS scores tend to be on the lower end of the spectrum (mean standard score = 58) and, certainly within the range that suggests a positive association between the severity of these core symptoms and outcome. The relationship between adaptive behaviours and language outcome may be predictable on the bases of the previous discussion of the impact of many nonverbal-social and adaptive behaviours on language (e.g. Luyster et al., 2008; Sallows & Graupner, 2005), as these types of behaviour are covered in the VABS.

There are actually few mediators of the impact of intake-adaptive behavioural skills. When the studies of behavioural interventions are divided into those with lower and higher child-age, lower and higher weekly intensity and lower and higher programme duration and the correlation between intake-VABS and gains are calculated (see Figure 6.6 for a representation of these correlations for each group), the only factor that moderates the results is weekly intensity. Those studies with a higher weekly intensity (greater than 30 hours) show a stronger relationship between initial adaptive behaviour levels and the gains made over the course of the intervention, compared to the studies with relatively lower weekly intensities of programme intervention.

Thus, overall there appears to be a positive relationship between the individuals adaptive behavioural functioning at intake and their outcomes on behavioural interventions – the greater their initial skills, the greater the gains. This partly corresponds to the impact of the other mediators discussed. However, it should be remembered that the VABS is a parent-rated measure, rather than being objectively assessed and this may introduce a range of other factors that impact this measure (such as parent perceptions), as were discussed previously when considering the impact of interventions on this domain.

Summary

The forgoing discussion has suggested that there are several child-predictors of outcomes for behavioural interventions for ASD, which may shape the degree to which these interventions are used and also limit their generality. Surprisingly, these predictors and limits are not of the types that are typically discussed in the literature (e.g. Mudford et al., 2001; Perry et al., 2011) and are also subject to a number of moderators, themselves. The following summarizes the key findings regarding the characteristics of the individuals with ASD who will benefit most from this form of intervention:

1. Surprisingly, ASD severity has little directly demonstrable relationship to the outcomes of behavioural interventions. To the extent that any relationship is noted, those with more severe levels of ASD tend to benefit more than those with less severe ASD.
2. Individuals who are younger at the start of the programme (up to around 3 years old) will tend to have more consistently positive outcomes than those who are older. The latter group still benefit from the intervention, but not as consistently. However, this relationship is more pronounced for longer and more weekly intensive programmes.
3. Intellectual functioning has a complex relationship to outcomes, in that there is a positive relationship between increasing IQ ability and outcome up an IQ of about 70, where after the relationship reverses. However, it is unclear if this is actually a product of the ASD severity rather than IQ itself.
4. Both language ability and adaptive behaviour function appear to predict the outcome of the intervention, with higher functioning individuals producing greater gains than lower functioning individuals on these measures. Both of these relationships are also impacted by a range of moderators, such as the age of the child and the duration and intensity of the programme.

However, these relationships should not be taken to suggest that older and lower-functioning children are beyond hope of improvement. Ruble and Dalrymple (1996) conducted a 5-year study on 46 individuals with ASD (aged 2–19 years old) and found that participants who would have been predicted to do poorly as adults, because of their relatively low verbal and adaptive behavioural levels, were found to be leading

Interventions for Autism

satisfactory lives. In addition to these studies, there are plenty of case-reports and single-subject studies, showing improvement in specific behaviours for older and less highly functioning children with ASD. In fact, Stoddart (1999) has noted that, rather than any one factor, the developmental trajectory of the child may interact strongly with the success of the intervention, irrespective of the specifics of the intervention. This suggestion is corroborated by the results reported by Sallows and Graupner (2005), in that children with ASD, who made rapid progress between Year 1 and Year 2, had better outcomes at the end of the study, than those who did not – irrespective of the baseline levels of ability. This concept requires much more exploration, but may offer an important metric to explore in terms of whether or not a programme should be continued. Thus, the current data suggest a complex, but discernible, pattern of mediation for the effectiveness of behavioural programmes.

7

Teaching Environment Modification Techniques

The approaches to the treatment of Autism Spectrum Disorders (ASD) to be discussed in this chapter typically attempt to address the problems experienced by individuals with ASD by manipulating the teaching environment in which the person is placed. As such, they may be termed 'environmental' interventions. Although most are typically delivered by manipulating school settings, these programmes can sometime be applied in the home. The overall strategy of these interventions is to help the person with ASD by providing a better match between the types of learning style and abilities that people with ASD tend to exhibit and the demands that the teaching environment places on that individual. Adapting the environment to the limitations and abilities of the person with ASD is hoped to maximize the opportunity of the individual to acquire skills in that context. In this sense, these programmes are akin to the behavioural approaches, discussed earlier in the text, as these programmes also attempt to structure the learning environment.

Given the wide range of potential areas of difficulty for a person with ASD (see Chapter 2), there are a wide range of such environmental-manipulation approaches and each tends to focus on specific aspects of the teaching environment. For example, the Treatment and Education of Autistic and Related Communication Handicapped Children approach (TEACCH; e.g. Schopler & Reichler, 1971) primarily attempts the environmental modification through the use of highly structured instruction techniques in order to help the individual with ASD to better understand the demands of an otherwise potentially complex and confusing environment (e.g. the classroom). The Learning Experiences and Alternative Program for Preschoolers and Their Parents approach (LEAP, which was established in 1981; see Hoyson et al., 1984) attempts to improve the social functioning of people with ASD by providing clear social models for those individuals. The Higachi approach (e.g. Kitahara, 1983) attempts to alter the environment by providing clear and structured activities throughout the day. There are many such attempts to modify the environment of

Interventions for Autism: Evidence for Educational and Clinical Practice, First Edition. Phil Reed.
© 2016 John Wiley & Sons, Ltd. Published 2016 by John Wiley & Sons, Ltd.

people with ASD, but these three approaches are the best known and best documented and have a reasonable evidence base on which to draw some relatively solid conclusions.

As noted, these interventions are all united in that they share a common philosophy that a comprehensive approach to the treatment of ASD can best be delivered by targeting the environment of the person with ASD. Although there are clear differences between these three intervention approaches, they all share a number of features in common. Firstly, they are all primarily delivered by educational professionals, who often have extensive experience and higher-educational qualifications, rather than by parents, or by tutors with only some limited training in a particular technique (although this is not universally true). This places these educationally driven approaches in contrast to some of the interventions that have been discussed in the previous chapters (see Chapters 4–6) and also contrasts with some parent-mediated approaches that are to be discussed in subsequent chapters (see Chapters 8 and 9). Secondly, as these environmental-manipulation interventions focus on controlling the types of environmental input given to a person with ASD, they tend to place a main focus on the school, or centre, as the primary locus of delivery for the intervention, rather than the home (although, again, some programmes can be delivered in modified home settings). Thirdly, the three specific approaches to be discussed in this chapter are now all very well used and established across multiple sites (see Odom et al., 2010). However, many of these approaches started as local solutions to the provision for individuals with ASD by particular education authorities. For example, the TEACCH programme was started in North Carolina (Schopler & Reichler, 1971). The LEAP programme (Hoyson et al., 1984) was developed in Pennsylvania and the Higachi approach (Kitahara, 1983) was started in Tokyo.

Table 7.1 presents the three main interventions to be discussed in this chapter, along with an overview of their characteristics and references where further detailed information can be found about the nature of the programmes. From inspection of Table 7.1, it is apparent that there are actually many similarities between these environmental-manipulation strategies: for example, the main aims of the programmes in terms of the projected impact on the children and their use of naturalistic teaching procedures in order to reach these goals. These similarities will become more apparent during the discussions of the individual interventions given next. For each of the approaches, their background and philosophy will be given, along with a brief overview of its implementation strategies (and any evidence adduced in their support) and, finally, the results of the outcome-effectiveness studies will be presented.

Treatment and Education of Autistic and Related Communication Handicapped Children (TEACCH)

The TEACCH approach is a structured teaching method that was initially developed in the early 1970s (e.g. Schopler & Reichler, 1971), but which has been successively refined since this time (see Campbell et al., 1996; Mesibov et al., 2004, for further descriptions of the programme). As with the behavioural approaches (see Chapter 4),

Table 7.1 Characteristics of three commonly-employed 'environmental' manipulation techniques.

Programme	Origin	Principles	References
Treatment and Education of Autistic and Related Communication Handicapped Children (TEACCH)	North Carolina Schopler & Reichler (1971)	• Improve skills and abilities by adapting the environment. • Accept differences and develop individualised training methods for individual needs. • Assess and monitor skills by using well-established tools. • Employ validated teaching strategies to modify behaviours and skills. • Employ visual cues. • Multi-disciplinary working including parents and professionals to develop programme.	Campbell et al. (1996) Mesibov et al. (2004) Marcus & Schopler (2007)
Learning Experiences and Alternative Program for Preschoolers and Their Parents (LEAP)	Pennsylvania Strain (1981; described by Hoyson et al., 1984)	• All children benefit from inclusive education. • Benefit from education is maximal when the school and home cohere. • Pupils with ASD can learn from typically developing peers. • Typically developing peers can benefit from inclusion. • Teaching is most effective when delivered through behavioural principles.	Hoyson et al. (1984) Kohler et al. (1996)
Daily Living Skills Therapy (Higashi)	Tokyo Kitahara (1983)	• Vigorous physical activity to promote co-ordination. • Focus on group activities to develop emotional stability. • Intellectual stimulation through exposure to models (both teacher and peers).	Kitahara (1983) Tutt et al. (2006)

there is no specified teaching content to the TEACCH method but, rather, the content is tailored to suit each individual's needs and the skills and behaviours that are is targeted for a particular child depend upon the strengths displayed and difficulties experienced, by that person. Thus, to this extent, the TEACCH intervention can be said to be a 'person-centred' approach (see Marcus & Schopler, 2007; Mesibov et al., 2004, for overviews).

The TEACCH approach can be used either in the classroom (e.g. Lord & Schopler, 1989; Panerai et al., 2002), in the home (e.g. Panerai et al., 2009; Short, 1984), or in adult residential settings (e.g. Keel et al., 1997; Van Bourgondien et al., 2003). Moreover, TEACCH can be delivered either by clinicians, teachers or by trained parents. This programme does not suggest that a particular delivery placement (e.g. a mainstream or special school) is critical to the success of the programme (and, in this, it contrasts with the LEAP approach, see next), but holds that cooperation between all stake-holders (e.g. parents and professionals) is important to the success of the intervention. By developing cooperation, it is hoped to produce shared philosophies and goals, which are taken by TEACCH to be important to a successful intervention (Callahan et al., 2010; Jennett et al., 2003).

Background and implementation of TEACCH

The TEACCH approach is driven by a number of basic aims and philosophies regarding the education of a person with ASD (see Campbell et al., 1996; Gresham et al., 1999, for differing discussions of these aims), which are to:

1. Improve the individual's skills and abilities by adapting the environment to maximize those skills.
2. Accept the differences or deficits in the individual with ASD and develop individualized training methods to deal with these individual needs.
3. Assess and monitor individual skills by using well-established tools. To this end, the Childhood Autism Rating Scale (for measuring ASD severity) and the Psycho-Educational Profile (assessing cognitive and intellectual functioning) have been developed by the TEACCH programme.
4. Employ well-validated cognitive and behavioural teaching strategies in the intervention in order to modify the individual's behaviours and skills.
5. Employ visual cues that appear to be effective for ASD to help structure the learning environment. It is this aspect that plays a central role in the implementation of the TEACCH programme's philosophy (see next).
6. Work in a multi-disciplinary manner and involve both parents and professionals in the process of developing programmes for the children.

These aims are achieved through the implementation of four specific teaching principles (see Mesibov & Shea, 2010, for an overview). These teaching principles can be characterized as being concerned with enhancing the individuals' learning opportunities by: (i) using structure in the environment and daily activities; (ii) employing visual information in teaching materials; (iii) using the special interests of the person with ASD to motivate activities and (iv) promoting self-initiated communication skills. The precise ways in which these four teaching principles are operationalized vary from individual to individual, but the following section outlines these principles, in general and points to some of the evidence adduced to support the use of these strategies in the TEACCH approach.

The first two of these four principles ('structures' and 'visual guides') are strongly related to one another and form key aspects of the programme that differentiates TEACCH from many other approaches (e.g. compare this use of structure in learning with the Floortime® or Options approaches, described in Chapter 8). The 'structures' in a TEACCH programme encompass both the physical structure of the classroom and the organization of work schedules and tasks.

The TEACCH classroom environment is physically organized in a way designed to alleviate potential problems and difficulties for the people with ASD who are exposed to that environment (Hume et al., 2012). For example, the arrangement of the furniture in a classroom can help a child's independent functioning (Hume & Odom, 2007); lighting and visual wall displays can all be organized to reduce distraction and potential confusion (Bodfish, 2004) and these displays can also help the individual to recognize and comply with expected routines (Rutter & Bartak, 1973).

In terms of work organization, a TEACCH programme will employ visual activity schedules, as it is believed that clearly displayed timetables and routines give direction and clarity to classroom and school life (Mesibov & Shea, 2010; Quill, 1995). In particular, it is held that unclear organization of a school day can result in people with ASD not knowing where to be at a given time, or not knowing how to get there (Schmit et al., 2000). Additionally, difficulties with receptive language for people with ASD may contribute to those individuals misunderstanding school rules and it is thought that clear visual cues can support their understanding of such rules (Mesibov & Shea, 2010). Furthermore, surprise and unexpected change can be disturbing to an individual with ASD (see Chapter 2), whereas familiar scheduled activities and regular routines, are comforting and calming (Grandin, 2002). In this use of visual structure, TEACCH shares procedures with the behavioural approaches discussed earlier (see Chapter 4).

In addition to the use of structure and visual materials, the TEACCH approach attempts to use the individual's own strengths and interests to engage them in other activities, especially in terms of self-initiated communication – that is, the previously mentioned points (iii) and (iv). Again, the principle of using individually tailored reward system is one shared with behavioural approaches (see Chapter 4), as well as with many developmental approaches to be discussed in Chapter 8. The TEACCH approach, critically, attempts to employ these individual strengths and interests to support the use of self-initiated communication by the person with ASD. Typically, this is achieved by pairing visual labels with the individual's preferred activities and, once the association is learned, using these labels to offer choices to the individual conversations (Mesibov et al., 2005; see also Conallen & Reed, 2012, for a similar discussion within a behavioural framework).

Reviews of the effectiveness of TEACCH

The evidence relating to the impact of the specific components of the TEACCH approach has been reviewed in a number of places (see Mesibov & Shea, 2010, for an overview). However, it is the impact of the components as a whole, when placed together, that is the central focus of this text and a number of reviews of the overall effectiveness of the TEACCH programme also have been provided in the literature. Some of these reviews are narrative assessments of the effectiveness of the TEACCH approach in particular (e.g. Mesibov & Shea, 2010; Roberts & Prior, 2006), some are general narrative reviews of the field that include an assessment of TEACCH (e.g. Gresham et al., 1999; Odom et al., 2010; Smith, 1999; Vismara & Rogers, 2010) and some are meta-analyses of the field that include reference to TEACCH intervention assessments (e.g. Eikeseth, 2009; Ospina et al., 2008; Virués-Ortega et al., 2013a).

In general, these reviews of outcome-effectiveness suggest that the TEACCH approach is moderately effective in improving the functioning of the individuals that it targets. For example, Roberts and Prior (2006) are generally positive about the impact seen in the studies that have assessed TEACCH programmes; Ospina et al. (2008) note that there are helpful impacts of TEACCH on a number of domains of behavioural functioning and Mesibov and Shea (2010) report the outcomes of five studies with positive results in terms of the functioning of the people with ASD exposed to the programme. However, in a larger-scale meta-analysis, which included 13 studies, Virués-Ortega et al. (2013a) concluded that there was little strong evidence of the effectiveness of the TEACCH approach, except in its impact in the adaptive-social domain.

Despite the differences in the summaries regarding the impact of TEACCH, a consistent conclusion that can be drawn from these reviews is that the evidence from TEACCH outcome-effectiveness studies is sometime difficult to generalize to other situations than those studied. For instance, many studies are highly focused on the assessment of TEACCH-specific goals and many of them focus on measuring the impacts of TEACCH components on very specific behaviours, rather than on overall measures of functioning (Mesibov & Shea, 2010). As a consequence, Smith (1999) noted that many of the studies do not report the data either fully, or in a way that makes comparison with other reports straightforward. This trend has continued in more recent studies (see Virués-Ortega et al., 2013a, for further discussion). For example, in the report by Van Bourgondien et al. (2003), the mean values for the major outcome measures concerning adaptive behavioural functioning are not cited, although the impact of the programme is suggested as producing a statistically significant effect in this domain. Additionally, many of these studies do not report the standard scores from the instruments that they employ, but rely on the raw scores (e.g. Panerai et al., 2002), or use instruments that are not necessarily used in studies of other interventions, such as the Ankara Developmental Screening Inventory (Mukaddes et al., 2004). The overall impact of these methods of data reporting is to make direct comparison and, indeed, ease of understanding the results (see next for more detailed discussion), harder than it needs to be. The adoption of more standard tools in future work may go some way to overcome these problems of comparison.

Outcome-effectiveness of TEACCH

To explore the impact of TEACCH interventions more fully, the results of individual outcome-effectiveness studies were analysed in a meta-analysis, as conducted for the behavioural interventions in Chapter 5 and 6. These TEACCH studies were identified through a literature search and by cross checking with the previously published reviews, noted earlier. Studies that satisfied the minimum requirements of presenting data from one of the key functioning domains of cognitive, communication and adaptive-behavioural functioning, after exposure to a TEACCH programme were included in the current chapter. However, as noted earlier, several outcome-effectiveness studies of TEACCH did not report the use of standard scales for the measurement of these functioning domains, especially in the areas of communication and adaptive-social behaviour. For example, several of the studies employed subscales from autism-specific scales and it is unclear whether the results from these assessments map directly onto other standardized tools designed to assess these communication functioning domains. Some of the studies produced composite scores from standardized scales (e.g. Van Bourgondien et al., 2003) and some have relied on video analysis of behaviours and utterances (e.g. Aoyama, 1995), neither of which are readily understandable in terms of more conventional approaches to measuring outcome-effectiveness and these studies were not included in the current analysis.

Study characteristics   Table 7.2 shows the characteristics of the outcome-effectiveness studies that were included in the present analysis. There were 16 such studies, which comprised 18 different groups of individuals undergoing various TEACCH programmes (the study reported by Lord & Schopler, 1989, contained three differently aged groups of children undergoing TEACCH interventions). The studies had a mean of 25.5 (standard deviation = ±24.2; range = 5–70) participants. There were five observational studies (50%), seven controlled studies (39%) with a non-randomized control comparison and two Randomized Controlled Trials (11%). Of these reports, 13 (72%) were conducted either in a school or residentially based setting (the school settings also included a parent-training component, but this was not central to the delivery of the programme) and there were five (28%) home-based programmes, three of which were primarily driven by the parents, rather than professional clinical or educational staff.

There was a large variation ion the duration of these TEACCH programmes, with the programmes having a mean duration of 78.7 (±62.2) weeks, but with a range of between 8 and 182 weeks. The intensity of the programmes delivered, in terms of hours per week, is somewhat difficult to derive from many of the reports. However, the TEACCH programme typically runs throughout the school or residential-centre day and, on the basis of estimating a 5-hour school day, the mean level of intensity would be around 25.2 (±11.6; range = 1–25) hours a week (comparable with the behavioural programmes discussed in the previous chapters). For the home programmes, it is difficult to derive these data.

The average age of the participants at intake was around 112 (±109.2; range = 20–394) months, although the mean is a somewhat misleading, as the studies tended to fall into two distinct clusters: those conducted on younger children (e.g. Lord & Schopler, 1989; Tsang et al., 2007) and those conducted on adults (e.g. Persson, 2000; Siaperas & Beadle-Brown, 2006). The mean level of intellectual functioning of the participants (based on the studies where this information was reported) in terms of their standard IQ score was 52 (±15.5; range = 20–75). Unfortunately, few of the studies reported standardized measures of language and adaptive-social behaviour at baseline.

Table 7.2 Characteristics of studies assessing TEACCH programmes for individuals with ASD showing the number of participants (N), type of trial (Obs = observational; Cont = controlled; RCT = randomized control trial), location of programme, duration and weekly intensity of the programme, as well as the participants' baseline age and intellectual functioning.

Study	Year	N	Trial type	Location	Duration (months)	Intensity (h/week)	Intake age (mths)	Intake IQ
Aoyama	1995	5	Obs	School				41
Braiden et al.	2012	18	Obs	Home	8		38	
Fornasari et al.	2012	28	Obs	School	52	2	50	75
Lord & Schopler	1989	70	Obs	School	182	25	36	60
Lord & Schopler	1989	70	Obs	School	182	25	48	60
Lord & Schopler	1989	70	Obs	School	182	25	60	60
Mandell et al.	2013	59	RCT	School	34	25	76	58
McConkey et al.	2010	35	Cont	Home	39		34	59
Mukaddes et al.	2004	10	Cont	Home	13	1	43	
Ozonoff & Cathcart	1998	11	Cont	Home	74		53	40
Panerai et al.	2002	13	Cont	School	52	25	108	20
Panerai et al.	2009	8	Cont	School	156	35	108	20
Persson	2000	7	Obs	School	130	35	384	60
Siaperas & Beadle-Brown	2006	12	Obs	School	26	35	252	60
Siaperas et al.	2007	10	Obs	School	78	35	252	
Tsang et al.	2007	18	Cont	School	26	25	48	60
Van Bourgondien	2003	6	Cont	School	52	35	284	50
Welterin et al.	2012	10	RCT	Home	52		30	57

Change in functioning As noted previously, a problem in presenting the data derived from these studies is that many of them use different outcome measures from one another and also from studies of other programmes, some of which were not standardized and some studies only reported the raw scores from standardized measures. Given this, only the effect sizes for the three key functioning domains: intellectual, language and adaptive-social behaviours, rather than changes in the actual standard scores, are shown in Table 7.3. Two effect sizes are displayed: the mean change from baseline to follow-up as a function of the baseline standard deviation and the difference between the change score for the TEACCH and comparison group divided by the pooled standard deviation of these groups at baseline (see Chapter 1). These data are shaded using the system described in previous chapters (see Chapter 5), according to the strength of the effect as suggested by Cohen (1988): lighter shaded cells indicating a strong effect (i.e. an effect size >0.7), medium shaded cells indicate a moderate sized effect (effect size = 0.3–0.7) and dark shaded cells show a weak effect (an effect size <0.30).

Table 7.3 Outcomes of TEACCH studies, showing pre-to-post intervention effect sizes (ES_1) and comparison with the control group effect size (ES_2).

Study (Year)	Pre- to Post-change			Comparison with control		
	IQ ES_1	Lang ES_1	ASB ES_1	IQ ES_2	Lang ES_2	ASB ES_2
Aoyama (1995)			.91			
Braiden et al. (2012)		.28				
Fornasari et al. (2012)	.80	.61				
Lord & Schopler (1989)	.47					
Lord & Schopler (1989)	.20					
Lord & Schopler (1989)	.07					
Mandell et al. (2013)	.69	.48		−.02	−.28	
McConkey et al. (2010)		1.48	.74			
Mukaddes et al. (2004)		.89	.97		−1.89	−1.43
Ozonoff & Cathcart (1998)	1.21	.51		.68	.45	
Panerai et al. (2002)	.67			.54		
Panerai et al. (2009)	.58	.33	.96	.59	.37	.64
Persson (2000)	.39	.35	.67			
Siaperas & Beadle-Brown (2006)		.32	.49			
Siaperas et al. (2007)						
Tsang et al. (2007)	.72	1.69	−.21	.08	−.25	−.87
Van Bourgondien (2003)		1.69	1.28			
Welterin et al. (2012)	.40	.40	1.00	.10	.00	−.03

IQ = intellectual function, Lang = language function; ASB = adaptive and social behaviour. White = strong effect; light grey = moderate effect; dark grey = weak effect; black = no data.

Most of the studies give a measure of progress in intellectual functioning (usually derived from the PEP-R or the Mullin's Scales) and inspection of these data shows that the majority of the reports indicate a moderate impact on intellectual functioning. The mean effect size for the groups analysed (see Table 7.3) was 0.56 (±0.31; range 0.07–1.21). However, there was some variation in these outcomes, with three of the studies reporting strong impacts in this domain (Fornasari et al., 2012; Ozonoff & Cathcart, 1998; Tsang et al., 2007) and there were two reports of weak effects, both of which were from the older participant groups included in the report by Lord and Schopler (1989). In an early review, Smith (1999) estimated that the typical gain in intellectual functioning as a result of a TEACCH programme to be of the order of 3–7 IQ points and, if the standard deviation of a standardized IQ test is taken to be 15, these current data suggest that the upper region of that estimate given by Smith (1999) is about right.

In terms of the language functioning, very few of the studies actually employed a standardized test of language, such as the Peabody Picture Vocabulary Test and the current data are drawn mainly from the cognitive verbal functioning scores from the IQ tests used. In addition, a number of the studies relied on measures of functional communication drawn from the adult PEP-R (e.g. Tsang et al., 2007). They also reflect a combination of receptive and expressive language scores, where those data were available. Keeping in mind these provisos in terms of the range and type of tools employed, the effect size for these TEACCH programmes language were, again, in the moderate range, with a mean of 0.65 (±0.48, range 0.32–1.69). However, four studies did report particularly strong effect sizes (i.e. McConkey et al., 2010; Mukaddes et al., 2004; Tsang et al., 2007; Van Bourgondien et al., 2003) and none presented findings of weak effect sizes in this domain.

Several of the studies included measures of adaptive and social behaviours and most of these effect sizes could be regarded as strong. Although the mean effect size was 0.64 (±0.52, range –0.21–1.00), this mean value for the studies was brought down by the report from Tsang et al. (2007), which showed a reduction in functioning in this domain after exposure to the TEACCH programme. In addition to these reports, a number of other studies not included in the current meta-analysis have supported the notion that TEACCH impacts positively on adaptive behaviour (e.g. Short, 1984; Van Bourgondien et al., 2003) and it should be noted that this was the only domain with a positive conclusion reached in the meta-analysis by Virués-Ortega et al. (2013a).

In addition to these three domains, several studies have provided data, or comment, on a range of other longer-term outcome measures (noted to be lacking in many assessments of other programmes). For example, Keel et al. (1997) noted that, after exposure to an adult work-oriented TEACCH programme, employment rates rose from 63% at the start of the programme to 89% of people in retained employment at the end of the programme. Similarly, Schopler et al. (1982) noted that only 7% of individuals who had undergone a TEACCH programme were institutionalized, which compares very favourably with the rates described in Chapter 1. Although such long-term outcome are clearly important and their inclusion in outcome-effectiveness studies has been urged by multiple commentators (e.g. Matson & Konst, 2013; Mesibov & Shea, 2010), these indices are not without their problems. Prime among these difficulties are that such measures are subject to the full range of the changing political and social priorities, up to and including, the vagaries of the world economic climate (i.e. it is unclear whether 'high' or 'low' unemployment rates are related to the impact of the programme or the impact of the economy as a whole). As such, it is not always clear whether such outcomes reflect the impact of the programme or the local politico-economic context (see Gresham et al., 1998).

Comparison with controls The previous data suggest that the application of a TEACCH programme has moderate effects across the range of outcome variables. However, another critical comparison by which to assess the strength of an approach is to establish how it compares with the effects of comparison treatments, to see whether the impact of the programme is greater than that which might have been expected anyway. There are now a number of studies that have provided such data (Mandell et al., 2013; Mukaddes et al., 2004; Ozonoff & Cathcart, 1998; Panerai et al., 2002; 2007; Tsang et al., 2007; Welterlin et al., 2012).

When these comparison data are examined, the evidence for the differential impact of a TEACCH programme, compared to a comparison group, is somewhat less compelling than its impact over time. The mean effect sizes for the three functioning domains in comparison to the comparison groups were: intellectual = 0.33 (±0.31, range –0.02–0.68); language and communication = –0.27 (±0.85, range –1.89–0.45) and adaptive and social = –0.42 (±0.91, range –1.43–0.64).

The large standard deviations and ranges for the effects sizes for the language and adaptive behaviour, domains suggest that simple consideration of these means might be somewhat misleading and that a variety of other factors are probably impacting these outcomes. Certainly one of these factors is the nature of the control group employed. Only one of the reports employed a 'no treatment' control (Welterin et al., 2012) and the majority employed a 'treatment as usual approach', which usually comprised a school placement that did not involve the use of a TEACCH approach (Ozonoff & Cathcart, 1998; Panerai et al., 2002; 2007; Tsang et al., 2007). All of these latter comparisons produced either moderate or weak effect sizes. The study by Mandell et al. (2013) compared TEACCH for ASD versus TEACCH for Reactive Attachment Disorder – that is, the comparison group also received TEACCH – and this study is the one that produced the worst comparative outcomes. Thus, it might be suggested that the comparison groups for TEACCH were particularly strict. That said, the comparison data do suggest that the TEACCH approach is not relatively effective and this corresponds to the conclusions reached by Virués-Ortega et al. (2013a) in their meta-analysis.

Predictors of outcome

The studies reported in Table 7.3 also allow a number of variables to be studied in relation to the outcomes of the TEACCH programme. In particular, it is possible to examine a number of programme variables, such as the impact of the type of programme (school/clinic versus home), whether the programme was professionally lead or parent-led, the duration of the programme, as well as several child-related variables, like the child's age at intake and their baseline intellectual functioning. As there were relatively few studies, the current chapter analysed their impact on outcomes by creating two groups of studies for each of these predictor potential variables – a group with a relatively lower value on the predictor and a group with a relatively higher value for that variable.

Figure 7.1 shows the effect size outcomes (pre- to post-programme changes) in the three functioning domains (intellectual, language, adaptive-social) for each of the five potential predictor variables outlined previously, when the studies have been divided into two groups reflecting: the location of the programme (school vs home); whether the programme had a shorter (up to 24 months) or longer (greater than 24 months) duration; whether the participants included were relatively younger (up to 6 years old) or older (greater than 6 years old) and whether the participants had a lower (IQ of up to 59) or a higher (IQ of 60 or over) level of intellectual functioning at intake.

In terms of the location of the programme, when the intervention was delivered in a school or a clinic it had a greater impact on the intellectual and language functioning of the participants, than when it was delivered at home. However, the home-lead programmes produced greater gains in intellectual and adaptive and social skills. The shorter programmes (up to 24 months) impacted more strongly on intellectual functioning and

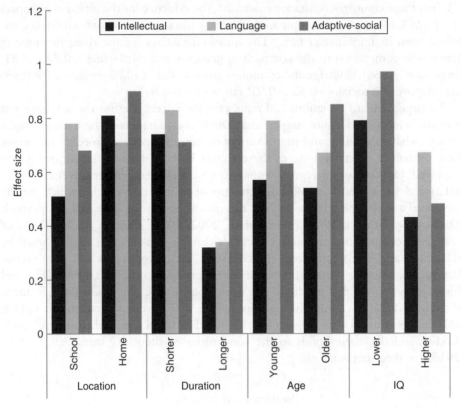

Figure 7.1 Effect sizes (pre-treatment to post-treatment change) for the studies examining TEACCH, divided into studies with below or above the sample mean for various aspects of the programme or participant characteristics.

language and less strongly on adaptive behaviours, than longer programmes (although this feature was highly confounded with the location of the programme).

In terms of the participant characteristics, when the group was split into studies conducted on relatively younger children and those employing older participants, the studies on younger and older participants did not display an effect on the intellectual functioning outcomes. However, the current comparison really reflects groups of children (the relatively younger group) and groups of adults (the relatively older group), being subjected to TEACCH and it contradicts several studies that have analysed the impact of age at intake when analysing studies purely conducted on differently aged school-age children. These studies have tended to find that, the younger the child at intake, the better the impact of the TEACCH programme on the intellectual functioning (see Smith, 1999, for a comment). For example, Lord and Schopler (1989) found much better gains for 3-year-old children than for 5-year-old children and Fornasari et al. (2012) noted good gains for children entering a programme before 40 months old, but not for those entering after 60 months.

The younger group shown in Figure 7.1 shows much greater language gain than the adult participants. This result might be expected on the basis of any number of theories of language development involving critical age periods and the adults developing nonverbal methods of communication that might interfere with acquiring typical language. In contrast, the reports of the effect of TEACCH on older participants tended to produce greater gains in adaptive-social behaviours.

Finally, in terms of the level of intellectual functioning at intake, Figure 7.1 shows that the lower functioning children showed stronger gains than the higher functioning children. This finding corroborates the reports suggesting that such gains are stronger for children with lower, than higher, intellectual functioning (Lord & Schopler, 1989; see also Venter et al., 1992).

Summary

These data show that there is evidence that a TEACCH approach can impact positively on the individual's functioning and that the typical gains in all three functioning domains are of moderate size. However, the data are still ambiguous regarding whether this programme offers benefits over and above alternative programmes and it would be a great help if future studies could employ more typical instruments in the assessment of the gains that can be made.

Although there are still relatively few data points that can be drawn on in order to assess the predictors of success, it might be concluded that programmes run in schools or clinics will tend to promote intellectual and linguistic functioning, whereas those run at home with parental input will tend to promote adaptive behaviour and social skills. Younger children will tend to fare better than older children on the programme for language gains, but that adults will derive benefit in terms of social and adaptive behavioural skills.

Learning Experiences and Alternative Programme for preschoolers and their parents (LEAP)

The LEAP programme was developed in the early 1980s (see Hoyson et al., 1984; Kohler et al., 1996) and reflects two important developments that were current at that time. The first of these developments was the emerging realization that behavioural principles could be used effectively to help individuals with ASD (see Lovaas, 1993; see Chapter 4). The second development was the growing force of the argument regarding including children with special needs within the mainstream classroom setting (e.g. Nirje, 1969; Warnock, 1978), an issue that will be documented and discussed more fully in the current Chapter 12.

Partly in response to both of these aspects of that educational zeitgeist, the LEAP approach suggested that educating children with ASD alongside their typically developing peers, while utilizing a set of behavioural strategies to facilitate this teaching, would help to improve the functioning of all of the children involved in the programme (those with ASD and their typically developing peers). It was hoped that these gains would be seen, especially in relation to the social skills of the individuals with ASD, who, it was thought, would benefit from the interactions with typically developing children (see also Boutot & Bryant, 2005; Connor, 2000, for similar suggestions). There have been a number of other interventions that similarly target manipulation of the school social milieu (see Ospina et al., 2008, for a summary), but LEAP is the most widely employed and best documented of these approaches.

The LEAP programme contrasts with the TEACCH approach in that it explicitly adopts an 'inclusionist' philosophy of education – holding that the education of individuals with ASD is best achieved when they are placed alongside their typically developing peers. To date, there has only been one study which has compared the TEACCH and LEAP approaches directly: Boyd et al. (2014) noted no difference in the extent to which the programmes impacted on the functioning outcomes of the participants. Unfortunately, the data presented by Boyd et al. (2014) were not reported in terms of gains in standardized measures of functioning, making definite interpretation problematic.

While the LEAP approach shares a behavioural orientation with the 'Lovaas' programme, it also explicitly suggests that a discrete-trial approach may not be optimal for teaching and instead uses a range of naturalistic teaching practices (e.g. Koegel et al., 2003; Stokes & Baer, 1977). In this aspect, LEAP is similar to the 'Verbal Behaviour' approach (Sundberg & Partington, 1998; see Chapter 4), although LEAP focuses more on the development of social skills, than language skills, as the key to unlocking the problems of ASD. To the extent that LEAP places a behavioural approach within a school setting, it also shares some features with the CABAS® programme (Greer, 1997; see Chapter 4), but, whereas the CABAS® intervention is neutral about the policy of inclusion, the LEAP approach requires an inclusive approach.

Background and implementation

The LEAP approach holds a number of basic tenets, which both describe the programme and also provide much of the framework for the evidence-base that is used to justify the implementation of this particular intervention. As with many other approaches developed for use in schools (e.g. CABAS®; TEACCH), much of the supporting evidence is not found in outcome-effectiveness studies, per se, as it is for behavioural approaches (see Chapter 5), but rather in small-scale studies that focus on particular aspects of the underlying tenets of the programme (Kohler et al., 1996; see previous text for a similar issue in relation to the TEACCH intervention). To this extent, the background assumptions of LEAP are important to outline and discuss in a little detail.

There are a number of places where the basic principles of the LEAP approach have been documented (see Hume et al., 2011; Kohler et al., 1996; Strain & Bovery, 2011). From these discussions, six main guiding principles may be abstracted and can be characterized as follows:

1. All children can benefit from inclusive education.
2. Benefit from education is maximal when the school and home cohere on shared principles and goals.
3. Parents and professionals need to work together to help the children.
4. Pupils with ASD can learn from typically developing peers, especially in terms of their social interactions.
5. Typically developing peers can benefit from the inclusion process.
6. Teaching is most effective when delivered through behavioural principles.

None of these principles are unique to the LEAP approach, but each has been subject to some degree of investigation in relation to the LEAP programme. In terms of the benefits of the inclusive approach to the education of individuals with ASD, this is a vast topic with much associated research (see Lindsay, 2003; Norwich, 2005; Reed & Osborne, 2014, for reviews) and which merits a chapter to itself (see Chapter 12). However, with respect to the LEAP approach, the particular model of inclusion proposed is quite specific and it is unclear whether, in general, the inclusion literature will generalize to this approach. In a typical LEAP classroom, there are about 10 typically developing children and usually about three children with ASD (Kohler et al., 1996). The classroom is structured to resemble a 'normal' room (Hoyson et al., 1984) and a teacher will co-teach with a learning support assistant (LSA; Kohler et al., 1996), using naturalistic teaching methods rather than discrete-trial procedures (Delprato, 2001).

Although it must be noted that not all studies of inclusive education have shown benefits to the children with ASD (e.g. Durbach & Pence, 1991; Harris et al., 1990; Reed et al., 2012; see Chapter 12), the particular model used in LEAP has been shown, in a few small-scale studies (e.g. see Strain et al., 1986; Strain & Hoyson, 2000) to produce benefits for children with ASD relative to the impact of placement in a special education classroom. Strain et al. (1986) noted that the gains in social functioning found for children with ASD were better after inclusion in a LEAP classroom than they were after a period of placement in a more typical special education setting. Moreover, Strain and Hoyson (2000) noted that there were significant improvements in social skills in a LEAP-inclusive setting; with around 50% of the children showing no signs of the developmental regression that might otherwise be expected over the period studied.

However, as mentioned previously, these studies were all relative small-scale and certainly need better documentation to allow fuller comparison with other intervention programmes. Moreover, it is unclear whether LEAP-induced gains also were observed in domains other than social development. In contrast to these positive results, Harris et al. (1990) compared children with ASD who were participating in a LEAP programme with children with ASD being educated in a special school setting and noted that, while the language skills of the children in the LEAP setting did improve over the time period employed, these improvements were no different to those noted in the children in the other special educational settings. However, again, this was a similarly relatively small-scale study, making reliance on these results as a general indication of outcome perilous.

The second and third principles of the LEAP programme, outlined previously, concern the relationship between the school and parents. Indeed, the role played by parents is recognized as pivotal to many treatments for children with ASD (Osborne et al., 2008a; Robbins et al., 1991). The development of this teacher-parent relationship is taken as central in a LEAP programme and it is approached in two ways. Firstly, by the establishment of a home-school alliance (Dawson & Osterling, 1997), present in order to facilitate communication and coherent planning between the parents and teachers. In this strategy, the LEAP programme shares much ground with many of the other educationally or professionally driven approaches, such as TEACCH (see Mesibov et al., 2004, and previously). Secondly, both parents and teachers receive training in a range of techniques for teaching individuals with ASD. For example, teachers and LSAs receive outreach training concerning various aspects of education for individuals with ASD, such as the need for individualized education plans (Kohler et al., 1996). Additionally, parents, receive training in behaviour management techniques (Strain et al., 1996).

A pivotal aspect of the inclusive programme for the LEAP approach is the adoption of 'peer-tutoring' procedures (Kohler et al., 1996; Strain & Bovey, 2011). The widespread use of the peer-tutor strategy underpins the earlier noted fourth and fifth elements of the LEAP approach. As with many of the individual components of any comprehensive approach, this is not a unique aspect of LEAP and many other interventions for the education of children with ASD share this approach (see McConnell, 2002, for a review). However, the LEAP approach proposes that, for those with ASD, many skills can be best learned from typically developing children. As with the issue of inclusive education, in general, this claim might be debatable within the broad context of interventions for individuals with ASD, but there have been a number of studies that have specifically examined the role of peer tutoring within the context of a LEAP classroom (Goldstein & Wickstrom, 1986; Odom & Strain, 1984; Strain & Bovey, 2008). All of these studies have pointed to the mutual benefits of learning for both the individuals with ASD who are taught through this medium (Odom & Strain, 1984), but also for the typically developing peers who act as peer-tutors. For example, Hoyson et al. (1984) describe an increase in the rate of learning for both the pupils with ASD and for their peer-tutors, after a peer-tutoring teaching approach was adopted in a LEAP classroom.

The final aspect of a LEAP classroom is it emphasis on a set of behavioural strategies to implement the teaching (Hume et al., 2011; Strain, 1981; Strain & Bovey, 2011). In particular, the LEAP approach relies on naturalistic teaching opportunities (Stokes & Baer, 1977) and pivotal response training (Koegel et al., 2003; see also the Early Start Denver Model described in Chapter 8), both of which strategies highlight the use of reinforcement for behaviours that occur in 'unforced' situations, rather than through discrete trail drills (see Chapter 4 for a discussion). In addition, communication skills are developed and facilitated through the use of the Picture Exchange Communication System (Frost & Bondy, 2002) and behaviours are managed through the application of positive behavioural support (see Grey et al., 2009). These procedures have been described in the context of LEAP in a number of articles, notably by Hume et al. (2011) and by Strain and Bovey (2011).

Outcome-effectiveness evidence

In contrast to the studies that have focused on particular components of the LEAP technique, there have been few studies that have specifically examined the overall outcomes produced from the adoption of a LEAP approach. A number of observational studies have noted that exposure to a LEAP intervention will reduce problems and promote a range of skills, for individuals with ASD. For example, Strain and Cordisco (1993) noted that children exposed to a LEAP programme showed a reduction in the severity of their ASD symptoms and Hoyson et al. (1984) noted that a LEAP programme improved the intellectual functioning (IQ scores) and language abilities of the individuals exposed to the scheme. Greater social skills in the children with ASD when they were at home were also reported by Hoyson et al. (1984) as a result of inclusion in a LEAP programme.

However, all of the previously discussed outcome-effectiveness studies were small scale and they did not report the results from a strong, or indeed any, comparison group, in order to evaluate the relative impact of the LEAP approach. In fact, there are very few such demonstrations of the effectiveness of a LEAP approach relative to a control condition.

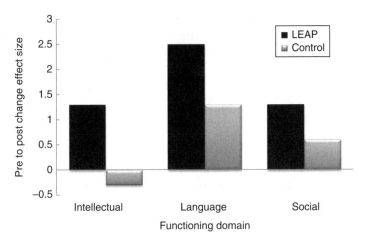

Figure 7.2 The pre- to post-intervention change effect sizes from three domains reported in an outcome-effectiveness study comparing a LEAP programme with a control group (Strain & Bovey, 2011).

One such study was reported by Strain and Bovey (2011), who compared children undergoing a LEAP approach, as described previously, for 3 hours a day, 5 days a week, over a period of 24 months, with the outcomes of matched children with ASD, whose teachers had been given access to the LEAP manual, but who had been given no formal instructions regarding setting up LEAP classrooms and so on. The effect sizes for the two groups this study in the three areas of functioning are shown in Figure 7.2. These results demonstrated a nine-point gain in the intellectual functioning of the children undergoing the LEAP programme, from a mean of 60–69, compared to a mean two-point loss in intellectual functioning for the pupils in the comparison condition. Moreover, there was a large gain in language skills, increasing from a standard score of 29–44, compared to a five-point gain in language for the comparison participants. In terms of language, it was noted that the gains in receptive language were greater than those in expressive language (which is similar to most intervention results for other programmes).

Certainly, these results are encouraging, although it is clearly the case that more studies will need to be conducted before the weight of evidence approaches that noted for the behavioural and TEACCH approaches. Moreover, there are no indications of the predictors of success for a LEAP approach and, given the controversies surrounding inclusive education for children with ASD (see Chapter 12), these aspects of the database for the LEAP programme will certainly need to be developed much more strongly.

Daily Living Skills Therapy (Higashi)

The 'Daily Living Skills' approach is based on educational principles that are in common use in Japan and is centred on the notion that every child has the potential to learn – indeed, the alternative and more commonly employed, name for this intervention technique, *higashi*, means 'hope'. The programme was initially developed in

Tokyo, in 1964 and was based on the experiences of teachers who attempted to accommodate children with ASD within this classroom. Subsequently, a school catering for 1800 pupils (approximately 25% of whom had ASD) has been established (see Kitahara, 1983). A second site in Boston, USA, was established in 1987, which caters for around 100 children with ASD and where around two-thirds of whom are residential at the school (Tutt et al., 2006).

The reports describing this technique and providing evidence regarding its effectiveness derive from the two Higachi cites (Tokyo and Boston). As a result of the relatively limited number of operational cites, there are rather few direct empirical examinations of this approach in the literature and a number of reviews of outcome-effectiveness often have chosen not to include the programme in the analyses (e.g. Kasari & Smith, 2013; Ospina et al., 2008). While acknowledging this as both a truth and a problem, there are a number of important reasons to provide an assessment of this programme: (i) there are widespread claims of effectiveness for the Higashi method (e.g. Brink, 1988); (ii) it is self-declaredly a 'comprehensive' approach to treatment of ASD (Kitahara, 1983) and (iii) its philosophy does rely on a package of well-known techniques that are similar to many of the approaches noted previously (see Tutt et al., 2006).

Philosophy

The Higashi method sets out to develop self-esteem, the ability to perform basic daily living skills and physical strength and coordination, in individuals with ASD (Cummins et al., 2005; Roberts, 2004). In these broad goals, the Higashi intervention manifests some differences from the other comprehensive packages that have been described earlier (such as ABA and TEACCH), which tend to focus on specific core problems of ASD, rather than on developing aspects of the 'whole child'. In fact, the Higashi website claims that the approach: '…provides the foundation which is at the core of a broad and full education rather than one directed as a piecemeal approach to remediating deficits.'

To reach these goals, the Higashi approach offers a broad-based school curriculum for children with ASD that mirrors the teaching provided for typically developing children and it encompasses teaching of subjects such as: literacy, mathematics, science and social studies. In addition, in the Higashi schools, there is a special focus on the teaching of music, art, physical education and also information technology. The teaching for this broad curriculum is provided in a consistent and structured manner and is facilitated through play-based means that are, more-or-less exclusively, focused on group-based activities.

The Higashi programme attempts to utilize the natural interests of the children to encourage their participation in these activities (similar to the strategies outlined above for the TEACCH and LEAP approaches). The programme also capitalizes on naturally occurring opportunities for teaching (similarly to that described above for the LEAP programme) and attempts to enhance 'positive' behaviours by encouraging such behaviours, rather than removing externalizing or inappropriate behaviours through the administration of aversive stimuli or medication. Thus, while the stated overall objectives of the approach are quite distinct from the other approaches discussed so far, the stated means of the Higashi approach to achieving these goals are highly similar to other programmes.

Implementation

There are three main pillars of the Higashi teaching technique that predominate in the daily teaching routines for the children and which might distinguish a Higashi classroom from other classrooms:

1. Vigorous physical activity (especially through music and dance) to promote strength and coordination.
2. A focus on group activities to help develop emotional stability through conformity to the group.
3. Intellectual stimulation through exposure to models (both teacher and peers).

In assessing the literature relating to the importance of these three strands of teaching strategy, it rapidly becomes apparent that these pillars of the Higashi education system correspond to some quite well-documented teaching strategies shared outside the Higashi schools.

Although there is little documented procedural detail regarding the use of physical activity in the Higashi classroom, the employment of music, dance, art and other physical intervention strategies (see Chapter 10), it is certainly true that each of these intervention strategies has been employed quite widely in other contexts and there is some evidence for the effectiveness of these approaches, which is outlined in Table 7.4. To the extent that these components of the intervention have some supporting evidence from other contexts, then it is possible that there will be some generalization to the Daily Living Skills programme. Moreover, the improvement of physical coordination, sensory issues and intellectual stimulation that sometimes accompanies these interventions certainly targets some key functioning areas of ASD (Dawson & Watling, 2000; Chapter 2).

There is some evidence to suggest that the physical activities which are undertaken in the Higashi schools do reduce self-stimulation in the children (Trevarthen et al., 1996), although it is not clear whether this reduction is better than that which would be achieved in alternative approaches (the role of physical therapies is further

Table 7.4 Brief outline of commonly used forms of 'physical therapies' for people with ASD.

Type	Description	References
Music Therapy	Uses singing, music-making and/or composition, to encourage engagement in musical activities. The response to music may lead to changes in behaviour and emotions.	Gold (2011) Kaplan & Steele (2005) Kern et al. (2012) Reschke-Hernández (2011)
Dance-Movement Therapy	Uses expressive elements of dance and movement to assess and intervene, developing attention to shared activity and social engagement.	Gunning & Holmes (1973) Koch et al. (2014) Ritter & Low (1996)
Art Therapy	Uses creative process of art to enhance physical, mental and emotional health. Aims to improve symbolic thinking, recognition of facial expressions and fine motor skills.	Emery (2004) Epp (2008) Evans & Dubowski (2001)

discussed in Chapter 10). Additionally, certain living skills, such as toilet training, have been noted to be promoted to a greater extent in a Higashi school, relative to other special school placements (see Richardson & Langley, 1997), although the mechanism whereby Daily Living Therapy promotes these behaviours is unclear. It may be that the improvement in physical coordination helps develop such skills, although it is equally possible that the physical activity reduces interfering levels of anxiety and hyperactivity in the children (Howlin, 1998), or that the highly structured and full curriculum it simply leaves the children no time to engage in ASD-typical behaviours (Baron-Cohen & Bolton, 1993). The suppressive effect of interfering activities remains a strong possibility, although one whose importance should not necessarily be discounted.

The focus on group activities, rather than on 1:1 teaching, is a defining characteristic of the Higashi approach and this is undertaken in the belief that it will help develop emotional stability in the children by allowing them to learn from others in the group (Tutt et al., 2006). The use of group teaching is not unique to Higashi and programmes such as LEAP also hope that peer-mediated learning may benefit the child with ASD (see Strain, 1983). The difference from programmes such as LEAP is that the group of individuals in a Higashi programme comprise other individuals with ASD and the teacher, rather than typically developing children. While this approach is at odds with an inclusionist philosophy, the use of peers with ASD to promote learning and social competencies resonates with much of the literature on school placement to be discussed in Chapter 12. The weight of such evidence currently suggests that exposure to other children with ASD, rather than to typically developing peers, may be better for this particular group (Ashburner et al., 2008; Humphrey & Symes, 2010; Chapter 12).

A concern about the Higashi method that should be commented upon is the focus placed on group conformity within the social context. Unless this aspect of the programme is very carefully managed, then, given the fundamental asocial nature of ASD and the potential for aversive experiences for the individual with ASD when confronted with large numbers of others (see Chapter 2), the strategy simply may not be effective (see Tutt et al., 2006, for further critique).

The final aspect of the implementation strategy for the Higashi programme is to provide a range of intellectual stimulation through exposure to a broad school curriculum. This stimulation is hoped to be facilitated by a reliance on the children imitating the teachers. Unfortunately, there is little evidence that such an 'imitation' mechanism is at work and it is unclear that imitation will spontaneous occur in the child with ASD (see Chapter 2). Certainly, such imitation skills would need to be explicitly taught to individuals with ASD (Lovaas, 1987).

Outcome-effectiveness evidence

Despite the similarity of some aspects of the Higashi approach to other interventions, there have been no large-scale examinations of the Higashi approach. Thus, while there are reasons not to dismiss the approach, there are also few reasons to actively endorse such an intervention. The one study regarding the outcome-effectiveness of Daily Living Skills Therapy that has been reported by Larkin and Gurry (1998) was a very small scale investigation (three children), conducted over a 2-year period, during which the participants received their education at a Higashi school. The children were observed for a series of eight, 1-hour sessions and their behaviours ('attention' and 'inappropriate') were recorded. Two years later the same observational processes were repeated. The investigators reported a six-fold increase in the number of attentional responses exhibited by the participants and a two-fold reduction in the emission of inappropriate behaviours. Although these data are encouraging, in the absence of standardized measures and of a comparison group, it is difficult to know exactly what to make of these reported improvements. Thus, it is wisest to conclude that the 'Higashi' approach does draw on some validated approaches and that it shows some similarities in procedure to range of alternative packages, but it requires far more empirical validation as an intervention in itself.

8

Developmental and Parent-Mediated Treatment Models

There is a family of approaches to treating Autism Spectrum Disorders (ASD) that can be termed 'developmental' (see McConachie & Diggle, 2007; Odom et al., 2010; Oono et al., 2013; Ospina et al., 2008, for overviews). This set of approaches can all be considered to be comprehensive, in that each could be offered as the sole intervention for the individual with ASD, although many are often used in conjunction with one another or with other forms of intervention (Stahmer et al., 2005). Furthermore, developmental programmes are very commonly occurring forms of intervention for ASD. For example, Stahmer et al. (2005; see also Matson et al., 2009) noted that around 80% of practitioners and parents report employ techniques from such developmental approaches with children with ASD. Figure 8.1 gives a representation of the percentage of therapists claiming to employ developmental approaches.

These interventions often purport to be based on particular theories regarding child development (Prizant et al., 2000; Rogers, 1998). However, in understanding the nature of these treatments, it is quite important to place the term 'developmental' into context. Although several of these approaches do refer to their bases in particular psychological developmental theory (such as Piagetian views), the nature of their foundation in such theories is somewhat unclear. For example, although a very early and influential developmental approach – the Denver Health Sciences Programme (see Rogers, 1998) – claims some relationship to Piagetian developmental theory, it is not clear how the specific strategies of the intervention (see next for fuller discussion) are related to those psychological principles. In fact, it could be claimed that examination of the nature of most developmental interventions shows that, rather than attempting to utilize the underlying psychological principles derived from stage models of child development, most developmental interventions focus on enhancing particular sets of skills and behaviours – such as, social communication and interactions (including joint attention and imitation), linguistic behaviours and also challenging behaviours. The approach taken to enhancing these skills mostly resides

Interventions for Autism: Evidence for Educational and Clinical Practice, First Edition. Phil Reed.
© 2016 John Wiley & Sons, Ltd. Published 2016 by John Wiley & Sons, Ltd.

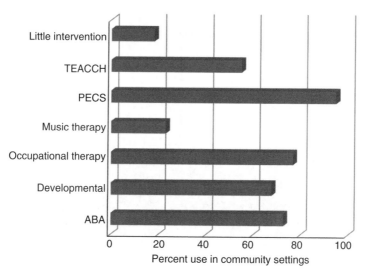

Figure 8.1 Percentage use of various forms of intervention for ASD by community providers, as reported by Stahmer et al. (2005).

in relating these behaviours closely to interactions with the child's parents and peers (e.g. Rogers et al., 1986; Wieder & Greenspan, 2003). This places these interventions in closer proximity to a Vygotskian social-developmental framework than a Piagetian stage model of development. The association between developmental approaches to ASD and social-learning views is not largely commented upon in the literature, but it certainly resonates with the discussion outlined in Chapter 2 of the present text, where it was argued that there was a lack of association between 'within-child' theories of ASD (such as Piagetian theory) and the production of interventions.

As noted earlier, developmental interventions focus on key aspects of child behaviour that are affected by insults to the typical developmental processes. In particular, these approaches often address the development of both social and functional communication abilities, such as in the Social Communication, Emotional Regulation and Transactional Support (SCERTS®; Prizant et al., 2003) programme and the 'Denver' models (Rogers et al., 1986; 2000). Alternatively, developmental approaches sometimes place a main focus on fostering the emergence of imitative behaviours and skills, as seen in the Intensive Interaction (Nind, 1999) and Options-Son-Rise (Kaufman, 1991) models. Given that such general categories of behaviours are considered to be core to the characterisation of ASD itself (Chapter 2), such an intervention focus is not wholly surprising for this population, although it should be noted that many of these treatments were not necessarily developed solely for use with children with ASD (see Kaufman, 1994).

In addition to their focus on key child behaviours, developmental interventions also often place the family at the centre of the approach in terms of their theoretical conceptualisation of the developmental process (see Williams & Wishart, 2003, for a discussion). Although there is a long history of incorporating family systems into models aiming to conceptualize ASD (Bronfenbrenner, 1979; Minuchin, 1974; Schopler, 1971; Chapter 3), as well as of addressing a number of aspects of functioning in families living with ASD (McCubbin & Patterson, 1983; Osborne, 2009),

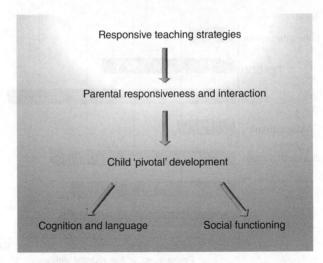

Figure 8.2   Representation of the assumed mechanisms of impact of a developmental intervention for ASD (Mahoney & Perales, 2003).

such family considerations are forming an increasingly important aspect of recent developments in the intervention field (see McConache & Diggle, 2007; Oono et al., 2013, for reviews). Placing the parents centrally in the conceptualization of the ways in which key child-developmental milestones (e.g. communication, imitation etc.) may be reached, unites many contemporary developmental interventions (Manolson, 1992; Rogers & Dawson, 2010) and many of these treatment approaches rely on parents as a main provider of the intervention: that is, they are also parent-mediated approaches (see Diggle & McConachie, 2002; Oono et al., 2013, for reviews). It is hoped, additionally, that the core incorporation of parents into the intervention will help to increase the number of treatment hours that can be provided for the child (Oono et al., 2013). To the extent that parents are involved in programme-delivery, many of these developmental approaches also involve strong initial degrees of parent training (see Matson et al., 2009). Thus, 'developmental' and 'parent-mediated' approaches are often discussed together in the literature (Diggle & McConachie, 2002; Oono et al., 2013). Figure 8.2 shows a schematic representation of the manner in which many developmental approaches assume the parent training will impact on child behaviours.

Nevertheless, while the theoretical stance of this family of programmes is relatively united in terms of the importance it places on the parents, it needs to be noted that there is some variance in the degree to which parent-mediation is employed across the different treatment regimes. Some types of developmental programme use parents almost exclusively to deliver the intervention, such as the Early Start Denver Model (ESDM; Rogers & Dawson, 2010), while some approaches employ a combination of parents and extra-familiar volunteers (e.g. the Options-Son-Rise model; see Williams, 2006). In contrast, some of these interventions are delivered exclusively by therapists and teachers, such as the Denver Health Science Programme (DHSP; Rogers & Lewis, 1989) or are typically employed in school settings, such as the SCERTS® approach (Prizant et al., 2003).

General Focus of Developmental Approaches

The advocates of developmental approaches tend to assume that a child's learning is driven by complex and dynamic processes, chiefly involving interactions between the child and their environment (particularly with their family and/or other key caregivers). As a consequence, these approaches often attempt to promote and enhance relationships between parents/caregivers and their children in order to facilitate the child's movement through the assumed typical stages of development: in particular, the development of social relationships and communication are central to many of these interventions. These areas of child functioning are not only thought to be important outcomes for the child in themselves, but are viewed also as the means by which the child may learn to communicate and interact with others, to regulate their behaviours and emotions and to develop symbolic thought.

In terms of the general teaching strategies that are employed by developmental interventions in order to promote these key skills, there are some common central features across the strategies. These strategies can be summarized, as follows:

1. The development of treatment goals are based on an analysis of an individual's developmental level.
2. Motivation is produced by building on the child's interests and strengths.
3. Naturally occurring teaching opportunities are pivotal for the programmes.
4. All attempts to communicate are important.

There are a wide range of approaches that appear to share many of these core beliefs and both Odom et al. (2010) and Ospina et al. (2008), have listed a number of developmentally based approaches that have both good documentation regarding the specifics of their conduct (e.g. the type of parent training to be given and intervention strategies to be employed) and also some evidence regarding their outcome-effectiveness. To the selection of approaches given by Odom et al. (2010) and Ospina et al. (2008) a number of other interventions can be added, derived from several substantial reviews of developmental and parent-mediated approaches (Diggle & McConachie, 2002; Matson et al., 2009; McConachie & Diggle, 2007; Oona et al., 2013).

Table 8.1 shows a number of developmental approaches and outlines their main focus of intervention (e.g. on the child's social skills, imitation abilities etc.), as well as giving further sources for their fuller description. Although there are some differences between these developmental interventions (as shall become clear in the later detailed reviews of some of these interventions), broadly these treatments can be categorized into those that involve application of 'behavioural' type approaches (e.g. the Early Start Denver Model; Pivotal Response Training), those that focus on specific cognitive skills (e.g. Parent-Mediated Communication-focused Treatment in Children with Autism), those that deal with parent-child interactions (e.g. Options-Son-Rise), those that attempt to train parents to manage specific challenging behaviours (e.g. Stepping Stones Triple-P) and those which make parent education or counselling (e.g. EarlyBird) the main focus of the approach.

Although it is apparent that there are a great number of developmental approaches that could be considered, the current chapter will focus only on describing the better-known and more widely employed techniques. This will serve to promote a general

Table 8.1　Commonly employed developmental interventions.

Approach	Programme	References	Website (where available)
Behavioural	Denver Health Sciences Programme Early Start Denver Model	Rogers et al. (1986) Rogers et al. (2000)	www.interacting withautism.com/ section/treating/ esdmod
	Pivotal Response Training	Koegel et al. (1999)	http://education.ucsb. edu/autism
Relationship-based	Developmental, Individual-difference, Relationship-based Model (Floortime)	Greenspan & Weider (1998)Wieder & Greenspan (2003)	www.floortime.org
	Intensive Interaction	Nind (1999)	www.intensive interaction.co.uk
	Responsive Teaching	Mahoney & Perales (2003)	www.responsive teaching.org
Emotion-Communication	Social Communication, Emotional Regulation Transactional Supports	Prizant et al. (2006)	www.scerts.com
	Early Social Interaction Project	Wetherby & Wood (2006)	http://esi.fsu.edu
	Improving Parents as Communication Teachers	Ingersoll & Dvortcsak (2009) Ingersoll & Wainer (2013)	http://psychology. msu.edu/autismlab/ projectimpact.html
Imitation	Options-Son-Rise Programme	Kaufman (1981)	www.autismtreat mentcenter.org
	Relationship Development Intervention	Gutstein et al. (2007)	www.rdiconnect.com
Communication	Hanen More Than Words Responsive Education and Prelinguistic Milieu Teaching	Manolson (1992) Sussman (1999) Yoder and Warren (2002) Yoder & Stone (2006)	www.hanen.org
Parent Education Training	Stepping Stones Triple P (Positive Parenting Program)	Sanders et al. (2003)	www.triplep.net/ glo-en/home
	EarlyBird	Smith (2000)	www.autism.org.uk/ earlybird

understanding of this type of approach and give some evidence about the effectiveness of specific approaches (the next chapter will consider the evidence for these approaches as a whole). It should be noted that, while some of these interventions are very commonly used, several of them do not have a strong evidence base for their effectiveness as comprehensive approaches for children with ASD. For example, Pivotal Response

Training (PRT; Koegel et al., 1999; Schreibman & Koegel, 1996) is widely employed alongside other interventions (see Chapter 3), forms part of the Early Start Denver Model (see Rogers et al., 2000) and it has a number of studies about its effects on specific behaviours (see Baker-Ericzén et al., 2007; Stahmer & Gist, 2001). However, the PRT intervention lacks reports concerning its impact on overall functioning when applied as a sole intervention for ASD. Some parent-training approaches to behaviour management, such as the Stepping Stones Triple-P approach have strong evidence for children without ASD (see Nowak & Heinrichs, 2008; Sofronoff et al., 2011; Wilson et al., 2012), but have little evidence for the impact on children with ASD (see Whittingham et al., 2006; 2009). Similarly, parent education and/or counselling programmes, such as EarlyBird (Shields, 2001; see also Pillay et al., 2011; Tonge et al., 2006) are widely employed, but have no substantial evidence in terms of their impact on child outcomes.

The following sections will provide an overview of the key aspects of the major developmental interventions. The major focus will be on those interventions that are well known and that have a more substantial evidence base regarding their effectiveness. However, in addition, approaches that share similar broad features to these major approaches will also be mentioned.

The Denver Models

Of the developmental approaches, the Denver models are among the most often assessed. It should quickly be noted that the Denver programme has evolved since its initial inception in 1981 (Rogers et al., 1986; Rogers & Lewis, 1989), from the original 'Denver Health Sciences Programme' (DHSP; Rogers et al., 1986) into the Early Start Denver Model programme (ESDM; Rogers et al., 2000). The transformation in the nature of the intervention is quite striking; the original conception being an approach that purported to be based on Piagetian principles (Rogers et al., 1986) and the later version (Rogers et al., 2000) being integrated with the behavioural PRT approach (Koegel et al., 1999).

However, although quite different in their theoretical underpinnings, the actual implementations of the two forms of the Denver intervention do share similarities with one another. Both versions of this intervention focus on the development of pragmatic language and of interpersonal relationships and both view ASD as a complex disorder impacting multiple domains of functioning. As such, both programmes suggest an interdisciplinary programme is needed to deal with this wide range of challenges.

The Denver Health Sciences Programme (DHSP)

The original DHSP was developed in 1981 to address the problems of children with a range of emotional and behavioural disorders (Rogers et al., 1986; Rogers & Lewis, 1989). The theoretical framework was based on prominent developmental theories (Rogers & DiLalla, 1991), such as Piaget's stage view of cognitive development (Piaget, 1954), the 'pragmatics' accounts of language acquisition (Weiss, 1981) and conceptualizations of social development through the 'attachment-separation-individuation' processes (Mahler et al., 1975). Thus, the underpinnings of the DHSP suggested the critical importance of social and emotional development and of communication, if any level of cognitive advancement in children is to be achieved (see Rogers et al., 1986; 1987, for further discussion).

The DHSP is typically implemented in a classroom setting, in which the child experiences about 20 hours of teaching a week (i.e. 4–5 hours a day, for 5 days a week) over the period of 1 year. A teacher-to-child ratio of 2:1, within a structured classroom environment, was thought to be ideal (Rogers & Lewis, 1989). The main focus of the programme is to improve pragmatic communication and social interactions, as well as to promote symbolic thought. The main teaching strategies occurred during 'play situations' that allowed the use of the resulting positive affect to increase motivation for engagement in an activities (see also TEACCH section in Chapter 7) and the DHSP also utilizes 'reactive language strategies' to facilitate communication and mental representation.

Evidence for the effectiveness of the DHSP

Four major studies of the DHSP have been reported (Rogers & DiLalla 1991; Rogers & Lewis 1989; Rogers et al., 1987). All of these reports are observational studies, using a pre-post design and noting changes in the development of the participants, although one of the reports did have a comparison group of children with other emotional-behavioural disorders (Rogers & DiLalla, 1991).

The studies reported by Rogers et al. (1987) and by Rogers and Lewis (1989), measured the progress of children with ASD, aged between 2 and 6 years old, over a 6 month period. Both of these studies noted gains in the participants' intellectual functioning and also in their motor skills. Rogers et al. (1987) evaluated 11 children with ASD and also noted positive changes in many developmental domains, including language and social development, beyond that which would have been projected on the basis of their previous developmental progress – although it has to be noted that extrapolating a developmental trajectory is not a particularly precise science. Rogers and DiLalla (1991) also noted similar gains over a 6–7 month period across all of the studied developmental domains for children with ASD undergoing the DHSP. Additionally, Rogers and DiLalla (1991) demonstrated that these children showed similar progress across the domains as comparison children undergoing the programme who did not have a diagnosis of ASD (and who might have been expected to show greater developmental progress in the areas of language and social skills).

Thus, there is some evidence to suggest that children with ASD will progress across many functioning domains when exposed to the DHSP. The gains reported in these four previously mentioned studies were all in the moderate effect size range (see Chapter 9 for a more detailed discussion), which suggests a reasonable degree of progress was made by the participants.

Notwithstanding this positive evidence, there are a number of limitations to these studies that should be noted. Almost all of the evidence for the DHSP is drawn from observational studies of groups undergoing the intervention and it is not known whether the progress of children receiving this treatment would be similar to those not receiving an intervention. To some extent, the fact that the children had made relatively little developmental progress previously (Rogers et al., 1987) and that their progress exceeded what might have been expected once they were established with the intervention (Rogers & DiLalla, 1991), goes some way to meeting this objection. However, the lack of comparison groups receiving no treatment or an alternative treatment is a limitation in assessing this intervention.

Early Start Denver Model (ESDM)

The DHSP has been expanded (see Eapen et al., 2013; Rogers et al., 2000) in order to both to address the needs of younger children with ASD (in the infant-toddler range) and also to utilize some of the advances seen in behavioural strategies for ASD (see Koegel et al., 1999). While still focusing on the areas of development outlined previously from the DHSP, the ESDM has introduced two notable departures from the preceding programme. Firstly, the children targeted by the ESDM are younger than those in DHSP treatments and, as a result, the ESDM is typically delivered in the home, rather than in the school classroom. Secondly, as the teaching in the ESDM programme often occurs along with family routines; such as during meals, family interactions and on visits, it relies on naturally occurring learning opportunities, facilitated by play-based techniques.

The key areas that are targeted are: promoting interpersonal exchanges, joint activity and shared engagement; increasing attention and motivation; developing imitation and joint attention and developing communication skills, both nonverbal and speech development. The ESDM also employs individualized functional analyses of the antecedents and consequences maintaining behaviour, as well as prompting, shaping and fading techniques (Rogers et al., 2012). Thus, the strategies used are consistent with the principles of ABA and in particular the ESDM uses strategies that have been derived from the behaviourally based PRT model (Koegel et al., 1999).

In fact, there are two delivery models for the ESDM: the programme can be delivered by therapists (Dawson et al., 2010; Eapen et al., 2013) or by parents (e.g. Rogers et al., 2012). In the former case, the therapists usually report delivering around 15 hours of intervention per week, with the parents providing an additional 15–16 hours (Dawson et al., 2010). The therapist sessions typically last 2 hours, twice a day, for 5 days each week. Parents are also provided with training during approximately monthly meetings and are asked to use ESDM strategies (see next) while conducting the daily activities with their child.

The parent-led model typically involves 12 1-hour sessions of initial parent training, with the therapist and parent working together in a clinic. A parent-training curriculum is followed, in which the parents are taught a number of intervention techniques from the ESDM programme (see previously). This training is usually provided in small groups (Estes et al., 2014; Rogers et al., 2012), but it can also be delivered at a distance though web-based training packages (Vismara et al., 2013). Following the training, the parents deliver the intervention in the home for around 15 hours a week.

Evidence for the effectiveness of the ESDM

A number of studies concerning the effectiveness of ESDM have been conducted; some are observational and have not employed a control group (Eapen et al., 2013; Vismara et al., 2009; Vivanti et al., 2013) and some have employed comparison groups (Dawson, et al., 2010; Rogers et al., 2006; 2012; Sullivan, 2013). Perhaps not surprisingly, given the range of different delivery methods, the results from these studies are somewhat mixed.

In terms of the impact of the approach itself, the two studies which have reported largest gains in child functioning (Dawson et al., 2010; Vivanti et al., 2013), have adopted a therapist-led approach – either using a 1:1 strategy (Dawson et al., 2010) or a small group approach (Vivanti et al., 2013) – and have delivered the programme in a relatively time-intense manner (for about 30 hours a week, including both therapist and parent input).

Dawson et al. (2010) recruited 48 individuals with ASD (aged 18 and 30 months), who were randomly assigned to either the ESDM intervention (receiving 15 hours of therapist-led input and 16 hours of parent led-input) or a treatment as usual group. The ESDM and comparison groups did not differ from one another at baseline, but, after 2 years of treatment, there was an 18 point increase in intellectual functioning for the ESDM group and a correspondingly large gain in language ability. However, there was little impact of the ESDM on adaptive behaviour. Similar substantial gains in cognition and language were noted by Vivanti et al. (2013) and also in the study reported by Sullivan (2013).

In contrast, studies that have used a largely parent-led approach, have reported only moderate impacts of the ESDM programme on children's intellectual functioning and language abilities. Of these studies, the results reported by Eapen et al. (2013) are noteworthy, as they did observed a 10-point gain in the children's developmental quotient, after using this approach for only a 3-month period, which is impressive – although there were no substantial gains in social behaviours reported in the same study. Similar sized increases in intellectual ability were also noted in the studies reported by Rogers et al. (2006; 2012).

The range of improvement in child functioning across these reports can be illustrated by comparison of the gains reported by Dawson et al. (2010), using a therapist-led approach for about 30 hours a week, with those reported by Rogers et al. (2012), who employed a parent-led approach for about 15 hours a week. The effect sizes for these two studies across the various domains of functioning studied are shown in Figure 8.3. These two studies are useful comparisons for one another, as both studies employed the same instruments to measure change: the Mullen Scales of Early Learning for intellectual/cognitive ability and the Vineland Adaptive Behavior Scales for social-adaptive behaviour. Inspection of Figure 8.3 shows the advantage derived in terms of functioning from the more intensive therapist-lead approach (i.e. Dawson et al., 2010).

However, in contrast to the moderately impressive gains in ability produced by exposure to the ESDM intervention, the impact of this programme relative to a control group has not been found to be so marked. In fact, the only study to record significant gains for the ESDM relative to a comparison group was reported by Dawson et al. (2010), which used the longest and most time-intense approach – even then, the gain relative to the control in terms of social behaviour, was a result of the control group going backwards over the 2 years and not to gains produced in the ESDM participants. Other comparisons between ESDM and control conditions, such as that noted in the small-scale study (five participants on the ESDM programme) reported by Rogers et al. (2006) and also in the larger-scale study (49 participants on the ESDM intervention) that was reported by Rogers et al. (2012), have failed to note any improvements relative to 'treatment as usual' control groups.

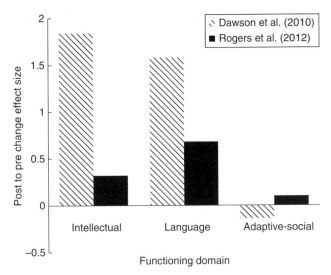

Figure 8.3 Comparison of the effect sizes noted in two studies of the Early Start Denver Model. Dawson et al. (2010) ran for 30 hours/week and was led by therapists; Rogers et al. (2012) ran for 15 hours/week and was led by parents. The therapist-lead programme was much more effective for intellectual and language functioning, but not for adaptive-social functioning.

In summary, as with the earlier DHSP, investigations into the effectiveness of the ESDM have established some evidence that this intervention can improve the functioning of children with ASD; certainly, in terms of their intellectual and linguistic skills, although less so in terms of their adaptive behaviour. These gains are more typically noted in programmes that are delivered by professionals, rather than parents (see also Chapter 5 for a similar discussion in relation to ABA).

There are also suggestions that these gains are moderated by a number of factors, including: the severity of the child's ASD, with mild and moderate cases responding better to treatment (Rogers et al., 2006); the child's ability to imitate and show joint attention at the start of the programme predicting greater improvements (Rogers et al., 2006; Vivanti et al., 2013) and by the degree to which parents can learn to utilize the techniques effectively (e.g. Eapen et al., 2013).

Social Communication, Emotional Regulation and Transactional Support (SCERTS®)

A number of developmental interventions attempt to target the social communication skills of children with ASD, along with aiding their ability to regulate their emotions (e.g. Aldred et al., 2004; Ingersoll & Dvortcsak, 2009; Prizant et al., 2003; Wetherby & Woods, 2006). This set of social-emotional intervention programmes start for the assumption that abilities and skills such as: joint attention (Mundy et al., 1986), functional and pragmatic communication (Prizant & Wetherby, 1987) and the ability to understand the social meanings of actions and so on (Sigman & Kasari, 1995;

Tager-Flusberg, 1993), help develop social and emotional functioning and, as such, should be the main focus of an intervention for ASD. As with other developmental approaches, these interventions highlight the importance of following the child's lead when engaging in teaching opportunities to develop these key skills (see Aldred et al., 2004).

There are a wide range of approaches that take this approach: the Early Social Interaction (ESI) Project (Wetherby & Wood, 2006); the Autism 1-2-3 Project (Wong & Kwan, 2010) and Project ImPACT (Improving Parents as Communication Teachers; see Ingersoll & Dvortcsak, 2009; Ingersoll & Wainer, 2013). However, the SCERTS® model (Prizant et al., 2003; 2006) of helping with social communication skills and emotional regulation for individuals with ASD (see Prizant et al., 2006) has become one of the better known of these programmes (see also Aldred et al., 2001).

In fact, the SCERTS® model is not only a relatively commonly practiced approach, in itself, but has formed the basis for a number of local-authority developed programmes (see Reed et al., 2013b, for a description of the one such intervention). As there is more evidence relating to the SCERTS® model and it is widely noted as a key approach in the literature, this approach will be the main focus of this section, although many other developmental interventions, as described previously, are highly similar (e.g. Salt et al., 2001; 2002; Wong & Kwan, 2010).

Characteristics of SCERTS®

SCERTS® is an individualized and multidisciplinary approach (Prizant et al., 2003; 2006) that focuses on two main areas that are central to many conceptions of the deficits seen in ASD: (i) Social Communication (SC) – particularly, independent functional communication and emotional expression, with the aim of producing strong adult-child relationships and (ii) Emotional Regulation (ER) – focusing on the ability to deal with stresses and regulate emotional states. These areas are facilitated through what is termed Transactional Support (TS) – which refers to a range of strategies aimed at helping teachers and parents: (i) identify and employ the child's needs and interests to encourage learning; (ii) alter the environment to maximize learning opportunities and minimize stresses and (iii) provide techniques to help with the learning process (e.g. picture communication, written schedules and sensory supports). In this broad sense, the SCERTS® programme is quite similar to the ESDM described previously.

Many of the SCERTS®-like programmes are structured so as to mirror the assumed developmental stages of pre-linguistic skills and their implementation is based on an assumed familiarity with developmental psycholinguistics and communication interventions. The initial focus of the intervention is to facilitate shared attention and also to promote parental sensitivity to the child's needs and attempts to communicate. In this way, the programme aims to improve parental adaptation to and communication with, their child (Aldred et al., 2001; Prizant et al., 2006). In a programme described by Aldred, et al., 2004), after a series of parent workshops, the parents and their children attend one treatment session each month for a period of 6 months, followed by 6 months of less frequent maintenance sessions. In each session, videotape of parent-child play is used to help the therapists work with the parents in order to plan the best parent-child interaction strategies to adopt over the coming month. Parents are then assumed to be able to implement these strategies for 30 minutes each day with their child, with the hope that these strategies would generalize across other daily routines.

Evidence of effectiveness of SCERTS®

The evidence presented in support of the SCERTS® programme is typically drawn from basic research work that shows the importance of the skills areas targeted by the interventions, such as joint attention (see O'Neill et al., 2010). This is, of course, a necessary set of evidence to present, but it is by no means sufficient to justify the approach.

A number of small-scale studies have directly evaluated the impact of emotional-communication strategies. For example, O'Neill et al. (2010) documented the impact of a school-based SCERTS® programme on the joint attention and adaptive and social abilities, of four pupils with ASD in a primary special school. The pupils all showed some progress in terms of increases in their joint attention and symbol use (based on tools developed for the SCERTS® programme) and two of the four participants showed gains in their adaptive and social behaviours, as measured by the VABS. However, the lack of a control group and the very small-scale nature of the project makes it unwise to place too much weight on these data.

The best documented study involving an intervention of a SCERTS®-type programme was described by Aldred et al. (2004). This study used a randomized control trial (RCT) design, in which children were assigned to either the SCERTS®-like intervention or to a 'treatment as usual' condition. The children were 50 months old at the start of the intervention and the intervention lasted for 12 months. The SCERTS®-like group showed relative improvements, compared to the control group, in terms of social interactions (as measured by the Autism Diagnostic Observation Schedule; ADOS) and also in their expressive language, initiation of communication and parent-child interactions. There were non-significant trends in improvement in adaptive-social behaviours as measured by the VABS.

The pattern of findings reported by Aldred et al. (2004) was also noted in two observational studies of SCERTS®-like approaches (Ingersoll & Wainer, 2013; Wetherby & Woods, 2006); which both noted gains in cognitive and communication functions, but not great gains in terms of social-adaptive behaviours. However, these findings stand in partial contrast to the results reported by Reed et al. (2013b), concerning a local-authority developed treatment package, which was based on the SCERTS® approach. In this latter study, children with ASD undergoing the SCERTS®-like treatment did demonstrate strong improvements in social and adaptive behaviour, over a 9-month period, as would be predicted on the basis of the model, but in contrast to the studies previously, they displayed little gain in cognitive function or language.

Summary

The SCERTS® approach and similar developmental interventions are certainly based on strong basic evidence regarding the key predictors of child development. There is also some evidence of their acceptability to staff and parents administering the programme (Aldred et al., 2007; O'Neill et al., 2010). However, at the present time, there is little clear evidence of their impact on functioning to draw strong conclusions about whether they will be effective across the range of skills needs. For example, while joint attention (O'Neill et al., 2010) and social interactional skills (Aldred et al., 2004), appear to be impacted positively by this type of intervention programme and there is some evidence regarding communication improvements, both in terms of linguistic and nonverbal aspects (Alfred et al., 2004; O'Neill et al., 2010), there is little evidence of impacts across a broader range of cognitive function to any greater extent than other treatments.

The Developmental, Individual-Difference, Relationship-Based Model (DIR® or Floortime Approach)

Several interventions have made their major target increasing the responsiveness of children with ASD to the social aspects of their environment through the use of play-based interactional procedures. These approaches often involve therapists and/or parents interacting with the children in order to enhance mutual social engagement with the child with ASD. In this broad bracket of interventions, a number of slightly different approaches have been attempted: Focused Playtime Intervention (FPI; Siller et al., 2013), Intensive Interaction (Nind, 1999) and, perhaps the most widely known – The Developmental, Individual-difference, Relationship-based model (DIR® or Floortime®; Greenspan & Wieder, 1998; Wieder & Greenspan, 2003). The latter of these approaches will be described in some detail in this section, as this approach is the best documented and has the highest number of studies of outcome-effectiveness. However, evidence from the other, somewhat similar play-responsiveness interventions will also be discussed.

Characteristics of the DIR-Floortime® approach

The DIR® model (Greenspan & Weider, 1998; Wieder & Greenspan, 2003) views ASD as resulting, primarily, from deficits in reciprocal social relating (Metz et al., 2005) and it aims to promote such relating, thinking and communicating (Kurtz, 2008). The DIR® approach is largely play-based and involves interactions between the parent and child, during which the parent follows the lead of the child and uses naturally occurring interactions and child interests, to promote the key skills that are assumed to be necessary for the child to develop. In truth, although the approach and ethos of the DIR® programme is radically different, these ideas are reminiscent of those outlined for the previous developmental interventions. The key difference between the latter mentioned approaches and the DIR® model being that the DIR® intervention is primarily child-led – in that the parent reacts to the child's behaviour and attempts to use that behaviour to develop important skills.

In terms of the actual components of the DIR® intervention, there are three main aspects of behaviour that the intervention considers critical: (i) Developmental, (ii) Interactional and (iii) Relationship and a key method of addressing these deficits (i.e. the Floortime® approach). The 'developmental' aspects of the programme focus on promoting six putative milestones in child development (Kurtz, 2008; Metz et al., 2005; Wieder & Greenspan, 2003). The DIR® model assumes that all children have to master these milestones, in sequence, to be able to achieve mastery of communication, thinking and emotional coping. These milestones are (see Wieder & Greenspan, 2003, for a fuller description):

1. Self-regulation and shared attention – often taught by involving the child in enjoyable social activities.
2. Engagement and relating – that is, emphasizing and encouraging social relationships.
3. Reciprocal two-way communication – facilitated by following the child's lead on behaviours and reinforcing any naturally occurring social gestures and so on.
4. Purposeful complex communication – involving the development of turn-taking activities.
5. Creating and elaborating symbols – fostered by play activities that allow the child to lead and express emotions.
6. Bridging between symbols (emotional thinking) – such as allowing the child to make connections between actions and feelings and helping them to understand the relationship between themselves and others.

The 'individual differences' aspect of DIR® refers to the assumed unique 'processing differences' for each person with ASD that may produce radically different impacts on their learning and behaviour based on the same input. That is, the approach is individualized for the particular learning styles of the child. Finally, 'relationship-based' aspect of the model refers to the relationship of the person with ASD with their parents and peers. In order to develop this aspect of functioning, the therapists provide training for the parents to allow them to become more effective teachers for their children and improve their interaction style (see previously for similar approaches in terms of the SCERTS® programme). DIR® programmes aim to aid parents to become the key organizer of their child's activities and environment, so that the environment can be structured to promote functional and emotional independence and capacity (Kurtz, 2008; Metz et al., 2005).

The Floortime® process is central to the conduct of the DIR® intervention and is the means by which these domains are developed as the child progresses through their developmental stages. During Floortime®, parents and therapists play, on a 1:1 basis, with the child with ASD. Through this means, it is assumed that the parents and therapists will be able to facilitate social interaction. The principles of Floortime® include creating an environment containing objects that are valued by the child, following the child's lead, engaging with the child at their developmental level and building on the child's interests in communication and motor and sensory activities (Kurtz, 2008; Metz et al., 2005). Again, although radically differently expressed, the components of the Floortime® approach mirror many of the techniques expressed in other approaches that employ natural teaching procedures, such as TEACCH (Chapter 7) and ABA procedures (Chapter 4).

Evidence for the effectiveness of DIR-Floortime®

Despite the components of the DIR® intervention approach being similar to many aspects of other interventions, there was, until recently, little evidence from outcome-effectiveness in favour of this approach (see Jacobson & Mulik, 2000; Metz et al.,

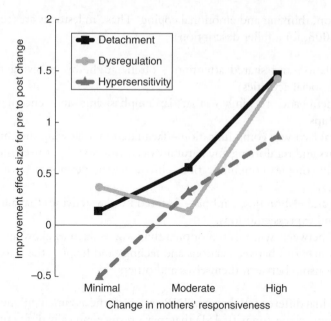

Figure 8.4   Results reported by Mahoney and Perales (2003) relating changes in child social functioning to changes in mothers' responsiveness to child behaviours. As the mothers become more responsive to the child's behaviours, the behaviours improved.

2005, for critical evaluations of this lack of evidence). However, over the last decade, some reports have emerged regarding the effectiveness of DIR®, although there is little doubt that this evidence is limited in scope and suffers from some methodological problems.

Hilton (2005; see also Hilton & Seal, 2007) reported the results of a small-scale RCT comparison between DIR® and the 'Lovaas' approach. In this trial, five children (aged 59 months) received a DIR® programme and five received a 'UCLA/Lovaas' intervention, for about 6 weeks. No difference was noted between these groups in the degree to which they progressed in terms of their communication skills or symbolic abilities. Similarly, Gonzalez (2006) reported a comparison between DIR® and treatment as usual for small groups ($n = 4$) of children with ASD. This study also found no difference between the interventions over an 8-week period. While both studies did assess DIR® against a comparison, the relatively short period of time used for the interventions really prevents any strong conclusions being drawn.

There have been four longer-term studies of the effectiveness of the DIR® approach; two observational studies (Mahoney & Perales, 2003; Soloman et al., 2007) and two RCT studies (Casenhiser et al., 2013; Pajareya & Nopmaneejumruslers, 2011). Mahoney and Perales (2003) followed 20 children with ASD (aged 32 months) over an 11-month exposure to DIR® and noted large effect size gains in their social interactions, but less strong gains in their social-emotional functioning. Mahoney and Perales (2003) also reported that maternal responsiveness to the DIR® programme was associated with gains in the children's social interactions – suggesting that the assumed mechanism of action of the programme was operative. Figure 8.4 shows the gains in children's functioning across a range of domains as a product of the level of alteration in the mother's responsiveness to the DIR® (the mothers were grouped into low, moderate and high responders). Of course, these data show what amounts to a correlation between changes in parent behaviour and changes in child behaviour and it is not clear which of these variables causes the other to alter.

Solomon et al. (2000) studied a 10-month programme based on DIR® and assessed the improvements made across a range of functioning domains for 68 children with ASD (3–7 years old). This programme involved a 3-hour monthly visit to the parents and the parents delivering about 15 hours' intervention a week to the children. The study reported gains in social and pragmatic communication after exposure to the DIR® programme.

Although showing increases after exposure to DIR®, neither of these studies (Mahoney & Perales, 2003; Soloman et al., 2007) demonstrated that DIR® was more effective than any other treatment. However, Pajareya and Nopmaneejumruslers (2011) did compare children, aged 51 months at the start of the programme, who were randomly allocated into either DIR® or treatment as usual groups ($n = 16$). The DIR® group received a similar intervention programme to that described by Solomon et al. (2007), in terms of supervision and parental input and the study lasted for 3 months. There were moderately strong gains for the DIR® group, relative to the comparison group, for all three measures employed: the Functional Emotional Assessment Scale (FEAS), which assesses social and pragmatic development; the Functional Emotional Developmental Questionnaire (FEDQ), which assesses developmental level and the Childhood Autism Rating Scale, which assess symptom severity.

Similarly, Casenhiser et al. (2013) examined two groups of 26 children with ASD, who were 42 months old at the start of the intervention; one group received DIR® training and the other received 'community treatment'. There were strong gains in social behaviour for the DIR® group, which were better than those displayed in the comparison condition. However, there were only moderate gains in language ability for the DIR® participants and these were weaker than the gains seen in the control group.

Summary

It is clear that there is some growing evidence of the impact of the DIR® approach and also for similarly based developmental interventions (e.g. Siller et al., 2013). There is also some evidence that the approach does alter parenting styles and that there is at least a correlation between changes in parenting and child behaviours (Mahoney & Perales, 2003). However, an issue that needs to be borne in mind when interpreting these data, is that the measurement scales employed in these studies (e.g. Pajareya & Nopmaneejumruslers, 2011; Solomon et al., 2007) are based on the assumptions that are built into the Floortime® intervention regarding the key developmental milestones. This means that these tools are not as well-used or strongly validated, for this population as the more broadly employed and standard assessments used in reports concerning other interventions. Perhaps more importantly, these tools also reflect the teaching that will occur in the programme – that is, these tools assess the very things that the interventions attempt to develop. To this extent, they will measure the success of the intervention by its own standards and it may be that more general tools would have recorded a different level of progress, as they do not assess advances in skills that were directly taught. This is not a unique problem for the DIR® approach; the SCERTS®

and TEACCH models have both produced tools to assess individuals' progress on their own interventions. However, the fact that outcome measures are so tied to the actual curriculum represents a significant problem in the external validity of these data.

The Options-Son-Rise Model

Some developmental interventions employ the type of interactional strategies described previously for the DIR-Floortime® approach, but have a more specific focus on the importance of using imitation to improve the child's functioning. To some extent, the Intensive Interaction (Nind, 1999) model has this focus, however, of this broad category of intervention, the Options-Son-Rise method (Kaufman, 1991) is the most commonly used.

Characteristics of the Options-Son-Rise approach

This intervention has been described fully in several places (Kaufman, 1991; 1994). There is no particular set form to the Options-Son-Rise intervention, other than that the parent is encouraged to follow the lead of the child and to engage in (imitate) whatever activity or behaviours that the child emits. The purpose of these parent-child imitation-engagements is to develop a joint or shared interaction, which can then be used to promote social communication between the adult and the child with ASD. In order to conduct the intervention, which takes place largely in the home, the parents devote a room in their home to the therapy. This 'playroom' is constructed so as to minimize distractions and allow 1:1 interactions with the child.

Apart from a focus on accepting the child's behaviour and imitating this behaviour as a strategy to generate shared activity and learning opportunities for the child, the Options-Son-Rise model is quite similar to the DIR-Floortime® approach, described previously. However, a somewhat contentious point regarding the Options-Son-Rise strategy (see Tutt et al., 2006) is that imitation of the child is also extended to engagement in behaviours that might appear 'inappropriate' or 'challenging'.

Typically, parents are taught the basic engagement strategies to use with their child over two, 5-day courses, which are held some months apart from one another (see Jenkins et al., 2012). The parents are then encouraged to use these techniques with their child at home for 30 or more hours a week – making the Option-Son-Rise method of similar time intensity to the Intensive Interaction (Nind, 1999) and ABA approaches. Williams (2006) studied the degree to which this proposed intense level of interaction was continued over time by parents conducting the Options-Son-Rise programme. This study noted that, according to the parents' reports, at the start of the programme the typical weekly interaction with their child on the programme was about 34 hours (18 hours being delivered by a parent and the remaining 16 hours being tutor/therapist lead). After about 6 months on the programme, this level of interaction was reported as having reduced to about 21 hours a week – with the parents delivering around 12 hours interaction and tutors delivering about 9 hours a week. These figures are broadly in line with those reported by Jenkins et al. (2012), whose sample of 34 parents had a median value of weekly Options-Son-Rise interactions with their child of between 10–19 hours.

Evidence for the Options-Son-Rise approach

Powell and Jordan (1997) review early teaching interventions and commented favourably on the level of child spontaneity that the Options-Son-Rise programmed delivered, relative to ABA programmes, but they presented no evidence in support of its effectiveness. However, Tutt et al. (2006), while favourably disposed to the use of imitation-promoting strategies for this population, noted that many teachers viewed the approach as having some severe limitations – especially in regard to imitating challenging or self-injurious behaviours. Parents' views of the utility of the programme also differ across studies. For example, Williams (2006) noted that most parents questioned were favourably disposed toward the approach. However, in contrast to this positive parental assessment, Williams and Wishart (2003) noted that, in a sample of 87 parents using the approach, most noted more drawbacks of implementing the system (e.g. the level of time input needed) and only 25% of the parents noted some benefits of the approach.

In fact, there are only two studies that have provided data on the outcome-effectiveness of the Options-Son-Rise approach (Houghton et al., 2013; Jenkins et al., 2012). The data in the study reported by Jenkins et al. (2012) came from parent-reported outcomes for their children using the Autism Treatment Evaluation Checklist (ATEC; Rimland & Edelson, 1999), which covers symptoms of ASD in the domains of: (i) speech, language and communication, (ii) sociability and (iii) sensory and cognitive awareness. The parents were surveyed at baseline and then again about 3–4 months later (during their attendance at the Options-Son-Rise training programmes). The parents also gave information on the amount of intervention time that they had engaged on and were divided into three groups on the basis of their responses: those who had delivered no treatment, those delivering between 10–19 hours a week and those delivering over 20 hours of treatment a week. The data on the effect sizes in a number of functioning domains (i.e. language, social and sensory) for these three groups are shown in Figure 8.5. These data show that the children in the two groups receiving some level of Options-Son-Rise intervention did better than the group receiving no intervention – although there was little difference between the two groups that received the intervention for varying levels of time during a week.

Houghton et al. (2013) reported the results from a very-short term study (1 week) of the Options-Son-Rise programme. During the week, six 5-year-old participants received 40 hours of the intervention. The changes in functioning noted in those participants, as measured by video analysis of their communication and social interactions with their parents, were compared to six comparison participants who did not receive the intervention. Both the measure of communication and of social behaviour, showed strong improvements for the Options-Son-Rise group compared to the control group. However, a number of problems with these data should be noted. Firstly, they are based on a very small sample. Secondly, they are not based on a standardized assessment scale, but on observations of behaviours and it is difficult to fully equate such data with those derived from standard assessment tests (see also Chapter 9 for a discussion of this point). Thirdly, it is unclear whether the changes were simply the result of increased attention in the target Options-Son-Rise group rather than the intervention itself, as the control group received no treatment during that week. In summary,

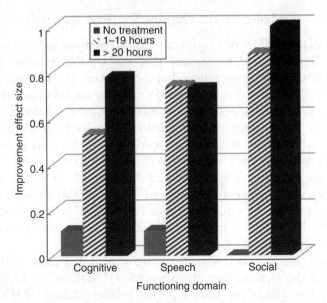

Figure 8.5 Improvement in children with ASD from pre- to post-treatment, for three functioning domains, in a study of Options-Son-Rise reported by Jenkins et al. (2012), depending on the weekly treatment intensity.

although there is clearly a large demand for this programme among parents, there is only a little evidence available on its impact either on the parents or on the child.

The Hanen More Than Words model

A number of interventions place their main focus on developing functional communication skills in children with ASD. For example, the 'More Than Words' (MTW) approach, developed by The Hanen Centre (Manolson, 1992; Sussman, 1999), attempts to help parents and teachers promote the communication of children with ASD. In this focus, the MTW approach is somewhat similar to that of the Responsive Education and Prelinguistic Milieu Teaching model described by Yoder and Warren (2002; see also Yoder & Stone, 2006). This general class of intervention does not treat spoken language as the key form of communication, but treats social behaviour and social interactions as methods by which communication can be made. This approach is designed to suit individuals with ASD who find difficulty with spoken forms of language (Chapter 2). Although there are a number of such general functional-communication approaches, as noted previously (see also the review by Ospina, 2008), the MTW programme has attracted the most attention.

Characteristics of the MTW programme

The MTW programme is based on three principles that are common across many developmental interventions: (i) the pivotal role of parents and caregivers; (ii) the importance of early intervention and (ii) the power of naturally occurring teaching opportunities. However, a key-teaching element in the MTW intervention is an initial parent training programme that attempts to promote practical strategies to help parents to increase the communication ability of their children (see Manolson, 1992; Sussman, 1999, for detailed descriptions). A typical MTW parent-training programme involves eight sessions with parents (usually conducted in a group setting), along with three home-based parent-child sessions that are witnessed by a therapist, usually a speech and language therapist (McConachie et al., 2005). This training aims to enhance parental responsiveness to their children's attention and communication attempts and, as a consequence, to enhance the number and quality of parent-child interactions during daily life.

The parent training sessions cover aspects of early child communication (see also the SCERTS® programme, previously): (i) two-way interaction, (ii) conventional ways of communicating, (iii) social communication and (iv) language comprehension. The training sessions also cover the promotion of the key child-skills needed for the development of effective social communication and the types of parental interaction that might help to develop such child communication, such as: responding to communicative attempts, following the child's lead and joint action and play. During this training, the MTW programme highlights the importance of positive affect being associated with interactions, the role of predictability and structure and the use of visual supports to enhance learning in children with ASD (as in the TEACCH approach, among others, see Chapter 7). As with many of the other developmental approaches noted earlier, the MTW programme teaches parents to use their child's interests to build communication skills during every-day routines and activities, employing naturally occurring opportunities for teaching.

Evidence for the MTW approach

There have been two controlled investigations of the Hanen MTW approach (Carter et al., 2011; McConachie et al., 2005). McConachie et al. (2005) reported the outcomes of an 8-month comparison between a group ($n = 26$) of 36-month-old children with ASD who received either MTW or were on a waiting-list. The parents of the children in the MTW group received a programme similar to that described previously (eight sessions of parent training and three home visits). Both groups then experienced similar additional provision as one another. Over the course of the intervention period, the size of the MTW group's vocabulary increased more than the comparison group, but there were no differences in the changes noted in the social or the behavioural problems of the two groups. One issue that should also be noted in interpreting these results is that the MTW programme lasted 3 months longer than the comparison condition.

Carter et al. (2011) conducted an RCT over a 9-month period comparing the MTW programme to a 'no treatment' group (which presumably was actually receiving 'treatment as usual', although this was not fully specified in the report). The children in this study were approximately 21 months old and the MTW programme was similar to that described by McConachie et al. (2005). In terms of the gains noted by the MTW group, there were substantial increases in expressive language (17 points in terms of a prorated mental age) and receptive language (a prorated increase of 15 points); both of which gains represented large effect sizes. These gains were mediated by the child's object-interest at baseline, in that the more stereotyped and restricted interests that were shown by the child, the less strong were the gains. However, there was a two-point decrease in adaptive-social behaviour as measured by the VABS. Whilst these gains over the course of exposure to the MTW programme are impressive, it should be noted that there were no significant differences between the gains for the MTW programme group and those for the comparison group. Moreover, there was no measured impact of the MTW group on the parents functioning and interaction with their children.

In summary, the studies of the Hanen MTW programme show that this programme can have an impact on language ability, but that there is less evidence that it will impact on social and adaptive behaviours. Moreover, there is no compelling evidence that exposure to this programme will accelerate development over and above exposure to other forms of treatment.

Overview of Developmental Interventions

The overview here of five commonly used developmental interventions has suggested two things: (i) that these programmes, with the possible exception of the Denver models, have not been evaluated to the degree that an individual sort of developmental intervention could be recommended or not and (ii) it would be quite difficult to discriminate between the interventions as all contain very similar components to on another – such as, a focus on social-communication, the use of naturally occurring teaching opportunities and the use of parents as leaders or collaborators in the treatment. As there are many commonalities between the approaches and in order to further assess the effectiveness of developmental approaches as a whole, Chapter 9 reviews the evidence for the outcome-effectiveness across all of the approaches combined.

There are also a number of further commonalities to many of the developmental programmes that require some comment. It is clear that many developmental interventions have particularly good websites, which are laden with testimonials from parents concerning the usefulness of the approach. It is also clear that some of these approaches have received substantial research funding to examine their outcome-effectiveness. However, few of these approaches have a great deal of substantiating evidence drawn from outcome-effectiveness studies in their favour.

Most of the evidence in favour of these approaches alluded on the websites is related to three sources. Firstly, appeal to the validity of the principles on which the approach is based (e.g. communication is important in ASD, therefore, any approach that tackles this is supported by the literature). Although such relationships may be necessary for a valid intervention, they are nowhere near sufficient to justify a particular approach. Secondly, from the experience of teachers and parents in delivering the intervention (Prizant & Rubin, 1999; Stahmer et al., 2005); while such evidence-based practice data is not to be disregarded lightly it is difficult to use to formulate a usable overview of an intervention's effectiveness. Finally, many of these interventions are well regarded by parents (Stahmer et al., 2005; Williams, 2006) and, thus, have a degree of ecological and social validity, which is important for any intervention and not to be dismissed lightly.

9

Outcome-Effectiveness for Developmental and Parent-Mediated Treatment Models

Reviews of the outcome-effectiveness studies for developmental and parent-mediated approaches (Diggle et al., 2002; McConachie & Diggle, 2007; Oono et al., 2013; Ospina et al., 2008) have reached a variety of conclusions. The earlier conducted reviews (e.g. Diggle et al., 2002; Ospina et al., 2008) suggest that there is little evidence in favour of these approaches. In contrast, some of the later reviews suggest that there is a growing degree of evidence for the effectiveness of the approaches (Oono et al., 2013), especially in the areas of language and communication (McConachie & Diggle, 2007) and also in developing some aspects of parenting skills (Oono et al., 2013). Given these apparent contradictions and the rather mixed picture of evidence that emerged when individual developmental intervention programmes were considered (Chapter 8), the current chapter will examine the evidence from quantifiable studies of these developmental approaches.

Table 9.1 displays the characteristics of 40 outcome-effectiveness studies of developmental interventions, which produce 42 separate conditions. These studies were identified from a search of the literature involving developmental approaches. They report the outcome-effectiveness of developmental programmes when they are used as the main intervention for participants with ASD and they also provide data on at least one of the global aspects of functioning, such as cognitive improvement (classed as IQ or developmental gains), communication gains (either language or functional communication) and/or adaptive behavioural gains. These studies also contained sufficient information to allow the calculation of effect sizes (see Chapter 1 for a discussion of the importance of these issues).

The programmes studied in each of the reports are characterized in Table 9.1 according to their general type of approach, such as: behavioural (e.g. Denver Health Science Programme, DHSP and Early Start Denver Model, ESDM), social-communication

---

Interventions for Autism: Evidence for Educational and Clinical Practice, First Edition. Phil Reed.
© 2016 John Wiley & Sons, Ltd. Published 2016 by John Wiley & Sons, Ltd.

Table 9.1 Characteristics of studies assessing developmental programmes, showing type of programme (Soc Com = social communication; Fun Com = functional communication; Play = play responsiveness; JA = joint attention; Beh = Denver; Spec Beh = programmes targeting only one behaviour), type of trial (Obs = observational; Cont = controlled; RCT = randomized control trial), number of participants (N), scope of programme, and who lead the programme (Par = parent; Ther = therapist; Comb = combination).

Study	Year	Type	Trial	N	Scope	Lead
Aldred et al.	2004	Soc Com	RCT	14	Broad	Comb
Carter et al.	2011	Fun Com	RCT	32	Focused	Par
Casenhiser et al.	2013	Play	RCT	26	Focused	Comb
Dawson et al.	2010	Beh	RCT	24	Broad	Ther
Drew et al.	2002	JA	RCT	12	Focused	Par
Eapen et al.	2013	Beh	Obs	26	Broad	Comb
Frankel et al.	2010	Play	RCT	35	Focused	Ther
Green et al.	2010	JA	RCT	77	Focused	Par
Houghton et al.	2013	Imit	Cont	6	Focused	Par
Ingersoll & Wainer	2013	Soc Com	Obs	8	Broad	Comb
Jenkins	2012	Imit	Cont	24	Focused	Par
Joycelyn et al.	1998	Soc Com	RCT	16	Broad	Comb
Kaale et al.	2014	JA	RCT	34	Focused	Ther
Kasari et al.	2010	JA	RCT	19	Focused	Comb
Mahoney & Perale	2003	Play	Obs	20	Focused	Comb
McConachie et al.	2005	Fun Com	Cont	26	Focused	Par
O'Neill et al.	2010	Soc Com	Obs	4	Broad	Comb
Oosterling et al.	2010	JA	RCT	31	Focused	Par
Pajareya & Napma	2011	Play	RCT	14	Focused	Par
Reed et al.	2013a	Port	Cont	16	Broad	Comb
Reed et al.	2007b	Port	Cont	16	Broad	Comb
Reed et al.	2013b	Soc Com	Cont	16	Broad	Comb
Rickards et al.	2007	Spec Beh	RCT	28	Focused	Comb
Roberts et al.	2011	Spec Beh	RCT	29	Focused	Ther
Roberts et al.	2011	Spec Beh	RCT	27	Focused	Comb
Rogers & DiLalla	1991	Beh	Cont	49	Broad	Ther
Rogers et al.	1989	Beh	Obs	31	Broad	Ther
Rogers et al.	1987	Beh	Obs	11	Broad	Ther
Rogers et al.	2006	Beh	RCT	5	Broad	Comb
Rogers et al.	2012	Beh	Cont	49	Broad	Comb
Salt et al.	2002	Soc Com	Cont	12	Broad	Comb
Schertz et al.	2013	JA	RCT	11	Focused	Comb
Shin et al.	2009	Port	RCT	16	Broad	Comb
Siller et al.	2013	Play	RCT	34	Focused	Par
Solomon et al.	2007	Play	Obs	68	Focused	Comb
Tonge et al.	2014	Spec Beh	RCT	33	Focused	Par
Tonge et al.	2014	Spec Beh	RCT	35	Focused	Comb
Vismara et al.	2013	Beh	Obs	8	Broad	Comb
Vivanti et al.	2013	Beh	Obs	21	Broad	Comb
Wetherby & Wood	2006	Soc Com	Obs	17	Broad	Comb
Wong & Kwan	2010	Soc Com	RCT	9	Broad	Comb
Yoder & Stone	2009	Fun Com	RCT	17	Focused	Par

(e.g. Social Communication, Emotional Regulation and Transactional Support; SCERTS®), joint attention (e.g. PArent-mediated Communication-focused Treatment in Children with Autism; PACTS), functional communication (e.g. Hanen More Than Words; MTW), play responsiveness (e.g. Developmental, Individualized-Difference, Relationship-based Model; DIR-Floortime®), imitation (e.g. Options-Son-Rise) and those focused on specific behaviours (e.g. Stepping Stones Triple-P). The natures of some of these individual approaches were described in Chapter 8.

Table 9.1 also shows the nature of the methodology employed in each study. There were 10 (24%) observational studies, 9 (21%) controlled studies and 22 (52%) randomized control trials. The relative higher proportion of RCTs compared to other approaches is noteworthy. The mean number of participants in each studied developmental programme was 24 (range 4–77). The programmes were evenly split between those that had a very-focused approach on one set of skills or behaviours (22 or 52%) or those that had a broader scope, addressing a range of problems associated with ASD (20 or 48%). The programmes were also coded into those that were largely therapist-led (7 or 17%), largely parent-led (12 or 29%) or those that were delivered by a combination of therapist, often supervising, the parent who did most of the actual delivery (23 or 55%).

Overall Outcomes for Developmental Approaches

Table 9.2 outlines the characteristics of the interventions in terms of their duration in weeks, the number of hours of intervention conducted per week, the number of weeks of parent training and the numbers of hours of parent training per week. Table 9.2 also shows the effect sizes of the programme for the three main areas of functioning (intellectual, language and adaptive-social behaviour), both in terms of the impact (pre- to post-intervention) of the programme itself and also against any comparison groups employed in the reports (see Chapter 1). As in previous chapters, these effect sizes are shaded (light shaded cell background = strong effect size of greater than 0.7; medium shaded background = effect size of 0.30 to 0.69 and dark shaded cell background = weak effect size of less than 0.30). The effect size was always calculated by obtaining the mean difference (either pre- to post-intervention or change in intervention versus change in control) and dividing this difference by the standard deviation of the sample (either pre-intervention for the programme effect or pooled for the two groups pre-intervention for the comparison with the control group).

It should be noted that, as for the other of intervention for ASD discussed in the previous chapters, there were a multitude of different scales employed by these studies and the reader is encouraged to examine each study for a full description. Nevertheless this issue is particularly pertinent in the case of developmental interventions, as the range of scales used was very wide: seven for intellectual functioning, mainly the Early Intervention Profile and Preschool Profile (EIDP), the Mullen Early Scales of Learning (MESL) and the Leiter International Performance Scale; nine for language functioning, mainly the EIDP, MESL and the MacArthur Communication Developmental Inventory (MCDI) and seven scales for adaptive behavioural functioning, mainly the Vineland Adaptive Behavior Scales (VABS). There are four issues that require some comment in this regard. Firstly, a number of studies have

Table 9.2 Outcomes of studies of developmental interventions showing pre-to-post intervention change effect sizes, and comparisons with control group effect sizes.

Study	Duration (wks)	Intensity (h/wk)	Parent Train (h/wk)	Parent Train (wks)	Pre- to Post-ES			Versus Control ES		
					Cog	Com	Soc	Cog	Com	Soc
Aldred et al. (2004)	52	3	.25	52		0.21	1.05		0.14	0.38
Carter et al. (2011)	39			15		0.05	.05		0.15	0.14
Casenhiser et al. (2013)	52	21	2	52		0.45	1.03		-0.46	0.74
Dawson et al. (2010)	104	31		8	1.84	1.58	-.14	1.19	1.34	1.50
Drew et al. (2002)	52	14	3	8	-0.91	2.52	-.43	-0.74	1.53	-0.29
Eapen et al. (2013)	42	18	1	12	0.47	0.44	.12			
Frankel et al. (2010)	24	1.5				0.62	.97			
Green et al. (2010)	56	3	2	18		0.62	.93		0.05	0.24
Houghton et al. (2013)	1	40		12		0.81	.86		1.03	2.04
Ingersoll & Wainer (2013)	16	1.5	1.5	2		1.44				
Jenkins et al. (2012)	17	20	30	2	0.65	0.74	.94	0.55	0.62	0.94
Joycelyn et al. (1998)	12	18	4	12		0.60			0.66	-0.40
Kaale et al. (2014)	52	36				0.71			-0.05	0.28
Kasari et al. (2010)	8		2	8			.84			0.87
Mahoney & Perales (2003)	50	19	1	50			.82			
McConachie et al. (2005)	37		2	12		0.60	-1.00		0.95	0
O'Neill et al. (2010)	52	20	2.5	16			.27			
Oosterling et al. (2010)	52		8	1	0.60	0.56	.55	0.53	0.19	0.40
Pajareya & Napma (2011)	3	15	1	39	0.08	-0.41	-2.00	0.01	-0.70	-3.56
Reed et al. (2013b)	39	8.5	1	30	0.09		-.23	-0.60		-0.68
Reed et al. (2007b)	39	8.5	1	30						
Reed et al. (2013b)	39	6	1	6	0.04	0.30	1.00	-0.05	0.60	2.30
Rickards et al. (2007)	52	6	1		0.26		.17	0.42		-0.07
Roberts et al. (2011)	40	2		40		0.29	.59		0.41	0.15

Study										
Roberts et al. (2011)	40	1		20	2	−0.25	.08		0.04	−0.24
Rogers & DiLalla (1991)	30	15				0.71	0.83	.52	0	.0	−0.12
Rogers et al. (1989)	29	25				0.34	0.36	.33			0
Rogers et al. (1987)	18	19				0.12	0.30	.40	0.19	
Rogers et al. (2006)	12	6	1	12		0.53		−0.01		−0.01
Rogers et al. (2012)	12	16	1	12		0.32	0.68	.10	0.19	−0.05	−0.19
Salt et al. (2002)	43	15	8	20		0.80	−.05		0.01	1.36
Schertz et al. (2013)	17	12	1	15		1.84	1.29		1.15	1.35
Shin et al. (2009)	52		1	52		.62			0.52
Siller et al. (2013)	52		1	12		0.73		0.26
Solomon et al. (2007)	43	10	2	10		0.53
Tonge et al. (2014)	52		1	20		0.24	0.73	.11	0.03	0.01	−0.42
Tonge et al. (2014)	52		1	20		0.27	0.21	.38	0.11	−0.05	0.05
Vismara et al. (2013)	26	5	1.5	12		0.46	.25
Vivanti et al. (2013)	52	20				1.50	1.10
Wetherby & Wood (2006)	78	9				1.36	.91
Wong & Kwan (2010)	2	5	2.5			0.44	.36		0.15	0.28
Yoder & Stone (2009)	52	16	15	26		0.36		0.15	0

Cog = cognitive function, Com = communication; Soc = social behaviour. White = strong effect; light grey = moderate effect; dark grey = weak effect; black = no data.

employed scales that were specifically designed for the intervention under investigation (e.g. the Functional Emotional Development Questionnaire, which is developed for DIR-Floortime® intervention; see Greenspan & Greenspan, 2002). Secondly, several of the studies employed subscales from autism specific scales, such as the Autism Diagnostic Observation Schedule, to assess some areas of functioning (e.g. Green et al., 2010; Wong & Kwok, 2010). It is unclear whether the results from this ASD specific assessment map directly onto other standardized tools designed to assess these functioning domains. Thirdly, many of these tools do not produce a standard score, but rely on counts of words produced (e.g. MCDI). Finally, a number of these studies relied on video analysis of behaviours and utterances (e.g. Houghton et al., 2013; Vismara et al., 2009). For this reason, Table 9.2 does not give changes in standard scores for these studies, but confines itself to reporting effects sizes.

The last two points also contribute to an issue in the calculation and interpretation of effect sizes. Non-standardized scales or observations of numbers of events (e.g. utterances), both often range from a zero baseline, indicating an absence of an ability, to a potentially very high or unconstrained upper limit. This means that baseline standard deviations are often much lower than they are when employing standardized scales, as they report very low means and changes can be much higher than for the standardized tools. Hence, when calculating change effect sizes, it is easier to obtain larger effect sizes using the non-standardized measures.

This suggestion can be corroborated by examining the mean effect sizes for the 'standard' and 'non-standard' methods of assessing functioning in each of the three domains. In terms of intellectual functioning, 88% of the studies employed a standard test and produced a mean effect size = 0.40; compared to the studies with a nonstandard measure that had a mean effect size of 0.57. In terms of language functioning, only 37% of the studies employed a standard test of language ability and they produced a mean effect size of 0.61; compared to a mean effect size of 0.75 for the nonstandard tests. Finally, 78% of the studies employed a standardized test of social-adaptive functioning and reported a mean effect size of 0.34, compared to the nonstandard assessments of this domain that reported a mean effect size of 0.76. Given these findings, the issue of assessment type should be kept in mind when interpreting the results from these studies.

As noted previously, the developmental programmes can be divided into those which had a broad scope (i.e. focused on multiple behaviours) and those that had a narrower focus on a single form of behaviour (e.g. joint attention or adaptive behaviours). They can also be split into programmes that are primarily therapist-led and those that are primarily parent-led or delivered jointly by therapist and parent. Figure 9.1 shows the mean effect sizes for the three outcome domains as a function of these aspects of the programme and these data will be discussed in detail in the following sections.

Cognitive functioning

Most of the studies reported assessments using standardized tools for measuring intellectual functioning in terms of IQ or developmental quotients. However, some of the reports employed assessments that could more properly be said to be concerned with general cognitive function, rather than that type of data that is generated by tests of IQ. For this reason, the term 'cognitive function' might better be applied to this set of measures.

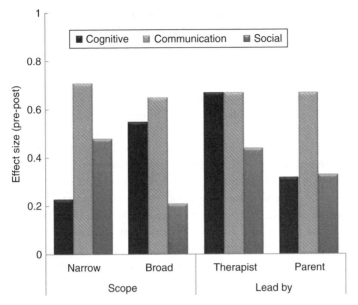

Figure 9.1   Effect sizes for pre-to-post interventions changes in three functioning domains for developmental programmes, split by their scope in targeting behaviours (narrow focus or broad focus), and whether they were led solely by therapists or by parents with therapists.

Pre- to post-intervention changes   In terms of the actual gains in cognitive functioning made over the course of the intervention, the effect size results of these studies were moderate. Cognitive function improvement had a mean effect size of 0.42 (standard deviation = ±0.60; r ange = –0.91–1.84). However, as can be seen from these summary data, there was a large range in the effect sizes: 47% of the studies reporting weak effects; 35% reporting moderate effects and only 18% reporting strong effect sizes (all from the DHSP or ESDM).

The mean change in intellectual function was moderate for the broad approaches: 0.55 (±0.63; range = 0.04–1.84), but weak for the narrow approaches: 0.23 (±0.53; range = –0.91–0.65). Splitting the studies into those lead by therapists (mean effect size = 0.73 ± 0.77; range = 0.12–1.84) and those led by parents either alone or with supervision (mean effect size = 0.32 ± 0.53; range = 0.91–1.50), revealed a large advantage for programmes led mainly by therapists.

Comparison with control conditions   The relative improvements in cognitive function for the developmental interventions when compared against a control group were weak, with a mean effect size of 0.14 (±0.51, range = –0.74–1.19). Indeed, 25% of the studies showed an advantage to the comparison group (e.g. Drew et al., 2002), 41% showed a weak effect size, 25% a moderate effect size and only 9% of the studies (one study of the ESDM) showing a strong effect size.

There was little difference in the relative effect sizes compared to the comparison groups depending on whether the programme was broad (mean effect size = 0.12 ± 0.59, range = –0.60–1.19) or narrow (mean effect size = 0.15 ± 0.49, range = –0.74– 0.55) in focus. There was, however, a strong advantage for therapist-led (mean effect size = 0.60 ± 0.84, range = 0.12–1.84), compared to parent-led or combination approaches (mean effect size = 0.05 ± 0.44, range = –0.74–0.55).

Communication abilities

Measures of functioning in this domain were not always taken from a standardized test of expressive and/or receptive language skills, but could include counts of the numbers of words understood or spoken, taken either from tests such as the MESL or from direct observation of the child's language. These measures were also taken by a number of different raters – some by therapists/assessors and some by parents. Importantly, in this regard, a number of studies have noted a difference in the size of outcome depending on whether language ability was parent-rated or objectively assessed (Casenhiser et al., 2013; Green et al., 2010); with there being an advantage in terms of parent-assessed measures. This may reflect either: the consequences of parental involvement in the programme changing the way in which they rate the language of their own children; changes in the way in which parents perceive their child's behaviours and attempts to communicate or alterations in the way in which the child behaves in their parents' presence or in the presence of others. It is currently impossible to distinguish between these possibilities.

Pre- to post-intervention changes   In terms of the gains made in communication over the course of the intervention, the results of these studies were moderate, bordering on strong: mean effect size of 0.68 (±0.57; range = –0.41–2.52). Only 18% of the studies reported a weak effect size (e.g. Aldred et al., 2004; Rogers et al., 1987), 39% reported a moderate effect size and almost half of the studies (43%) reported a strong effect size for communication (e.g. Dawson et al., 2010; Houghton et al., 2013; Rogers & DiLalla, 1991).

If the programmes were divided into those that had a broad scope (i.e. focused on multiple behaviours) and those that had a narrower focus (see Figure 9.1), the mean change in communication was moderate for the broad approaches: mean effect size = 0.66 (±0.49; range = –0.41–1.58) and strong for the narrow approaches: mean effect size 0.71 (±0.68; range = –0.25–2.52). Dividing the programmes into those lead by therapists (mean effect size = 0.68 ± 0.65; range 0.29–1.58) and those lead by parents either alone or with supervision (mean effect size = 0.68 ± 0.60; range –0.41–2.52), revealed little difference between the types of programmes in terms of their effect on the children's communication skills.

Comparison with control conditions   The relative improvements in communication ability after exposure to a developmental approach compared to a control condition were moderate (mean effect size = 0.33 ± 0.54, range = –0.70–1.53). Of the studies, 22% revealed an advantage to the comparison group (e.g. Casenhiser et al., 2013; Kaale et al., 2014; Reed et al., 2013b), 41% showed a weak effect size (e.g. Aldred et al., 2004; Wong & Kwan, 2010), 14% a moderate effect size and 23% of the studies reported a strong effect size in favour of the developmental approach (e.g. Dawson et al., 2010; Drew et al., 2002).

There was little difference in the relative effect sizes depending on whether the programme was broad (mean effect size = 0.28 ± 0.56, range = –0.70–1.34) or narrow (mean effect size = 0.36 ± 0.54, range = –0.46–1.53) in focus. Neither was there an advantage for therapist led (mean effect size = 0.43 ± 0.64, range = –0.05–1.34) compared to parent-led or combination approaches (mean effect size = 0.31 ± 0.54, range = –0.70–1.53).

Adaptive-social behaviour

For most studies of developmental interventions, this area of functioning was measured by the VABS, although some reports used other measures of this domain, such as modified versions of the Child Behaviour Rating Scale (e.g. Casenhiser et al., 2013; Mahoney & Perales, 2003).

Pre- to post-intervention changes   In terms of the gains made over the course of the intervention, the results of these studies were moderate – adaptive-social behaviour improvement had a mean effect size of 0.36 (±0.64; range = –2.00–1.29): 18% of the studies reported a reduction in this domain of functioning (e.g. Drew et al., 2002; McConachie et al., 2005), 23% noted a weak effect size, 26% reported a moderate effect size and 33% reported a strong effect size (e.g. Casenhiser et al., 2013; Frankel et al., 2010).

Figure 9.1 shows how this domain was affected by the type of programme (i.e. scope and primary lead). If the programmes were divided into those that had a broad scope and those that had a narrower focus on a single form of behaviour, the mean change in adaptive-social functioning was weak for the broad approaches: mean effect size = 0.23 (±0.68; range = –2.00–1.05) and moderate for the narrow approaches: mean effect size = 0.48 (±0.59; range = –1.00–1.29). Dividing the programmes into those lead by therapists (mean effect size = 0.45 ± 0.36; range –0.14–0.97) and those that were parent-led either alone or with supervision (mean effect size = 0.36 ± 0.69; range –2.00–1.29), revealed little difference between the types of programmes.

Comparison with control conditions   The relative improvements for adaptive-social behaviour when compared against a control conditions were weak, but with a very large range (mean effect size = 0.28 ± 1.07, range = –3.56–2.30). Of the studies, 33% revealed an advantage to the comparison group (e.g. Reed et al., 2007b), 26% showed a weak effect size (e.g. Carter et al., 2011), 10% a moderate effect size and 30% of the studies showing a strong effect size in favour of the developmental approach (e.g. Houghton et al., 2013; Salt et al., 2002).

There was a difference in the relative effect sizes depending on whether the programme had a broad focus (mean effect size = 0.13 ± 1.51, range = –3.56–2.30) or narrow focus (mean effect size = 0.39 ± 0.66, range = –0.42–2.04), with these data favouring the narrow-focused approaches. There was also an advantage for therapist-led approaches (mean effect size = 0.45 ± 0.71, range = –0.12–1.51), compared to parent-led or combination approaches (mean effect size = 0.25 ± 1.13, range = –3.56–2.30).

Autism severity and associated behavioural problems

The impact of the developmental interventions on the level of ASD severity observed in the participants or on their levels of externalizing or challenging behaviours, has been assessed by a number of studies of developmental interventions.

Autism severity   This aspect of the child's functioning is often objectively assessed by the Autism Diagnosis Observation Schedule (ADOS) or through informant report via the Autism Diagnosis Interview (ADI) or a parent-rated questionnaire, like the Social Communication Questionnaire (SCQ). In the one review to address this issue, Oono et al. (2013) reported a borderline weak-moderate effect size in favour of the developmental interventions when compared to control conditions in reducing ASD symptoms (mean effect size = 0.30). This rather small effect is actually the result of a range of discrepant findings in the studies: four studies reporting improvements in ASD severity as a result of exposure to a developmental intervention (notably that of the ESDM reported by Dawson et al., 2010); in contrast, seven studies reported no change in ASD severity, including one study of ESDM by Rogers et al. (2012), which found greater improvements in ASD severity in the comparison group.

As mentioned previously, Dawson et al. (2010) using the ADOS noted that for a group of children with ASD exposed to the ESDM, 30% of these participants improved their diagnostic classification (e.g. moving from the DSM-IV-TR classification of Autism to PDD:NOS) and only 8% experienced a worsening of the classification; whereas, in the control group, only 5% of participants showed improvement and 23% showed a worsening of classification. Aldred et al. (2004) also employed the ADOS, in a study of the impact of a SCERTS® programme and noted that there were improvements in the ASD severity for the intervention group, in terms of the mean ADOS score, but did not note any changes in terms of their diagnostic classification. Two further studies also noted improvements in ASD symptoms using informant-report scales: Eapen et al. (2013) used the SCQ for an ESDM intervention and Pajareya and Nopmaneejumruslers (2011), used the CARS in a study of the DIR-Floortime® programme.

In contrast to these positive results, a somewhat larger set of studies have noted no impact of developmental interventions on ASD severity. For example, neither Vivanti et al. (2013), studying the effect of the ESDM programme, nor Siller et al. (2013), studying a DIR-Floortime® programme, noted any change in the ADOS scores for the participants undergoing the respective programme. This lack of an effect has also been seen in several studies of Joint Attention Programmes using the ADOS as a measure of severity (Green et al., 2010; Oosterling et al., 2010). Although Rogers et al. (2012) did note improvements in the ADOS score for a group of children undergoing an ESDM programme, it was also noted that, relative to a control group, these participants showed less improvement in their ASD severity. Finally, two studies employing informant-rated surveys of ASD severity noted no significant change in levels of ASD as a result of either a SCERTS®-like programme (Reed et al., 2013b) or of a Portage programme (Reed et al., 2007b).

Thus, the impact on ASD severity of developmental programmes is mixed, with no strong suggestion that any particular programme, or method of measurement of this domain, is associated with better or worse outcomes. This suggests that these results may largely be random in nature and that it cannot be concluded with any certainty that developmental approaches will have an impact on the overall ASD severity of children exposed to such interventions.

Behavioural problems   A sizable number of the studies (approximately 12) have reported the impact of the programme on the child behaviour problems, mainly through parent report measures of challenging behaviours. Overall, the effect size for improving behaviour problems from these studies was weak: a mean pre- to post-intervention effect size improvement in behaviour change of 0.23 (±0.47; range = −0.47–0.89). These data suggest that there was little overall impact of developmental approaches on behavioural problems. This finding may not be surprising as not all of the programmes set out to tackle such problems directly.

Of the studies that report such behavioural-problem data, 33% actually noted deterioration in these problems over the course of the treatment (e.g. McConachie et al., 2005; Reed et al., 2013b; Rickards et al., 2007; the home-based version of the programme reported by Roberts et al., 2011). These studies were of a variety of approaches, but they tended to be implemented in the home and conducted by parents. A further 17% of the studies of developmental interventions reported a weak effect size with respect to behavioural improvements (e.g. the clinic-based version of Roberts et al., 2011, intervention) and 33% reported a moderate effect size (the Joint Attention Programme, analysed by Green et al., 2010; the Denver programme reported by Rogers & DiLalla, 1991 and the Stepping Stone Triple-P project analysed by Sofronoff et al., 2011). Only 17% of the studies reported a strong effect size for improvements in behaviour problems (e.g. the DIR-Floortime programme reported by Mahoney & Perales, 2003 and the Stepping Stones Triple-P approach studied by Whittingham et al., 2009).

Summary

Overall, there are a number of conclusions that can be drawn from this analysis of the impact of developmental interventions on the main functioning outcomes for participants with ASD.

1. There is little evidence of strong impacts of the programmes as a whole on either ASD severity or behaviour problems.
2. The impact on intellectual functioning over the course of the intervention (e.g. pre- to post-intervention) is weak-to-moderate, but is better in therapist-led approaches that have a broad scope in terms of the behaviours that they tackle.
3. The programmes produce a moderate-to-strong effect on language, with bigger gains being made in those approaches with a specific focus on language or its precursors, such as joint attention.
4. The impact on adaptive-social behaviour was weak-to-moderate, in terms of pre- to post-intervention change.
5. The comparisons of developmental approaches with controls tended to produce only weak effect sizes in support of the developmental interventions, except for the area of linguistic functioning, which had moderate effect sizes relative to the comparison groups.

Child Predictors of Outcome

The relatively high level of RCT studies concerning developmental programmes, with their often tighter inclusion criteria for participants (and consequent lower variance at intake in the characteristics of the participants), mean that there are few studies that

Interventions for Autism

Table 9.3   Baseline characteristics of participants in studies of developmental interventions.

Study	Year	Age (months)	Cognitive	Communication	Social
Aldred et al.	2004	48			22
Carter et al.	2011	21		40	69
Casenhiser et al.	2013	42			
Dawson et al.	2010	23	61	60	70
Drew et al.	2002	21	88		
Eapen et al.	2013	50	37	30	62
Frankle et al.	2010	103	106		68
Green et al.	2010	45	27		
Houghton et al.	2013	70			22
Ingersoll & Wainer	2013	53	49	43	
Jenkins et al.	2012	60			
Joycelyn	1998	42	58		
Kaale et al.	2014	47	54	42	
Kasari et al.	2010	30	64		
Mahoney & Perales	2003	32	50	41	
McConachie et al.	2005	36			66
O'Neill et al.	2010				
Oosterling et al.	2010	35	58		
Pajareya & Napma	2011	51	44		24
Reed et al.	2013a	40	72	55	69
Reed et al.	2007	30	53		59
Reed et al.	2013a	43	83	60	70
Rickards et al.	2007	70	61		63
Roberts et al.	2011	43	66		69
Roberts et al.	2011	41	57		67
Rogers & DiLalla	1991	45	70	53	66
Rogers et al.	1989	45	68	53	64
Rogers et al.	1987	56	26	22	28
Rogers et al.	2006	41	47	35	
Rogers et al.	2012	18	65	48	77
Salt et al.	2002	42	39		49
Schertz et al.	2013	24		60	63
Shin et al.	2009	54			52
Siller et al.	2013	58	63	50	
Solomon et al.	2007	43			
Tonge et al.	2014	43	48	30	60
Tonge et al.	2014	46	64	44	67
Vismara et al.	2013	28			
Vivanti et al.	2012	38	57		
Wetherby & Wood	2006	19			
Wong & Kwan	2010	25	71		
Yoder & Stone	2009	34	51		

have directly examined the impact of child variables on developmental programmes. However, combining these data across the various developmental programmes allows some exploration of the factors related to the children in those programmes that might predict their effectiveness.

Table 9.4 Correlations between child characteristics at intake and pre-to-post intervention effect sizes in three functioning domains.

Intake	Cognitive	Communication	Social
Age	0.006	–0.298	0.240
Cognitive Function	–0.276	0.165	–0.041
Communication	0.347	0.280	0.002
Social Function	0.101	–0.005	–0.321

White = strong effect; light grey = moderate effect; dark grey = weak effect. No relationship is very strong.

Table 9.3 displays the characteristics of the participants, in the studies of these programmes for which these data were available. The participants can be characterized in terms of their age at intake, as well as in terms of the standard scores (mean of 100 and standard deviation of 15) for their intellectual ability, language ability (mean of expressive and receptive language) and their adaptive-social behaviours. The mean age of the participants at intake for these programmes was 42.3 (±16.0; range 18–103) months. The mean intellectual ability (standard score) of the included participants at baseline was 58.6 (±16.7; range 26–106); this score for language ability was a little lower than for intellectual functioning, being 45.1 (±11.4; range 22–60) and the mean pre-treatment standard score for the level of social adaptive behaviours was 57.6 (±16.9; range 22–77).

When these participant data shown in Table 9.4 are correlated with the outcome data (effect sizes for the pre- to post-intervention changes) for the three domains of functioning, displayed in Table 9.2, the pattern of relationships between the intake characteristics and programme effectiveness can be seen to be rather weak. The correlations between participant intake variables and outcomes all are relatively small, with only language ability at intake showing even borderline moderate relationships with improvements in intellectual functioning and language ability. However, as shall be seen in the next sections, this overall pattern of weak relationships obscures some rather more complex relationships.

Age at intake

The studies of developmental interventions can be divided into those that are conducted on very young children (i.e. those studies whose participants had a mean age at intake of less than 30 months old), those conducted on children between 30 and 48 months old and those conducted on relatively older children (who were more than 48 months old). The mean effect sizes for the three domains of functioning for these three age bands, along with the standard errors as a measure of variability, are displayed in Figure 9.2.

Inspection of these data reveals that, for intellectual functioning, there was relatively little impact of the age of the child at intake on the outcome. In part, this lack of relationship may be due to the rather larger variability in outcomes for intellectual functioning for the younger children than the older children, which can also be noted by observing the standard errors for the three age bands. However, a lack of clear effect of intake age on intellectual functioning outcomes was noted also by Vivanti et al. (2013) in their report concerning the predictors of success for the ESDM programme.

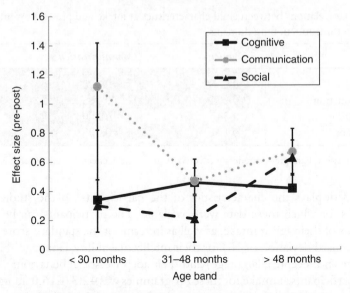

Figure 9.2 Effect sizes in three domains of functioning for studies of developmental interventions conducted with children of different ages at intake (error bars are the standard errors). The major advantage for younger children (<30 months) is in terms of improved communication – but there is a large variation in the outcomes.

Figure 9.2 shows that the impact of baseline age of the participants was much clearer for gains in language abilities, with greater gains being noted in the studies that employed the younger children (<30 months), than the studies that used older children. This finding was also noted by Rogers et al. (2012), in a study of the ESDM programme.

In contrast, to the effect on language, as the age of the children at intake increased, so did the impact of the programme on their social and adaptive behaviours. It might be noted that one of the few studies to directly examine this relationship did not find similar findings to that seen in the current meta-analysis. In a study of the impact of PRT, Baker-Ericzen et al. (2007) noted that younger children displayed better gains in social abilities (although they also found that the younger children in their study were also higher functioning).

Cognitive ability at intake

Figure 9.3 shows the mean effect sizes (and standard errors as a measure of variability), in the three functioning domains, for studies conducted on children who have relatively lower or greater intake levels of cognitive functioning, language ability and adaptive-social skills. In terms of intellectual functioning, dividing the studies at the mean and comparing those studies whose participants had an intellectual functioning standard score of 58 or less, with those whose participants had a score of 59 or greater shows a number of quite clear effects. Studies whose participants had relatively poor intellectual abilities at baseline displayed moderate gains in language, but those studies whose participants had relatively higher intellectual functioning at intake showed strong gains in language. This effect also was noted by Casenhiser et al. (2013), in a study of the DIR-Floortime® programme. The effect of baseline

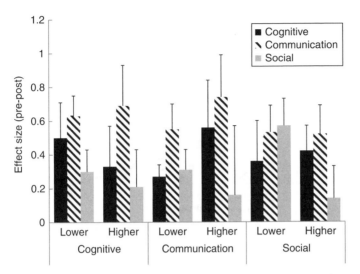

Figure 9.3 Pre-to-post intervention changes in three functioning domains for studies of developmental interventions, depending on the intake abilities of the sample in terms of their cognitive, communication and adaptive-social behaviours (error bars are standard errors).

intellectual functioning on gains in social and adaptive functioning was, however, opposite to the previously mentioned – those reports whose participants had relatively worse intellectual ability, displayed the greatest levels of gain.

The impact of intake intellectual ability on intellectual gains was much less clear. This is also reflected in individual studies that have attempted to assess this relationship: Rogers and DiLalla (1991), in a study of the DHSP; Vivanti et al. (2013), in a study of ESDM and Kaale et al. (2014), in a study of a Joint Attentional programme, all failed to note a relationship between these variables. However, a closer study of the relationship between baseline intellectual functioning and the effect size for the change in this variable reveals that, while there was no significant linear relationship, there was a significant bitonic relationship between the variables – shown in the scatter-plot in Figure 9.4 – with fewer gains for lower- and higher-functioning children as a result of the programme and greater gains in intellectual functioning for those children, peaking at an intake IQ of about 50–60.

A similar relationship between intake intellectual functioning and intellectual gains was also noted for the behavioural programmes and was discussed in some detail in Chapter 6. The reasons for the current bitonic relationship are not entirely clear; however, one possibility is worth a brief mention. Many of the developmental programmes rely, to some extent, on the child initiating the interactions and the parent/therapist using those child behaviours as teaching opportunities (e.g. DIR-Floortime® intervention, see Chapter 8 for a discussion), rather than the therapist driving the behaviours, as in a 'Lovaas' type ABA approach. If the child has lower intellectual abilities and initiates fewer interactions, then this may limit the number of engagement opportunities presented and, thus, limit the potential impact of the developmental approach. Of course, this is not true of all developmental programmes, but reliance on naturalistic teaching (see Chapter 8) may present such a problem, which has not been fully discussed or explored in the literature.

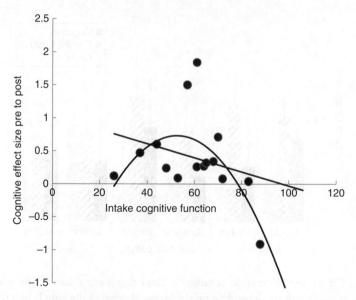

Figure 9.4 Relationship between intake cognitive function and the effect size for the change in cognitive function from before to after the developmental intervention. Lines show both the linear and quadratic trends in these data – the latter is a stronger fit than the former.

Language ability at intake

Figure 9.3 also displays the impact of language ability (expressive and receptive combined) on the gains made in each of the three functioning domains. In this instance, the studies were split at the mean for intake language ability, to create a lower-functioning intake group (with a language standard score of 45 or less) and a higher-functioning language group (with a language score of 46 or more at intake).

Those studies that employed children with relatively greater language abilities at intake showed greater gains in terms of intellectual functioning: the lower intake language groups produced weak effect size gains in intellectual functioning; whereas the higher language functioning group showed moderate effect sizes in intellectual gains. The relationship between language ability at baseline and intellectual functioning gains over the course of the programme mirrors that discussed previously for the impact of intake intellectual functioning on language gains. This relationship may, to some extent, reflect the close association between these domains in terms of their measurement.

The overall relationship between initial language ability and gains in that same domain was in the same direction as that for intellectual gains – higher ability groups producing greater gains – but this effect was less pronounced, with both studies of lower- and higher-functioning children at intake revealing moderate effect size gains in language. This less pronounced association is reflected in the outcomes of individual studies that have investigated this relationship, which have shown a mixed pattern of results. For example, Kaale et al. (2014), when studying a Joint Attention programme, noted no effect of baseline language on language outcomes; whereas, Siller et al. (2013), investigating a DIR-Floortime® intervention, reported an inverse relationship between these variables, with children with poorer language ability at intake making better progress in the language domain over the course of the programme.

In terms of the impact of language on adaptive-social functioning, the programmes with children of lower language ability showed relatively greater gains in social-adaptive behaviours, than those studies whose participants had relatively greater baseline language ability. Again, this may be partly because of a much greater variability in outcome for the higher language group of programmes than the lower language group of studies, although the precise reasons for this relationship are unclear.

Social-adaptive behaviour at intake

The programmes were divided into those that studied children with a baseline social-adaptive behaviour standard score of 57 or less (lower-functioning) and those that had an intake social-adaptive behaviour of 58 or more. The impact of initial social-adaptive functioning were clear on intellectual gains, with the higher functioning group of reports showing moderate effect sizes and the lower-functioning intake groups showing only weak effect sizes (see Figure 9.3). This overall result was mirrored in the reported by Vivanti et al. (2013) in a study of the predictors of the ESDM.

A similar relationship was noted between intake social-adaptive behaviours and language gain: the programmes employing participants with initially lower socially functioning showing weak gains in language; whereas the programmes with relatively socially higher-functioning participants, demonstrated moderate effect size gains in language. Again, this finding has been noted in many individual studies across a range of different developmental intervention programmes. For example, Rogers et al. (2006), Sullivan (2013) and Vivanti et al. (2013), in terms of the ESDM; Ingersoll et al. (2001) when studying PRT; Oosterling et al. (2010) investigation Joint Attention Programme; Casenhiser et al. (2013) in terms of DIR-Floortime®. Two studies have also noted that children with lower interest in object exploration and/or interaction (as opposed to non-object interaction), display greater language gains (Carter et al., 2011; Yoder & Stone, 2006 – again using different developmental approaches).

Finally, in terms of gains in social functioning, those programmes that studied children with a relatively lower social-adaptive ability at intake, demonstrated higher effects sizes in social gains following the intervention. This result corresponds with that reported by Tonge et al. (2014) in a study of a behaviour management training programme, who noted better social gains in those children who initially had lower social skills.

That there is a relatively strong relationship between social ability at intake and the outcome for this domain may reflect the importance of social interaction between the child and parent/therapist in many of the developmental approaches. Those children who are better at such interactions initially may well benefit more from such developmental programmes than those who are not so socially skilled at intake. This may reflect a limitation in the impact of some of these programmes.

Summary

The preceding discussion of the child moderators of the outcomes of developmental programmes has identified a number of predictors of success of those programmes, which are summarized next. However, it should be noted that some of these relationships are not strong, often reflecting the difference between obtaining a weak and a moderate effect size.

1. Intellectual functioning is promoted better in older children, who have initially higher language abilities and better social skills, but with moderate intellectual abilities.
2. Language functioning is better promoted with younger children who have higher intellectual, language and social abilities.
3. Social adaptive behaviour is promoted best in older children who have relatively poor intellectual language and social abilities.
4. The nature of the developmental programmes teaching strategy may well favour children who emit a greater range and level of behaviours and are more sociable, at intake.

Programme Predictors of Outcome

There are a number of characteristics of the programmes themselves that can be used to predict their impact on the participants' levels of functioning (effect size gains made pre- to post-intervention): the duration of the programme, the number of weekly hours of intervention received by the individuals with ASD on the programme and finally the number of weeks of training received by the parents and the number of hours training per week. These data are displayed in Table 9.1.

Of the conditions included in this review, the mean duration of the entire programme (including any parent training) was 37.9 weeks (±21.0; range = 1–104), with a mean of 13.9 hours (±9.9; range = 1–40) of intervention per week. Of these programmes, 30 (71%) provided parent training components at the commencement of the programme. The mean duration of this parent training was 19.6 weeks (±15.2; range = 1–52) and the mean number of hours a week of this parent training was 3.4 (±5.8; range = 0.25– 30). In addition, a number of studies have documented the impact of the parent training on the parents' behaviours and parenting skills and some studies have analysed the association between change in parenting behaviours and changes in child behaviours.

Programme duration and intensity

The programmes can be divided into those that ran for up to 6 months, those that ran for between 6 and 11 months and those, relatively few, that ran for a year or more. The impact on functioning can be seen in the left panel of Figure 9.5 for these three groups of programmes. In terms of programme duration, it can be seen from Figure 9.5 that there was actually little relationship between programme length and intellectual functioning gains. However, there was a clear positive relationship between this aspect of the programme and language gain – with longer programmes producing greater gains. In contrast, for adaptive-social behavioural functioning, the converse was true – programmes lasting 6 months or less producing the greatest gains in this area of functioning.

The right panel of Figure 9.5 shows the relationship between the programme intensity (weekly hours of intervention given to the person with ASD) and functioning gains. In this instance, the programmes were grouped into those that provided

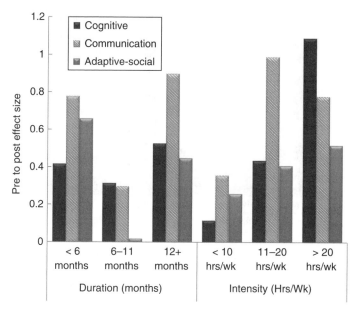

Figure 9.5   Pre- to post-intervention effect size for changes in functioning across three domains in studies using different monthly durations and weekly intensities. Gains tend to improve as the duration of the programme increases.

10 hours or less of intervention per week, those that provided between 11 and 20 hours per week and those that provided over 20 hours a week. Inspection of these data shows that there were positive relationships between the weekly intensity and outcomes in intellectual functioning and also for language functioning: with programmes providing 20 hours a week of intervention showing strong effect sizes.

The impact of weekly intensity on social functioning was less clear, although there were improvements when the weekly intensity was over 10 hours, compared to when it was less than this level.

These overall data on the relationship between weekly intensity and programme outcomes are borne out in the individual studies that have analysed this association. Soloman et al. (2007), investigating a DIR-Floortime® programme and Jenkins et al. (2012), for an Options-Son-Rise programme, both noted such effects. There was a partial effect of weekly intensity noted by Rogers et al. (2012) for an ESDM programme. In contrast, Vivanti et al. (2013) noted no such effect for the ESDM and Kasari et al. (2010) found no relationship for a Joint Attention programme. However, it should be noted that the number of hours of weekly intervention, in many cases, might be made up of additional types of therapy, such as ABA or special nursery placements (e.g. see Green et al., 2010). This makes the interpretation of these data somewhat uncertain.

Parent training

The programmes included in the current meta-analyses differed in terms of whether they provided parent training or not and, if so, how much they provided. To create sets of studies in order to analyse the impact of the length of such parent training, the programmes were divided into those that did not have a parent training component

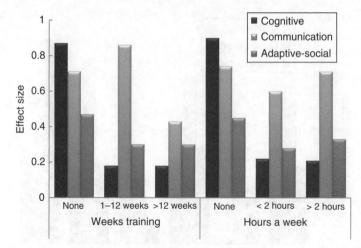

Figure 9.6   Pre- to post-intervention effect sizes in three functioning domains for studies of developmental interventions that gave different levels of parent training (in terms of weeks and hours per week). Studies without parent training (i.e. therapist-led) produced the strongest gains.

(i.e. the intervention was delivered by teachers or therapist), those programmes that gave up to 12 weeks of parent training (a number used by many models, such as the ESDM and Joint Attention programmes) and those programmes that gave more than 12 weeks parent training (often continuing the parent training throughout the course of the intervention). The left panel of Figure 9.6 shows the gains made in the three functioning domains (intellectual, language and social-adaptive) as a product of the number of weeks parent training.

These data show that the programmes without a parent component produced stronger gains for intellectual functioning. For those programmes with a parent-training aspect, better gains were made in terms of intellectual functioning with more weeks training. Gains in language and in social-adaptive behaviours were slightly better with up to 12 weeks parent training, than without such a parent-training component and both of these sets of studies produced better gains than those that gave more parent training.

The right panel of Figure 9.6 shows the impact on outcome effect sizes (pre- to post-intervention changes in functioning) of the amount of parent training per week. The studies were divided into programmes that gave no parent training, programmes that gave few parent-training hours per week (up to 2 hours) and those that gave greater amounts of parent training (over two per week). These data show an inverse relationship between parental training and intellectual functioning gains. For language and social-adaptive gains, the programmes without a parent training component worked better than those with a parent-training component, but for those programmes that involved the parents, the more training they received the better the gains in terms of language ad social-adaptive behaviours.

Impact on parents

A number of studies have examined the impact of parent training on the parents themselves and there are also some reports concerning the effect of the training on the parenting skills of the people who underwent the training. These data are important, as a critical aspect of the developmental approaches is that they assume that the child-benefits will be mediated by improved parental functioning and responsiveness to their child. However, these studies reveal that the impact on parental functioning of the training has been mixed.

In studies of how the programmes impact parental functioning, both Rickards et al. (2009) and Salt et al. (2002), in studies of home-based developmental programmes, noted no impact of the parent training on parental stress. In contrast, Wong and Kwan (2010), in study of a SCERTS®-like programme and Estes et al. (2014), in a study of ESDM, did report a reduction in parent stress as a result of the parent training. Further, Tonge et al. (2006), in a behaviour-management programme, noted some impact of the training on the health of some, but not all, of the parents involved.

There have been a large number of reports of the impact of such programmes on the parenting skills of the parents across many of the different types of developmental programme. For example, Casenhiser et al. (2013), studying a DIR® programme, noted an increase in parent skills after the parent training component of the intervention. Similarly, Sofronoff et al. (2011) and Whittingham et al. (2009), in reports about the Stepping Stones Triple-P programme (which targets parents' abilities to tackle challenging behaviours), noted reduced 'dysfunctional' parenting and such behaviour management programmes have been found to be more effective in this regard that parent counselling (e.g. Tonge et al., 2014).

A number of reports have noted increases in the responsiveness of parents towards their children or in the synchronization of parent-child behaviours. For example, Vismara et al. (2012), analysing the impact of a web-delivered version of ESDM, noted improved engagement of the parents with their children after the training programme. Green et al. (2010), investigating the PACT Joint Attention Programme, found increased synchronous parent-child responding after training, as did Aldred et al. (2004), who were studying a SCERTS®-like programme and also Mahoney and Perales (2003), investigating a DIR® model.

There is little evidence to bear on the issue of which parents will benefit from this training. One study, however, does offer some interesting possible insight into this issue. Siller et al. (2013), analysing a DIR®-like programme, noted that increases in parental responsiveness or parent-child synchronization in behaviours, may be mediated by the initial levels of parental insight into their behaviours, with parents with greater insight into their behaviours toward their children showing greater increases in responsiveness as a result of the training – as shown in Figure 9.7. 'Insight' in this context refers to the ability of the parents to understand the nature of their own social interactions with their children. This immediately raises two issues in terms of the generality of these programmes, which further research will need to address: (i) does this insight correlate with parental intelligence? And (ii) if many parents of children with ASD are high in the broad autistic phenotype (see Chapter 2), does this mean that they lack insight into their social behaviours?

Despite the evidence that such developmental programmes might have some impact on the parent's behaviours, it is still somewhat unclear as to whether this altered parent behaviour is the cause of the changes in the child functioning. In fact, several reviews of this area (Diggle et al., 2002; McConachie & Diggle, 2007; Oono et al., 2013) have suggested that there is little evidence to support the notion that changes in parent behaviours directly drive changes in child functioning in such developmental programmes.

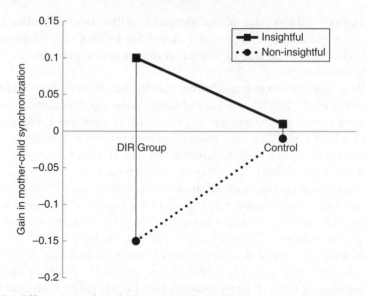

Figure 9.7   Effects on mother-child synchronization of behaviours of a DIR intervention and a control group depending on the initial levels of insight shown by the mother, as reported by Siller et al. (2013). The DIR intervention only produced strong effects if the mother had initially high insight into the child's problems.

Although there is little direct evidence of a causal relationship (McConachie & Diggle, 2007), there is growing evidence of an association (at least) between changes in parent behaviour and child functioning. This evidence has been obtained across a wide range of different developmental programmes. For example, Vismara et al., (2012; 2013), for different versions of the ESDM, have noted correlations between changes in parent behaviours and gains in child functioning. Kasari et al. (2010), for a Joint Attention Programme, noted that increases in parental involvement, as a result of the parent training, were related to child outcomes.

The most studied developmental intervention in this regard is the DIR® programme, for which there have been some mixed results. Casenhiser et al. (2013; see also Mahoney & Perales, 2003) noted that increases in parental social-communication were reflected in increased language ability for the children. In contrast, Siller et al. (2013; see also Carter et al., 2011, for the Hanen MTW Programme), found no relationship between increases in parent-child synchronous behaviours and language development in the children.

Summary

A number of programme predictors of child outcome can be discerned from these data, which appear reasonably consistent across the various programmes that have studied them.

1. Programme duration has a positive effect on language, a negative effect on social-adaptive behaviours and little effect on intellectual functioning.
2. The weekly intensity of the intervention is positively related to all areas of functioning – especially intellectual and language abilities.

3. Programmes delivered by therapists appear to be more effective than those delivered by parents, but, when they are delivered by parents, the more hours per week training received, the better.

4. Parent training does appear to have an impact on parenting behaviours and there is some correlational evidence to suggest that this may also be related to child behaviours. However, it is not clear whether all parents will benefit from such training.

Programme Comparison

To this point, the current chapter has examined the overall impact of the various developmental approaches, as well as the potential predictors of success. However, as outlined in Chapter 8, although there are a number of similarities between these approaches, the umbrella of 'developmental interventions' covers a wide range of treatments.

Figure 9.8 presents the pre- to post-intervention effects sizes for the changes in the main areas of functioning (cognitive, communication and social-adaptive behaviour) for each of the broad categories of developmental approach outlined in Table 9.1 (see also Chapter 8). Inspection of these data shows that the only approach that produces a strong effect size for change in cognitive functioning is the ESDM. However, the play-responsiveness based models (such as DIR-Floortime®) and the imitation-based programmes (such as Options-Son-Rise), also produce moderate sized gains in this domain. However, it might be noted that these moderate gains may be the product

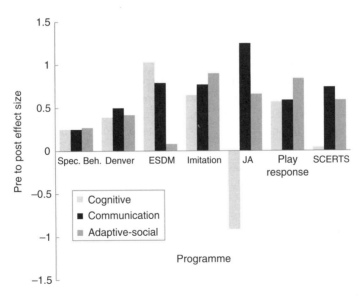

Figure 9.8　Pre- to post-intervention effect sizes in three functioning domains for different types of developmental intervention: Spec Beh = programmes targeting one form of behaviour; ESDM = Early Start Denver Model; JA = Joint Attention; Play Resp = play responsiveness.

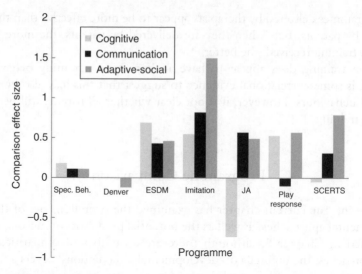

Figure 9.9 Effect sizes relative to a control group in three functioning domains for different types of developmental intervention. Spec. Beh. = programmes targeting one form of behaviour; ESDM = Early Start Denver Model; JA = Joint Attention; Play Resp = play responsiveness.

of the use of nonstandard tests for this domain, which tends to inflate the estimate of the impact (see Chapter 8 for a fuller discussion).

Inspection of the communication changes suggests that many of the programmes produce either strong effects sizes (Joint Attention Programmes and ESDM) or moderate-strong effects (SCERTS®, Play-Responsiveness, Imitation). It is worth noting that the former two sets of approaches (Joint Attention and ESDM) specifically target behaviours that are taken as precursors as language – such as joint or shared attention and the latter set of programmes target communication behaviours (see Chapter 2 and 5 for further discussion).

The Play-Responsiveness and imitation-based approaches also produce strong effect sizes in terms of the changes in social-adaptive behaviour (but, again, interpretation of these data is made difficult by the use of nonstandard tests for these domains). The SCERTS® and Joint Attention programmes produce moderate effects sizes in this domain.

The relative impacts of these programmes are displayed in Figure 9.9, which presents the effect sizes for the various broad types of developmental programme relative to the comparison groups. Of the approaches, only the ESDM programme has a large effect size for cognitive functioning, although the Play-Responsiveness (e.g. DIR-Floortime®) and imitation-based (e.g. Options-Son-Rise), models also produce moderate effect size relative to the controls. In terms of communication, the imitation-based approaches produce large effect sizes relative to comparison groups, with Joint Attention programmes having a moderate effect size in this domain.

Many of the programmes reveal either moderate or strong levels of success in the social-adaptive behaviour domain. The imitation-based set of interventions has a very strong effect size in this area, although many of the studies of this intervention have used nonstandard measures. The SCERTS® type of approach also demonstrates a large effect size for social adaptive behaviour. The ESDM, Play-Responsiveness and Joint Attention programmes all show moderate effect sizes, in comparison to the control groups included in their studies.

Overview

In summary, if the discussions of Chapters 8 and 9 are combined, it can be said that developmental approaches are clearly widely used and have a high degree of acceptance for authorities, teachers and parents. To this extent, they are important programmes of intervention for people with ASD. There is also some evidence that exposure to these types of programmes does impact positively on functioning. These gains are moderate in terms of the communication domains, with weaker impacts in terms of the cognitive and social-adaptive, functioning domains. Although the gains produced by the programmes themselves are respectable, the size of the gains, when compared to control conditions, is rather weaker. However, it does need to be stressed that a significant limitation for many these studies of 'developmental' approaches is the lack of use of standard instruments of cognitive and language developments – many reports use tools developed for and by, the programme itself.

Much more information is also needed regarding the optimum conditions for the success of these developmental interventions. These programmes seem to be better suited to promoting cognitive and social functioning in older children and language gains in younger children. The longer the duration of the programme (especially programmes lasting for around 12 months) and the more programme hours (around 20 hours per week), the better the gains seem to be, especially in terms of in cognitive and language functioning. The fact that many of the developmental programmes studied actually have rather shorter and less-intense characteristics may be limiting their effectiveness.

In fact, the programme that has several of these key characteristics – the ESDM programme – is also the programme that appears most effective across a range of domains of functioning. However, these considerations raise a question over developmental approaches: in that the more successful programmes share many features with the behavioural programmes discussed in Chapters 4–6. This also raises an issue as to the mechanism of action of these developmental approaches; that is, do they work due to the suggested processes or through other means (i.e. simple reinforcement, see Osborne & Reed, 2008 for some analysis of this issue).

A key consideration for developmental approaches was that they should be mediated, to some extent, by the parents – that is, changes is parent behaviour should be reflected in changes in child behaviour. The ability to utilize parents as the means of delivery of the intervention also endows 'developmental' approaches with an immediate financial attractiveness, compared to more professional-time intense programmes (see Carter et al., 2011, for a discussion), although the longer-term financial implications are somewhat unclear (Jacobson & Mulick, 2000). However, the child gains that are noted tend to be more pronounced in the more therapist-led approaches, with there being less evidence for the effectiveness of parent-led approaches. Moreover, there is only moderate evidence that the changes that are effected by the programme are the product of parent-mediation (i.e. that they occur as a result of changes in parent behaviour) – and they could result directly from the impact of the programme on the child.

This summary of studies of developmental interventions broadly coheres with the conclusions drawn in two other reviews (Oono et al., 2013; Ospina et al., 2008). For example, Ospina et al. (2008) suggested that it is difficult to draw firm conclusions regarding 'developmental' approaches, but suggest that they may impact language development to a greater extent than social development. While, Oono et al. (2013; see also Diggle et al., 2002) suggested that there is little direct evidence for the role of parent-mediation as a mechanism of action for these approaches.

10

Sensory and Physical Stimulation Treatments

The set of interventions for Autism Spectrum Disorders (ASD) to be discussed in this chapter can be termed 'sensory and physical stimulation' treatments. These interventions target the sensory problems that are often experienced by individuals with ASD across a number of different modalities (see Chapter 2). As might be expected, there is a very broad range of such sensory treatment programmes: sensory integration therapy (SIT; Ayres, 1972); auditory integration therapy (AIT; Berard, 1993); visual stimulation therapies (VST; Kaplan et al., 1998) and a range of direct physical stimulation approaches, such as various forms of Massage Therapy (MT; e.g. Silva et al., 2011). Of these approaches, SIT is very commonly adopted as a treatment for ASD and MT is gaining increasing currency as an intervention for this population (Lee et al., 2011).

In general, such interventions aim to improve the functioning of individuals with ASD across a wide spectrum of domains, mainly by attempting to alleviate the assumed central sensory-physical deficits responsible for those ASD symptoms. Thus, these intervention approaches take the position that many ASD symptoms, especially those associated with either externalizing behaviours (e.g. challenging behaviours) or internalizing behaviours (e.g. anxiety), may result from sensory processing problems. Certainly, the presence of such sensory processing difficulties in those with ASD has been noted to be associated with stereotypical and repetitive behaviours (Baranek et al., 1997). As a consequence, it is thought by many promoters of these treatment regimes that processing abnormalities hold a key to reducing the symptoms of ASD (Dawson & Watling, 2000). In particular, sensory therapies speculate that providing particular types of sensory stimulation may facilitate the development or integration of the nervous system and enable it to process sensory stimuli more effectively (Ayres & Tickle, 1980; Baranek, 2002; Lang et al., 2012; Schaaf & Miller, 2005, for reviews and discussion); thus, allowing the resulting behavioural symptoms to reduce in severity (Baranek 2002; Lane et al., 2010; Schaaf & Miller, 2005). However, it should

Interventions for Autism: Evidence for Educational and Clinical Practice, First Edition. Phil Reed.
© 2016 John Wiley & Sons, Ltd. Published 2016 by John Wiley & Sons, Ltd.

be noted that the nature of the putative sensory impairment and the influence of this impairment over the symptoms of ASD, is the subject of some theoretical speculation (see Lane & Schaaf, 2010; Smith et al., 2005).

As outlined in Chapter 2, it is certainly true that people with ASD can display abnormal sensory reactivity to external and internal stimulation. Leekam et al. (2007) noted that as many as 90% of individuals with ASD present with a sensory problem and Billstedt et al. (2007) suggested that inappropriate responses to sensory stimulation were one of the most enduring symptoms across the life of a person with ASD. In fact, such sensitivity to sensory stimulation can take one of two forms: *hypo-reactivity* to stimuli, such as an attenuated reaction to speech, noise or pain or *hyper-reactivity*, such as agitation, distress or withdrawal, on the presentation of a stimulus (see Liss et al., 2006; Ornitz, 1974). Given this range of potential problems, the nature of the sensory therapy applied (e.g. physical, auditory or visual), will depend on the precise nature of the individual's particular sensory issue (Dunn, 1999; Lang et al., 2012, for a discussion).

As many individuals with ASD display sensory problems, and as these problems are associated with a range of ASD-relevant symptoms, sensory-stimulation approaches are actually very widely adopted (see Devlin et al., 2011; Lang et al., 2012). For example, Watling et al. (1999) found that almost all Occupational Therapists working with children with ASD regularly implemented Sensory Integration Therapy (SIT; see also Case-Smith & Miller, 1999). The evidence provided by Watling et al. (1999), coupled with the data reported by Stahmer et al. (2005), which suggests over 75% of children with ASD receive occupational therapy, implies that sensory therapies must be very widespread in their implementation. This is an inference corroborated by the results of a survey conducted by Green et al. (2006), who reported that 70% of parents of children with ASD stated that their child had received some form of sensory therapy. It should probably be noted that such sensory therapies are not often used as the sole intervention for ASD – as many of these therapies are often used along with other approaches – however, an assumption underlying these interventions is that the symptoms of ASD are a result of sensory deficits and so such therapies could be used as a sole comprehensive intervention. Taken together, these considerations mean that a documentation of the evidence relating to the effectiveness of sensory therapies is called for in any review of intervention techniques for ASD.

Review Evidence for Sensory Therapies

There have been a number of narrative and meta-analytic reviews of the effectiveness of sensory therapies for individuals with ASD (and other developmental disorders) published over the last 30 years. Unfortunately, these reviews have produced a mixed set of conclusions regarding the effectiveness of sensory therapies (Baranek, 2002; Hoehn & Baumeister, 1994; May-Benson & Koomar, 2010; Lang et al., 2012; Lee et al., 2011; Ottenbacher, 1982; Stephenson & Carter, 2005; Vargas et al., 1999; Zimmer & Desch, 2012). In fact, the conclusions of these reviews have ranged from being positively disposed to sensory treatments (Lee et al., 2011; Ottenbacher, 1982), to being extremely critical of the application of these techniques (Lang et al., 2012). It is entirely unclear why there is a such a variety in the recommendations provided regarding the use of these sensory approaches, save to say that the studies included in these reviews are highly variable in terms of the nature of the participants, the nature and amount of the sensory therapy received and the outcome measures employed, which are very rarely validated standardized measures of functioning (Baranek, 2002; May-Benson & Koomar, 2010).

One set of these reviews suggests that participants undergoing SIT show better functioning than control groups who did not receive this therapeutic approach (May-Benson & Koomar, 2010; Ottenbacher, 1982). However, these reviews were not specifically related to individuals with ASD, but incorporated participants with many forms of developmental and intellectual disability. Given the specific problems associated with ASD, compared to many developmental and intellectual disorders, the generality of these conclusions for an ASD population may be questioned. Notwithstanding this proviso, May-Benson and Koomar (2010) concluded that SIT can produce positive benefits for individuals, which may be sustained over relatively long periods of time (of up to 2 years). The review concluded that these gains were especially noticeable in terms of sensorimotor skills and motor planning and also in terms of social skills, play, attention and behavioural regulation of the individuals. A similar positive conclusion was reached by Lee et al. (2011) in a meta-analysis of the effects of massage therapy for participants with ASD. However, it was also noted by both May-Benson and Koomar (2010) and Lee et al. (2011) that this overall conclusion may be limited for a number of reasons: (i) the small sample sizes employed in many of the studies included in the review; (ii) the inconsistent levels of intervention given across the studies; (iii) difficulties with establishing the treatment fidelity of the intervention and (iv) the frequent use of outcome measures that may not be clinically meaningful.

A second set of reviews of sensory therapies have produced more muted supported for sensory therapies; concluding that, while there may be some indication of effectiveness, there is not yet enough strong data available to ensure that the suggested outcomes can be relied upon. For example, Stephenson and Carter (2005) suggested that there was a case for more research into the effectiveness of a particular form of sensory therapy (the use of a weighted vest) for individuals with ASD, but that there was insufficient evidence to recommend the treatment for clinical application. Similarly, in a review conducted across multiple sensory treatments for individuals with ASD, Baranek (2002) concluded that sensory therapies were safe for individuals with ASD, but that the evidence for their effectiveness was not yet well established. The third article in this category of moderately supportive reviews, by Vargas et al. (1999), drew several conclusions from their meta-analysis of sensory treatments for participants with a variety of disorders. On the positive side, they noted that SIT interventions were as effective as a variety of comparison groups, but that this effectiveness was greater for psycho-educational and motor functioning domains, than they were for sensory functioning – suggesting the mechanism of action may not be as expected for these treatments (if the symptoms are moderated by sensory processing, then reductions in sensory problems should be seen in any groups that shows improvements in other symptoms). However, on the negative side, Vargas et al. (1999) also noted that such positive effects were much more pronounced in the earlier studies of the intervention (typically conducted in the 1980s), compared to the later studies, which did not show overall positive effects on functioning.

Finally, a number of reviews have suggested, very strongly in some cases, that sensory therapy techniques are not effective and, in fact, should not be employed.

Hoehn and Baumeister (1994) suggested that their review of the impact of SIT for people with learning disabilities raised serious concerns about the use of sensory integration. In particular, they suggested that the research, to that point in time, was sufficient to conclude not only that sensory integration was of unproven effectiveness (see also Baranek, 2002; Stephenson & Carter, 2005), but that it was 'demonstrably ineffective'. As a result, Hoehn and Baumeister (1994) suggested that SIT not be employed, either as a main therapy or as part of a broader treatment, for learning and developmental disabilities. Nearly 20 years later, Lang et al. (2012) arrived at a similar conclusion for individuals with ASD, suggesting that the evidence does not support the use of sensory integration for the treatment of ASD and that this approach should not be employed outside research studies until evidence of outcome-effectiveness is provided.

As a result of such a mixed and confused pattern of data, Zimmer and Desch (2012, p. 1186), in a policy statement for the American Academy of Pediatrics, concerning sensory integration therapies for developmental and behavioural disorders, concluded that:

> Occupational therapy with the use of sensory-based therapies may be acceptable as one of the components of a comprehensive treatment plan. However, parents should be informed that the amount of research regarding the effectiveness of sensory integration therapy is limited and inconclusive.

However, as there are a number of different sensory approaches, the following sections review the evidence for each sensory intervention, in turn, focusing on those treatments with the greatest amount of evidence relating to their effectiveness.

Sensory Integration Therapy

Sensory Integration Therapy (SIT; Ayres, 1972; 1979) attempts to promote processing of sensory information by providing a variety of tactile stimulation in order to facilitate learning in the client. It should be noted that the neurological assumptions that were originally taken to underpin this treatment model have been heavily criticized (see Baranek, 2002; Lang et al., 2012, for discussion). However, more recent work in this field has reconceptualized the bases for SIT (Bundy & Murray, 2002) and this debate should not be taken as a reason for ignoring this form of intervention.

Implementation

There are a number of ways in which SIT is delivered for an individual with ASD (Baranek, 2002; Parham & Ecker, 2007). Traditionally, the interventions are usually conducted by an Occupational Therapist and delivered on a 1:1 basis between therapist and client with ASD, with the interactions following a child-lead play-based approach. The treatment is conducted in a clinic that has the needed specialized equipment (e.g. suspended swings, pressure vests, sensory brushes etc.). The SIT sessions usually last for 1 hour and are conducted 1–3 times per week, over the course of several months.

Implementation of the treatment typically involves a combination of the application of a weighted vest (Cox et al., 2009), sensory brushes (Davis et al., 2011), swinging

(Bonggat & Hall, 2010), sitting on a bouncy ball (Devlin et al., 2011) and/or being squeezed between exercise pads (Bonggat & Hall, 2010; Devlin et al., 2009). However, the SIT treatment plans are highly individualized (as are many treatments for ASD, see previous chapters in the current text) and the precise nature of the stimulation depending on the sensory needs of the individual (Dunn, 1999).

It should be noted that several types of SIT deviate from the previous 'classical' approach. For example, some SIT programmes may provide stimulation, but not use any suspended equipment; alternatively, the treatment may be more structured and not follow the child's play-lead or the treatment may feature more cognitively demanding tasks for the client. Two examples of such modified sensory integration tasks are the: 'Sensory Diet' (Devlin et al., 2011), which is delivered at home or at school and which is integrated into the daily routines of the client and the 'Alert Programme' (Williams & Shellenberger, 1996), in which higher-functioning children with ASD are given additional cognitive strategies to assist with arousal modulation.

Outcome-effectiveness evidence for SIT

The reviews of SIT effectiveness, mentioned previously, offer a mixed picture of outcomes. Of these reviews, only one provided any effect sizes for the impact of the treatment (Vargas et al., 1999) and these data suggested a mean effect size improvement in functioning across multiple domains of 0.29 (a weak strength effect according to the accepted criteria of Cohen, 1988). However, this effect size figure was based not only on programmes that studied the impact of SIT for participants with ASD, but also included studies that involved participants with a range of other disabilities.

In order to compile further evidence regarding the effectiveness of SIT for ASD specifically, this chapter examines the 31 studies of SIT for this population mentioned in two thorough reviews (Baranek, 2002; Lang et al., 2012). Due to the nature of the measures used in many of these studies (which rarely adopted standardized instruments and which often used idiosyncratic observational methods), the evidence provided by each of these studies was classified as either 'positive', 'mixed' or 'negative' (see Lancioni et al., 1996; Lang et al., 2012, for discussion of this approach). The results were classified as 'positive' if all of the dependent variables employed in the study showed some improvement. The outcomes were said to be 'mixed' if there were improvements in some of the outcome variables, but outcomes were classed as 'negative' if there were no improvements in any domain or if there was deterioration in functioning.

Table 10.1 presents the studies that were included in these reviews of SIT and classifies them according to outcome and also in terms of the primary domains of the outcome variables. Inspection of the data in Table 10.1 reveals that 6 of these 31 studies (20%) were classified as having 'positive' outcomes. However, of these six studies, the one by Linderman and Stewart (1999) used only two participants and Edelson et al. (1999) employed qualitatively judged outcome measures, making these positive results less strong than they appear. Another 11 studies (26%) were classed as having 'mixed' results, as they showed some improvement in functioning across the outcome measures. The remaining 14 studies (45%) were classified as showing 'negative' outcomes, because no benefit on any dependent measure was found. Of the 14 studies with a 'negative' outcome, five (16%) actually suggested a worsening of symptoms after the intervention (i.e. Carter, 2005; Davis et al., 2011; Devlin et al., 2009; 2011; Kane et al., 2004).

Table 10.1 Studies of Sensory Integration Therapy, including the functioning domains investigated and their outcomes.

Study	Year	Domains Investigated	Outcome
Ayers & Tickle	1980	Behaviour, Social	Mixed
Bagatell et al.	2010	Behaviour	Mixed
Bonggat & Hall	2010	Behaviour, Cognition	Negative
Carter	2005	Behaviour	Negative
Case-Smith & Bryan	1999	Social	Mixed
Cox et al.	2009	Behaviour	Negative
Davis et al.	2011	Behaviour	Negative
Devlin et al.	2009	Behaviour	Negative
Devlin et al.	2011	Behaviour	Negative
Edelson et al.	1999	Social	Mixed
Fazlioglu & Baron	2008	Sensory	Positive
Fertel-Daly et al.	2001	Behaviour	Mixed
Field et al.	1997	Behaviour, Sensory	Mixed
Hodgetts et al.	2011a	Behaviour, Social	Mixed
Hodgetts et al.	2011b	Behaviour	Negative
Kane et al.	2004	Behaviour	Negative
Larrington	1987	Behaviour, Social	Positive
Leew et al.	2010	Behaviour, Cognition	Negative
Linderman & Stewart	1999	Social	Positive
McClure & Holtz-Yotz	1990	Behaviour, Social	Positive
Pfeiffer et al.	2011	Sensory, Social	Mixed
Piravaj et al.	2009	Behaviour	Mixed
Quigley et al.	2011	Behaviour	Negative
Ray et al.	1988	Social	Negative
Reichow et al.	2010	Behaviour	Negative
Reilly et al.	1983	Social	Negative
Stagnitti et al.	1999	Behaviour, Sensory	Positive
Thompson	2011	Cognition	Positive
Van Rie & Heflin	2009	Cognition	Mixed
Watling & Dietz	2007	Sensory	Negative
Zisserman	1992	Behaviour	Mixed

White = strong effect; light grey = moderate effect and dark grey = weak effect.

Overall, these results seem to suggest that there is only limited evidence of strong SIT effectiveness for a population with ASD. This view corresponds to that arrived at by both Baranek (2002) and Lang et al. (2012). However, although the evidence is not particularly strong in terms of the positive outcomes for SIT, there

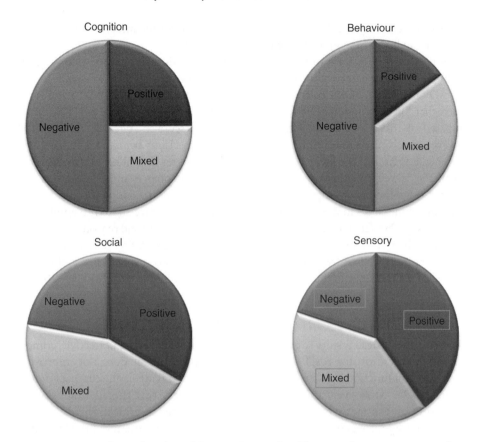

Figure 10.1   Numbers of studies of Sensory Integration Therapy whose outcomes on the various domains displayed can be defined as positive, mixed or negative. Social and sensory outcomes appear to be better impacted than cognition or language.

was only a minor suggestion across these studies of any contra-indication for its use (see Hoehn & Baumeister, 1994).

In addition to examining the overall impacts of SIT for people with ASD, it is also possible to investigate the specific effects of this treatment for particular aspects of functioning. In fact, there are some discernible patterns in terms of the functioning domains that SIT appears to impact most strongly. The percentages of studies that could be classified as having 'positive', 'mixed' or 'negative' outcomes for the domains of: cognition, behaviour, social-emotional functioning (including language) and sensory processing, can be seen in the pie charts displayed in Figure 10.1. For the cognition domain (top left panel), only one of the four studies that assessed this domain produced a 'positive' result, one produced a 'mixed' result and two studies produced 'negative' results. A broadly similar pattern was noted for behavioural problems (such as self-injury, stereotyped behaviours), which can be seen in the top right panel of Figure 10.1 – with most studies showing no impact of SIT on these problems and some studies also showing a potential deleterious effect (e.g. Devlin et al., 2011). A majority of the studies that included measures relating to social-emotional functioning, produced either 'positive' or 'mixed' results (see bottom left panel of Figure 10.1) – a finding that concurs with the conclusions of the review produced by Vargas et al. (1999). Finally, the studies were relatively evenly split in terms of the impact of the intervention on sensory processing abilities (bottom right panel of Figure 10.1).

This rather mixed pattern of results across the various domains may be a consequence of the very different nature of the sensory problems presented by the participants in these studies. For example, on the basis of the review conducted by Baranek (2002), it was concluded that SIT may function better for those individuals with sensory hyper-sensitivity, compared to those individuals with hypo-sensitivity (see also Ayres & Tickle, 1980). However, much more research is needed prior to such claims being accepted as having any generality. In fact, the literature relating to SIT requires several key additions. Firstly, as with the 'developmental' approaches reviewed in Chapters 8 and 9, there is a great need for outcome-effectiveness studies of this programme to adopt the use of more standardized measures in assessing outcomes. Some studies have started to employ such measures (e.g. Pfeiffer et al., 2011; Thompson, 2011), but most still rely on observational measures of behaviour or on experimenter-ratings of behaviours. Secondly, there is a clear need to expand the time-frame over which these interventions are studied and to assess the level of maintenance in the behaviours examined (May-Benson & Koomar, 2010).

Summary

Taken together, these results suggest that SIT will not serve as an effective 'comprehensive' intervention for ASD – the evidence implies that it does not improve all (if any) areas of functioning with any consistency (see also Lang et al., 2012; Zimmer & Dresh, 2012). Moreover, there is little evidence that this therapeutic approach works through the mechanisms that have been suggested as critical, that is, in terms of alleviating symptoms by altering the sensory processing capacities of the individuals (Ayers, 1972), as there is little consistent evidence that such sensory processing capacities are impacted by the intervention. Neither is there strong evidence that SIT reduces behavioural problems in those with ASD. However, neither is there the strong evidence, as is claimed by some (Hoehn & Baumeister, 1994), that the intervention should not be employed as it can worsen the symptoms.

One aspect of the effect of SIT is worth some brief comment is that the available evidence suggests that SIT does have a possible (albeit relatively weak) impact on the social and emotional functioning of individuals with ASD (e.g. social interactions, anxiety levels etc.). There are, of course, many caveats to this conclusion regarding social-emotional functioning, but the fact that there is some positive impact in this domain, while there is no strong sign of impact on sensory processing, suggests that SIT may be operating through a very different mechanism to that initially suggested (i.e. through alteration of neural processing of sensory stimuli).

As this intervention appears to impact those with sensory hyper-sensitivity most strongly (see Ayres & Tickle, 1980) and it improves social-emotional function best, it may be that what is being witnessed is a form of exposure therapy to the stimuli that previously produced internalized behaviours (fear, anxiety). In turn, this fear would cause a withdrawal from particular situations involving those stimuli and a reduction in this sensitivity to the stimuli would remove this problem. This is, of course, is conjectural, but there is evidence to suggest that exposure therapy will work for social anxieties for individuals with ASD (Wood et al., 2009).

Auditory Integration Training

Auditory Integration Training (AIT) was developed by Berard (1982) to help 'normalize' hearing and improve the processing of auditory information. The approach was developed initially for individuals with depression, as it was thought that improvement in reactions to auditory cues may improve social engagement, but AIT subsequently became used also as an intervention for a variety of developmental disorders. The basic assumption of AIT is that distortions in auditory processing may be associated with difficulties in learning about the environment and in modulating behaviour. Consequently, 'normalizing' the hearing process was thought to improve the individuals' attention to auditory cues and help to promote social engagement, which often involves multiple types of auditory stimulation (Bettison, 1996; Porges, 1998). Thus, although improved sound processing is a primary treatment goal, potentially more important goals of AIT include promoting attention, arousal, language and social skills. As noted previously, individuals with ASD can show altered sensitivities to auditory stimulation (see also Dawson et al., 2000; present Chapter 2) and such disruptions to processing auditory stimuli (e.g. hyper-sensitivity to sound) has also been suggested to lead to the development of social difficulties.

There are a number of different forms of AIT (e.g. Berard, 1982; Porges, 1998; Tomatis, 1991), but all of these approaches follow a similar basic pattern to one another. For example, auditory tests may indicate that an individual has auditory hyper-sensitivities to particular frequencies, but their perception of other frequencies is normal. If this is the case, then that individual may be a candidate for AIT, as they may become distressed in the presence of those sounds with the frequencies to which they are hyper-sensitive. In these cases, the goal of AIT would be to 'normalize' the hearing response across all frequencies in an effort to overcome these problems.

To rectify these sensitivities, the 'Berard' treatment (Berard, 1982) consists of the participant listening to music that has been modified to remove the frequencies to which there are hyper-sensitivities. The AIT also attempts to reduce the predictability of the auditory patterns in order to promote generalization of attention to sounds. Sometimes the volume level for the left ear is reduced, as it is thought that this will stimulate language development in the left hemisphere of the brain.

The 'Tomatis' method (Tomatis, 1991; see Gilmor, 1999, for a review) is similar to the Berard treatment, but it integrates a psycho-physiological aspect that utilizes filtered maternal-voice sounds, in addition to music, as well as exposing the participant to language and audio-vocal exercises, to reinforce 'normal' auditory perception in these domains. Another variation of AIT, which often is applied to children with ASD, is the 'Porges Acoustic Intervention' (Porges, 1998). In this latter approach, filtered sounds, produced by a human voice, are presented to the individual; a procedure that is designed to repeatedly 'challenge' and 'relax' the muscles of the middle ear, with the aim of facilitating speech perception. Irrespective of whether or not any of the alleged physiological responses are involved in any of these treatments, it can be seen that all of them involve the presentation of manipulated sounds to a client in order to improve their reactions to that sound.

Service delivery models

The 'Bernard' form of AIT is typically provided on a 1:1 basis, in a sound-proof quiet room, for 30-minute sessions, usually with two sessions a day, over a period of 10–20 days. Most often the procedure is conducted in a clinic setting, but, occasionally, such auditory treatments can be provided within a school setting. The equipment used comprises a modulating and filtering device (e.g. 'Ears Education & Retraining System', Audiokinetron), which transforms auditory stimuli by randomly modulating high and low frequencies and filtering out the targeted frequencies.

The Tomatis method is performed in a similar way to that described previously, but often involves repeated blocks of auditory intervention and with longer overall intervention durations – sometimes spanning a period of years. The Porges intervention typically employs five, 45-minute sessions. There have been no direct comparison studies of the impact of these different auditory integration techniques and there are not enough studies of each procedure to allow a picture of their relative effectiveness to be developed.

Outcome-effectiveness evidence for AIT

A number of reviews have gauged the strength of the evidence regarding the outcome-effectiveness of AIT (Baranek, 2002; Dawson & Watling, 2000; Sinha et al., 2006; 2011). These reviews have typically concluded that the evidence for AIT for individuals with ASD is, at best, equivocal (Baranek, 2002; Dawson & Watling, 2000). For example, Sinha et al. (2006; see also Goldstein, 2000; Sinha et al., 2011) concluded that, although there were no contra-indications for the use of AIT, there was not sufficient evidence to support its use for people with ASD.

As with the studies relating to SIT, a problem in collating the evidence from the various outcome-effectiveness studies relating to this programme, is that, while many studies of this intervention actually do employ standardized instruments (e.g. Bettison, 1996; Mudford et al., 2000) and there are also a high proportion of RCTs in these reports (Bettison, 1996; Corbett et al., 2008; Edelson et al., 1999; Mudford et al., 2000; Rimland & Edelson, 1995; Veale, 1993; Zollweg et al., 1997), the manner in which the data is presented in many of these studies does not lend itself to any form of meta-analysis (see Sinha et al., 2011, for further discussion of this problem). To overcome such issues, a similar approach to that used previously in categorizing the outcomes of SIT studies was employed for AIT: that is, the studies were classified as reporting 'positive', 'mixed' or 'negative' outcomes.

Table 10.2 shows the studies reported for AIT for people with ASD that are described in the various reviews of sensory treatments. Table 10.2 also presents the functioning domains examined in the individual studies (i.e. cognitive, behaviour and sensory processing). The outcomes associated with each intervention study are shaded, such that a light shaded background implies a positive outcome, a medium shaded background implies a mixed outcome and a dark shaded background implies a negative outcome.

The studies included participants with a wide range of ages (from 3 to 39 years of age) and the data were taken following a variety of periods after the treatment, from 3 months to 14 months, with the majority of post-intervention measures being around 3–6 months

Table 10.2 Studies of Auditory Integration Therapy, including the functioning domains investigated and their outcomes.

Study	Year	Domains Investigated	Outcome
Bettison	1996	Behaviour, Cognition, Sensory, Social	Mixed
Brown	1999	Sensory	Positive
Corbett et al.	2008	Cognition. Social	Negative
Gillberg et al.	1997	Behaviour	Negative
Link	1997	Behaviour, Sensory	Mixed
Mudford et al.	2000	Behaviour, Cognition	Negative
Neysmith-Roy	2001	Behaviour	Mixed
Rimland & Edelson	1995	Behaviour, Sensory	Mixed
Rimland & Edelson	1994	Behaviour, Sensory	Positive
Veale	1993	Behaviour, Sensory	Negative
Zollweg et al.	1997	Sensory	Negative

White = strong effect; light grey = moderate effect; and dark grey = weak effect.

after the treatment. The analysis in Table 10.2 shows that, of these studies, three out of 11 (27%) showed a positive result – although one of these positive studies presented case reports from a very small sample (Brown, 1999). Another three of the studies (27%) demonstrated a mixed set of outcomes, showing improvements in some but not all, of the functioning domains that were measured. The remaining five studies (46%) showed no evidence of improvement in any domain, although none of these studies indicated any adverse effects of the auditory integration training (Sinha et al., 2011).

This pattern of results supports the conclusions form the majority of reviews of this treatment and suggests that AIT has only marginal and inconsistent results with regard to its outcomes for ASD (Dawson & Watling, 2000; Sinha et al., 2006; 2011). Moreover, in terms of the specific areas of functioning assessed, the pattern for the impact of AIT was also unclear, with none of the domains (cognitive, behaviour or sensory processing) showing consistent positive or negative outcomes.

Particularly problematic for this intervention is that, although some of these studies did show improvement in functioning as a result of exposure to the AIT, none of the studies that included a comparison group demonstrated any consistent patterns of benefit from AIT relative to that comparison group. The study that demonstrated the greatest level of gain relative to the comparison was reported by Bettison (1996), with the vast majority of the other studies showing equivalent performance across the intervention and comparison groups. This pattern of results has suggested to some that it may be the 'peripheral' aspects of the treatment, such as the attention given to the client, its impact on the parents' functioning and their abilities to manage their child and so on, which are responsible for any improvements noted (Baranek, 2002). However, it should be noted that the majority of these studies employed RCT techniques, which, from examination of the ABA programmes reported in Chapter 5, have been shown to produce the lowest levels of gain versus a comparison group and a different set of study designs may have come to a different conclusion.

Visual Therapies

'Visual therapies' focus on enhancing different aspects of visual processing or rectifying deficits in visual-spatial perception, in the client (Rapin, 1996b). These therapies often include the use of ocular-motor exercises, prism lenses and Irlen lenses (which filter certain colours). There are a number of examples of 'visual therapy' being attempted for people with ASD (see Baranek, 2002, for a review). According to the proponents of these interventions, visual processing deficits are related to certain symptoms of ASD, such as coordination and attention problems and the intervention aims to rectify these sensory problems in order to alleviate these ASD-related symptoms.

However, of the various forms of sensory therapy, this form is the least extensively investigated and probably the least administered, in the context of ASD. In part, this lack of application may simply reflect the long-standing notion that visual routes to learning are actually favoured in individuals with ASD (Behrmann et al., 2006; Quill, 1997) and that there is rather limited evidence that vision is a major area of impairment associated with ASD. However, there are some reports of impaired visual-motor abilities for individuals with ASD (Rapin, 1996b; Rumsey & Hamburger, 1990), but it is difficult to know whether these deficits are the product of the co-ordination and ataxic problems that are also associated with ASD (Dawson & Watlin, 2000) rather than being visual problems *per se*. Similarly, there are numerous reports of differences in the eye-gaze patterns in people with ASD compared to non-ASD comparison groups (e.g. Bal et al., 2010; Klin et al., 2002), which might reflect visual processing deficits. However, these differences may well reflect other issues, such as aversions to the socially related cues that are often used in these eye-tracking studies.

Of the available visual therapy approaches, the use of prism lenses appears to be intervention that has attracted some research activity in the context of ASD (Baranek, 2002). The prism lenses used in this visual therapy alter the passage of light through particular angles, which results in a shift in the visual field. Theoretically, this produces greater stability in the individual's perception and removes the distortions in stimuli that may lead to impaired performance or, in some cases, behavioural problems (Kaplan et al., 1996).

Two studies of the impact of prism lenses for individuals with ASD have been reported, which, unfortunately, have produced different results from one another. The study with the strongest evidence for the effectiveness of the treatment was reported by Carmody et al. (2001), who tested prism lenses for 24 people with ASD (aged 3–18 years). All of the participants were assessed for their spatial orientation and spatial abilities in three conditions: (i) no lenses; (ii) prisms using 'upward' visual deflections and (iii) prisms using 'downward' deflections. One of the lens conditions (upward or downward) was the participant's correct condition and the other was an interfering lenses condition. The results suggested that orientation and visual-spatial abilities, improved in the correct lens condition, as opposed to the no lens condition or the interfering lens condition. However, no standardized assessments of ability were employed in this study and there was no indication of the long-term effects of the treatment.

A less positive set of findings was reported by Kaplan et al. (1998; see also Kaplan et al., 1996, for an initial report on the same data), who randomly allocated 18 individuals with ASD (aged approximately 6–18 years) into one of two conditions: (i) a lens treatment group and (ii) a placebo lens group. The lenses were worn for 3 months and then the group assignment was reversed and changes in the participants' posture, vision, cognitive abilities (attention) and behaviour were measured. It was noted that the behavioural measures improved in the short-term after the application of the lenses, but that this improvement in behaviour diminished over time. However, there was no difference between the conditions regarding improvement in posture or visual-spatial tasks. That the central mechanism of the lenses is taken to be through improving vision and that this did not occur, suggests that any behavioural improvements that may have occurred could have been the result of extra-intervention factors (e.g. attention, effects on the family).

Thus, there is little consistent evidence either that visual difficulties reflects a serious problem for many people with ASD, that any such problems that do exist result in a worsening of symptoms of ASD or that correcting for visual problems remedies these symptoms.

Physical Stimulation Therapies

There are a wide variety of interventions that fall under the general rubric of 'physical stimulation therapies'; all of these treatments share a belief that some form of physical contact with the person with ASD will be beneficial for the client, although there are a very wide range of theories about why this form of intervention might be successful. One of the earliest recommended interventions for ASD could be said to fall under this category of treatment: 'holding therapy' (Tinbergen & Tinbergen, 1983; see Welsh, 1989) assumed that a fundamental deficit in ASD related to poor parental attachment and that this could be overcome through a reduction in the anxiety produced by physical contact (see Chapter 3). Although the theoretical basis for the development of such an intervention has been repeatedly challenged and many reviews do not consider this approach as contemporary (Ospina et al., 2008), there has recently been a resurgence in the use of physical stimulation techniques (see Lee et al., 2011, for a recent discussion). For example, Grandin (1984; Grandin & Scariano, 1986) developed a 'holding' or 'squeeze' machine for use with people with ASD (see also Edelson et al., 1999, for a related approach). Moreover, there are increasing uses of 'massage therapies' (e.g. Escalona et al., 2001) or 'touch therapies' (e.g. Field et al., 1997), in the context of ASD.

In fact, Green et al. (2006; see also Hess et al., 2008) reports that between 4% and 8% of parents report use of some such 'physical stimulation' approach to the treatment of their children with ASD and there are now a number of reviews of this area (e.g. Lee et al., 2011). Given the relatively widespread usage of such treatments, but acknowledging their espoused philosophical differences, the main forms of these contemporary physical stimulation interventions will be reviewed separately from one another next. While this preserves the theoretical differences between them, it also has the effect of reducing the numbers of outcome-effectiveness studies that each sort of approach can draw upon and the following review will be of a narrative rather than analytic nature.

Holding or squeezing therapies

These forms of intervention derive from a variety of theoretical perspectives (see Heflin & Simpson, 1998, for a review), most involving some suggestion that ASD is, either in whole or in large part, the product of an attachment problem (see Raz, 2013;

Tinbergen & Tinbergen, 1972; Zaslow & Breger, 1969, for discussion of some of the underlying attachment work). As briefly mentioned in Chapter 3, the original holding therapy was suggested as a means of re-bonding the child with the parent by Tinbergen and Tinbergen (1983), but has since been developed and popularized by Welsh (1989) and, in an altered form, by Grandin (1992; see also Blairs et al., 2007). The inclusion of the latter form of intervention (the 'squeeze machine' or 'deep-touch therapy') in the same section as holding therapy might appear somewhat controversial (see Raz, 2013) and others have avoided drawing such comparisons (Heflin & Simpson, 1998). However, it seems to be the case that Grandin (1992) does consider there to be some similarities between the two and so the current work combines the two approaches. It should also be noted that, as holding therapy is based on notions of attachment disorder, it is not exclusively viewed as a treatment for ASD (Heflin & Simpson, 1998), but has been applied in the context of people with attachment disorder itself (Dozier, 2003; Magid & McKelvey, 1987), people with high levels of aggression (Myeroff et al., 1999) and otherwise vulnerable children (Dozier, 2003).

Implementation   Original holding therapy involves forced contact with the person with ASD for a fixed period of time or until the person with ASD (usually a child) looks at the therapist (usually a parent) who is administering the intervention (Stades-Veth, 1988; Welsh, 1989). Given the aversion to social and physical contact often exhibited by individuals with ASD, this process is often accompanied by a deal of anxiety and emission of externalizing behaviours on the part of the child with ASD, which, according to holding therapy, must be resisted by the therapist, who should continue with the hold until these behaviour reduce in intensity and frequency and the person looks at the therapist (see Stades-Veth, 1988, for a description). This physical contact – termed 'holding time' (Welsh, 1989) – is suggested to occur for long periods of the day, with no more than a 2-hour break between each session. In this way, it is hoped to restore the bond between parent and child (see Heflin & Simpson, 1998, for a less than sympathetic description).

   The 'squeeze machine' approach outlined by Grandin (1992) shares some features with holding therapy, although it is essentially asocial in nature. This intervention involves the person with ASD being placed in a machine that applies pressure to the individual, over most of their body, for a set period for between 5 and 15 minutes (see Grandin, 1984, 1992, for a description). The procedure connected to the use of this machine involves the individual controlling the pressure that is applied to them-selves through the use of controls. More recent implementations of such a form of therapy have been termed 'deep-touch therapies' and involve short-term physical pressure being applied to the person, usually provided by rolling them in a blanket, under non-aversive circumstances and accompanied by engagement in social activities such as being read to (see Blairs et al., 2007; Zissermann, 1992, for case reports).

Outcome-effectiveness evidence   There is a limited amount of evidence available on the impacts of either holding therapy or of the squeeze machine (see Grandin, 1992; Heflin & Simpson, 1998, for reviews), although there are rather more case reports for the latter of these approaches than for the former (e.g. Blairs et al., 2007, see Grandin, 1992, for further examples).

   In terms of holding therapy, most of the evidence presented concerning the approach comes from a paper published by Stades-Veth (1988), although there are

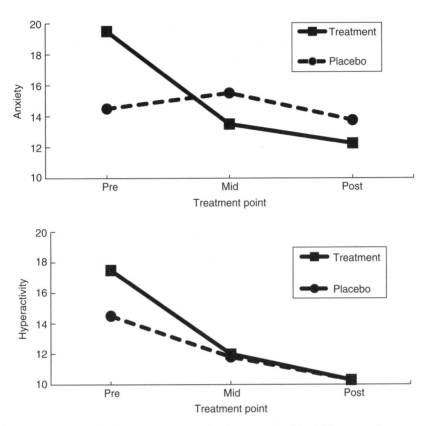

Figure 10.2 Effect of exposure to an operative 'squeeze machine' (Treatment) versus exposure to the non-operative apparatus (Placebo), reported by Edelson et al. (1999). Top panel shows parent-rated anxiety for the children with ASD and the bottom panel shows parent-rated hyperactivity for the children.

anecdotal reports of success contained in the works on the topic published by Tinbergen and Tinbergen (1983) and also by Welsh (1989). Stades-Veth (1988) reported the results of one large-scale observational study conducted using this approach for 104 individuals. These participants had a variety of disorders, including some with ASD. It was reported that 30% of the sample reported clinically significant changes in social relatedness, with some reports of people with ASD appearing 'cured'. Unfortunately, the details of the report are extremely vague from an evaluation viewpoint and it is difficult to know what to conclude on the bases of these data (see also Heflin & Simpson, 1998, for similar concerns).

The squeeze machine (Grandin, 1984) or more recently deep-touch therapy (Blairs et al., 2007; Zissermann, 1992), has produced a number a case reports suggesting that this procedure results in reductions in anxiety resulting from physical contact or, in some cases, from social contact. However, there is still only one outcome-effectiveness study that has been conducted on this approach. Edelson et al. (1999) compared the impact of the squeeze machine with that of exposure to a non-operative squeeze machine using an RCT procedure. Participants received the treatment or apparatus exposure for two 20-minute sessions over a 6-week period and the changes in a range of physiological and informant rated indices of anxiety were noted. Figure 10.2 shows the outcomes for this study.

Participants in the squeeze-machine group demonstrated significantly greater reductions in levels of parent-rated anxiety and tension, compared to the comparison group who received only apparatus-exposure (see Figure 10.2). However, this mainly reflected the increased anxiety of the treatment group prior to their experience of being 'squeezed'. The pattern of outcomes when the physiological data were explored were less clear, suggesting that the technique did improve some aspects of this measure of anxiety (i.e. GSR responses), which corroborates the impressions given by Grandin (1992). However, this effect was much more pronounced in the participants who had high levels of physiological-indexed anxiety initially. This latter finding chimes with the comments of Blairs et al. (2007) on the basis of their case report, who suggest the procedure may help with highly anxious individuals.

Massage therapies

Massage therapy has been widely applied for a large variety of different problems and has received a number of reviews in terms of its general effectiveness (Field, 1988; Field et al., 2007). Most of these uses have been for physical problems, often including as part of the management strategy for chronic pain (Field et al., 2007). However, more recently these techniques have been applied for psychological issues and have been effective especially in the area of anxiety-related problems (see Jackson et al., 2008, for an example).

Perhaps due to the prevalence of co-morbid anxiety with ASD (Bradley et al., 2004), rather than its similarity to the touch therapies, discussed previously, massage therapies have begun to be used in the treatment of ASD (Escalona et al., 2001; Silva et al., 2007; see Lee et al., 2011, for a review). A number of different approaches to massage therapy have been adopted, including traditional massage therapy as typically employed in physiotherapy and occupational therapy (Field et al., 2007) and increasing uses of traditional Thai (Piravej et al., 2009) and Qigong (Silva, 2011) massage techniques. These techniques are briefly outlined next, but it is currently impossible to determine if any one of them is superior to any other, nor, indeed, to determine if they operate on different principles – other than their underlying philosophies. Nor is it possible to isolate which are the key ingredients of the different processes. Given this situation and that, basically, all massage techniques involve the social application of physical stimulation, the outcomes of these approaches will be discussed together.

Implementation

Traditional massage A typical intervention using this approach was described by Field et al. (1997), from which the following description has been summarized. Participants are typically given two, 15-minute sessions of massage per week, for about 8 weeks. The massage technique involves a number of 'stroking' movements across the client's head and neck, arms and hands, torso and legs and feet. Each of the 'stroking' movements lasts about 10–15 s and each region of the body is 'stroked' about five or six times in a set order, according to a prescribed sequence. During this period the client is in a prone position.

Traditional Thai massage This variant of massage therapy was described by Piravej et al. (2009). The practitioner leans on the client's body with their arms locked to allow the application of pressure and the client's body can be held still with the legs (mirrored in the deep touch approach noted previously, see Blairs et al., 2007). During a session, there would be pressing and stretching of the entire body, which, is given according to a pre-set order. A full session typically lasts two hours or more, but it can be delivered during a shorter session and the treatment sessions for people with are typically given over an 8-week period (Piravej et al., 2009).

Qigong massage   Silva (2011) has outlined the use of this form of treatment for people with ASD ('Qigong Massage for Your Child with Autism: A Home Program from Chinese Medicine'). Although the massage has traditionally been performed by therapists, in the context of ASD, it has been adapted to be used by parents. The protocol takes 15 minutes for the parents to deliver, usually just prior to the child going to sleep. The massage comprises a pre-specified sequence of 12 movements, which have assumed theoretical mechanisms of action to: promote circulation to the brain; clear functional impediments of the ear; promote social interaction, speech and self-regulation; strengthen digestion and to calm the child and improve sleep. Although these are all areas noted as in need of attention in ASD, there is little evidence to suggest that specific movement do indeed impact on these precise areas. Such a qigong programme can be followed for up to 5 months (Silva et al., 2007).

Outcome-effectiveness results   The results of studies of massage therapies have often been reported in terms of case studies, but there are a number of reports of controlled studies of their impact. These were reviewed by Lee et al. (2011), who noted some evidence of effectiveness across the studies, especially in terms of the improvement of sensory responsiveness and adaptive-social functioning, but they also noted that most of these investigations adopted different procedures from one another and employed relatively small sample sizes. In addition, it was noted that many of the outcome measures were informant-rated indices of functioning and that these could have been influenced by expectations of improvement. Nevertheless, some of these studies do appear to tell a converging story in terms of the areas of impact of massage therapy.

Impact of intervention   As noted in a number of reviews (Lee et al., 2011) there are now a number of studies that have assessed the impact of massage therapies, across a number of functioning domains, for people with ASD. These studies have primarily been delivered to children with ASD between the ages of 3 and 6 years old, who have a range of functioning abilities – although they tend to fall on the higher-range of functioning (Escalona et al., 2001; Field et al., 1997). The interventions, typically, for about 4–5 months in duration and involve between two and seven weekly sessions during this time.

These studies are shown in Table 10.3, which shows the nature of the study (RCT, controlled trial or observational study), the type of massage therapy and whether the massage therapy was delivered primarily by a therapist or by a combination of therapist and parent. Inspection of these data shows that most of these studies have been conducted by two groups of researchers, which is not in itself a problem, although it is always stronger to see a number of replications across different sites. Table 10.3 also shows the effect sizes (Cohen's *d*) for pre-therapy to post-therapy change in the

Table 10.3 Outcomes of studies of massage therapies, showing type of massage (MT = Traditional; QM = Qigong; TM = Thai), whether the therapy was therapist or parent delivered, as well as the pre- to post-intervention changes effect sizes (ES).

Study	Year	Trial Type	Massage Type	Lead By	Autism ES	Social ES	Behaviour ES	Sensory ES
Escalona et al.	2001	RCT	MT	Par			0.44	
Field et al.	1997	Cont	MT	Ther	0.53	0.55	0.44	0.69
Piravaj et al.	2008	Cont	TM	Ther			0.22	
Silva & Cignolini	2005	Obs	QM	Par	1.21	0.67		0.67
Silva et al.	2007	Cont	QM	Par	0.64	0.80		1.44
Silva et al.	2008	RCT	QM	Par	0.96	0.75		1.11
Silva et al.	2008	Obs	QM	Ther	0.66	0.41		0.84
Silva et al.	2009	RCT	QM	Par	0.71	0.31	0.66	0.90
Silva et al.	2011	RCT	QM	Par	1.03	0.27	0.66	0.79
Silva & Schalock	2013	RCT	QM	Par			0.99	0.62

Autism = autistic severity; Social = social functioning; Behaviour = challenging behaviours; Sensory = sensory sensitivities. White = strong effect; light grey = moderate effect; dark grey = weak effect; black = no data.

different domains assessed (shaded so that a light cell background is a strong effect size $d > 0.70$; a medium cell background is a moderate effect size, $d = 0.31$ to 0.69 and a dark cell background is a weak effect size, $d < 0.30$).

These studies differ somewhat in nature from assessments of other interventions, in that they rarely focus on intellectual or linguistic functioning and instead focus on the impact of the therapy on the ASD symptomatology, social communication abilities, behaviour problems and sensory sensitivities of the participants. In terms of the ASD symptoms, these were almost always measured by the parent-rated Autism Behaviour Checklist (ABC) rather than objective assessments such as the Autism Diagnostic Observation Schedule. However, adaptive-social functioning was typically assessed using the VABS and behaviour problems frequently measured by the Connor's Rating Scales. The sensory sensitivities were assessed by a variety of direct observations and parent ratings. The focus on core ASD problems is, of course, a strength in that the reports assess the impacts of therapy on ASD itself, but it is also a limitation in that the lack of objective data from standardized assessments makes their interpretation more vulnerable to bias effects (Lee et al., 2011).

The effect sizes were calculated on the basis of the data provided in the papers – sometimes this did not include the standard deviations of the samples, in which case the known population standard deviation of the scale was employed and sometimes the effect size was constructed from the statistical test result. Hence, these effect sizes should be used only as estimates of this statistic for these studies. It would be helpful in future studies if all of the basic data were presented to allow these calculations.

Looking at the impact on ASD severity, it can be seen that most of the studies that measured this aspect of functioning (e.g. Silva & Cignolini, 2005; Silva et al., 2008; 2011) produced moderate to large size effects (mean = 0.85 ± 0.21; range = 0.64–1.11). This result is quite striking, as it stands in contrast to the results from many other

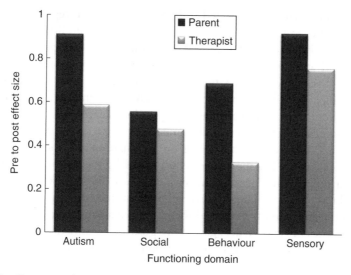

Figure 10.3 Outcomes for studies of massage therapies that were delivered primarily by parents or by therapists. Parent-delivered massage produced greater gains.

intervention studies, which have shown this aspect of functioning to be somewhat resistant to intervention-produced change (see Chapters 5, 7 and 8).

Adaptive-social behavioural functioning showed a range of different effect sizes from weak (e.g. Silva et al., 2011), through moderate (e.g. Field et al., 1997), to large (e.g. Silva et al., 2008). The mean effect size for adaptive-social functioning was 0.54 (±0.23; range = 0.27–0.80). Similarly, there was a range in the effect sizes for improvements in behavioural functioning (mean = 0.57 ± 0.26; range = 0.22–0.99), with most of the studies showing moderate effect sizes, except (Pirajev et al., 2008 – weak and Silva & Schalock, 2013 – strong).

Almost all of the studies demonstrated moderate to strong changes in sensory processing over the course of the treatment; mean effect size = 0.89 (±0.30; range = 0.62–1.44). However, a noteworthy feature of these data is that there is no association between the size of the effect on sensory processing and any of the other variables (correlations between the sensory effect size and: ASD severity effect size = –0.271; social-adaptive behaviour effect size = 0.548 and behavioural functioning effect size = –0.358). If the massage therapy were working on sensory processing, as sometimes suggested (see previous), then stronger correlations between these variables might be expected.

One distinction that can be drawn between the studies is whether the massage was primarily delivered by a therapist (e.g. Field et al., 1997; Piravej et al., 2008; Silva et al., 2008) or by a combination of a therapist and the parents. Separating out these two sets of studies and calculating the mean effect size shows a rather striking difference in the mean effect sizes depending on the primary deliverer of the treatment, which are shown in Figure 10.3. These data show a much greater improvement in ASD severity and in behaviour problems, in the parent-led groups compared to the therapist-led groups. There was a smaller advantage to the parent-led group in terms of social-adaptive behaviour and sensory processing. These overall findings were also mirrored in the one report that directly compared the two approaches. Silva et al. (2008) reported data for the same massage technique, administered for the same duration and so on, by either parents or a therapist (although they were collected at different times). This report noted that there was twice the effect size of ASD severity (1.21 versus 0.66) and 30% greater effect size for adaptive-social behaviour (0.84 versus 0.67), for the parent-led approaches. However, the therapist-led approach had a stronger effect on sensory processing (0.84 versus 0.67). Coupled with the considerations previously regarding the lack of relationship between the impact of the therapy on sensory processing and the other variables, this suggests that some other factors may be at play in this intervention.

One possibility is that the intervention impacts as much on the parents who administer the massage intervention, as it does on the children and the superiority of the parent- versus therapist-led approaches is explained by this factor. Indeed, there are some data to support this suggestion. Silva et al. (2011; see also Silva & Schalock, 2013) noted reductions in parenting stress after administering the intervention. This might mean that the parents perceived their children's behaviours in a more positive light (see Fong, 1991) and, hence, gave more positive assessments of the same behaviours after the intervention. Alternatively, improvements in parenting stress are associated with improvements in limit setting abilities of parents (Osborne & Reed, 2010), which could have resulted in the improved child behaviour problems after the massage. In line with this suggestion, Lee (2008) have noted that parent-led massage promotes levels of attachment in those parents, as did both Cullen-Powell et al. (2005) and also Zhou and Zhang (2008) or increases in the degree to which parent-child behaviours become synchronized (see Chapters 8 and 9). The fact that Figure 10.3 shows larger improvements in child behaviour for parent-led massage therapies might tend to support this view. Whichever of these alternatives proves correct (and they are not mutually exclusive), coupled with a lack of evidence for modulation by sensory processing, it suggests that the mechanism of action may not be through neurological mechanisms (see also the rather pithy, if accurate, comment by Wiwanitkit, 2010).

Outcomes compared to control conditions   A number of the studies of massage therapy have also included comparison groups and have shown typically positive findings in favour of the massage therapy. These comparison groups have included waiting list controls (Silva et al., 2009; 2011), alternative treatment groups, such as sensory integration therapy (Piravej et al., 2008) and attention-matched groups (Escalona et al., 2001; Field et al., 1997). The studies vary tremendously from one another in terms of the measures employed, making summative analysis of the effect size data difficult. However, in no case did the control group outperform the massage therapy group.

In terms of traditional massage, Field et al. (1997) compared the effects of massage therapy with relaxation techniques (playing a game with the child) for 11 children with ASD (aged 4–5 years old) per group. The treatments were given twice a week, for 15 minutes a session, by a therapist over a 4-week period. The group receiving the massage intervention showed improvements in their ASD severity, as measured by the parent-rated ABC and also showed reduced levels of aversion to physical contact and stereotyped movements. However, both groups improved in terms of their 'attentiveness' to task. Escalona et al. (2001) reported the results of an RCT which compared the impact of a parent-led traditional massage therapy versus attention (reading). The interventions were each given for 15 minutes a day by the parents, just prior to bedtime, for 1 month, on 10 children with ASD (aged 3–6 years old). The results demonstrated less hyperactivity, stereotyped movement and sleep disturbance in the children undergoing the massage therapy relative to the control group.

Silva and colleagues (Silva et al., 2007; 2009; 2011) have compared groups of children (aged 3–6 years) receiving Qigong massage therapy to matched children in a waiting list control. The therapy is, typically, delivered over a 5-month period and the results have variously noted advantages for the massage therapy group in terms of sensory and adaptive-social behaviours (Silva et al., 2007), social skills and behaviour problems (Silva et al., 2009) and in terms of parent-rated ASD symptoms (Silva et al., 2011). Many of these comparisons have used RCT (see Table 10.3) and so are regarded as methodological strong in that regard.

However, as noted by Lee et al. (2011), there is a high risk of bias in many of these studies of massage therapy, as very few studies have yet demonstrated an advantage over a control condition in terms of an objectively assessed measure. In this regard, Field et al. (1997) did report an advantage of massage therapy over attention-matched control in terms of assessor-rated early social communication skills. However, it is unclear if the raters in this study were blind to the nature of the intervention being presented.

Summary

The previous review of physical stimulation therapies has suggested that some of these approaches appear to have some evidence suggesting that they are effective. Although there is no evidence of impact on intellectual or linguistic functioning, there are apparent impacts on social and behavioural functioning. The degree to which the interventions are effective appears to be moderated by the levels of anxiety initially experienced by the participant – with the interventions appearing to have greater effects on more anxious individuals. The interventions also appear somewhat better suited to higher functioning individuals with ASD.

However, the effects of these treatments may be mediated through alteration of the social aspects of the interaction, rather than on their assumed physiological impacts. In no cases are there any clear links between improved physiological responding and improvements in other areas of function, nor is there any strong evidence that such a theoretical link is substantiated. This leaves the suggestion, initially made by Tinbergen and Tinbergen (1983), that such therapies improve bonding between parent and child as potentially viable. Indeed, despite the outcry that this suggestion initially was greeted with, the evidence from these studies suggests that the impact on the parents may be as important to the success of the therapy (either perceived or actual) as the impact on the child. This discussion will be taken up in the final section that follows.

Overview of Sensory Therapies

The previous discussion indicates that sensory therapies, as 'comprehensive' interventions, will not suffice. It would be unfair to claim that many current practitioners believe that this is the case – although it is certainly the case that many proponents of these approaches do indicate that this is a possibility. Nevertheless, they could form an important component of many treatment packages and so it is important to understand their effectiveness; especially as strong advice against their use has been offered by some professional bodies and reports. There is no evidence to suggest that either auditory therapies, visual therapies or the initial forms of holding therapy help individuals with ASD. However, there is some indication that sensory integration therapy, to a lesser extent and massage therapies, to a greater extent, may help in developing social abilities of people with ASD – although not for the reasons suggested by its proponents. These interventions may also be better suited for slightly higher-functioning individuals with high levels of social anxiety.

These interventions could be unkindly described as 'poking and prodding' therapies, although from the perspective of a person with ASD this is how they may appear. Nevertheless, whether the participant is being rubbed in a massage therapy, squeezed in Grandin's machine or even being hosted in a suspension apparatus and poked with a stick, as in sensory integration therapy – the essential description is accurate. To summarize, those therapies that involve physical stimulation with a social aspect, which are non-aversive, fare better than those sensory interventions that do not fit this description. Moreover, those which involve the parent, fare better than those which involve only a therapist.

This suggests a two-pronged mechanism for these interventions. Firstly, they reduce sensory sensitivities to touch on the part of the person with ASD, through some form of exposure therapy, which makes social contact and interactions less aversive. Secondly, they can serve to improve attachment between a parent and their child, which would produce behavioural improvements due to improved parenting. The importance of the latter issue should not be overlooked – having parents provide such a form of intrusive therapy would be far more preferable for many reasons.

11

Eclectic Interventions

'Eclectic' interventions remain one of the most controversial approaches to the treatment of Autism Spectrum Disorders (ASD), both in terms of identifying their precise nature and in establishing their effectiveness. The term 'eclectic intervention' will be employed in the present text to refer to the use of a combination of treatment strategies, which are sometimes drawn from different comprehensive intervention approaches and sometimes from a variety of single-strategy approaches (see Chapter 1 for a discussion of such distinctions). This form of 'mixed' approach to the development of an intervention strategy for ASD does not necessarily follow a specific treatment ethos, as do many 'brand name' approaches, other than to help the person with ASD by tailoring an intervention specifically for that individual (see Lord & McGee, 2001; Stahmer & Mandell, 2007, for discussions). Despite the lack of 'branding' and some difficulties in establishing an 'identity', it has clearly been the case, for some time, that the majority of practitioners employ such eclectic approaches for individuals with ASD (Jordan et al., 1998; Kasari & Smith, 2013; Stahmer et al., 2005; Stahmer & Mandell, 2007) and this sort of approach is also very commonly used within school provisions for children with ASD (Frederickson et al., 2010; Kasari & Smith, 2013; Reed et al., 2007b).

Although in widespread use for ASD-related problems, the evidence-base in support of eclectic approaches is not as systematically documented or well publicized, as it is for some of the branded comprehensive interventions. It is undoubtedly this tension between the high degree of usage of eclectic interventions (see Jordan et al., 1998), coupled with the support for this usage provided by many education authorities (Lord & McGee, 2001; Parsons et al., 2009) and the lack of systematically presented evidence regarding their effectiveness (Dillenberger, 2011), which has caused a great deal of the argument surrounding the use of eclectic treatments.

Much of the debate surrounding the use of eclectic approaches has centred on the arguments presented by behavioural psychologists, who often contrast the evidence

---

base for behavioural programmes with the lack of widely available and clear evidence for eclectic programmes and who also point out that many of the components for eclectic approaches have little support in themselves (Dillenberger, 2011; Stahmer & Ingersoll, 2004). The tenor of such debates is perhaps not helped by the characterization of eclectic approaches as 'generic' (e.g. Lovaas, 1987), which certainly has some pejorative overtones. Neither is it aided by the frequent relegation of the study of eclectic approaches to control conditions within studies of other interventions (e.g. Eldevik et al., 2006). Leaving aside the heated nature of some of exchanges, it appears important to set out the basic cases for and against the use of eclectic interventions, as this will inform reading the evidence that the rest of the chapter presents.

The case against the use of eclectic interventions, as noted previously, is that it is difficult to know what such an approach comprises and, hence, almost impossible to establish an evidence base by which to judge its effectiveness (Dillenberger, 2011). Certainly, it is important to note that there are no specific characteristics or components that must be applied within an eclectic intervention; there are no limits on what types of strategies may be combined or on the number of approaches that may be adapted to fit with an eclectic package. For example, an eclectic treatment might combine elements from just two approaches, such as the Treatment and Education of Autistic and Related Communication Handicapped Children (TEACCH; Schopler & Reichler, 1971) programme and an Applied Behaviour Analysis (ABA) approach (Farrell et al., 2005; Jónsdóttir et al., 2007) or the approach could combine multiple methods drawn from Speech and Language Therapy, Occupational Therapy, Physiotherapy and Portage (Drew et al., 2002).

Some examples of these combinations may serve to illustrate the nature of the approach and the problems it presents for determining effectiveness. Of course, there are many eclectic interventions that employ well-validated components. For example, within the intervention studied by Akstinas (2006), the Picture Exchange Communication System (PECS®; Frost & Bondy, 2002) was included and improvements in speech and social behaviour, as well as a reduction in problematic behaviour, was noted for three participants with ASD (Charlop-Christy et al., 2002). Social Stories™ (Karkhaneh et al., 2010) can often be found within eclectic approaches (Reed et al., 2007b) and this approach been reported to both decrease disruptive behaviour (Crozier & Tincani, 2005) and to increase appropriate social interaction, for some individuals with ASD (Scattone et al., 2006). Similarly, Speech and Language Therapy (SLT) is commonly found within eclectic interventions (Gabriels et al., 2001; Howard et al., 2005; Stahmer & Ingersoll 2004; Tsang et al., 2007) and the number of hours of SLT received at an early age is a predictor of later language skills (Stone & Yoder, 2001; but see Osborne & Reed, 2008).

Although it is certainly the case that positive results have been documented for many of the strategies that are often employed within an eclectic intervention, for some other elements that often are included in these programmes there is not such clear positive evidence. For example, facilitated communication, auditory integration and Holding Therapy, which are included in some eclectic intervention programmes, have little support in the context of ASD (see Chapter 10). Occupational Therapy also is often included in eclectic intervention (Drew et al., 2002; Sallows & Graupner, 2005; Sheinkopf & Siegel, 1998; Tsang et al., 2007), however, as an ASD-intervention alone, it remains largely unsupported (Dawson & Watling, 2000; Chapter 10).

Importantly for many critiques of eclectic approaches, there is little clear evidence that the combination of successful individual strategies does not actually dilute their impact when they are presented in 'compound'. Certainly, this degree of strategy inclusiveness can result in a wide variation between different eclectic programmes and, as a result, make it difficult to know whether such 'packages' may hold any validity. For example, McConkey et al. (2007, p.20) have argued that: '...within the literature on ASD, the meaning of the term "eclectic" is not always clear and it is not always possible to identify what theories or models, are being used to support practice.' Given the diverse nature of eclectic packages and the patchy evidence relating to the often-employed components, it is unclear how much of a scientific base many of these treatments can claim to possess. At the extreme of this line of argument, it is often suggested that there is little evidence for the effectiveness of *any* eclectic package (Dillenberger, 2011; Howard et al., 2005). Moreover, the lack of clear evidence in support of the impact of these interventions has also been related to the short- and long-term cost-effectiveness of eclectic approaches, which have been compared unfavourably with behavioural interventions (Chasson et al., 2007; Jacobson et al., 1998).

Although at the conclusion of the case against eclectic approaches, there is little to recommend the use of these approaches for ASD, the situation facing most practitioners is certainly not so simple or straightforward as the research literature would suggest. There are a number of important additional considerations relating to the continued widespread usage of eclectic approaches that need to be presented and these form the basis for the case for eclectic interventions.

Firstly, as Kasari and Smith (2013) have argued, although many comprehensive 'brand name' approaches to the treatment of ASD may have a degree of systematized evidence-base in their favour, such approaches may not fit well with the constraints under which many practitioners operate. For example, brand name approaches may not fit comfortably with legislation surrounding the education of individuals. It is often not a straightforward task to integrate many national curriculum requirements with the needs of implementing a comprehensive approach for ASD; for example, there may be problems in accommodating aspects of the Options-Son-Rise Programme (Kaufman, 1994) or perhaps even the Developmental, Individual-Difference, Relationship-Based Model (DIR®; see Wieder & Greenspan, 2003), into a school curriculum (although see Pajareya & Nopmaneejumruslers, 2011, for one such attempt). Of course, there are some comprehensive approaches that focus on behavioural change strategies, which would lend themselves to delivery in any curriculum, such as the Complete Application of Behaviour Analysis to Schooling (CABAS®; Greer, 1997) or TEACCH (Schopler & Reichler, 1971). However, many of these interventions require a degree of staff training and orientation that may not be possible to achieve within the confines of an organization with limited resources.

Secondly, it has been pointed out that eclectic approaches may offer a degree of flexibility for the professional or organization (Jordan, 2008; Lord & McGee, 2001). By their nature and lack of adherence to a single philosophy or a particular set of techniques, eclectic interventions allow professionals a greater opportunity to produce a treatment package that fits the constraints of the organization in which the professionals work. This flexibility may also allow the stronger pursuance of a person-centred intervention, that is to say an intervention that is tailored to the individual needs of the person with ASD (Jordan, 2008).

Finally and ultimately of more critical importance than the considerations previously, it should be recognized that there is actually growing evidence relating to the effectiveness of eclectic programmes for individuals with ASD. There are now in excess of 20 reports that have involved a group of individuals with ASD (mostly children) receiving an eclectic intervention. Admittedly, some of these programmes have been used as controls for comprehensive brand name approaches (e.g. Eldevik et al., 2006), but some of these programmes were actually the primary focus of the report (e.g. Farrell et al., 2005; Magiati et al., 2007). Thus, the characterization of eclectic approaches as having no evidence base is not as certain as it was some years ago – of course, the mere existence of an evidence base does not mean that the evidence-base is supportive.

Given this set of ongoing issues and debates, the current chapter has three main aims: firstly, to present clarification regarding the types of components that are typically seen in eclectic approaches; secondly, to collate the evidence relating to the outcome-effectiveness of these approaches in terms of their impact on the major functioning domains usually studied in such reports (intellectual, language, social and ASD symptoms) and finally, to highlight the predictors of the success of such programmes, including the characteristics of the individuals who benefit most and also regarding the components that seem to produce the best outcomes.

The Nature of Eclectic Interventions

Most contemporary proponents of an eclectic approach define this form of intervention as comprising the careful selection of evidence-based strategies in response to the needs of the child as revealed by on-going assessment (Stahmer & Mandell, 2007). While this might sound vague in terms of a programme specification, it should be noted that it is not dissimilar to the overarching philosophy of an applied behavioural approach (Chapter 4). Indeed, programmes operating according to this approach have recently been characterized as 'technical eclectic' programmes (Odom et al., 2012), in recognition of their focus on data-driven strategy.

However, Rogers (1998) made the strong point that what gets studied under the term eclectic in outcome-effectiveness reports may not actually adhere to this type of technical approach. In fact, the understanding of eclectic programmes is hindered by the widespread tendency to use the term eclectic (often 'treatment as usual') to describe intervention packages employed as controls for the study of other comprehensive interventions (e.g. Eldevik et al., 2006; Tsang et al., 2007). Many of the eclectic groups that are included in such outcome-effectiveness studies are not only eclectic, in the sense that a single programme employing a combination of different component strategies is being examined, but also are eclectic in that the sample may cover a range of different 'technical eclectic' strategies being conducted cross multiple locations (Remington et al., 2007; Stahmer & Mandell, 2007) and, thus, may not reflect the operation of a designed 'technical eclectic' approach (Mandell et al., 2013; Reed et al., 2010).

There may be, then, at least three separate meanings subsumed within the literature concerning outcome-effectiveness of eclectic approaches: treatment as usual (a sampling of all potential strategies across different locations), generic (a combination of available methods) and technical eclectic (involving evidence-based individualized strategies). These distinctions will be addressed in this section – and understanding the diversity in the way such terms are used, goes some way to unpicking the range of evidence relating to this type of approach.

Given this it seems important to summarize what is known about the types of strategies that are most commonly used within eclectic approaches. There are two sources of evidence regarding what an eclectic approach typically comprises: firstly, there are a number of surveys that have been conducted in this regard (Frederickson et al., 2010; Machalicek et al., 2008; Stahmer et al., 2005; Stahmer & Mandell, 2007) and secondly, there are a range of reasonably well-documented eclectic packages that have been outlined in some detail (Eldevik et al., 2006; Farrell et al., 2005; Magiati et al., 2007; Reed et al., 2010).

Treatment as usual

The term *treatment as usual* can be taken to have pejorative connotations, but it is not meant to be understood in this way in the present context, where it refers to a grouping together of a number of approaches (often delivered across different centres). This group of eclectic treatments is often observed in studies where it acts as a control for another specific intervention package (Eldevik et al., 2006; Tsang et al., 2007). On the negative side, this means that the results of such programmes do not reflect the operation of a single intervention strategy – and, as such, they may not form the strongest comparison group available (see Reed et al., 2007b, for discussion). Consequently, this also could mean that some of the studies that employ such eclectic groups may confer an advantage to the target group (e.g. Remington et al., 2007). However, despite this concern, it is important to note that such groups may well reflect the true likelihood of improvement of an individual with ASD in the absence of a specific approach. Indeed, Stahmer and Mandell (2007) noted that the majority of services provided would fall within this type (see also Jordan, 1998).

A number of reviews have identified the key types of treatment that are typically presented to individuals with ASD – usually during their pre-school or school years (Frederickson et al., 2010; Machalicek et al., 2008; Stahmer et al., 2005). Two of these studies, Frederickson et al. (2010) and Stahmer et al. (2005) used practitioner interviews to characterize typical eclectic provision for children with ASD. In the study reported by Stahmer et al. (2005), four focus groups, involving early intervention providers, were conducted with participants in the USA and included both home-based and centre-based provisions. In a similar study conducted in the UK, Frederickson et al. (2010) interviewed staff working in mainstream schools that catered for individuals with ASD. One member of staff in each school was identified as the professional with the best overview of provision in that school and this person provided the information.

Figure 11.1 shows the main types of strategy employed in the two different studies (Frederickson et al., 2010; Stahmer et al., 2005). The differences between the results of these two studies are readily apparent from even a cursory inspection of the results. The study conducted in the USA suggested that strategies which were primarily focused on behavioural and language aspects were more predominant in these eclectic approaches, whereas, the UK-based study reported by Frederickson et al. (2010)

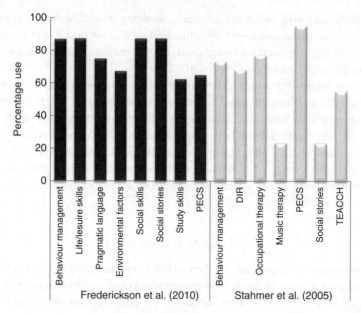

Figure 11.1   Results of two surveys of uses of intervention strategies for pupils with ASD in educational settings: in the UK (Frederickson et al., 2010) and in the USA (Stahmer et al., 2005).

suggested a greater focus on social interactions. Over and above these differences, the data presented by Stahmer et al. (2005) suggest that the professionals were combining existing strategies in different proportions across the treatment sites. The main approaches suggested as being employed were the use of PECS, Occupational Therapy and either Floortime® or ABA. However, the data presented by Frederickson et al. (2010) suggest that it was not necessarily the approaches themselves that were being combined, but rather the goals that the approaches might have stressed. So, for example, personalized training (i.e. using the person with ASD's interests to motivate them) was very commonly adopted, as were behaviour management strategies.

It is not precisely clear what underlies the differences between the results of these two studies. It could have reflected the range of professionals consulted – which was much wider in Stahmer et al. (2005), compared to Frederickson et al. (2010) who restricted their study to mainstream schools. Alternatively, the discrepancies could reflect cultural differences between the UK and USA. However, two studies that have involved a treatment as usual eclectic group (Eldevik et al., 2006; Remington et al., 2007), which were not conducted in the USA, have described the range of approaches employed in these treatments and these descriptions show some similarities with the strategies outlined by Stahmer et al. (2005). For instance, Eldevik et al. (2006) reported that, of the participants in their treatment as usual eclectic group, 53% received some form of ABA, 47% received PECS and 27% received TEACCH and Occupational Therapy. Similarly, Remington et al. (2007) reported that, for their group, 67% received PECS, 57% speech therapy, 38% TEACCH and 24% sign language. Irrespective of the reason for differences in the descriptions of eclectic treatments, what does emerge from these data is that treatment as usual groups cover a large and varied number of strategies (Eldevik et al., 2006) and that this may well reflect what actually happens in the treatment of most individuals with ASD (Stahmer & Mandell, 2007).

Generic treatments

As with the previously discussed treatment as usual category, the use of the term generic is not meant to be dismissive, but simply to refer to interventions that do not carry a 'brand name'. In the current usage, 'generic treatment' interventions can be thought of as being constructed from multiple elements (sometimes from brand name interventions) and are typically conducted either at one site (e.g. Zachor et al., 2010) or across a number of sites which share the same general approach as one another (e.g. Reed et al., 2007b). Given that these groups of individuals are given the same type of intervention as one another (in potential contrast to the treatment as usual groups, earlier), the generic treatment group may be a stronger comparison group in studies of branded therapies. On the positive side, it has greater internal consistency than a treatment as usual group, but, on the other side, it may lack the generality of extrapolation that a treatment as usual group may possess.

A number of studies have specifically focused on generic intervention groups (Eikeseth et al., 2002; Howard et al., 2005; Magiati et al., 2007; Reed et al., 2007b; Zachor et al., 2010). All of these studies suggest that similar components are present in these generic approaches as were outlined for treatment as usual groups, albeit all of the individuals undergoing such a generic intervention would receive similar treatments to one another. For example, Eikeseth et al. (2002) report that their generic intervention comprised strategies from TEACCH, sensorimotor treatments, as well as from ABA interventions. Howard et al. (2005) similarly describe a generic group as receiving input based on ABA, TEACCH and PECS interventions. Other generic programmes do not contain ABA elements, but combine strategies from TEACCH and PECS (Magiati et al., 2007) or TEACCH, Occupational Therapy, Social Stories™ and Floortime (Reed et al., 2007b; Zachor et al., 2010).

Technical eclectic approaches

Some eclectic approaches are more than the combination of strategies from brand name programmes, but are developed with their own specific goals and particular rationales – such approaches have been termed technical eclectic approaches (Odom et al., 2012). There are many technical eclectic packages that have been developed by educational professionals for use in their own local authority (Mandell et al., 2013; Reed et al., 2013b; Webster-Stratton et al., 2010) and such approaches are increasingly being evaluated in the published literature. The evidence regarding these programmes is worth brief mention, as many will resemble the types of provision offered by other local authorities.

Table 11.1 gives a brief overview of some of these approaches, in terms of their content, information sources and relative effectiveness across functioning domains. This limited overview shows that many of these programmes are beginning to cohere in the components that they offer. They focus on younger children, generally between 4 and 6 years old and combine some form of parent-education about

Table 11.1 Description of a selection of 'technical eclectic' approaches to treating ASD.

Approach	Source	Description	Assessments
Strategies for Teaching based on Autism Research (STAR)	Arick et al. (2004)	Teaching techniques from ABA – discrete trial training, pivotal response training, and teaching in functional routines: DTT and PRT designed for one-to-one instruction, and functional routines designed for use with groups. Techniques address: receptive, expressive, and spontaneous language; functional routines; and pre-academic, play, and social concepts. Lesson choice is guided by the student learning profile. Teachers implement the lesson with the student until the student is able to correctly use the skill to criterion without prompting. Classrooms include visual schedules, labels, and cues.	Arick et al. (2003) Mandell et al. (2013)
Barnet Early Autism Model (BEAM)	Reed et al. (2013b)	Delivered on a 1:1 basis by therapists in collaboration with parents to address social communication, and emotional regulation. Uses structure and routine, visually-supported learning, and operates within the SCERTS framework. Targets communication and social interaction through PECS, and behaviour problems through ABA-like techniques.	Reed et al. (2013a)
Scottish Centre for Autism Preschool Treatment	Salt et al. (2001)	Developmental approach tailored to individual needs. Children get 8 hours treatment every 2 weeks for 11 months. Parents receive training in behaviour management, and strategies developed in therapy sessions, and implement these outside the formal sessions.	Salt et al. (2002)
The Incredible Years Program	Webster-Stratton & Reid (2010)	Series of training programmes for children, parents, and teachers, designed to work jointly to promote emotional, social, and academic competence, and to treat behavioural and emotional problems.	Webster-Stratton et al. (2011)

ASD, with 1:1 delivered teaching for the child for about 10 hours a week. The programmes typically commence in the home, but often attempt to facilitate a transfer to a school placement on termination of the programme, most usually after about 1 or 2 years.

The outcome-effectiveness evidence regarding these approaches presents a mixed pattern of data, but typically shows that whatever aspect of child's functioning is the primarily focus of the intervention often shows some improvement. These levels of improvement are not as consistent as shown in other, more well-developed approaches and these local authority packages certainly need further development (see Reed et al., 2013b, for a discussion of this in the context of the BEAM approach). However, the emerging data suggests that some of these approaches may offer promise for helping individuals with ASD.

Characteristics of Studied Eclectic Programmes

In order to explore the effectiveness of these types of programme, the current chapter sought to perform a meta-analysis on the results of outcome-effectiveness studies that have included eclectic interventions. There are new reports of such studies almost weekly and the current sample was collected from period between 1987 and 2014, which broadly corresponds with the data considered in the preceding chapters on branded approaches. The studies were included if they provided outcome data in one of the key functioning domains (intellectual, language, social-adaptive). In total 31 studies were identified, that produced a total of 33 different eclectic programmes (the studies by Howard et al., 2005 and Reed et al., 2010, involved more than one eclectic programme). Thus, it cannot be claimed that there is a lack of evidence relating to these forms of interventions.

Table 11.2 summarizes lists these studies and gives details of the nature of the report, the characteristics of the programme, in terms of its overall duration and weekly intensity; as well as the characteristics of the individuals who experienced the programme, in terms of their ages and baseline functioning abilities.

Nature of the studies

Of the outcome-effectiveness reports listed in Table 11.2, nine (27%) were observational studies, involving only a pre-intervention and post-intervention measure of functioning (e.g. Charman et al., 2004; Jónsdóttir et al., 2007; Stahmer & Ingersoll, 2004). There were 19 (58%) reports of controlled studies, involving comparison between an eclectic and alternative intervention, but with no random allocation of the participants to the groups (e.g. Magiati et al., 2007; Reed et al., 2007b; Zachor et al., 2010). In addition, there were five (15%) randomized control trials (Aldred et al., 2004; Dawson et al., 2010; Drew et al., 2002; Pajareya & Nopmaneejumruslers, 2011; Rogers et al., 2012). The mean number of participants involved in these studies was 21.5 (+13.6; range 9–65). Overall, the types of methodology employed to establish the outcome-effectiveness of eclectic programmes and the numbers of participants included in the studies were highly similar to those conducted for other intervention programmes discussed earlier in this book.

Table 11.2 Characteristics of studies assessing eclectic programmes, showing type of trial (Obs = observational; Cont = controlled; RCT = randomised control trial), location of programme, whether programme was the target (T) or a control (N), number of participants (N), duration, weekly intensity and total intervention hours, as well as participants' mean age, intellectual (IQ), language (lang) and adaptive-social (ASB), functioning at intake.

Study	Year	Type	Location	Target	N	Duration (weeks)	Intensity (h/week)	Age (months)	IQ	Lang	ASB
Aldred et al.	2004	RCT	Home	N	14	12	25.00	51			20
Charman et al.	2004	Obs	School	T	57	12	25.00	56			53
Cohen et al.	2006	Cont	School	N	19	36	20.00	33	59	52	70
Dawson et al.	2010	RCT	School	N	21	24	18.00	23	59	60	69
Drew et al.	2002	RCT	School	N	12	12	33.00	23	66		
Eikeseth et al.	2002	Cont	School	N	12	12	29.00	65	65	60	60
Eldevik et al.	2006	Cont	School	N	15	21	24.00	49	47	42	52
Farrell et al.	2005	Cont	School	T	9	20	25.00	69	31		26
Gabriels et al.	2001	Obs	School	T	17	22	23.00	30	57	42	
Howard et al.	2005	Cont	School	N	16	14	25.00	39	53	44	69
Howard et al.	2005	Cont	School	N	16	14	15.00	34	59	48	71
Jonsdottir et al.	2007	Obs	School	T	41	28	31.00	41	56		
Magiati et al.	2007	Cont	School	T	16	24	21.00	42	65		57
Makrygianni et al.	2010	Cont	School	T	14	9	21.00	121	41		29
Makrygianni et al.	2010	Cont	School	T	13	9	29.00	128	39		52
Osborne & Reed	2008	Obs	School	T	65	9	15.00	36	53		56
Pajareya & Nopmaneejumruslers	2011	RCT	Home	N	16	3		51	40		23
Paynter et al.	2012	Obs	School	T	10	15	25.00	53	66	56	77
Peters-Scheffer et al.	2013	Cont	School	N	20	24	35.00	23	40	21	20
Reed et al.	2013b	Cont	Home	T	16	10	6.00	43	83	60	70
Reed et al.	2011	Obs	School	T	39	9	25.00	74			50
Reed et al.	2010	Obs	Home	T	13	9	12.00	40	49		56

Reed et al.	2007b	Cont	School	T	20	9	12.00	43	51			53
Reed et al.	2010	Obs	School	T	20	9	14.00	43	52			53
Remington et al.	2007	Cont	Home	N	21	24	16.00	38	62			
Rogers et al.	2012	RCT	Home	N	49	3	11.00	18	63		44	78
Sallows & Graupner	1999	Cont	School	N	19	36	12.00	33	59			
Salt et al.	2002	Cont	School	T	12	10	38.00	42	39			49
Sheinkopf & Siegel	1998	Cont	School	N	11	18	11.00	35	61			
Stahmer & Ingersoll	2004	Obs	School	T	20	9	17.00	27	67			75
Tsang et al.	2007	Cont	School	N	16	6	25.00	48	74			
Waddington & Reed	2009	Cont	School	N	18	10	25.00	74				43
Zachor et al.	2010	Cont	School	N	33	12	19.00	26	73		30	68

However, a major difference between the nature of the studies of eclectic programmes and the study of other forms of intervention is that the eclectic programmes included in these reports were not always the primary focus of the study. In fact, the reports documented in Table 11.2 are approximately evenly divided between those that primarily sought to investigate the eclectic intervention (16 programmes or 49%) and those that included the eclectic programme as a comparison group for another intervention (17 programmes – 51%). There are some differences in this regard across the three types of eclectic intervention (i.e. treatment as usual, generic and technical eclectic – see Table 11.3). When a treatment as usual programme was included in a study, it was almost always used as a comparison (non-target) programme for another type of intervention (10/12; with the exceptions being reported by Charman et al., 2004 and Gabriels et al., 2001). Generic programmes were split evenly between those that were the target of the report (7/14) and those that were a non-target comparison condition. Technical eclectic programmes were always studied as the target of the outcome-effectiveness report.

Programme characteristics

The majority of the eclectic programmes studied (82%) were conducted in a centre or school setting, with only a few being home-based. The typical duration of the eclectic programme was 15 months (+8.4; range 3–36), with a typical weekly intensity of 21 hours (+7.7; range 6–38) per week. This range of durations and intensities is broadly similar to that studied in relation to the comprehensive programmes discussed in the previous chapters of this book. There was a slight difference in the observed programme characteristics of the three types of eclectic programmes: the treatment as usual programmes tended to have a longer duration (mean = 19 + 11; range 3–36 months), than either the generic (mean = 13 + 6.3; range 6–28 months) or technical eclectic programmes (mean = 12 + 4.2 range 9–20 months). This tended to be because many of the treatment as usual groups were included in longer-term studies of behavioural programmes (e.g. Cohen et al., 2006; Sallows & Graupner, 2005). However, the mean weekly intensity of the three types of eclectic programme was similar: treatment as usual = 22 hours per week (+7.7; range 11–35); generic = 21 hours per week (+6.5; range 11–31) and technical eclectic = 20 hours per week (+10.6; range 6–38).

The composition of the eclectic programmes, in terms of the components that they included: for example, those drawn from ABA or TEACCH programmes, strategies aimed at improving social functioning (e.g. Circle of Friends, Social Stories™), those aimed at language (e.g. PECS, sign language) or whether they included Speech and Language Therapy or Occupational Therapy (often including Sensory Integration Therapy) and whether they involved a parent training component, are shown in Table 11.3. Inspection of this table shows that the strategies mentioned in the studies of eclectic programmes broadly correspond to those suggested as occurring in the survey reported by Stahmer et al. (2005), although the match to the procedures reported by Frederickson et al. (2010) is harder to discern: 52% of the currently included reports used ABA; 58% used TEACCH; 73% social; 36% communication; 61% speech and language therapy; 33% Occupational Therapy and 21% employed parental training.

Table 11.3 Type of eclectic programme (TAU = treatment as usual; G = generic; TE = technical eclectic), and components of the programmes: ABA = applied behaviour analysis; Social = social functioning; Com = communication; SLT = speech and language therapy; OT = occupational therapy; Parent = parental training (white = present; black = absent).

Study	Type	ABA	TEACCH	Social	Com	SLT	OT	Parent
Aldred et al. (2004)	TAU				■		■	
Charman et al. (2004)	TAU	-	-	-	-	-	-	-
Cohen et al. (2006)	TAU		■				■	■
Dawson et al. (2010)	TAU		■		■		■	■
Drew et al. (2002)	TAU		■		■			■
Eikeseth et al. (2002)	G							■
Eldevik et al. (2006)	TAU							■
Farrell et al. (2005)	TE			■				■
Gabriels et al. (2001)	TAU		■	■	■			■
Howard et al. (2005)	G	■		■			■	■
Howard et al. (2005)	G	■	■		■			■
Jonsdottir et al. (2007)	G			■			■	■
Magiati et al. (2007)	G	■		■		■		■
Makrygianni et al. (2010)	G			■	■	■	■	
Makrygianni et al. (2010)	G	■				■		■
Osborne & Reed (2008)	G		■		■			■
Pajareya & Nopmaneejumruslers (2011)	TAU	-	-	-	-			-
Paynter et al. (2012)	TE		■			■		■
Peters-Scheffer et al. (2013)	TAU		■					■
Reed et al. (2013b)	TE			■		■	■	
Reed et al. (2011)	G	■						■
Reed et al. (2010)	TE		■					

(Continued)

Table 11.3 *(Continued)*

Study	Type	ABA	TEACCH	Social	Com	SLT	OT	Parent
Reed et al. (2007b)	G	■						■
Reed et al. (2010)	TE	■						■
Remington et al. (2007)	TAU	■						■
Rogers et al. (2012)	TAU				■	■		■
Sallows & Graupner (1999)	TAU	■						
Salt et al. (2002)	TE			■	■	■	■	■
Sheinkopf & Siegel (1998)	G	■	■					
Stahmer & Ingersoll (2004)	TE				■	■		■
Tsang et al. (2007)	G	■	■	■	■	■	■	
Waddington & Reed (2009)	G							■
Zachor et al. (2010)	G	■		■		■		■

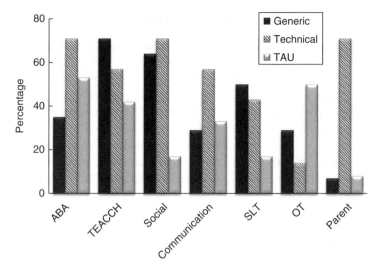

Figure 11.2 Percentage of different types of eclectic programme (generic, technical or treatment as usual) employing strategies from various approaches. ABA = applied behaviour analysis; Social = social functioning targeted; Com = communication targeted; SLT = speech and language therapy; OT = occupational therapy; Parent = parental training.

There were differences in the proportions of strategies adopted by the three different types of eclectic programme and the percentage of the programmes from each of these three types of eclectic intervention that employed various component strategies is shown in Figure 11.2. The treatment as usual programmes placed more reliance on strategies designed to promote social functioning and also on Speech and Language Therapy and Occupational Therapy, than either of the other two forms of eclectic intervention. Generic programmes tended to employ TEACCH-based strategies, in preference to ABA strategies; whereas technical eclectic programmes tended to employ more ABA strategies, than the other two types of eclectic approach and also placed more emphasis on parent training as part of the programme. Of course, it is difficult to place too much weight on these generalizations, given the nature of the descriptions of the programmes from which they were drawn, but these data are certainly suggestive that what may be termed eclectic provision is, indeed, a very broad spectrum approach.

The manner in which these strategies were delivered (i.e. mainly in group settings, individual settings or through a mixture of both) was also determined from the information provided in the reports. Of the programmes, 11 (33%) delivered the intervention primarily in a group-based setting, 5 (15%) were delivered primarily on a 1:1 basis and 16 (49%) delivered the intervention through a mixture of group and individual work. There were some differences between the three types of eclectic intervention in this regard, with around 30–35% of the treatment as usual and generic approaches being delivered mainly in a group setting, 7–8% through 1:1 means and 50–60% of these programmes using a combination approach to treatment delivery. However, the technical eclectic programmes were more often delivered through 1:1 means (42%). This difference may reflect the greater utilization of ABA strategies in technical eclectic interventions, although some caution is needed in offering this interpretation, as the reports are often not particularly detailed in this regard.

Child characteristics

The characteristics of the participants in these studies are displayed in Table 11.2 and an inspection of their ages, intellectual, linguistic and social-adaptive functioning, when the programme commenced, show that these participants were highly similar to those in the outcome-effectiveness reports of the other forms of intervention. The mean age of the participants at intake was 47 (+24.7; range 18–128) months. The intellectual functioning of the participants, as measured by standardized tools, was 56 (+12.1; range 31–83) and their mean standardized language functioning was 47 (+12.2; range 21–60). The standardized adaptive and social behavioural functioning, typically measured by the Vineland Adaptive Behavior Scales (VABS), was 54 (+17.8; range 20–78).

Results from Outcome-Effectiveness Studies

The results for the individual outcome-effectiveness studies are presented in Table 11.4. These data show the change in the levels of functioning in those studies in terms of the absolute change in the standard score of the measure in question (i.e. intellectual, language, adaptive behaviour) and the associated effect size. The outcomes are shaded, so that: strong effects are seen in light shaded cells – an increase of 15 points in the standard score or of greater than 0.7 in terms of effect size; moderate impacts are shown in medium shaded cells – changes of between 10 and 14 points and effect sizes of between 0.3 and 0.7) and weak impacts are shown in dark shaded cells – changes of less than 10 or effect sizes of less than 0.3.

As in previous chapters, these impacts are shown for two metrics: (i) between the baseline (pre-test) and follow-up (post-test) measures and (ii) the difference in the pre- to post-test scores in the eclectic programme group and any control groups in the report (see Chapter 1 for description). The first of these metrics of impact is straightforward to interpret; however, the comparison with control groups is not so straightforward, as this needs consideration of exactly what the control group received, which varies a large amount between the studies. Of the 33 conditions included, 25 provide comparison data from an alternative group. In all cases, the control group was assessed over the same time period as the eclectic group, however, what they received during that period varied widely.

As noted previously, the eclectic programmes differed in terms of the amount of intervention that was given to the participants: in particular, in terms of the duration of the study (how long the programme was conducted) and the intensity of the intervention (how many hours per week the intervention was delivered). The impact of these quantifiable variables on the effect sizes of the changes in the three functioning domains can be seen in Figure 11.3, which displays the correlations between these programme variables and the effect sizes.

Intellectual functioning

Intellectual functioning was typically assessed using well-used standardized instruments; most commonly, the Bayley Scale of Infant Development (e.g. Eikeseth et al., 2002; Farrell et al., 2005), the Mullen Scales of early Learning (e.g. Dawson

Table 11.4 Outcomes of eclectic programmes, showing pre-to-post intervention change in standard scores and the effect size (ES$_1$), and comparisons with control group standard score and effect size (ES$_2$).

Study	Pre- to Post-change						Comparison with control					
	IQ	Lang	ASB	IQ ES$_1$	Lang ES$_1$	ASB ES$_1$	IQ	Lang	ASB	IQ ES$_2$	Lang ES$_2$	ASB ES$_2$
Aldred et al. (2004)			8.00		0.05	0.81			−5.60		−0.13	−0.47
Charman et al. (2004)			1.00			0.06						
Cohen et al. (2006)	14.00	13.00	−4.00	0.95	0.88	−0.42	−11.00	.00	−13.00	−0.72	0	−1.50
Dawson et al. (2010)	6.90	10.70	−10.8	0.80	1.15	−1.48	−10.60	−12.60	−10.40	−1.19	−1.38	−1.60
Drew et al. (2002)	0			0	1.09		10.30			0.74	−1.61	
Eikeseth et al. (2002)	4.30	1.08	0.17	0.29	0.05	0.01	−13.13	−25.92	−11.06	−0.99	−1.25	−1.00
Eldevik et al. (2006)	−2.90	−7.05	−4.80	−0.20	−0.43	−0.50	−11.10	−15.95	−3.90	−0.74	−1.15	−0.56
Farrell et al. (2005)	2.00		16.00	0.13		1.07	−5.00		2.00	−0.33		−0.13
Gabriels et al. (2001)	5.10	14.98		0.20	0.93							
Howard et al. (2005)	8.44	4.17	−0.56	0.63	0.39	−0.05	−11.70	−4.82	−4.31	−0.75	−0.34	−0.39
Howard et al. (2005)	8.93	−0.89	−3.37	0.60	−0.07	−0.32	−10.96	−12.41	−8.53	−0.71	−0.95	−0.78
Jonsdottir et al. (2007)	4.22			0.24								
Magiati et al. (2007)	0		−5.30	0	1.65	−0.96	4.70		−4.70	0.23	−0.27	−0.96
Makrygianni et al. (2010)	−0.29		−3.39	−0.03	0.20	−0.43	−0.07		−7.92	0	−0.04	−0.77
Makrygianni et al. (2010)				0.37	0.21	0.77				0.22	−0.09	0.72
Osborne & Reed (2008)	8.10		1.10	0.48		0.16						
Pajareya & Nopmaneejumruslers (2011)	0.80		1.90	0.05		0.15	−6.80		−5.10	−0.48		−0.40
Paynter et al. (2012)	1.00	−3.00	2.00	0.07	−0.20	0.15						
Peters-Scheffer et al. (2013)	−1.00	9.00	7.00	−0.04	1.83	1.46	−9.00	0	−12.00	−0.47	0.70	−2.96
Reed et al. (2013b)	0.70	6.00	5.00	0.03	0.31	1.22	−0.01	12.00	16.50	0	0.70	3.27
Reed et al. (2011)			18.00			0.95						

(Continued)

Table 11.4 (*Continued*)

	Pre- to Post-change						Comparison with control					
Study	IQ	Lang	ASB	IQ ES$_1$	Lang ES$_1$	ASB ES$_1$	IQ	Lang	ASB	IQ ES$_2$	Lang ES$_2$	ASB ES$_2$
Reed et al. (2010)	6.50		-0.50	0.50		-0.10						
Reed et al. (2007b)	10.20		3.30	0.51		0.72	2.60		2.55	0.16		0.41
Reed et al. (2010)	10.50		3.00	0.66		1.00						
Remington et al. (2007)	-2.00			-0.13			-14.00			-0.85		
Rogers et al. (2012)	4.84	9.90	2.11	0.30	0.49	0.24	-0.10	1.03	1.14	-0.01	0.05	0.12
Sallows & Graupner (1999)	-8.00			-0.53			-30.00			-2.00		
Salt et al. (2002)			-0.17			-0.05						
Sheinkopf & Siegel (1998)	2.60			0.13			-24.30		14.30	-1.03		3.33
Stahmer & Ingersoll (2004)	7.40		3.22	0.50		0.29						
Tsang et al. (2007)				0.43	0.48	0.19				-0.64	-1.40	0.40
Waddington & Reed (2009)			7.00			0.27			.20			0.01
Zachor et al. (2010)	2.50	8.00	4.00	0.17	0.53	0.63	2.50	1.50	6.00	0.16	0.10	.74

IQ = intellectual function, Lang = language function; ASB = adaptive and social behaviour. White = strong effect; light grey = moderate effect; dark grey = weak effect; black = no data.

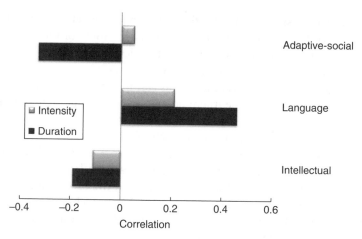

Figure 11.3 Correlations between programme duration (weeks), and intensity (hours per week), with changes in standardised scores for three outcome domains over the course of the intervention. Longer and more intensive programmes produce better language outcomes.

et al., 2010; Paynter et al., 2012) and the Merrill–Palmer Scales (e.g. Cohen et al., 2006; Tsang et al., 2007). These scales cover a wide range of intellectual functioning, which, although not in themselves central to the definition of ASD, do cover many of the behaviours and cognitions implicated as being associated with ASD (see Chapter 5). A variety of other scales were also employed (e.g. the Leiter International Performance Scale, Psycho-Educational profile), but all of these have been relatively well-employed in the literature previously and all tend to cover the same types of functioning domains as those more widely used tests mentioned previously. A common issue that needs brief mention is that a variety of measurement scales were often employed within each study (usually dependent upon the ability of individual children). The problems of employing different scales have been discussed previously and include a reduction in the reliability of the measurement (see Chapter 4). Nevertheless, this is not a unique issue for the assessment of intervention outcomes.

Change in functioning　The mean increase in the standardized intellectual functioning score following the programmes shown in Table 11.4 was 3.6 points (+4.9; range −8–14). This change cannot be considered as particularly large and does not compare well with the mean increases in standardized measures of intellectual functioning noted for many comprehensive programmes reviewed in earlier chapters. A similarly relatively weak pattern of increase in intellectual functioning is reflected when the mean effect size of these studies is considered. This metric shows a mean effect size of 0.25 (+0.33, range −0.53–0.95). The mean change effect size can be said to fall into the 'small' effect size category.

However, it is also clear that there was a large variation in the size of these increases (a range of 22 points, with the standard deviations in both the standardized score increase and the effect size, being similar to the mean for those measures). In fact, of the 26 programmes that provided these data, 10 show an increase in the moderate to large range, 13 in the small range and 5 showed a decrease in functioning over time.

This suggests that the studies do not reflect a homogenous set of data and that there may be a range of factors that mediate these findings. Some of these predictors will be discussed in detail later (such as the characteristics of the children and the nature of the programme). However, of the basic categorical differences between the types of eclectic programme: that is, whether it was run in a clinic/school or in the home or the type of eclectic programme, there do appear to be some suggestions of effectiveness moderators.

When the programme was led by a clinic/school, the mean increase in the intellectual functioning score was 4.0 points (mean effect size = 0.28), which was twice the mean increase observed in home-based programmes (standard score change = 2.2, ES = 0.15). There was also an advantage noted when the programme was a generic (standard score improvement = 4.9, effect size 0.32) or technical eclectic (standard score improvement = 4.7, effect size 0.32), compared to a treatment as usual group (standard score improvement = 1.8, effect size 0.14).

In terms of the impact on intellectual functioning of some of the quantitative aspects of the eclectic programmes, there was little impact of the duration of the programme on the outcome (see Figure 11.3). Similarly, there was little impact of the intensity of the programme (hours per week) on the intellectual gains made across the studies reported. However, it might be noted that this overall result does contrast with the results of several individual reports of the effect of intensity. For example, Reed and Osborne (2012) and Reed et al. (2012) both noted that increases in the number of hours per week of an eclectic programme run in a nursery school resulted in an increase in the gains made by the participants.

Figure 11.4 shows the mean effect sizes for all three functioning domains depending on whether the instruction in the programme was mainly given individually (1:1), in a group or using mixed group and 1:1 strategies. Inspection of these data show that the gains in intellectual functioning were better than when the programme was delivered in mixed settings, than when it was delivered mainly 1:1 or mainly in a group.

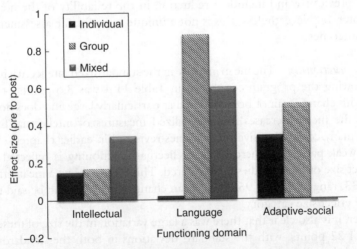

Figure 11.4 Effect size for pre-to-post programme change in three functioning domains for eclectic programmes delivered mainly individually (1:1), in group settings, or using a mixture of the two teaching approaches.

Comparison with control group   The other metric to consider is the effectiveness of the intervention in comparison to other programmes. The data from the studies in Table 11.4 shows (with some exceptions) that intellectual functioning increased less after exposure to an eclectic programme than in the alternative groups. In fact, the change over time for the eclectic programmes compared to the various comparison groups was –7.4 standard points (+9.9, range –30–10), with a mean effect size of –0.45 (+0.62, range –2.00–0.74). Overall, these data suggest that eclectic approaches were less effective than alternative treatments in terms of improving intellectual functioning. This was true irrespective of whether the eclectic approach was conducted in a clinic/school (comparative standard score change = –7.8; effect size = –0.47) or at home (comparative standard score change = –5.2; effect size = –0.34).

However, there were large differences in the performance of the types of eclectic programme relative to their various comparisons. The treatment as usual groups showed the worst relative performance (comparative standard score change = –9.1; effect size = –0.64); the generic programmes (standard score = –6.3; effect size = –0.33) showed intermediate levels of performance and the technical eclectic approaches (standard score = –2.5; effect size = –0.17) showed the best (least bad) performance relative to a comparison group. In fact, in the meta-analysis reported by Reichow and Wolery (2009) noted that the weakest evidence for the effectiveness of behavioural programmes was when they were compared to eclectic programmes that consisted of a single approach, rather than being constructed of any available participants, who may be receiving different procedures to one another (Magiati et al., 2007; Reed et al., 2007b; Zachor & Ben-Itzchak, 2010; but see Howard et al., 2005). These differences may reflect the 'quality' or 'internal integrity' of the eclectic group that was employed in the study. However, it should be noted that none of these three approaches showed superior performance than the controls.

Language functioning

Typically, assessments of language functioning were conducted using the Reynell Scales of Development (e.g. Cohen et al., 2006) or the Peabody Scales (e.g. Makrygianni et al., 2010c) and most scales employed provided an expressive and receptive language score, although the data in Table 11.4 is a mean of these measures. There were a number of cases where a standardized test of language ability was not reported, but rather the number of words employed or recognized was assessed (e.g. Aldred et al., 2004) and, in these cases, effect sizes, but not standard scores, were calculated.

Change in functioning   The mean increase in the standardized language functioning score following exposure to the eclectic programmes was 5.5 (+6.8; range –7–15) points. Although this average change in standardized language ability cannot be considered large, the mean effect size for the improvement was 0.53 (+0.62, range: –0.43–1.83), which is a moderately sized increase. The receptive language scores improved consistently more than the expressive language scores in these studies, but neither measure generally attained the levels of improvement noted for the programmes discussed in previous chapters. Nevertheless, there was a considerable range in the outcomes of the studies of eclectic approaches (a range of 22 points), with some showing very weak improvements or even reductions, in language ability (e.g. Eldevik et al., 2006; Paynter et al., 2010) and some showing rather large gains (e.g. Cohen et al., 2006; Rogers et al., 2012).

The differential impact of the eclectic programme on language when it was conducted in a clinic or school (standard score = 4.9, effect size = 0.58), compared to when it was conducted in the home (standard score = 8.0, effect size = 0.28), was not great. There was a difference between the impacts of the various forms of eclectic programmes. Treatment as usual programmes displayed the largest increase in language functioning (standard score = 8.4, effect size = 0.75), with generic approaches (standard score = 3.1, effect size = 0.43) displaying moderate gains and technical eclectic approaches displaying the weakest improvement in language (standard score = 1.5, effect size = 0.06).

Figure 11.3 shows that eclectic programmes offer a greater improvement in language skills when they are conducted for a longer period of time and with a greater intensity. This pattern of results with respect to programme duration and language gain was noted for almost all other forms of intervention (see previous chapters). There were also greater gains in language when the programme was delivered in a group or mixed setting (in fact, these effect sizes could be considered as large), compared to when the programmes were delivered 1:1.

Comparison with control groups The data with respect to the relative impact of eclectic programmes on the language functioning of the participants, shown in Table 11.4, suggests that language functioning increased less after exposure to the eclectic programme than after exposure to the comparison groups. The mean change in the language standard score for the eclectic programmes compared to that change in the comparison groups was –5.7 standard points (+11.0, range –26–12), with a mean effect size of –0.49 (+0.69, range –1.60–0.70). However, when comparing the relative improvements produced by eclectic approaches conducted in different locations, those conducted in the home (comparative standard score change = 6.5, effect size = 0.21) produced better relative results, than those conducted in a clinic/school (comparative standard score change = –8.8, effect size = –0.65). This may reflect the importance for the children's language of conducting the programme in a home setting with the parents involved for language development.

Neither the treatment as usual (comparative standard score change = –5.5, effect size = –0.65), nor the generic (comparative standard score change = –10.4, effect size = –0.53), approaches fared well in comparison with their various control groups. There was only one technical eclectic approaches which provided such data (Reed et al., 2013b) and that study showed a large gain in language relative to the control (comparative standard score change = 12.0, effect size = 0.70).

Adaptive social behaviours

These behaviours were measured using the parent-reported VABS and the results reported here come from the composite score from the VABS (which includes indication of the daily living skills, communication, socialization and motor skills).

Change in functioning The studies that provided data for this aspect of functioning, demonstrated a mean increase in the adaptive behaviour standard score of 2.00 (+6.3, range: −11–18), with an associated mean effect size of 0.22 (+0.67, range: −1.48–1.46). Although this was only a relatively small mean improvement, it should be noted that many interventions show difficulty influencing this aspect of functioning and, in fact, it often shows less change compared to intellectual functioning and language scores. Despite this, of the studies conducted with eclectic interventions, 10 reported a moderate to large increase in adaptive behaviour (effect sizes >0.30) and particularly impressive increases were noted in the studies by Farrell et al. (2005), Peters-Scheffer et al. (2013) and Reed et al. (2013b). Of the remaining reports, nine showed smaller improvement effects and nine showed decreased VABS scores.

Those eclectic interventions that were conducted in a school or clinic produced a mean improvement in adaptive behavioural functioning of 1.7 points (mean effect size = 0.16) and the programmes conducted at home produced a mean improvement in the standard score of 3.3 (mean effect size = 0.46). These data suggest that this aspect of functioning is more likely to be improved if the programme includes home component and this has been suggested by many previously with respect to behavioural programmes. In terms of the type of eclectic programme adopted, the technical eclectic approaches produced he largest mean increase in adaptive-social behavioural functioning (standard score = 4.1; effect size = 0.51), with generic approaches producing an intermediate level of improved functioning in this domain (standard score = 2.1; effect size = 0.16) and treatment as usual groups displaying little increase (standard score = 0.1; effect size = 0.04).

Figure 11.3 shows that there was little effect of any of the programme characteristics (duration, intensity) on the effectiveness of the treatment on adaptive behavioural functioning, whereas Figure 11.4 shows that these skills are best promoted in a group setting, compared to mixed or 1:1 settings.

Comparison with control groups Relative to the gains made in the alternative treatment groups in these studies, eclectic programmes showed a slightly worse performance in terms of impact on adaptive behavioural skills. The mean relative effect of an eclectic programme on adaptive behaviour standard score was −2.4 (+8.4, range: −13–16), with a mean effect size of −0.13 (+1.46, range: −2.96–3.33). Clearly, these results reflect some degree of variation in the relative effectiveness of eclectic programmes; with some studies showing very strong effects of the eclectic programme over and above the comparison groups (e.g. Reed et al., 2013b) and some showing the opposite pattern of outcome (Dawson et al., 2010; Peters-Scheffer et al., 2013).

As with the changes in adaptive functioning over time, programmes conducted in a home setting demonstrated greater relative gains in adaptive functioning than the controls (standard score = 1.74, effect size = 0.63), compared to those conducted in a school/clinic (standard score = −3.62, effect size = −0.32). These data suggest the importance of the home in developing social and adaptive skills.

There was an extremely pronounced difference between the varieties of eclectic programmes that were studied in these outcome-effectiveness reports. The treatment as usual groups had particularly poor comparative performance (comparative standard score change = –7.0, effect size = –1.05). The generic programmes also had poor performance relative to a comparison group (comparative standard score change = –3.5, effect size = –0.16). However, the technical eclectic programmes showed an advantage over the comparison groups (comparative standard score change = 10.9, effect size = 2.16). This difference in the impact between the types of eclectic programme studied is largely the result of two studies in which a technical eclectic intervention produced very large effect size gains over and above those produced by a comparison group (Reed et al., 2013b; Salt et al., 2002).

Autism symptoms

A number of the studies of eclectic programmes have attempted to measure the improvement in the core ASD symptoms as a result of exposure to the treatment. These core symptoms were measured in some studies by objective observational assessment of the children, using the Autism Diagnosis Observational Schedule (ADOS) and, in other studies, through parent-rated measures, such as the Gillian Autism Rating Scale (GARS). The overall pattern of results suggests that, irrespective of the scales employed, the interventions did not typically reduce the level of ASD symptoms.

Several studies have attempted to look at possible shifts in the diagnostic categories of the participants as a result of the eclectic treatment (Dawson et al., 2010; Gabriels et al., 2001; Jonsdottir et al., 2007; Zachor et al., 2007). Few of these studies showed any significant shift in the diagnostic category from baseline to follow-up assessment. The patterns of change in the studies can be seen in Figure 11.5 and these data reveal that there was a mixed pattern of change across the studies, usually between a diagnosis of 'autism' and a diagnosis of an 'ASD' or PDD:NOS (which requires the presence of fewer symptoms). However, this change was restricted to only around 10–15% of the participants involved and, for the most part, the participants left the study with the same diagnostic category with which they entered.

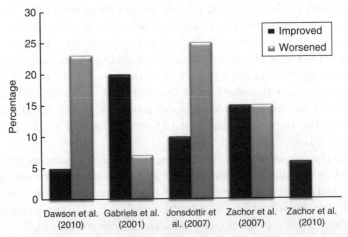

Figure 11.5 Percentage of participants in eclectic programmes who showed a diagnostic improvement or a diagnostic worsening, of their condition after the treatment, for several studies where these data were reported.

In terms of the level of severity of the ASD symptoms, three reports noted a reduction in the severity of ASD symptoms over the period of exposure to the eclectic programme. For example, Stahmer and Ingersoll (2004) reported a reasonable level of change in the severity of the ASD symptoms, as assessed by parents through the GARS. Rogers et al. (2012) noted a strong improvement in the participants' social affect scores, as measured by the ADOS and Jónsdóttir et al. (2007) also reported some symptom improvement, using a mixture of direct observation (CARS) and parent-report (ADI). However, another four studies (Aldred et al., 2004; Drew et al., 2002; Makrygianni et al., 2010b; Reed et al. 2007b) found no alteration in the level of ASD symptomatology using a variety of measurement tools.

Summary of outcome-effectiveness

The preceding overview has established a number of findings regarding the impact of eclectic programmes. This goes some way to help resolve the debate that has revolved around such interventions discussed at the outset of this chapter. The evidence relating to 'eclectic' programmes may be summarized as follows:

- They produce only weak improvements in intellectual functioning and adaptive-social behavioural domains (but the latter is improved with group-based teaching).
- They have a moderate overall effect size for language functioning, which is more pronounced in longer duration programme and with some group-based teaching.
- Clinic or school based programmes produce better gains in intellectual functioning, but that home-based programmes produce better outcomes for language and adaptive-social functioning.
- Technical eclectic approaches fared best for intellectual and adaptive-social functioning, while treatment as usual groups produced the best improvements in language.
- Eclectic programmes do not fare well in comparison with a range of alternative treatment programmes in these outcome domains. However, technical eclectic programmes do appear to have success in the area of adaptive social behaviour.

These conclusions tend to support the impression that has gained credence in the behavioural literature that eclectic programmes are not particularly effective, certainly not in comparison with alternative intervention programmes. However, a key question that these data do not address, and which is critical for any professional, is whether there are any indicators of potential success for particular programmes and whether or not eclectic interventions are any different in the degree to which this question is of importance.

Programme Characteristics as Moderators of Effectiveness

A key aspect of exploring the impact of eclectic programmes is to consider their composition, in terms of their various components; that is, whether they include components of ABA, TEACCH, SLT, OT or focus on communication and social behaviours. The following section examines these components as predictors of the outcome of these programmes.

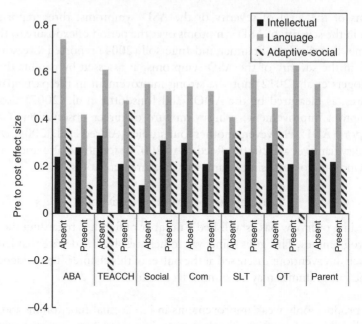

Figure 11.6   Pre- to post-intervention effect sizes for changes in three domains for eclectic programmes that did or did not include various teaching components.

Figure 11.6 shows the mean effect sizes for the change between baseline and follow-up measurement points, in the three outcome domains, for eclectic programmes that did (or did not) contain each of the elements listed previously. Unfortunately, there are actually very few clear indications in these data to suggest whether the presence or absence of any element in an eclectic programme is helpful. Those differences that are present can be summarized briefly. The presence of an ABA component promotes intellectual functioning, but not either of the other two functioning domains. This finding corroborates that noted in the study reported by Osborne and Reed (2008), which noted that the numbers of hours a week of ABA in an eclectic therapy predicted growth in intellectual functioning, but not adaptive-social functioning. The presence of a TEACCH element appears to promote social-adaptive behaviour, but not intellectual and linguistic functioning. In terms of a focus on either social and communication behaviours in the eclectic intervention, the only domain impacted was an increase in intellectual functioning promoted by the presence of a social focus – an effect that is not entirely easy to explain. As might be expected, the presence of Speech and Language Therapy promoted language abilities, but it also tended to hinder social abilities, as did the presence of Occupational Therapy. This latter finding contrasts with the review of sensory-integration therapy provided in Chapter 10, which is a major component of occupational therapy. The use of parent training and parents as major contributors to the programme did not produce any particular benefits – which does resonate with the findings reported in Chapter 9.

The lack of major associations between particular components is in line with the findings reported by Gabriels et al. (2001), who divided their sample of participants exposed to eclectic treatments into those showing 'good' or 'poor' outcomes and noted almost no difference in the components of the programmes experienced by those two groups. This lack of clear evidence that an eclectic programme functions best when it is constructed in a particular way might result from a number of factors. Firstly, it is not straightforward to extract detailed information about the nature of the eclectic programmes from many of the reports and a simple present versus absent dichotomy is not a particularly sharp scalpel with which to dissect such data. The issue of specifying the nature of eclectic programmes remains problematic for assessment of this area. Secondly, it may well be that combining certain types of strategy may either facilitate or inhibit their individual effectiveness. That is, ABA, on its own, may promote intellectual functioning, but when paired with TEACCH, this benefit may be reduced. Thirdly, it may be that combining these data across all types of participant may obscure important information; that is, some components or combinations thereof may be effective for certain types of individual.

It is possible to explore the relationship between the combinations of all of the component strategies and outcomes and not just the presence or absence of the strategies individually. In order to do this, a cluster analysis was conducted on the composition of the studies, which produced three main clusters of eclectic programmes, based on the combinations of components that they comprised. The studies in each of these clusters are shown in the bottom right panel of Figure 11.7. None of the clusters adhere to one form of eclectic intervention (i.e. treatment as usual, generic or technical eclectic), but their characteristics are shown in the pie charts in the remaining panels of Figure 11.7. The studies in Cluster 1 (top left panel) all use ABA, TEACCH and Social strategies, with some use of Communication strategies, but little or no use of the other components. The studies in Cluster 2 (top right panel) tend to employ Social, SLT and OT strategies, with some use of ABA and TEACCH and little employment of Communication or Parent strategies. The final cluster of studies (Cluster 3; bottom left panel), tend to employ Social, Communication and TEACCH strategies, with some use of Social and little use of ABA, OT or parent strategies.

The impact of these clusters of reports on the effects sizes for the three outcome domains are shown in the top panel of Table 11.5 – the importance of these effect sizes is shaded so that a light shaded cell = strong; a medium shaded cell = moderate and a dark shaded cell = weak. Inspection of these data shows that Cluster 1 impacts most on adaptive-social functioning and it does so more than the other clusters. Cluster 2 impacts most on language skills and does this more than the other clusters. Finally, Cluster 3 impacts to the greatest extent on intellectual and language functioning. The bottom panel presents the effect sizes when the studies are compared to control conditions. These values are all weak, with the exception of adaptive-social functioning for Cluster 1 (the ABA and TEACCH cluster). The use of these two components can be singled out, not only because of their individual evidence-base, but also as some studies have explored their joint effectiveness. For instance, Makrygianni et al. (2010c) noted that, for an older sample of individuals with ASD (mean age around 10–11 years), a programme involving both ABA and TEACCH was more effective than an ABA programme on its own, in terms of adaptive-social behaviour.

Figure 11.8 presents the data from the three clusters of eclectic programmes, split for the studies in which the individuals involved had a lower than the mean age for these studies as a whole (47 months) and those studies where the mean age at baseline was higher than this sample mean. On this basis, Cluster 1 programmes had a much

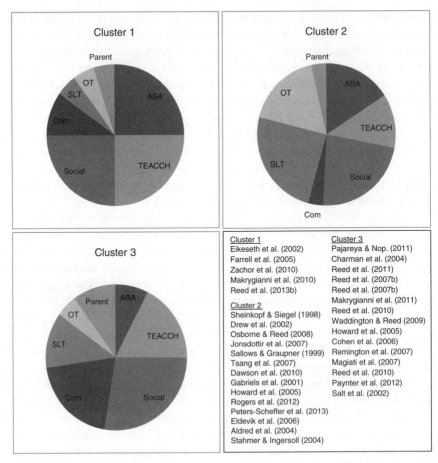

Figure 11.7 Results of cluster analysis for eclectic programmes. Pie charts show percentage of programmes in each cluster adopting particular teaching approaches and the bottom right panel lists the programmes included in each cluster.

Table 11.5 Effect sizes for clusters, for three functioning domains, for both pre to post changes and in comparison with control groups.

	Pre- to Post-change			*Comparison with control*		
	Intellectual	*Language*	*Adaptive*	*Intellectual*	*Language*	*Adaptive*
Cluster 1	0.12	0.27	0.50	−0.23	−0.12	0.42
Cluster 2	0.22	0.66	0.12	−0.68	−0.75	−0.78
Cluster 3	0.35	0.49	0.17	−0.30	−0.32	0.10

White = strong effect; light grey = moderate effect; dark grey = weak effect; black = no data.

stronger impact on older children, especially in terms of adaptive-social behaviours. For Cluster 2 and 3 programmes, there was little difference in the outcome of the interventions for younger or older children in terms of intellectual functioning or language outcomes, but they promoted adaptive-social behaviour better in younger

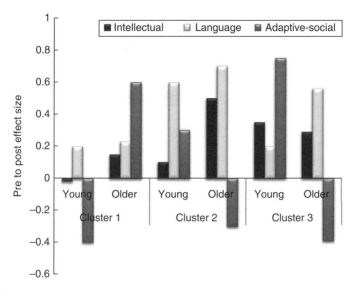

Figure 11.8 Pre-to-post intervention effect sizes for three functioning domains, for the three clusters, divided into studies that used younger or older participants. See text for discussion.

than older children. This finding of better social adaptive functioning being produced in older participants resonates with findings in Chapter 7 relating to TEACCH programmes.

Thus, it can be seen that the composition of the eclectic programme may have some impact, but that this impact is not necessarily easily attributed to a single component. These analyses hint at some potentially useful combinations of components and some that some combinations may produce effective results, especially in particular domains. Moreover, there is some evidence that eclectic programmes should not be dismissed out of hand on the bases of their overall effectiveness. While such dismissals can be legitimately made on the bases of some research data (Howard et al., 2007), it is dangerous to ignore the data taken as a whole.

Child Moderators of Eclectic Programme Outcomes

Four characteristics of the participants in the outcome-effectiveness studies are shown in Table 11.2: age, intellectual functioning, language ability and social-adaptive behaviour functioning. It is possible to relate these intake measures to the change in the standard scores for the three outcome domains (intellectual functioning, language and social-adaptive behaviour) presented in Table 11.3.

Figure 11.9 shows the strength of the relationships (determined by Pearson correlation coefficients) between the four child intake variables and the three outcome domains. In terms of predictors of intellectual functioning, having good language skills and good social-adaptive behaviour, at intake appears to be associated with greater gains over the course of the treatment (see also Magiati et al., 2011; Peters-Scheffer et al., 2013). Change in language ability is predicted by the level of intellectual

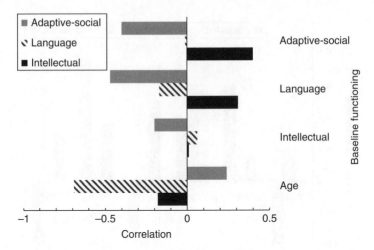

Figure 11.9   Correlations between four baseline functioning domains and the standard score changes (pre-to-post intervention) following eclectic interventions.

functioning at intake (see also Magiati et al., 2011; Peters-Scheffer et al., 2013), but seems to be inversely related to social and adaptive skills at baseline. Adaptive and social skills are predicted by age (the older the child the better the progress) and negatively predicted by language ability. These data show that there are indications of potential predictors of outcome, but that this pattern is rather complex and only a few of the levels of linear association are strong. These overall impressions, however, do cover a range of somewhat more subtle effects that are discussed in some more detail next for each predictor in turn.

Age at intake

The data in Figure 11.9 show a clear relationship between age at intake and the change in language and adaptive-social behaviours of the participants, but there is a less strong relationship between this intake variable and changes in intellectual functioning. A similar pattern of results can be seen when considering the mean effect sizes for these outcome domains when the studies are split into those whose mean intake age was less than the median for the sample (<47 months) and those studies with a higher than median mean age intake (>47 months). The mean effect sizes for the outcome domains for these two groups are shown in Figure 11.10.

From the data in Figure 11.10, it can be seen that younger participants at intake make stronger gains in language ability; suggesting that the younger the children are at intake. Similar findings have been reported across a number of individual studies of eclectic programmes that have assessed this relationship (Magiati et al., 2011; Peters-Scheffer et al., 2013; Rogers et al., 2012). In contrast, there is an indication of a positive relationship between the age of the participant at intake and gains in social-adaptive behaviour – suggesting that older children benefit more from eclectic programmes in this domain than younger children. This finding was also noted by Peters-Scheffer et al. (2012).

One domain where starting the programme at a younger age might have been expected to produce stronger gains is that of intellectual functioning. However, this

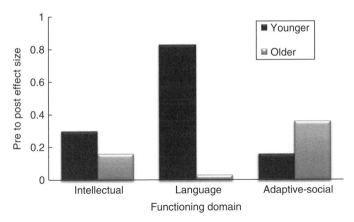

Figure 11.10 Effect sizes for the pre-to-post intervention changes in three functioning domains following an eclectic intervention for studies involving participants younger or older than the sample mean (47 months). Younger participants at baseline fair better in terms of intellectual and language gains, whereas older participants make more adaptive-social gains.

relationship was only marginal when the changes in standard scores across the studies as a whole were considered (Figure 11.9), although the effect size data shown in Figure 11.10 suggest the presence of some such relationship. Paralleling this rather varied picture, there is some disagreement in the literature on this point with respect to eclectic programmes: Rogers et al. (2012) noted a strong negative relationship between intake age and intellectual function gain, whereas Peters-Scheffer et al. (2012) noted the converse relationship. It should be noted that the ages of the children in the Rogers et al. (2012) study were very young (around 18 months old) and different relationships may exist for such exceptionally young samples.

Intellectual functioning at intake

A number of individual studies of eclectic interventions have suggested that the higher the participants' intake intellectual functioning, the better will be the outcomes (Gabriels et al., 2001; Magiati et al., 2007; 2011). However, this is not a universally noted finding and several studies have either failed to note such a relationship (Zachor et al., 2007). The data presented in Figure 11.9 relating to intake intellectual functioning show little relationship between this variable and outcome, supporting the findings of Zachor et al. (2007). However, when the effect sizes for the change in the three functioning domains were plotted against the intellectual functioning of the participants at intake for the studies (see Figure 11.11), then it can be seen that this relationship is not straightforward.

Figure 11.11 presents the scatterplots for intake intellectual functioning and effect size in terms of the three outcomes. For intellectual functioning and language ability there is little relationship (if anything, the relationship is slightly negative). However, for the social-adaptive functioning effect size, there is quite a clear quadratic relationship between these variables; with greater gains being seen for those participants who enter the programme with low or high levels of intellectual functioning.

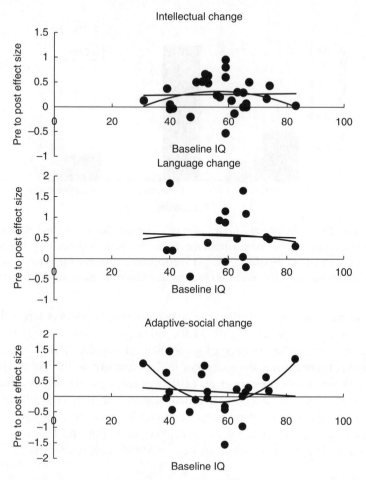

Figure 11.11 Relationship between baseline intellectual functioning (standard score) and the effect size for changes in three functioning domains after exposure to an eclectic intervention. Lines represent the linear and quadratic trends in these data. See text for full discussion.

Language functioning at intake

The data presented in Figure 11.9 show that the greater the language ability of the participants at intake, the better will be the outcome in terms of intellectual functioning, but that this relationship was not pronounced for language functioning gains and that there was a clear reverse relationship between gains in adaptive-social functioning and language ability at intake. With respect to the relationship between language ability and intellectual ability gains, this has been noted in a number individual studies of eclectic programmes, such as that reported by Magiati et al. (2011; see also Gabriels et al., 2001). However, the overall findings regarding social-adaptive behaviours have not been reported in any individual study.

These findings with regard to standard score increases are also noted in terms of effect sizes of change when the sample of studies is split into lower language ability (standard score <46) and those studies where participants entered treatment with a

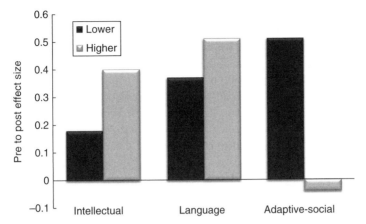

Figure 11.12 Pre-to-post effect sizes for changes in functioning domains following eclectic intervention for studies whose participants had a lower or higher than mean VAB score (57) at baseline. Higher scorers performed better in terms of intellectual and language gains, but not in terms of adaptive-social gains.

greater then mean language abilities. The effect size for intellectual functioning gain for the studies whose participants had a higher mean language ability at intake (ES = 0.46) was much greater than for the studies with a lower than average language ability at intake (ES = 0.18). In contrast, studies with a mean lower language ability at intake showed nearly three times the gain in social-adaptive behaviours (ES = 0.35) than those reports whose participants had a higher mean language ability at intake (ES = -0.14). Unfortunately, it is unclear what underlies this pattern of data. Moreover, it should be noted that the split between lower and higher language abilities at intake is based on only six reports in each group, making the data less powerful than they might have been with greater numbers of studies.

Adaptive-social behaviour and ASD severity at intake

Figure 11.12 shows the mean effect sizes for the three outcome domains (intellectual, language, social-adaptive, functioning) for the groups with lower than mean intake VABS scores (VABS standard score < 53) and the groups with greater than mean for the sample VABS scores at intake (VABS > 54). The findings in terms of the impact of adaptive-social behaviours (as measured by the VABS) on the three outcome domains are quite straightforward. As Figure 11.12 shows for gains in effect sizes (and Figure 11.9 shows for standard score changes), the greater the intake adaptive-social behaviour of the participants, the greater the outcome, in terms of the intellectual functioning gains produced by the programme. This pattern of results is also noted in terms of the language effect sizes (although this is not so apparent for the change in standard scores represented in Figure 11.9). The relationship between initial VABS scores and gain in functioning for this domain over the course of the eclectic programme is actually negative, but this finding more than likely reflects the greater scope for increase in participants with lower VABS scores at intake. The finding that stronger gains can be achieved with participants with greater adaptive-social behaviours is consistent with the results reported by the few individual studies that have analysed this association (e.g. Magiati et al., 2011; Peters-Scheffer et al., 2012).

There have been relatively few studies that have examined the relationship between ASD severity at intake and the outcomes of eclectic programmes, although the relatively strong relationship between the VABS domain and ASD severity goes some way to address this issue as these two measures are often related to one another. However, the two reports that have directly examined the impact of ASD severity on outcome have come to similar conclusions to one another (Reed & Osborne, 2013; Zachor et al., 2007). In the study of a technical eclectic programme reported by Zachor et al. (2007), it was noted that greater gains were made in their eclectic programme by participants with less severe ASD symptoms. This was also shown by Reed and Osborne (2013), who found that fewer gains were made by the more severe ASD participants in a generic eclectic programme.

Summary

This review of the impact of various child characteristics that may serve as moderators of the effectiveness of eclectic interventions has revealed that there are some circumstances in which, at least, moderate effect size gains can been observed. In particular:

- Intellectual functioning is promoted with more language-skilled and more socially able, individuals.
- Language ability is promoted to a larger degree in younger individuals.
- Social skills are better promoted in older participants.

The suggestion that there are sets of individuals with ASD who may benefit from eclectic programmes has not gone unnoticed in the literature. Indeed, in response to the accusation that there is little evidence for the effectiveness of such eclectic programmes (see Howard et al., 2005), Zachor et al. (2007) suggested that, with appropriate participants, there may be little difference between the impacts of eclectic programmes and brand name interventions. Indeed, there are some individual studies that have shown such effects for particular areas of functioning, especially in terms of social functioning (Magrygianni et al., 2010; Reed et al., 2007b; Zachor et al., 2007).

To explore this suggestion further, the data presented in Table 11.4 with respect to the effect sizes of eclectic programmes in comparison to control groups were further analysed. The comparative effect sizes were plotted against the potential child intake moderator variables and these plots can be seen in Figure 11.13. Inspection of these data suggest that there were few cases where the eclectic programmes outperformed the comparison groups in any of the domains (all mean effect sizes were negative). However, it can be seen that there was some suggestion that for higher functioning and for older, children the effect sizes approaches zero – suggesting no difference between the eclectic and comparison programme. Of course, it should be remembered that many brand name interventions typically have positive comparative effect sizes.

This suggestion that there are circumstances under which eclectic programmes will be successful is strengthened further when the three forms of eclectic programme are analysed separately (unfortunately this cannot be done for each separate outcome variable, as there are too few studies of each eclectic type to produce reliable data).

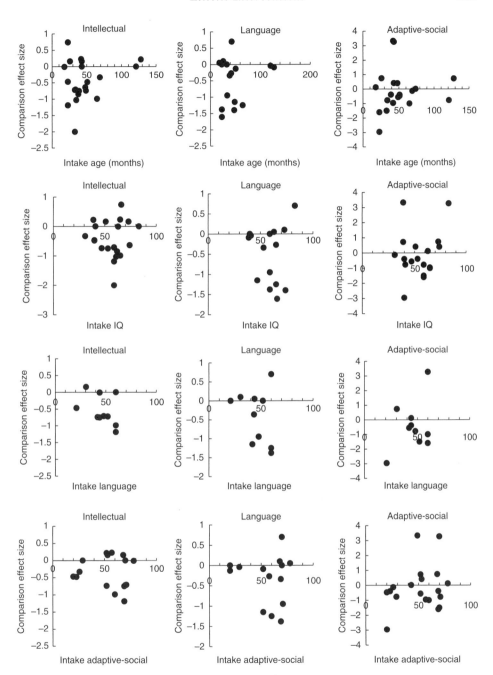

Figure 11.13 Scatterplots relating baseline child characteristics (age, IQ, language, adaptive-social) to three outcome domains (intellectual, language, adaptive-social) for the relative effect of eclectic programmes versus their comparison conditions.

When the mean comparative effect size (eclectic versus control) across all the outcome domains is calculated for each study, to produce an overall comparative effect size and the means for the three types of programme are calculated, it can be seen that treatment as usual approaches are, indeed, less successful than their comparisons for this measure (ES = −0.81) and generic programmes also have a poor relative effect size (−0.33). These are the types of programme that have typically prompted concerns about eclectic interventions. However, technical eclectic interventions have a positive effect size (1.47), meaning that they are more effective than the comparisons in those reports. Of course, the nature of the comparison groups in an issue (e.g. technical eclectic programmes have not been compared directly with strong behavioural programmes), but the previous discussion suggests that there is more to be done in terms of evaluating these programmes.

Theory, Perception and Commitment

Many of the differences between brand name comprehensive intervention packages and eclectic programmes have been discussed previously – but one major difference has remained unaddressed, that is, the fact that much of the data relating to eclectic programmes are drawn from interventions that have not been specifically set up for test. That is, these programmes have been included as control programmes for other interventions, perhaps because they were available to the researchers at the time and, in fact, the practitioners may not be committed to these approaches in the way that they may be committed to a brand name intervention.

It may well be that having a greater commitment to an approach will produce greater motivation on the part of the therapist and this greater motivation may translate into greater progress on the part of the person receiving the treatment. The notion of commitment to the intervention has received some study in the literature and there are a number of scales that have been designed to measure commitment to particular philosophies of treatment (Coman et al., 2013; Hume et al., 2011; Jennett et al., 2003).

The issue of commitment to a particular treatment philosophy is also associated with another potentially important area for consideration. The degree to which staff training predicts outcomes in such ASD programmes has been the subject of investigation in relation to behavioural programmes (see Chapter 6 for further discussion). The general consensus on this issue is that greater levels of training produce more effective interventions and better outcomes. However, the numerous issues revolving around the problem of how such training is measured render this generally held view open to question. Nevertheless, if there is no particular central coherence to the theory or philosophy underlying the treatment, then providing training in the implementation of this theory is, of course, not easy. This is a further reason why many eclectic programmes could fail to produce the improvements seen in some brand name interventions.

If all of this holds some credibility as an argument, then it follows that the eclectic programmes, which were the target of the outcome-effectiveness studies, should show signs of greater effectiveness than those programmes that were merely included as a useful comparison group. To investigate this possibility, the studies outlined in Table 11.3, which were the specific target of the investigation and those that were not the target intervention of the report, were analysed separately in terms of their outcomes. The change between baseline to follow-up measures in the standard scores and the associated effect sizes, from these two groups of eclectic programmes, are presented in Figure 11.14.

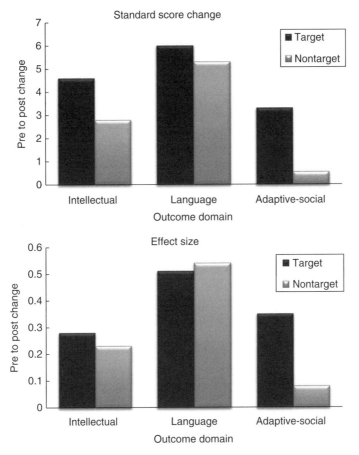

Figure 11.14 Outcomes of eclectic interventions that were the target of the study (Target) or included in the study as a control condition for another intervention (Nontarget). Top panel = change in standard score; bottom panel = pre-to-post effect sizes.

Inspection of these data, show that for intellectual functioning and adaptive-social behaviours, the target eclectic programmes produced around twice the gain in standard score as those programmes that were not the subject of the report. There was a less pronounced difference in terms of language between these two groups. The effect sizes show two findings of importance for this discussion: firstly, they are in line with the standard score changes and secondly, even when considering the target interventions, these effect sizes were not strong, although the target eclectic interventions could be considered to have produced moderate effect sizes – in line with some 'brand name' interventions discussed previously.

If the target and non-target eclectic programmes are considered separately against their control groups, a somewhat different pattern of relative effect sizes emerges for the two groups. For the non-target programmes, effect sizes across all functioning domains are universally negative and all in the moderately negative zone, suggesting that the alternative treatment is more effective. However, none of these comparative effect sizes are negative for the target eclectic programmes; intellectual functioning = 0.05; language ability = 0.07 and adaptive-social behaviour skills = 0.83. Of course, the former two domains are not particularly striking and only suggest that such programmes are no worse than comparisons. However, the strong effect size for adaptive-behaviour skills is worthy of attention, as it rivals most effect sizes seen previously for brand name approaches and surpasses many.

There are a number of provisos to these data that do need to be considered. Importantly, it is difficult to directly compare effect sizes across programmes when the effect sizes are based on comparisons with different control groups. There have been very few direct comparisons between a 'target' eclectic approach and a target behavioural approach, for instance. The only study which has attempted this was reported by Reed et al. (2007b) and they found that the behavioural approach had the advantage for intellectual functioning, but that there was slight advantage for the eclectic approach in terms of adaptive-social skills. This was commented on in Chapter 5 in relation to the more unanimous support given by Howard et al. (2005) for behavioural programmes. However, the latter report was focused on the behavioural approach as the target and, as such, could not be considered to offer a comparison between 'equals'. These considerations mean that the exact nature of the eclectic intervention is of importance, a finding that should come as no surprise at all, but one that tends to be overlooked when considering the impact of other programmes against such eclectic controls.

Summary

The current chapter has overviewed the effectiveness of a range of eclectic provisions for the treatment of ASD and there are a number of clear conclusions that have emerged from this overview, which can be summarized as follows:

- Eclectic approaches offer a diverse set of strategies that need to be considered in some detail rather than making blanket observations about their effectiveness.
- In the main, there is little support for the impact of eclectic programmes on intellectual functioning; either in themselves or in comparison with other programmes.
- Eclectic programmes often fare reasonably well in terms of language development.
- There is reason to suggest that some particular eclectic strategies offer as good progress as some brand name interventions, especially in terms of adaptive-social behaviours.
- Children who are younger with higher functioning improve most in terms of intellectual and language functioning (especially on programme with SLT and social skills), but older and higher functioning often fare well for adaptive behaviour (especially those involving both ABA and TEACCH principles).
- It is important to consider the nature of programme – with technical eclectic programmes that are the predominant target of the outcome-effectiveness report producing the best changes.

Thus, there are some theoretical reasons and some empirical reasons, to suggest that eclectic approaches may offer some gains to some participants. However, much greater understanding of the nature of the programmes is needed before such conclusions can be firmly verified.

12

Inclusive or Special Education

As with many of the questions regarding the effectiveness of particular interventions raised in the previous chapters, whether children with Autism Spectrum Disorders (ASD) should be educated in mainstream or special schools has been hotly debated (see Mesibov, 1990; Warnock, 1978; 2005). Although critical for much contemporary educational policy, questions regarding the efficacy of 'inclusive' education for individuals with ASD are not straightforward to answer – and cannot be addressed simply by reference to effect sizes and significant changes in functioning. The issue of placing individuals with ASD into mainstream education is beset with helpful politicians (see Bricker, 1995; Kauffman, 1989), poorly thought-out agendas (Warnock, 2005) and, as shall be observed in the current chapter, sparse evidence on which to base such decisions.

The practice of educating children with special educational needs (SEN) in mainstream schools has been driven by a philosophical human rights agenda (Lindsay, 2003; Norwich, 2005). At its core, the 'rights-based' view asserts that inclusion of children with SEN into mainstream schools is a moral and social imperative that is necessary to remove discrimination and exclusion (Novick & Glanz, 2011; UNESCO, 1994). This drive has greatly impacted educational placement and provision for children with ASD and, as it turns out, not always positively. The counter-position to the 'rights-based' view is that education should be based on individual needs, rather than social imperatives (see Ravet, 2011, for a discussion of the 'rights' versus 'needs' agendas).

It is these issues that frame the central discussions of the current chapter, which will involve consideration of the effect of school placement on the reduction of stigma and the development of equality of educational provision, as well as how to promote educational effectiveness within these constraints. The first of these concerns involves the impacts on the individual of the perceived stigma often attached to being educated in a special school. Related to this is the suggestion that the labels associated with 'special education' follow the individual through their life, reducing their

Interventions for Autism: Evidence for Educational and Clinical Practice, First Edition. Phil Reed.
© 2016 John Wiley & Sons, Ltd. Published 2016 by John Wiley & Sons, Ltd.

opportunities, feeding prejudices and limiting choices (Gray, 2002). The second issue is whether different school provisions ever produce the possibility of equivalent outcomes – and this is the aspect of the debate that underlies and prompts much of the 'rights agenda' regarding inclusive education (see *Brown versus Board of Education* 1954). This second issue, of course is intimately related to the third issue, which concerns the effectiveness of mainstream and special educational.

Historical Development of Segregated Education

Understanding these issues of school placement involves, in part, grasping the various changes to educational policy that have occurred over the past 100 years or so. It is these policy-driven changes that have created the major points of debate in this area. The current section summarizes these changes and what they have meant for the study of the education of individuals with ASD. Most of what follows is based around policy in the UK, but, as has been argued elsewhere (Reed & Osborne, 2014), the UK has tended to produce a lead in the education of children with SEN that other countries have followed (see Table 12.1 for a timeline).

Concerns about the appropriate school placement for children dates to changes in UK educational policy at the end of the nineteenth century (Reed & Osborne, 2014). In fact, the proliferation of special schools that followed this period of intensive change in educational policy produced the key issues connected to inclusion that still provoke debate. After the UK Education Act of 1870, increasing numbers of children were admitted to school, but increasing numbers of these newly admitted pupils were also then excluded due to alleged learning and behaviour problems. Yet as these pupils were legally entitled to an education by this Act, the solution was an expansion of the special school sector by which to educate them. Prior to this point, special schools had a prime focus on physically and sensory-impaired children and began to appear around 1865 (Gillard, 2011), after the 1870 Act these schools took pupils, who were quickly termed 'feeble minded' (i.e. intellectually disabled individuals who were thought able to benefit from education). The subsequent UK Mental Deficiency Act (1913) cemented the term 'feeble-minded' and this led to further increases in the use of special schools for these pupils (Simmons, 1978).

Half a century later, many noted that impact of special schools on the progress of children in their charge had been minimal. Certainly, in the context of ASD, special schools had not improved the prognosis of individuals with ASD (Howlin, 1997; Rutter & Lockyer, 1967; Chapter 1). This recognition prompted a drive to 'normalization' in education (Nirje, 1969) and to 'mainstream' children with SEN (UNESCO, 1994; Warnock, 1978; Wedell, 2008). The Warnock Report (1978) began the wholesale movement of pupils with SEN (including ASD) into mainstream schools, which, it was argued, would combat discriminatory attitudes (Peck et al., 1992), create welcoming communities (Bogdan & Taylor, 1989; Murray-Seegert, 1989) and improve the efficiency and cost effectiveness of the educational system (Affleck et al., 1988; Piuma, 1989).

Unfortunately, subsequent research found that mainstreamed SEN children often had very low levels of acceptance in the schools (Nabuzoka & Smith, 1993) and the anticipated educational gains did not emerge (Davis et al., 2004b). The lacklustre

Table 12.1 Timeline of developments across the world in terms of education of pupils with special educational needs.

Date	UK	USA and elsewhere
1860s	First special schools for physical problems	
1870	*Education Act (1970)* Expands right to education to working classes.	
1900–1950	*Mental Deficiency Act (1913)* Introduces concept of 'feeble-minded' but educable *Brock Committee (1930)* Rejects sterilization for those with learning difficulties.	60 000–70 000 individuals with learning disabilities sterilized. *Law for the Prevention of Progeny with Hereditary Diseases* (Germany, 1933)
1950–1979	*Warnock Report (1978)* Calls for inclusive education for all.	20% of individuals with SEN receive an education. *Rehabilitation Act (1973)* Introduces notion of right to education for persons with disabilities *Rolf v Weinberger (1974)* Reveals around 100 – 150,00 people with SEN sterilized *Education of all Handicapped Children Act (1975)*
1980	*Education Act (1981)* Introduces SEN statements and right to help with mainstream education	
1990s		*Individuals with Disabilities Education ACT (1990)* *U.N. Salamanca Statement (1994)*
2000s	*Education Act (2001)* Mainstream placements should be the norm *Warnock Report (2005)* Concludes inclusive education is not working	*No Child Left Behind Act (2001)*

empirical evidence was coupled with emerging philosophical views suggesting that trying to force all students into 'mainstream' schools was as coercive as trying to force all SEN students into special education (Lindsey, 2003; Norwich, 2005). A further barrier confronting mainstreaming was that children with SEN, especially those with ASD (Lord & McGee, 2001), were a very heterogeneous population, with very different needs from one another and not all suited to the same teaching methods (as has been highlighted by all successful interventions for ASD). Such considerations prompted Warnock (2005; see also Tomlinson, 1996) to recant the earlier views and conclude that inclusion, as an SEN policy, was not working and that the strategies underlying the policy of equity needed to be revised (see also Booth & Ainscow, 2000; Humphrey, 2008).

Placement of Pupils with ASD in Mainstream and Special Schools

Even given these concerns, individuals with ASD are the only SEN group to be increasingly represented in mainstream schools (UK Office of National Statistics, 2004; 2009). A decade ago, approximately 50% of children with ASD received mainstream placements in the UK (Barnard et al., 2000; Keen & Ward, 2004). In the intervening decade and despite the previous argument against inclusion, there has been around a 15% increase in the placement of children with ASD into mainstream schools (Frederickson et al., 2010). There are many potential reasons for ASD bucking this particular trend: diagnostic substitution (Matson & Shoemaker, 2009; Chapter 1); closure of special schools (Department for Education and Skills, 2006; Chapter 1) or school selection policies that make it harder for children with ASD to be accepted in mainstream placement (West & Hind, 2006). Whatever the reasons for this trend, it stresses the importance of school placement for children with ASD.

The placement of children with ASD in mainstream settings varies greatly across different countries. For example just over 25% of children with ASD are in mainstream education in the USA (*27th Annual Report to Congress on the Implementation of the Individuals with Disabilities Education Act*, 2007), whereas, at least twice this number of children with ASD are in mainstream schools. Waddington and Reed (2015) surveyed several authorities in the UK with a combined population of around one million pupils and noted that, although practice across the individual authorities varied, 60% of pupils with ASD in these authorities combined were placed in a mainstream school (see Table 12.2) – a figure that translates into between 0.5 and 1% of the entire mainstream school population.

Although these data suggest that there are large numbers of individuals with ASD in mainstream settings, there also imply a sizable minority of children with ASD are in special schools. Several investigations have attempted to determine whether there are any characteristics that predict school placement (Buysse et al., 1994; Eaves & Ho, 1997; Waddington & Reed, 2015). Perhaps not surprisingly, these reports have noted that those placed in special schools have more severe ASD symptoms. Eaves and Ho (1997; Buysse et al., 1994) assessed that the likelihood of a child with ASD being placed in a mainstream school, a unit attached to a mainstream school or a special school and found that this varied with their level of intellectual functioning as measured by the Wechsler Intelligence Scale for Children – Revised (see Figure 12.1).

Table 12.2 Percentage of pupils with different types of ASD diagnoses who were placed in different educational establishments in the UK (Waddington & Reed, 2015).

		School placement			
		Mainstream	*Special*	*Special unit in mainstream*	*Home*
Diagnosis	*Autism*	59%	35%	6	0
	Autism spectrum	61%	28%	11	0
	ASD/co-morbid	33%	42%	8	17

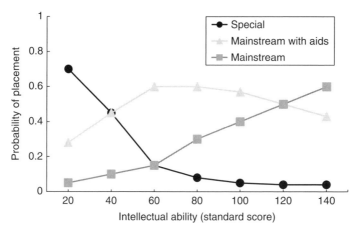

Figure 12.1 Probability of placement within various types of school depending upon the intellectual ability of the pupil with ASD, based on figures reported by Eaves and Ho (1997). Mainstream placement is more likely for pupils with higher intellectual ability.

Waddington and Reed (2015) noted that social skills and self-help skills also predicted placement in a mainstream school.

It should be noted that these figures only represent those children with a clear ASD diagnosis. Often, children with ASD will be recognized as such and will have been deliberately placed into a particular school setting. However, there are individuals with ASD who have not been diagnosed (Humphrey, 2008) and this group presents an 'invisible problem' (Connor, 2000). In fact, Baron-Cohen et al. (2009) estimated that as many as 40% of ASD cases were unrecognized. These individuals may be placed in a mainstream school and receive no help, even though it may be necessary (Kim et al., 2011; Lord, 2011). As this 'invisible' group receive no support, they may be vulnerable to the range of co-morbid issues that can beset high-functioning individuals with ASD (Barnhill & Myles, 2001; Ghaziuddin et al., 2002; Humphrey & Symes, 2010; see Chapter 1).

Impacts of Educational Placement on Children with ASD

Although the mainstream education of pupils with ASD is an issue that has merited special consideration due to their peculiar needs (Norwich & Lewis, 2005), there is very little direct evidence regarding the impact of school placement (see Von der Embse et al., 2011, for a review). However, what is known is that, in the mainstream school, pupils with ASD are 20 times more likely to be excluded from a mainstream school than typically developing children (Department of Education and Skills, 2006) and have a 20% probability of being excluded or suspended from school at least once (Barnard et al., 2000). However, how headline findings such as these should be interpreted, and what their implications for the policy of inclusion may be, is not at all clear – whether they reflect a failure of inclusive education or a failure to implement policies appropriately is still debated.

Successful inclusion

Without the foundation of a definition of successful inclusion, then neither the evidence regarding effectiveness of educational placement, nor the practices that facilitate that practice, can be developed. In order to understand what would constitute successful inclusion, Frederickson et al. (2004; see also Sansosti & Sansosti, 2012) sought the views of educational professionals (mainstream school teachers, special school teachers, educational psychologists) regarding what pupil skills were important in achieving successful inclusion. Table 12.3 presents a summary of the responses from the different groups.

The key areas that were suggested as being needed for a successful inclusion were: academic progress; social progress; the child's views and happiness and discipline and compliance with school rules (see also Eldar et al., 2010; Sansosti & Sansosti, 2012). These findings highlight the key domains of functioning that need to be considered in exploring inclusive education for pupils with ASD. However, although the participants from the various professions tended to agree that academic and social progress were paramount; mainstream teachers placed more emphasis on discipline and special school teachers placed more weight on the child's happiness. This discrepancy may go some way towards explaining the different perspectives that have emerged when discussing the success of inclusion as a policy (Ravet, 2011). The following sections review the evidence of whether placement in mainstream schools facilitates these key areas of functioning in pupils with ASD.

Academic and intellectual progress

Mainstreaming individuals with ASD initially was premised on the suggestion that special schools did not facilitate their academic performance (Lockyer & Rutter, 19709; Rutter, 1968; see Chapter 1). The current situation with respect to academic and intellectual progress for pupils with ASD in mainstream placements presents a mixed pattern of data and several reviews relevant to ASD have reached contradictory conclusions from one another (Freeman & Alkin, 2000; Ruijs & Peetsma, 2009; Schneider & Leroux, 1994. Two of these reviews (Freeman & Alkin, 2000; Ruijs & Peetsma, 2009) concluded that mainstream placements produced small advantages in terms of academic development for children with mild intellectual disabilities (although both reports acknowledge that there are a number of studies that report no difference between these placements). In contrast, Schneider and Leroux (1994) suggested that greater academic gains were made for children with behavioural difficulties in special schools. The difference between the conclusions of these reviews may be connected with the difference in the populations included – intellectual disabilities versus behavioural problems – as interference with academic progress may be produced by the presence of challenging behaviours (Koegel et al., 2012). Such interference with school progress may be quite pronounced in mainstream schools, where discipline and compliance are seen as key to success (Frederickson et al., 2004). The high levels of externalizing behaviours in individuals with ASD (Smith & Matson, 2010; Wacker et al., 2009; see the present Chapter 2) also may imply a problem for the mainstream education of such individuals.

Table 12.3 Percentage of responses falling into various categories regarding key elements for judging successful inclusion into a mainstream school (from Frederickson et al., 2004).

	Effects on other pupils	Attendance	Child views and happiness	Parental support and happiness	Disciplinary compliance and behaviour	Learning and academic progress	Social progress	School support systems	Methods and monitoring
Special School	1	8	19	4	9	25	21	9	4
Primary Mainstream	6	4	5	5	19	20	28	7	7
Secondary Mainstream	4	6	13	3	14	21	22	12	5
Professional Support	5	4	16	4	4	18	25	17	7

Several studies have investigated the effects of mainstream school placement on the academic and intellectual development of children with ASD, but these studies also have reported mixed results. Two observational studies (Stahmer et al., 2011; Webb et al., 2012) followed the progress of a cohort of children with ASD over a period of a school year; Stahmer et al. (2011) for very young children and Webb et al. (2012) for older children. Both reports were of specially designed inclusive mainstream placements and both studies noted small to moderate improvements in intellectual functioning and communication. However, although Stahmer et al. (2011) presented comparison data on expected developmental trajectories for these children over the period of time and demonstrated greater than expected improvement in the mainstreamed ASD pupils, the absence of a control group in these studies make definitive conclusions difficult.

Kurth and Mastergeorge (2010) reported the results of a comparative study of children with ASD (aged 12–14 years old), who had been continuously in the same school setting for some time. These data noted an advantage for the mainstream schools in terms of academic/intellectual gains; pupils in both settings demonstrated gains, but pupils who were placed in a mainstream school for more than 80% of their school day, obtained higher levels of reasoning ability, than the pupils who spent less than 50% of their school day in these mainstream settings.

In contrast, two further studies reported no benefit of mainstreaming for pupils with ASD. Harris et al. (1990) assessed increases in the ratio between developmental level and the rate of language use and found no differences between the developmental level and the rate of language gain between students with ASD in the two settings. Waddington and Reed (2015) assessed the records of 108 children with ASD (aged 5–16 years), who were exclusively educated in special or mainstream school (with no particular modifications in teaching approach provided for the pupils with ASD). There were no differences in the ASD severity or type of ASD diagnoses, between the two groups. The mean level of academic achievement, based on National Curriculum results, are displayed in Figure 12.2, which reveals that the overall level was around the UK P-level 8 (a scale with 8 levels that is used for children working below that expected of children in the first year of primary school – usually 5–6 years old). This performance is much lower than would be expected for a cohort of this age, but there was a slight advantage for pupils in the special placements over the mainstream schools. However, these differences were not great in magnitude and suggest no great impact on the academic achievement of the children.

It is important to remember that, in many of the studies reported previously (e.g. Kurth & Mastergeorge, 2010; Waddington & Reed, 2015) there would be differences in the teaching strategies adopted in the mainstream and special schools, making difficult the direct comparison of the effect of placement, itself. However, the results from a study reported by Panerai et al. (2009) partially address this issue: the developmental progress of children with ASD was compared across mainstream and special schools that were employing the same teaching technique as one another (Treatment and Education of Autistic and related Communication handicapped Children; TEACCH). The academic/intellectual outcomes were virtually identical in these two groups and were higher than those noted in a mainstream class lacking this structured teaching approach.

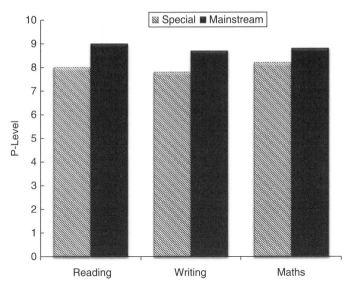

Figure 12.2 Differences in attainment in three aspects of the UK national curriculum (P-Level) by pupils with ASD in either a mainstream or special school setting.

In summary, there is no great reason to suppose that one educational placement will produce greater academic gains than another. The mixed results complicates the interpretation of this set of results and make it difficult to provide any clear guidance on which children will benefit most from inclusion in a mainstream school. The reviews by Freeman and Alkin (2000) and Ruijs and Peetsma (2009), coupled with the results from Stahmer et al. (2011), suggest that better intellectual skills at intake predict academic development in mainstream school. It also might be suggested that those with lower intellectual functioning probably fare slightly better in special schools (Waddington & Reed, 2009; 2015). However, as will be seen later in this chapter, there are many additional factors that mitigate any impact of mainstream schools on academic progress. These issues include the interaction between any perceptual sensitivities and the noisy environment of the school (Ashburner et al., 2010), the teaching style adopted in mainstream classes (Panerai et al., 2009), the pupil's level of disruptive behaviour (Kupersmidt & DeRosier, 2004) and the teacher perceptions about inclusion and pupils with ASD (Ashburner et al., 2010). Thus, in terms of academic progress, the safest conclusion is that this will be a product of the interaction between the individual and the school and not simply a function of school placement alone.

Social progress

A major reason presented in favour of inclusive education was the assumed more beneficial impact of a mainstream placement on social skills and peer acceptance (Connor, 2000; Harris & Handlemann, 1997). For the general population of children with SEN, there may be some evidence to support this position (see Baker et al., 1994; McGregor & Vogelsberg, 1998, for reviews). However, as Kurth and Mastergeorge (2010) have noted, the primary deficit for many children with SEN is not social, as it

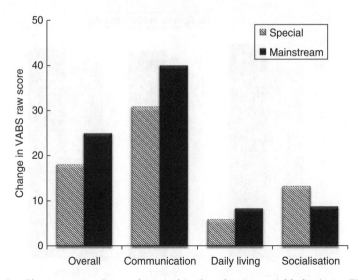

Figure 12.3 Changes over a 9-month period in the adaptive-social behaviours (VABS) by pupils with ASD who were placed in either a mainstream or a special school setting reported by Reed et al. (2012).

usually is for pupils with ASD and this may make generalization to ASD from the broad SEN literature difficult (Hilton et al., 2008; Knight et al., 2010).

Strain (1983a) focused on preschool and primary school children with ASD and found that pupils in mainstream schools exhibited more pro-social behaviours than those in special schools. Similarly, Buysse and Bailey (1993) documented greater improvements in social and play skills for children with ASD in inclusive settings, as did Webb et al. (2012). Both of these studies were conducted in mainstream classroom settings that were highly managed with regard to their ASD-sensitive teaching strategies.

In contrast to these positive reports, several other studies have shown no social gains for children with ASD in more typical mainstream placements (Durbach & Pence, 1991; Harris et al., 1990; Reed et al., 2012). Reed et al. (2012) assessed 54 children with ASD attending mainstream school and 86 children with ASD attending special school. The two groups of children were matched for age, gender, ASD severity. Figure 12.3 shows the gains made in terms of adaptive-social behaviours in the study reported by Reed et al. (2012), as measured by the Vineland Adaptive Behavior Scale (VABS), which shows that both groups made similar improvements to one another. Similarly, Boyd et al. (2014) noted no difference between the social gains made by pupils with ASD in a mainstream or special school placement.

Importantly, several studies have reported high levels of social exclusion suffered by children with ASD when placed in mainstream settings. Humphrey and Symes (2010; 2011, see also Ashburner et al., 2008) found that children with ASD in mainstream schools reported more social rejection, lower acceptance and more reactive aggression than other SEN children (dyslexia) and matched typically developing groups (see also Koster et al., 2010). In fact, several authors have suggested that social isolation and loneliness are more typical in mainstream schools for this population than enhanced social interaction (see also Bauminger & Kasari, 2000; Knight et al., 2009; Ochs

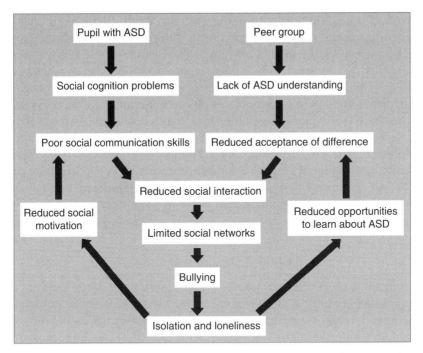

Figure 12.4 The Reciprocal Effects Peer Interaction Model (REPIM) from Humphrey and Symes (2011), describing the negative social outcomes sometimes experienced by pupils with ASD when placed in a mainstream school setting.

et al., 2001). Similarly, Koster et al. (2010) found that children with SEN (including those with ASD) reported having fewer friendships with children in mainstream placements than their typically developing peers (see also Cairns & Cairns, 1994).

Findings that corroborate this picture of social exclusion are also reported from the perspective of the child with ASD (Browning et al., 2009; Humphrey & Lewis, 2008). For example, at the extreme, the experience of bullying is reported as being high by pupils with ASD in mainstream schools (Attwood, 2007; Rowley et al., 2012). These findings are especially pronounced in higher-functioning individuals with ASD – potentially jeopardizing any potential benefits that this group might have in terms of academic/intellectual gains that they may make in inclusive settings (see previous). Such results have been summarized by Humphrey and Symes (2011) in a model of the impact of mainstream placement on social progress of children with ASD, which is displayed in Figure 12.4.

A key hope for inclusion in mainstream schools was to promote social skills in those included children, as it was assumed that children with SEN would learn these skills through imitation of their typically developing peers (Boutot & Bryant, 2005). However, in mainstream placements which do not explicitly focus on these aspects of development, this view encounters three problems that may explain the lack of clear benefit of inclusion in this functioning domain. Firstly, individuals with ASD have deficits in their ability to model and imitate without special training (Rogers & Pennington, 1991; see Chapter 2). Secondly, imitation is stronger when the model has a number of characteristics, such as being: perceived as similar to the observer

(DiSalvo & Oswald, 2002); familiar to the observer (Birch, 1980) and socially agreeable rather than dominating (Marinho, 1940). These findings suggest that imitation may be stronger when the models are other children with similar SEN problems – a suggestion that is consistent with findings reported by Osborne and Reed (2011), showing that children with ASD perform better in mainstream settings when there are more children with SEN in the school. Finally, even if imitation were to occur, there is little evidence that typically developing children in mainstream settings spontaneously will model strong pro-social behaviours and, in fact, are more likely to engage in aggressive behaviours (Attwood, 2007; Humphrey & Symes, 2010). Thus, the evidence in regard to social progress is variable, but with its preponderance suggesting that problems can emerge in this domain from unmanaged inclusive programmes and that social progress will not spontaneously occur by mere placement in a mainstream setting.

Child views and happiness

Whether mainstream placement improves a child's psychological state and self-concept is a fraught and complex area. For example, the assessments of the impact of that placement on the child's state that are expressed by parents, teachers and the included pupil, are often mutually contradictory (Rowley et al., 2012) and this section attempts to summarize this literature.

There is still a relatively widespread view that education in special school provision is stigmatizing (Gray, 2002; Whittaker, 2001). Overall, a majority of parents of children with ASD express a wish for a mainstream placement for their child, not least, as they believe that it will help their child develop a stronger self-concept by avoiding the 'special school' label (Barnard et al., 2000; Resch et al., 2010). Indeed, child-related stress reported by parents has been noted to decrease after their toddlers had been placed in mainstream education (Baker-Ericzén et al., 2005). However, this rather broad characterization of parental views about the positive aspects of inclusion actually obscures the existence of a range of opinion with respect to the impacts of the placement on their child (see. Leyser & Kirk, 2004; Resch et al., 2010; Russell & Norwich, 2012). For example, Leyser and Kirk (2004) noted that, while parents expressed support for inclusion of their children with SEN in mainstream schools, this support was much more pronounced if their child had milder special needs and most parents expressed worries about the deleterious impacts on the child's psychological state and self-concept caused by the potentially negative social reactions of their peers.

There have been few quantitative studies of the impact of school inclusion on child depression and anxiety using typical psychometric tools. Hebron and Humphrey (2014) compared included pupils with ASD to both a matched dyslexic group and a group of typically developing children. They noted greater levels of depression, anxiety and a lower self-concept in the children with ASD compared to either of the other two groups. This evidence resonates with many qualitative studies that have addressed pupils' views of mainstream placement (Bauminger & Kasari, 2000; Browning et al., 2009; Humphrey & Lewis, 2008; Ochs et al., 2001). While many children with ASD in these reports want to be included in mainstream schools (Humphrey & Lewis, 2008; Schneider & Leroux, 1994; Struab, 1995), many also express great concerns over the negative social reactions of their peers (Humphrey & Lewis, 2008) and about bullying (Browning et al., 2009); the latter issue strongly diminished their self-concept (Bauminger & Kasari, 2000) and produce negative affect (Bauminger & Kasari, 2000; Ochs et al., 2001). These qualitative data are drawn from higher-functioning individuals with ASD (see Browning et al., 2009, for a discussion), which may highlight concerns over social-interaction induced problems to a greater extent than they are present for other less high-functioning included children (although, as noted previously, it is the higher functioning children who do tend to be included; Eaves & Ho, 1997; Waddington & Reed, 2015).

These negative impacts can lead to the development of co-morbid psychiatric problems (Barnhill & Myles, 2001; Ghaziuddin & Greden, 1998; Hebron & Humphrey, 2012), especially around the time of transition to secondary education (Ghaziuddin & Greden, 1998) when social comparison becomes more of an issue (Bellini, 2006; Humphrey & Lewis, 2008). These co-morbid problems may be especially pronounced for those with higher functioning ASD (Ghaziuddin et al., 1998; Chapter 2). However, as these are the very sorts of children with ASD who are likely to be included (see Buysee et al., 1994; Eaves & Ho, 1997; Waddington & Reed, 2015), this aspect of education in a mainstream setting must remain a serious concern.

Behaviour and compliance

An area that makes some groups of children with ASD particularly challenging in a school setting is their levels of externalizing behaviours (Eisenhower et al., 2005; Lecavalier et al., 2006; Osborne & Reed, 2009a; Chapter 2). In fact, by the time that their children reach school age, it is the externalizing problems, rather than other facets of ASD, that parents report as being most problematic (Osborne & Reed, 2009b) and it is the presence of such challenging behaviours that often defines successful inclusion (Eldar et al., 2010; Frederickson et al., 2004). The statistics on school exclusion for children with ASD (Department for Education and Skills, 2006) suggest that it is externalizing behaviours that are the key instigator of suspensions and permanent exclusions from school.

Both parent and teacher ratings of problem behaviours emitted by pupils in mainstream schools are higher for children with ASD than for matched typically developing peers (Ashburner et al., 2010; Gadow et al., 2005; MacIntosh, & Dissanayake, 2006). Ashburner et al. (2010) found that teachers rated the levels of problem behaviours emitted by higher-functioning ASD pupils as greater than those emitted by age- and gender-matched typically developing children educated in the same mainstream classrooms. Similarly, MacIntosh and Dissanayake (2006) compared problems behaviours emitted by higher-functioning ASD pupils with matched typically developing peers in the same mainstream classrooms, as rated by both teachers and parents and found that both sets of informants rated the ASD group as having more social-skill deficits and greater numbers of problem behaviours (see Figure 12.5).

It is unclear whether the same issues apply to those lower-functioning pupils with ASD who are included in mainstream classes. There are actually very few studies that bear on this issue, although Gadow et al. (2005) noted that higher-functioning children with ASD who were included had more severe psychiatric symptoms, including oppositional defiant disorder, compared to lower-functioning included pupils. This finding was also indicated in a comparison made by Osborne and Reed (2011)

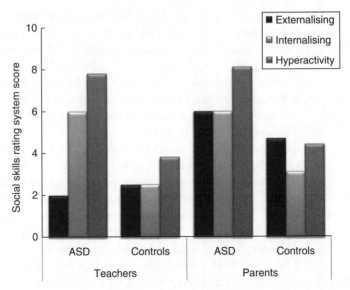

Figure 12.5 Severity of the problem behaviours displayed by pupils with high-functioning ASD and a control group of typically developing peers, as rated by their teachers and by their parents (Macintosh & Dissanayake, 2006).

between children with Asperger syndrome (who tended to be higher functioning) and those with ASD (lower functioning), who were being educated in mainstream schools; the former group showed more co-morbid problems than the latter.

Another important issue in regard to the impact of mainstreaming on the behavioural problems of children with ASD is whether the same levels of behavioural challenge as noted in many mainstream settings would also have been noted in a special school. Unfortunately, few controlled studies have been conducted that have made this direct comparison. One such study was reported by Reed et al. (2012) who measured the teacher-rated change in the behaviour problems emitted by matched children with higher-functioning ASD who attended either mainstream or special schools. The study noted that both sets of participants improved in both placements over the course of a year; however, children with ASD in specialist provision made greater improvements in area of conduct problems.

Of course, there are many reasons why mainstream and special schools would differ from one another and any number of these differences could explain these findings. However, when children undergo the same curriculum (the Preschool Inventory of Repertoires for Kindergarten, PIRK®) in special or mainstream schools, greater reductions in conduct disorders and hyperactivity are noted in the special school participants (Waddington & Reed, 2009). In this study, the group attending the special schools had more severe ASD symptoms and higher levels of behaviour problems, at intake, than those in the mainstream setting, but the latter difference had disappeared at the end of the year's placement.

Thus, it is clear that children with ASD in typical mainstream settings exhibit a large number of externalizing behaviours, which appear to be greater than matched groups in special educational settings. In part, these increased levels of externalizing behaviours may be a consequence of reactive aggression to peer bullying in mainstream schools. It may also be that, as these behavioural problems are almost always measured through teacher ratings, such teacher ratings may be influenced by the teachers' perceptions of their own ability to deal with those behaviours, which may not always be high (Avramidis et al., 2000; Reed & Osborne, 2013). This latter perception of efficacy may well be weaker in mainstream schools than in special schools, causing some over-estimation of the behaviour problems in the former setting.

Summary

From the available evidence on the impact of various school placements (which is far from complete), the key findings to emerge are that children with ASD educated in mainstream settings exhibit higher levels of emotional problems and display more behavioural problems, than both their typically developing peers and their ASD-peers educated in special schools. There is some limited evidence in support of the expected greater academic and social progress in the mainstream setting. However, if higher academic achievement is the goal of inclusive education for children with ASD, then there may be a heavy price to pay in terms of depression and reduced self-concept. As a whole, the evidence actually suggests that mere placement in a mainstream school will not promote performance, as initially hoped for by the 'inclusive movement' (Nirje, 1969; Warnock, 1978). In contrast to this hope, there are several areas of functioning for which there reasons to be highly concerned about inclusive placements being detrimental (see also Humphrey & Symes, 2011).

Factors Promoting Mainstream Success

The findings discussed here are mainly derived from reports of the impact of general educational curricula, which are often not heavily modified for the ASD pupils that include (Brown & McIntosh, 2012). The instructional methods adopted by mainstream and special education teachers are quite different from one another (Frederickson et al., 2010; Fuchs et al., 1992; Kauffman et al., 1985) and this may account for the differences noted for each provision – that is to say, if some of the approaches adopted in special school were also utilized for mainstream settings that include pupils with ASD, the differences in outcome between the placements may well reduce. For example, class sizes in special school are typically smaller than those in mainstream classrooms (Office of Special Education Programs, 1994; Reed et al., 2012). Smaller teacher-to-student ratios may lead to more individualized teaching, which may, in turn, foster children's performance (Hocutt, 1996). Moreover, the curricula in special schools tend to focus more on functional and daily living skills and they are also implemented at a slower pace (Gersten & Woodward, 1999). Any one of these differences may be responsible for the differences or lack of difference, between the outcomes from the schools and it may be that the problems encountered by children with ASD in mainstream settings could be ameliorated if appropriate support for their needs were given in a mainstream setting.

Given such concerns, a number of reviews have outlined several factors that may be used to help develop a more successful approach to the mainstream education for children with ASD (Crosland & Dunlap, 2012; Von der Embse et al., 2011; Morewood et al., 2012; Symes & Humphrey, 2011). The factors that have been highlighted in these reviews bear some similarity to one another and include: organizational and school factors, such as positive attitudes and clear leadership (Crosland & Dunlap, 2012; Von der Embse et al., 2011; Symes & Humphrey, 2011); teacher factors, such as attitude and training (Morewood et al., 2012) and the development of individualized teaching procedures, often including functional assessment (Crosland & Dunlap, 2012; Embse et al., 2011). These broad categories of factors that might mediate the success of an inclusive placement will be discussed in this section.

School factors

There are a range of school factors that may play a role in successful inclusion in a mainstream setting for children with ASD (Crosland & Dunlap, 2012; Symes & Humphrey, 2011). Unfortunately, many of these issues (e.g. 'leadership' and 'appropriate organizational factors') are extremely difficult to measure. However, the impact on ASD inclusion of a range of measurable school factors can be assessed (Osborne & Reed, 2011) and these include aspects of the school such as the number of other included children with SEN, the number of pupils in the school and the size of the classes. Such factors are important to consider, as many of the inclusive placements that have produced successes not only adopt particular teaching strategies in the inclusive classroom, but also the classrooms in such studies are usually much smaller and much more highly managed, than in an unmodified mainstream classroom (Stahmer et al., 2011).

Osborne and Reed (2011) noted that the number of other pupils with an identified SEN in the school was a positive factor in promoting progress for children with ASD. This may imply that the greater the experience of the school in dealing with such pupils may play a role in the pupils' success. However, it should be noted that this was not true for those pupils with a diagnosis of Asperger syndrome (who would now be classed as having an ASD diagnosis but being higher functioning). This latter finding suggests that an explanation of successful inclusion based on greater experience of the school in dealing with children with SEN (see Osler & Osler, 2002) cannot be a full account of these data, as this should have positively correlated with progress in both groups of children.

Osborne and Reed (2011) also noted that the size of the school and of the classes both impacted positively on the pupils with ASD in the mainstream setting. In addition to improvements in behaviour, the report by Osborne and Reed (2011) also found that the size of the school was correlated with increases in the level of self-reported school belonging in the children seen over the course of a year's placement in that setting (see Figure 12.6). Although this relationship may appear counter-intuitive, it actually corresponds to research that suggests small class sizes are not necessarily optimal for progress. It has been speculated that this reflects the potential for the smaller class size to more strongly highlight differences between the included child and their peers as they are more visible with fewer other pupils (Blatchford et al., 2007). Similarly, there are data which show that school size is inversely related to the numbers and levels of behaviour problems observed in the pupils at that school (Cotton, 1996); a finding that holds true, at least, up to medium-sized schools (Blatchford, 2009; Newman et al., 2006). However, it should be noted that very

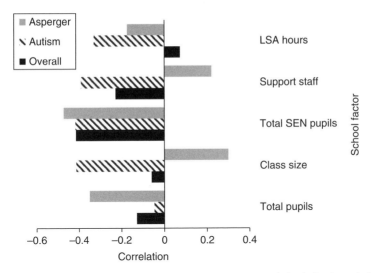

Figure 12.6 Correlations between a range of school factors and the behavioural change observed in included secondary school aged pupils with ASD (both for the whole sample and broken down by Autism and Asperger diagnoses), as reported by Osborne and Reed (2011).

large schools may well produce the opposite pattern of data. Carrington and Graham (2001) presented results showing that ASD pupils find large schools stressful and anxiety-provoking environments. This stress, however, may not be associated with school-size *per se*, but with other factors associated with the school size; for example, large numbers of transitions between classes (Myles & Simpson, 1998) – a factor related to a preference for routine in children with ASD (Adreon & Stella, 2001) and high levels of noise (Mesibov & Shea, 1996) – possibly related to the sensory sensitivities of these children (Ashburner et al., 2010).

These data suggest a few school factors might be important in helping the progress of children with ASD in the mainstream and that some procedures put in place by the school can limit the negative impact of mainstream placements on the included children with ASD (Gibbons & Goins, 2008). However, the variety and pattern of data also prompts the conclusion that, whatever the school factor, it will certainly be mediated by a range of within-child factors (see Newman et al., 2006, for a review). The full range of these interactions would be difficult to document, but the key point is that they will exist and will need consideration for each pupil with ASD and for each school, separately.

Teacher factors

The level of training and experience that teachers in a mainstream school have regarding the potential problems that children with ASD included in their classrooms may experience is widely regarded as critical to the success of a child with ASD in that setting (Koegel et al., 2012; Morewood et al., 2012; Symes & Humphrey, 2011). Many teachers in mainstream schools report that they are poorly prepared to deal with children with ASD (McGregor & Campbell, 2001; Robertson et al., 2003; Smith & Smith, 2000). The extent to which this impacts on a belief in an inclusive educational strategy was outlined by Wishart and Manning (1996), who found that many teachers believed in the abstract concept of inclusion, but only 13% actually believed it would work in practice and only 6% felt qualified to deal with a child with SEN. This finding was mirrored two decades later by Segall and Campbell (2012) who found that mainstream teachers still had significantly less knowledge than special school teachers about ASD.

These perceptions of mainstream teaching staff regarding their training to deal with children with ASD are supported by two important sets of findings. Firstly, teaching staff with little training in ASD experience large amounts of stress and 'occupational burnout' when placed in inclusive mainstream settings (Farber, 1991; Reddy, 2008). Secondly, staff training regarding ASD can lead to more informed expectations about child prospects (Avramidis et al., 2000; Jindal-Snape et al., 2005; McConkey et al., 2012). However, it is important to note that not all training is seen as helpful (Brown & McIntosh, 2012). In particular, staff training appears to be successful when it reduces expectations of potential progress – meaning that it reduces perceptions of inclusive placements as failures (Frederickson et al., 2004). On a more positive note, there is a link between more accurate teacher expectations and increased success of children with ASD in the mainstream school (Burack et al., 1997).

One of the more important aspects of increasing teacher knowledge is in allowing the development of strong pupil-teacher relationships (Brown & McIntosh, 2012; Morewood et al., 2012). It is often the case that children with ASD do not form great numbers of social relationships with their typically developing peers in mainstream settings (Humphrey & Symes, 2011). As a result of this impoverished social peer-network, the teacher–pupil relationship becomes more critical in guiding the success of a mainstream placement for pupils with ASD (Donnellan, 1984; Robertson et al., 2003). For example, Robertson et al. (2003) found that when teachers perceived their relationships with the included pupils to be positive, the behavioural problems exhibited by the child reduced and the children with ASD were more socially included in the classroom. Similarly, Osborne and Reed (2011) found a positive correlation between teachers' perceived preparation for inclusion and improvement in the included pupils' social behaviours and sense of school belonging, measured over the year (see Figure 12.7).

Child characteristics

Although an anathema to those on the extreme of the inclusive movement, some child characteristics may predict the success of a particular educational placement for a pupil with ASD. Differential school placement according to characteristics, such as intellectual ability or ASD severity (Eaves & Ho, 1997; Waddington & Reed, 2015), indicates that these factors are already established in practice. Similarly, mainstream placement is predicted if the child is younger rather than older (Hocutt, 1996) – although this may also be confounded with the impact of behavioural problems, which are greater for older children (Osborne & Reed, 2009a; b). However, there are several other child factors that also appear to predict successes and problems in mainstream placement that are covered in the following section.

The specific ASD diagnosis and symptoms and an individual's reaction to a mainstream placement, are associated with one another (Osborne & Reed, 2011).

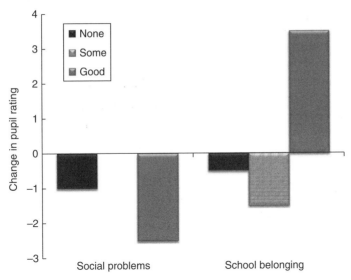

Figure 12.7 Changes in pupils' with ASD ratings of their own social problems (a decrease is good) and feelings of school belonging (an increase is good) over a 1-year period of inclusion in a mainstream secondary school as a product of their teachers' assessments of their own ability to deal with pupils with ASD (Osborne & Reed, 2011).

Although it is much more likely that a child with a DSM-IV-TR Asperger diagnosis will be placed in a mainstream school than a child with Autism Disorder (Waddington & Reed, 2015), the former group also more likely to show increased problems as a result of the placement. As noted previously, foremost amongst these problems are the negative impacts on the social and behavioural functioning of the mainstream placement (Gadow et al., 2005). This finding could be related to differences in intellectual functioning between these broad groups (MacIntosh, & Dissanayake, 2006) and the consequent likelihood of making negative social comparisons (Bellini, 2006; Humphrey & Lewis, 2008). Certainly, the latter issue is seen to a large extent in those individuals with diagnoses as Asperger's (Chapter 2).

There are also indications that social and communication abilities predict mainstream success (McIntyre et al., 2006; Stahmer et al., 2011; Whitney et al., 1994) and that social-communication skills may also impact on subsequent academic performance (Kupersmidt & DeRosier, 2004). These findings chime with predictions derived from models of emotional and social self-regulation that imply early skills in social interactions are associated with better subsequent school outcomes (Parker & Asher, 1987). Jones and Frederickson (2010) found that if parents rated their child's social ability as low, this predicted a lower level of acceptance for those children in a mainstream school setting. Similarly, McIntyre et al. (2006) noted that pre-school self-regulation (i.e. impulse inhibition) and social skills both predicted school adaptation, even when the level of IQ was controlled (see also Zingerevich & LaVesser, 2009).

Another symptom often associated with ASD is the presence of sensory processing problems (see Chapters 2 and 10) and this symptom is quite strongly associated with poor mainstream success (Ashburner et al., 2008; Baranek et al., 2006). Reynolds et al. (2011) reported that pupils with ASD who had greater sensory sensitivities had poorer social competence and suggested that such sensory issues could be negatively impacting social participation. Certainly, Ashburner et al. (2008; 2010) have related these sensory problems to both conduct and social problems in school environments. Ashburner et al. (2008; see also Jasmin et al., 2009) noted that sensory difficulties explained about half of the variance in academic performance for children with ASD in mainstream school settings; there being substantial negative relationships between both auditory filtering problems and tactile hypersensitivity and inattention problems and also between movement sensitivity and oppositional behaviour problems.

In addition to the core ASD deficits, a range of problem behaviours are associated with children with ASD (see Chapter 2), which also impact on the success of a mainstream placement. Prime among these potential problems are the levels of externalizing behaviours emitted during the period in the mainstream school. The negative impact of these behaviours on mainstream success is very well documented (Department for Education and Skills, 2006; Kauffman et al., 1987 and the previous sections of the current chapter). It might be noted that there is one study that appears to show that the level of externalizing behaviour positively predicts gain over the inclusive period (Stahmer et al., 2011). However, this study was conducted in a highly managed mainstream placement and it may be that externalizing behaviours, in themselves, correlate with intellectual ability (see previously) and this latter relationship underlies that association.

Summary

The evidence concerning predictors of successful mainstream inclusion suggests that older and higher-functioning children with ASD, who are placed into medium-sized classrooms in medium-sized mainstream schools, with high levels of individualized support, delivered by staff who have training and confidence in their own abilities, will fare best. Of course, this is not really saying that much beyond what common sense implies would work for any child, either with or without special educational needs. However, a logical problem for the inclusive movement emerges if mainstream settings are modified to accommodate the presence of pupils with ASD: if the mainstream setting were altered to provide all of the support seen in a special school, then that mainstream setting would be a special school setting. Moreover, it is uncertain whether any 'improved performances' would represent anything more than a return to the performance that would have been seen if the child had not been included in the mainstream in the first place, as the special school already provides this support. The other question that this issue raises, is what would then happen to the majority of children in such a mainstream setting who are without an SEN and who are taught in this manner – and there is little to no evidence to draw on in order to assess this issue.

Mainstream or Special? An Overview

This chapter has outlined the state of knowledge regarding the education of a child with ASD in mainstream- and special-school placements. At the moment, it is impossible to say with certainty that education in a mainstream environment is either good or bad for individuals with ASD, as the evidence is not present in any great quantity or great quality (Davis et al., 2004a; Humphrey & Parkinson, 2006). However, contemporary evidence regarding the impacts of mainstream education on the academic, social, psychological and behavioural functioning of a pupil with ASD, gives little support to support the view that mainstream placements are inherently superior to those at special schools. In fact, there is much evidence that poorly managed mainstream placements can be harmful and it is difficult not to conclude that the problems produced by simple and unmanaged placement in mainstream school may well outweigh the benefits; the general mainstream education will not be appropriate for all children with ASD and, in many cases, it may be against the child's best interests.

If the motivation behind mainstreaming a child with ASD is purely 'rights-driven', then those determining policy need to be certain that they are not imposing their set of values on others to the detriment of those to whom it is being done. The concept of imposing a wholesale policy on a whole group of individuals, merely because they share a highly variable diagnostic label (Lord & McGee, 2001), may be just another form of inappropriate discrimination. If the motivation behind mainstreaming is economic, then this view may well be deluded, as either it will be very expensive to produce effective strategies for the appropriate mainstream education of children with ASD or even more expensive to sort out the problems that the experience has left the child with later in life. While the proponents of inclusion argued that inclusive education is of value in itself, others noted that there are other important values with which a commitment to inclusion in mainstream schools may be in conflict, such as a commitment to the best education for the individual (see Lindsay, 2003; Norwich, 2005).

13

Interventions – What is Known about What Works?

The previous chapters have illustrated the degree to which various forms of intervention for Autism Spectrum Disorders (ASD) impact on a range of functioning domains. Each chapter has addressed the evidence for the effectiveness and the potential predictors of success, of those individual types of treatment programmes. However, the as yet unrecognized elephant in this particular book's room is the question: 'does one of these approaches work better than the others?' The final chapter will attempt to summarize the previously presented evidence in an attempt to answer this question, but also in order to focus attention on the subsidiary and possibly more sensible question regarding: 'for whom do the interventions work best?'

It is the question about the best intervention that has provided the heat in the debate alluded to in Chapter 1 and that has provided the impetus behind much of the empirical evaluation of these interventions – to this extent, if for no other reason, such a comparative question has proved useful. For example, it has been the proud claim of some in the applied behaviour analytic (ABA) field that behavioural treatments are 'the best' (and sometimes, more strongly, 'the only') scientifically validated interventions for ASD (see Keenan, 2004; Levy et al., 2009). Such a claim to uniqueness for behavioural treatments was always one that was unlikely to be free of criticism with the ASD community (see Prizant, 2009, for a discussion of this suggestion) and the critiques of this suggestion tend to fall into one of two camps. There are the strong, challenging and wrong claims that there is no evidence that behavioural treatments are at all effective (see Morris, 2009, for a discussion of such views). However, there is another argument regarding this claim, which is more sensible and is based on current practice and the available evidence (see Levy et al., 2009). The current book, from both an historical perspective (see Chapter 3) and from an empirical standpoint, has suggested that ABA is not (nor has it ever really been) the only game in town for ASD – however, the issue that remains is whether ABA is the best game in town.

Interventions for Autism: Evidence for Educational and Clinical Practice, First Edition. Phil Reed.
© 2016 John Wiley & Sons, Ltd. Published 2016 by John Wiley & Sons, Ltd.

The debate over behavioural treatments is an important one given their relatively high use in the field, but it is not the only comparison that needs to be made and the current text has attempted to broaden this debate across a wider range of approaches to ASD treatment. This chapter places the questions of regarding what we know about effective intervention for ASD into this broader context by presenting the comparative evidence for a number of approaches, examining the differential impacts of programmes and also outlining the mediators of these approaches. In the light of this it will, finally, make some recommendations about treatment choices for people with ASD.

Comprehensive Approaches

As outlined in Chapter 1, there is a range of five or so broad treatment categories for ASD about which there are adequate data and good grounds to discuss their impact: behavioural (Chapters 4–6); environment-alterations/systems (Chapter 7); developmental (Chapters 8 and 9); sensorimotor (Chapter 10) and eclectic (Chapters 11 and 12). These various forms of treatment each have been discussed in detail in their own particular chapters and all of this evidence will not be rehearsed here. However, the current chapter will provide summaries of the data from a number of the more often assessed approaches, in order to address the questions of comparative effectiveness and moderators of that effectiveness.

There are, of course, many such interventions that were not covered in this book and some of those that were discussed in individual chapters concerning particular approaches will not be covered in this final chapter, as they lack the necessary substantial body of evidence to allow discussion. The interventions that were selected for discussion were chosen on the bases of the range of evidence available for them and on the degree to which they are known in the field. In summary, the behavioural approaches will be taken as one set of treatments (see Chapter 4 for discussion of the various alternatives within this broad category). The Treatment and Education of Autistic and Related Communication Handicapped Children (TEACCH) programme will be employed from the systems treatments section, discussed in Chapter 7, as this programme has the most evidence available. The developmental interventions will be split into those employing variants of the Denver programmes (e.g. Denver Health Sciences Programme and the Early Start Denver Model, ESDM) and the other developmental approaches, as the former rely to a much greater extent on ABA components than the others. The massage therapies from the sensorimotor treatments (Chapter 10) are considered as having some usable comparative evidence. Although Sensory Integration Therapy has a lot of evidence, much of it is unusable in this present comparative context. Finally, the eclectic programmes, examined in Chapter 11, will used in these comparisons.

It should be pointed out that despite being classified into different broad types of treatment approaches, many of these interventions actually share similar features with one another. These overarching characteristics of interventions for ASD will not come as a surprise to anybody working in the field and they have been repeated in many articles outlining best practice in ASD interventions (Dunst et al., 2012; Iovannone et al., 2003). In particular, the following commonalities may be extracted from many comprehensive intervention strategies:

- An individualized approach to intervention and teaching – focusing on identifying the needs of the person and assessing the types of activities that can be used to encourage learning for that individual.
- A focus on the assumed core deficits of ASD – especially language and communication abilities and adaptive-social skills, as well as on the broader issues of intellectual and cognitive functioning.
- The use of naturalistic teaching opportunities for teaching these skills – although this is not universally encouraged by some interventions.
- The involvement of both professionals and parents in the treatment – although the degree of parental involvement does differ between programmes.

Some examples of the commonalities may further serve to briefly highlight these shared features. For example, the specific and explicit adoption of the behavioural Pivotal Response Training by the ESDM model (see Chapter 8) and use of functional assessment and analysis to determine individualized treatment plans and discover appropriate reinforcing activities across many forms of approaches is also striking (see Chapters 4, 7 and 8). Moreover, the similarity between the theoretical underpinning of some developmental treatments that discuss 'developmental steps' in ASD (Chapter 8) and some recent trends in behavioural approaches (Chapter 4), are surprisingly clear. These similarities suggest that, apart from the languages employed and perhaps the methodological rigour with which these goals are sought, there is a growing rapprochement in approaches between these various programmes and this makes any comparison made between broad approaches need to be treated with appropriate caution given that they may be comparing interventions that are not as dissimilar to one another as they sound.

Given these considerations, perhaps there is some truth in the view that comparison between these interventions is somewhat invidious and the tendency of such comparisons has been to establish unproductive rivalries between the various adherents of different approaches. However, such comparison can serve to highlight best practices and to signpost the way ahead and it is in this light that the current chapter presents these data. To go some way towards offsetting any impression that the current data provides a 'once and for all' solution to the question what works best, Table 13.1 presents studies of the individual programmes from within each form of treatment approach that provided a 'good' outcome result – that is, where at least two domains showed a strong effect and there were no indications of poor effects elsewhere. These data may serve to illustrate that many interventions can be effective (even if they are so to different degrees) and also to spotlight the characteristics of successful intervention programmes of every hue.

Overall Outcomes for 'Comprehensive' Treatments

To allow comparison between the different forms of approach, the effect sizes from each of the broad forms of treatment approach were calculated. In doing so, the pre- to post-treatment effect sizes were used, rather than the effect sizes derived from

Table 13.1 Individual outcome effectiveness studies of various types of intervention that demonstrated a good pre- to post-change outcome (i.e. two functioning domains with strong effects sizes, and no poor effect sizes), along with the domains in which there were successes.

Approach	Study	Intellectual	Language	Adaptive-social
ABA	Anan et al. (2008)	√		√
	Anderson et al. (1987)		√	√
	Cohen et al. (2006)	√	√	√
	Eikeseth et al. (2002)	√	√	√
	Eikeseth et al. (2007)	√	√	√
	Eldevik et al. (2012)	√		√
	Hayward et al. (2009)	√		√
	Howard et al. (2005)	√	√	√
	Matos & Mustaca (2006)	√	√	√
	Sallows & Graupner (2005)	√	√	√
	Smith et al. (2000)	√	√	
	Smith et al. (1997)	√	√	
TEACCH	McConkey et al. (2010)		√	√
	Mukaddes et al. (2004)		√	√
	Van Bourgondie (2003)		√	√
Developmental	Dawson et al. (2010)	√	√	
	Jenkins et al. (2012)		√	√
	Rogers & DiLalla (1991)	√	√	
	Schertz et al. (2013)		√	√
	Vivanti et al. (2012)	√	√	
	Weatherby & Woods (2006)		√	√
Massage	Silva et al. (2008)			√

comparisons between a treatment and a control group. The former effect sizes are more numerous across the approach types, allowing a bigger basis for comparison. Moreover, the comparative effect sizes are affected not only by the nature of the target intervention, but also by the nature of the comparison group, which differs a great deal across the different studies and introduces a confound when comparing the impact of the interventions.

Table 13.2 displays these mean pre- to post-intervention change effect sizes for each of the three main domains of functioning (intellectual/cognitive; linguistic/communication and adaptive-social behaviours). These effect sizes are shaded, as in the previous chapters, to highlight in light shaded cells strong effect sizes (greater than 0.70), moderate effect sizes in medium shaded cells (between 0.30 and 0.69) and weak effect sizes in dark shaded cells (less than 0.30). It should be noted that these effect sizes are derived from a variety of different instruments – some of which are not standardized – but, in general, to translate these effect size figures back to a growth in ability – each 0.3 of an effect size equates to about 5 points on a standardized test of

Table 13.2 Mean effect sizes (along with standard deviations and ranges) for the pre- topost-intervention changes produced by different types of intervention across three outcome domains.

Intervention	Intellectual	Language	Adaptive-Social
ABA	0.93 (±0.56; −0.35–2.23)	0.88 (±0.56; 0.02–2.38)	0.67 (±0.87; −0.78–4.13)
Denver	0.76 (±0.66; 0.12–1.84)	0.70 (±0.42; 0.30–1.58)	0.23 (±0.22; −0.14–0.52)
Developmental	0.19 (±0.94; −0.91–0.65)	0.67 (±0.65; −0.41–2.52)	0.39 (±0.74; −2.00–1.29)
Eclectic	0.25 (±0.33; −0.53–0.95)	0.53 (±0.62; −0.43–1.83)	0.22 (±0.67; −1.48–1.46)
Massage			0.54 (±0.23; 0.27–0.80)
TEACCH	0.56 (±0.31; 0.07–1.21)	0.65 (±0.48; 0.32–1.69)	0.64 (±0.52; −0.21–1.00)

White = strong effect; light grey = moderate effect; dark grey = weak effect; black = no data.

ability. Of course, as noted in Chapter 1, there are problems with effect sizes – they are only an approximate reflection of the impact of the intervention, given the constraints of calculating them. However, when the impacts of those treatments over the course of the intervention are compared with one another, these data do allow some answers to the issue of which approach has the strongest evidence in its support.

The answer to the question that triggered much of the field; whether ABA is the best approach, is a qualified – 'apparently, but it depends on what aspect of functioning is studied'. Certainly, inspection of the effect sizes for the behavioural interventions for intellectual/cognitive functioning displayed in Table 13.2 reveals the effect sizes for ABA interventions are typically greater than those seen for these alternative comprehensive approaches – although there is some strong growth in this domain provided by the Denver programmes. This domain of functioning that provides the strongest evidence for the overall greater effectiveness of behavioural approaches and it has formed the basis for most arguments in its favour (see Chapters 5 and 6).

Although there is a case to be made for the importance of intellectual functioning in ASD (see Chapters 2 and 4), it has to be recognized that it is not a core aspect of ASD in itself (Chapter 2). Areas that are more associated with the central ASD problems, such as language and/or communication function (although not necessarily always perceived as central – see DSM-5 criteria) and adaptive-social functioning, are also shown in Table 13.2. Inspection of these data shows that the effect size for language is usually greater for behavioural approaches, but, there are some indications of moderate to large effect sizes in this domain for all of the types of programme. In contrast, the area in which there is no strong advantage for the behavioural approaches, compared to some of the other intervention types, is in terms of the adaptive-social development of the individuals with ASD. Measures of progress in this domain are as large for the TEACCH approach and also for the massage therapies. However, there is a long way to go in the validation process for these latter interventions and it cannot

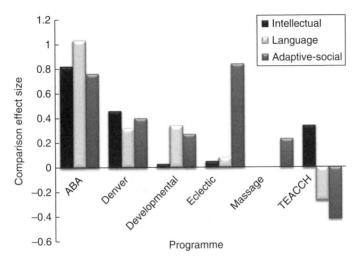

Figure 13.1 Mean effect sizes for the different programme types in comparison to control groups for three main outcome domains.

be said that the evidence for these treatments comes close, either in breadth or depth, to that for the behavioural interventions.

Aggregating results in this way does give a reasonable estimate of the impact of these various approaches. The variation in study and participant characteristics across the component reports allows a reasonably broad and ultimately similar, sample form each programme type. However, such cross-experimental comparison is fraught with some difficulty – and it is always reassuring to have some data from individual studies to back up these general assertions. Unfortunately, there have been relatively few individual studies that have provided direct comparisons between interventions drawn from each of these treatment categories.

The comparative outcome data, as they relate to these functioning domains, from the individual studies that have directly compared different interventions using a true alternative treatment design, where each intervention is a target in itself and not included merely as a 'control' (e.g. Boyd et al., 2014; Howard et al., 2005; Mandell et al., 2013; Reed et al., 2007b), are presented in Figure 13.1. These effect size data tend to support the results of these meta-analysis; the behavioural programmes studied in these reports tend to show the greatest gains in intellectual and language functioning, when directly compared to other treatments within the same study (see also the comparative effect sizes in each chapter). However, there is a less clear beneficial impact of ABA on adaptive-social functioning relative to the other forms of intervention.

Thus, from these overall data, it is clear that behavioural approaches are effective for intellectual and language functioning, but it is also apparent that non-behavioural comprehensive programmes can impact positively on some domains of functioning. In particular, these approaches can rival behavioural programmes in terms of their impacts on social functioning. This may well be the result of greater emphasis on group work in these latter programmes. Given this, there may be situations where other comprehensive approaches may have at least as much to offer as behavioural programmes. Moreover, there are all sorts of reasons, not directly related to intervention-teaching style, why behavioural programmes outperform many non-behavioural

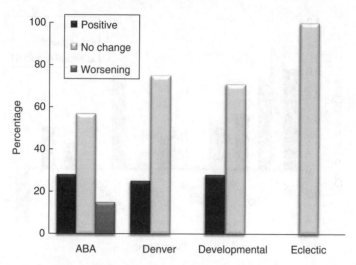

Figure 13.2 Percentage of studies from several intervention types that report an overall improvement, no change or worsening of ASD diagnosis following the intervention. No intervention can be said to show substantial impacts on diagnostic category.

interventions (see Connor, 1998) – for instance, their typically longer duration, greater time intensity, as well as staff commitment and so on and some of these issues will be addressed next when attempting to determine the differential predictors of programme success for the different interventions.

Of course, the data presented in Table 13.2 and Figure 13.1 relate to a range of domains that, while strongly associated with ASD, are not measures of the severity of ASD itself. A question that many parents want answered and, indeed, one that sparked much of the contemporary furore about behavioural approaches (see Chapter 4), is whether any approach can improve functioning and reduce ASD severity to such an extent that the individual is 'cured' or at least becomes undifferentiable from their peers without ASD. Figure 13.2 presents the data on the percentage of studies from each broad type of intervention that show an overall improvement, no change or an overall worsening, in the classification or diagnosis of the participants (unfortunately, these data could not be calculated for Massage or TEACCH interventions). For example, where the bulk of the participants moved from a diagnosis of ASD to not having such a diagnosis or from a severe form of ASD to a less severe form of the disorder (e.g. Autism to Pervasive Developmental Disorder under the DSM-IV-TR system), this would be classed as an improvement.

Unfortunately, inspection of the data presented in Figure 13.2 shows that none of the approaches have a strong impact on the classification of the ASD severity itself. At best, around one quarter of the studies for any particular type of approach show an improvement in ASD classification, with the bulk of studies showing no overall impact of the intervention on this aspect of outcome. It should be noted that many of the studies were only conducted for 1 year or so; hence, may have not been conducted for long enough to generate substantial changes in the ASD classification. Moreover, these data represent the overall and general impact of a study and not the percentage change at the participant level within these studies. These considerations may have tended to produce an underestimation of the impact of a programme – although when individual studies have reported such data they almost universally note little change in ASD severity (Reed et al., 2007b; Zachor et al., 2007).

These data lead to the conclusion that, while some programmes may improve various aspects of an individual's functioning, there is no evidence of a cure for ASD. This is an area that will require much more study and a word about measurement of this domain is also needed to qualify this somewhat depressing conclusion. Although there are signs that ASD functioning is now more often being measured directly and objectively in outcome-effectiveness studies, using tools such as the Autism Diagnostic Observation Schedule (e.g. Drew et al., 2002), many reports are still either not measuring this aspect of functioning or are relying on non-standardized (if validated) informant-rated tools, such as the Autism Behaviour Checklist. Indeed, this was an issue in the assessment of the impact of massage therapies (Chapter 10) on ASD severity. Thus, while there has been some improvement in this area of assessment, there is still some way to go before a full picture of the impacts of interventions on ASD severity can be given.

Impact of Programme Characteristics

There is layer of complexity in comparing across approaches that the meta-data described in Table 13.2 obscures. These overall effect size data are the mean figures for a number of individual studies from each type of approach, but, when aggregated, each approach has somewhat different programme characteristics that are quite separate from the differences in intervention content. These differences are often noted in variations in the duration of the programme (months conducted) and in the intensity of the programme (hours per week) actually experienced. This introduces a confound in comparing the various approaches, in that any outcome differences, putatively attributable to differences in the intervention type, might actually be attributable to the length of the treatment or to the numbers of hours of intervention received. Any intervention using the same levels of treatment input might have produced the same results.

The differences between the various forms of approach in this regard have been pointed out in the context of the relative advantage often noted for behavioural approaches. To investigate the possibility that such factors are impacting on the results, the mean data for the duration (in months) and intensity (in hours per week) of the various forms of treatment are shown in Figure 13.3. These data show that the behavioural and TEACCH programmes typically run for longer than the other forms of intervention and that the developmental approaches (including the Denver models) were typically less intensive than the other forms of intervention.

In order to affect a better comparison between the impacts of the various types of approaches and to determine whether there were any differences in the mediating effect of programme duration on treatment outcome, the mean effect sizes for each of the three functioning domains (intellectual/cognitive, linguistic/communication and adaptive-social) were calculated for each type of programme, depending on the programme duration. These effect sizes are shown in Table 13.3 and are shaded for strong (light shaded cell), moderate (medium shaded cell) and weak (dark shaded cell) effect sizes.

These data in Table 13.3 show a number of different patterns of outcome effectiveness that deserve comment. In very general terms, the longer that the programmes run, the more improvement is seen, although this is not universally true. These

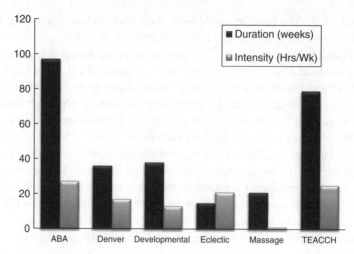

Figure 13.3 Mean durations of different intervention programmes (weeks) and their mean weekly intensities (hours).

Table 13.3 Mean effect sizes for the various forms of intervention for three outcome domains (IQ = intellectual; L = language; ASB = adaptive-social behaviour) as a product of the duration of the programme.

	<1 Year			*1–2 Years*			*2–3 Years*			*>3 Years*		
	IQ	L	ASB	IQ	L	ASB	IQ	L	ASB	IQ	L	ASB
ABA	0.88	0.89	0.46	0.93	0.77	0.69	0.91	0.96	0.90	1.00	1.30	0.51
Denver	0.40	0.53	0.16	1.67	1.34	-0.14						
Developmental	0.33	0.56	0.32	0.03	0.81	0.50						
Eclectic	0.35	0.33	0.38	0.21	0.26	0.21	0.18	1.40	-0.35			
Massage			0.54									
TEACCH	0.65	0.87	0.71	1.21	0.51	1.28	0.48	0.34	0.82			

White = strong effect; light grey = moderate effect; dark grey = weak effect; black = no data.

improvements get less pronounced as the length of time on the programme increases and this issue was discussed in detail for some of the individual approaches (e.g. see Chapter 6).

However, some programmes displayed a slightly different pattern of effects related to programme duration. For the behavioural programmes, it is clear that as the duration of the intervention increases, the stronger the effect sizes become for all functioning domains. For the other types of approach, there were fewer longer-duration studies, so some caution is needed in interpreting these data, but the positive duration-outcome result noted for the behavioural programmes was not always replicated. The Denver approach shows a similar result – which might reflect the largely behavioural nature of these programmes. However, although a similar 1–2-year effect size increase is seen for the TEACCH approach, it is not seen for the developmental or eclectic programmes, which both tend to show a decreased effect size with prolonged duration (this is also true of TEACCH after the third year of the programme duration).

Table 13.4 Mean effect sizes for the various forms of intervention for three outcome domains (IQ = intellectual; L = language; ASB = adaptive-social behaviour) as a product of the weekly intensity of the programme.

	<15 h/wk			16–20 h/wk			21–30 h/wk			>30 h/wk		
	IQ	L	ASB	IQ	L	ASB	IQ	L	ASB	IQ	L	ASB
ABA	0.67	0.61	0.38	0.77	0.68	0.36	0.89	1.41	0.56	1.13	0.94	1.15
Denver	0.71	0.46	0.25				0.34	0.36	0.33	1.84	1.58	-0.14
Developmental	0.10	0.71	0.31	0.65	0.67	0.68		0.45	1.03		0.76	0.86
Eclectic	0.30	0.24	0.41	0.45	0.85	-0.25	0.19	0.33	0.18	0.07	1.46	0.71
TEACCH	0.80	0.75	0.97	0.47	1.09	-0.21				0.48	0.67	0.85

White = strong effect; light grey = moderate effect; dark grey = weak effect; black = no data.

The net result of these different overall changes for the various broad programme categories is that, when the programme is conducted for up to 1 year, there is a clear advantage for the behavioural programmes in terms of intellectual and linguistic functioning (although not for adaptive-social behaviour). This difference reduces in comparison with some programmes (i.e. TEACCH and Denver) after two years, but becomes larger again for all domains after 3 or more years. This pattern of results might go some way toward explaining the apparent difference in the relative effectiveness of behavioural and eclectic programmes noted between the studies reported by Reed et al. (2007b) and by Howard et al et al. (2005). The former noted less difference between behavioural and eclectic treatments in terms of adaptive-social behaviours than the latter study (see Figure 13.1). The study that noted a less pronounced difference in this domain (Reed et al., 2007b) was conducted for less than 1 year, whereas the interventions studied by Howard et al. (2005) ran for 3 years. Clearly, further comparative work is needed to consolidate these findings with regard to programme duration and to the offer some explanation of this differential pattern, but they do suggest that the programme duration should be fixed with regard to the type of approach being taken and the level of improvement in functioning that is being sought.

The effect sizes for the various types of intervention, when conducted for different weekly intensities (hours of per week), are shown in Table 13.4. With the proviso that some of these means are based on rather few data studies, these data show that as the weekly intensity increases, the effect sizes for the functioning domains tend to increase across all the programmes. However, there are differential impacts of increasing the programme intensity between programme types that need comment. When a programme is conducted for less than 15 hours a week, there is a small advantage to the behavioural and Denver programmes, compared to some of the other approaches, especially in terms of adaptive-social behaviour outcomes. However, as the programme intensity increases, the relative advantage to the behavioural and Denver approaches also increases.

It should be noted that, within each of the individual studies, there may well be a different effect programme intensity, which such aggregate data may obscure. It is possible for the general trend to show a positive relationship between a variable such as intensity and the outcomes, but for individual studies to show a different pattern of

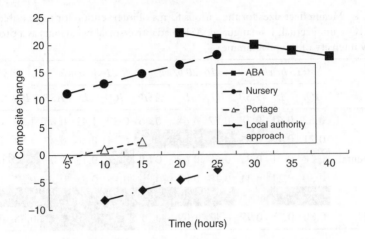

Figure 13.4   Effect of weekly intensity (hours per week) of various programmes on the composite gain score (PEP-R, BAS and VABS) for four interventions reported by Reed and Osborne (2012). For all but ABA, as intensity increases outcome gets stronger.

results. For example, two studies may be conducted: one has a mean intensity of 10 hours a week, with a range of 6–14 hours and show a mean outcome effect size of 0.50 and a second study may be conducted for a mean of 20 hours a week, with a range of 16–24 hours and have a mean effect size of 1.00. When the overall data are considered, there is a positive relationship between mean intensity and mean effect size, but it is perfectly possible that each separate study has a negative relationship between programme intensity and outcome (there are theoretical reasons how this could happen, see next).

The relationship between programme intensity and outcome within a study was explored by Reed and Osborne (2012), in which the participants received either exposure to a behavioural programme, Portage, special nursery placement or a Local Authority Approach (combining parts of ABA and special nursery). The gains made by the participants over a 9-month period were plotted as a function of the weekly intensity of the intervention. The gains were a composite measure of intellectual functioning (measured by the Psycho-Educational Profile, educational functioning (British Abilities Scale) and adaptive-social behaviour (Vineland Adaptive Behavior Scales). These data revealed that the ABA programme had the best overall outcomes. However, for all of the treatments, except for the behavioural intervention, as the weekly time input increased, the gains increased. In contrast, over the range of weekly intensities employed, as the teaching hours increased in the behavioural programme, the gains reduced (see Figure 13.4).

There are a number of possible explanations for an increasing weekly intensity impacting negatively on outcome for ABA, including the lessening impact of reinforcers as training sessions increase in length. As there are a limited number of reinforcers than can be chosen for an individual with ASD (given their restricted range of interests), then this reduction in their effectiveness over time may well be quite pronounced for this population. This is already a well-known phenomenon in operant conditioning (McSweeney & Murphy, 2000) and it suggests that the effect should not be limited to ABA, but should be seen in most interventions with a heavy reliance on reinforcement-based learning. However, more research is needed into whether

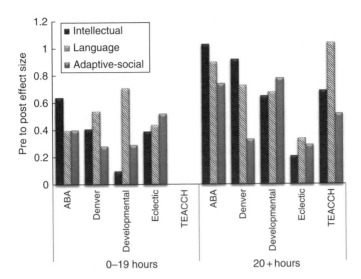

Figure 13.5 Mean pre- to post-intervention effect sizes for the three outcome domains for different intervention types that were conducted for up to 1 year, split by the weekly intensity of the programme.

this is assertion of generality is true and whether this is a reasonable explanation of the effect in the context of ASD treatment.

Although organizing these data in these manners makes it easier to see the impacts of the different programme characteristics on the outcomes of the various interventions, this approach still suffers from one interpretive problem: dividing the programmes into those with different durations still allows variation of the intensity within each duration band (e.g. it is possible that the longer duration programmes were also the most time intensive). To partially accommodate this issue, the programmes were divided into those that had weekly intensities of less than 20 hours and those with weekly intensities of greater than this level. Programmes that were conducted for up to 1 year were then divided into these two groups: 1 year was chosen, as most of the programme types had a reasonable number of individual studies lasting for this length of time. The effect sizes for the three functioning domains for each for these intensity groups are shown in Figure 13.5.

When this fairer (like-for-like) comparison was made between the various interventions, allowing the issues raised about confounds in the comparisons to be addressed, it can be seen that there was an advantage for the behavioural programmes for intellectual functioning at both levels of weekly time input. However, there was no consistent advantage for the behavioural programme in the other two outcome domains. For example, while language functioning improved with greater intensity for the behavioural approach, it was slightly less effective than the TEACCH approach at the greater weekly intensity. Similarly, although adaptive-social functioning improved with more weekly time input for the behavioural treatments, it also did so in the developmental approaches. Thus, when the programme characteristics are equated, there is still an advantage for the behavioural approach, but not as pronounced as the overall data might suggest. Of course, these data are only based on programmes that were conducted for less than 1 year and the situation may change as the duration increases.

However, there are currently insufficient data for most approaches to determine whether or not this pattern of data holds at longer durations.

Impact of Participant Characteristics

In addition to the overall success of the various intervention types, it was apparent in each individual chapter that there were a range of participant characteristics that mediated the effects of the interventions, such as the age and functioning abilities of the clients at intake. The effects of these participant-mediators on each programme might make particular interventions more or less successful with particular types of individual. In order to explore whether this is the case, the mediating relationships that were discussed in detail in each of the individual chapters were summarized with respect to the impact of the participant characteristics at intake on the observed outcomes.

Table 13.5 shows the relationship between the various intake participant characteristics and the intervention outcomes for the three functioning domains (intellectual/cognitive, language/communication and adaptive-social functioning). These data show the nature of the relationship: positive – as the intake variable increases, the outcome gets stronger; no relationship and negative – as the intake variable gets larger, the outcome gets smaller. The strength of these effects is also shown for each relationship – with those in light shaded cells being very strong, those in medium shaded cells being reasonable and those in dark shaded cells being weak.

Inspection of the Table 13.5 shows a number of different impacts of the intake variables on outcomes, which highlight the types of individuals who might benefit most from each form of intervention. The impact of the participants' language abilities and adaptive-social skills at intake is quite straightforward, in that there was a positive relationship between both intake variables and treatment outcomes for most of the functioning domains for all of the different treatment types. That is, all of the intervention types, these tend to work better with participants who had greater levels of language ability and better adaptive-social skills, at the start of the intervention.

The other two intake predictors (age and intellectual functioning) present a rather more complex picture. In terms of age at intake, this variable was strongly negatively

Table 13.5 Nature of the relationship (+ = positive, – = negative, Q = quadratic; 0 = no relationship) between child intake characteristics and three outcome domains (IQ = intellectual; L = language; ASB = adaptive-social behaviour).

	ABA			Denver			Developmental			TEACCH		
	IQ	L	ASB	IQ	L	ASB	IQ	L	ASB	IQ	L	ASB
Age	+	+	+	0	+	–	0	+	–	0	+	–
Autism Severity										+		
Intellectual	Q	Q	Q	0	+	–	Q	+	+	0	0	+
Language	+	+	+				+	+	–	+	0	–
Adaptive-social	+	+	+				+	+	–	+	+	–

White = strong effect; light grey = moderate-weak effect; black = no data) for the different types of intervention.

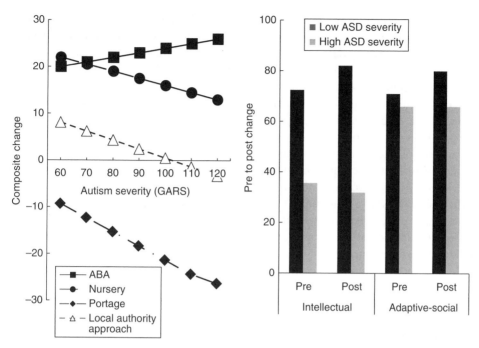

Figure 13.6 Outcomes for eclectic interventions as a function of ASD severity Left panel = results of a study reported by Reed and Osborne (2012) showing gain in outcomes across intellectual and adaptive-social domains. Right panel = results of a study reported by Zachor and Ben-Itzchak (2010) showing pre- and post-scores in intellectual and adaptive-social domains for a low and high functioning ASD group.

associated with gains in language for all of the interventions – such that younger participants at intake demonstrated the greatest gains. Younger participants also tended to show greater intellectual and adaptive-social gains for behavioural programmes, but older individuals demonstrated greater adaptive-social gains for both developmental and eclectic programmes.

The differential pattern of age mediation of adaptive-social behaviour may explain some of the differences in the outcome-effectiveness literature. For example, Eikeseth et al. (2002) used participants who were aged 4–7 years at the start of the study and compared behavioural and eclectic programmes. There was a greater improvement in all three functioning domains in the behavioural intervention compared to the special education group. In contrast, Makrygianni and Reed (2010c) studied the effectiveness of behavioural and eclectic intervention programmes for an older age group (6.5–14 years old) and noted that the eclectic programme demonstrated greater improvement in adaptive behaviour (see Figure 13.6). That the pattern of relative effectiveness changed between these two studies with the age of the participants is consistent with the data from Table 13.5.

Table 13.5 also shows that the relationship between baseline intellectual functioning and outcome was not straightforward. As discussed at some length in Chapters 6 and 8, there was a bitonic relationship between this predictor and intellectual gain for the behavioural and Denver models – both less- and more-able individuals fared worse in terms of intellectual and language gains. What other relationships there were

in this data, were all in the positive direction – with more intellectually able participants showing greater adaptive-social gains for the Denver and eclectic models.
Overall, this pattern of data suggests that more intellectually able participants might
tend to fare better on programmes other than behaviourally based interventions.

Unfortunately, there is less data available regarding the impact of the initial ASD
severity on the outcomes of the treatments. Reed and Osborne (2012) provided some
comparative data regarding this potential mediator on the impact of a number of
programmes (including behavioural, eclectic and developmental approaches). These
data were collected on children aged 2–4 years old and are shown in the left panel of
Figure 13.6. These data show the improvement over a 9-month period from baseline to
follow-up in a composite outcome measure (intellectual, educational and adaptive
behavioural skills) as a function of the child's parent-rated ASD symptoms at baseline.
These data suggest that the behavioural programme worked best overall, but that the
differential impact of the programmes is greatest at higher ASD severities and that
milder cases fare similarly well on all the programmes studied.

In a study that compared children (around 2 years old) with either low and high
severity ASD symptoms (measured using the ADOS) and who received either a behavioural or eclectic treatment placement, Zachor and Ben-Itzchak (2010) noted greater
gains in intellectual functioning and adaptive behaviours with the low severity ASD
group in both programmes. However, they also noted that the less severe ASD group
performed better when given the eclectic treatment in terms of social-communication
tasks, but not in terms of intellectual functioning (see right panel of Figure 13.6).
This enhanced effect of an eclectic programme for higher-functioning ASD clients
was also mentioned previously in the study reported by Makryginani and Reed
(2010b). Thus, in both cases, the eclectic group outperformed the behavioural group
in terms of adaptive behaviour (but not intellectual functioning) when the sample had
less severe ASD symptoms.

Thus, there are indications that participant characteristics at intake can differentially
impact the outcomes of these interventions. Taken as a whole, the previous data suggest that those with more severe ASD symptoms and/or who are lower functioning,
will tend to fare better with a behavioural programme, certainly for intellectual and
language functioning. However, the situation for adaptive-social skills is not as clear.
Data on participant mediation of adaptive-social outcomes tend to imply that behavioural
programmes may not be optimal, with the preponderance of evidence suggesting
that, while more severe ASD cases benefit from behavioural programmes, less severe
cases may benefit from eclectic or school-based programmes.

Involving Parents in Treatment

Many of the treatment programmes have been designed to be presented by parents in
addition to therapists. This is especially true for the developmental programmes (see
Chapter 8), but parents can also play a significant role in the delivery of other treatments programmes also, such as behavioural (Chapter 5), TEACCH (Chapter 7) and
the sensorimotor treatments (Chapter 10). Given that treatment programmes might
be delivered either by professionals or parents prompts the question as to whether the
intervention is improved by the use of parents as therapists.

Table 13.6 Mean effect sizes for different intervention types, split by whether those interventions were led primarily by parents or by professionals.

	ABA			Denver			Eclectic			TEACCH		
	IQ	L	ASB	IQ	L	ASB	IQ	L	ASB	IQ	L	ASB
Parent-led	0.73	0.59	0.46	0.32	0.68	0.36	0.15	0.28	0.46	0.40	0.52	0.98
Professional-led	1.07	0.98	0.82	0.73	0.68	0.45	0.28	0.58	0.16	0.58	0.83	0.69

IQ = intellectual; L = language; ASB = adaptive-social behaviour. White = strong effect; light grey = moderate effect; dark grey = weak effect.

Table 13.6 presents the mean effect sizes for the three outcome domains, for each programme type for which these data are available. These effect sizes are calculated depending on whether the intervention was primarily delivered by therapists/professionals or by parents and are shaded to represent: strong effects (light shaded cells), moderate effects (medium shaded cells) and weak effects (dark shaded cells). Inspection of Table 13.6 shows a very clear pattern of results for the different outcome variables. Professional-led programmes have a better impact on intellectual/cognitive gain than parent-led programmes for all of the different intervention types. This relationship is also noted for language/communication gains for both the behavioural and eclectic approaches, but not for the TEACCH and Denver models of treatment. However, the pattern of data for adaptive-social behaviour is not so clear. Although professionally led approaches appear to show an advantage for the behavioural intervention (and to a lesser extent for the Denver model), having the programme led by parents was more beneficial for adaptive-social functioning gains for the TEACCH and eclectic programmes. Involvement of the parents was also seen to be highly beneficial for this domain in the massage therapies discussed in Chapter 10.

The reasons for this pattern of data, where professionally led approaches appear to offer a clear advantage for most programmes in terms of the intellectual and language gains for the child but not necessarily for the adaptive-social skills, is not fully understood and certainly requires further investigation in terms of its mechanisms. However, the effect is consistent with findings regarding the impact of parenting stress levels on the child improvements noted for an eclectic programme reported by Osborne et al. (2008a). In this study, levels of parenting stress were measured at baseline and the children were then exposed to 9 months of an eclectic programme. Those children having a more intense weekly treatment demonstrated greater gains over the course of the intervention, but this advantage for more intensive programmes was reduced by high levels of parenting stress (see Figure 13.7).

These data imply that parental functioning may impact on the outcomes of the intervention, with the children of highly stressed parents showing weaker gains as a result of the intervention. The reasons for this effect have been discussed at length in a number of places (Osborne, 2009; Reed & Osborne, 2014) but appear to involve a number of aspects of the parent-child interaction: highly stressed parents find it more difficult to engage with an intervention programme; highly stressed parents have less ability to effectively limit set for their children and this creates further behavioural problems for the child (Osborne & Reed, 2009a) and there may be some difficulty in

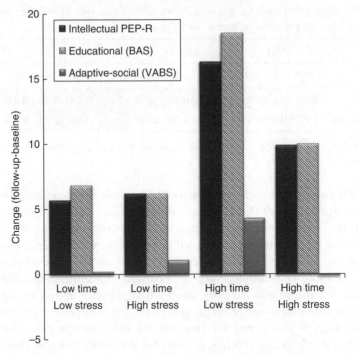

Figure 13.7 Pre- to post-change in several functioning domains for an eclectic programme reported by Osborne et al. (2008a), as a function of pre-intervention parent stress levels and the weekly intensity (time) of the programme (above or below 25 hours).

forming attachment with a very challenging individual (see Chapter 10 for a discussion in the context of massage therapy).

Thus, involving parents in the intervention may prove to be something of a double-edged sword. For some parents, with some intervention programmes, their involvement may improve adaptive-social outcomes for their children, perhaps because the parents' ability to manage their children increases, their responsiveness to their child's behaviour improves or the levels of attachment improve (see Chapters 8 and 10). If any of these aspects of parenting do improve, then the inclusion of the parents may well help with adaptive-social skills of the child undergoing the therapy as it helps the parent to understand better their child. However, highly stressed parents may not be able to engage to an extent that allows them to be helped and, until the parents themselves are helped, then their involvement in the intervention may then be detrimental to the outcome of the treatment.

Overview

In bringing together the evidence for each intervention it was hoped to do more than merely contribute to the arguments concerning which of the treatment programmes are the most effective. Clearly, this is an important question and one that has exercised many researchers and practitioners over the last 25 years. However, it is not the only question, nor possibly the best question to ask; rather, the current chapter also was hoping to address the issue of which intervention works best for whom. That is, it hoped to address whether there is any evidence that would allow treatment decisions to be made that are tailored to the needs of the individual with ASD and their families.

In overviewing the evidence, the current book has established a number of things that we now do know about the treatment of ASD. For instance, it is very apparent that within-person models of ASD have largely failed to make an impression on the development of treatments – certainly not any developments that have led to real world impacts of any note. In contrast, the views of ASD that place at their core the interplay between the person with ASD and their environment have fared much better in terms of establishing interventions and also in understanding the nature of the disorder. Focus on the implications of these latter views has produced a wide variety of interventions for ASD, which were outlined in detail in the preceding chapters, along with the evidence that has been compiled for their effectiveness.

At this point, with the evidence that is available, it is possible to start to develop a tentative set of decision rules that might help to match the treatment given to the individual. In terms of the decision rules, the initial question has to be about the individual's severity of ASD, along with an examination of the other levels of functioning presented by that person. This suggestion is nothing particularly new, as many treatments espouse starting from the assessment of the individual and developing individualized therapy based on this assessment. The evidence about what to do next, as presented in this text, is quite clear: if the individual has severe ASD, perhaps also coupled with low levels of functioning in other domains, then a behavioural approach appears to be the best option. An alternative to this option might be a Denver model, which employs a good deal of ABA within it. The ESDM version of this treatment model typically tends to be delivered for less time per week than ABA, if that is a consideration. The other forms of intervention do not appear to perform as well for very severely autistic individuals.

The nature of the behavioural programme will depend on the specific requirements of the individual, both in terms of the areas needing to be developed, but also in terms of its duration and weekly intensity. If the needs of the individual include intellectual and linguistic problems, then behavioural programmes will work well. However, if the need is purely in the adaptive-social domain (and other aspects of functioning are reasonably strong), then other programmes might be good options (see next). With regard to the appropriate programme duration for a behavioural programme, it will depend just how severe the individual's problems are; the longer the programme, the more gains will be made in terms of intellectual and linguistic functioning, but the law of diminishing returns applies – gains in the latter years will not be as pronounced as in the initial years. Given this, it would be wise to set some exit-point strategy, with a clear goal in mind in terms of the level of improvement needed in these domains and then to think about moving to another form of therapy to impact on adaptive-social functioning, when the more basic needs are met. The same issues of diminishing returns are broadly true of the weekly intensity of behavioural programmes, with the additional gains after increasing the programme much beyond the 25 hours a week mark being less certain.

If the individual has less severe ASD or is less severely impaired intellectually and/ or if their needs are broadly in the adaptive-social domain, then a programme, such as a TEACCH approach, might be useful to employ initially. Alternatively, when the intellectual goals are reached in a behavioural approach, then a TEACCH programme might be thought of as being helpful in order develop the adaptive-social skills. Similarly, a developmental approach, conducted for a reasonable amount of time each week, would also serve to help these skills. In both cases, it would be advisable to place the child into a social situation – that is, to conduct the intervention within a school setting – probably in a special school with appropriately trained staff working closely with parents (although this latter issue is not entirely straightforward).

If the person with ASD has a reasonable degree of intellectual functioning, but has social anxiety problems, then the use of a massage therapy along with the other approaches may also be considered. In fact, this might be a way to involve more-stressed parents in the treatment, without placing the extra teaching burdens on them that come with a parent-led behavioural or developmental approach. This part of the intervention should last for no more than 1–2 years, as, after that period of time, the impact appears to get worse – and this aspect of the programme may need to be supported by behavioural interventions as well, especially for less highly functioning individuals.

The issue of whether parents or caregivers should be involved in delivering the treatment (as opposed to agreeing its nature) also raises the question of how to help the parents. The parents/caregivers are clearly a major part of the person with ASD's environment and, as such, will have a major impact on that person's functioning. Providing help to the parents also appears to be very important. This is not just about providing parents with behaviour management strategies to use with their child or with information about ASD, but also directly targeting their very legitimate concerns about their child. Without this, they will not be helped not will they be able to help their child.

Thus, the current review has produced some answers to the issues of treating individuals with ASD. Obviously, much more needs to be done in this area and this will only be achieved by careful collaboration between basic and applied researchers. As a parting message of some hope, there may well be no cure for ASD – but there are certainly some things that will help and some, we now know, will help particular types of individual more than others.

References

Adreau, D. & Stella, J. (2001). Transition to middle and high school. *Interventions in School and Clinic, 36*, 266–271.

Adreon, D., & Stella, J. (2001). Transition to middle and high school: Increasing the success of students with Asperger syndrome. *Intervention in School and Clinic, 36*, 266–271.

Affleck, J. Q., Madge, S., Adams, A., & Lowenbraun, S. (1988). Integrated classroom versus resource model: academic viability and effectiveness. *Exceptional Children, 54*, 339–358.

Akstinas, M. (2006). *When is a child too young to attend IAC: The relationship of age at entry on cognitive, language, social and behavioural development.* Interagency Assessment Centre: Laguna Niguel.

Albers, A., & Greer, R. D. (1991). Is the three term contingency trial a predictor of effective instruction? *Journal of Behavioral Education, 1*, 337–354.

Aldred, C., Green, J., & Adams, C. (2004). A new social communication intervention for children with autism: pilot randomised controlled treatment study suggesting effectiveness. *Journal of Child Psychology and Psychiatry, 45*(8), 1420–1430.

Aldred, C., Phillips, R., Pollard, C., & Adams, C. (2001). Multidisciplinary social communication intervention for children with autism and pervasive developmental disorder: the Child's Talk project. *Educational and Child Psychology, 18*(2), 76–87.

American Psychiatric Association (1994). *DSM-IV.* Washington, DC: Author.

American Psychiatric Association (2013). *The Diagnostic and Statistical Manual of Mental Disorders: DSM 5.* bookpointUS.

Anan, R. M., Warner, L. J., McGillivary, J. E., Chong, I. M., & Hines, S. J. (2008). Group Intensive Family Training (GIFT) for preschoolers with autism spectrum disorders. *Behavioral Interventions, 23*, 165–180.

Anderson, S. R., Avery, D. L., DiPietro, E. K., Edwards, G. L., & Christian, W. P. (1987). Intensive home-based intervention with autistic children. *Education and Treatment of Children, 10*, 352–366.

Aoyama, S. (1995). The efficacy of structuring the work system: Individualization of the work format and the use of a 3-level paper rack in a special education class. *Japanese Journal of Special Education, 32*, 1–5.

Interventions for Autism: Evidence for Educational and Clinical Practice, First Edition. Phil Reed.
© 2016 John Wiley & Sons, Ltd. Published 2016 by John Wiley & Sons, Ltd.

Arick, J. R., Loos, L., Falco, R., & Krug, D. A. (2004). *The STAR Program: Strategies for teaching based on autism research, levels I, II, & III.* Austin. TX: PRO-ED.

Arno, P. S., Levine, C., & Memmott, M. M. (1999). The economic value of informal caregiving. *Health Affairs, 18*(2), 182–188.

Ashburner, J., Ziviani, J., & Rodger, S. (2008). Sensory processing and classroom emotional, behavioral, and educational outcomes in children with autism spectrum disorder. *American Journal of Occupational Therapy, 62*(5), 564–573.

Ashburner, J. K., Ziviani, J. M., & Rodger, S. (2010). Surviving in the mainstream: Capacity of children with autism spectrum disorders to perform academically and regulate their emotions and behavior at school. *Research in Autism Spectrum Disorders, 4,* 18–27.

Ashwood, P., & Van de Water, J. (2004). Is autism an autoimmune disease? *Autoimmunity Reviews, 3*(7), 557–562.

Asperger, H. (1944). Die 'Autistischen Psychopathen' in Kindesalter [Autistic psychopathy in childhood]. *Archiv fur Psychiatrie und Nervenkrankheiten, 117,* 76–136.

Attwood, T. (2007). *The complete guide to Asperger's syndrome.* London: Jessica Kingsley Publishers.

Avramidis, E., Bayliss, P., & Burden, R. (2000). A survey into mainstream teachers' attitudes towards the inclusion of children with special educational needs in the ordinary school in one local education authority. *Educational Psychology, 20,* 191–121.

Ayres, A. J. (1972). Improving academic scores through sensory integration. *Journal of Learning Disabilities, 5*(6), 338–343.

Ayres, J. A. (1979). *Sensory integration and the child.* Los Angeles: Western Psychological Services.

Ayres, A. J., & Tickle, L. S. (1980). Hyper-responsivity to touch and vestibular stimuli as a predictor of positive response to sensory integration procedures by autistic children. *The American journal of occupational therapy: official publication of the American Occupational Therapy Association, 34*(6), 375–381.

Baer, D. M., Wolf, M. M., & Risley, T. R. (1968). Some current dimensions of applied behaviour analysis. *Journal of Applied Behavior Analysis, 1*(1), 91–97.

Bagatell, N., Mirigliani, G., Patterson, C., Reyes, Y., & Test, L. (2010). Effectiveness of therapy ball chairs on classroom participation in children with autism spectrum disorders. *American Journal of Occupational Therapy, 64,* 895–903.

Baird, G., Charman, T., Baron-Cohen, S., Cox, A., Swettenham, J., Wheelwright, S., & Drew, A. (2000). A screening instrument for autism at 18 months of age: a 6-year follow-up study. *Journal of the American Academy of Child & Adolescent Psychiatry, 39*(6), 694–702.

Baird, G., Simonoff, E., Pickles, A., Chandler, S., Loucas, T., Meldrum, D., & Charman, T. (2006). Prevalence of disorders of the autism spectrum in a population cohort of children in South Thames: the Special Needs and Autism Project (SNAP). *The Lancet, 368,* 210–215.

Baker, E. T., Wang, M. C., & Walberg, H. J. (1994). The effects of inclusion on learning. *Educational Leadership, 52,* 33–35.

Baker-Ericzén, M. J., Brookman-Frazee, L., & Stahmer, A. (2005). Stress levels and adaptability in parents of toddlers with and without Autism Spectrum Disorders. *Research and Practice for Persons with Severe Disabilities, 30,* 194–204.

Baker-Ericzén, M. J., Stahmer, A. C., & Burns, A. (2007). Child demographics associated with outcomes in a community-based pivotal response training program. *Journal of Positive Behavior Interventions, 9*(1), 52–60.

Bal, E., Harden, E., Lamb, D., Van Hecke, A. V., Denver, J. W., & Porges, S. W. (2010). Emotion recognition in children with autism spectrum disorders: Relations to eye gaze and autonomic state. *Journal of Autism and Developmental Disorders, 40*(3), 358–370.

Baranek, G. T. (2002). Efficacy of sensory and motor interventions for children with autism. *Journal of Autism and Developmental Disorders, 32*(5), 397–422.

Baranek, G. T., David, F. J., Poe, M. D., Stone, W. L., & Watson, L. R. (2006). Sensory Experiences Questionnaire: Discriminating sensory features in young children with autism, developmental delays, and typical development. *Journal of Child Psychology and Psychiatry*, 47(6), 591–601.

Baranek, G. T., Foster, L. G., & Berkson, G. (1997). Tactile defensiveness and stereotyped behaviors. *American Journal of Occupational Therapy*, 51, 91–95.

Barbera, M. L. & Rasmussen, T. (2007). *The Verbal Behavior Approach: How to teach children with autism and related disorders.* London: Jessica Kingsley Publishers.

Barnard, J., Prior, A., & Potter, D. (2000). *Inclusion and autism: Is it working?* National Autistic Society, London.

Barnhill, G. P. & Myles, B. (2001). Attributional style and depression in adolescents with Asperger syndrome. *Journal of Positive Behavioral Intervention*, 3, 175–190.

Baron, I.S. (2008). Autism Spectrum Disorder: Complex, controversial, and confounding. *Neuropsychology Review*, 18, 271–272.

Baron-Cohen, S. (1988). Social and pragmatic deficits in autism: Cognitive or affective? *Journal of Autism and Developmental Disorders*, 18(3), 379–402.

Baron-Cohen, S. (1989). The autistic child's theory of mind: A case of specific developmental delay. *Journal of Child Psychology and Psychiatry*, 30(2), 285–297.

Baron-Cohen, S. (2000). Theory of mind and autism: A fifteen year review. In S. Baron-Cohen, H. Tager-Flusberg, & D. J. Cohen (Eds.), *Understanding other minds: Perspectives from developmental cognitive neuroscience* (2nd ed.), (pp. 3–20). New York, NY: Oxford University Press.

Baron-Cohen, S. (2002). The extreme male brain theory of autism. *Trends in Cognitive Sciences*, 6(6), 248–254.

Baron-Cohen, S. (2003). *Mind reading: the interactive guide to emotions.* London: Jessica Kingsley Publishers.

Baron-Cohen, S. (2009). Autism: The Empathizing–Systemizing (E-S) Theory. *Annals of the New York Academy of Sciences*, 1156(1), 68–80.

Baron-Cohen, S., & Bolton, P. (1993). *Autism: the facts.* Oxford: Oxford University Press.

Baron-Cohen, S., Golan, O., & Ashwin, E. (2012). Teaching emotion recognition to children with autism spectrum conditions. *BJEP Monograph Series II, Number 8-Educational Neuroscience*, 1(1), 115–127.

Baron-Cohen, S., Leslie, A. M., & Frith, U. (1985). Does the autistic child have a 'theory of mind'? *Cognition*, 21(1), 37–46.

Baron-Cohen, S., Scott, F. J., Allison, C., Williams, J., Bolton, P., Matthews, F. E., & Brayne, C. (2009). Prevalence of autism-spectrum conditions: UK school-based population study. *The British Journal of Psychiatry*, 194(6), 500–509.

Baron-Cohen, S., & Wheelwright, S. (1999). 'Obsessions' in children with autism or Asperger syndrome. Content analysis in terms of core domains of cognition. *The British Journal of Psychiatry*, 175(5), 484–490.

Baron-Cohen, S., Wheelwright, S., Hill, J., Raste, Y., & Plumb, I. (2001). The 'Reading the Mind in the Eyes' test revised version: A study with normal adults, and adults with Asperger syndrome or high-functioning autism. *Journal of Child Psychology and Psychiatry*, 42(2), 241–251.

Bartak, L., & Rutter, M. (1974). The use of personal pronouns by autistic children. *Journal of Autism and Childhood Schizophrenia*, 4(3), 217–222.

Bartman, S., & Freeman, N. (2003). Teaching language to a two-year-old with autism. *Journal on Developmental Disabilities*, 10(1), 47–53.

Bauminger, N., & Kasari, C. (2000). Loneliness and friendship in high-functioning children with autism. *Child Development*, 71, 447–456.

Behrmann, M., Thomas, C., & Humphreys, K. (2006). Seeing it differently: Visual processing in autism. *Trends in Cognitive Sciences*, 10(6), 258–264.

Begeer, S., Gevers, C., Clifford, P., Verhoeve, M., Kat, K., Hoddenbach, E., & Boer, F. (2011). Theory of mind training in children with autism: A randomized controlled trial. *Journal of Autism and Developmental Disorders, 41*(8), 997–1006.

Begeer, S., Rieffe, C., Terwogt, M. M., & Stockmann, L. (2006). Attention to facial emotion expressions in children with autism. *Autism, 10*(1), 37–51.

Bellini, S. (2006). The development of social anxiety in adolescents with autism spectrum disorders. *Focus on Autism and Other Developmental Disabilities, 21*(3), 138–145.

Ben-Itzchak, E., Lahat, E., Burgin, R., & Zachor, A. D. (2008). Cognitive, behavior and intervention outcome in young children with autism. *Research in Developmental Disabilities, 29*(5), 447–458.

Ben-Itzchak, E., & Zachor, D. A. (2007). The effects of intellectual functioning and autism severity on outcome of early behavioral intervention for children with autism. *Research in Developmental Disabilities, 28*(3), 287–303.

Bertrand, J., Mars, A., Boyle, C., Bove, F., Yeargin-Allsopp, M., & Decoufle, P. (2001). Prevalence of autism in a United States population: the Brick Township, New Jersey, investigation. *Pediatrics, 108*(5), 1155–1161.

Bettelheim, B. (1967). *Empty fortress.* Simon and Schuster.

Bettison, S. (1996). The long-term effects of auditory training on children with autism. *Journal of Autism and Developmental Disabilities, 26*, 361–374.

Berard, G. (1982). *Audition egale comportement.* Sainte-Ruffine: Maisonneuve.

Berard, G. (1993). *Hearing equals behavior.* New Canaan, CT: Keats.

Bibby, P., Eikeseth, S., Martin, N. T., Mudford, O. C., & Reeves, D. (2001). Progress and outcomes for children with autism receiving parent-managed intensive interventions. *Research in Developmental Disabilities, 22*(6), 425–447.

Billstedt, E. (2000). Autism and Asperger syndrome: coexistence with other clinical disorders. *Acta Psychiatrica Scandinavica, 102*(5), 321–330.

Billstedt, E., Gillberg, C., & Gillberg, C. (2005). Autism after adolescence: population-based 13-to 22-year follow-up study of 120 individuals with autism diagnosed in childhood. *Journal of Autism and Developmental Disorders, 35*(3), 351–360.

Billstedt, E., Gillberg, C., & Gillberg, C. (2007). Autism in adults: symptom patterns and early childhood predictors. Use of the DISCO in a community sample followed from childhood. *Journal of Child Psychology and Psychiatry, 48*(11), 1102–1110.

Birch, L. L. (1980). Effects of peer models' food choices and eating behaviors on preschoolers' food preferences. *Child Development, 51*, 489–496.

Birnbrauer, J. S., & Leach, D. J. (1993). The Murdoch Early Intervention Program after 2 years. *Behaviour Change, 10*(2), 63–74

Blairs, S., Slater, S., & Hare, D. J. (2007). The clinical application of deep touch pressure with a man with autism presenting with severe anxiety and challenging behaviour. *British Journal of Learning Disabilities, 35*(4), 214–220.

Blatchford, P. (2009). Class size. In E. Anderman (Ed.), *Psychology of classroom learning: An encyclopedia.* Detroit: Macmillan Reference.

Blatchford, P., Russell, A., Bassett, P., Brown, P., & Martin, C. (2007). The role and effects of teaching assistants in English primary schools (Years 4 to 6) 2000–2003. Results from the Class Size and Pupil–Adult Ratios (CSPAR) KS2 Project. *British Educational Research Journal, 33*, 5–26.

Boakes, R. (1984). *From Darwin to behaviourism: Psychology and the minds of animals.* CUP Archive.

Bodfish, J. W. (2004). Treating the core features of autism: Are we there yet? *Mental Retardation and Developmental Disabilities Research Reviews, 10*, 318–326

Bodfish, J. W., Symons, F. J., Parker, D. E., & Lewis, M. H. (2000). Varieties of repetitive behavior in autism: Comparisons to mental retardation. *Journal of Autism and Developmental Disorders, 30*(3), 237–243.

Bogdan, R., & Taylor, S. J. (1989). Relationships with severely disabled people: The social construction of humanness. *Social Problems*, *36*, 135–148.

Bolles, R.C. (1979). *Learning theory*. New York: Holt, Rinehart and Winston.

Bölte, S., & Poustka, F. (2002). Intervention bei autistischen Störungen: Status quo, evidenz-basierte, fragliche und fragwürdige Techniken. *Zeitschrift für Kinder-und Jugendpsychiatrie und Psychotherapie*, *30*(4), 271–280.

Bonggat, P. W. & Hall, L. J. (2010). Evaluation of the effects of sensory integration-based intervention by a preschool special education teacher. *Education and Training in Autism and Developmental Disabilities*, *45*, 294–302.

Booth, T., & Ainscow, M. (2000). *The index for inclusion*. Bristol: Centre for Studies on Inclusive Education.

Boucher, J., Mayes, A., & Bigham, S. (2012). Memory in autistic spectrum disorder. *Psychological Bulletin*, *138*(3), 458.

Boutot, E. A. & Bryant, D. P. (2005). Social integration of students with autism in inclusive settings. *Education and Training in Developmental Disabilities*, *401*, 14–23.

Boyd, R. D. (1998). Sex as a possible source of group inequivalence in Lovaas (1987). *Journal of Autism and Developmental Disorders*, *28*(3), 211–215.

Boyd, R. D., & Corley, M. J. (2001). Outcome survey of early intensive behavioral intervention for young children with autism in a community setting. *Autism*, *5*(4), 430–441.

Boyd, B. A., Hume, K., McBee, M. T., Alessandri, M., Gutierrez, A., Johnson, L., Sperry, L., & Odom, S. L. (2014). Comparative efficacy of LEAP, TEACCH and non-model-specific special education programs for preschoolers with autism spectrum disorders. *Journal of Autism and Developmental Disorders*, *44*(2), 366–380.

Bradley, E. A., Summers, J. A., Wood, H. L., & Bryson, S. E. (2004). Comparing rates of psychiatric and behavior disorders in adolescents and young adults with severe intellectual disability with and without autism. *Journal of Autism and Developmental Disorders*, *34*(2), 151–161.

Braiden, H.J., McDaniel, B., McCrudden, E., & Hanes, M., & Crozier, B. (2012). A practice-based evaluation of Barnardo's forward steps early intervention programme for children diagnosed with autism. *Child Care in Practice*, *18*, 227–242.

Bricker, D. (1995). The challenge of inclusion. *Journal of Early Intervention*, *19*, 179–194.

Brink, S. (1988). Japanese ideas helping autistic children in U.S. *Boston Herald (6 June)*, pp. 25, 26.

Bronfenbrenner, U. (1979). *The ecology of human development: Experiment in nature and design*. Cambridge, MA: Harvard University Press.

Brown versus Board of Education (1954). 347, US 483, 492.

Brown, J. A., & McIntosh, K. (2012). Training, Inclusion, and Behaviour: Effect on Student-Teacher and Student-SEA Relationships for Students with Autism Spectrum Disorders. *Exceptionality Education International*, *22*(2), 77–88.

Brown, M. M. (1999). Auditory integration training and autism: Two case studies. *British Journal of Occupational Therapy*, *62*, 13–17.

Browning, J., Osborne, L. A., & Reed, P. (2009). A qualitative comparison of perceived stress and coping in adolescents with and without autistic spectrum disorders as they approach leaving school. *British Journal of Special Education*, *36*(1), 36–43.

Brugha, T., McManus, S., Meltzer, H., Smith, J., Scott, F. J., Purdon, S., Harris, J. & Bankart, J. (2009). *Autism spectrum disorders in adults living in households throughout England: Report from the adult psychiatric morbidity survey 2007*. Leeds: The NHS Information Centre for Health and Social Care.

Buitelaar, J. K. (1995). Attachment and social withdrawal in autism: Hypotheses and findings. *Behaviour*, *319–350*.

Bundy, A. C., & Murray, E. A. (2002). Sensory integration: A. Jean Ayres' theory revisited. In A. C. Bundy, E. A. Murray, & S. J. Lane (Eds.), *Sensory integration: Theory and practice* (2nd ed.), (pp. 3–33). Philadelphia: F. A. Davis.

Burack, J. A., Root, R., & Zigler, E. (1997). Inclusive education for students with Autism: Reviewing ideological, empirical and community considerations. In D. Cohen & F.R. Volkmar (Eds.), *Handbook of autism and pervasive developmental disorders*, (2nd ed.), (pp. 796–807). New York: John Wiley & Sons, Inc.

Buysse, V., & Bailey, D. B. (1993). Behavioural and developmental outcomes in young children with disabilities in integrated and segregated settings: A review of comparative studies. *Journal of Special Education, 26*, 434–461.

Buysse, V., Bailey, D. B., Smith, T. M., & Simeonsson, R. J. (1994). The relationship between child characteristics and placement in specialized vs. inclusive early childhood programs. *Topics in Early Childhood Special Education, 14*, 419–435.

Cairns, R. B., & Cairns, B. D. (1994). *Lifelines and risks: pathways of youth in our time.* New York: Cambridge University Press.

Callahan, K., Shukla-Mehta, S., Magee, S., & Wie, M. (2010). ABA versus TEACCH: the case for defining and validating comprehensive treatment models in autism. *Journal of Autism and Developmental Disorders, 40*(1), 74–88.

Campbell, M., Schopler, E., Cueva, J. E., & Hallin, A. (1996). Treatment of autistic disorder. *Journal of the American Academy of Child & Adolescent Psychiatry, 35*(2), 134–143.

Canitano, R. (2007). Epilepsy in autism spectrum disorders. *European Child & Adolescent Psychiatry, 16*(1), 61–66.

Capps, L., Kehres, J., & Sigman, M. (1998). Conversational abilities among children with autism and children with developmental delays. *Autism, 2*(4), 325–344.

Carbone, P. S., Behl, D. D., Azor, V., & Murphy, N. A. (2010). The medical home for children with autism spectrum disorders: Parent and pediatrician perspectives. *Journal of Autism and Developmental Disorders, 40*(3), 317–324.

Carmody, D. P., Kaplan, M., & Gaydos, A. M. (2001). Spatial orientation adjustments in children with autism in Hong Kong. *Child Psychiatry and Human Development, 31*, 233–247.

Caron, C., & Rutter, M. (1991). Comorbidity in child psychopathology: concepts, issues and research strategies. *Journal of Child Psychology and Psychiatry, 37*, 1063–1080.

Carpenter, M., Pennington, B. F., & Rogers, S. J. (2001). Understanding of others' intentions in children with autism. *Journal of Autism and Developmental Disorders, 31*(6), 589–599.

Carr, E. G., Newsom, C. D., & Binkoff, J. A. (1980). Escape as a factor in the aggressive behavior of two retarded children. *Journal of Applied Behavior Analysis, 13*(1), 101–117.

Carr, E. G., & Durand, V. M. (1985). Reducing behavior problems through functional communication training. *Journal of Applied Behavior Analysis, 18*(2), 111–126.

Carr, J. E., & Firth, A. M. (2005). The Verbal Behavior Approach to early and intensive behavioral intervention for autism: a call for additional empirical support. *Journal of Early and Intensive Behavior Intervention, 2*(1), 18–27.

Carrington, S. & Graham, L. (2001). Perceptions of school by two teenage boys with Asperger syndrome and their mothers: a qualitative study. *Autism, 5*, 37–48.

Carter, S. L. (2005). An empirical analysis of the effects of a possible sinus infection and weighted vest on functional analysis outcomes of self-injury exhibited by a child with autism. *Journal of Early and Intensive Behavior Intervention, 2*, 252–258.

Carter, A. S., Messinger, D. S., Stone, W. L., Celimli, S., Nahmias, A. S., & Yoder, P. (2011). A randomized controlled trial of Hanen's 'More Than Words' in toddlers with early autism symptoms. *Journal of Child Psychology and Psychiatry, 52*(7), 741–752.

Cascio, C., McGlone, F., Folger, S., Tannan, V., Baranek, G., Pelphrey, K. A., & Essick, G. (2008). Tactile perception in adults with autism: a multidimensional psychophysical study. *Journal of Autism and Developmental Disorders, 38*(1), 127–137.

Casenhiser, D. M., Shanker, S. G., & Stieben, J. (2013). Learning through interaction in children with autism: Preliminary data from asocial-communication-based intervention. *Autism, 17*(2), 220–241.

Case-Smith, J., & Bryan, T. (1999). The effects of occupational therapy with sensory integration emphasis on preschool-age children with autism. *American Journal of Occupational Therapy, 53,* 489–497.

Case-Smith, J., & Miller, H. (1999). Occupational therapy with children with pervasive developmental disorders. *American Journal of Occupational Therapy, 53*(5), 506–513.

Cashin, A., Sci, D. A., & Barker, P. (2009). The triad of impairment in autism revisited. *Journal of Child and Adolescent Psychiatric Nursing, 22*(4), 189.

Catania, A. C. (2007). *Learning* (4th ed.). Sloan Publishing.

Cederlund, M., Hagberg, B., Billstedt, E., Gillberg, I. C., & Gillberg, C. (2008). Asperger syndrome and autism: A comparative longitudinal follow-up study more than 5 years after original diagnosis. *Journal of Autism and Developmental Disorders, 38*(1), 72–85.

Celani, G., Battacchi, M. W., & Arcidiacono, L. (1999). The understanding of the emotional meaning of facial expressions in people with autism. *Journal of Autism and Developmental Disorders, 29*(1), 57–66.

Chakrabarti, S., & Fombonne, E. (2001). Pervasive developmental disorders in preschool children. *JAMA, 285*(24), 3093–3099.

Chan, J. M., O'Reilly, M. F., Lang, R. B., Boutot, E. A., White, P. J., Pierce, N., & Baker, S. (2011). Evaluation of a Social Stories™ intervention implemented by pre-service teachers for students with autism in general education settings. *Research in Autism Spectrum Disorders, 5*(2), 715–721.

Charlop-Christy, M. H., LeBlanc, L. A., & Carpenter, M. H. (1999). Naturalistic Teaching Strategies (NaTS) to teach speech to Children with Autism: Historical perspective, development, and current practice. *The California School Psychologist, 4*(1), 30–46.

Charlop-Christy, M. H., Carpenter, M., Le, L., LeBlanc, L. A., & Kellet, K. (2002). Using the picture exchange communication system (PECS) with children with autism: assessment of PECS acquisition, speech, social-communicative behavior, and problem behavior. *Journal of Applied Behaviour Analysis, 35,* 213–31.

Charman, T., Howlin, P., Berry, B., & Prince, E. (2004). Measuring developmental progress of children with autism spectrum disorder on school entry using parent report. *Autism, 8*(1), 89–100.

Charman, T., Pickles, A., Chandler, S., Wing, L., Bryson, S., Simonoff, E., Loucas, T., & Baird, G. (2009). Commentary: Effects of diagnostic thresholds and research vs service and administrative diagnosis on autism prevalence. *International Journal of Epidemiology, 38*(5), 1234–1238.

Chasson, G. S., Harris, G. E., & Neely, W. J. (2007). Cost comparison of early intensive behavioral intervention and special education for children with autism. *Journal of Child and Family Studies, 16*(3), 401–413.

Cheely, C. A., Carpenter, L. A., Letourneau, E. J., Nicholas, J. S., Charles, J., & King, L. B. (2012). The prevalence of youth with autism spectrum disorders in the criminal justice system. *Journal of Autism and Developmental Disorders, 42*(9), 1856–1862.

Chomsky, N. (1957). *Syntactic structures.* Princeton, NJ: Mouton and Co.

Clark, T. F., Winkielman, P., & McIntosh, D. N. (2008). Autism and the extraction of emotion from briefly presented facial expressions: stumbling at the first step of empathy. *Emotion, 8*(6), 803.

Cohen, H., Amerine-Dickens, M., & Smith, T. (2006). Early intensive behavioral treatment: Replication of the UCLA model in a community setting. *Journal of Developmental & Behavioral Pediatrics, 27*(2), S145–S155.

Cohen, J. (1988). *Statistical power analysis for the behavioral sciences* (2nd ed.). Hillsdale, NJ: Erlbaum.

Coman, D., Alessandri, M., Gutierrez, A., Novotny, S., Boyd, B., Hume, K., Sperry, L., & Odom, S. (2013). Commitment to classroom model philosophy and burnout symptoms among high fidelity teachers implementing preschool programs for children with autism spectrum disorders. *Journal of autism and developmental disorders, 43*(2), 345–360.

Conallen, K., & Reed, P. (2012). The effects of a conversation prompt procedure on independent play. *Research in Autism Spectrum Disorders, 6*(1), 365–377.

Connor, M. (1998). A review of behavioural early intervention programmes for children with autism. *Educational Psychology in Practice, 14,* 109–117.

Connor, M. (2000). Asperger syndrome (autistic spectrum disorder) and the self reports of comprehensive school students. *Educational Psychology in Practice, 16,* 285–296.

Constantino, J. N., Gruber, C. P., Davis, S., Hayes, S., Passanante, N., & Przybeck, T. (2004). The factor structure of autistic traits. *Journal of Child Psychology and Psychiatry, 45*(4), 719–726.

Conti-Ramsden, G., Simkin, Z., & Botting, N. (2006). The prevalence of autistic spectrum disorders in adolescents with a history of specific language impairment (SLI). *Journal of Child Psychology and Psychiatry, 47*(6), 621–628.

Cooper, J. O., Heron, T. E., & Heward, W. L. (2007). *Applied behavior analysis.* Upper Saddle River, NY: Pearson.

Corbett, B. A., Shickman, K., & Ferrer, E. (2008). Brief report: the effects of Tomatis sound therapy on language in children with autism. *Journal of Autism and Developmental Disorders, 38*(3), 562–566.

Cotton, K. (1996). *School size, school climate, and student performance.* (School Improvement Research Series (SIRS), Close-up #20). Portland, OR: Northwestern Regional Educational Laboratory (NWREL).

Couturier, J. L., Speechley, K. N., Steele, M., Norman, R., Stringer, B., & Nicolson, R. (2005). Parental perception of sleep problems in children of normal intelligence with pervasive developmental disorders: prevalence, severity, and pattern. *Journal of the American Academy of Child & Adolescent Psychiatry, 44*(8), 815–822.

Cox, A. L., Gast, D. L., Luscre, D., & Ayres, K. M. (2009). The effects of weighted vests on appropriate in-seat behaviors of elementary-age students with autism and severe to profound intellectual disabilities. *Focus on Autism and Other Developmental Disabilities, 24,* 17–26.

Croen, L. A., Grether, J. K., Hoogstrate, J., & Selvin, S. (2002). The changing prevalence of autism in California. *Journal of autism and developmental disorders, 32*(3), 207–215.

Crosland, K., & Dunlap, G. (2012). Effective strategies for the inclusion of children with autism in general education classrooms. *Behavior Modification, 36*(3), 251–269.

Crozier, S., & Tincani, M. (2007). Effects of social stories on prosocial behavior of preschool children with autism spectrum disorders. *Journal of Autism and Developmental Disorders, 37*(9), 1803–1814.

Cullen-Powell, L. A., Barlow, J. H., & Cushway, D. (2005). Exploring a massage intervention for parents and their children with autism: the implications for bonding and attachment. *Journal of Child Health Care, 9*(4), 245–255.

Cummins, A., Piek, J. P., & Dyck, M. J. (2005). Motor coordination, empathy, and social behaviour in school-aged children. *Developmental Medicine & Child Neurology, 47*(7), 437–442.

Davis, P. S., Florian, L., Ainscow, M., Dyson, A., Farrell, P., Hick, P., Humphrey, N., Jenkins, P., Kaplan, I., Palmer, S., Parkinson, G., Polat, F., Reason, R., Byers, R., Dee, L., Kershner, R. & Rouse, M. (2004a). *Teaching strategies and approaches for pupils with special educational needs: a scoping study.* Research Report 516, Nottingham: DfES Publications.

Davis, P. S., Fox, S., & Farrell, P. T. (2004b). Factors associated with the effective inclusion of primary- aged pupils with Down's syndrome. *British Journal of Special Education, 31,* 184–190.

Davis, T. N., Durand, S., & Chan, J. M. (2011). The effects of a brushing procedure on stereo-typical behavior. *Research in Autism Spectrum Disorders, 5,* 1053–1058.

Davison, G. C. (1965). The training of undergraduates as social reinforcers for autistic chil-dren. *Case studies in behavior modification* (pp. 146–148). New York: Holt, Rinehart & Winston.

Dawson, G. (2008). Early behavioral intervention, brain plasticity, and the prevention of autism spectrum disorder. *Development and psychopathology, 20*(03), 775–803.

Dawson, G., & Fernald, M. (1987). Perspective-taking ability and its relationship to the social behavior of autistic children. *Journal of Autism and Developmental Disorders, 17*(4), 487–498.

Dawson, G., & Osterling, J. (1997). Early intervention in autism: Effectiveness and common elements of current approaches. In M. J. Guralnick (Ed.), *The effectiveness of early inter-vention: Second generation research* (pp. 307–326). Baltimore, MD: Paul H. Brookes.

Dawson, G., Osterling, J., Meltzoff, A., & Kuhl, P. (2000). Case study of the development of an infant with autism from birth to 2 years of age. *Journal of Applied Developmental Psychology, 21,* 299–313.

Dawson, G., Rogers, S., Munson, J., Smith, M., Winter, J., Greenson, J., Donaldson, A., & Varley, J. (2010). Randomized, controlled trial of an intervention for toddlers with autism: the Early Start Denver Model. *Pediatrics, 125*(1), e17–e23.

Dawson, G., & Watling, R. (2000). Interventions to facilitate auditory, visual, and motor integration in autism: A review of the evidence. *Journal of Autism and Developmental Dis-orders, 30*(5), 415–421.

Dawson, G., Webb, S. J., & McPartland, J. (2005). Understanding the nature of face processing impairment in autism: insights from behavioral and electrophysiological studies. *Develop-mental Neuropsychology, 27*(3), 403–424.

de Bruin, E. I., Ferdinand, R. F., Meester, S., de Nijs, P. F., & Verheij, F. (2007). High rates of psychiatric co-morbidity in PDD-NOS. *Journal of Autism and Developmental Disorders, 37*(5), 877–886.

Delprato, D. J. (2001). Comparisons of discrete-trial and normalized behavioral language intervention for young children with autism. *Journal of Autism and Developmental Disor-ders, 31*(3), 315–325.

Department for Education and Skills. (2006). *Ethnicity and education. the evidence on minority ethnic pupils aged 5–16.* Nottingham: DfES Publications.

Dettmer, S., Simpson, R. L., Myles, B. S., & Ganz, J. B. (2000). The use of visual supports to facilitate transitions of students with autism. *Focus on Autism and Other Developmental Disabilities, 15*(3), 163–169.

DeMyer, M. K., Barton, S., DeMyer, W. E., Norton, J. A., Allen, J., & Steele, R. (1973). Prog-nosis in autism: A follow-up study. *Journal of Autism and Childhood Schizophrenia, 3*(3), 199–246.

Deprey, L., & Ozonoff, S. (2009). Assessment of comorbid psychiatric conditions in autism spectrum disorders. *Assessment of Autism Spectrum Disorders, 290–317.*

De Villiers, J., Myers, B., & Stainton, R. J. (2010). Differential pragmatic abilities and autism spectrum disorders: The case of pragmatic determinants of literal content. In: M. Macau-lay and P. Garces-Blitvich (Eds.), *Pragmatics and context.* Toronto, Canada: Antares.

Devlin, S., Healy, O., Leader, G., & Hughes, B. M. (2011). Comparison of behavioral inter-vention and sensory-integration therapy in the treatment of challenging behavior. *Journal of Autism and Developmental Disorders, 41*(10), 1303–1320.

Devlin, S., Leader, G., & Healy, O. (2009). Comparison of behavioral intervention and sensory-integration therapy in the treatment of self-injurious behavior. *Research in Autism Spectrum Disorders, 3,* 223–231.

Dewey, M. A., & Everard, M. P. (1974). The near-normal autistic adolescent. *Journal of Autism and Childhood Schizophrenia, 4*(4), 348–356.

Department of Health and Social Security (1981). *The Primary Health Care Team. Report of a Joint Working Group of the Standing Medical Advisory Committee and the Standing Nursing and Midwifery Advisory Committee. The Harding Report.* HMSO, London.

Diggle, T., McConachie, H. R., & Randle, V. R. L. (2002). Parent-mediated early intervention for young children with autism spectrum disorder. *Cochrane Database Syst Rev, 2.*

Dillenburger, K. (2011). The emperor's new clothes: eclecticism in autism treatment. *Research in Autism Spectrum Disorders, 5,* 1119–1128.

DiSalvo, C. A., & Oswald, D. P. (2002). Peer-mediated interventions to increase the social interaction of children with autism consideration of peer expectancies. *Focus Autism Other Developmental Disabilities, 17,* 198–207.

Donnellan, A. M. (1984). The criterion of the least dangerous assumption. *Behavior Disorders, 9,* 141–150.

Donnellan, A. M., Hill, D. A., & Leary, M. R. (2012). Rethinking autism: implications of sensory and movement differences for understanding and support. *Frontiers in Integrative Neuroscience, 6,* 46.

Dover, C. J., & Le Couteur, A. (2007). How to diagnose autism. *Archives of Disease in Childhood, 92*(6), 540–545.

Dozier, M. (2003). Attachment-based treatment for vulnerable children. *Attachment & Human Development, 5*(3), 253–257.

Drash, P. W., High, R. L., & Tudor, R. M. (1999). Using mand training to establish an echoic repertoire in young children with autism. *The Analysis of Verbal Behavior, 16,* 29.

Drash, P. W., & Tudor, R. M. (2004). An analysis of autism as a contingency-shaped disorder of verbal behavior. *The Analysis of Verbal Behavior, 20,* 5.

Drasgow, E., Halle, J. W., & Sigafoos, J. (1999). Teaching communication to learners with severe disabilities: Motivation, response competition, and generalisation. *Australasian Journal of Special Education, 23,* 47–63.

Drew, A., Baird, G., Baron-Cohen, S., Cox, A., Slonims, V., Wheelwright, S., Sweetenham, J., Berry, B., & Charman, T. (2002). A pilot randomised control trial of a parent training intervention for pre-school children with autism. *European Child & Adolescent Psychiatry, 11*(6), 266–272.

Dube, W. V. (2009). Stimulus overselectivity in discrimination learning. In P. Reed (Ed.) *Behavioral theories and interventions for autism* (pp. 23–46). New York: Nova.

Dube, W. V., & McIlvane, W. J. (1999). Reduction of stimulus overselectivity with non-verbal differential observing responses. *Journal of Applied Behavior Analysis, 32*(1), 25–33.

Dunn, W. (1999). *The Sensory Profile: User's manual.* San Antonio, TX: Psychological Corporation.

Dunst, C. J., Trivette, C. M., & Hamby, D. W. (2012). Effect of interest-based interventions on the social-communicative behavior of young children with autism spectrum disorders. *Center for Early Literacy Learning, 5*(6).

Durbach, M., & Pence, A. R. (1991). A comparison of language production skills of pre-schoolers with special needs in segregated and integrated settings. *Early Child Development and Care, 68,* 49–69.

Durkin, K., & Conti-Ramsden, G. (2007). Language, social behavior, and the quality of friendships in adolescents with and without a history of specific language impairment. *Child Development, 78*(5), 1441–1457.

Dziuk, M. A., Larson, J. C., Apostu, A., Mahone, E. M., Denckla, M. B., & Mostofsky, S. H. (2007). Dyspraxia in autism: association with motor, social, and communicative deficits. *Developmental Medicine & Child Neurology, 49*(10), 734–739.

Eapen, V., Črnčec, R., & Walter, A. (2013). Clinical outcomes of an early intervention program for preschool children with Autism Spectrum Disorder in a community group setting. *BMC Pediatrics, 13*(1), 3.

Eaves, L. C., & Ho, H. H. (1997). School placement and academic achievement in children with Autistic Spectrum Disorders. *Journal of Developmental and Physical Disabilities, 9*, 227–291.

Eaves, L. C., & Ho, H. H. (2008). Young adult outcome of autism spectrum disorders. *Journal of Autism and Developmental Disorders, 38*(4), 739–747.

Eaves, L. C., Ho, H. H., & Eaves, D. M. (1994). Subtypes of autism by cluster analysis. *Journal of Autism and Developmental Disorders, 24*(1), 3–22.

Edelson, S. M., Edelson, M. G., Kerr, D. C., & Grandin, T. (1999). Behavioral and physiological effects of deep pressure on children with autism: A pilot study evaluating the efficacy of Grandin's Hug Machine. *American Journal of Occupational Therapy, 53*(2), 145–152.

Eikeseth, S. (2009). Outcome of comprehensive psycho-educational interventions for young children with autism. *Research in Developmental Disabilities, 30*(1), 158–178.

Eikeseth, S., & Smith, D. P. (2013). An analysis of verbal stimulus control in intraverbal behavior: Implications for practice and applied research. *The Analysis of Verbal Behavior, 29*(1), 125.

Eikeseth, S., Smith, T., Jahr, E., & Eldevik, S. (2002). Intensive behavioral treatment at school for 4-to 7-year-old children with autism a 1-year comparison controlled study. *Behavior Modification, 26*(1), 49–68.

Eikeseth, S., Smith, T., Jahr, E., & Eldevik, S. (2007). Outcome for children with autism who began intensive behavioral treatment between ages 4 and 7 a comparison controlled study. *Behavior Modification, 31*(3), 264–278.

Eisenhower, A. S., Baker, B. L., & Blacher, J. (2005). Preschool children with intellectual disability: Syndrome specificity, behaviour problems, and maternal well-being. *Journal of Intellectual Disability Research, 49*, 657–671.

Eldar, E., Talmor, R., & Wolf-Zukerman, T. (2010). Successes and difficulties in the individual inclusion of children with Autism Spectrum Disorder (ASD) in the eyes of their coordinators. *The International Journal of Inclusive Education, 14*, 97–114.

Eldevik, S., Eikeseth, S., Jahr, E., & Smith, T. (2006). Effects of low-intensity behavioral treatment for children with autism and mental retardation. *Journal of Autism and Developmental Disorders, 36*(2), 211–224.

Eldevik, S., Hastings, R. P., Hughes, J. C., Jahr, E., Eikeseth, S., & Cross, S. (2009). Meta-analysis of early intensive behavioral intervention for children with autism. *Journal of Clinical Child & Adolescent Psychology, 38*(3), 439–450.

Eldevik, S., Hastings, R. P., Jahr, E., & Hughes, J. C. (2012). Outcomes of behavioral intervention for children with autism in mainstream pre-school settings. *Journal of Autism and Developmental Disorders, 42*(2), 210–220.

Emery, M. J. (2004). Art therapy as an intervention for autism. *Art Therapy, 21*(3), 143–147.

Engelmann, S., & Carnine, D. (1982). *Theory of instruction*. New York: Irvington.

Epp, K. M. (2008). Outcome-based evaluation of a social skills program using art therapy and group therapy for children on the autism spectrum. *Children & Schools, 30*(1), 27–36.

Escalona, A., Field, T., Singer-Strunck, R., Cullen, C., & Hartshorn, K. (2001). Brief report: improvements in the behavior of children with autism following massage therapy. *Journal of Autism and Developmental Disorders, 31*(5), 513–516.

Estes, A., Vismara, L., Mercado, C., Fitzpatrick, A., Elder, L., Greenson, J., … & Rogers, S. (2014). The impact of parent-delivered intervention on parents of very young children with autism. *Journal of Autism and Developmental Disorders, 44*(2), 353–365.

Evans, K., & Dubowski, J. (2001). *Art therapy with children on the autistic spectrum: Beyond words*. London: Jessica Kingsley Publishers.

Falter, C. M., Plaisted, K. C., & Davis, G. (2008). Visuo-spatial processing in autism – testing the predictions of extreme male brain theory. *Journal of Autism and Developmental Disorders*, *38*(3), 507–515.

Farber, B.A. (1991). *Crisis in education: Stress and burnout in the American teacher*. San Francisco; Jossey-Bass.

Farley, M. A., McMahon, W. M., Fombonne, E., Jenson, W. R., Miller, J., Gardner, M., Block, H., Pingree, C.B., Ritvo, E.R., Ritvo, R.A. & Coon, H. (2009). Twenty-year outcome for individuals with autism and average or near-average cognitive abilities. *Autism Research*, *2*(2), 109–118.

Farrell, P., Trigonaki, N., & Webster, D. (2005). An exploratory evaluation of two early intervention programmes for young children with autism. *Educational and Child Psychology*, *22*, 29–40.

Fazlioglu, Y., & Baran, G. (2008). A sensory integration therapy program on sensory problems for children with autism. *Perceptual and Motor Skills*, *106*, 115–422.

Fenske, E. C., Krantz, P. J., and McClannahan, L. E. (2001). Incidental teaching: A not discrete-trial teaching procedure. In C. Maurice, G. Green, and R. Foxx (Eds.) *Making a difference: Behavioral intervention for autism* (pp. 75–82). Austin, TX: PRO-ED.

Fenske, E. C., Zalenski, S., Krantz, P. J., McClannahan, L. E. (1985). Age at intervention and treatment outcome for autistic children in a comprehensive intervention program. *Analysis and Intervention in Developmental Disabilities*, *5*, 49–58.

Fernell, E., Hedvall, Å., Westerlund, J., Höglund Carlsson, L., Eriksson, M., Barnevik Olsson, M., Holm, A., Norrelgen, F., Kjellmer, L., & Gillberg, C. (2011). Early intervention in 208 Swedish preschoolers with autism spectrum disorder. A prospective naturalistic study. *Research in Developmental Disabilities*, *32*(6), 2092–2101.

Ferster, C. B. (1961). Positive reinforcement and behavioral deficits of autistic children. *Child Development*, *32*, 437–456.

Ferster, C. B., & DeMyer, M. K. (1961). The development of performances in autistic children in an automatically controlled environment. *Journal of Chronic Diseases*, *13*(4), 312–345.

Ferster, C. B., & Skinner, B. F. (1957). *Schedules of reinforcement*. New York: Appleton Century Crofts.

Fertel-Daly, D., Bedell, G. & Hinojosa, J. (2001). Effects of a weighted vest on attention to task and self-stimulatory behaviors in preschoolers with pervasive developmental disorders. *American Journal of Occupational Therapy*, *55*, 629–640.

Field, T. (1988). Stimulation of preterm infants. *Pediatrics Review*, *10*, 149–154.

Field, T., Diego, M., & Hernandez-Reif, M. (2007). Massage therapy research. *Developmental Review*, *27*(1), 75–89.

Field, T., Lasko, D., Mundy, P., Henteleff, T., Kabot, S., Talpins, S., & Dowling, M. (1997). Autistic children's attentiveness and responsivity improve after touch therapy. *Journal of Autism and Developmental Disorders*, *27*, 333–338.

Fisher, N., & Happé, F. (2005). A training study of theory of mind and executive function in children with autistic spectrum disorders. *Journal of Autism and Developmental Disorders*, *35*(6), 757–771.

Flanagan, H. E., Perry, A., & Freeman, N. L. (2012). Effectiveness of large-scale community-based intensive behavioral Intervention: a waitlist comparison study exploring outcomes and predictors. *Research in Autism Spectrum Disorders*, *6*(2), 673–682.

Fodor, J. A. (1983). *The modularity of mind: An essay on faculty psychology*. MIT Press.

Fombonne, E. (2003). Epidemiological surveys of autism and other pervasive developmental disorders: an update. *Journal of Autism and Developmental Disorders*, *33*(4), 365–382.

Fong, P. L. (1991). Cognitive appraisals in high-and low-stress mothers of adolescents with autism. *Journal of Consulting and Clinical Psychology*, *59*(3), 471.

Fornasari, L., Garzitto, M., Fabbro, F., Londero, D., Zago, D., Desinano, C., Rigo, S., Molteni, M., & Brambilla, P. (2012). Twelve months of TEACCH-oriented habilitation on an Italian population of children with autism. *International Journal of Developmental Disabilities, 58*(3), 145–158.

Frankel, F., Myatt, R., Sugar, C., Whitham, C., Gorospe, C. M., & Laugeson, E. (2010). A randomized controlled study of parent-assisted children's friendship training with children having autism spectrum disorders. *Journal of Autism and Developmental Disorders, 40*(7), 827–842.

Frederickson, N., Jones, A.P., & Lang, J. (2010). Inclusive provision options for pupils on the autistic spectrum. *Journal of Research in Special Educational Needs, 10*, 63–73.

Frederickson, N., Osborne, L. A., & Reed, P. (2004). Judgments of successful inclusion by education service personnel. *Educational Psychology, 24*(3), 263–290

Freedman, A. M., Ebin, E. V., & Wilson, E. A. (1962). Autistic schizophrenic children: An experiment in the use of D-lysergic acid diethylamide (LSD-25). *Archives of General Psychiatry, 6*(3), 203–213.

Freeman, S. F. N. & Alkin, M. C. (2000). Academic and social attainments of children with mental retardation in general education and special education settings. *Remedial and Special Education, 21*, 3–18.

Frith, U. (1989). *Autism: Explaining the enigma.* Oxford: Blackwell.

Frith, U. (1991). *Autism and Asperger syndrome.* Cambridge: Cambridge University Press.

Frith, U., & Happé, F. (1994). Autism: Beyond 'theory of mind'. *Cognition, 50*(1), 115–132.

Frost, L., & Bondy, A. (2002). *The picture exchange communication system training manual.* Pyramid Educational Products, Inc.

Fuchs, D., Fuchs, L. S, & Bishop, N. (1992). Teaching planning for students with learning disabilities: differences between general and special educators. *Learning Disabilities: Research and Practice, 7*, 120–128.

Gabriels, R. L., Hill, D. E., Pierce, R. A., Rogers, S. J., & Wehner, B. (2001). Predictors of Treatment Outcome in Young Children with Autism A Retrospective Study. *Autism, 5*(4), 407–429.

Gadow, K. D., DeVincent, C. J., Pomeroy, J. (2005). Comparison of DSM-IV symptoms in elementary school aged children with PDD versus clinic and community samples. *Autism, 9*, 392–415.

Ganz, M. L. (2007). The lifetime distribution of the incremental societal costs of autism. *Archives of Pediatrics & Adolescent Medicine, 161*(4), 343–349.

Gepner, B., Deruelle, C., & Grynfeltt, S. (2001). Motion and emotion: A novel approach to the study of face processing by young autistic children. *Journal of Autism and Developmental Disorders, 31*(1), 37–45.

Gersten, R., & Woodward, J. (1999). Rethinking the regular education initiative: Focus on the classroom teacher. *Remedial and Special Education, 11*, 7–16.

Ghaziuddin, M., & Butler, E. (1998). Clumsiness in autism and Asperger syndrome: A further report. *Journal of Intellectual Disability Research, 42*(1), 43–48.

Ghaziuddin, M., Ghaziuddin, N., & Greden, J. (2002). Depression in persons with autism: Implications for research and clinical care. *Journal of Autism and Developmental Disorders, 32*(4), 299–306.

Ghaziuddin, M., & Greden, J. (1998). Depression in children with autism/pervasive developmental disorders: A case-control family history study. *Journal of Autism and Developmental Disorders, 28*(2), 111–115.

Ghaziuddin, M., Tsai, L., & Ghaziuddin, N. (1991). Brief report: violence in Asperger syndrome, a critique. *Journal of Autism and Developmental Disorders, 21*(3), 349–354.

Ghaziuddin, M., Tsai, L., & Ghaziuddin, N. (1992). Comorbidity of autistic disorder in children and adolescents. *European Child & Adolescent Psychiatry, 1*(4), 209–213.

Ghaziuddin, M., Weidmer-Mikhail, E., & Ghaziuddin, N. (1998). Comorbidity of Asperger syndrome: A preliminary report. *Journal of Intellectual Disability Research, 4,* 279–283.

Gibbons, M. M., & Goins, S. (2008). Getting to know the child with Asperger syndrome. *Professional School Counseling, 11,* 347–352.

Gibson, E. J. (1969). *Principles of perceptual learning and development.* New York: Appleton-Century-Crofts.

Gibson, E. J., & Walk, R. D. (1956). The effect of prolonged exposure to visually presented patterns on learning to discriminate them. *Journal of Comparative and Physiological Psychology, 49*(3), 239.

Gillard, D. (2011). *Education in England: a brief history.* Website (available at www.educationengland.org.uk/history, accessed 7 July 2015).

Gillberg, C. (1990). Autism and pervasive developmental disorders. *Journal of Child Psychology and Psychiatry, 31*(1), 99–119.

Gillberg, C. (1998). Asperger syndrome and high-functioning autism. *The British Journal of Psychiatry, 172*(3), 200–209.

Gillberg, C., & Coleman, M. (2000). *The biology of autistic syndromes.* London: Cambridge University Press.

Gillberg, C., Johansson, M., Steffenburg, S., & Berlin, O. (1997). Auditory integration training in children with autism: Brief report of an open pilot study. *Autism, 1*(1), 97–100.

Gillberg, C., Steffenburg, S., & Schaumann, H. (1991). Is autism more common now than ten years ago? *British Journal of Psychiatry, 158,* 403–409.

Gilliam J. E., (1995). *Gilliam autism rating scale.* Austin, TX: PRO-ED.

Gillott, A., & Standen, P. J. (2007). Levels of anxiety and sources of stress in adults with autism. *Journal of Intellectual Disabilities, 11*(4), 359–370.

Gilmor, T. (1999). The efficacy of the Tomatis Method for children with learning and communication disorders: A meta-analysis. *International Journal of Listening, 13*(1), 12–23.

Goldstein, S., & Schwebach, A. J. (2004). The comorbidity of pervasive developmental disorder and attention deficit hyperactivity disorder: results of a retrospective chart review. *Journal of Autism and Developmental Disorders, 34*(3), 329–339.

Golan, O., Ashwin, E., Granader, Y., McClintock, S., Day, K., Leggett, V., & Baron-Cohen, S. (2010). Enhancing emotion recognition in children with autism spectrum conditions: An intervention using animated vehicles with real emotional faces. *Journal of Autism and Developmental Disorders, 40*(3), 269–279.

Gold, C. (2011). Special section: music therapy for people with autistic spectrum disorder. *Nordic Journal of Music Therapy, 20*(2), 105–107.

Goldsmith, T. R., LeBlanc, L. A., & Sautter, R. A. (2007). Teaching intraverbal behavior to children with autism. *Research in Autism Spectrum Disorders, 1*(1), 1–13.

Goldstein, H. (2000). Commentary: Interventions to facilitate auditory, visual, and motor integration: 'Show me the data'. *Journal of Autism and Developmental Disorders, 30*(5), 423–425.

Goldstein, H., & Wickstrom, S. (1986). Peer intervention effects on communicative interaction among handicapped and nonhandicapped preschoolers. *Journal of Applied Behavior Analysis, 19,* 209–214.

Gómez, J. C. (2009). Embodying meaning: Insights from primates, autism, and Brentano. *Neural Networks, 22*(2), 190–196.

Gonzalez, J. S. (2006). *Parent implementation of the developmental, individual difference, relationship-based (DIR) program: changes in the repetitive behaviors of children with autism.* Pan American: The University of Texas.

Gopnik, A., & Astington, J. W. (1988). Children's understanding of representational change and its relation to the understanding of false belief and the appearance-reality distinction. *Child Development, 59*(1), 26–37.

Grandin, T. (1984). My experiences as an autistic child. *Journal of Orthomolecular Psychiatry*, *13*, 144–174.

Grandin, T. (1992). An inside view of autism. In *High-functioning individuals with autism* (pp. 105–126). New York: Springer US.

Grandin, T. (2002). *Teaching tips for children and adults with autism*. Fort Collins, Colorado/ EUA.

Grandin, T., & Scariano, M. (1986). *Emergence: Labelled autistic*. Novato, CA: Arena.

Granpeesheh, D., Tarbox, J., & Dixon, D. R. (2009). Applied behavior analytic interventions for children with autism: a description and review of treatment research. *Annals Clinical Psychiatry*, *21*(3), 162–173.

Gray, D. E. (2002). Ten years on: A longitudinal study of families of children with autism. *Journal of Intellectual and Developmental Disability*, *27*(3), 215–222.

Gray, J. A. (1980). *Ivan Pavlov*. New York: Viking Press.

Grecucci, A., Brambilla, P., Siugzdaite, R., Londero, D., Fabbro, F., & Rumiati, R. I. (2013). Emotional resonance deficits in autistic children. *Journal of Autism and Developmental Disorders*, *43*(3), 616–628.

Green, G. (2004). *The 'Verbal Behavior' approach to autism: Where are the data?* An invited address to the annual meeting of the Experimental Analysis of Behavior Group, London, England.

Green, G., Brennan, L. C., & Fein, D. (2002). Intensive behavioral treatment for a toddler at high risk for autism. *Behavior Modification*, *26*, 69–102.

Green, J., Charman, T., McConachie, H., Aldred, C., Slonims, V., Howlin, P., ... & Pickles, A. (2010). Parent-mediated communication-focused treatment in children with autism (PACT): a randomised controlled trial. *The Lancet*, *375*(9732), 2152–2160.

Green, V. A., Pituch, K. A., Itchon, J., Choi, A., O'Reilly, M., & Sigafoos, J. (2006). Internet survey of treatments used by parents of children with autism. *Research in Developmental Disabilities*, *27*(1), 70–84.

Greenspan, J. & Greenspan, S. I. (2002) 'Functional Emotional Developmental Questionnaire for childhood: A preliminary report on the questions and their clinical meaning', *Journal of Developmental and Learning Disorders*, *6*, 71–116.

Greenspan, S. I., & Wieder, S. (1998). *The child with special needs*. Reading, MA: Addison-Wesley.

Greer, R. D. (1997). The Comprehensive Application of Behavior Analysis to Schooling (CA-BAS®). *Behavior and Social Issues*, *7*(1), 25–42.

Greer, R. D. (2002). *Designing teaching strategies, an applied behavioural analysis systems approach*. New York: Academic Press.

Greer, R. D., & Keohane, D. (2004). A real science and technology of education. In J. Moran & R. Malott, (Eds.), *Evidence-based educational methods* (pp. 23–46). New York: Elsevier/Academic Press.

Greer, R. D., & Keohane, D. D. (2009). CABAS® contributions to identifying, inducing, and sequencing verbal development. In P. Reed (Ed.), *Behavioral theories and interventions for autism* (pp. 235–271). New York: Nova.

Greer, R. D., Keohane, D. D., & Healy, O. (2002). Quality and comprehensive applications of behavior analysis to schooling. *The Behavior Analyst Today*, *3*(2), 120–132.

Greer, R. D., & McCorkle, N. P. (2003). International curriculum and inventory of repertoires for children from preschool through kindergarten (PIRK). *Yonkers, NY: The Fred S. Keller School and CABAS*.

Greer, R. D., McCorkle, N., & Williams, G. (1989). A sustained analysis of the behaviors of schooling. *Behavioral Residential Treatment*, *4*, 113–141.

Greer, R. D., & Ross, D. E. (2008). *Verbal behavior analysis: Inducing and expanding new verbal capabilities in children with language delays*. Allyn & Bacon.

Grelotti, D. J., Gauthier, I., & Schultz, R. T. (2002). Social interest and the development of cortical face specialization: what autism teaches us about face processing. *Developmental Psychobiology, 40*(3), 213–225.

Gresham, F. M., Beebefrankenberger, M. E., & MacMillan, D. L. (1999). A selective review of treatments for children with autism: Description and methodological considerations. *School Psychology Review, 28*(4), 559–575.

Gresham, F. M., & MacMillan, D. L. (1997). Autistic recovery? An analysis and critique of the empirical evidence on the early intervention project. *Behavioral Disorders, 22*(4), 185–201.

Gresham, F. M., & MacMillan, D. L. (1998). Early intervention project: Can its claims be substantiated and its effects replicated? *Journal of Autism and Developmental Disorders, 28*(1), 5–13.

Grey, I., McClean, B., & McCauley, N. (2009). Positive Behavior Support: Supporting children and adults with Autistic Spectrum Disorders and challenging behaviors. In P. Reed (Ed.) *Behavioural theories and interventions for autism.* New York: Nova.

Griffith, G. M., Totsika, V., Nash, S., Jones, R. S., & Hastings, R. P. (2012). 'We are all there silently coping.' The hidden experiences of parents of adults with Asperger syndrome. *Journal of Intellectual and Developmental Disability, 37*(3), 237–247.

Grossman, R. B., Bemis, R. H., Skwerer, D. P., & Tager-Flusberg, H. (2010). Lexical and affective prosody in children with high-functioning autism. *Journal of Speech, Language, and Hearing Research, 53*(3), 778–793.

Grossman, J. B., Klin, A., Carter, A. S., & Volkmar, F. R. (2000). Verbal bias in recognition of facial emotions in children with Asperger syndrome. *Journal of Child Psychology and Psychiatry, 41*(3), 369–379.

Gunning, S. V., & Holmes, T. H. (1973). Dance therapy with psychotic children. *Archives of General Psychiatry, 28,* 707–713.

Gusi, N., Olivares, P. R., & Rajendram, R. (2010). The EQ-5D quality of life questionnaire. In V. Preedy (Ed.) *Handbook of disease burdens and quality of life measures.* (pp. 88–99). London: Springer.

Gutstein, S. E., Burgess, A. F., & Montfort, K. (2007). Evaluation of the relationship development intervention program. *Autism, 11*(5), 397–411.

Hall, G., & Sundberg, M. L. (1987). Teaching mands by manipulating conditioned establishing operations. *The Analysis of Verbal Behavior, 5,* 41.

Hanley, G. P., Iwata, B. A., & McCord, B. E. (2003). Functional analysis of problem behavior: A review. *Journal of Applied Behavior Analysis, 36*(2), 147–185.

Happé, F. (1995). *Autism: An introduction to psychological theory.* Harvard University Press.

Happé, F. G. (1997). Central coherence and theory of mind in autism: Reading homographs in context. *British Journal of Developmental Psychology, 15*(1), 1–12.

Happé, F., & Ronald, A. (2008). The 'fractionable autism triad': a review of evidence from behavioural, genetic, cognitive and neural research. *Neuropsychology Review, 18*(4), 287–304.

Happé, F., Ronald, A., & Plomin, R. (2006). Time to give up on a single explanation for autism. *Nature Neuroscience, 9*(10), 1218–1220.

Harris, S. L., & Handleman, J. S. (1997). Helping children with autism enter the mainstream. In D. Cohen & F. R. Volkmar (Eds.), *Handbook of autism and pervasive developmental disorders: 2nd. edition,* (pp. 665–675). New York: John Wiley & Sons, Inc.

Harris, S. L., & Handleman, J. S. (2000). Age and IQ at intake as predictors of placement for young children with autism: A four-to six-year follow-up. *Journal of Autism and Developmental Disorders, 30*(2), 137–142.

Harris, S. L., Handleman, J. S., Gordon, R., Kristoff, B., & Fuentes, F. (1991). Changes in cognitive and language functioning of preschool children with autism. *Journal of Autism and Developmental Disorders, 21,* 281–290.

Harris, S. L., Handleman, J. S., Kristoff, B., Bass. L., & Gordon, R. (1990). Changes in language development among autistic and peer children in segregated and integrated preschool setting. *Journal of Autism and Developmental Disorders, 20,* 23–31.

Hart, B., & Risley, T. R. (1975). Incidental teaching of language in the preschooll. *Journal of Applied Behavior Analysis, 8*(4), 411–420.

Hartley, S. L., Sikora, D. M., & McCoy, R. (2008). Prevalence and risk factors of maladaptive behaviour in young children with autistic disorder. *Journal of Intellectual Disability Research, 52*(10), 819–829.

Hastings, R. P., & Johnson, E. (2001). Stress in UK families conducting intensive home-based behavioral intervention for their young child with autism. *Journal of Autism and Developmental Disorders, 31*(3), 327–336.

Hatton, D. D., Sideris, J., Skinner, M., Mankowski, J., Bailey, D. B., Roberts, J., & Mirrett, P. (2006). Autistic behavior in children with fragile X syndrome: prevalence, stability, and the impact of FMRP. *American Journal of Medical Genetics Part A, 140*(17), 1804–1813.

Hawkins, E., Charnock, J., & Gautreaux, G. (2007). The Jigsaw CABAS® School: protocols for increasing appropriate behaviour and evoking verbal capabilities. *European Journal of Behavior Analysis, 8*(2), 203.

Hayashida, K., Anderson, B., Paparella, T., Freeman, S. F., & Forness, S. R. (2010). Comorbid psychiatric diagnoses in preschoolers with autism spectrum disorders. *Behavioral Disorders, 35*(3), 243–254.

Hayes, G. R., Hirano, S., Marcu, G., Monibi, M., Nguyen, D. H., & Yeganyan, M. (2010). Interactive visual supports for children with autism. *Personal and Ubiquitous Computing, 14*(7), 663–680.

Hayward, D., Eikeseth, S., Gale, C., & Morgan, S. (2009). Assessing progress during treatment for young children with autism receiving intensive behavioural interventions. *Autism, 13*(6), 613–633.

Healy, O., Leader, G., & Reed, P. (2009). Applied Behavior Analysis and the Treatment of Autism Spectrum Disorders in the Republic of Ireland. In L. V. Berhardt (Ed.), *Advances in Medicine and Biology. Volume 8.* New York: Nova Science Publishers, Inc.

Hebron, J., & Humphrey, N. (2014). Exposure to bullying among students with autism spectrum conditions: A multi-informant analysis of risk and protective factors. *Autism, 18,* 618–630.

Heflin, L. J., & Simpson, R. L. (1998). Interventions for children and youth with autism prudent choices in a world of exaggerated claims and empty promises. Part I: Intervention and treatment option review. *Focus on Autism and Other Developmental Disabilities, 13*(4), 194–211.

Hergenhahn, B. R., & Olson, M. H. (2009). *Theories of learning.* Terjemahan Tri Wibowo. Jakarta: Kencana Prenada Media Group.

Hess, K. L., Morrier, M. J., Heflin, L. J., & Ivey, M. L. (2008). Autism treatment survey: Services received by children with autism spectrum disorders in public school classrooms. *Journal of Autism and Developmental Disorders, 38*(5), 961–971.

Hewett, F. M. (1966). The autistic child learns to read. *The Slow Learning Child, 13*(2), 107–121.

Hill, E. L. (2004). Executive dysfunction in autism. *Trends in Cognitive Sciences, 8*(1), 26–32.

Hilton, C. L., Crouch, M. C., & Israel, H. (2008). Out of school participation in children with high functioning autism spectrum disorder, *American Journal of Occupational Therapy, 62,* 554–563.

Hilton, J. C. (2005). Communication skills of young children diagnosed with autism: comparative effectiveness of applied behavior analysis and developmental, individual-difference, relationship-based interventions [dissertation]. Harrisonburg: James Madison University.

Hilton, J. C., & Seal, B. C. (2007). Brief report: comparative ABA and DIR trials in twin brothers with autism. *Journal of Autism and Developmental Disorders, 37*(6), 1197–1201.

Hobson, R. P. (1986). The autistic child's appraisal of expressions of emotion: A further study. *Journal of Child Psychology and Psychiatry, 27*(5), 671–680.

Hobson, R. P. (2005). Autism and emotion. In F. R. Volkmar, R. Paul, A. Klin & D. Cohen (Eds.), *Handbook of autism and pervasive developmental disorders* (3rd Ed.), *Volume 1.* Chapter 15. New York: John Wiley & Sons, Inc.

Hobson, R. P., Lee, A., & Hobson, J. A. (2010). Personal pronouns and communicative engagement in autism. *Journal of Autism and Developmental Disorders, 40*(6), 653–664.

Hobson, R. P., Ouston, J., & Lee, A. (1988). Emotion recognition in autism: Coordinating faces and voices. *Psychological Medicine, 18*(04), 911–923.

Hocutt, A. M. (1996). Effectiveness of special education: Is placement the critical factor? *The Future of Children, 6,* 77–102.

Hodgetts, S., Magill-Evans, J., & Misiaszek, J. E. (2011a). Weighted vests, stereotyped behaviors and arousal in children with autism. *Journal of Autism and Developmental Disorders, 41,* 805–814.

Hodgetts, S., Magill-Evans, J., & Misiaszek, J. (2011b). Effects of weighted vests on classroom behavior for children with autism and cognitive impairments. *Research in Autism Spectrum Disorders, 5,* 495–505.

Hoehn, T. P., & Baumeister, A. A. (1994). A critique of the application of sensory integration therapy to children with learning disabilities. *Journal of Learning Disabilities, 27*(6), 338–350.

Hofvander, B., Delorme, R., Chaste, P., Nydén, A., Wentz, E., Ståhlberg, O., Herbrecht, E., Stopin, A., Anckarsäter, H., Gillberg, C., Råstam, M., & Leboyer, M. (2009). Psychiatric and psychosocial problems in adults with normal-intelligence autism spectrum disorders. *BMC Psychiatry, 9*(1), 35.

Houghton, K., Schuchard, J., Lewis, C., & Thompson, C. K. (2013). Promoting child-initiated social-communication in children with autism: Son-Rise Program intervention effects. *Journal of Communication Disorders, 46*(5), 495–506.

Howard, J. S., Sparkman, C. R., Cohen, H. G., Green, G., & Stanislaw, H. (2005). A comparison of intensive behavior analytic and eclectic treatments for young children with autism. *Research in Developmental Disabilities, 26*(4), 359–383.

Howlin, P. (1997). Prognosis in autism: do specialist treatments affect long-term outcome? *European Child & Adolescent Psychiatry, 6*(2), 55–72.

Howlin, P. (1998). *Children with autism and Asperger Syndrome.* Chichester: John Wiley & Sons, Ltd.

Howlin, P., Goode, S., Hutton, J., & Rutter, M. (2004). Adult outcome for children with autism. *Journal of Child Psychology and Psychiatry, 45*(2), 212–229.

Howlin, P., Magiati, I., & Charman, T. (2009). Systematic review of early intensive behavioral interventions for children with autism. *American Journal on Intellectual and Developmental Disabilities, 114*(1), 23–41.

Hoyson, M., Jamieson, B., & Strain, P. S. (1984). Individualized group instruction of normally developing and autistic-like children: The LEAP curriculum model. *Journal of Early Intervention, 8*(2), 157–172.

Hubert, B. E., Wicker, B., Monfardini, E., & Deruelle, C. (2009). Electrodermal reactivity to emotion processing in adults with autistic spectrum disorders. *Autism, 13*(1), 9–19.

Hubert, B., Wicker, B., Moore, D. G., Monfardini, E., Duverger, H., Da Fonseca, D., & Deruelle, C. (2007). Brief report: recognition of emotional and non-emotional biological motion in individuals with autistic spectrum disorders. *Journal of Autism and Developmental Disorders, 37*(7), 1386–1392.

Hughes, C., Russell, J., & Robbins, T. W. (1994). Evidence for executive dysfunction in autism. *Neuropsychologia, 32*(4), 477–492.

Hume, D. (1748). *An enquiry concerning human understanding.* Available online at www. davidhume.org/texts/ehu.html (accessed 24 June, 2015).

Hume, K., Boyd, B., McBee, M., Coman, D., Gutierrez, A., Shaw, E., Sperry, L., Alessandri, M., & Odom, S. (2011). Assessing implementation of comprehensive treatment models for young children with ASD: Reliability and validity of two measures. *Research in Autism Spectrum Disorders, 5*(4), 1430–1440.

Hume, K., & Odom, S. (2007). Effects of an individual work system on the independent functioning of students with autism. *Journal of Autism and Developmental Disorders, 37*(6), 1166–1180.

Hume, K., Plavnick, J., & Odom, S. L. (2012). Promoting task accuracy and independence in students with autism across educational setting through the use of individual work systems. *Journal of Autism and Developmental Disorders, 42*(10), 2084–2099.

Humphrey, N. (2008). Including pupils with autistic spectrum disorders in mainstream schools. *Support for Learning, 23*, 41–47.

Humphrey, N., & Lewis, S. (2008). 'Make me normal': The views and experiences of pupils on the autistic spectrum in mainstream secondary schools. *Autism, 12*(1), 23–46.

Humphrey, N., & Parkinson, G. (2006). Research on interventions for children and young people on the autistic spectrum: a critical perspective. *Journal of Research in Special Educational Needs, 6*, 76–86.

Humphrey, N., & Symes, W. (2010). Perceptions of social support and experience of bullying among pupils with autistic spectrum disorders in mainstream secondary schools. *European Journal of Special Needs Education, 25*(1), 77–91.

Humphrey, N., & Symes, W. (2011). Peer interaction patterns among adolescents with autistic spectrum disorders (ASDs) in mainstream school settings. *Autism, 15*, 397–419.

Ingersoll, B. (2012). Brief report: Effect of a focused imitation intervention on social functioning in children with autism. *Journal of Autism and Developmental Disorders, 42*(8), 1768–1773.

Ingersoll, B., & Dvortcsak, A. (2009). *Teaching social communication to children with autism: a practitioner's guide to parent training and a manual for parents.* New York: Guilford Press.

Ingersoll, B., Schreibman, L., & Stahmer, A. (2001). Brief report: Differential treatment outcomes for children with autistic spectrum disorder based on level of peer social avoidance. *Journal of Autism and Developmental Disorders, 31*(3), 343–349.

Ingersoll, B. R., & Wainer, A. L. (2013). Pilot study of a school-based parent training program for preschoolers with ASD. *Autism, 17*(4), 434–448.

Ingham, P., & Greer, R. D. (1992). Changes in student and teacher responses in observed and generalized settings as a function of supervisor observations. *Journal of Applied Behavior Analysis, 25*, 153–164.

Ionasiu, L., Lungu, C., Iosit, S., & Cupcea, S. (1936). Contributiuni la studiul experimental al perceptiei vizuale la bolnavii mintali. / Experimental contributions to the psychology of perception of demented people. *Bul-Spital Boli-Ment-Nerv-Sibiu, 1936*, 28–35.

Iovannone, R., Dunlap, G., Huber, H., & Kincaid, D. (2003). Effective educational practices for students with autism spectrum disorders. *Focus on Autism and Other Developmental Disabilities, 18*(3), 150–165.

Jackson, E., Kelley, M., McNeil, P., Meyer, E., Schlegel, L., & Eaton, M. (2008). Does therapeutic touch help reduce pain and anxiety in patients with cancer? *Clinical Journal of Oncology Nursing, 12*(1), 113–120.

Jacobson, J. W., & Mulick, J. A. (2000). System and cost research issues in treatments for people with autistic disorders. *Journal of Autism and Developmental Disorders, 30*(6), 585–593.

Jacobson, J. W., Mulick, J. A., & Green, G. (1998). Cost–benefit estimates for early intensive behavioral intervention for young children with autism—general model and single state case. *Behavioral Interventions, 13*(4), 201–226.

James, R. (2011). *An evaluation of the 'Circle of Friends' intervention used to support pupils with autism in their mainstream classrooms* (Doctoral dissertation, University of Nottingham).

Järbrink, K., & Knapp, M. (2001). The economic impact of autism in Britain. *Autism, 5*(1), 7–22.

Jasmin, E., Couture, M., McKinley, P., Reid, G., Fombonne, E. & Gisel, E. (2009). Sensorimotor and daily living skills of preschool children with Autism Spectrum Disorders. *Journal of Autism and Developmental Disorders, 39,* 231–241.

Jemel, B., Mottron, L., & Dawson, M. (2006). Impaired face processing in autism: fact or artifact? *Journal of Autism and Developmental Disorders, 36*(1), 91–106.

Jenkins, T., Schuchard, J., & Thompson, C. K. (2012). Training parents to promote communication and social behavior in children with Autism: The Son-Rise Program. Available at: www.autism treatmentcenter.org

Jennett, H. K., Harris, S. L., & Delmolino, L. (2008). Discrete trial instruction vs. mand training for teaching children with autism to make requests. *The Analysis of Verbal Behavior, 24*(1), 69.

Jennett, H. K., Harris, S. L., & Mesibov, G. B. (2003). Commitment to philosophy, teacher efficacy, and burnout among teachers of children with autism. *Journal of Autism and Developmental Disorders, 33*(6), 583–593.

Jindal-Snape, D., Douglas, W., Topping, K. J., Kerr, C., & Smith, E. F. (2005). Effective education for children with Autistic Spectrum Disorder: Perceptions of parents and professionals. *The International Journal of Special Education, 20,* 77–87.

Jocelyn, L. J., Casiro, O. G., Beattie, D., Bow, J., & Kneisz, J. (1998). Treatment of children with autism: a randomized controlled trial to evaluate a caregiver-based intervention program in community day-care centers. *Journal of Developmental & Behavioral Pediatrics, 19*(5), 326–334.

Jones, A. P., & Frederickson, N. (2010). Multi-informant predictors of social inclusion for students with Autism Spectrum Disorders attending mainstream school. *Journal of Autism and Developmental Disorders, 40,* 1094–1103.

Johnson, S. A., Filliter, J. H., & Murphy, R. R. (2009). Discrepancies between self and parent-ratings of autistic traits in high functioning children and adolescents on the autism spectrum. *Journal of Autism and Developmental Disabilities, 39,* 1706–1714.

Jónsdóttir, S. L., Saemundsen, E., Ásmundsdóttir, G., Hjartardóttir, S., Ásgeirsdóttir, B. B., Smáradóttir, H. H., Sigurdardóttir, S., & Smári, J. (2007). Follow-up of children diagnosed with pervasive developmental disorders: stability and change during the preschool years. *Journal of Autism and Developmental Disorders, 37*(7), 1361–1374.

Jordan, R. (2008). Autistic spectrum disorders: A challenge and a model for inclusion in education. British Journal of Special Education, *35,* 11–15.

Jordan, R., Jones, G., & Murray, D. (1998). *Educational interventions for children with autism: A literature review of recent and current research.* London: DfEE.

Kaale, A., Fagerland, M. W., Martinsen, E. W., & Smith, L. (2014). Preschool-based social communication treatment for children with autism: 12-month follow-up of a randomized trial. *Journal of the American Academy of Child & Adolescent Psychiatry, 53*(2), 188–198.

Kane, A., Luiselli, J. K., Dearborn, S., & Young, N. (2004). Wearing a weighted vest as intervention for children with autism/pervasive developmental disorder: Behavioral assessment of stereotypy and attention to task. *The Scientific Review of Mental Health Practice: Objective Investigations of Controversial and Unorthodox Claims in Clinical Psychology, Psychiatry, and Social Work, 3,* 19–24.

Kanner, L. (1943). Autistic disturbances of affective contact. *Nervous Child, 2*(3), 217–250.

Kanner, L. (1944). Early infantile autism. *The Journal of Pediatrics, 25*(3), 211–217.

Kanner, L. (1949). Problems of nosology and psychodynamics of early infantile autism. *American Journal of Orthopsychiatry, 19,* 416–426.

Kanner, L., & Eisenberg, L. (1956). Early infantile autism, 1943–1955. *American Journal of Orthopsychiatry, 26,* 55.

Kaplan, M., Carmody, D. P., & Gaydos, A. (1996). Postural orientation modifications in autism in response to ambient lenses. *Child Psychiatry and Human Development, 27*(2), 81–91.

Kaplan, M., Edelson, S. M., & Seip, J. L. (1998). Behavioral changes in autistic individuals as a result of wearing ambient transitional prism lenses. *Child Psychiatry and Human Development, 29,* 65–76.

Kaplan, R. S., & Steele, A. L. (2005). An analysis of music therapy program goals and outcomes for clients with diagnoses on the autism spectrum. *Journal of Music Therapy, 42*(1), 2–19.

Kaplan, M., Edelson, S. M., & Seip, J. A. L. (1998). Behavioral changes in autistic individuals as a result of wearing ambient transitional prism lenses. *Child Psychiatry and Human Development, 29*(1), 65–76.

Karkhaneh, M., Clark, B., Ospina, M. B., Seida, J. C., Smith, V., & Hartling, L. (2010). Social Stories™ to improve social skills in children with autism spectrum disorder: A systematic review. *Autism, 14,* 641–662.

Kasari, C. (2002). Assessing change in early intervention programs for children with autism. *Journal of Autism and Developmental Disorders, 32*(5), 447–461.

Kasari, C., Gulsrud, A. C., Wong, C., Kwon, S., & Locke, J. (2010). Randomized controlled caregiver mediated joint engagement intervention for toddlers with autism. *Journal of Autism and Developmental Disorders, 40*(9), 1045–1056.

Kasari, C., & Patterson, S. (2012). Interventions addressing social impairment in autism. *Current Psychiatry Reports, 14*(6), 713–725.

Kasari, C., & Smith, T. (2013). Interventions in schools for children with autism spectrum disorder: Methods and recommendations. *Autism, 17*(3), 254–267.

Kaufman B. N. (1991). *Happiness is a choice.* New York: Fawcett.

Kaufman B. N. (1994). *Son-Rise: The miracle continues.* Tiburon, CA: H.J. Kramer.

Kauffman, J. M. (1989). The regular education initiative as Reagan–Bush education policy: A trickle-down theory of education of the hard-to-teach. *Journal of Special Education, 23,* 256–278.

Kauffman, J. M., Cullinan, D., & Epstein, M. H. (1987). Characteristics of students placed in special programs for the seriously emotionally disturbed. *Behavioral Disabilities, 12,* 175–184.

Kauffman, J. M., Agard, T. A., & Semmel, M. I. (1985). *Mainstreaming: Learners and their environment.* Cambridge, MA: Brookline Books.

Keel, J. H., Mesibov, G. B., & Woods, A.V. (1997). TEACCH supported employment program. *Journal of Autism and Developmental Disorders, 27,* 3–9.

Keen, D. & Ward, S. (2004). Autistic spectrum disorder: a child population profile. *Autism, 8,* 39–48.

Keenan, M. (2004). Autism in N. Ireland: The tragedy and the shame. *The Psychologist, 17,* 72–75.

Keller, F. S. (1968). Good-bye teacher. *Journal of Applied Behavior Analysis, 1*(1), 79–89.

Kern, P., Humpal, M. E., & Humpal, M. (Eds.). (2012). *Early childhood music therapy and autism spectrum disorders: developing potential in young children and their families.* London: Jessica Kingsley Publishers.

Kestenberg, J. S. (1954). The history of an autistic child; clinical data and interpretation. *The Journal of Child Psychiatry, 3*(1), 5.

Khalfa, S., Bruneau, N., Rogé, B., Georgieff, N., Veuillet, E., Adrien, J. L., Barthelemy, C., & Collet, L. (2004). Increased perception of loudness in autism. *Hearing Research, 198*(1), 87–92.

Kim, Y. S., Leventhal, B. L., Koh, Y. J., Fombonne, E., Laska, E., Lim, E. C., Cheon, K.; Kim, S-J M.D.; Kim, Y-K., Lee, H.K., Song, D., & Grinker, R. R. (2011). Prevalence of autism spectrum disorders in a total population sample. *American Journal of Psychiatry, 168*(9), 904–912.

Kim, J. A., Szatmari, P., Bryson, S. E., Streiner, D. L., & Wilson, F. J. (2000). The prevalence of anxiety and mood problems among children with autism and Asperger syndrome. *Autism*, *4*(2), 117–132.

Kitahara, K. (1983). *Daily life therapy, (Volume. 1)*. Tokyo: Musashino Higashi Gakuen School.

King, M., & Bearman, P. (2009). Diagnostic change and the increased prevalence of autism. *International Journal of Epidemiology*, *38*(5), 1224–1234.

Klin, A., Jones, W., Schultz, R., Volkmar, F., & Cohen, D. (2002). Visual fixation patterns during viewing of naturalistic social situations as predictors of social competence in individuals with autism. *Archives of General Psychiatry*, *59*(9), 809–816.

Klintwall, L., Holm, A., Eriksson, M., Carlsson, L. H., Olsson, M. B., Hedvall, Å., Gillberg, C., & Fernell, E. (2011). Sensory abnormalities in autism: a brief report. *Research in Developmental Disabilities*, *32*(2), 795–800.

Knapp, M., Romeo, R., & Beecham, J. (2009). Economic cost of autism in the UK. *Autism*, *13*(3), 317–336.

Knight, A., Petrie, P., Zuurmond, M., & Potts, P. (2009). 'Mingling together': promoting the social inclusion of disabled children and young people during the school holidays. *Child and Family Social Work*, *14*, 15–24.

Koch, S., Kunz, T., Lykou, S., & Cruz, R. (2014). Effects of dance movement therapy and dance on health-related psychological outcomes: A meta-analysis. *The Arts in Psychotherapy*, *41*(1), 46–64.

Koegel, R. L., Koegel, L. K., & Brookman, L. I. (2003). Empirically supported pivotal response interventions for children with autism. In A. E. Kazdin & J. R. Weisz (Eds.), *Evidence-based psychotherapies for children and adolescents* (pp. 341–357). New York: Guilford Press.

Koegel, L. K., Koegel, R. L., Harrower, J. K., & Carter, C. M. (1999). Pivotal response intervention I: Overview of approach. *Research and Practice for Persons with Severe Disabilities*, *24*(3), 174–185.

Koegel, L., Matos-Freden, R., Lang, R., & Koegel, R. (2012). Interventions for children with autism spectrum disorders in inclusive school settings. *Cognitive and Behavioral Practice*, *19*(3), 401–412.

Koegel, R. L., O'Dell, M. C., & Koegel, L. K. (1987). A natural language teaching paradigm for nonverbal autistic children. *Journal of Autism and Developmental Disorders*, *17*(2), 187–200.

Kohen-Raz, R., Volkman, F. R., & Cohen, D. J. (1992). Postural control in children with autism. *Journal of Autism and Developmental Disorders*, *22*(3), 419–432.

Kohler, F. W., Strain, P. S., & Shearer, D. D. (1996). Examining levels of social inclusion within an integrated preschool for children with autism. In R. L. Koegel, R. L. Koegel, & G. Dunlap (Eds.), *Positive behavioral support: including people with difficult behavior in the community* (pp. 305–332), Baltimore, MD: Brookes.

Koning, C., & Magill-Evans, J. (2001). Social and language skills in adolescents with Aspergers syndrome. *Autism*, *5*, 23–36.

Korkmaz, B. (2011). Theory of mind and neurodevelopmental disorders of childhood. *Pediatric Research*, *69*, 101R–108R.

Koster, M., Pijl, S.J., Nakken, H., & Van Houten, E. (2010). Social participation of students with special needs in regular primary education in the Netherlands. *International Journal of Disability: Development and Education*, *57*, 59–75.

Kovach, J., Fabricius, E., & Falt, L. (1966). Relationships between imprinting and perceptual learning. *Journal of Comparative and Physiological Psychology*, *61*(1966), 449–454.

Krug, D. A., Arick, J. R., & Almond, P. J. (1980). Behavior checklist for identifying severely handicapped individuals with high levels of autistic behavior. *Journal of Child Psychology and Psychiatry*, *21*, 221–229.

Kupersmidt, J. B., & DeRosier, M. E. (2004). How peer problems lead to negative outcomes: An integrative mediational model. In J. B. Kupersmidt & K. A. Dodge (Eds.), *Children's peer relations: From development to intervention* (pp. 119–138). Washington, D.C: American Psychological Association.

Kurth, J. & Mastergeorge, A. (2010). Academics and cognitive profiles of students with autism: Implications for classroom practice and placement. *International Journal of Special Education, 25*, 8–14.

Kurtz, L. A. (2008). *Understanding controversial therapies for children with autism, attention deficit disorder, and other learning disabilities: a guide to complementary and alternative medicine.* London: Jessica Kingsley Publishers.

Lacava, P. G., Rankin, A., Mahlios, E., Cook, K., & Simpson, R. L. (2010). A single case design evaluation of a software and tutor intervention addressing emotion recognition and social interaction in four boys with ASD. *Autism, 14*, 161–178.

Laidler, J. R. (2005). US Department of Education data on 'autism' are not reliable for tracking autism prevalence. *Pediatrics, 116*(1), e120–e124.

La Malfa, G., Lassi, S., Bertelli, M., Salvini, R., & Placidi, G. F. (2004). Autism and intellectual disability: a study of prevalence on a sample of the Italian population. *Journal of Intellectual Disability Research, 48*(3), 262–267.

Lainhart, J. E., & Folstein, S. E. (1994). Affective disorders in people with autism: A review of published cases. *Journal of Autism and Developmental Disorders, 24*(5), 587–601.

Lancioni, G. E., O'Reilly, M., & Emerson, E. (1996). A review of choice research with people with severe and profound developmental disabilities. *Research in Developmental Disabilities, 17*, 391–411.

Lang, R., O'Reilly, M., Healy, O., Rispoli, M., Lydon, H., Streusand, W., ... & Giesbers, S. (2012). Sensory integration therapy for autism spectrum disorders: A systematic review. *Research in Autism Spectrum Disorders, 6*(3), 1004–1018.

Lane, S. J., & Schaaf, R. C. (2010). Examining the neuroscience evidence for sensory driven neuroplasticity: Implications for sensory-based occupational therapy for children and adolescents. *The American Journal of Occupational Therapy, 64*, 375–390.

Lane, A. E., Young, R. L., Baker, A. E. Z., & Angley, M. T. (2010). Sensory processing subtypes in autism: Association with adaptive behavior. *Journal of Autism and Developmental Disorders, 40*, 112–122.

Larkin, A. S., & Gurry, S. (1998). Brief report: Progress reported in three children with autism using daily life therapy. *Journal of Autism and Developmental Disorders, 28*(4), 339–342.

Larrington, G. G. (1987). A sensory integration based program with a severely retarded/autistic teenager: An occupational therapy case report. In Z. Mailloux (Ed.), *Sensory integration approaches* (pp. 101–117). New York: Hawthorn Press.

Leader, G., Loughnane, A., McMoreland, C., & Reed, P. (2009). The effect of stimulus salience on over-selectivity. *Journal of Autism and Developmental Disorders, 39*(2), 330–338.

Leaf, R., & McEachin, J. (1999). *A work in progress: Behavior management strategies and a curriculum for intensive behavioral treatment of autism.* New York: DRL Books.

LeBlanc, L. A., Esch, J., Sidener, T. M., & Firth, A. M. (2006). Behavioral language interventions for children with autism: Comparing applied verbal behavior and naturalistic teaching approaches. *The Analysis of Verbal Behavior, 22*(1), 49.

Lecavalier, L., Leone, S., & Wiltz, J. (2006). The impact of behaviour problems on caregiver stress in young people with autism spectrum disorders. *Journal of Intellectual Disability Research, 50*(3), 172–183.

Lee, H. K. (2008). Effects of massage and attachment promotion program on social maturity, child autism and attachment of children with autism and their mothers. *Journal of Korean Academy of Child Health Nursing, 14*(1), 14–21.

Lee, M. S., Kim, J. I., & Ernst, E. (2011). Massage therapy for children with autism spectrum disorders: a systematic review. *The Journal of Clinical Psychiatry, 72*(3), 406–411.

Leekam, S. R., Nieto, C., Libby, S. J., Wing, L., & Gould, J. (2007). Describing the sensory abnormalities of children and adults with autism. *Journal of Autism and Developmental Disorders, 37*(5), 894–910.

Leew, S. V., Stein, N. G., & Gibbard, W. B. (2010). Weighted vests' effect on social attention for toddlers with autism spectrum disorders. *Canadian Journal of Occupational Therapy/ Revue Canadienne D'Ergotherapie, 77*, 113–124.

Leslie, A. M. (1987). Pretense and representation: The origins of 'theory of mind'. *Psychological Review, 94*(4), 412.

Levy, A., & Perry, A. (2011). Outcomes in adolescents and adults with autism: A review of the literature. *Research in Autism Spectrum Disorders, 5*(4), 1271–1282.

Levy, S. E., Mandell, D. S., & Schultz, R. T. (2009). Autism. *The Lancet, 374*, 1627–1638.

Leyfer, O. T., Folstein, S. E., Bacalman, S., Davis, N. O., Dinh, E., Morgan, J., Tager-Flusberg, H., & Lainhart, J. E. (2006). Comorbid psychiatric disorders in children with autism: interview development and rates of disorders. *Journal of Autism and Developmental Disorders, 36*(7), 849–861.

Leyser, Y., & Kirk, R. (2004). Evaluating inclusion: An examination of parent views and factors influencing their perspectives. *International Journal of Disability, Development and Education, 51*, 271–285.

Linderman, T. M., & Stewart, K. B. (1999). Sensory integrative-based occupational therapy and functional outcomes in young children with pervasive developmental disorders: A single-subject study. *American Journal of Occupational Therapy, 53*, 207–213.

Lindsay, G. (2003). Inclusive education a critical perspective. *British Journal of Special Education, 30*, 3–12.

Lindsley, O. R. (1990). Precision teaching: By teachers for children. *Teaching Exceptional Children, 22*(3), 10–15.

Link, H. M. (1997). Auditory integration training (AIT): Sound therapy – Case studies of three boys with autism who received AIT. *British Journal of Learning Disabilities, 25*, 106–110.

Lipsey, M. W. & Wilson, D. B. (2001). *Practical meta-analysis*. Thousand Oaks, CA: Sage publications.

Liss, M., Saulnier, C., Fein, D., & Kinsbourne, M. (2006). Sensory and attention abnormalities in autistic spectrum disorders. *Autism, 10*(2), 155–172.

Lockyer, L., & Rutter, M. (1969). A five-to fifteen-year follow-up study of infantile psychosis. *The British Journal of Psychiatry, 115*(525), 865–882.

Lockyer, L., & Rutter, M. (1970). a five-to fifteen-year follow-up study of infantile psychosis: IV. Patterns of cognitive ability. *British Journal of Social and Clinical Psychology, 9*(2), 152–163.

Lopez, B. R., Lincoln, A. J., Ozonoff, S., & Lai, Z. (2005). Examining the relationship between executive functions and restricted, repetitive symptoms of autistic disorder. *Journal of Autism and Developmental Disorders, 35*(4), 445–460.

Lord, C. (2011). How common is autism? *Nature, 474*, 166–168.

Lord, C., Kim, S. H., & Dimartino, A. (2011). Autism spectrum disorders: general overview. In *The Sage handbook of developmental disorders* (pp. 287–305). Los Angeles: Sage.

Lord, C., & McGee, J. (2001). *Educating children with autism*. Washington, DC: National Academy Press.

Lord, C., Petkova, E., Hus, V., Gan, W., Lu, F., Martin, D. M., ... & Risi, S. (2012). A multisite study of the clinical diagnosis of different autism spectrum disorders. *Archives of General Psychiatry, 69*(3), 306–313.

Lord, C., Rutter, M., DiLavore, P., & Risi, S. (1999). *Autism diagnostic observation schedule (ADOS)*. Los Angeles, CA: Western Psychological Services.

Lord, C., Rutter, M., & Le Couteur, A. (1994). Autism Diagnostic Interview-Revised: a revised version of a diagnostic interview for caregivers of individuals with possible pervasive developmental disorders. *Journal of Autism and Developmental Disorders*, 24(5), 659–685.

Lord, C., & Schopler, E. (1989). The role of age at assessment, developmental level, and test in the stability of intelligence scores in young autistic children. *Journal of Autism and Developmental Disorders*, 19(4), 483–499.

Losh, M., & Capps, L. (2006). Understanding of emotional experience in autism: insights from the personal accounts of high-functioning children with autism. *Developmental Psychology*, 42(5), 809.

Lotter, V. (1966). Epidemiology of autistic conditions in young children. *Social Psychiatry*, 1(3), 124–135.

Lotter, V. (1974a). Factors related to outcome in autistic children. *Journal of Autism and Childhood Schizophrenia*, 4(3), 263–277.

Lotter, V. (1974b). Social adjustment and placement of autistic children in Middlesex: A follow-up study. *Journal of Autism and Childhood Schizophrenia*, 4(1), 11–32.

Lotter, V. (1978). Follow-up studies. In *Autism* (pp. 475–495). New York: Springer US.

Lovaas, O. I. (1960). The relationship of induced muscular tension, tension level, and manifest anxiety in learning. *Journal of Experimental Psychology*, 59(3), 145.

Lovaas, O. I. (1966). A program for the establishment of speech in psychotic children. In J. K. Wing (Ed.), *Early childhood autism* (pp. 115–144). London: Pergamon.

Lovaas, O.I. (1981). *Teaching developmentally disabled children: The ME book (1981)*. Austin, TX: PRO-ED.

Lovaas, O. I. (1987). Behavioral treatment and normal educational and intellectual functioning in young autistic children. *Journal of Consulting and Clinical Psychology*, 55(1), 3–9.

Lovaas, O. I. (1993). The development of a treatment-research project for developmentally disabled and autistic children. *Journal of Applied Behavior Analysis*, 26(4), 617–630.

Lovaas, O. I. (2003). *Teaching Individuals with developmental delays: basic intervention techniques*. Austin, TX: PRO-ED.

Lovaas, O. I., Koegel, R., Simmons, J. Q., & Long, J. S. (1973). Some generalisation and follow-up measures on autistic children in behaviour therapy 1. *Journal of Applied Behavior Analysis*, 6(1), 131–165.

Lovaas, O. I., & Newsom, C. D. (1976). Behavior modification with psychotic children. *Handbook of behavior modification and behavior therapy* (pp. 303–360). Englewood Cliffs, NJ: Prentice-Hall.

Lovaas, O. I., & Smith, T. (1989). A comprehensive behavioral theory of autistic children: Paradigm for research and treatment. *Journal of Behavior Therapy and Experimental Psychiatry*, 20(1), 17–29.

Love, J. R., Carr, J. E., Almason, S. M., & Petursdottir, A. I. (2009). Early and intensive behavioral intervention for autism: A survey of clinical practices. *Research in Autism Spectrum Disorders*, 3(2), 421–428.

Luiselli, J. K., Cannon, B. O. M., Ellis, J. T., & Sisson, R. W. (2000). Home-based behavioral intervention for young children with autism/pervasive developmental disorder a preliminary evaluation of outcome in relation to child age and intensity of service delivery. *Autism*, 4(4), 426–438.

Lutchmaya, S., Baron-Cohen, S., & Raggatt, P. (2002). Foetal testosterone and eye contact in 12-month-old human infants. *Infant Behavior and Development*, 25(3), 327–335.

Luyster, R. J., Kadlec, M. B., Carter, A., & Tager-Flusberg, H. (2008). Language assessment and development in toddlers with autism spectrum disorders. *Journal of Autism and Developmental Disorders*, 38(8), 1426–1438.

Lydon, S., Healy, O., Reed, P., Mulhern, T., Hughes, B. M., Goodwin, M. S. (2015). Physiological reactivity in autism spectrum disorder: a systematic review. *Neurodevelopmental Rehabilitation.* In press.

Mace, F. C. (1994). The significance and future of functional analysis methodologies. *Journal of Applied Behavior Analysis, 27*(2), 385–392.

MacDuff, G. S., Krantz, P. J., & McClannahan, L. E. (2001). Prompts and prompt-fading strategies for people with autism. In C. Maurice, G. Green, & R. M. Foxx (Eds.), *Making a difference: Behavioral intervention for autism* (pp. 37–50). Austin, TX: PRO-ED.

Machalicek, W., O'Reilly, M. F., Beretvas, N., Sigafoos, J., Lancioni, G., Sorrells, A., ... & Rispoli, M. (2008). A review of school-based instructional interventions for students with autism spectrum disorders. *Research in Autism Spectrum Disorders, 2*(3), 395–416.

MacIntosh, K., & Dissanayake, C. (2006). Social skills and problem behaviours in school aged children with high-functioning autism and Asperger's disorder. *Journal of Autism and Developmental Disorders, 36,* 1065–1076.

MacNeil, B. M., Lopes, V. A., & Minnes, P. M. (2009). Anxiety in children and adolescents with autism spectrum disorders. *Research in Autism Spectrum Disorders, 3*(1), 1–21.

MacCorquodale, K. (1969). BF Skinner's *Verbal Behavior*: A retrospective appreciation 1. *Journal of the Experimental Analysis of Behavior, 12*(5), 831–841.

Maenner, M. J., & Durkin, M. S. (2010). Trends in the prevalence of autism on the basis of special education data. *Pediatrics, 126*(5), e1018–e1025.

Magiati, I., Charman, T., & Howlin, P. (2007). A two-year prospective follow-up study of community-based early intensive behavioural intervention and specialist nursery provision for children with autism spectrum disorders. *Journal of Child Psychology and Psychiatry, 48*(8), 803–812.

Magiati, I., & Howlin, P. A. (2001). Monitoring the progress of preschool children with autism enrolled in early intervention programmes: Problems in cognitive assessment. *Autism, 5,* 399–406.

Magiati, I., Moss, J., Charman, T., & Howlin, P. (2011). Patterns of change in children with Autism Spectrum Disorders who received community based comprehensive interventions in their pre-school years: A seven year follow-up study. *Research in Autism Spectrum Disorders, 5*(3), 1016–1027.

Magid, K., & McKelvey, C. A. (1987). *High risk.* Random House LLC.

Magnuson, K. M., & Constantino, J. N. (2011). Characterization of depression in children with autism spectrum disorders. *Journal of Developmental and Behavioral Pediatrics, 32*(4), 332.

Mahler, M., Pine, E, & Bergman, A. (1975). *The psychological birth of the human infant.* New York: Basic Books.

Mahoney, G., & Perales, F. (2003). Using relationship-focused intervention to enhance the social – emotional functioning of young children with autism spectrum disorders. *Topics in Early Childhood Special Education, 23*(2), 74–86.

Makrygianni, M. K., Gena, A., & Reed, P. (2010c). The effectiveness of behavioural and eclectic intervention programmes for 6.5–14 year old children with Autistic Spectrum Disorders: A cross-cultural study. *Journal of Education Research, 4*(4), 295–316.

Makrygianni, M. K., & Reed, P. (2010a). A meta-analytic review of the effectiveness of behavioural early intervention programs for children with Autistic Spectrum Disorders. *Research in Autism Spectrum Disorders, 4*(4), 577–593.

Makrygianni, M. K., & Reed, P. (2010b). Factors impacting on the outcomes of Greek intervention programmes for children with autistic spectrum disorders. *Research in Autism Spectrum Disorders, 4*(4), 697–708.

Mandell, D. S., Stahmer, A. C., Shin, S., Xie, M., Reisinger, E., & Marcus, S. C. (2013). The role of treatment fidelity on outcomes during a randomized field trial of an autism intervention. *Autism, 17*(3), 281–295.

Mandler, G. (2002). *Consciousness recovered: Psychological functions and origins of conscious thought.* Amsterdam/Philadelphia: John Benjamins.

Mandy, W. P., & Skuse, D. H. (2008). Research Review: What is the association between the social-communication element of autism and repetitive interests, behaviours and activities?. *Journal of Child Psychology and Psychiatry, 49*(8), 795–808.

Manolson, A. (1992). *It takes two to talk: A parent's guide to helping children communicate* (2nd ed.). Toronto: Hanen Centre.

Marcus, L. M., Rubin, J. S., & Rubin, M. A. (2000). Benefit–cost analysis and autism services: a response to Jacobson and Mulick. *Journal of Autism and Developmental Disorders, 30*(6), 595–598.

Marcus, L.M., & Schopler, E. (2007). Educational approaches for autism – TEACCH. In E. Hollander & E. Anagnostou (Eds.), *Autism spectrum clinical manual for the treatment of autism* (pp. 211–233). Washington, DC: American Psychiatric Publishing, Inc.

Mari, M., Castiello, U., Marks, D., Marraffa, C., & Prior, M. (2003). The reach–to–grasp movement in children with autism spectrum disorder. *Philosophical Transactions of the Royal Society of London. Series B: Biological Sciences, 358*(1430), 393–403.

Marinho, H. (1940). Social influence in the formation of enduring preferences. *Journal of Abnormal Social Psychology, 37,* 448–468.

Marion, C., Martin, C. L., Yu, C. T., & Buhler, C. (2011). Teaching children with autism spectrum disorder to mind 'what is it?'. *Research in Autism Spectrum Disorders, 5,* 1584–1597.

Mason, J., & Scior, K. (2004). Diagnostic overshadowing amongst clinicians working with people with intellectual disabilities in the UK. *Journal of Applied Research in Intellectual Disabilities, 17,* 85–90.

Matos, M. A., & Mustaca, A. E. (2005). Análisis Comportamental Aplicado (ACA) y Trastornos Generalizados del Desarrollo (TGD): Su evaluación en Argentina [Applied behavior analysis and pervasive developmental disabilities: Assessment in Argentina]. *Interdisciplinaria, 22,* 59–76.

Matson, J. L., Barrett, R. P., & Helsel, W. J. (1988). Depression in mentally retarded children. *Research in Developmental Disabilities, 9,* 39–46.

Matson, J. L., Benavidez, D. A., Stabinsky Compton, L., Paclawskyj, T., & Baglio, C. (1996). Behavioral treatment of autistic persons: A review of research from 1980 to the present. *Research in Developmental Disabilities, 17*(6), 433–465.

Matson, J. L., & Konst, M. J. (2013). What is the evidence for long term effects of early autism interventions? *Research in Autism Spectrum Disorders, 7*(3), 475–479.

Matson, M. L., Mahan, S., & Matson, J. L. (2009). Parent training: A review of methods for children with autism spectrum disorders. *Research in Autism Spectrum Disorders, 3*(4), 868–875.

Matson, J. L., & Newbel-Schwalm, M. S. (2007). Comorbid psychopathology with autism spectrum disorder in children: An overview. *Research in Developmental Disabilities, 24,* 341–352.

Matson, J. L., & Rivet, T. T. (2008). Characteristics of challenging behaviours in adults with autistic disorder, PDD-NOS, and intellectual disability. *Journal of Intellectual and Developmental Disability, 33*(4), 323–329.

Matson, J. L., & Shoemaker, M. (2009). Intellectual disability and its relationship to autism spectrum disorders. *Research in Developmental Disabilities, 30*(6), 1107–1114.

Matson, J. L., Smiroldo, B. B., & Bamburg, J. W. (1998). The relationship of social skills to psychopathology for individuals with severe or profound mental retardation. *Journal of Intellectual and Developmental Disability, 23,* 137–145.

Matson, J. L., & Smith, K. R. (2008). Current status of intensive behavioral interventions for young children with autism and PDD-NOS. *Research in Autism Spectrum Disorders, 2*(1), 60–74.

Matson, J. L., Wilkins, J., & Macken, J. (2008). The relationship of challenging behaviors to severity and symptoms of autism spectrum disorders. *Journal of Mental Health Research in Intellectual Disabilities, 2*(1), 29–44.

May, R. J., & Dymond, S. (2014). Facilitating emergent verbal repertoires in individuals with autism spectrum disorders and other developmental disorders. *Communication in Autism, 11*, 29.

May-Benson, T. A., & Koomar, J. A. (2010). Systematic review of the research evidence examining the effectiveness of interventions using a sensory integrative approach for children. *The American Journal of Occupational Therapy, 64*, 403–414.

McClure, M. K., & Holtz-Yotz, M. (1990). The effects of sensory stimulatory treatment on an autistic child. *American Journal of Occupational Therapy, 45*, 1138–1145.

McConachie, H., & Diggle, T. (2007). Parent implemented early intervention for young children with autism spectrum disorder: a systematic review. *Journal of Evaluation in Clinical Practice, 13*(1), 120–129.

McConachie, H., Randle, V., Hammal, D., & Le Couteur, A. (2005). A controlled trial of a training course for parents of children with suspected autism spectrum disorder. *The Journal of Pediatrics, 147*(3), 335–340.

McConkey, R., Kelly, G., & Cassidy, A. (2007). An evaluation of the need and early intervention support for children (aged 2–4 years) with an autistic spectrum disorder in Northern Ireland (No. 44). Belfast, NI: Department of Education.

McConkey, R., Mullan, A., & Addis, J. (2012). Promoting the social inclusion of children with autism spectrum disorders in community groups. *Early Child Development and Care, 182*(7), 827–835.

McConkey, R., Truesdale-Kennedy, M., Crawford, H., McGreevy, E., Reavey, M., & Cassidy, A. (2010). Preschoolers with autism spectrum disorders: evaluating the impact of a home-based intervention to promote their communication. *Early Child Development and Care, 180*(3), 299–315.

McConnell, S. R. (2002). Interventions to facilitate social interaction for young children with autism: Review of available research and recommendations for educational intervention and future research. *Journal of Autism and Developmental Disorders, 32*(5), 351–372.

McCubbin, H. I., & Patterson, J. (1983). The family stress process: The double ABCX model of adjustment and adaptation. In H. I. McCubbin, M. B. Sussman, & J. M. Patterson (Eds.), *Social stress and the family: Advances and developments in family's stress theory and research*. New York: Haworth.

McDuffie, A., Yoder, P., & Stone, W. (2005). Prelinguistic predictors of vocabulary in young children with autism spectrum disorders. *Journal of Speech, Language, and Hearing Research, 48*, 1080–1097.

McEachlin, J. J., Smith, T., & Lovaas, O. I. (1993). Long-term outcome for children with autism who received early intensive behavioral treatment. *American Journal on Mental Retardation, 97*, 359–372.

McGarrell, M., Healy, O., Leader, G., O'Connor, J., & Kenny, N. (2009). Six reports of children with autism spectrum disorder following intensive behavioral intervention using the Preschool Inventory of Repertoires for Kindergarten (PIRK®). *Research in Autism Spectrum Disorders, 3*(3), 767–782.

McGreevy, P. (2009). Teaching verbal behavior to children and adults with developmental disabilities, including autism spectrum disorder. In P. Reed (Ed.) *Behavioral theories and intervention for autism* (pp. 133–168). New York: Nova.

McGregor, E., & Campbell, E. (2001). The attitudes of teachers in Scotland to the integration of children with Autism into mainstream schools. *Autism, 5*, 189–207.

McGregor, G., & Vogelsberg, R. T. (1998). *Inclusive schooling practices: pedagogical and research foundations*. Paul H. Brookes Publishing Co., Inc.

McGregory, E., Whiten, A., & Blackburn, P. (1998). Teaching theory of mind by high-lighting intention and illustrating thoughts: A comparison of their effectiveness with 3-year-olds and autistic individuals. *British Journal of Developmental Psychology*, 16(3), 281–300.

McIntosh, D. N., Reichmann-Decker, A., Winkielman, P., & Wilbarger, J. L. (2006). When the social mirror breaks: deficits in automatic, but not voluntary, mimicry of emotional facial expressions in autism. *Developmental Science*, 9(3), 295–302.

McIntyre, L. L., Blacher, J., & Baker, B. L. (2006). The transition to school: Adaptation in young children with and without intellectual disability. *Journal of Intellectual Disability Research*, 50(5), 349–361.

McLeish, J. (1975). *Soviet psychology: History, theory, content.* Methuen.

McSweeney, F. K., & Murphy, E. S. (2000). Criticisms of the Satiety Hypothesis as an Explanation for Within-Session Decreases in Responding. *Journal of the Experimental Analysis of Behavior*, 74(3), 347–361.

Mesibov, G. B. (1990). Normalization and its relevance today. *Journal of Autism and Developmental Disorders*, 20, 379–390.

Mesibov, G. B., & Shea, V. (1996). Full inclusion and students with autism. *Journal of Autism and Developmental Disorders*, 26, 337–346.

Mesibov, G. B., & Shea, V. (2010). The TEACCH program in the era of evidence-based practice. *Journal of Autism and Developmental Disorders*, 40(5), 570–579.

Mesibov, G., Shea, V., & Schopler, E. (2005). *The TEACCH approaches to Autism Spectrum Disorders.* Raleigh, NC: The Autism Society of North Carolina.

Mesibov, G. B., Shea, V., Schopler, E., Adams, L., Merkler, E., Burgess, S., Mosconi, M., Chapman, S.M., Tanner, C., & Bourgondien, M. E. (2004). *The TEACCH approach to autism spectrum disorders.* New York, NY: Springer.

Metz, B., Mulick, J. A., & Butter, E. M. (2005). Autism: A late-20th-century fad magnet. In: J. W. Jacobson, R. M. Foxx, & J. A. Mulick (Eds.), *Controversial therapies for developmental disabilities: Fad, fashion and science in professional practice*, (pp. 237–263). Mahwah, NJ: Lawrence Erlbaum Associates Publishers.

Militerni, R., Bravaccio, C., Falco, C., Fico, C., & Palermo, M. T. (2002). Repetitive behaviors in autistic disorder. *European Child & Adolescent Psychiatry*, 11(5), 210–218.

Miller, N. E. (1944). Experimental studies of conflict. In J. McV. Hunt (Ed.), *Personality and the behavior disorders* Vol. 1 (pp. 431–465). New York: Ronald Press.

Miltenberger, R. (2011). *Behavior modification: Principles and procedures.* Cengage Learning.

Minderaa, R. B., Volkmar, F. R., Hansen, C. R., Harcherik, D. F., Akkerhuis, G. W., & Cohen, D. J. (1985). Brief report: Snout and visual rooting reflexes in infantile autism. *Journal of Autism and Developmental Disorders*, 15(4), 409–416.

Ming, X., Brimacombe, M., & Wagner, G. C. (2007). Prevalence of motor impairment in autism spectrum disorders. *Brain and Development*, 29(9), 565–570.

Minshew, N. J., Sung, K., Jones, B. L., & Furman, J. M. (2004). Underdevelopment of the postural control system in autism. *Neurology*, 63(11), 2056–2061.

Minuchin, S. (1974). *Families and family therapy.* Cambridge, MA: Harvard University Press.

Miyahara, M., Tsujii, M., Hori, M., Nakanishi, K., Kageyama, H., & Sugiyama, T. (1997). Brief report: motor incoordination in children with Asperger syndrome and learning disabilities. *Journal of Autism and Developmental Disorders*, 27(5), 595–603.

Miyake, A., Friedman, N., Emerson, M., Witzki, A., Howerter, A., & Wager, T. (2000). The unity and diversity of executive functions and their contributions to complex 'frontal lobe' tasks: a latent variable analysis. *Cognitive Psychology*, 41, 49–100.

Moore, D. G. (2001). Reassessing emotion recognition performance in people with mental retardation: A review. *American Journal on Mental Retardation*, 106(6), 481–502.

Mordre, M., Groholt, B., Knudsen, A. K., Sponheim, E., Mykletun, A., & Myhre, A. M. (2012). Is long-term prognosis for pervasive developmental disorder not otherwise specified different from prognosis for autistic disorder? Findings from a 30-year follow-up study. *Journal of Autism and Developmental Disorders, 42*(6), 920–928.

Morewood, G., Humphrey, N., & Symes, W. (2011). Mainstreaming autism: making it work. *Good Autism Practice, 12,* 62–8.

Morris, E. K. (2009). A case study in the misrepresentation of applied behavior analysis in autism: The Gernsbacher lectures. *The Behavior Analyst, 32*(1), 205.

Mouridsen, S. E. (2012). Current status of research on autism spectrum disorders and offending. *Research in Autism Spectrum Disorders, 6,* 79–86.

Mowrer, O. H. (1939). A stimulus-response analysis of anxiety and its role as a reinforcing agent. *Psychological Review, 46*(6), 553.

Mowrer, O. H. (1952). Speech development in the young child: 1. The autism theory of speech development and some clinical applications. *Journal of Speech & Hearing Disorders, 17,* 263–268.

Mowrer, O. H. (1958). Hearing and speaking: An analysis of language learning. *Journal of Speech and Hearing Disorders, 23*(2), 143–152.

Mudford, O. C., Cross, B. A., Breen, S., Cullen, C., Reeves, D., Gould, J., & Douglas, J. (2000). Auditory integration training for children with autism: no behavioral benefits detected. *American Journal on Mental Retardation, 105*(2), 118–129.

Mudford, O. C., Martin, N. T., Eikeseth, S., & Bibby, P. (2001). Parent-managed behavioral treatment for preschool children with autism: Some characteristics of UK programs. *Research in Developmental Disabilities, 22*(3), 173–182.

Mukaddes, N. M., Kaynak, F. N., Kinali, G., Besikci, H., & Issever, H. (2004). Psychoeducational treatment of children with autism and reactive attachment disorder. *Autism, 8*(1), 101–109.

Mundy, P., Sigman, M., & Kasari, C. (1990). A longitudinal study of joint attention and language development in autistic children. *Journal of Autism and developmental Disorders, 20*(1), 115–128.

Mundy, P., Sigman, M., & Kasari, C. (1994). Joint attention, developmental level, and symptom presentation in autism. *Development and Psychopathology, 6*(03), 389–401.

Mundy, P., Slgman, M., Kasarl, C., & Ylrmlya, N. (1988). Nonverbal communication skills in Down Syndrome children. *Child Development, 59,* 235–249.

Mundy, P., Sigman, M., Ungerer, J., & Sherman, T. (1986). Defining the social deficits of autism: The contribution of nonverbal communication measures. *Journal of Child Psychology and Psychiatry, 27,* 657–669.

Munson, J., Dawson, G., Sterling, L., Beauchaine, T., Zhou, A., Koehler, E., Lord, C., Rogers, S., Sigman, M., Estes, A., & Abbott, R. (2008). Evidence for latent classes of IQ In young children with Autism Spectrum Disorder. American Journal on Mental Retardation, *113,* 439–452.

Murray-Seegert, C. (1989). *Nasty girls, thugs, and humans like us: Social relations between severely disabled and nondisabled students in high school.* Baltimore, MD: Paul H. Brookes

Myeroff, R., Mertlich, G., & Gross, J. (1999). Comparative effectiveness of holding therapy with aggressive children. *Child Psychiatry and Human Development, 29*(4), 303–313.

Myles, B. S., & Simpson, R. L. (1989). Regular educators' modification preferences for mainstreaming mildly handicapped children. *Journal of Special Education, 22,* 479–492.

Nabuzoka, D., & Smith, P. K. (1993). Sociometric status and social behaviour of children with and without learning difficulties. *Journal of Child Psychology and Psychiatry, 34,* 1435–1448.

Newman, M., Garrett, Z., Elbourne, D., Bradley, S., Noden, P., Taylor, J., & West, A. (2006). Does secondary school size make a difference? A systematic review. *Educational Research Review, 1,* 41–61.

Newschaffer, C. J., Falb, M. D., & Gurney, J. G. (2005). National autism prevalence trends from United States special education data. *Pediatrics, 115*(3), e277–e282.

Neysmith-Roy, J. M. (2001). The Tomatis method with severely autistic boys: Individual case studies of behavioral changes. *South African Journal of Psychology, 31*, 19–28.

Nind, M. (1999). Intensive Interaction and autism: a useful approach? *British Journal of Special Education, 26*(2), 96–102.

Nirje, B. (1969). The normalization principle and its human management implications. In R. Kugel and W. Wolfensberger (Eds.), *Changing Patterns in Residential Services for the Mentally Retarded*, Washington, D.C.: Government Printing Office.

Nordin, V., & Gillberg, C. (1998). The long-term course of autistic disorders: update on follow-up studies. *Acta Psychiatrica Scandinavica, 97*(2), 99–108.

Norwich, B. (2005). Inclusion: is it a matter of evidence about what works or about values and rights? *Education, 33*, 51–56.

Noterdaeme, M., Mildenberger, K., Minow, F., & Amorosa, H. (2002). Evaluation of neuromotor deficits in children with autism and children with a specific speech and language disorder. *European Child & Adolescent Psychiatry, 11*(5), 219–225.

Novick, R. M., & Glanz, J. (2011). Special education: 'and you shall do that which is right and good …'. *Jewish special education in North America: From exclusion to inclusion. International Handbook of Jewish Education, 5*, 1021–1040.

Nowak, C., & Heinrichs, N. (2008). A comprehensive meta-analysis of Triple P-Positive Parenting Program using hierarchical linear modeling: Effectiveness and moderating variables. *Clinical Child and Family Psychology Review, 11*(3), 114–144.

O'Brien, G., & Pearson, J. (2004). Autism and learning disability. *Autism, 8*(2), 125–140.

O'Connor, A. B., & Healy, O. (2010). Long-term post-intensive behavioral intervention outcomes for five children with Autism Spectrum Disorder. *Research in Autism Spectrum Disorders, 4*(4), 594–604.

Odom, S. L., Boyd, B. A., Hall, L. J., & Hume, K. (2010). Evaluation of comprehensive treatment models for individuals with autism spectrum disorders. *Journal of Autism and Developmental Disorders, 40*(4), 425–436.

Odom, S., Hume, K., Boyd, B., & Stabel, A. (2012). Moving beyond the intensive behavior treatment versus eclectic dichotomy evidence-based and individualized programs for learners with ASD. *Behavior Modification, 36*(3), 270–297.

Odom, S. L., & Strain, P. S. (1984). Peer-mediated approaches to promoting children's social interaction: A review. *American Journal of Orthopsychiatry, 54*, 544–557.

Office of National Statistics (2004). *Special Educational Needs in England 2004.* London: DfES.

Office of National Statistics (2009). *Special Educational Needs in England 2009.* London: DfES.

Office of Special Education Programs (1994). *Implementation of the Individuals with Disabilities Education Act:* Sixteenth annual report to Congress. Washington, D.C.: U.S. Department of Education.

Ogletree, B. T., Oren, T., & Fischer, M. A. (2007). Examining effective intervention practices for communication impairment in autism spectrum disorder. *Exceptionality, 15*(4), 233–247.

O'Neill, J., Bergstrand, L., Bowman, K., Elliott, K., Mavin, L., Stephenson, S., & Wayman, C. (2010). The SCERTS model: Implementation and evaluation in a primary special school. *Good Autism Practice, 11*(1), 7–15.

Ochs, E., Kremer-Sadlik, T., Solomon, O. & Sirota, K. G. (2001). Inclusion as social practice: views of children with autism. *Social Development, 10*, 399–419.

Oono, I. P., Honey, E. J., & McConachie, H. (2013). Parent-mediated early intervention for young children with autism spectrum disorders (ASD). *Evidence-Based Child Health: A Cochrane Review Journal, 8*(6), 2380–2479.

Oosterling, I., Visser, J., Swinkels, S., Rommelse, N., Donders, R., Woudenberg, T., Roos, S, van der Gaag, R., & Buitelaar, J. (2010). Randomized controlled trial of the focus parent training for toddlers with autism: 1-year outcome. *Journal of Autism and Developmental Disorders*, *40*(12), 1447–1458.

Ornitz, E. M. (1974). The modulation of sensory input and motor output in autistic children. *Journal of Autism and Childhood Schizophrenia*, *4*, 197–215.

Osborne, L. A. (2009). A dynamic transactional model of parent-child interactions. In P. Reed (Ed.), *Behavioral theories and interventions for autism*. New York: Nova Science Publishers.

Osborne, L. A., McHugh, L., Saunders, J., & Reed, P. (2008a). Parenting stress reduces the effectiveness of early teaching interventions for autistic spectrum disorders. *Journal of Autism and Developmental Disorders*, *38*(6), 1092–1103.

Osborne, L. A., Noble, G.J., Maramba, I. D., Jones, K. H., Middleton, R. M., Lyons, R. A., Ford, D., & Reed, P. (2014). Outcome measures for multiple sclerosis. *Physical Therapy Reviews*, *19*(1), 24–38.

Osborne, L. A., & Reed, P. (2008). An evaluation of the role of reinforcement-based interventions in determining the effectiveness of 'eclectic' approaches for teaching children with Autistic Spectrum Disorders. *Behavioral Development Bulletin*, *14*, 30–39.

Osborne, L. A., & Reed, P. (2009a). The role of the family in Autistic Spectrum Conditions: Theory and practical implications. In P. H. Krause, & T. M. Dailey (Eds.), *Handbook of parenting: styles, stresses, and strategies*. New York: Nova Science Publishers.

Osborne, L. A., & Reed, P. (2009b). The relationship between parenting stress and behavior problems of children with autistic spectrum disorders. *Exceptional Children*, *76*(1), 54–73.

Osborne, L. A., & Reed, P. (2010). Stress and self-perceived parenting behaviors of parents of children with autistic spectrum conditions. *Research in Autism Spectrum Disorders*, *4*(3), 405–414.

Osborne, L. A., & Reed, P. (2011). School factors associated with mainstream progress in secondary education for included pupils with Autism Spectrum Disorders. *Research in Autism Spectrum Disorders*, *5*(3), 1253–1263.

Osgood, C. E. (1979). *Focus on Meaning: Explorations in Semantic Space*. Mouton Publishers.

Osler, A., & Osler, C. (2002). Inclusion, exclusion and children's rights: a case study of a student with Asperger syndrome.' *Emotional and Behavioural Difficulties*, *7*, 35–54.

Ospina, M. B., Seida, J. K., Clark, B., Karkhaneh, M., Hartling, L., Tjosvold, L., Vandermeer, B, & Smith, V. (2008). Behavioural and developmental interventions for autism spectrum disorder: a clinical systematic review. *PloS One*, *3*(11), e3755.

Ottenbacher, K. (1982). Sensory integration therapy: Affect or effect. *American Journal of Occupational Therapy*, *36*, 571–578.

Ozonoff, S., & Cathcart, K. (1998). Effectiveness of a home program intervention for young children with autism. *Journal of Autism and Developmental Disorders*, *28*(1), 25–32.

Ozonoff, S., Rogers, S. J., & Pennington, B. F. (1991). Asperger's syndrome: Evidence of an empirical distinction from high-functioning autism. *Journal of Child Psychology and Psychiatry*, *32*(7), 1107–1122.

Ozonoff, S., South, M., & Provencal, S. (2005). Executive Functions. In F. R. Volkmar, R. Paul, A. Klin, & D. Cohen (Eds.) *Handbook of autism and developmental disorders*, (3rd ed.), (pp. 606–627). New York: John Wiley & Sons, Inc.

Pajareya, K., & Nopmaneejumruslers, K. (2011). A pilot randomized controlled trial of DIR/ Floortime™ parent training intervention for pre-school children with autistic spectrum disorders. *Autism*, *15*(5), 563–577.

Panerai, S., Ferrante, L., & Zingale, M. (2002). Benefits of the Treatment and Education of Autistic and Communication Handicapped Children (TEACCH) programme as compared with a non-specific approach. *Journal of Intellectual Disability Research*, *46*(4), 318–327.

Panerai, S., Zingale, M., Trubia, G., Finocchiaro, M., Zuccarello, R., Ferri, R., & Elia, M. (2009). Special education versus inclusive education: the role of the TEACCH program. *Journal of Autism and Developmental Disorders, 39*(6), 874–882.

Parham, L. D., & Ecker, C. (2007). *Sensory Processing Measure Manual.* Los Angeles: Western Psychological Services.

Parker, J., & Asher, S. R. (1987). Peer acceptance and later personal adjustment: Are low accepted children 'at risk'? *Psychological Bulletin, 102*, 357–389.

Parsons, S., Lewis, A., & Ellins, J. (2009). The views and experiences of parents of children with autistic spectrum disorder about educational provision: comparisons with parents of children with other disabilities from an online survey. *European Journal of Special Needs Education, 24*(1), 37–58.

Pavlov, J. P. (1926). *Conditioned reflexes.* Mineola NJ: Dover Publications.

Paynter, J., Scott, J., Beamish, W., Duhig, M., & Heussler, H. (2012). A pilot study of the effects of an Australian centre-based early intervention program for children with autism. *The Open Pediatric Medicine Journal, 6*, 7–14.

Peck, C., Carlson, P., & Helmstetter, E. (1992). Parent and teacher perceptions of outcomes for typically-developing children enrolled in integrated early childhood programs: A state-wide survey. *Journal of Early Intervention, 16*, 53.

Peppé, S., Cleland, J., Gibbon, F., O'Hare, A., & Castilla, P. M. (2011). Expressive prosody in children with autism spectrum conditions. *Journal of Neurolinguistics, 24*(1), 41–53.

Pérez González, L. A., & Williams, G. (2006). Comprehensive program for teaching skills to children with autism. *Psychology in Spain, 10*(1), 37–51.

Perry, A., Blacklock, K., & Dunn Geier, J. (2013). The relative importance of age and IQ as predictors of outcomes in Intensive Behavioral Intervention. *Research in Autism Spectrum Disorders, 7*(9), 1142–1150.

Perry, A., Condillac, R. A., Freeman, N. L., Dunn-Geier, J., & Belair, J. (2005). Multi-site study of the Childhood Autism Rating Scale (CARS) in five clinical groups of young children. *Journal of Autism and Developmental Disorders, 35*(5), 625–634.

Perry, A., Cummings, A., Geier, J. D., Freeman, N. L., Hughes, S., Managhan, T., Reitzel, J-A., & Williams, J. (2011). Predictors of outcome for children receiving intensive behavioral intervention in a large, community-based program. *Research in Autism Spectrum Disorders, 5*(1), 592–603.

Persson, B. (2000). Brief report: A longitudinal study of quality of life and independence among adult men with autism. *Journal of Autism and Developmental Disorders, 30*(1), 61–66.

Peters-Scheffer, N., Didden, R., Korzilius, H., & Sturmey, P. (2011). A meta-analytic study on the effectiveness of comprehensive ABA-based early intervention programs for children with Autism Spectrum Disorders. *Research in Autism Spectrum Disorders, 5*(1), 60–69.

Peters-Scheffer, N., Didden, R., Korzilius, H., & Matson, J. (2012). Cost comparison of early intensive behavioral intervention and treatment as usual for children with autism spectrum disorder in The Netherlands. *Research in Developmental Disabilities, 33*(6), 1763–1772.

Peters-Scheffer, N., Didden, R., Mulders, M., & Korzilius, H. (2013). Effectiveness of low intensity behavioral treatment for children with autism spectrum disorder and intellectual disability. *Research in Autism Spectrum Disorders, 7*(9), 1012–1025.

Pfeiffer B.A., Koenig K., Kinnealey M., Sheppard M., & Henderson L. (2011). Effectiveness of sensory integration interventions in children with autism spectrum disorders: A pilot study. *American Journal of Occupational Therapy, 65*, 76–85.

Phillips, E. L. (1957). Contributions to a learning theory account of childhood autism. *The Journal of Psychology, 43*(1), 117–124.

Piaget, J. (1954). *The construction of reality in the child.* New York: Basic Books.

Piaget, J. (1968). *Genetic epistemology.* New York: Columbia University Press.

Pillay, M., Alderson-Day, B., Wright, B., Williams, C., & Urwin, B. (2011). Autism Spectrum Conditions-Enhancing Nurture and Development (ASCEND): An evaluation of intervention support groups for parents. *Clinical Child Psychology and Psychiatry, 16*(1), 5–20.

Piuma, F. (1989). *A benefit-cost analysis: the economic impact of integrated educational service delivery models on the employment of individuals with severe disabilities.* San Francisco: National Institute on Disability and Rehabilitation Research.

Place, U. T. (1981). Skinner's 'Verbal Behavior I' – Why we need it. *Behaviorism, 9*(1), 1–24.

Plaisted, K., O'Riordan, M., & Baron-Cohen, S. (1998). Enhanced visual search for a conjunctive target in autism: A research note. *Journal of Child Psychology and Psychiatry, 39*(05), 777–783.

Pinker, S. (1994). *The language instinct: The new science of language and mind.* London: Penguin UK.

Piravej, K., Tangtrongchitr, P., Chandarasiri, P., Paothong, L., & Sukprasong, S. (2009). Effects of Thai traditional massage on autistic children's behavior. *The Journal of Alternative and Complementary Medicine, 15*(12), 1355–1361.

Powell, S. D. & Jordan, R. R. (1997). *Autism and learning,* London: David Fulton.

Porges, S. W. (1998). Love: an emergent property of the mammalian autonomic nervous system. *Psychoneuroendocrinology, 23,* 837–861.

Premack, D., & Woodruff, G. (1978). Does the chimpanzee have a theory of mind?. *Behavioral and Brain Sciences, 1*(04), 515–526.

Prinsen, H. (1954). Der fruehkindliche Autismus; Versuch einer heilpaedagogischen Behandlung/ Early autism; experiment in educational therapy. *Heilpaedagogische-Werkblaetter, 23,* 2–11.

Prizant, B. M. (2009). Is ABA the only way? *Social Thinking. Spring,* 28–32.

Prizant, B. M., & Rubin, E. (1999). Contemporary Issues in Interventions for Autism Spectrum Disorders: A commentary. *Journal of the Association for Persons with Severe Handicaps, 24*(3), 199–208.

Prizant, B. M., & Wetherby, A. M. (1987). Communicative intent: A framework for understanding social-communicative behavior in autism. *Journal of the American Academy of Child & Adolescent Psychiatry, 26*(4), 472–479.

Prizant, B. M., Wetherby, A. M., Rubin, E., & Laurent, A. C. (2003). The SCERTS Model: A transactional, family-centered approach to enhancing communication and socioemotional abilities of children with autism spectrum disorder. *Infants & Young Children, 16*(4), 296–316.

Prizant, B. M., Wetherby, A. M., Rubin, E., Laurent, A. C., & Rydell, P. J. (2006). *The SCERTS™ model. Volume I: Assessment; Volume II: Program planning and intervention.* Baltimore, MD: Brookes Publishing.

Prizant, B., Wetherby, A., Rydell, P., Wetherby, A., & Prizant, B. (2000). Communication intervention issues for children with autism spectrum disorders. *Autism spectrum disorders: A transactional developmental perspective, 9,* 193–224.

Quigley, S. P., Peterson, L., Frieder, J. E., & Peterson, S. (2011). Effects of a weighted vest on problem behaviors during functional analyses in children with pervasive developmental disorders. *Research in Autism Spectrum Disorders, 5,* 529–538.

Quill, K. A. (1995). Visually cued instruction for children with autism and pervasive developmental disorders. *Focus on Autism and Other Developmental Disabilities, 10*(3), 10–20.

Quill, K. A. (1997). Instructional considerations for young children with autism: The rationale for visually cued instruction. *Journal of Autism and Developmental Disorders, 27*(6), 697–714.

Rapin, I. (1996a). Practitioner review: Developmental language disorders: A clinical update. *Journal of Child Psychology and Psychiatry, 37*(6), 643–655.

Rapin, I. (1996b). Preschool children with inadequate communication. *Clinics in Developmental Medicine* (No. 139). London: MacKeith.

Rapin, I., & Dunn, M. (1997). Language disorders in children with autism. In *Seminars in Pediatric Neurology*, 4, 86–92.

Råstam, M., Gillberg, C., & Wentz, E. (2003). Outcome of teenage-onset anorexia nervosa in a Swedish community-based sample. *European Child & Adolescent Psychiatry*, 12(1), i7–i90.

Ravet, J. (2011). Inclusive/exclusive? Contradictory perspectives on autism and inclusion: the case for an integrative position. *International Journal of Inclusive Education*, 15(6), 667–682.

Ray, T. C., King, L. J., & Grandin, T. (1988). The effectiveness of self-initiated vestibular stimulation in producing speech sounds in an autistic child. *Occupational Therapy Journal of Research*, 8, 186–190.

Raz, M. (2013). Deprived of touch: How maternal and sensory deprivation theory converged in shaping early debates over autism. *History of the Human Sciences*, 0952695113512491.

Reddy, G. L. (2008). *Special education teachers: Occupational stress, professional burnout and job satisfaction.* New Dehli: Discovery Publishing House.

Reed, P. (1999). Managing dyslexia is understanding dyslexia: implicit functional and structural approaches in the articles by Cameron and his critics. *Educational and Child Psychology*, 16, 51–69.

Reed, P. (2009). *Behavioral theories and interventions for autism.* Nova Science.

Reed, P. (2011). Discrimination learning process in Autism Spectrum Disorders. In T. R. Schachtman & S. Reilly (Eds), *Associative Learning and Conditioning Theory: Human and Non-human Applications* (p. 168). Oxford: Oxford University Press.

Reed, P. (2014). Learning, not instinct, determines behaviour: social or otherwise. In S. Nolen-Hoeksema, B. Fredrickson, G. R. Loftus and C. Lutz (Eds.), *Atkinson and Hilgard's introduction to psychology* (16th ed.). Andover, UK: Cengage.

Reed, P., & Gibson, E. (2005). The effect of concurrent task load on stimulus over-selectivity. *Journal of Autism and Developmental Disorders*, 35(5), 601–614.

Reed, P., & Osborne, L. (2012). Impact of severity of autism and intervention time-input on child outcomes: comparison across several early interventions. *British Journal of Special Education*, 39(3), 130–136.

Reed, P., & Osborne, L. A. (2013). The role of parenting stress in discrepancies between parent and teacher ratings of behavior problems in young children with Autism Spectrum Disorder. *Journal of Autism and Developmental Disorders*, 43(2), 471–477.

Reed, P., & Osborne, L. A. (2014). Mainstream education for children with Autism Spectrum Disorders. In *Handbook of Early Intervention for Autism Spectrum Disorders* (pp. 565–616). New York: Springer.

Reed, P., Osborne, L. A., & Corness, M. (2007a). Brief report: relative effectiveness of different home-based behavioral approaches to early teaching intervention. *Journal of Autism and Developmental Disorders*, 37(9), 1815–1821.

Reed, P., Osborne, L. A., & Corness, M. (2007b). The real-world effectiveness of early teaching interventions for children with autism spectrum disorder. *Exceptional Children*, 73(4), 417–433.

Reed, P., Osborne, L. A., & Corness, M. (2010). Effectiveness of special nursery provision for children with autism spectrum disorders. *Autism*, 14(1), 67–82.

Reed, P., Osborne, L. A., Makrygianni, M., Waddington, E., Etherington, A., & Gainsborough, J. (2013b). Evaluation of the Barnet Early Autism Model (BEAM) teaching intervention programme in a 'real world' setting. *Research in Autism Spectrum Disorders*, 7(6), 631–638.

Reed, P., Osborne, L. A., & Waddington, E. M. (2012). A comparative study of the impact of mainstream and special school placement on the behaviour of children with Autism Spectrum Disorders. *British Educational Research Journal*, *38*(5), 749–763.

Reed, P., Watts, H., & Truzoli, R. (2013a). Flexibility in young people with autism spectrum disorders on a card sort task. *Autism*, *17*(2), 162–171.

Reichow, B. (2012). Overview of meta-analyses on early intensive behavioral intervention for young children with autism spectrum disorders. *Journal of Autism and Developmental Disorders*, *42*(4), 512–520.

Reichow, B., Barton, E. E., Sewell, J. N., Good, L., & Wolery, M. (2010). Effects of weighted vests on the engagement of children with developmental delays and autism. *Focus on Autism and Other Developmental Disabilities*, *25*, 3–11.

Reichow, B., & Wolery, M. (2009). Comprehensive synthesis of early intensive behavioral interventions for young children with autism based on the UCLA young autism project model. *Journal of Autism and Developmental Disorders*, *39*(1), 23–41.

Reid, T. (1785). *Essays on the intellectual powers of man*. Available at https://books.google.co.uk/books?id=2A4cAQAAMAAJ&printsec=frontcover&source=gbs_ge_summary_r&cad=0#v=onepage&q&f=false (accessed 31 July 2015).

Reiersen, A. M., & Todd, R. D. (2008). Co-occurrence of ADHD and autism spectrum disorders: phenomenology and treatment. *Review of Neurotherapeutics*, *8*, 657–669.

Reilly, C., Nelson, D. L., & Bundy, A. C. (1983). Sensorimotor versus fine motor activities in eliciting vocalizations in autistic children. *Occupational Therapy Journal of Research*, *3*, 199–212.

Remington, B., Hastings, R. P., Kovshoff, H., degli Espinosa, F., Jahr, E., Brown, T., Alsford, P., Lemaic, M., & Ward, N. (2007). Early intensive behavioral intervention: outcomes for children with autism and their parents after two years. *American Journal on Mental Retardation*, *112*(6), 418–438.

Resch, J.A., Mireles, G., Benz, M.R., Grenwelge, C., Peterson, R., & Zhang, D. (2010). Giving parents a voice: A qualitative study of the challenges experienced by parents of children with disabilities. *Rehabilitation Psychology*, *55*, 139–150.

Reschke-Hernández, A. E. (2011). History of music therapy treatment interventions for children with autism. *Journal of Music Therapy*, *48*(2), 169–207.

Reynolds, G. S. (1961). Attention in the pigeon. *Journal of the Experimental Analysis of Behavior*, *4*, 203–208.

Reynolds, S., Bendixen, R.M., Lawrence, T., & Lane, S.J. (2011). A pilot study examining activity participation, sensory responsiveness, and competence in children with high functioning Autism Spectrum Disorder. *Journal of Autism and Developmental Disorders*, *41*, 1496–1506.

Richardson, H., & Langley, T. (1997). The potential benefits of daily life therapy for children with autism. *International Journal of Autism*, *1*(2), 237.

Rickards, A. L., Walstab, J. E., Wright-Rossi, R. A., Simpson, J., & Reddihough, D. S. (2007). A randomized, controlled trial of a home-based intervention program for children with autism and developmental delay. *Journal of Developmental & Behavioral Pediatrics*, *28*(4), 308–316.

Rimland, B. (1964). *Infantile autism: The syndrome and its implications for a neural theory of behavior*. East Norwalk, CT: Appleton-Century-Crofts.

Rimland, B., & Edelson, R. (1994). The effects of auditory integration training on autism. *American Journal of Speech and Language Pathology, May*, 18–24.

Rimland, B., & Edelson, S. M. (1995). Brief report: A pilot study of auditory integration training in autism. *Journal of Autism and Developmental Disorders*, *25*(1), 61–70.

Rimland, B. & Edelson, M. (1999). *The Autism Treatment Evaluation Checklist (ATEC)*. San Diego: Autism Research Institute.

Rinehart, N. J., Bellgrove, M. A., Tonge, B. J., Brereton, A. V., Howells-Rankin, D., & Bradshaw, J. L. (2006). An examination of movement kinematics in young people with high-functioning autism and Asperger's disorder: further evidence for a motor planning deficit. *Journal of Autism and Developmental Disorders, 36*(6), 757–767.

Ritter, M., & Low, K. G. (1996). Effects of dance/movement therapy: A meta-analysis. *The Arts in Psychotherapy, 23*(3), 249–260.

Robbins, F. R., Dunlap, G., & Plienis, A. J. (1991). Family characteristics, family training, and the progress of young children with autism. *Journal of Early Intervention, 15*(2), 173–184.

Roberts, J. M. A. (2004). *A review of the research to identify the most effective models of best practice in the management of children with autism spectrum disorders.* Sydney, NSW: Centre for Developmental Disability Studies, University of Sydney.

Roberts, J. M. A., & Prior, M. (2006). *A review of the research to identify the most effective models of best practice in the management of children with Autism Spectrum Disorders.* Sydney, NSW, Australia: Australian Government Department of Health and Ageing.

Roberts, J., Williams, K., Carter, M., Evans, D., Parmenter, T., Silove, N., Clark, T., & Warren, A. (2011). A randomised controlled trial of two early intervention programs for young children with autism: Centre-based with parent program and home-based. *Research in Autism Spectrum Disorders, 5*(4), 1553–1566.

Robertson, A. E., & Simmons, D. R. (2013). The relationship between sensory sensitivity and autistic traits in the general population. *Journal of Autism and Developmental Disorders, 43*(4), 775–784.

Robertson, K., Chamberlain, B., & Kasari, C. (2003). General education teachers' relationships with included students with Autism. *Journal of Autism and Developmental Disorders, 33*, 123–130.

Rogers, S. J. (1998). Empirically supported comprehensive treatments for young children with autism. *Journal of Clinical Child Psychology, 27*(2), 168–179.

Rogers, S. J., & Dawson, G. (2010). *Early start Denver model for young children with autism: Promoting language, learning, and engagement.* New York: Guilford Press.

Rogers, S. J., & DiLalla, D. L. (1991). A comparative study of the effects of a developmentally based instructional model on young children with autism and young children with other disorders of behavior and development. *Topics in Early Childhood Special Education, 11*(2), 29–47.

Rogers, S. J., Estes, A., Lord, C., Vismara, L., Winter, J., Fitzpatrick, A., Guo, M., & Dawson, G. (2012). Effects of a brief Early Start Denver Model (ESDM)–based parent intervention on toddlers at risk for autism spectrum disorders: a randomized controlled trial. *Journal of the American Academy of Child & Adolescent Psychiatry, 51*(10), 1052–1065.

Rogers, S. J., Hall, T., Osaki, D., Reaven, J., & Herbison, J. (2000). A comprehensive, integrated, educational approach to young children with autism and their families. In S. L. Harris & J. S. Handleman (Eds.), *Preschool education programs for children with autism* (2nd ed.). Austin, TX: PRO-ED.

Rogers, S. J., Hayden, D., Hepburn, S., Charlifue-Smith, R., Hall, T., & Hayes, A. (2006). Teaching young nonverbal children with autism useful speech: A pilot study of the Denver model and PROMPT interventions. *Journal of Autism and Developmental Disorders, 36*(8), 1007–1024.

Rogers, S. J., Hepburn, S. L., Stackhouse, T., & Wehner, E. (2003). Imitation performance in toddlers with autism and those with other developmental disorders. *Journal of Child Psychology and Psychiatry, 44*(5), 763–781.

Rogers, S. J., Herbison, J. M., Lewis, H. C., Pantone, J., & Reis, K. (1986). An approach for enhancing the symbolic, communicative, and interpersonal functioning of young children with autism or severe emotional handicaps. *Journal of Early Intervention, 10*(2), 135–148.

Rogers, S. J., & Lewis, H. A. L. (1989). An effective day treatment model for young children with pervasive developmental disorders. *Journal of the American Academy of Child & Adolescent Psychiatry, 28*(2), 207–214.

Rogers, S. J., Lewis, H. C., & Reis, K. (1987). An effective procedure for training early special education teams to implement a model program. *Journal of the Division of Early Childhood, 11*, 180–188.

Rogers, S. J., & Ozonoff, S. (2005). Annotation: What do we know about sensory dysfunction in autism? A critical review of the empirical evidence. *Journal of Child Psychology and Psychiatry, 46*(12), 1255–1268.

Rogers, S. J., & Pennington, B. (1991). A theoretical approach to the deficits in infantile autism. *Developmental Psychology, 3*, 137–162.

Rogers, S. J., & Vismara, L. A. (2008). Evidence-based comprehensive treatments for early autism. *Journal of Clinical Child & Adolescent Psychology, 37*(1), 8–38.

Rogers-Warren, A., & Warren, S. F. (1980). Mands for verbalization facilitating the display of newly trained language in children. *Behavior Modification, 4*(3), 361–382.

Ronald, A., Happé, F., Price, T. S., Baron-Cohen, S., & Plomin, R. (2006). Phenotypic and genetic overlap between autistic traits at the extremes of the general population. *Journal of the American Academy of Child & Adolescent Psychiatry, 45*(10), 1206–1214.

Rowley, E., Chandler, S., Baird, G., Simonoff, E., Pickles, A., Loucas, T., & Charman, T. (2012). The experience of friendship, victimization and bullying in children with an autism spectrum disorder: Associations with child characteristics and school placement. *Research in Autism Spectrum Disorders, 6*(3), 1126–1134.

Ruble, L. A., & Dalrymple, N. J. (1996). An alternative view of outcome in autism. *Focus on Autism and Other Developmental Disabilities, 11*(1), 3–14.

Ruijs, N. M., & Peetsma, T. T. D. (2009). Effects of inclusion on students with and without special educational needs reviewed. *Educational Research Review, 4*, 67–79.

Rumsey, J. M., & Hamburger, S. D. (1990). Neuropsychological divergence of high-level autism and severe dyslexia. *Journal of Autism and Developmental Disorders, 20*(2), 155–168.

Russell, G., & Norwich, B. (2012). Dilemmas, diagnosis and de-stigmatization: Parental perspectives on the diagnosis of autism spectrum disorders. *Clinical child psychology and psychiatry, 17*(2), 229–245.

Rutter, M. (1968). Concepts of autism: A review of research. *Journal of Child Psychology and Psychiatry, 9*(1), 1–25.

Rutter, M. (1970). Autistic children: Infancy to adulthood. *Seminars in Psychiatry, 2*, 435–450.

Rutter, M. (1978). Diagnosis and definition of childhood autism. *Journal of Autism and Childhood Schizophrenia, 8*(2), 139–161.

Rutter, M., & Bartak, L. (1973). Special educational treatment of autistic children: A comparative study – II. Follow-up findings and implications for services. *Journal of Child Psychology and Psychiatry, 14*, 241–270.

Rutter, M., Bailey, A., & Lord, C. (2003). *The social communication questionnaire: Manual.* Western Psychological Services.

Rutter, M., Greenfeld, D., & Lockyer, L. (1967). A five to fifteen year follow-up study of infantile psychosis II. Social and behavioural outcome. *The British Journal of Psychiatry, 113*(504), 1183–1199.

Rutter, M., & Lockyer, L. (1967). A five to fifteen year follow-up study of infantile psychosis I. Description of sample. *British Journal of Psychiatry, 113*, 1169–1182.

Salt, J., Sellars, V., Shemilt, J., Boyd, S., Coulson, T., & McCool, S. (2001). The Scottish Centre for Autism preschool treatment programme I: A developmental approach to early intervention. *Autism, 5*(4), 362–373.

Salt, J., Shemilt, J., Sellars, V., Boyd, S., Coulson, T., & McCool, S. (2002). The Scottish Centre for autism preschool treatment programme II: the results of a controlled treatment outcome study. *Autism, 6*(1), 33–46.

Sallows, G. O., & Graupner, T. D. (2005). Intensive behavioral treatment for children with autism: Four-year outcome and predictors. *American Journal on Mental Retardation, 110*(6), 417–438.

Sanders, M. R., Cann, W., & Markie-Dadds, C. (2003). The Triple P-Positive Parenting Programme: a universal population-level approach to the prevention of child abuse. *Child Abuse Review, 12*(3), 155–171.

Sansosti, J. M., & Sansosti, F. J. (2012). Inclusion for students with high-functioning Autism Spectrum Disorders: Definitions and decision making. *Psychology in the Schools, 49*(10), 917–931.

Sarafino, E. P. (1996). *Principles of behavior change: Understanding behavior modification techniques.* New York: John Wiley & Sons, Inc.

Sauri, J. J., & De-Onorato, A. (1955). Las esquizofrenias y la dietilamida del acido Dlisergico (LSD 25): I. Variaciones del estado de animo/Schizophrenia and lysergic acid diethylamide (LSD 25): I. Variations in mental state. *Acta Neuropsiquiatrica Argentina, 1,* 469–476.

Sautter, R. A., & LeBlanc, L. A. (2006). Empirical applications of Skinner's analysis of verbal behavior with humans. *The Analysis of Verbal Behavior, 22*(1), 35.

Scanlon, J. B., Leberfeld, D. T., & Freibrun, R. (1963). Language training in the treatment of the autistic child functioning on a retarded level. *Mental Retardation, 1,* 305–310.

Scattone, D., Tingstrom, D. H., & Wilczynski, S. M. (2006). Increasing appropriate social interactions of children with autism spectrum disorders using Social Stories™. *Focus on Autism and Other Developmental Disabilities, 21*(4), 211–222.

Scattone, D., Wilczynski, S. M., Edwards, R. P., & Rabian, B. (2002). Decreasing disruptive behaviors of children with autism using social stories. *Journal of Autism and Developmental Disorders, 32*(6), 535–543.

Schaaf, R. C., & Miller, L. J. (2005). Occupational therapy using a sensory integrative approach for children with developmental disabilities. *Mental Retardation and Developmental Disabilities Research Reviews, 11,* 143–148.

Schafer, R., & Murphy, G. (1943). The role of autism in a visual figure-ground relationship. *Journal of Experimental Psychology, 32*(4), 335.

Schertz, H. H., Odom, S. L., Baggett, K. M., & Sideris, J. H. (2013). Effects of Joint Attention Mediated Learning for toddlers with autism spectrum disorders: An initial randomized controlled study. *Early Childhood Research Quarterly, 28*(2), 249–258.

Schmit, J., Alper, S., Raschke, D., & Ryndak, D. (2000). Effects of using a photographic cueing package during routine school transitions with a child who has autism. *Mental Retardation, 38*(2), 131–137.

Schneider, B. H., & Leroux, J. (1994). Educational environments for the pupil with behavioural disorders: A 'best evidence' synthesis. *Behavioral Disorders, 19,* 192–204.

Schopler, E. (1971). Parents of psychotic children as scapegoats. *Journal of Contemporary Psychotherapy, 4,* 17–22.

Schopler, E., Mesibov, G., & Baker, A. (1982). Evaluation of treatment for autistic children and their parents. *Journal of the American Academy of Child Psychiatry, 21*(3), 262–267.

Schopler, E., & Reichler, R. J. (1971). Parents as cotherapists in the treatment of psychotic children. *Journal of Autism and Childhood Schizophrenia, 1*(1), 87–102.

Schopler, E., Reichler, R. J., & Renner, D. R. (1988). *The childhood autism rating scale (CARS).* Los Angeles: Western Psychological.

Schopler, E., Short, A., & Mesibov, G. (1989). Relation of behavioral treatment to' normal functioning': Comment on Lovaas. *Journal of Consulting and Clinical Psychology, 57,* 162–164.

Schreibman, L. E. (2005). *The science and fiction of autism.* Harvard University Press.

Schreibman, L. (2000). Intensive behavioral/psychoeducational treatments for autism: Research needs and future directions. *Journal of Autism and Developmental Disorders, 30*(5), 373–378.

Schreibman, L., & Koegel, R. L. (1996). Fostering self-management: Parent-delivered pivotal response training for children with autistic disorder. In E. D. Hibbs, & P.S. Jensen (Eds.), *Psychosocial treatments for child and adolescent disorders: Empirically based strategies for clinical practice* (pp. 525–552). Washington, DC, US: American Psychological Association,

Schroeder, S. R., Schroeder, C. S., Smith, B., & Dalldorf, J. (1978). Prevalence of self-injurious behaviors in a large state facility for the retarded: A three-year follow-up study. *Journal of Autism and Childhood Schizophrenia, 8*(3), 261–269.

Schuler, A. L. (1979). Echolalia: Issues and clinical applications. *Journal of Speech and Hearing Disorders, 44*(4), 411–434.

Segall, M. J., & Campbell, J. M. (2012). Factors relating to education professionals' classroom practices for the inclusion of students with autism spectrum disorders. *Research in Autism Spectrum Disorders, 6*(3), 1156–1167.

Selinske, J. E., Greer, R. D., & Lodhi, S. (1991). A functional analysis of the comprehensive application of behavior analysis to schooling. *Journal of Applied Behavior Analysis, 24*(1), 107–117.

Senju, A., & Johnson, M. H. (2009). Atypical eye contact in autism: models, mechanisms and development. *Neuroscience & Biobehavioral Reviews, 33*(8), 1204–1214.

Shah, A., & Frith, U. (1993). Why do autistic individuals show superior performance on the block design task? *Journal of Child Psychology and Psychiatry, 34*(8), 1351–1364.

Sharda, M., Subhadra, T. P., Sahay, S., Nagaraja, C., Singh, L., Mishra, R., Sen, A., Singh, N., Ericson, D., & Singh, N. C. (2010). Sounds of melody – Pitch patterns of speech in autism. *Neuroscience Letters, 478*(1), 42–45.

Shattuck, P. T. (2006). The contribution of diagnostic substitution to the growing administrative prevalence of autism in US special education. *Pediatrics, 117*(4), 1028–1037.

Shattuck, P. T., Seltzer, M. M., Greenberg, J. S., Orsmond, G. I., Bolt, D., Kring, S., ... & Lord, C. (2007). Change in autism symptoms and maladaptive behaviors in adolescents and adults with an autism spectrum disorder. *Journal of Autism and Developmental Disorders, 37*(9), 1735–1747.

Sharpe, D. L., & Baker, D. L. (2007). Financial issues associated with having a child with autism. *Journal of Family and Economic Issues, 28*(2), 247–264.

Sheinkopf, S. J., & Siegel, B. (1998). Home-based behavioral treatment of young children with autism. *Journal of Autism and Developmental Disorders, 28*(1), 15–23.

Shields, J. (2001). The NAS EarlyBird Programme Partnership with parents in early intervention. *Autism, 5*(1), 49–56.

Shin, J. Y., Nhan, N. V., Lee, S. B., Crittenden, K. S., Flory, M., & Hong, H. T. D. (2009). The effects of a home-based intervention for young children with intellectual disabilities in Vietnam. *Journal of Intellectual Disability Research, 53*(4), 339–352.

Short, A. B. (1984). Short-term treatment outcome using parents as co-therapists for their own autistic children. *Journal of Child Psychology and Psychiatry, 25*(3), 443–458.

Siaperas, P., & Beadle-Brown, J. (2006). The effectiveness of the TEACCH approach programme for people with autism in Greece. *Autism, 10*(4), 330–43.

Siaperas, P., Higgins, S., & Proios, P. (2007). Challenging behaviours on people with autism: A case study on the effect of a residential training programme based on structured teaching and TEACCH method. *Psychiatriki, 18*(4), 343–350.

Siegel, B., Anders, T. F., Ciaranello, R. D., Bienenstock, B., & Kraemer, H. C. (1986). Empirically derived subclassification of the autistic syndrome. *Journal of Autism and Developmental Disorders, 16*(3), 275–293.

Sigman, M., & Kasari, C. (1995). Joint attention across contexts in normal and autistic children. In C. Moore & P. Dunham (Eds.) *Joint attention: Its origins and role in development* (pp. 189–203). London: Psychology Press.

Sigman, M. D., Kasari, C., Kwon, J. H., & Yirmiya, N. (1992). Responses to the negative emotions of others by autistic, mentally retarded, and normal children. *Child Development*, *63*(4), 796–807.

Siller, M., Hutman, T., & Sigman, M. (2013). A parent-mediated intervention to increase responsive parental behaviors and child communication in children with ASD: a randomized clinical trial. *Journal of Autism and Developmental Disorders*, *43*(3), 540–555.

Silva, L. (2011). *Qigong massage for your child with autism: a home program from Chinese medicine*. Singing Dragon.

Silva, L. M., Ayres, R., & Schalock, M. (2008). Outcomes of a pilot training program in a qigong massage intervention for young children with autism. *American Journal of Occupational Therapy*, *62*(5), 538–546.

Silva, L. M., & Cignolini, A. (2005). A medical qigong methodology for early intervention in autism spectrum disorder: a case series. *The American Journal of Chinese Medicine*, *33*(02), 315–327.

Silva, L. M., Cignolini, A., Warren, R., Budden, S., & Skowron-Gooch, A. (2007). Improvement in sensory impairment and social interaction in young children with autism following treatment with an original Qigong massage methodology. *The American journal of Chinese Medicine*, *35*(03), 393–406.

Silva, L., & Schalock, M. (2013). Treatment of tactile impairment in young children with autism: Results with Qigong Massage. *International Journal of Therapeutic Massage & Bodywork*, *6*(4), 12.

Silva, L. M., Schalock, M., & Gabrielsen, K. (2011). Early intervention for autism with a parent-delivered qigong massage program: A randomized controlled trial. *American Journal of Occupational Therapy*, *65*(5), 550–559.

Simmons, D. R., Robertson, A. E., McKay, L. S., Toal, E., McAleer, P., & Pollick, F. E. (2009). Vision in autism spectrum disorders. *Vision Research*, *49*(22), 2705–2739.

Simmons, H. G. (1978). Explaining social policy: The English Mental Deficiency Act of 1913. *Journal of Social History*, *11*, 387–403.

Simmons, J. Q., Leiken, S. J., Lovaas, O. I., et al. (1966). Modification of autistic behavior with LSD-25. *American Journal of Psychiatry*, *122*, 1201–1211.

Simonoff, E., Pickles, A., Charman, T., Chandler, S., Loucas, T., & Baird, G. (2008). Psychiatric disorders in children with autism spectrum disorders: prevalence, comorbidity, and associated factors in a population-derived sample. *Journal of the American Academy of Child & Adolescent Psychiatry*, *47*(8), 921–929.

Sinha, Y., Silove, N., Hayen, A., & Williams, K. (2011). Auditory integration training and other sound therapies for autism spectrum disorders (ASD). *Cochrane Database of Systematic Reviews*, *12*.

Sinha, Y., Silove, N., Wheeler, D., & Williams, K. (2006). Auditory integration training and other sound therapies for autism spectrum disorders: a systematic review. *Archives of Disease in Childhood*, *91*(12), 1018–1022.

Sirota, K. G. (2004). Positive politeness as discourse process: Politeness practices of high-functioning children with autism and Asperger syndrome. *Discourse Studies*, *6*(2), 229–251.

Skinner, B. F. (1938). *The behavior of organisms: An experimental analysis*. New York: Appleton-Century-Crofts.

Skinner, B. (1957). *Verbal Behavior*. New York: Appleton-Century-Crofts.

Skinner, B. F. (1984). The shame of American education. *American Psychologist*, *39*(9), 947.

Skuse, D. H. (2009). Is autism really a coherent syndrome in boys, or girls? *British Journal of Psychology*, *100*(1), 33–37.

Sluckin, W., & Salzen, E. A. (1961). Imprinting and perceptual learning. *Quarterly Journal of Experimental Psychology*, *13*(2), 65–77.

Smith, D. E., & Hochberg, J. E. (1954). The effect of 'punishment' (electric shock) on figure-ground perception. *The Journal of Psychology, 38*(1), 83–87.

Smith, K. R. M., & Matson, J. L. (2010). Psychopathology: Differences among adults with intellectually disabled, comorbid autism spectrum disorders and epilepsy. *Research in Developmental Disabilities, 31*, 743–749.

Smith, L., & von Tetzchner, S. (1986). Communicative, sensorimotor and language skills of young children with Down syndrome. *American Journal of Mental Deficiency, 91*, 57–66.

Smith, M.K., & Smith, K.E. (2000). 'I believe in inclusion, but...': Regular education early childhood teachers' perceptions of successful inclusion. *Journal of Research in Childhood Education, 14*, 161–180.

Smith, T. (1999). Outcome of early intervention for children with autism. *Clinical Psychology: Science and Practice, 6*(1), 33–49.

Smith, T. (2001). Discrete trial training in the treatment of autism. *Focus on Autism and Other Developmental Disabilities, 16*(2), 86–92.

Smith, T., Mruzek, D. W., & Mozingo, D. (2005). Sensory integrative therapy. In J. W. Jacobson, R. M. Foxx, & J. A. Mulick (Eds.), *Controversial therapies for developmental disabilities: Fad, fashion and science in professional practice* (pp. 331–350). Mahwah, NJ: Lawrence Erlbaum Associates Publishers.

Smith, T., Eikeseth, S., Klevstrand, M., & Lovaas, O. I. (1997). Intensive behavioral treatment for preschoolers with severe mental retardation and pervasive developmental disorder. *American Journal on Mental Retardation, 102*(3), 238–249.

Smith, T., Groen, A. D., & Wynn, J. W. (2000). Randomized trial of intensive early intervention for children with pervasive developmental disorder. *American Journal on Mental Retardation, 105*(4), 269–285.

Solley, C. M., & Engel, M. (1960). Perceptual autism in children: The effects of reward, punishment, and neutral conditions upon perceptual learning. *The Journal of Genetic Psychology, 97*(1), 77–91.

Sparrow, S. S., Balla, D. A. & Cicchetti, D. V. (1984) *Vineland Adaptive Behavior Scales.* Circle Pines, MN: American Guidance Service, Inc.

Speers, R. W., & Lansing, C. (1965). *Group therapy in childhood psychosis.* North Carolina: The University of North Carolina Press.

Spratt, E. G., Nicholas, J. S., Brady, K. T., Carpenter, L. A., Hatcher, C. R., Meekins, K. A., Furlanetto, R.W., & Charles, J. M. (2012). Enhanced cortisol response to stress in children in autism. *Journal of Autism and Developmental Disorders, 42*(1), 75–81.

Spreckley, M., & Boyd, R. (2009). Efficacy of applied behavioral intervention in preschool children with autism for improving cognitive, language, and adaptive behavior: a systematic review and meta-analysis. *The Journal of Pediatrics, 154*(3), 338–344.

Sofronoff, K., Jahnel, D., & Sanders, M. (2011). Stepping Stones Triple P seminars for parents of a child with a disability: a randomized controlled trial. *Research in Developmental Disabilities, 32*(6), 2253–2262.

Solomon, R., Necheles, J., Ferch, C., & Bruckman, D. (2007). Pilot study of a parent training program for young children with autism The PLAY Project Home Consultation program. *Autism, 11*(3), 205–224.

Stades-Veth, J. (1988). [Holding. 2. Prevention of autistiform behavior]. *TVZ: het vakblad voor de verpleging, 42*(5), 150–153.

Stagnitti, K., Raison, P., & Ryan, P. (1999). Sensory defensiveness syndrome: A paediatric perspective and case study. *Australian Occupational Therapy Journal, 46*, 175–187.

Stahmer, A. C., Akshoomoff, N., & Cunningham, A. B. (2011). Inclusion for toddlers with autism spectrum disorders: the first ten years of a community program. *Autism, 15*, 1–17.

Stahmer, A. C., Collings, N. M., & Palinkas, L. A. (2005). Early intervention practices for children with autism: Descriptions from community providers. *Focus on Autism and Other Developmental Disabilities, 20*(2), 66–79.

Stahmer, A. C., & Gist, K. (2001). The effects of an accelerated parent education program on technique mastery and child outcome. *Journal of Positive Behavior Interventions, 3*(2), 75–82.

Stahmer, A. C., & Ingersoll, B. (2004). Inclusive programming for toddlers with Autism Spectrum Disorders: Outcomes from the children's toddler school. *Journal of Positive Behavior Interventions, 6*(2), 67–82.

Stahmer, A. C., & Mandell, D. S. (2007). State infant/toddler program policies for eligibility and services provision for young children with autism. *Administration and Policy in Mental Health and Mental Health Services Research, 34*(1), 29–37.

Steel, S., Joseph, R. M., & Tager-Flusberg, H. (2003). Brief report: Developmental change in theory of mind in children with autism. *Journal of Autism and Developmental Disorders, 33*, 461–467.

Stephenson, J., & Carter, M. (2005). The use of weighted vests with children with autism spectrum disorders and other disabilities. *Journal of Autism and Developmental Disorders, 39*, 105–114.

Stewart, M. E., McAdam, C., Ota, M., Peppé, S., & Cleland, J. (2013). Emotional recognition in autism spectrum conditions from voices and faces. *Autism, 17*(1), 6–14.

Stock, R., Mirenda, P., & Smith, I. M. (2013). Comparison of community-based verbal behavior and pivotal response treatment programs for young children with autism spectrum disorder. *Research in Autism Spectrum Disorders, 7*(9), 1168–1181.

Stoddart, K. P. (1999). Adolescents with Asperger Syndrome Three Case Studies of Individual and Family Therapy. *Autism, 3*(3), 255–271.

Stokes, T. F., & Baer, D. M. (1977). An implicit technology of generalization1. *Journal of Applied Behavior Analysis, 10*(2), 349–367.

Stone, W. L., Ousley, O. Y., & Littleford, C. D. (1997). Motor imitation in young children with autism: What's the object? *Journal of Abnormal Child Psychology, 25*(6), 475–485.

Stone, W. L., & Yoder, P. J. (2001). Predicting spoken language level in children with autism spectrum disorders. *Autism, 5*(4), 341–361.

Strain, P. (1983a). Generalisation of autistic children's social behaviour change: Effects of developmentally integrated and segregated settings. *Analysis and Intervention in Developmental Disabilities, 3*, 23–24.

Strain, P. S. (1983b). Identification of social skill curriculum targets for severely handicapped children in mainstreamed preschools. *Applied Research in Mental Retardation, 4*, 369–382.

Strain, P. S., & Bovey, E. (2008). LEAP preschool. In J. Handleman & S. Harris (Eds.), *Preschool education programs for children with autism* (pp. 249–280). Austin, TX: PRO-ED.

Strain, P. S., & Bovey, E. H. (2011). Randomized, controlled trial of the LEAP model of early intervention for young children with autism spectrum disorders. *Topics in Early Childhood Special Education, 31*(3), 133–154.

Strain, P. S., & Cordisco, L. (1993). The LEAP preschool model: Description and outcomes. In S. Harris & J. Handleman (Eds.), *Preschool education programs for children with autism* (pp. 224–244). Austin, TX: PRO-ED.

Strain, P. S., & Hoyson, M. (2000). The need for longitudinal, intensive social skill intervention: LEAP follow-up outcomes for children with autism. *Topics in Early Childhood Special Education, 20*(2), 116–122.

Strain, P. S., Jamieson, B. J., and Hayson, M. H. (1986). Learning experiences...An alternative program for preschoolers and parents: A comprehensive service system for mainstreaming of autistic-like preschoolers. In C. J. Meisel (Ed.), *Mainstreaming Handicapped Children-Outcomes, Controversies and New Directions*. Hillsdale, NJ: Erlbaum.

Strain, P. S., Kohler, F. W., & Goldstein, H. (1996). Learning experiences... an alternative program: Peer-mediated interventions for young children with autism. In E. D. Hibbs and P. S. Jensen (Eds.) *Psychosocial treatments for child and adolescent disorders: empirically based strategies for clinical practice* (2nd ed.) (pp. 573–587). Washington D.C.: APA.

Strain, P. S., & Schwartz, I. (2001). ABA and the development of meaningful social relations for young children with autism. *Focus on Autism and Other Developmental Disabilities, 16*(2), 120–128.

Straub, D. (1995). Qualitative research on school inclusion: What do we know? What do we need to find out? *Paper presented at the Annual Conference of the Association for Persons with Severe Handicaps.*

Strauss, K., Mancini, F., & Fava, L. (2013). Parent inclusion in early intensive behavior interventions for young children with ASD: a synthesis of meta-analyses from 2009 to 2011. *Research in Developmental Disabilities, 34*(9), 2967–2985.

Sullivan, K. (2013). *The Early Start Denver Model: Outcomes and moderators of an intervention for toddlers with Autism.* PhD. Dissertation University of Washington.

Sulzer-Azaroff, B., & Mayer, G. R. (1986). *Achieving educational excellence using behavioural strategies.* New York: Holt, Rinehart, & Winston.

Sundberg, M. L. (2007). Verbal behavior. *Applied Behavior Analysis, 2*, 526–547.

Sundberg, M. L., & Michael, J. (2001). The benefits of Skinner's analysis of verbal behavior for children with autism. *Behavior Modification, 25*(5), 698–724.

Sundberg, M. L., & Partington, J. W. (1998). *Teaching language to children with autism and other developmental disabilities.* Pleasant Hill, CA: Behavior Analysts.

Sundberg, M. L., Michael, J., Partington, J. W., & Sundberg, C. A. (1996). The role of automatic reinforcement in early language acquisition. *The Analysis of Verbal Behavior, 13*, 21.

Sussman, F. (1999). *More than words: The Hanen program for parents of children with autism spectrum disorder.* Toronto, ON, Canada: The Hanen Centre.

Symes, W., & Humphrey, N. (2011). The deployment, training and teacher relationships of teaching assistants supporting pupils with autistic spectrum disorders (ASD) in mainstream secondary schools. *British Journal of Special Education, 38*(2), 57–64.

Szatmari, P., Archer, L., Fisman, S., Streiner, D. L., & Wilson, F. (1995). Asperger's syndrome and autism: Differences in behavior, cognition, and adaptive functioning. *Journal of the American Academy of Child & Adolescent Psychiatry, 34*(12), 1662–1671.

Tager-Flusberg, H. (1981). On the nature of linguistic functioning in early infantile autism. *Journal of Autism and Developmental Disorders, 11*(1), 45–56.

Tager-Flusberg, H. (1992). Autistic children's talk about psychological states: Deficits in the early acquisition of a theory of mind. *Child Development, 63*(1), 161–172.

Tager-Flusberg, H. (1993). What language reveals about the understanding of minds in children with autism. In S. Baron-Cohen, H. Tager-Flusberg, & D. J. Cohen *Understanding other minds: Perspectives from autism* (pp. 138–157). Oxford: OUP.

Tager-Flusberg, H. (2000). Language and understanding minds: Connections in autism. *Understanding other minds: Perspectives from Developmental Cognitive Neuroscience, 2*, 124–149.

Tager-Flusberg, H. (2007). Evaluating the theory-of-mind hypothesis of autism. *Current Directions in Psychological Science, 16*(6), 311–315.

Tantam, D. (1991) 'Asperger Syndrome in Adulthood'. *in* U. Frith (ed.) *Autism and Asperger's Syndrome.* Cambridge: Cambridge University Press.

Tantam, D. (2000). Psychological disorder in adolescents and adults with Asperger syndrome. *Autism, 4*(1), 47–62.

Tapper, K. (2005). Motivating operations in appetite research. *Appetite, 45*(2), 95–107.

Taylor, B., Miller, E., Farrington, C., Petropoulos, M. C., Favot-Mayaud, I., Li, J., & Waight, P. A. (1999). Autism and measles, mumps, and rubella vaccine: no epidemiological evidence for a causal association. *The Lancet, 353*(9169), 2026–2029.

Taylor, J. L., & Seltzer, M. M. (2011). Employment and post-secondary educational activities for young adults with autism spectrum disorders during the transition to adulthood. *Journal of Autism and Developmental Disorders, 41*(5), 566–574.

Teitelbaum, P., Teitelbaum, O., Nye, J., Fryman, J., & Maurer, R.G. (1998). Movement analysis in. infancy may be useful for early diagnosis of autism. *Proc Natl Acad Sci U S A, 95*(1998), 13982–13987.

Thompson, C. J. (2011). Multisensory intervention observational research. *International Journal of Special Education, 26*, 202–214.

Thrum, A., Lord, C., Lee, L., & Newschaffer, C. (2007). Predictors of language acquisition in preschool children with autism spectrum disorders. *Journal of Autism and Developmental Disorders, 37*, 1721–1734.

Tinbergen, E. A., & Tinbergen, N. (1972). *Early childhood autism: An ethological approach.* Berlin: Parey.

Tinbergen, N., & Tinbergen, E. A. (1983). *Autistic children: New hope for a cure.* London: Allen & Unwin.

Tomatis, A. A. (1991). *The conscious ear.* New York: Station Hill.

Tomlinson, P. (1996). *Inclusive Learning; the report of the Learning Difficulties and/or Disabilities Committee of the Further Education Funding Council.* London: HMSO.

Tonge, B., Brereton, A., Kiomall, M., Mackinnon, A., King, N., & Rinehart, N. (2006). Effects on parental mental health of an education and skills training program for parents of young children with autism: A randomized controlled trial. *Journal of the American Academy of Child & Adolescent Psychiatry, 45*(5), 561–569.

Tonge, B., Brereton, A., Kiomall, M., Mackinnon, A., & Rinehart, N. J. (2014). A randomised group comparison controlled trial of 'preschoolers with autism': A parent education and skills training intervention for young children with autistic disorder. *Autism, 18*(2), 166–177.

Tordjman, S., Anderson, G. M., Botbol, M., Brailly-Tabard, S., Perez-Diaz, F., Graignic, R., Carlier, M., Schmit, G., Trabado, S., Roubertoux, P., & Bronsard, G. (2009). Pain reactivity and plasma β-endorphin in children and adolescents with autistic disorder. *PLoS One, 4*(8), e5289.

Trevarthen, C., Aitken, K., Papoudi, D., & Robarts, J. (1996). *Children with autism.* London: Jessica Kingsley Publishers.

Tsang, S. K., Shek, D. T., Lam, L. L., Tang, F. L., & Cheung, P. M. (2007). Brief report: application of the TEACCH program on Chinese pre-school children with autism – Does culture make a difference? *Journal of Autism and Developmental Disorders, 37*(2), 390–396.

Turner, L. M., & Stone, W. L. (2007). Variability in outcome for children with an ASD diagnosis at age 2. *Journal of Child Psychology and Psychiatry, 48*(8), 793–802.

Tutt, R., Powell, S., & Thornton, M. (2006). Educational approaches in autism: What we know about what we do. *Educational Psychology in Practice, 22*(1), 69–81.

UNESCO (United Nations Educational, Scientific and Cultural Organisation) (1994). *The Salamanca Statement and Framework for Action on Special Needs Education.* Paris: UNESCO.

Van Bourgondien, M. E., Reichle, N. C., & Schopler, E. (2003). Effects of a model treatment approach on adults with autism. *Journal of Autism and Developmental Disorders, 33*(2), 131–140.

van Lang, N. D., Bouma, A., Sytema, S., Kraijer, D. W., & Minderaa, R. B. (2006). A comparison of central coherence skills between adolescents with an intellectual disability with and without comorbid autism spectrum disorder. *Research in Developmental Disabilities, 27*(2), 217–226.

Van Rie, G.L., & Heflin, L.J. (2009). The effect of sensory activities on correct responding for children with autism spectrum disorders. *Research in Autism Spectrum Disorders, 3,* 783–796.

Vargas, S., Kean, C., & Camilli, G. (1999). A meta-analysis of research on sensory integration treatment. *American Journal of Occupational Therapy, 53,* 189–198.

Veale, T. (1993). Effectiveness of AIT using the BCG device (Clark method): a controlled study. In *Proceedings of the World of Options International Autism Conference. Canada: Toronto* (Vol. *16*).

Venter. A., Lord, C., & Schopler, E. (1992). A follow-up study of high-functioning autistic children. *Journal of Child Psychology and Psychiatry, 33,* 489–507.

Verhoeff, B. (2012). What is this thing called autism?; A critical analysis of the tenacious search for autism's essence. *BioSocieties, 7*(4), 410–432.

Vismara, L. A., Colombi, C., & Rogers, S. J. (2009). Can one hour per week of therapy lead to lasting changes in young children with autism? *Autism, 13*(1), 93–115.

Vismara, L.A., McCormick, C., Young, G.S., Nadhan, A., & Monlux, K. (2013). Preliminary findings of a telehealth approach to parent training in autism. *Journal of Autism and Developmental Disorders, 43*(12), 2953–2969.

Vismara, L. A., & Rogers, S. J. (2010). Behavioral treatments in autism spectrum disorder: what do we know? *Annual Review of Clinical Psychology, 6,* 447–468.

Vismara, L. A., Young, G. S., & Rogers, S. J. (2012). Telehealth for expanding the reach of early autism training to parents. *Autism Research and Treatment, 2012,* doi: http://dx.doi.org/10.1155/2012/121878.

Virués-Ortega, J. (2010). Applied behavior analytic intervention for autism in early childhood: Meta-analysis, meta-regression and dose–response meta-analysis of multiple outcomes. *Clinical Psychology Review, 30*(4), 387–399.

Virués-Ortega, J., Julio, F. M., & Pastor-Barriuso, R. (2013). The TEACCH program for children and adults with autism: A meta-analysis of intervention studies. *Clinical Psychology Review, 33*(8), 940–953.

Virués-Ortega, J., Rodríguez, V., & Yu, C. T. (2013). Prediction of treatment outcomes and longitudinal analysis in children with autism undergoing intensive behavioral intervention. *International Journal of Clinical and Health Psychology, 13*(2), 91–100.

Vivanti, G., Dissanayake, C., Zierhut, C., & Rogers, S. J. (2013). Brief report: predictors of outcomes in the early start Denver model delivered in a group setting. *Journal of Autism and Developmental Disorders, 43*(7), 1717–1724.

Volkmer, F. R., Klin, A., & Cohen, D. J. (1997). Diagnosis and classification of autism and related conditions: Consensus and issues. In D. Cohen and F. Volkmar (Eds.), *Handbook of autism and pervasive developmental disorders* (2nd ed.). New York: John Wiley & Sons, Inc.

Volkmar, F. R., & Mayes, L. C. (1990). Gaze behavior in autism. *Development and Psychopathology, 2*(01), 61–69.

Von der Embse, N., Brown, A., & Fortain, J. (2011). Facilitating inclusion by reducing problem behaviors for students with autism spectrum disorders. *Intervention in School and Clinic, 47*(1), 22–30.

Vygotsky, L. S. (1987). Thinking and speech. *The collected works of LS Vygotsky, 1,* 39–285.

Wacker, D. P., Berg, W. K., Harding, J. W., & Cooper-Brown, L. J. (2009). Matching treatment to the function of destructive behavior. In P. Reed (Ed.) *Behavioral theories and interventions for autism* (pp. 3–21). New York: Nova.

Waddington, E. M., & Reed, P. (2009). The impact of using the 'Preschool Inventory of Repertoires for Kindergarten' (PIRK ®) on school outcomes of children with Autistic Spectrum Disorders. *Research in Autism Spectrum Disorders, 3*(3), 809–827.

Waddington, E. M., & Reed, P. (2015). Comparison of the effects of mainstream and special school placements on outcomes in children with ASD: An archive-based analysis. *Journal of Research in Special Educational Needs,* In Press.

Walters, R. H. (1958). Conditioning of attention as a source of autistic effects in perception. *The Journal of Abnormal and Social Psychology*, *57*(2), 197.

Wang, L. W., Tancredi, D. J., & Thomas, D. W. (2011). The prevalence of gastrointestinal problems in children across the United States with autism spectrum disorders from families with multiple affected members. *Journal of Developmental & Behavioral Pediatrics*, *32*(5), 351–360.

Warnock, M. (1978). *Special educational needs (The Warnock Report)*. Department for Education and Science. London: Her Majesty's Stationery Office.

Warnock, M. (2005). *Special educational needs: A new outlook*. London: Philosophy of Education Society of Great Britain.

Watling, R. L., & Dietz, J. (2007). Immediate effect of Ayres' sensory integration-based occupational therapy intervention on children with autism spectrum disorders. *American Journal of Occupational Therapy*, *61*, 574–583.

Watling, R., Deitz, J., Kanny, E. M., & McLaughlin, J. F. (1999). Current practice of occupational therapy for children with autism. *American Journal of Occupational Therapy*, *53*, 498–505.

Watson, J. B. (1913). Psychology as the behaviorist views it. *Psychological Review*, *20*(2), 158.

Webb, N. J., Candreva, I. A., Strum, D. H., Richter, A., & Dwelle, T. (2012). Evaluating community inclusion: A novel treatment program for children with Autism Spectrum Disorders. Social Science Research Network. Available at: http://papers.ssrn.com/sol3/papers.cfm?abstract_id=2146862 (accessed 31 July 2015).

Weber, D. (1978). 'Toe-walking' in children with early childhood autism. *Acta Paedopsychiatrica: International Journal of Child & Adolescent Psychiatry*, *43*, 73–83.

Webster-Stratton, C., & Reid, M. J. (2010). The Incredible Years Program for children from infancy to pre-adolescence: Prevention and treatment of behaviour problems. In R. Murrihy, A. Kidman, & T. Ollendick (Eds.), *Clinician's handbook for the assessment and treatment of conduct problems in youth* (pp. 117–138). Heidelberg: Springer Press.

Webster-Stratton, C., Rinaldi, J., & Reid, J.M. (2011). Long term outcomes of the Incredible Years parenting program: Predictors of adolescent adjustment. *Child and Adolescent Mental Health*, *16*(1), 38–46.

Wedell, K. (2008). Confusion about inclusion: patching up or system change? *British Journal of Special Education*, *35*, 27–135.

Weiss, M. J. (1999). Differential rates of skill acquisition and outcomes of early intensive behavioral intervention for autism. *Behavioral Interventions*, *14*(1), 3–22.

Weiss, R. S. (1981). INREAL intervention for language handicapped and bilingual children. *Journal of Early Intervention*, *4*(1), 40–51.

Welsh, M.G. (1989). *Holding time*. New York: Fireside.

Welterlin, A., Turner-Brown, L. M., Harris, S., Mesibov, G., & Delmolino, L. (2012). The home TEACCHing program for toddlers with autism. *Journal of Autism and Developmental Disorders*, *42*(9), 1827–1835.

West, A., & Hind, A. (2006). Selectivity, admissions and intakes to 'comprehensive' schools in London, England. *Educational Studies*, *32*, 145–155.

Wetherby, A., Watt, N., Morgan, L., & Shumway, S. (2007). Social communication profiles of children with autism spectrum disorders late in the second year of life. *Journal of Autism and Developmental Disorders*, *37*, 960–975.

Wetherby, A., & Woods, J. (2006). Early social interaction project for children with ASD spectrum disorders beginning in the second year of life: A preliminary study. *Topics in Early Childhood Special Education*, *26*, 67–82.

Wheeler, J. J., Baggett, B. A., Fox, J., & Blevins, L. (2006). Treatment Integrity A Review of Intervention Studies Conducted With Children With Autism. *Focus on Autism and Other Developmental Disabilities*, *21*(1), 45–54.

Whitaker, P., Barratt, P., Joy, H., Potter, M., & Thomas, G. (1998). Children with autism and peer group support: using 'circles of friends'. *British Journal of Special Education, 25*(2), 60–64.

White, S. W., Keonig, K., & Scahill, L. (2007). Social skills development in children with autism spectrum disorders: A review of the intervention research. *Journal of Autism and Developmental Disorders, 37*(10), 1858–1868.

White, S. W., Oswald, D., Ollendick, T., & Scahill, L. (2009). Anxiety in children and adolescents with autism spectrum disorders. *Clinical Psychology Review, 29*(3), 216–229.

Whitney, I., Smith, P. K. & Thompson, D. (1994) Bullying and children with special educational needs. In P. K. Smith & S. Sharp (Eds.) *School bullying: insights and perspectives* (pp. 213–240). New York: Routledge.

Whittaker, J. (2001). Segregated special schools must close. *Greater Manchester of Disabled People's Magazine Coalition, 2001,* 12–16.

Whittingham, K., Sofronoff, K., & Sheffield, J. K. (2006). Stepping Stones Triple P: a pilot study to evaluate acceptability of the program by parents of a child diagnosed with an Autism Spectrum Disorder. *Research in Developmental Disabilities, 27*(4), 364–380.

Whittingham, K., Sofronoff, K., Sheffield, J., & Sanders, M. R. (2009). Stepping Stones Triple P: an RCT of a parenting program with parents of a child diagnosed with an autism spectrum disorder. *Journal of Abnormal Child Psychology, 37*(4), 469–480.

Wieder, S., & Greenspan, S. I. (2003). Climbing the symbolic ladder in the DIR model through floor time/interactive play. *Autism, 7*(4), 425–435.

Wiggins, L. D., Robins, D. L., Bakeman, R., & Adamson, L. B. (2009). Brief report: sensory abnormalities as distinguishing symptoms of autism spectrum disorders in young children. *Journal of Autism and Developmental Disorders, 39*(7), 1087–1091.

Williams, G., & Greer, R. D. (1993). A comparison of verbal behavior and linguistic curricula. *Behaviorology, 1,* 31–46.

Williams, J. H., Whiten, A., Suddendorf, T., & Perrett, D. I. (2001). Imitation, mirror neurons and autism. *Neuroscience & Biobehavioral Reviews, 25*(4), 287–295.

Williams, J. G., Higgins, J. P., & Brayne, C. E. (2006). Systematic review of prevalence studies of autism spectrum disorders. *Archives of Disease in Childhood, 91*(1), 8–15.

Williams, K. R. (2006). The Son-Rise Program® intervention for autism Prerequisites for evaluation. *Autism, 10*(1), 86–102.

Williams, K. R., & Wishart, J. G. (2003). The Son-Rise Program1 intervention for autism: an investigation into family experiences. *Journal of Intellectual Disability Research, 47*(4–5), 291–299.

Williams, M. S., & Shellenberger, S. (1996). *How does your engine run?: A leader's guide to The Alert Program for self-regulation.* Therapy Works, Inc.

Wilson, D. B., & Lipsey, M. W. (2001). The role of method in treatment effectiveness research: evidence from meta-analysis. *Psychological Methods, 6*(4), 413.

Wilson, P., Rush, R., Hussey, S., Puckering, C., Sim, F., Allely, C. S., Doku, P., McConachie, A., & Gillberg, C. (2012). How evidence-based is an 'evidence-based parenting program'? A PRISMA systematic review and meta-analysis of Triple P. *BMC Medicine, 10*(1), 130.

Wimmer, H., & Perner, J. (1983). Beliefs about beliefs: Representation and constraining function of wrong beliefs in young children's understanding of deception. *Cognition, 13*(1), 103–128.

Wing, L. (1981). Asperger's syndrome: a clinical account. *Psychological Medicine, 11*(01), 115–129.

Wing, L., & Gould, J. (1979). Severe impairments of social interaction and associated abnormalities in children: Epidemiology and classification. *Journal of Autism and Developmental Disorders, 9*(1), 11–29.

Wing, L., Gould, J., & Gillberg, C. (2011). Autism spectrum disorders in the DSM-V: better or worse than the DSM-IV? *Research in Developmental Disabilities, 32*(2), 768–773.

Wing, L., Leekam, S. R., Libby, S. J., Gould, J., & Larcombe, M. (2002). The diagnostic interview for social and communication disorders: Background, inter-rater reliability and clinical use. *Journal of Child Psychology and Psychiatry, 43*(3), 307–325.

Wishart, J. G., & Manning, G. (1996). Trainee teachers' attitudes to inclusive education for children with Down's syndrome. *Journal of Intellectual Disability Research, 40*, 56–65.

Wiwanitkit, V. (2010). Thai massage and autism: correlation? *The Journal of Alternative and Complementary Medicine, 16*(6), 613.

Wong, V. C., & Kwan, Q. K. (2010). Randomized controlled trial for early intervention for autism: a pilot study of the autism 1-2-3 project. *Journal of Autism and Developmental Disorders, 40*(6), 677–688.

Wood, J. J., Drahota, A., Sze, K., Har, K., Chiu, A., & Langer, D. A. (2009). Cognitive behavioral therapy for anxiety in children with autism spectrum disorders: A randomized, controlled trial. *Journal of Child Psychology and Psychiatry, 50*(3), 224–234.

Woodard, C. R., Goodwin, M. S., Zelazo, P. R., Aube, D., Scrimgeour, M., Ostholthoff, T., & Brickley, M. (2012). A comparison of autonomic, behavioral, and parent-report measures of sensory sensitivity in young children with autism. *Research in Autism Spectrum Disorders, 6*(3), 1234–1246.

Wolery, M., & Garfinkle, A. N. (2002). Measures in intervention research with young children who have autism. *Journal of Autism and Developmental Disorders, 32*(5), 463–478.

World Health Organization. (1992). *The ICD-10 classification of mental and behavioural disorders: clinical descriptions and diagnostic guidelines.* Geneva: WHO.

Worley, J. A., & Matson, J. L. (2012). Comparing symptoms of autism spectrum disorders using the current DSM-IV-TR diagnostic criteria and the proposed DSM-V diagnostic criteria. *Research in Autism Spectrum Disorders, 6*(2), 965–970.

Yarmolenko, A.V. (1926). Change of environment as a factor determining an anomaly of behavior (autism in uncontrolled children). *Voprosy Izucheniya i Vospitaniya Lichnosti/ Problems in the Study and Education of Personality, 1*, 38–46.

Yarmolenko, A. V. (1930). *Obsledovanie dvisheniy normalnikh i anormalnikh detey./*[A study of the movements of normal and abnormal children]. Oxford: Gosudarstvennoe Medizinskoe Izdatel.

Yarmolenko, A. V. (1935a). The exactness of hand movements in psychoneurotic children. *Novosti Psikhonevrologii Detskogo Vozrasta* (pp. 129–138).

Yarmolenko, A. V. (1935b). The motor sphere of psychoneurotic children. *Novosti Psikhonevrologii Detskogo Vozrasta* (pp. 149–167).

Yerys, B. E., Wallace, G. L., Harrison, B., Celano, M. J., Giedd, J. N., & Kenworthy, L. E. (2009). Set-shifting in children with autism spectrum disorders reversal shifting deficits on the Intradimensional/Extradimensional Shift Test correlate with repetitive behaviors. *Autism, 13*(5), 523–538.

Yoder, P., & Stone, W. L. (2006). Randomized comparison of two communication interventions for preschoolers with autism spectrum disorders. *Journal of Consulting and Clinical Psychology, 74*(3), 426.

Yoder, P. J., & Warren, S. F. (2002). Effects of prelinguistic milieu teaching and parent responsivity education on dyads involving children with intellectual disabilities. *Journal of Speech, Language, and Hearing Research, 45*(6), 1158–1174.

Zachor, D. A., & Ben Itzchak, E. (2010). Treatment approach, autism severity and intervention outcomes in young children. *Research in Autism Spectrum Disorders, 4*(3), 425–432.

Zachor, D. A., Ben-Itzchak, E., Rabinovich, A. L., & Lahat, E. (2007a). Change in autism core symptoms with intervention. *Research in Autism Spectrum Disorders, 1*(4), 304–317.

Zaslow, R., & Breger, L. (1970). A Theory and Treatment of Autism. In L. Breger (Ed.) *Clinical-cognitive psychology: models and integrations*, (pp. 246–291). Englewood Cliffs, NJ: Prentice-Hall.

Zhou, H.C., & Zhang, P.D. (2008). Language therapy combined with acupoints massage on communication disability in autistic children. *Chinese Medicine, 23*, 24–26.

Zissermann, L. (1992). The effects of deep pressure on self-stimulating behaviors in a child with autism and other disabilities. *American Journal of Occupational Therapy, 46*(6), 547–550.

Zimmer, M., & Desch, L. (2012). Sensory integration therapies for children with developmental and behavioral disorders. *Pediatr, 129*(6), 1186–1189.

Zingerevich, C., & Lavesser. P. (2009). The contribution of executive functions to participation in school activities of children with high functioning autism spectrum disorder. *Research in Autism Spectrum Disorders, 3*, 429–437.

Zollweg, W., Palm, D., & Vance, V. (1997). The efficacy of auditory integration training: A double blind study. *American Journal of Audiology, 6*, 39–47.

Zwaigenbaum, L., Bryson, S., Rogers, T., Roberts, W., Brian, J., & Szatmari, P. (2005). Behavioral manifestations of autism in the first year of life. *International Journal of Developmental Neuroscience, 23*(2), 143–152.

Index

Note: Page numbers in *italics* refer to Figures; those in **bold** to Tables.

Interventions for Autism: Evidence for Educational and Clinical Practice, First Edition. Phil Reed.
© 2016 John Wiley & Sons, Ltd. Published 2016 by John Wiley & Sons, Ltd.